Employment law

an adviser's handbook

Tamara Lewis is a solicitor who works in the employment unit of the Central London Law Centre and has written and lectured extensively on employment law.

The purpose of the Legal Action Group is to promote equal access to justice for all members of society who are socially, economically or otherwise disadvantaged. To this end, it seeks to improve law and practice, the administration of justice and legal services.

Employment law

an adviser's handbook

EIGHTH EDITION

Tamara Lewis

 Legal Action Group
2009

This edition published in Great Britain 2009
by LAG Education and Service Trust Limited
242 Pentonville Road, London N1 9UN
www.lag.org.uk

First published 1991
Second edition 1994
Third edition 1996
Fourth edition 2000
Fifth edition 2003
Sixth edition 2005
Sixth edition reprinted 2007
Seventh edition 2007
Seventh edition reprinted 2008 and 2009

British Library Cataloguing in Publication Data
a CIP catalogue record for this book is available from the British Library.

ISBN 978 1 903307 69 4

Typeset and printed in Great Britain by Hobbs the Printers, Totton,
Hampshire SO40 3WX

Recent developments

Since the first printing of the eighth edition of this book, the Equality Act (EA) 2010 received Royal Assent on 8 April 2010 and is being implemented in stages, with the core provisions coming into force from 1 October 2010.

The Equality Act 2010 replaces the Equal Pay Act 1970, Sex Discrimination Act (SDA) 1975, Race Relations Act 1976, Disability Discrimination Act (DDA) 1995, Employment Equality (Religion or Belief) Regulations 2003, Employment Equality (Sexual Orientation) Regulations 2003 and Employment Equality (Age) Regulations 2006. Although the employment provisions are similar, they are not identical. The differences will be fully explored in the ninth edition (due Autumn 2010). Meanwhile, here are some key points to look out for.

The term 'protected characteristics' is now used to refer to the different strands, ie race, sex, disability etc. There are uniform definitions of direct discrimination, indirect discrimination and victimisation which apply to all the protected characteristics.[1] These are almost identical to the existing definitions, except that the phrase 'because of' is used instead of 'on grounds of' in the definition of direct discrimination. This is intended to mean the same thing. Also, in respect of all the characteristics, it is unlawful to directly discriminate against a worker because s/he has the protected characteristic or because s/he is perceived to have it or because someone else has the protected characteristic. As at present, there is a unique justification defence available to employers in respect of direct age discrimination.

From 2011, there will be a new offence of combined discrimination: dual characteristics.[2] This will apply where an employer directly discriminates against a worker because s/he has combined characteristics, eg the worker is a black woman.

The definition of harassment is carried over to all the protected characteristics with uniform wording, ie unwanted conduct related to a protected characteristic which has the purpose or effect of violating the worker's dignity or creating an intimidating, hostile, degrading,

---

1 EA 2010 ss13, 19 and 27 respectively.
2 EA 2010 s14.

humiliating or offensive environment for him/her.[3] There are still the additional definitions of sexual harassment originally in SDA 1975. The offence of third party harassment, previously applicable only under SDA 1975, will now apply to each of the protected characteristics.[4]

Disability discrimination law has changed the most. In addition to direct discrimination, victimisation and harassment, indirect discrimination now applies in respect of disability. This is unlikely to be needed very often as the much wider duty to make reasonable adjustments still applies. There is a new offence of 'discrimination from disability'.[5] This is intended to restore the concept of 'disability-related discrimination' as applied under the DDA 1995 before it was rendered useless by the case of *Lewisham LBC v Malcolm*. There is no longer a list of possible reasonable adjustments or of criteria which determine whether an adjustment is reasonable to carry out or not. This should not change the way the law is applied. As regards the definition of 'disability', there is no longer a closed list of 'capacities', within which any adversely affected normal day-to-day activities must fall. This should make it easier to apply the definition. There is to be revised statutory Guidance on the definition of disability to reflect this change. The final item of interest in regard to disability discrimination is the new restriction on pre-employment enquiries about disability and health.[6] This is not quite as effective as it could be, but should still offer some protection.

The public sector race, sex and disability equality duties will be replaced in 2011 with a single public sector equality duty. Unfortunately, the new specific duties are likely to be considerably weaker than the previous model.

Tamara Lewis
September 2010

---

3   EA 2010 s26.
4   EA 2010 s40.
5   EA 2010 s15.
6   EA 2010 s60.

Preface

This book was first written because Thomas Kibling and I were constantly asked to recommend a book which covered the wide range of employment problems in a clear and practical form. There was no obvious book to recommend and we wrote this book to fill the gap. In particular, we have aimed to provide lay advisers, trade union officials and lawyers with a handbook which is a real support in identifying the relevant law and issues of evidence and which can be used as a self-contained guide while running unfair dismissal and discrimination cases. The book therefore devotes as much space to evidence, precedents and checklists as to setting out the law. Due to this practical emphasis, further research may be necessary on the law itself in new, developing, specialist or complex areas.

For a clear overview of the contents and lay-out of the book, it is best to look at the contents list on pages ix-xiv.

Employment law is a large subject, which has simply exploded in recent years, especially as a result of European influence. The book now is almost twice as long as the first edition. It is not possible to cover the whole of employment law and all the rules and permutations in a small textbook. Inevitably there are some omissions and certain topics have been covered in more detail than others. I have tried to deal most thoroughly with subjects which frequently come up for advisers of low-paid workers. Because of its complexity, the law on race, sex and disability discrimination has been treated in the greatest detail.

In 2004, the government introduced statutory dispute resolution procedures, requiring employers and employees to go through internal disciplinary and grievance procedures before bringing employment tribunal claims. The procedures were universally unpopular and formally abolished with effect from 6 April 2009. Unfortunately they still apply in many transitional situations, so chapter 22 has expanded rather than contracted. The procedures have been replaced by a new ACAS compensation regime which is likely to give rise to its own complications and is as yet untested.

At the time of writing, a single Equality Bill, to replace all the separate discrimination legislation is going through parliament. It remains to be seen how much new law this introduces in practice, or whether it will end up being little more than a consolidating statute. All should be clear by the next edition.

Some employment rights are available only to employees working under a contract of employment, others are available to workers generally. In early editions, we used the generic word 'worker'. Since the fifth edition, I have tried to use the appropriate terminology when dealing with each right. However, this can become awkward in some contexts and it is most important to check the start of each section to see who is covered. Unless specified, where the word 'worker' is used, it is not confined to the definition of 'worker' followed in certain legislation.

The internet is now an invaluable access source for reports, guidance and Codes. As these are often badly sign-posted and hard to find on the host websites, I have tried to give the exact web addresses. Unfortunately these tend to be long and cumbersome and very frequently change. If you find they are out of date, try looking through the sitemap. The internal search engines rarely help, but it sometimes works if you type in the full name of a report. Suprisingly often, it works to type the name of what you want into Google. Disappointingly, all the wonderful guidance previously on the DTI (then BERR) site has been broken up and divided between two separate sites, Directgov for employees and Business Link for employers. In many cases, this has reduced its scope and weakened its authority.

I should say that all the names used in the case precedents in the appendices are fictional and any resemblance to real names is purely coincidental.

The law is stated as known at 26 June 2009. Where possible, reference has been made to more recent law at proof stage.

Tamara Lewis
Central London Law Centre
June 2009

While every attempt has been made to ensure the accuracy of the contents of this book, the author can accept no responsibility for advice given in reliance on its contents.

Acknowledgements

The development of Central London Law Centre's employment unit has been greatly assisted by a small group of volunteers who have shown remarkable commitment over the years. Particular thanks to barristers Nick O'Brien and Martin Westgate for being such staunch supporters of the law centre for as long as I have been here. Thanks also to Thomas Kibling, my first inspiration in employment law, who conceived the idea of this book with me many years ago.

In relation to the book, many thanks to Martin Westgate for checking various sections over the various editions and for being my first port of call for all the trickiest queries. Special thanks to Philip Tsamados, my long-standing colleague at the law centre, for providing continual support and for making countless useful suggestions which have improved this and past editions enormously.

Finally I would like to thank all at LAG for their encouragement and support over the years.

Contents

Table of cases

Table of statutes

Table of statutory instruments

Table of European legislation

Abbreviations

ACAS	Advisory, Conciliation and Arbitration Service
AML	Additional maternity leave
BERR	Business, Enterprise and Regulatory Reform
CA	Court of Appeal
CCO	Continuation of contract order
CEHR	Commission for Equality and Human Rights
CPR 1998	Civil Procedure Rules 1998
CRE	Commission for Racial Equality
DDA 1995	Disability Discrimination Act 1995
DDP	Dismissal and disciplinary procedures
DPA 1998	Data Protection Act 1998
DRC	Disability Rights Commission
DTI	Department of Trade and Industry
DWP	Department for Work and Pensions
EA 2002	Employment Act 2002
EAT	Employment Appeal Tribunal
EAT PD	EAT Practice Direction of December 2004
ECHR	European Convention on Human Rights
ECJ	European Court of Justice
ECtHR	European Court of Human Rights
EDT	Effective date of termination
EE(A) Regs 2006	Employment Equality (Age) Regulations 2006
EE(RB) Regs 2003	Employment Equality (Religion or Belief) Regulations 2003
EE(SO) Regs 2003	Employment Equality (Sexual Orientation) Regulations 2003
EHRC	Equality and Human Rights Commission
EOC	Equal Opportunities Commission
EOP	Equal opportunities policy
EOR	Equal Opportunities Review
EPD	Equal Pay Directive
EqPA 1970	Equal Pay Act 1970
ERA 1996	Employment Rights Act 1996
ERelA 1999	Employment Relations Act 1999
ET	Employment tribunal
ET Regs 2001	Employment Tribunal (Constitution and Rules of Procedure) Regulations 2001

ET Regs 2004	Employment Tribunal (Constitution and Rules of Procedure) Regulations 2004
ET1	Application to an employment tribunal
ET3	Response to a claim to an employment tribunal
ET5	Standard acknowledgement form from an employment tribunal
ETA 1996	Employment Tribunals Act 1996
ETAD	Equal Treatment Amendment Directive
ETD	Equal Treatment Directive
ETO	Economic, technical or organisational
ETS	Employment Tribunals Service
EWC	Expected week of childbirth
FEA	Fair Employment Acts (1976 and 1989)
FIA 2000	Freedom of Information Act 2000
FTE Regs 2002	Fixed-term Employees (Prevention of Less Favourable Treatment) Regulations 2002
GOQ	Genuine occupational qualification
GOR	Genuine and determining occupational requirement
GP	Grievance procedure
GRA 2004	Gender Recognition Act 2004
HL	House of Lords
HMRC	Her Majesty's Revenue and Customs
HRA 1998	Human Rights Act 1998
HSE	Health and Safety Executive
ICR	Industrial Cases Reports
IRLR	Industrial Relations Law Reports
JES	Job evaluation scheme
JSA	Jobseeker's Allowance
JSB	Judicial Studies Board
LIFO	Last in, first out
MOD	Ministry of Defence
MPL Regs 1999	Maternity and Parental Leave etc Regulations 1999
NMWA 1998	National Minimum Wage Act 1998
NRA	Normal retirement age
OML	Ordinary maternity leave
OPSI	Office of Public Sector Information
PAL Regs 2002	Paternity and Adoption Leave Regulations 2002
PHA 1997	Protection from Harassment Act 1997
PI	Personal injury
PIDA 1998	Public Interest Disclosure Act 1998
PTW Regs 2000	Part-time Workers (Prevention of Less Favourable Treatment) Regulations 2000
RDO	Register deletion order
RIPA 2000	Regulation of Investigatory Powers Act 2000
RR(A)A 2000	Race Relations (Amendment) Act 2000
RRA 1976	Race Relations Act 1976

RRO	Restricted reporting order
SDA 1975	Sex Discrimination Act 1975
SOSR	Some other substantial reason
SSCBA 1992	Social Security Contributions and Benefits Act 1992
SSP	Statutory sick pay
TUC	Trades Union Congress
TULR(C)A 1992	Trade Union and Labour Relations (Consolidation) Act 1992
TUPE Regs 1981	Transfer of Undertakings (Protection of Employment) Regulations 1981
TUPE Regs 2006	Transfer of Undertakings (Protection of Employment) Regulations 2006
WA 1986	Wages Act 1986
WTR 1998	Working Time Regulations 1998

Introduction

CHAPTER 1

Terms and conditions of employment

continued

Chapter 1: Key points

- All employees have a contract of employment. Verbal contracts have the same status as written contracts, but are harder to prove.
- Contract terms may be express, implied or inserted by statute. Express terms are written or verbally agreed. Where there is no express term, an implied term may fill the gap. Terms may be implied because they are obvious or by looking at what has happened in practice, but not just because they are reasonable.
- Also, general implied terms apply in most employment contracts, eg the obligation not to destroy trust and confidence.
- Under the Employment Rights Act 1996 s1, certain contract terms must be put in writing. A written statement of these particulars does not necessarily constitute the contract in itself, but often amounts to strong evidence of what the contract is. Changes in terms should be confirmed in a section 4 statement.
- Contract terms are often varied during employment, but this can only occur by agreement (express or implied). Where the employer tries to enforce changes to the contract without agreement, this is called 'unilateral variation'.
- An employee must respond quickly where the employer tries to impose contract changes unilaterally, otherwise s/he may be taken to have agreed the change by inaction. There are various options for an employee in this situation, but most of them risk dismissal. If an employee is dismissed for refusing to accept a contract change, the dismissal will not necessarily be unfair.
- There are special regulations protecting employees working on fixed-term contracts from unjustified less favourable treatment.
- In theory, an employer can be sued for defamation, malicious falsehood or negligent misstatement if s/he writes a misleading or inaccurate reference. In practice, these claims are difficult to bring.
- Under the Data Protection Act 1998, workers have access to their own personal data and can seek corrections of inaccurate information held on them.
- Monitoring and privacy at work are covered by various specialist legislation as well as the Human Rights Act 1998 and Part 3 of the Data Protection Code.
- The Freedom of Information Act 2000 provides access to information held by public authorities.

General guide to useful evidence

- The letter of appointment, written contract of employment or statement of particulars under section 1 of the Employment Rights Act 1996, the staff handbook, any collective agreement (if unionised) or other written procedures, pay-slips.
- If there is no written contract: the job advertisement; what was said at interview and immediately on starting; custom and practice at the workplace.
- Having established the original contractual agreement, look for any variations which were applicable at the material time: further documents; verbal agreements; changes in practice.

The contract of employment

1.1   Depending on the circumstances, people may work on a variety of arrangements, eg as self-employed, as a 'worker' or as an 'employee'. As will be clarified throughout this book, their status will affect the extent of their employment rights. Whatever the basis for their employment, they are likely to be working under some kind of contract. Paras 1.1–1.40 of this chapter specifically concern the contractual rights of employees. For the definition of an employee in the context of unfair dismissal law, and global contracts, see paras 6.4–6.12. Every employee has a contract *of* employment, which consists of a number of terms, some of which are express terms, some implied and some statutory. Express terms are those agreed between the employer and employee whether in writing or orally. Implied terms are not expressly agreed but are implied from surrounding circumstances into the contract of employment by the tribunals and courts. Some implied terms are universal (ie they apply to all contracts of employment) and others are implied as a natural consequence of a specific contract of employment, either because the term is so obvious that the employer and employee would have agreed to the term if asked to consider it, or because the contract could not work without the term being incorporated. Statutory terms are inserted into the contract by Acts of Parliament. For example, the Equal Pay Act 1970 inserts an equality clause into contracts.

Express terms

1.2   An express term is one which has been the subject of discussion and acceptance by the employer and employee. These terms are usually put in writing but this is not necessary.[1] The main express terms are usually found in the letter of appointment or in the written contract of employment. Sometimes they are found in other documents such as the staff handbook, the rule book or collective agreement. Also watch for memos, notices on a notice board and e-mails, although these documents may or may not have contractual status. Pay-slips can provide good evidence of contractual pay rates and the name of the employer, although they are unlikely to amount to contractual documents in themselves. The contract of employment often expressly incorporates the provisions of the staff handbook as part of the employment contract. The main express terms are usually:

- the rate of pay, and how often the employee will be paid;
- the hours of work;
- any terms and conditions relating to holidays and holiday pay;
- sick pay;
- notice pay; and
- the disciplinary rules and grievance procedure.

Implied terms

1.3   In the absence of express terms, employment contracts need terms to be implied into them in order to make them workable, meaningful and complete. Implied terms of fact are used to fill a gap where there is no express term on a particular point. The courts will imply a term only if it is absolutely necessary to do so, or if it is clear that the employer and employee would have agreed to the term if it had been discussed.[2] The courts will not intervene and imply a term just because it is reasonable or convenient.[3] The idea is to give effect to the parties' presumed intentions. There are four common ways of trying to work out what an implied term might be:

- the 'business efficacy' test;
- the 'officious bystander' test;
- the behaviour of the parties in practice; and
- custom and practice.

1.4   The 'business efficacy' test is where a term is implied to make the contract workable. For example, it may be an implied contract term that

---

1 Though there is a separate right to have certain terms in writing. See para 1.24.
2 See *Lister v Romford Ice and Cold Storage Co Ltd* [1957] 1 All ER 125, HL.
3 *Aparau v Iceland Frozen Foods plc* [1996] IRLR 119, EAT.

a chauffeur holds a valid driving licence, even though this has never been explicitly discussed. The 'officious bystander' test is where a term is so obvious that both parties would instantly have agreed it at the outset, had they been asked. This test works for the driving licence example too. However, these tests do not always give an answer where there is no express term on a point.

1.5   A term can sometimes be implied by looking at what has happened between the particular employee and the employer in practice. For example, if the employer has given seven weeks' holiday every year to the employee without exception this may indicate an unspoken agreement at the outset for seven weeks' holiday. This way of implying a contractual term can be confusing, because behaviour and the contractual position can change over time.

1.6   Custom and practice across the workplace or the industry may also give rise to an implied term if the custom and practice is reasonable, notorious and certain. 'Reasonable' means that the term is fair, 'notorious' requires the term to be well known, and 'certain' requires the term to be sufficiently precise so that the term is possible to state.[4] For example, the employer always closes the factory for a trade holiday and gives all staff paid holidays for that week.[5] Depending on the facts, a policy which is adopted unilaterally by management, eg to pay travel expenses or to give enhanced redundancy pay, can sometimes become implied into an employee's contract by custom and practice.[6]

Universal implied terms

Mutual trust and confidence

1.7   As employment contracts involve personal contact between the parties, it is necessary to have certain terms implied into them so that they can operate smoothly, such as the implied term of mutual trust and confidence. This is the most widely applied and influential of all the implied terms. The employer must not, without reasonable and proper cause, conduct him/herself in a manner likely to destroy or seriously damage the relationship of trust and confidence with the employee.[7] This term applies to the employee as well. The following are

4 *Sagar v Ridehalgh and Sons Ltd* [1931] 1 Ch 310, CA.

5 *Quinn v Calder Industrial Materials Ltd* [1996] IRLR 126, EAT.

6 *Quinn v Calder Industrial Materials Ltd* [1996] IRLR 126, EAT; *Albion Automotive Ltd v Walker and others* (2002) 718 IDS Brief 5, EAT.

7 *Woods v WM Car Services (Peterborough)* [1982] ICR 693, CA.

examples of breaches of this implied term by the employer:

- physical or verbal abuse;[8]
- sexual harassment[9] and the failure to support someone who has been the victim of harassment at work;[10]
- imposing a disciplinary penalty when unwarranted or where the disciplinary procedure is not followed.[11]

Breach of the implied term of trust and confidence may cause an employee to resign and claim constructive dismissal.[12]

1.8   In very limited circumstances, employers may use an express term in a way which breaches the implied term of trust and confidence. For example, in one case the employers were in breach of this term when they invoked a mobility clause to insist an employee move workplace to a distant town on extremely short notice.[13] Usually, however, employers are able to rely on express terms, however unreasonable the result.

Not to act arbitrarily, capriciously or inequitably

1.9   There is an implied term that an employer will not treat an employee arbitrarily, capriciously or inequitably without good reason. Failing to give an employee a pay increase without good cause when other employees are given an increase has been held to be a breach of this term.[14]

Good faith and fidelity

1.10   This implied term lasts during employment but not after its termination.[15] Any action by an employee which seriously harms the employer's business will be in breach of this term,[16] (although whistle-blowing authorised by the Public Interest Disclosure Act 1998 would override this).[17] Likewise, an employer who discloses to a third party

---

8 *Western Excavating (ECC) v Sharp* [1978] ICR 221; [1978] IRLR 27, CA.

9 *Western Excavating (ECC) v Sharp* [1978] ICR 221; [1978] IRLR 27, CA.

10 *Wigan BC v Davies* [1979] ICR 411, EAT.

11 *Post Office v Strange* [1980] IRLR 515, EAT.

12 See paras 6.35–6.44.

13 *United Bank Ltd v Akhtar* [1989] IRLR 507, EAT.

14 *FC Gardiner Ltd v Beresford* [1978] IRLR 63, EAT.

15 *Faccenda Chicken Ltd v Fowler* [1986] IRLR 69, CA.

16 *Boston Deep Sea Fishing and Ice Co v Ansell* (1888) 39 Ch D 339, CA.

17 See para 6.91.

information about an employee without good reason or consent will be in breach of this term. Examples are:

- carrying on business in competition with the employer;[18]
- the use of the employer's list of customers including his/her business requirements.[19]

Employees cannot use confidential information for their own personal benefit during their employment.

1.11   The employee may also have agreed express contract terms, eg not to set up in competition after leaving the employment or not to poach staff or customers for a specified period of time. These are known as 'restrictive covenants'. If they are too restrictive in their ambit, they may not be enforceable, because it can be against the public interest to restrain trade more than is reasonably required to protect legitimate business interests. This is a complex area of law.

Not to disclose trade secrets/confidentiality

1.12   It is implied that the employee cannot disclose, either during employment or after it has ended, the employer's trade secrets or highly confidential information.[20] Most employees will not have access to information which would amount to a trade secret. The true nature of a trade secret is something which the outside world does not or could not ascertain, such as a process or a chemical formula, eg the ingredients of Coca Cola, and not just lower level confidential information which the employer does not want the employee to use after s/he leaves.[21]

To obey reasonable and lawful orders

1.13   The employee is obliged to obey reasonable and lawful orders. Lawful means both a requirement of parliament as well as an order given within the ambit of the employment contract. If the employee is asked to perform a function outside the employment contract which is unreasonable, s/he can, in theory, refuse. The employee needs to be careful because a small degree of flexibility is often taken to be within the

18 *Hivac Ltd v Park Royal Scientific Instruments* [1946] 1 All ER 350; [1946] Ch 169, CA.
19 *Faccenda Chicken Ltd v Fowler* [1986] IRLR 69, CA.
20 *Faccenda Chicken Ltd v Fowler* [1986] IRLR 69, CA. This is subject to protected whistleblowing, see para 6.91.
21 *Faccenda Chicken Ltd v Fowler* [1986] IRLR 69, CA.

contract. Also, if the employee is dismissed over the issue, it is still possible that the dismissal will be fair.[22]

Care of employer's equipment

1.14 The employee owes the employer a duty to look after the employer's equipment and machinery. The failure to exercise due care, leading to loss to the employer, could constitute a disciplinary matter. This will arise if the employee has injured a third party, as any claim by the latter will usually be against the employer.

To employ a competent workforce

1.15 The employer owes a duty to employ a competent and safe workforce,[23] safe plant and equipment, to have a safety system at work and to pay attention to employees' complaints in relation to safety matters.[24]

To provide a safe working environment

1.16 The employer owes a contractual duty to provide a safe working environment. (There are also detailed statutory rules about health and safety at work.[25])

To deal promptly with grievances

1.17 The employer is under a duty to afford employees an opportunity to obtain, reasonably and promptly, redress of any grievance that they may have.[26]

Statutory terms

1.18 Due to the unequal bargaining power between workers and employers, successive governments have found it necessary to incorporate into the employment contract certain terms protecting workers during, and on termination of, employment, for example minimum notice pay, an equality clause under the Equal Pay Act 1970 and the national minimum wage.

---

22 See paras 7.55-7.60.
23 *Hudson v Ridge Manufacturing Co* [1957] 2 All ER 229, QBD.
24 *British Aircraft Corporation v Austin* [1978] IRLR 332, EAT.
25 See also para 17.144 onwards.
26 *W A Goold (Pearmak) Ltd v McConnell* [1995] IRLR 516, EAT.

1.19   Generally speaking, clauses which exclude an employee's various statutory rights are void, though there are special rules when claims are settled.[27]

Varying the terms of employment

1.20   Any term of the employment contract can be varied by consent of the parties (except for certain statutory minimum terms). If the employer tries to vary a term of the employment contract but does not get the employee's consent, that variation is not recognised as lawful.[28] However, the courts and tribunals will treat the employee as having consented to the variation if s/he does not object to the change within a reasonable period of time. This is often referred to as a variation by affirmation. It is therefore important that the employee objects to any proposed variation as soon as possible. It is not necessary for the employee to keep repeating his/her objection; once is sufficient if it is clear and unequivocal. But an objection cannot hold all the options open forever without taking further action.

1.21   Where an employer insists on varying terms without the employee's consent, the employee's refusal to agree will rarely be the end of the matter. The employer may impose the changes anyway, such that the employee's normal options are to resist, resign[29] or, if relevant, sue for any unlawful deduction from wages or breach of contract. Alternatively, if the change is very radical, an employee may claim that s/he has in reality been dismissed and is now working under an alternative contract.[30] The employee can then claim unfair dismissal, while still working in the new employment. There are other options too, eg claiming discrimination, whether or not the employee actually leaves the employment. A checklist of the options is in appendix A.[31]

1.22   Many of the options may lead to the employee's dismissal. Whether or not an employee will succeed in an unfair dismissal case depends on eligibility to claim and the normal principles of fairness.[32] It does not necessarily follow that dismissal for opposing a change of contract

---

27 See para 20.161.

28 *Rigby v Ferodo Ltd* [1987] IRLR 516; [1988] ICR 29, HL.

29 For constructive dismissal, see paras 6.35–6.44.

30 *Hogg v Dover College* [1990] ICR 39, EAT; *Alcan Extrusions v Yates and others* [1996] IRLR 327, EAT.

31 See p728.

32 In particular, see paras 7.72–7.77.

will be unfair, or even if it is, the employee may not get much by way of compensation. In some circumstances, the dismissal will be automatically unfair, eg if on the facts it is due to the employee having asserted a statutory right such as to have written particulars of the terms and conditions of employment or not to have an unlawful deduction from wages.[33]

1.23   The employer cannot effect a change in the contract simply by notifying the employee that after a period of time the contract will be treated as having been varied. Employers have been known to terminate the original employment contract and offer a new contract which contains the variation as a means of getting round the employee's lack of consent to the variation. This approach is only lawful under the contract if the full contractual period of notice is given to terminate the employment contract and it is clear that the original contract is being terminated. If this happens, the employee can probably claim unfair dismissal in respect of the first contract and continue to work under the second contract. Where the employer effects mass dismissals in this way, the duty to consult trade union or employee representatives regarding collective redundancies also applies.[34]

The right to written particulars of employment

1.24   Employees are entitled to receive, within two months of the start of their employment,[35] a written statement of particulars of their employment. This is often known as a section 1 statement.[36] The particulars must include:

- the names of the employer and employee;
- the date on which employment began, including any period of continuous employment with a previous employer;
- rates of pay or methods of calculating pay and frequency of payment;
- hours of work, including normal working hours and compulsory overtime;[37]

33 See paras 6.73–6.76.

34 See para 2.17.

35 Employment Rights Act (ERA) 1996 s1(2).

36 Temps seeking work through a temp agency who are not employees of that agency, should be given a slightly different statement of terms under the Conduct of Employment Agencies and Employment Businesses Regulations 2003 SI No 3319 reg 15.

37 *Lange v Georg Schünemann GmbH* [2001] IRLR 244, ECJ Case C-350/99.

- terms relating to holidays, including public holidays and holiday pay;
- the employee's job title or a brief description of the work for which s/he is employed;
- place of work, including details of any mobility clause, and the employer's address;
- rules relating to sickness or injury and sick pay;
- pension arrangements;
- the length of notice required by each party;
- if employment is not intended to be permanent, the period for which it is expected to continue, or if a fixed-term contract, its expiry date;
- any collective agreements which directly affect the terms and conditions of employment;
- certain details[38] if the employee is required to work outside the UK for a period of more than one month;
- the disciplinary rules and procedure;[39]
- the name of a person to whom the employee can apply if s/he is dissatisfied with any disciplinary decision or seeking redress of any grievance relating to his/her employment; and
- any other term which, in view of its importance, is an essential part of the contract.[40]

Where there are no particulars on a point, this should be stated. If there is a change in any of the terms, the employer is required to notify the employee in writing within one month of the change.[41] Employers do not always make this written notification of contract variations, but an agreed variation will nevertheless be valid (provided it can be proved).

1.25   At least the first seven items listed above must be contained in a single document (the principal statement). Regarding notice, the statement can refer to the legal position (see para 1.38) or a reasonably accessible collective agreement. The other particulars may be contained in separate documents such as the staff handbook, provided these are reasonably accessible and referred to in the principal statement. Where an employer has supplied a written contract of employment or letter of engagement containing all the required particulars within the relevant time, this will be sufficient.[42]

---

38 ERA 1996 s1(4)(k).
39 ERA 1996 s3(1).
40 *Lange v Georg Schünemann GmbH* [2001] IRLR 244, ECJ Case C-350/99.
41 ERA 1996 s4.
42 ERA 1996 s7A.

1.26   The statement of terms is not itself the contract. It is strong but not conclusive evidence of what the contractual terms are.[43] If no proper statement is supplied within two months, the employee can apply to an employment tribunal (ET) during employment or within three months after termination of employment.[44] An employee can make an ET claim for a determination of particulars even if s/he left within the first two months of employment, as long as s/he has worked at least one month. The application can ask the ET to decide all the particulars which ought to have been given in a statement, or simply one or two specific particulars which have been omitted. The ET cannot award compensation in itself for failure to supply the particulars, but it can award 2–4 weeks' gross pay (subject to the same cap as for statutory redundancy pay) as extra compensation where the employee has also brought and won certain claims, eg unfair dismissal or discrimination.[45] Unless there are exceptional circumstances, this award must be made if, at the time such proceedings were started, the employer was in breach of his/her duty to supply a section 1 or section 4 statement.[46]

1.27   In practice employees tend not to apply to the ET unless there is a dispute over their entitlement to, eg holidays. There is always a risk that the employee will not be happy with the ET's findings on what the true contractual position is. It is useful to remember that it is automatically unfair to dismiss an employee, regardless of length of service, because s/he has demanded a section 1 statement.[47]

1.28   The duty on the ET is to determine what has in fact been agreed by the employer and the employee (including any term which needs to be implied), but not to remake a contract or decide what should have been agreed. The ET may have to make findings as to the terms and conditions of the contract when initially made and then consider whether there have been subsequent variations.

Wrongful dismissal

1.29   Unlike unfair dismissal, which is a statutory right, wrongful dismissal is a contractual claim. It arises when an employer terminates the

---

43 *Robertson and Jackson v British Gas Corporation* [1983] IRLR 302, CA.

44 ERA 1996 s11.

45 This covers claims listed in Schedule 5 of the Employment Act 2002 (see para 22.78) – essentially those covered by the statutory dispute resolution procedures and the new ACAS regime.

46 Employment Act 2002 s38. See also p757.

47 See paras 6.73–6.76.

employment contract contrary to the terms of the contract (eg failure to give proper notice, or breach of another contractual term such as failure to follow the contractual disciplinary procedure).

1.30   The general rule is that either party can end the contract by giving the appropriate notice and without cause or reason. Where an employee has committed an act of gross misconduct, the employer may end the contract without giving notice. What amounts to gross misconduct depends on the facts of each case, but it is an act which completely undermines the employment contract. Some employment contracts define what amounts to gross misconduct; some acts such as theft and physical assault are obvious acts of gross misconduct and do not need stating. Although gross misconduct entitles the employer to dismiss without giving notice, whether the dismissal is fair is a separate question under the general unfair dismissal provisions of the ERA 1996.[48]

1.31   A wrongfully dismissed employee can recover damages for breach of contract. The idea is to put the employee in the position s/he would have been in if the employer had not broken the contract. Where the breach of contract is failure to give proper notice, compensation will usually be the loss of earnings (pay and other benefits, eg use of a company car) for the notice period, subject to mitigation. The employee is expected to take reasonable steps to reduce his/her loss by seeking alternative employment. Any earnings received in the notice period will be set off against the claim.[49] It is also possible that any Jobseeker's Allowance received will be set off if it amounted to a net gain; similarly if the employee unreasonably failed to claim it.[50]

1.32   The tribunal or court will award compensation net of tax up to £30,000[51] and after that, should award a grossed-up sum to allow for tax on the award. Despite this, it is common practice for employers to pay employees a gross sum in lieu of notice, which in many situations will not be taxable up to £30,000.[52] However, if the contract explicitly allows for termination on payment of a sum in lieu of notice, there is probably no breach of contract, in which case the sum must be paid net as an emolument from the employment. This can become complicated. Matters of tax are beyond the scope of this book and where there is an issue, advisers should check specialist sources.

48 See also paras 22.15–22.16.

49 *Cerberus Software Ltd v Rowley* [2001] IRLR 160, CA.

50 *Secretary of State for Employment v Stewart* [1996] IRLR 334, EAT; *Westwood v Secretary of State for Employment* [1984] IRLR 209, HL.

51 Though a tribunal claim is subject to a £25,000 ceiling, see para 1.37 below.

52 Income Tax (Earnings and Pensions) Act (ITEPA) 2003 s401.

1.33   It is not possible to recover compensation for mental distress or injury to feelings caused by the wrongful dismissal,[53] although it might be possible to get stigma damages, but this will only arise in very limited circumstances.[54] It may, however, be possible to claim damages for breach of the implied term of trust and confidence if this takes place before and is unconnected with the dismissal.[55] It may be difficult to know on the facts whether the breach was part of the process of dismissal. For example, distress caused by a lengthy suspension which is followed by a disciplinary process ending with dismissal, may or may not be connected with the dismissal.[56]

1.34   Where the wrongful dismissal is because the employer fails to follow a contractual disciplinary procedure prior to dismissal, compensation should include wages for the length of time it would have taken to go through the compulsory disciplinary procedure.[57]

1.35   Surprisingly, if failure to give contractual notice or follow a contractual disciplinary procedure means the employee falls short of the necessary service for a statutory right (eg falls short of one year's service to claim unfair dismissal), the value of the employee's claim does not include compensation for the lost opportunity of bringing an unfair dismissal claim.[58]

1.36   Claims for breach of contract based on failure to follow disciplinary procedures are hard to prove and should be approached with caution. Most disciplinary procedures are not contractual but offer guidance rather than impose mandatory obligations, and failure to hold a disciplinary hearing or give a warning prior to dismissal will not necessarily be a breach of contract.

1.37   An employee who has been wrongfully dismissed can claim in the ET, county court or High Court, subject to the value of the claim. The court rules are complex and should be checked.[59] As a rough guide, most claims can only be started in the High Court if worth more than £25,000 (£50,000 if there is also a personal injury claim). Otherwise they

---

53 *Addis v Gramophone* [1909] AC 488; *Johnson v Unisys Ltd* [2001] IRLR 279, HL. See also para 17.154.

54 *Bank of Credit and Commerce International SA v Ali* [1999] IRLR 508, HL.

55 *McCabe v Cornwall CC* [2003] IRLR 87, CA.

56 *McCabe v Cornwall CC* [2003] IRLR 87, CA.

57 *Gunton v Richmond LBC* [1980] IRLR 321, CA.

58 *Harper v Virgin Net Ltd* [2004] IRLR 390, EAT; May 2004 *Legal Action* 34, CA; *The Wise Group v Mitchell* UKEAT/0693/04.

59 See the Practice Direction on How to Start Proceedings supplementary to the Civil Procedure Rules 1998 SI No 3132 Part 7, available on www.justice.gov.uk/civil/procrules_fin/index.htm

must be started in the county court. There are different allocation tracks for both county court and High Court claims according to the type, value and complexity of the claim. One of these is the small claims track (previously known as 'the small claims court') which covers most claims for damages up to £5,000 (other than certain housing and personal injury claims). Unlike the usual position in the civil courts, there is only a limited costs risk on the small claims track if the employee loses.[60] Alternatively, certain contract claims arising or outstanding on the termination of an employee's employment may be brought in an ET, currently for up to £25,000.[61]

Statutory minimum notice

1.38   ERA 1996 s86 sets out minimum notice periods though the contract may require more. An employer must give at least:

- one week's notice to an employee who has been continuously employed for one month or more but less than two years;
- one week's notice for each whole year of continuous employment for an employee employed for two years or more, but less than 12 years. For example, an employee employed for 5 years 11 months, would be entitled to at least five weeks' notice of dismissal;
- 12 weeks' notice for continuous service of 12 years or more. For example, an employee employed for 16 years would be entitled to at least 12 weeks' notice.

An employee employed for one month or more need give only one week's notice when resigning. In some situations, neither contractual nor statutory notice needs to be given,[62] eg an instant or summary dismissal for gross misconduct or a resignation due to the employer's fundamental breach of contract (constructive dismissal).

1.39   An employee must be paid for the statutory notice period even if s/he is off sick and has exhausted his/her normal entitlement to sick pay, or if s/he is absent due to pregnancy, childbirth, adoption leave, parental leave or paternity leave.[63] Oddly, if the employee has a contractual entitlement to notice which is at least one week longer than the

---

60 See Civil Procedure Rules (CPR) 27.14 (website, n59).
61 Employment Tribunals Act 1996 s3; Industrial Tribunals Extension of Jurisdiction (England and Wales) Order 1994 SI No 1623 article 10.
62 ERA 1996 s86(6).
63 ERA 1996 ss87–88.

statutory minimum, s/he entirely loses the right to statutory notice pay in these circumstances.[64]

1.40 An employee can claim for wrongful dismissal including the failure to give notice in the ET within three months of the effective date of termination.

Fixed-term employees

1.41 The Fixed-term Employees (Prevention of Less Favourable Treatment) Regulations (FTE Regs) 2002[65] implement the EC Fixed-term Work Directive[66] and grant additional rights concerning pay and pensions. The government has produced guidance on the FTE Regs 2002 which can be downloaded via links to Directgov and Business Link on the website for the Department for Business Innovation & Skills (BIS) (previously BERR).[67] This guidance has no legal status, but it is a useful reference point. In a related area, the government has been consulting on the implementation of the EC Temporary Agency Workers Directive[68] which must be introduced by 5 December 2011.

1.42 The FTE Regs 2002 only cover employees, but it is arguable that the Fixed-Term Work Directive also protects other workers.[69] A fixed-term employee is someone who is employed under a contract of employment that will terminate on a specific date, or on completion of a particular task, or when a specific event does or does not happen.[70] This can include employees on short contracts to do seasonal work (eg agricultural workers or working in children's summer camps or shop assistants taken on purely for Christmas), and employees employed as maternity or sickness locums.[71] It is still a fixed-term contract, even if it contains a clause allowing the employer or employee to terminate it on notice during its course.[72] A permanent employee is one who is

---

64 ERA 1996 s87(4); *Scott Company (UK) Ltd v Budd* [2003] IRLR 145, EAT.

65 SI No 2034.

66 No 99/70.

67 www.berr.gov.uk/employment/employment-legislation/employment-guidance/page18475.html

68 No 2008/104.

69 See scope defined by ECJ in *Del Cerro Alonso v Osakidetza-Servicio Vasco de Salud* [2007] IRLR 911, ECJ.

70 FTE Regs 2002 reg 1(2).

71 See Directgov guidance (n67).

72 *Allen v National Australia Group Europe Ltd* [2004] IRLR 847, EAT.

not employed on a fixed-term contract.[73] The FTE Regs 2002 do not apply where the employee is an agency worker.[74] Apprentices and employees on certain government training or work experience schemes are also excluded.[75]

1.43   A fixed-term employee has the right not to be treated less favourably than a comparable permanent employee just because s/he is a fixed-term employee as regards contract terms or by being subjected to any other detriment.[76] A comparable permanent employee is someone who, at the time of the less favourable treatment, is employed by the same employer on broadly similar work (having regard to similar levels of qualification and skills), and who is based at the same establishment or if there is no one comparable at the same establishment, then based at a different establishment.[77] Subject to the defence of justification (below) an employer must not give a fixed-term employee less favourable access than a permanent employee to benefits such as Christmas bonuses, free gym membership, travel loans, training courses or occupational pension schemes, or deny him/her promotion opportunities or select him/her first for redundancy, purely because s/he works fixed-term. However, it is not contrary to the FTE Regs 2002 to dismiss full-time employees just short of the one year qualifying period for unfair dismissal protection, even though no similar action is taken against permanent employees.[78] Where the fixed-term employee does the same work as several permanent employees whose contract terms are different, s/he may choose who to compare him/herself with.

1.44   Employers have a defence if the less favourable treatment can be justified on objective grounds.[79] An employer should balance the rights of individual employees against business objectives and consider justification on a case-by-case basis. The Directgov guidance says the treatment will be justified if it is to achieve a legitimate objective, if it is necessary to achieve that objective and if it is an appropriate way to achieve that objective. This is similar to the test used for justifying indirect race or sex discrimination, although arguably a higher

73 FTE Regs 2002 reg 1(2).
74 FTE Regs 2002 reg 19. Note that reg 19(1) repeals the exclusion of agency workers on contracts shorter than 3 months from SSP entitlement from 27th October 2008.
75 FTE Regs 2002 regs 20 and 18.
76 FTE Regs 2002 reg 3.
77 FTE Regs 2002 reg 2.
78 *DWP v Webley* [2005] IRLR 288, CA.
79 FTE Regs 2002 reg 3(3)(b).

threshold. Another way an employer can justify less favourable treatment is if the terms of the fixed-term employee's contract, taken as a whole, are at least as favourable as the terms of the comparable permanent employee's contract.[80] This 'package approach' may not be lawful under the Directive.[81] It will also not necessarily amount to less favourable treatment where the pro rata principle applies,[82] eg where an employer pays for annual health insurance and an employee on a six-month fixed-term contract is offered half the subscription cost.

1.45   A fixed-term employee has the right to be informed of any available permanent vacancies. It is sufficient if the vacancy is contained in an advertisement which the employee has a reasonable opportunity of reading in the course of his/her employment.[83] Also, once an employee has been continuously employed on two or more fixed-term contracts for four years (excluding any employment before 10 July 2002), the contract becomes permanent unless keeping the employee on a fixed-term contract is objectively justified.[84] Unfortunately the wording of the FTE Regs 2002 is clumsy as to the date on which this takes effect. The FTE Regs 2002 may simply mean that the employee becomes permanent as soon as s/he has been employed for four years (on at least two contracts). But some commentators believe that the employee only becomes permanent on the next occasion (after four years) when a new contract is offered or the previous fixed-term contract is renewed. A collective or workforce agreement can modify the rule.[85] Continuous employment for this purpose is calculated in the same way as it is to qualify for unfair dismissal protection.[86] so that certain breaks between fixed-term contracts may be counted in. For example, teachers employed on nine-month or term-time only contracts may be able to claim permanent status after four years if they can show their service through the breaks is continuous by reason of custom and arrangement or as temporary cessation only, and the employer cannot justify keeping them on fixed-term contracts.

1.46   An employee can request a written statement confirming his/her new status as permanent employee or, if this is disputed, explaining the

---

80 FTE Regs 2002 reg 4.
81 The ECJ in *Del Cerro Alonso v Osakidetza-Servicio Vasco de Salud* [2007] IRLR 911, ECJ seems to require a more precise defence.
82 FTE Regs 2002 regs 2(1) and 3(5).
83 FTE Regs 2002 reg 3(6) and (7).
84 FTE Regs 2002 reg 8.
85 FTE Regs 2002 reg 8(5).
86 FTE Regs 2002 reg 8(4); see paras 6.21–6.23.

justification for the contract remaining fixed term.[87] Employees place great value on being given 'permanent' status, but it is not always as important as they think. Employees qualify for unfair dismissal protection as soon as they build up one year's service, whether they are employed on a permanent or fixed-term contract.[88] Admittedly, having permanent status as opposed to working on a short-term contract may make the employee less vulnerable to dismissal in practice.

Enforcement

1.47   An employee who thinks s/he may have been less favourably treated, may make a written request to the employer to supply written reasons for the treatment within 21 days.[89] If the employer fails to answer or is evasive, the ET may draw an adverse inference in any subsequent tribunal proceedings. If the treatment concerned is dismissal, the employee cannot make a request under the FTE Regs 2002, but can make an equivalent request for written reasons for dismissal under ERA 1996 s92.[90]

1.48   If a fixed-term employee believes s/he has been less favourably treated than a comparable permanent employee, or that his/her rights have been infringed under the FTE Regs 2002 in any other way, s/he can bring an ET claim within three months.[91] Late claims may be allowed if it is just and equitable to do so. The ET has power to make a declaration as to the employee's rights, to order compensation and to make recommendations that the employer take certain action.[92] The amount of compensation will be what the ET thinks is just and equitable having regard to the infringement and any loss attributable to it. No award may be made for injury to feelings.

1.49   It is automatic unfair dismissal to dismiss an employee because s/he has done anything under the FTE Regs 2002 including alleging, eg in a grievance, that the employer has infringed the Regulations (except where the allegation is false and not made in good faith), bringing ET proceedings, giving evidence or requesting a written statement, or because the employer believes or suspects the employee has done or

---

87 FTE Regs 2002 reg 9.
88 See para 6.26.
89 FTE Regs 2002 reg 5.
90 See para 20.11.
91 FTE Regs 2002 reg 7.
92 FTE Regs 2002 reg 7.

intends to do any of these things.[93] It is also unlawful to submit an employee to a detriment for these reasons.[94]

References

1.50   There is usually no obligation on an employer to provide a worker with a reference on termination of the employment contract. An exception is where a reference is required by a regulatory body such as the Financial Service Authority (FSA) to ensure that financial services are only handled by authorised and competent persons.

1.51   If an employer does provide a reference to a third party, that employer owes a duty of care to the person to whom the reference is provided. Furthermore, a corresponding duty is owed to the worker who is the subject matter of the reference. It is necessary for the reference to be true, accurate and fair. Also the reference must not give an unfair or misleading impression overall, even if the discrete components are factually correct.[95]

1.52   A worker can sue an employer if s/he has suffered loss due to a negligent reference, either for breach of an implied term of the contract or in negligence.[96] The duty imposed on the employer is to ensure that the reference is fair, just and reasonable and the author of the reference should take all reasonable care to ensure that there is no misstatement. Negligent misstatement is where the employer, honestly but carelessly, makes a false statement of fact or opinion in the reference. Employers should confine unfavourable statements about the employee to those matters into which they had made reasonable investigation and had reasonable grounds for believing to be true.[97] It is also possible to sue an employer for defamation or malicious falsehood in the provision of a reference.

1.53   In practical terms, it can be hard for a worker to do anything if s/he suspects a bad reference has been given. It may be hard to obtain a copy of the reference, even from the proposed new employer. The Data Protection Act 1998 is rather a mixed blessing in this respect. However, the worker could make a subject access request[98] of the

93 FTE Regs 2002 reg 6.
94 FTE Regs 2002 reg 6.
95 *Bartholomew v Hackney LBC* [1999] IRLR 246.
96 *Spring v Guardian Assurance plc* [1994] IRLR 460.
97 *Cox v Sun Alliance Life Ltd* [2001] IRLR 448, CA.
98 See paras 1.61–1.63.

prospective/new employer (but not of his/her ex-employer)[99] and enlist the Information Commissioner's assistance if disclosure is refused. The Commissioner has issued a short Good Practice Note: 'Subject access and employment references', which encourages disclosure.[100] Although the reference will doubtless disclose the identity of the author, this can sometimes be concealed. Any claim for a negligent or false reference would usually only be enforceable in the county court or High Court. If s/he has been unable to get the reference any other way and has sufficient grounds, the worker may be able to get pre-action disclosure. Realistically, the worker will not want to bring a case in the civil courts unless public funding (legal aid) is available. This depends on the nature of the claim and whether the worker is eligible. It may be available for negligent misstatement, but not for defamation or malicious falsehood. Sometimes the best and simplest thing to do is to send a solicitor's letter to the former employer warning him/her of the consequences of unjustified references. This may prevent the employer doing it again.

1.54   An employer may give a discriminatory reference or victimise a worker by giving an adverse reference or no reference because the worker alleged discrimination during his/her employment or brought a case after leaving.[101] The advantage of a discrimination claim, if it can be brought, is that it is run in an ET and the questionnaire procedure can be used to obtain details and possibly a copy of the reference before starting any case.

1.55   These days, many employers give a purely factual reference confirming dates of employment and job title, to avoid any possibility of action being taken against them. Unfortunately such a reference can be of limited value to the worker. Because of the above difficulties, it is usually important to obtain an agreed reference as part of any settlement negotiated on an unfair dismissal or discrimination case.

---

99 Data Protection Act (DPA) 1998 Sch 7 para 1.

100 Available at
   www.ico.gov.uk/upload/documents/library/data_protection/detailed_specialist_guides/subject_access_and_employment_references.pdf

101 See para 13.85 for a definition of victimisation under the discrimination legislation.

The Data Protection Act 1998

The legal framework

1.56   The Data Protection Act (DPA) 1998 implements the EC Data Protection Directive.[102] Various statutory instruments have also added requirements. There is an Information Commissioner with powers to enforce the DPA 1998 and issue Codes and Guidance. The Commissioner has issued an Employment Practices Data Code of Practice. He has also issued 'Supplementary Guidance' and a 'Quick Guide to the Employment Practices Code: Ideal for Small Businesses'.[103] The Code has four parts. Part 1 concerns recruitment and selection; Part 2 concerns employment records; Part 3 concerns monitoring at work; and Part 4 concerns medical information. The Code does not constitute the law but it provides useful guidelines on how the Commissioner will interpret the law. The DPA 1998 also needs to be interpreted in the context of the Human Rights Act 1998, especially the potentially conflicting provisions of article 8, the right to private life, and article 10, freedom of expression.[104] The rules under the DPA 1998 are detailed and complex. The following is only a summary of the main rules applicable in an employment context. A guide to the DPA 1998 and the Freedom of Information legislation (below) in the context of discrimination cases is available on the EHRC website.[105]

1.57   The DPA 1998 provides data protection controls in all fields of life. It contains a lot of jargon which cannot be avoided. In the employment context, the 'data controller', ie the person who collects and processes the data, is usually the employer. The 'data subject', whose rights are protected, may be a job applicant, trainee, existing employee or other worker. 'Processing' data or information means obtaining, recording or holding data or carrying out any operation on the data, including use, disclosure or destruction of the data.[106]

---

102 No 95/46/EC.

103 All available from the Information Commissioner's website via www.ico.gov.uk/what_we_cover/data_protection/guidance/codes_of_practice.aspx

104 See paras 3.13–3.25.

105 *Using the Data Protection Act and Freedom of Information Act in Employment Discrimination Cases* by Tamara Lewis at www.equalityhumanrights.com/uploaded_files/dpa_and_foi_in_employment_discrim_cases.doc

106 DPA 1998 s1(1).

Which data is protected

1.58   'Data' is information which is stored on automated systems, eg computers, CCTV or telephone logging systems, or manual information which forms part of an 'accessible record' including health records[107] or a relevant filing system.[108] A relevant filing system is defined as a set of non-automated information structured in such a way that specific information related to a particular individual is readily accessible.[109] This would cover, for example, manual personnel files stored in alphabetical order with the contents of each file in indexed categories. It only covers manual filing systems which are broadly equivalent to computerised systems in ready accessibility to relevant information.[110] It would not cover a disorganised filing system where the contents of individual files are thrown together in a completely random order. Workers' rights to see their files may therefore depend on how tidy and organised their employers are. The test is whether the file is so well organised that a new temp would be able to extract specific information without leafing through the whole file.[111] Employees of a public authority have an additional right to see unstructured manual personal data about themselves, provided it is not too expensive to search out.[112] This may cover information held on an unstructured personnel file, someone else's file, or generally elsewhere. Some workers may also have a right in their contracts to see their files.

1.59   'Personal data' means data related to a worker who can be identified from the data alone or taken together with other information which the employer has. It includes an expression of opinion about the worker or indication of anyone's intentions towards him/her, eg a manager's view on a worker's promotion prospects.[113] CCTV footage from which the worker could be identified would also be personal data. However, it is not enough that the data simply refers to the worker. The information must significantly focus on the worker with content which

---

107 DPA 1998 s68.

108 DPA 1998 s1(1).

109 DPA 1998 s1(1).

110 *Durant v Financial Services Authority* [2003] EWCA Civ 1746.

111 This is the Information Commissioner's interpretation of Durant [2003] EWCA Civ 1746.

112 DPA 1998 ss7(1) and 9A.

113 DPA 1998 s1(1). *Common Services Agency v Scottish Information Commissioner* 2008 UKHL 47 could be problematic in that it extends the scope of identifiable personal data.

would affect his/her personal or professional privacy.[114] 'Sensitive personal data' means personal data containing information on a worker's race or ethnic origin, religious belief, political opinions, trade union membership, health, sexual life or the commission of any offence.[115]

The data protection principles

1.60 At the heart of the DPA 1998 are eight data protection principles, with which employers must comply.[116] In summary, these are:

1) To process personal data fairly and lawfully and to meet at least one of the conditions set out in DPA 1998 Schedule 2. The Schedule 2 conditions are that the worker's specific, unpressurised and informed consent has been obtained, or if not, the processing is necessary:
   - for the performance of the worker's contract; or
   - to meet any non-contractual obligations of the employer (eg record keeping for the minimum wage); or
   - to protect the vital interests of the worker; or
   - for the administration of justice, etc; or
   - to protect the legitimate interests of the employer or parties to whom the data is disclosed, unless this prejudices the worker's legitimate interests.

   For sensitive personal data, at least one of the conditions set out in Schedule 3 must also be met. These include explicit consent and exemptions in connection with legal rights and proceedings.[117]

2) To obtain and process data only for specified and lawful purposes.

3) To hold data only where it is relevant and not excessive to the purpose.

4) Data should be accurate and up to date. It is sufficient if the employer took reasonable steps to ensure the accuracy of the data and if the worker has notified the employer that the data is inaccurate, that a note of this is made.

5) Not to keep data for longer than necessary.

---

114 *Durant v Financial Services Authority* [2003] EWCA Civ 1746, CA.
115 DPA 1998 s2.
116 DPA 1998 s4(4) and Schedule 1.
117 See para 1.68 below.

6) To process data in accordance with the rights of data subjects. (See below for workers' rights.)

7) To take measures to prevent unauthorised processing of data and against accidental loss. This means taking appropriate security measures and also ensuring that other employees or even external companies such as those set up to pay wages who have access to data are reliable.

8) Not to transfer data outside the European Economic Area unless to a country which has adequate data protection and controls.

Workers' rights

Access to the data

1.61   Workers have a right of access to their own personal data, eg their computerised personnel information, if they make a written request and pay a fee up to £10.[118] This is called a 'subject access request'. Employers must comply promptly and within 40 days at the latest. Repeated requests for access can only be made at reasonable intervals.[119] If the employer refuses to give access, the worker can apply to the High Court or county court for an order[120] or to the Information Commissioner for an assessment.[121] The employer must not tamper with the information before disclosure, except to conceal identity where required.[122]

1.62   The worker is entitled to a description of any personal data held on him/her, its purposes and the recipients to whom the data may be disclosed. The employer must show the data to the worker in an intelligible form and, provided it is possible, give the worker a hard copy to keep.[123] The employer must provide information on the source of the data except where it identifies an individual.

1.63   Where the data reveals information about any other individual including an individual who is the source of the information (eg the author of an appraisal or reference), the employer can conceal his/her identity or, if that is impossible, withhold the data. This is the posi-

118 DPA 1998 s7.
119 DPA 1998 s8.
120 DPA 1998 s7(9).
121 See para 1.73 below.
122 See para 1.63.
123 DPA 1998 ss7(1)(c) and 8.

tion unless the individual consents or it is reasonable for the employer to dispense with his/her consent.[124] It may be unreasonable of the employer to refuse to dispense with consent where s/he has not even tried to get it.[125] In addition, workers are not entitled to see employment and certain other references given by their own employers.[126] They can ask their current or prospective employer to show them a reference written by someone else, eg their former employer. Although this will probably fall within the rules about concealing an individual's identity, the Information Commissioner encourages employers to reveal as much information as possible.[127]

1.64   There are other exceptions to the right of access including documents which are legally privileged (ie confidential documents between the employer and legal advisers), and information revealing the employer's intentions in any situation where s/he is negotiating with the worker.[128] There is no right to data processed for management planning if it would prejudice the conduct of the business, eg confidential plans regarding future staff reorganisations. There is also no right of access to data processed for assessing suitability for a Crown or ministerial appointment.[129]

1.65   There are special rules regarding whether data relating to the worker's health needs to be disclosed if it would be likely to cause serious harm to his/her health or anyone else's.[130]

1.66   It is permitted for employers to disclose information to others in connection with actual or prospective legal proceedings or for establishing legal rights. This can be important, for example, in the context of the questionnaire procedure under the discrimination legislation where employers often use the DPA 1998 as an excuse not to answer.[131]

1.67   Section 35(2) says:

> Personal data are exempt from the non-disclosure provisions where the disclosure is necessary –
> (a) for the purpose of, or in connection with, any legal proceedings (including prospective legal proceedings), or

---

124 DPA 1998 s7(4)(5).
125 DPA 1998 s7(6)
126 DPA 1998 Sch 7.
127 See '*Data Protection Good Practice Note: Subject access and employment references*' on www.ico.gov.uk
128 DPA 1998 Sch 7.
129 Data Protection (Crown Appointments) Order 2000 SI No 416.
130 Data Protection (Subject Access Modification) (Health) Order 2000 SI No 413.
131 See para 21.10 on this.

(b) for the purpose of obtaining legal advice, or is otherwise necessary for
the purpose of establishing, exercising or defending legal rights.

1.68   With regard to disclosure of sensitive information, this exception is
repeated at paragraph 6 of Schedule 3. Paragraph 9(1) may also be
useful in obtaining access to monitoring results. It says:

> The processing –
> (a) is of sensitive personal data consisting of information as to racial or
>   ethnic origin,
> (b) is necessary for the purpose of identifying or keeping under review
>   the existence or absence of equality of opportunity or treatment between
>   persons of different racial or ethnic origins, with a view to enabling such
>   equality to be promoted or maintained, and
> (c) is carried out with appropriate safeguards for the rights and freedoms
>   of data subjects.

Correcting inaccurate data

1.69   It is contrary to the fourth Data Protection Principle to hold inaccurate
data. If the worker finds that inaccurate data is held on him/herself,
s/he can complain to the Information Commissioner. The Commissioner can serve an enforcement notice requiring the data to be rectified or erased, or that the data be supplemented with a statement of the
true facts.[132] Alternatively, if the worker has suffered resulting damage
and there is a substantial risk of a further breach of the DPA 1998,
s/he can apply to the High Court or county court for an order to rectify
or erase the inaccurate information.[133] The court can also order the
employer to correct the information with any third party to whom the
employer has disclosed it. If the employer was relying on inaccurate
records given to him/herself, the court may simply order that the data
be supplemented by a court approved statement of the true facts.
Compensation can be awarded for any damage suffered by the worker
as a result of a breach of the fourth Data Protection Principle.[134]

Rights in relation to automated decision-making

1.70   If data is automatically processed for evaluating matters such as the
worker's performance, reliability or conduct and solely relied on as a
basis for any decision significantly affecting him/her, the worker is

---

132 DPA 1998 s40. See also paras 1.73–1.74 below.
133 DPA 1998 s14.
134 DPA 1998 s13.

entitled to be told of the logic involved in the decision-taking.[135] In many situations, where an adverse decision is made on this basis, the DPA 1998 gives workers a right to have the decision reconsidered and make representations.[136]

Preventing processing causing damage or distress

1.71 Where a worker believes the employer is processing personal data in a way likely to cause substantial unwarranted damage or distress (not merely irritation or annoyance), s/he can send a 'data subject notice' asking the employer to stop.[137] If that fails, s/he can go to the Information Commissioner or to court.[138] There are a number of exceptions to this right and it will rarely apply.

Criminal records

1.72 As a general rule, employers must not require existing employees or job applicants to supply records of criminal convictions, unless it is in the public interest or required or authorised by law.[139] Where it is proper for employers to know if the worker has a criminal record, they can do so with the worker's consent through the Criminal Records Bureau. For details as to when disclosure is appropriate and how to apply to the Criminal Records Bureau, see Part 1 of the Employment Practices Data Protection Code and the Bureau's website.[140]

Enforcement

1.73 If any of the Data Protection Principles are not complied with, the worker can either go directly to court or approach the Information Commissioner. To ask the Commissioner to investigate, the worker must request an 'assessment' under DPA 1998 s42 as to whether the employer is complying with the DPA 1998. The Commissioner must notify the worker of how he is going about the assessment and the outcome. The Commissioner has power to serve an information notice on the employer requiring information for the investigation and an

---

135 DPA 1998 s7(1)(d).
136 See the exact wording of the complicated DPA 1998 s12.
137 DPA 1998 s10.
138 See enforcement at para 1.73 below.
139 DPA 1998 s56.
140 www.crb.gov.uk

enforcement notice if he finds the employer has contravened the DPA 1998. The enforcement notice can require the employer to take or stop taking specified steps or to refrain from processing certain data. However, the Commissioner is not obliged to take action on each occasion he believes there has been a breach of the DPA 1998, and he says he will only do so if he considers it is a serious contravention or if it affects a large number of people and is an ongoing breach. The Commissioner has no power to order compensation. The worker can also go to the High Court or a county court if any of his/her rights under the DPA 1998 are breached and claim compensation if, as a result, s/he has suffered any damage, or damage plus distress.[141]

1.74   There is a notification scheme and register under the DPA 1998 on which employers should have registered. With a few exceptions, it is generally an offence to process data if the employer is not registered. For a small fee, members of the public can get a copy of the data entries, which should include details of what sort of data the employer holds, its purposes and to whom it may be disclosed.[142]

Monitoring at work

1.75   Some employers may monitor their workers, eg by CCTV, by opening e-mails, examining logs of internet websites visited, checking telephone logs for calls to premium lines, and even arranging video evidence outside the workplace to check whether a worker is genuinely sick. It is potentially a breach of the first data principle in the DPA 1998[143] to carry out this monitoring. In theory it could also breach the Human Rights Act 1998 (see below). However, there does not seem to be an absolute right not to be monitored, especially if the worker has been informed in advance that monitoring will take place. Part 3 of the Data Protection Code concerns monitoring at work and provides useful guidelines, although it does not amount to the law in itself. The Code seeks to balance the rights of workers with the needs of employers. Part 3 of the Code and supplementary guidance are available on the Information Commissioner's website.[144]

1.76   The Code stresses that workers have a legitimate expectation to a degree of privacy in the workplace. Monitoring of private information

141 DPA 1998 ss15 and 13.
142 DPA 1998 s19.
143 See para 1.60 above.
144 www.ico.gov.uk

is intrusive and should be avoided if possible. Even a ban on private e-mail and internet use does not in itself allow the employer to access messages that are clearly private. Any monitoring which is carried out should be for a clear purpose and, ideally, justified by an impact assessment. This means the employer should have, formally or informally, weighed up his/her business needs against the adverse impact of monitoring and alternative ways of meeting the needs. Workers should be made aware of the nature, extent and reasons for any monitoring, except in exceptional circumstances where covert monitoring is justified, eg where there are grounds for suspecting criminal activity. The Code notes that continuous video and audio monitoring is particularly intrusive and only justifiable in rare situations, eg where security is a particular issue. Employers should also avoid opening workers' personal e-mails as this is especially intrusive. Workers should be told if their e-mails are to be opened and checked in their absence. If workers are to be monitored on their use of telephones, e-mails and internet, there should be a clear policy as to the permitted use of such systems (eg how much personal use is allowed; what kind of use is prohibited) and the penalties for breaching the policy. For a worker's rights if the DPA 1998 is broken, see para 1.73. Most employers will not like the prospect of the Information Commissioner investigating their data arrangements. A threat by workers to request a Commissioner assessment may be a useful way to persuade an employer to reduce or abandon the idea of monitoring.

1.77   Where employers intercept electronic communications (eg telephone, e-mail, fax, internet), the most relevant additional legislation is the Regulation of Investigatory Powers Act (RIPA) 2000[145] and the Telecommunications (Lawful Business Practice) (Interception of Communications) Regulations 2000.[146] Section E of the Information Commissioner's 'Supplementary Guidance' (above) contains a useful explanation of these Regulations, which cover interceptions such as listening in on telephone calls or opening e-mails before they reach the intended recipient. Interception without consent is generally unlawful. The Regulations set out a number of exceptions, such as monitoring (though not recording) communications to see if they are business-related, eg opening an absent workers' e-mails to check if they need dealing with. Employers may also intercept in connection with the

---

145 For limits to RIPA 2000's usefulness in challenging covert surveillance, see *C v (1) The Police (2) Secretary of State for the Home Department* (2007) 823 IDS Brief 11, Investigatory Powers Tribunal 14.11.06.
146 SI No 2699.

operation of a telecommunications service, including their own network, so an IT department could open e-mails to prevent blockages to the system. There have been few claims directly under this legislation because it is so easy for employers to fit into one of the exceptions.

1.78   Article 8 of the European Convention on Human Rights (respect for private and family life) and possibly article 10 (freedom of expression) may provide protection in some circumstances. Interception of calls made on a worker's office telephone without his/her prior knowledge is a breach of the right to privacy.[147] All the legislation mentioned above would need to be interpreted in line with the Convention as far as possible.[148] These principles will also be relevant in an unfair dismissal case where an employee is dismissed for improper use of telephone, e-mail or internet.[149] For the use in ET cases of evidence obtained from covert surveillance, see para 3.20 below. The law on privacy is a developing area and the above is just a brief introduction.

Freedom of information

1.79   The Freedom of Information Act (FIA) 2000 and the Freedom of Information (Scotland) Act (FI(S)A) 2002 came into effect on 1 January 2005. The FIA 2000 applies to public authorities in England, Wales and Northern Ireland, UK government departments, Parliament and the Welsh and Northern Ireland assemblies. The FI(S)A 2002 applies to Scottish public authorities, the Scottish Executive and Scottish Parliament. It is similar to the FIA 2000, but gives slightly better rights.

1.80   Schedule 1 to the FIA 2000 lists the public authorities to which it applies and this list is updated every October. Some authorities are listed by category and others are precisely described. The list includes central and local government, the health sector, the education sector, the Employment Tribunals Service (ETS) and the police. The UK Information Commissioner has produced very useful guidance notes on his website[150] and the Scottish Information Commissioner also has a helpful site[151]. There is also interesting information on the website of the Campaign for Freedom of Information.[152]

---

147 *Halford v United Kingdom* [1997] IRLR 471, ECtHR.
148 See para 3.13.
149 See para 7.67.
150 www.ico.gov.uk/what_we_cover/freedom_of_information/guidance.aspx
151 www.itspublicknowledge.info/home/ScottishInformationCommissioner.asp
152 www.cfoi.org.uk

1.81   Under FIA 2000 s19, all public authorities must produce a publication scheme, which sets out what kinds of information the public authority will proactively make available, how it can be accessed and the cost. Very often these schemes are published on the authorities' websites. The scheme must be approved by the Information Commissioner.

1.82   A member of the public can request any information held by the public authority,[153] whether or not it appears on the published scheme. 'Information' is wider than 'data' covered by the DPA 1998. It covers information which is recorded in any form, including paper records, handwritten notes, computer information and information on audio cassettes and videos. Information which is purely in the knowledge of the authority but unrecorded is not covered.

1.83   A request should be in writing, state clearly what information is required, and state the name of the applicant and an address for correspondence.[154] The request should be sent to someone appropriate, eg the authority's Freedom of Information Officer, if it has one, or the chief executive. The authority must respond as soon as possible and no later than 20 working days after receiving the request.[155] The response must either provide the information or explain why it has not been provided, quoting an exemption under the FIA 2000.

1.84   There are two categories of exempt information: information which is absolutely exempt and information which is exempt if the authority can prove the public interest in keeping it exempt is greater than the public interest in its disclosure. Absolute exemptions include information contained only in court documents, personal data about the applicant (because there is a right of access under the DPA 1998) or about another individual, if disclosure would breach the DPA 1998, and information whose disclosure would be a breach of confidence at common law. Public interest exemptions include information covered by legal professional privilege and information whose disclosure is likely to prejudice commercial interests. It is advisable to look at the full list of exemptions before making a request.[156]

1.85   The authority may charge a fee of £25 per hour, but it cannot charge (except for photocopying and post) for requests costing less than £450 to answer (£600 for requests to central government). If it costs more than these figures to search out the information, the authority can

---

153 FIA 2000 s1 gives the general right of access.
154 FIA 2000 s8.
155 FIA 2000 s10.
156 FIA 2000 Pt II.

either charge or refuse to supply the information altogether.[157] In Scotland, the maximum fee is £15/hour with no charge at all for the first £100 and thereafter only 10 per cent of charges over £100 and up to £600.

1.86   If a request is refused, it is possible to apply for an internal review of the decision (reviews are compulsory only in Scotland). If the review also fails, the Information Commissioner can be asked to review the decision.

1.87   Workers or trade unions may be able to use Freedom of Information requests to get information from public authorities which they cannot get in any other way. There is a guide to making Freedom of Information requests in the context of employment discrimination cases on the Equality and Human Rights Website.[158] The FIA 2000 does not place restrictions on how the information supplied under it may be used, although certain types of confidential information may be exempt from disclosure. However, if the information sought by the worker concerns him/herself, s/he must apply under the DPA 1998, which involves a different procedure.[159]

---

157 FIA 2000 s12.

158 *Using the Data Protection Act and Freedom of Information Act in Employment Discrimination Cases,* by Tamara Lewis, bibliography Appendix F, at www.equalityhumanrights.com/uploaded_files/dpa_and_foi_in_ employment_discrim_cases.doc

159 See para 1.61.

CHAPTER 2

Collective consultation and trade union rights

Chapter 2: Key points

- It is unlawful to subject a worker to a detriment including dismissal for joining or not joining a trade union or participating in trade union activities in various ways.
- A worker must not be offered an inducement to join or not join a trade union or to surrender trade union rights.
- Trade union officials, learning representatives and members are entitled to time off for trade union duties or activities in strictly defined circumstances.
- An employer must inform and consult the trade union or, if none, employee representatives, when proposing to make redundant or substantially change the terms and conditions of 20 or more employees.
- An employer must inform and consult the trade union or, if none, employee representatives, prior to a transfer of an undertaking.
- The Information and Consultation of Employees Regulations cover wider areas of consultation with employees.
- Under these Regulations, employers with at least 50 employees must set up an information and consultation mechanism if requested by 10 per cent of employees. The employees can choose their negotiating representatives and then their information and consultation representatives, who need not be trade union representatives.

Inducements related to trade union membership

2.1 It is unlawful for an employer to make a worker an offer for the purpose of inducing him/her to become or not to become a trade union member, or not to take part in trade union activities or, as a trade union member, not to use its services at an appropriate time.[1] This includes a member consenting to a trade union raising a matter on his/her behalf. It is also unlawful for the employer to make offers which, if accepted, would mean that the worker's terms of employment, or any of those terms, will no longer be determined by collective agreement negotiated on behalf of the union.[2]

2.2 Before the introduction of this legislation, the House of Lords had said it was lawful for an employer to offer pay increases only to staff who

1 Trade Union and Labour Relations (Consolidation) Act (TULR(C)A) 1992 s145A.
2 TULR(C)A 1992 s145B.

agree to sign personal contracts and relinquish their right to union representation in pay negotiations.[3] However, the European Court of Human Rights (ECtHR) said that, by allowing employers to use financial incentives to induce employees to surrender important union rights, the UK was in breach of article 11 of the European Convention on Human Rights.[4] The ECtHR said it is the essence of the right to join a trade union that employees should be free to instruct or permit the union to make representations to their employers or take action in support of their interests on their behalf. If workers are prevented from doing so, their freedom to belong to a union for the protection of their interests becomes illusory. As a result of this case, the government made the above changes to the law in 2004.

Detriment or dismissal for trade union reasons

2.3   It is unlawful for an employer to subject a worker to a detriment including dismissal or to fail to confer a benefit which would otherwise be conferred, because of the worker's refusal to accept an inducement as set out in para 2.1 above. It is also unlawful to subject a worker to a detriment by any act or deliberate failure to act for the purpose of:

- preventing or deterring the worker from being or seeking to become a member of a trade union, or penalising him/her for doing so;[5]
- preventing or deterring the worker from taking part in the activities of a trade union at an appropriate time, or penalising him/her for doing so;[6]
- preventing or deterring the worker from making use of the services of his/her trade union at an appropriate time, or penalising him/her for doing so;[7]
- compelling the worker to become a member of a trade union or a particular trade union.[8]

---

3 *Wilson v Associated Newspapers; Palmer v Associated British Ports* [1995] IRLR 258, HL.
4 *Wilson and National Union of Journalists v United Kingdom; Palmer, Wyeth and National Union of Rail, Maritime and Transport Workers v United Kingdom; Doolan and others v United Kingdom* [2002] IRLR 568, ECtHR.
5 TULR(C)A 1992 s146(1)(a).
6 TULR(C)A 1992 s146(1)(b).
7 TULR(C)A 1992 s146(1)(ba).
8 TULR(C)A 1992 s146(1)(c).

2.4   Where the worker is an employee, it is automatically unfair to dismiss him/her or select him/her for redundancy if the sole or principal reason for dismissal is that the employee:

- was or proposed to become a member of a trade union;[9]
- had taken part in or proposed to take part in the activities of a trade union at an appropriate time;[10]
- had made use of or proposed to make use of his/her trade union's services at an appropriate time, including giving consent to the union to raise a matter on his/her behalf, or the trade union raised a matter on his/her behalf with or without his/her consent;[11]
- had refused to accept an inducement as set out at para 2.1 above.[12]

2.5   There is only protection for activities which the worker did, or services which s/he used, at the 'appropriate time'. Appropriate time is defined as a time which is either outside a worker's working hours or is within hours at a time which, in accordance with arrangements agreed with, or consent given by, the employer, it is permissible for the worker to take part in union activities.[13] Working hours are those hours which the worker is contractually required to be at work. Lunch and tea breaks are usually outside working hours.[14]

2.6   The protection on taking part in the activities of an independent trade union applies even if the union is not recognised. The type of protected activity depends on whether it is a union official or ordinary member claiming the protection. Both officials and members would need to be acting within union rules and approved practices for their role. Depending on their role, protected activities could be recruitment and organisation, acting or being involved in grievances and complaints,[15] meetings and voting, and organising industrial action.[16]

---

9 TULR(C)A 1992 s152(1)(a).

10 TULR(C)A 1992 s152(1)(b).

11 TULR(C)A 1992 s152(1)(ba) and (2B).

12 TULR(C)A 1992 s152(1)(bb).

13 TULR(C)A 1992 ss152(2) and 146(2).

14 *Post Office v Union of Post Office Workers and another* [1974] ICR 378, HL.

15 *Brennan and Ging v Ellward (Lancs) Ltd* [1976] IRLR 378, EAT. See also special rules on the right to representation at para 22.80.

16 *Britool Ltd v Roberts and others* [1993] IRLR 481, EAT. But see *Crowther v British Railways Board* EAT 762/95. See also para 6.77 for health and safety representatives.

Industrial action

2.7   There are special rules regarding whether a worker dismissed while taking industrial action can claim unfair dismissal.[17]

Time off for trade union duties and activities

Officials

2.8   Regard must be had to provisions of the Advisory, Conciliation and Arbitration Service (ACAS) Code of Practice, Time Off for Trade Union Duties and Activities 2003[18] which aims to aid and improve the effectiveness of relationships between employers and trade unions. The Code of Practice may be taken into account by employment tribunals when considering a claim which concerns the subject matter of the Code.[19]

2.9   An employer must allow an employee who is an official of an independent trade union to take paid time off during working hours to carry out his/her union duties.[20] The duties are:[21]

- negotiations connected with collective bargaining matters set out in TULR(C)A 1992 s178(2) in respect of which the union is recognised;
- the performance on behalf of employees of functions related to the collective bargaining matters set out in s178(2) which the employer has agreed may be so performed by the union;
- receipt of information and consultation for collective redundancies or the Transfer of Undertakings (Protection of Employment) Regulations 2006[22] (TUPE Regs 2006).

The matters set out in TULR(C)A 1992 s178(2) include terms and conditions or physical conditions of employment; disciplinary issues; work allocation; trade union membership and facilities; machinery for negotiation, consultation and other procedures. The ACAS Code gives guidance on the scope of these.

---

17 See paras 6.100–6.102.
18 Available from the ACAS website at www.acas.org.uk See also state of play on the draft revised Code (December 2008).
19 TULR(C)A 1992 ss168 and 170.
20 TULR(C)A 1992 ss168–169.
21 TULR(C)A 1992 s168.
22 SI No 246.

2.10   Employers must also allow a trade union official paid time off for industrial relations training[23] relevant to carrying out his/her duties.[24] This training must be approved by the Trades Union Congress (TUC) or by the official's own trade union.[25] The ACAS Code provides further guidance as to the type of training covered.

2.11   The amount of time off for duties or training must be reasonable in all the circumstances. The ACAS Code provides guidance as to what is reasonable and regard must be had to the size of the organisation, the production process, the need to maintain a public service, and safety considerations. The test is objective and requires the balancing of the competing interests of both parties.[26]

2.12   Where time off is given during working hours the employee is entitled to be paid and the employer cannot allow time off if the employee agrees it will not be paid.[27]

2.13   Note also that the Employment Relations Act (ERelA) 1999 entitles a worker, where there is a reasonable request, to be accompanied by a work colleague or trade union official at disciplinary and grievance hearings.[28] The companion must be allowed reasonable paid time off during working hours to attend the hearing.[29] A trade union official must be certified by the union as being capable of acting as a worker's companion.

Members

2.14   An employee who is a member of a recognised independent trade union is entitled to a reasonable amount of unpaid time off to take part in any activities of the union or activities in relation to which s/he is acting as a representative of the union.[30] The ACAS Code gives examples of union activities, eg meeting and voting on the outcome of negotiations with the employer; meeting full-time officials to discuss workplace issues; voting in strike ballots and union elections; representation at the union's annual conference or regional committees. Industrial action is excluded.[31]

23 TULR(C)A 1992 s168.
24 TULR(C)A 1992 s168(2).
25 TULR(C)A 1992 s168(2).
26 *Chloride Silent Power Ltd v Cash* EAT 95/86.
27 *Beecham Group Ltd v Beal* [1983] IRLR 317.
28 ERelA 1999 ss10–15, particularly s10(7). See also paras 22.80–22.83 below.
29 ERelA 1999 s10(6)–(7). See para 22.81.
30 TULR(C)A 1992 s170(1).
31 TULR(C)A 1992 s170(2).

Remedies

2.15   An employee can complain to an employment tribunal (ET) about the failure to permit time off for trade union duties or activities, or, in the case of trade union duties, failure to pay for any time off which is permitted.[32] The claim must be presented within three months of the refusal or failure to pay.[33] Where there has been a failure to give time off the ET can award compensation which it considers just and equitable.[34]

Time off for union learning representatives

2.16   Employees who are members of an independent trade union recognised by the employer can take reasonable paid time off to undertake the duties of a union learning representative, provided the union has given the employer written notice that the employee is a learning representative and has undergone sufficient training for the role.[35] Activities covered include providing information and advice about learning or training matters and analysing needs, promoting the value of training and learning, arranging it and consulting with the employer. Learning representatives are also allowed reasonable paid time off to undergo training relevant to their functions.[36] The ACAS Code[37] gives further guidance.

The statutory duty to consult in respect of collective redundancy dismissals

2.17   Sections 188–198 of TULR(C)A 1992 contain rules regarding consultation with trade union or employee representatives where redundancies of 20 or more employees are proposed. Certain employees are excluded, eg those in Crown employment (working in a government department, etc), the police and army, and those employed on fixed-term contracts of three months or less.[38] Redundancy in this context includes

---

32 TULR(C)A 1992 ss168(4), 170(4) and 169(5).
33 TULR(C)A 1992 s171.
34 TULR(C)A 1992 s172(2).
35 TULR(C)A 1992 ss168A and 170.
36 TULR(C)A 1992 s169.
37 See para 2.8 above.
38 TULR(C)A 1992 ss273, 280, 274 and 282 respectively.

dismissals for any reason not related to the individuals concerned, eg reorganisation or in order to harmonise terms and conditions, as opposed to dismissals for redundancy in the normal sense (as in paras 8.2–8.8 below).[39] Therefore consultation is required where the employer proposes to vary employees' contracts in order to offer new contracts on different terms.[40] It will also be required where the proposal is to redeploy staff following redundancy on substantially different contracts.[41] Non-renewal of fixed-term contracts for redundancy reasons is also covered.[42]

2.18   The relevant sections in TULR(C)A 1992 are intended to implement the Collective Redundancies Directive.[43] In some respects, the wording in the Directive is more generous than that of TULR(C)A 1992. If this becomes crucial, public sector employees may be able to claim directly under the Directive.[44] The Department for Business Innovation & Skills (BIS) has produced guidance, although this has no legal status, entitled Redundancy consultation and notification – Guidance.[45]

2.19   Consultation must take place with the appropriate representatives of any employees who may be affected by the proposed dismissals or by measures taken in connection with those dismissals.[46] This means the representatives of the recognised trade union, or if there is none, correctly elected employee representatives.[47] Affected employees could include employees who are not going to be made redundant, but may experience a change in their working conditions as a result of the redundancies. There are rules covering the position where there is no trade union and employee representatives have not been elected.[48]

2.20   The duty arises when an employer is proposing to dismiss as redundant 20 or more employees at one establishment within a period of 90 days or less.[49] Volunteers who were selected for redundancy can be

39 TULR(C)A 1992 s195(1); *GMB v Man Truck & Bus UK Ltd* [2000] IRLR 636, EAT.

40 *GMB v Man Truck & Bus UK Ltd* [2000] IRLR 636, EAT; *TGWU v Manchester Airport plc* (2005) 755 IRLB 16, EAT.

41 *Hardy v Tourism South East* [2005] IRLR 242, EAT.

42 Under TULR(C)A 1992, though not necessarily under EU law.

43 98/59/EC consolidating previous Directives.

44 See paras 3.8–3.11 for more detail.

45 Available at www.berr.gov.uk/employment/employment-legislation/employ-ment-guidance/page13852.html

46 TULR(C)A 1992 s188(1).

47 TULR(C)A 1992 ss188(1B) and 188A(1).

48 See TULR(C)A 1992 ss188, 188A and 189.

49 TULR(C)A 1992 s188(1).

counted in.[50] Legally it is not clear what an 'establishment' is. Employers sometimes try to avoid their consultation obligations by claiming that the employees are spread across several establishments, arguing that different buildings, departments or even floors are separate establishments. Unfortunately the test case before the European Court of Justice (ECJ) on the meaning of 'establishment' involved Danish law, where defining 'establishment' as a small unit, produced a result that encouraged consultation.[51] In that case, the ECJ said that 'establishment', albeit depending on the circumstances, meant the unit to which employees were assigned to carry out their duties, and the unit need not have independent management. Following this decision, the Employment Appeal Tribunal (EAT) decided that separate branch offices of an insurance company, which constituted separate costs centres with staff assigned to each of them, were separate establishments.[52] Arguably cases under TULR(C)A 1992, which is worded differently to Danish law, need not be decided in this restrictive way; each case should be looked at on its facts and tribunals are likely to make findings which encourage consultation.[53] Relevant factors to consider are geographical separation, permanence, exclusivity of employees, managerial and administrative independence. Centralised decision-making is likely to be the most important factor. In a more positive case, a nationwide sales team was considered one establishment, even though the individual employees were located at various sites around the country.[54]

2.21   Under TULR(C)A 1992, consultation must begin in good time and in any event, where the employer is 'proposing' to dismiss 100 or more employees, at least 90 days before the first dismissals take effect; where the employer is proposing to dismiss at least 20 but fewer than 100 employees, then at least 30 days before.[55] A dismissal takes effect in this context when notice is given.[56] Unlike TULR(C)A 1992, under the directive, consultation should start when the employer is 'contemplating' collective redundancies.[57] This suggests an earlier stage, ie

---

50 *Optare Group Ltd v Transport and General Workers Union* UKEAT/0143/07; [2007] IRLR 931, EAT.

51 *Rockfon A/S v Special arbejderforbunet i Danmark, acting for Nielsen and others* [1996] IRLR 168, ECJ.

52 *MSF v Refuge Assurance plc and another* [2002] IRLR 324, EAT.

53 The earlier case of *Barratt Developments (Bradford) Ltd v UCATT* [1977] IRLR 403, EAT is preferable.

54 *Mills and Allen Ltd v Bulwich* (2000) 670 IDS Brief 8, EAT.

55 TULR(C)A s188(1A).

56 *Junk v Kühnel* [2005] IRLR 310, ECJ.

57 Collective Redundancies Directive 98/59/EC article 2(1).

when the employer first envisages the possibility of redundancies and has some sort of optional plan, as opposed to a later stage when the employer has a specific proposal.[58] Moreover, under the directive the consultation must be completed before notice of any dismissal is given.[59] Where dismissals will inevitably arise from a workplace closure, there should be consultation over the decision to close.[60]

2.22   Consultation is supposed to be with a view to reaching agreement.[61] This means negotiation.[62] It is strongly arguable that for meaningful consultation to take place, it should start as early as possible. However, employers do not need to consult on the economic decisions forming the background to redundancies, eg decisions to close certain branches of a chain.[63]

2.23   Consultation must at least cover ways of avoiding or reducing the numbers of dismissals and mitigating the consequences of the dismissals.[64] To be meaningful, it should take place when the proposals are still at a formative stage; the representatives must have sufficient information and adequate time in which to respond; and the employer must give conscientious consideration to the response.[65] However, the employer cannot be forced to agree with the representatives or change any plans.

2.24   For the purposes of consultation, the employer must disclose in writing to the representatives: the reason for the redundancy proposals, the numbers and descriptions of the workers whom it is proposed to dismiss as redundant, the total number of workers employed at the establishment in question, the proposed method of selection, the manner in which the dismissals are to be carried out and the proposed method of calculating the redundancy payments.[66] Where there is no trade union and the employees have failed to elect representatives

---

58 *MSF v Refuge Assurance plc* [2002] IRLR 324; *Scotch Premier Meat Ltd v Burns* [2000] IRLR 639, EAT.

59 *Junk v Kühnel* [2005] IRLR 310, ECJ.

60 *UK Coal Mining Ltd v National Union of Mineworkers (Northumberland Area) and another* UKEAT/0397/06 and 0141/07; [2008] IRLR 4, EAT.

61 TULR(C)A 1992 s188(2).

62 *Junk v Kühnel* [2005] IRLR 310, ECJ.

63 *Securicor Omega Express Ltd v GMB* [2004] IRLR 9, EAT.

64 TULR(C)A 1992 s188(2); *Middlesbrough BC v TGWU and another* [2002] IRLR 332, EAT.

65 *R v British Coal Corporation and Secretary of State for Trade and Industry ex p Price* [1994] IRLR 72, CS; *Middlesbrough BC v TGWU and another* [2002] IRLR 332, EAT; *TGWU v Ledbury Preserves (1928) Ltd* [1986] IRLR 492, EAT.

66 TULR(C)A 1992 s188(4).

after being invited to do so, the employer must give each affected employee this information.[67]

2.25 The employer must also give the Department for Business Innovation & Skills (BIS) written notification of his/her proposal to make 20 or more employees redundant at least 30 days before, and 100 or more employees redundant at least 90 days before. The employer must give copies of the notice to the trade union or employee representatives.[68] Failure to notify is a criminal offence.

2.26 Employers are excused from the duty to consult or provide information only in special circumstances, eg a very sudden disaster. However, tribunals are unlikely to consider it special circumstances where there have been financial difficulties over a long period, or where redundancies would seem to be inevitable. Even if special circumstances exist, the employer must still do as much as is reasonably practicable.[69]

Collective consultation on business transfers

2.27 The employer's duty to consult on a transfer is similar, although not identical, to the duty to consult on mass redundancies. The EC Business Transfers Directive[70] is implemented by the TUPE Regs 2006.[71]

2.28 The employer of any affected employees must inform and consult either the trade union or, if there is none, with correctly elected employee representatives.[72] If the employees fail to elect any representatives within a reasonable time, the employer must give each affected employee the relevant information.[73] The affected employees may be those of the transferor or transferee, whether or not employed in the undertaking to be transferred, who may be affected in some way by the transfer or measures taken in connection with it.[74]

---

67 TULR(C)A 1992 s188(7B).
68 TULR(C)A 1992 s193.
69 TULR(C)A 1992 s188(7).
70 Now EC Directive 2001/23 consolidating previous directives.
71 See chapter 10 on TUPE Regs 2006 generally.
72 TUPE Regs 2006 regs 13(2) and (3) and 10A.
73 TUPE Regs 2006 reg 13(11); *Howard v Millrise t/a Colourflow (in liquidation) and another* [2005] IRLR 84, EAT.
74 TUPE Regs 2006 reg 13(1).

2.29   The employer must provide the following information long enough before the transfer occurs to enable consultation to take place:[75]

- the fact of the transfer, its approximate date and the reasons for it;
- the legal, economic and social implications of the transfer for the affected employees; the legal implications need not be correct as long as the employer expresses a genuinely held view (though it is unlikely to excuse a complete failure to inform or consult that an employer genuinely believes TUPE does not apply);[76]
- whether the employer envisages taking measures in relation to the affected employees and if so, what these are;
- if the employer is the transferor, s/he must also pass on any measures which the transferee envisages. The transferee must give the transferor this information.[77]

2.30   The obligation to inform is wider than the obligation to consult. There is no obligation on employers to consult with regard to the fact and reasons for the transfer. However, if employers envisage they will take measures in connection with the transfer, they must consult with a view to seeking the representatives' agreement. Employers should consider and reply to any representations made by the representatives, giving reasons if they reject the suggestions.[78] It appears that there is no duty on the transferee to consult with the transferred employees after the transfer, which does seem to undermine the duty to consult.[79]

2.31   As with redundancy consultation, delay or failure to consult can only be justified in special circumstances, which will be hard for the employer to prove.[80]

Remedies for failure to consult on redundancies or transfers

2.32   If the employer fails to inform or consult, the remedy is to complain to an ET. If the appropriate representative is the trade union then the

75 TUPE Regs 2006 reg 13(2).
76 *Royal Mail Group Ltd v Communication Workers Union* UKEAT/0338/08; [2009] IRLR 108, EAT.
77 TUPE Regs 2006 reg 13(2)(d) and 13(4).
78 TUPE Regs 2006 reg 13(6) and (7).
79 *UCATT v AMICUS and others* UKEATS/0007/08 and *AMICUS and others v UCATT and others* UKEATS/0007/08.
80 TUPE Regs 2006 reg 13(9); *Clarks of Hove v Bakers' Union* [1979] 1 All ER 152.

complaint is made by the trade union, and otherwise, by the employees' representative.[81] The remedy is in two stages. The first stage is a declaration that the employer has failed to consult and an ET may award compensation to each affected employee.[82] The second stage applies if the employer fails to pay, in which case the individual employee must apply to an ET.[83] Where there is no trade union, if the employer has failed to take the correct steps in relation to the election of employee representatives, an individual employee can claim compensation.[84]

2.33 Where an ET declares that there has been inadequate consultation on collective redundancies, it can make a protective award, ordering the employer to pay remuneration to individual employees for the protected period. This period starts when the first dismissal takes effect (or the date of the ET award if earlier), and lasts for as long as the ET thinks just and equitable having regard to the seriousness of the employer's default. It cannot exceed 90 days' pay.[85] There are a few circumstances in which an award cannot be made, eg for unreasonably refusing an offer of suitable alternative employment by the employer.[86] The purpose of the award is to ensure consultation takes place, and not to compensate individual workers. In deciding how much to award, the emphasis is therefore on the extent of the employer's failure to consult, whether it was deliberate and whether legal advice was available.[87] It is irrelevant if the employer becomes insolvent.[88] The starting point is to consider the 90-day maximum and to reduce it only if there are appropriate mitigating circumstances.[89] The award is not confined to 30 days simply because the employer was proposing to dismiss fewer than 100 employees.[90]

2.34 Where there is a failure to give information or consult under the TUPE Regs 2006 on information and consultation, an ET can order the employer to pay appropriate compensation to individual employees up to a maximum of 13 weeks' pay for each employee. Again the ET

81 TULR(C)A 1992 s189(2); TUPE Regs 2006 reg 15(1).

82 TULR(C)A 1992 s189(2); TUPE Regs 2006 reg 15(7)–(9).

83 TULR(C)A 1992 s192; TUPE Regs 2006 reg 15(10).

84 TULR(C)A 1992 s189(1)(a); TUPE Regs 2006 reg 15(1)(a).

85 TULR(C)A 1992 ss189(4) and 190.

86 See TULR(C)A 1992, s190(4) and (6) and s191 for the exceptions.

87 *Susie Radin v GMB* [2004] IRLR 400, CA.

88 *Smith and another v Cherry Lewis Ltd (in receivership)* [2005] IRLR 86, EAT.

89 *Susie Radin v GMB* [2004] IRLR 400, CA; *Leicestershire County Council v UNISON* [2006] IRLR 810, CA.

90 *TGWU v Morgan Platts Ltd (in administration)* EAT/646/02; *Hutchins v Permacell Finesse Ltd (in administration)* UKEAT/0350/07.

must take account of the seriousness of the employer's failure.[91] Actual financial loss need not be shown.

The Information and Consultation of Employees Regulations

2.35   The Information and Consultation of Employees Regulations 2004[92] (ICE Regs 2004) came into force on 6 April 2005, to implement the EC Directive on Information and Consultation in the Workplace.[93] The former DTI provided detailed guidance when the regulations came into force,[94] but this does not have legal status. There were two comprehensive guidance notes in Industrial Relations Law Bulletin, issues 758 and 759.[95]

2.36   The ICE Regs 2004 apply to undertakings with 50 or more employees.[96] An undertaking means a public or private undertaking carrying out an economic activity, whether or not operating for gain. It is unclear whether certain parts of the public sector carry out economic as opposed to purely administrative activities. Providers of healthcare services and some educational establishments are probably covered. Central and local government are likely to follow similar rules under internal guidance. According to the DTI (BIS) Guidance, in the case of a company, an undertaking means a separately incorporated legal entity as opposed to a division or business unit.

2.37   Except in unionised workplaces, there will usually be no existing mechanisms for information and consultation to take place. There are two ways under the ICE Regs 2004 for starting negotiations to set up such mechanisms. Either the employer voluntarily starts negotiations to set up an ICE agreement[97] or 10 per cent of the employees (subject to a minimum of 15 and maximum of 2,500) put in a written request for an agreement.[98] In the latter case, the employer must start

---

91 TUPE Regs 2006 reg 16(3).

92 SI No 3426.

93 No 2002/14.

94 Available at www.berr.gov.uk/files/file25934.pdf There is also a large amount of current guidance accessible via
www.berr.gov.uk/whatwedo/employment/employment-legislation/ice/index.html

95 April 2005. Published by IRS (Tel: 020 7400 2500).

96 ICE Regs 2004 reg 3.

97 ICE Regs 2004 reg 11.

98 ICE Regs 2004 reg 7.

negotiations within three months with negotiating representatives.[99] Where there is a valid pre-existing agreement,[100] eg a trade union collective agreement which satisfies the conditions, the employer has the option of balloting the workforce as to whether they endorse the request for a new ICE agreement, or – in effect – would prefer to leave things as they are. Even if the workforce votes for a new ICE agreement, any collective agreement would remain in force for other purposes.

2.38   When there is no approved pre-existing agreement, a new one must be negotiated. The employer must make arrangements for all employees to take part in the election or appointment of their negotiating representatives.[101] Any number of representatives may be chosen, but there must be enough of them to represent all the employees from different parts of the undertaking and different sections of the workforce. Where there is a recognised trade union, the union representatives may or may not be selected as the negotiating representatives.

2.39   Negotiations to set up an ICE agreement may take up to six months or longer if agreed, and should be conducted in a co-operative spirit. The eventual agreement must meet the minimum requirements set out in ICE Regs 2004 reg 16(1). It must provide for the appointment or election of information and consultation representatives (ICE representatives), or for information and consultation to be carried out directly with the employees, or both. The ICE representatives need not be the same people as the negotiating representatives. They must be elected in a ballot organised by the employer in accordance with the rules. The number of representatives is proportional to the number of employees – one per 50 employees or part, but no fewer than two or more than 25.[102]

2.40   The negotiated agreement must set out the circumstances in which employers will inform and consult their employees. The subject matter, method, frequency and timing of information and consultation should be agreed. If no agreement is reached or if the employer fails to initiate negotiations altogether, the standard ICE procedures apply by default. Under these, the employer must give information on:

1) the recent and probable development of the undertaking's activities and economic situation;

---

99 ICE Regs 2004 reg 14(3).
100 Meeting the requirements of ICE Regs 2004 reg 8(1); *Stewart v Moray Council* [2006] IRLR 592, EAT.
101 ICE Regs 2004 reg 14.
102 ICE Regs 2004 reg 19.

2) the situation, structure and probable development of employment within the undertaking and any anticipatory measures envisaged, particularly where there is a threat to employment within the undertaking; and

3) decisions likely to lead to substantial changes in work organisation or in contractual relations.

2.41   The information must be given at an appropriate time to enable the representatives to conduct an adequate study and to prepare for consultation on categories 2 and 3. The DTI Guidance at paragraph 55 expands on what kind of information should be provided under these categories. Employers can insist that representatives do not pass on information to anyone else, or can withhold information altogether on grounds of confidentiality.[103] This covers price-sensitive or other information which would seriously harm the functioning of the undertaking or be prejudicial to it.

2.42   Category 3 includes decisions on collective redundancies and business transfers. Employers need not consult on these matters under the ICE Regs 2004 if they notify the ICE representatives on a case-by-case basis that they will be consulting under the legislation specific to those matters.[104] Similarly, consultation over certain changes to pension schemes should be dealt with under the Occupational and Personal Pension Schemes (Consultation by Employers and Miscellaneous amendment) Regulations 2006.[105]

2.43   The DTI Guidance points out that consultation is more than simply providing information and carrying on regardless. Although ultimately it is for the employer to make decisions, there should be genuine consideration of the views of the ICE representatives and a reasoned response should be given. The employer must meet the representatives with an appropriate level of management – presumably a level capable of changing the decisions under discussion. There is no obligation on the representatives to obtain the employees' views and report back to them, but the DTI says this would be good practice.

2.44   The ICE Regs 2004 do not say how often or when information and consultation must take place. The DTI Guidance says it should be ongoing and regular, not solely on one-off occasions when there is a problem. Ideally the representatives should agree frequency and timing with the employer, but a lot will depend on how and when issues actually arise.[106]

103 ICE Regs 2004 regs 25–26.
104 See paras 2.17–2.34.
105 SI No 349; ICE Regs 2004 reg 17A.
106 See para 61 of the DTI (BIS) Guidance for further guidelines.

2.45   Negotiating and ICE representatives are entitled to reasonable paid time off during working hours to perform their functions.[107] This right does not apply to representatives paid under a pre-existing agreement. It is automatically unfair to dismiss an employee or subject him/her to a detriment for seeking paid time off or performing the functions of a representative (including standing as candidate) or for a number of other reasons connected with these rights.[108]

2.46   The Central Arbitration Committee (CAC) adjudicates on breaches of the general rights in the ICE Regs 2004, eg what amounts to an undertaking; whether the appointment or election of representatives is valid; whether an employer has failed to comply with the terms of a negotiated or default arrangement. A claim can be brought by a relevant applicant, ie an ICE representative or, if none has been elected or appointed, by an employee or an employee's representative.[109] The CAC can make an order requiring the employer to take specified steps within a specific period. The relevant applicant may then apply to the EAT for a penalty notice of up to £75,000.

2.47   The ICE Regs 2004 represented a culture change in the UK, where traditionally worker representation is carried out through trade union recognition. It is still early days and there is a risk that the ICE Regs 2004 undermine trade unions in unionised workplaces by setting up alternative structures. There is a worry that negotiating or ICE representatives who do not have trade union experience will not be sufficiently experienced or supported to negotiate effectively.

107 ICE Regs 2004 regs 27–29.
108 ICE Regs 2004 regs 30 and 32.
109 ICE Regs 2004 reg 22.

European law and human rights

Chapter 3: Key points

- EU law has greatly influenced certain areas of employment law, eg TUPE, collective consultation, equal pay, pregnancy rights and discrimination.
- Member states must usually pass legislation to implement EU Directives into domestic law.
- If member states inadequately implement an EU Directive, public sector employees may be able to rely on the Directive directly where it gives better rights.
- Where EU law applies, cases are sometimes referred to the European Court of Justice to lay down guidelines.
- The Human Rights Act 1998 incorporates articles of the European Convention on Human Rights into domestic law where possible.
- Employment tribunals and courts must take account of applicable Convention rights.
- The Human Rights Act 1998 has not made great impact on employment cases because most of the Convention articles are subject to qualifications and exceptions.
- Article 6, the right to a fair hearing, has had the most impact.
- Under article 14, there must be no discrimination on any ground in any of the Convention rights, but there is no free-standing right not to be discriminated against.

European law

3.1   The law of the European Union (EU) has become increasingly influential in the employment field, most obviously in the fields of discrimination, transfers of undertakings and health and safety. The following is only a brief and simplified outline of the basic principles as to how individuals in member states including the UK may rely on legislation and case-law from the EU.[1] It is an extremely complex area.

3.2   The advantage of EU law is that its ambit is often wider than the equivalent UK legislation. Wherever possible, UK legislation should be interpreted consistently with any relevant EU Directive.[2] Arguably this

---

1 See also the relevant subject areas.

2 *Pickstone v Freemans* [1988] IRLR 357; [1988] ICR 697, HL; *Litster v Forth Dry Dock and Engineering Co* [1989] IRLR 161; [1989] ICR 341, HL; *Finnegan v Clowney Youth Training Programme* [1990] IRLR 299, HL; *Marleasing SA v La Commercial Internacional de Alimentacion SA* [1992] 1 CMLR 305, ECJ; *Webb v EMO Air Cargo (UK) Ltd* [1993] IRLR 27, HL.

may go as far as implying extra words into the national legislation, provided these are consistent with the scheme of the legislation and not explicitly contradicted.[3] Where there is an irreconcilable conflict between UK and EU law, the latter can be applied to individual cases in the employment tribunal (ET) only in the limited circumstances described below.

3.3   Where a question arises as to the interpretation or applicability of EU law, any UK court or tribunal can ask the European Court of Justice (ECJ) to give a preliminary ruling. UK courts and tribunals can choose to interpret EU law themselves, but where there is no further route of appeal, ie beyond the House of Lords, the case must be referred to the ECJ. The referring court/tribunal asks the ECJ a series of questions relevant to the principles in its case. The ECJ's judgment takes the form of answers to those questions. The ECJ then sends the matter back to the referring court/tribunal for it to apply the guidelines to the facts of the particular case. Before it reaches a decision, the ECJ seeks an opinion from an Advocate General. The opinion tends to get published before the final judgment and is usually, but not always, followed by the ECJ. There is now a large body of ECJ case-law developed from cases referred by the various member states, in areas such as equal pay, pregnancy and transfers of undertakings.

The Treaty of Rome and its articles

3.4   The European Economic Community (EEC)[4] was established by the Treaty of Rome and it is this Treaty which provides the original basis for the establishment of employment rights. On 1 May 1999, the Treaty of Amsterdam came into force, renumbering the articles of the Treaty of Rome and making other amendments.

3.5   On the whole, the Treaties impose obligations on member states which are enforceable only by other member states. However, some key articles are 'directly applicable' and have 'horizontal direct effect'. This means they can be used in claims brought by individual citizens of the member states, even though they may not have been implemented by the relevant member state. If necessary, such articles override conflicting national law.

3.6   Under the Treaty of Rome, the articles with direct effect were article 119 requiring men and women to receive equal pay for equal work,

3 Taking principles from a Human Rights Act 1998 case, *Ghaidan v Godin-Mendoza* [2004] 3 All ER 411.
4 Subsequently renamed the EU.

and article 48 prohibiting discrimination in work on grounds of nationality against nationals of other member states.

3.7   The Treaty of Amsterdam amended the Treaty of Rome in a number of ways and renumbered the articles. Most importantly for employment law, article 119 was renumbered as article 141 and expanded to include a reference in the Treaty to equal treatment for the first time. Article 48 was renumbered article 39. There was also a new article 13 to enable the EU to issue directives and take other action to combat discrimination based on sex, racial or ethnic origin, religion or belief, disability, age or sexual orientation. Following this, the EU Council issued two important directives: a directive on equal treatment between persons irrespective of racial or ethnic origin, ('the Race Discrimination Directive'),⁵ and a directive establishing a general framework for equal treatment in employment and occupation ('the General Framework Directive').⁶

Directives

3.8   The European Parliament, together with the Council and the Commission, can make regulations, issue directives and make recommendations.⁷ An increasing number of directives are being issued. Examples of important directives issued over the years are:

- Directive 76/207/EEC on the implementation or the principle of equal treatment for men and women as regards access to employment, vocational training and promotion, and working conditions. This is known as the Equal Treatment Directive.⁸ In 2006 this was consolidated into the Recast Directive.⁹
- Directive 2001/23/EC safeguarding employees' rights on transfers of undertakings, businesses or parts of businesses. This is known as the Business Transfers Directive.¹⁰
- Directive 93/104/EEC concerning certain aspects of the organisation of working time. This is known as the Working Time Directive.¹¹

A member state must implement the contents of a directive into its own national law by a given date. In the years between a directive coming

5 Council Directive 2000/43/EC.
6 Council Directive 2000/78/EC.
7 Treaty of Rome article 249 (formerly article 189).
8 See para 13.8 below.
9 No 2006/54. See para 5.8 below.
10 See para 10.2 below.
11 See para 4.61 below.

into force and the implementation date, the courts and tribunals of the member states must refrain as far as possible from interpreting domestic law in a way which might seriously compromise attainment of the directive's objective after the period for implementation has expired.[12] If a member state fails to implement the directive by the relevant date, the European Commission can bring enforcement proceedings against the defaulting member state. In one UK case, the former Equal Opportunities Commission brought a judicial review to force the government to redraft some of the definitions in the Sex Discrimination Act 1975 so as to comply with the wording in the Equal Treatment Directive.[13] An individual may be able to claim rights given by a directive in an ET, but only if the directive has 'direct effect'.[14] For this, the directive, and the relevant provision, must be clear, precise and allow no exceptions.[15]

3.9   Where a directive has 'vertical direct effect', a worker employed by the state or an 'emanation' of it, can claim against his/her employer the rights given by the directive. This is to prevent the state, in any of its guises, taking advantage of its own failure to comply with EU law. Unfortunately a worker who is not employed by an 'emanation of the state' cannot claim under the directive against his/her employer. It now seems that an ET cannot hear free-standing claims under EU law which are unconnected to a claim under any relevant UK statute.[16] This is important for time-limit purposes,[17] but it may not make much difference in other respects, since an ET can extend the relevant national legislation under which the worker claims or disapply any restrictions, so as to make it compatible with the directive.[18] For example, the Court of Appeal has disapplied the requirement under the Equal Pay Act 1970 to have a male comparator, in a case where a woman was paid less on grounds of pregnancy.[19]

3.10   A worker who is not employed by an emanation of the state may be able to sue the government for compensation in the county court or

---

12 *Adelener and others v Ellinikos Organismos Galaktos* [2006] IRLR 716, ECJ.
13 *Equal Opportunities Commission v Secretary of State for Trade and Industry* [2007] EWHC 483 (Admin); see para 17.102.
14 And if the conditions in the next paragraph apply.
15 *Van Duyn v Home Office* [1975] 3 All ER 190, ECJ.
16 *Biggs v Somerset County Council* [1996] IRLR 203, CA; *Barber v Staffordshire County Council* [1996] IRLR 209, CA.
17 See para 21.32.
18 *R v Secretary of State for Employment ex p EOC* [1994] IRLR 176, HL.
19 *Alabaster v Barclays Bank plc and the Secretary of State for Social Security* (No 2) [2005] IRLR 576, CA; and see para 5.11 below.

High Court (but not the ET) if s/he suffers loss as a direct result of the UK government's failure to implement a directive.[20]

3.11   On the whole, the UK has now implemented most EU directives by national legislation. However, there may still be a few areas where a directive has not been fully implemented. In such cases, it is unsatisfactory that private sector workers may have lesser rights than their public sector colleagues. In the area of discrimination, there are still several legal definitions in the national statutes and regulations which do not match the corresponding definitions in the directives. The government has adopted an unsatisfactory piecemeal approach by amending each piece of legislation only when it is specifically challenged, so that the discrimination statutes no longer read in a uniform way.[21] See chapter 12 for an overview of EC directives in the discrimination field and common principles of implementation.

What is an emanation of the state?

3.12   A useful definition of 'emanation of the state' is in *Foster v British Gas*,[22] where the ECJ said that the Equal Treatment Directive could be used by individuals employed by any body made responsible by the state for providing a public service under the control of the state and which has special powers for that purpose. An 'emanation of the state' includes local government, health authorities,[23] the police,[24] the Post Office and nationalised industries.[25] In some circumstances, privatised industries may remain an 'emanation of the state'. A useful case is *Griffin v South West Water Services Ltd.*[26] In stating that a privatised water

---

20 *Francovich v Italian Republic* [1992] IRLR 84, ECJ; (1) *Brasserie du Pecheur SA v Federal Republic of Germany;* (2) *R v Secretary of State for Transport ex p Factortame Ltd* [1996] IRLR 267, ECJ; *R v HM Treasury ex p British Telecommunications plc* [1996] IRLR 300, ECJ; *Secretary of State for Employment v Mann and others* [1996] IRLR 4, EAT; *Dillenkofer and others v Federal Republic of Germany* [1997] IRLR 60, ECJ; *Potter and others v Secretary of State for Employment* [1997] IRLR 21, CA.

21 As in the redrafting of the definition of harassment under the SDA 1975 – see para 17.102.

22 [1991] IRLR 268, HL.

23 *Marshall v Southampton and South-West Hampshire AHA* [1986] IRLR 140; [1986] ICR 335.

24 *Johnston v Chief Constable of the Royal Ulster Constabulary* [1986] IRLR 263; [1987] ICR 83, ECJ.

25 *Foster v British Gas* [1991] IRLR 268, HL. But see also *Doughty v Rolls-Royce plc* [1992] IRLR 126, CA.

26 [1995] IRLR 15, HC.

company was an emanation of the state, the court emphasised that it is the service, not the body, which needs to be under state control. The Foster case gives indicators as to when an employer may be considered an emanation of the state, but these will not always apply, for example, it is not necessary to be under the control of central government.[27] The governing body of a voluntary aided school can be considered an emanation of the state for these purposes.[28]

The Human Rights Act 1998

3.13   The Human Rights Act (HRA) 1998 was passed in order to incorporate the European Convention on Human Rights[29] into domestic law. It came into force on 2 October 2000. Until incorporation the only redress under the Convention was to claim against the UK in the European Court of Human Rights (ECtHR) in Strasbourg. The Convention was ratified by the Labour Government in 1951 and came into force in 1953.

3.14   The HRA 1998 requires the courts to interpret domestic legislation so far as is possible to give effect to the rights imposed by the articles of the Convention.[30] Where it is not possible to do so, the domestic legislation remains unaltered thereby preserving parliamentary sovereignty. However, Convention rights can generally be enforced directly against public authorities (see below). The Equality and Human Rights Commission (EHRC)[31] has a remit to promote human rights, but no power to take up individual cases.

The articles of the Convention

3.15   The HRA 1998 incorporates articles 2 to 12 and 14 of the Convention, but not article 13.[32] The important articles which are most likely to have an impact in the employment field include article 4 (the right

---

27 *NUT v Governing Body of St Mary's Church of England (Aided) Junior School* [1997] IRLR 242, CA.

28 *NUT v Governing Body of St Mary's Church of England (Aided) Junior School* [1997] IRLR 242, CA.

29 European Convention for the Protection of Human Rights and Fundamental Freedoms 1950 ('the Convention').

30 HRA 1998 s3; *Ghaidan v Godin-Mendoza* [2004] UKHL 30, CA illustrates how this works in practice.

31 See para 12.25.

32 HRA 1998 s1.

not to be held in slavery and to be protected against forced or compulsory labour), article 5 (the right to liberty and security of the person), article 6 (the right to a fair and public hearing within a reasonable period of time), article 8 (the right to respect for private and family life), article 9 (freedom of religion),[33] article 10 (the right to freedom of expression) and article 11 (the right to peaceful assembly and the freedom of association with others).

3.16   Importantly, article 14 declares:

> The enjoyment of the rights and freedoms set forth in this Convention shall be secured without discrimination on any ground such as sex, race, colour, language, religion, political or other opinion, national or social origin, association with a national minority, property, birth or other status.

There is a defence of objective justification. 'Other status' could include any category, eg sexual orientation, age, education or trade union status. Article 14 does not give a free-standing right not to be discriminated against in any sphere of employment. It only forbids discrimination in areas covered by the other Convention rights. The Council of Europe has adopted Protocol 12 to the Convention, which does give a free-standing right against discrimination. Unfortunately the government is unwilling to sign and ratify the protocol on grounds that it is 'too general and open-ended'.

3.17   Many of the rights and fundamental freedoms under the Convention are qualified, ie have exceptions. For example, articles 8 to 11 may be subject to restrictions on a number of grounds 'in accordance with the law' which are deemed 'necessary in a democratic society', eg for public safety, for the protection of health or morals, or for the protection of the rights and freedoms of others. There should be a fair balance between protecting individual rights and the interests of the community at large. This is called the principle of 'proportionality'. Unfortunately many cases have failed because of the exceptions.

3.18   Employment cases under the Convention have not been particularly successful so far.[34] Future developments will depend on imaginative lawyers and more flexible courts, but advisers must be careful not to risk costs awards against them by raising far-fetched arguments. Article 6 has proved to be the most useful, in challenging the conduct of court and tribunal processes. This is because 'public authorities' are defined to include courts and tribunals.[35] Article 6 starts by saying: 'In the

33 See paras 17.49-17.73.
34 For a useful round up to April 2005, see 779 IDS Brief 11.
35 HRA 1998 s6(3)(a). See para 3.23 below.

determination of his civil rights and obligations ..., everyone is entitled to a fair and public hearing within a reasonable time by an independent and impartial tribunal established by law.' Article 6 does not usually apply to internal disciplinary hearings, though it may apply to those held by professional bodies which can affect a worker's right to practice or to an internal disciplinary, where the employer's decision would have similar effect, because it would lead to a statutory ban on, or otherwise prevent, future practice.[36] In such exceptional cases, it may be a basis for arguing there is a right to legal representation at the disciplinary hearing. The UK rules on state immunity preventing employees at diplomatic missions from claiming in courts and tribunals apparently do not breach article 6.[37]

3.19   Under article 6, a worker may be able to challenge restrictions on his/her access to bringing or processing a claim, eg the requirement to pay a deposit following a pre-hearing review or the lack of legal aid for complex ET hearings. Refusing adjournments[38] or putting artificial limits in advance on cross-examination time may also be challengeable, as would failing to make necessary adjustments to ensure disabled claimants or those with language difficulties are able to give evidence to the best of their ability. Article 6 has been used successfully to challenge the appearance of bias where an employer's representative at an Employment Appeal Tribunal (EAT) hearing was a part-time judge at the EAT. He had previously chaired a panel where one of the current lay members had also sat as a lay member.[39]

3.20   Article 8 has been used in several reported cases. Article 8(1) states: 'Everyone has the right to respect for his private and family life, his home and his correspondence.' This right is qualified by article 8(2), which allows an exception if it is 'in accordance with the law and is necessary in a democratic society in the interests of national security, public safety or the economic well-being of the country, for the prevention of disorder or crime, for the protection of health or morals, or for the protection of the rights and freedoms of others'. The right to respect for private life includes sexual activity, eg the ECtHR said that

36 See *Tehrani v UK Central Council for Nursing, Midwifery and Health Visiting* [2001] IRLR 208, CS; *Preiss v Genera Dental Council* [2001] IRLR 696, PC; *R v Securities and Futures Authority Ltd and another ex p Fleurose* [2002] IRLR 297, CA; *Kulkarni v Milton Keynes Hospital NHS Trust and the Secretary of State for Health* [2009] EWCA Civ 789; *R on the application of G v the Governors of X School and Y City Council* [2009] EWHC 504 (Admin).

37 *Fogarty v UK* [2002] IRLR 148, ECHR.

38 *Teinaz v L B Wandsworth* [2002] IRLR 721, CA. See also para 20.81.

39 *Lawal v Northern Spirit Ltd* [2003] IRLR 538, HL.

the discharge of lesbians and gay men from the armed forces and investigations into their homosexuality were breaches of article 8.[40] However, where an employee is dismissed for sexual activity in a public place, this does not fall within article 8 because it does not concern privacy.[41] Even where article 8 does apply, it may be a justified interference with employees' privacy to dismiss them if knowledge of their sexual activities has become public and could impair their ability effectively to carry out their duties.[42] Article 8 has also proved useful in connection with the rights of transsexuals to legal recognition of their gender reassignment.[43] Where the employer obtains evidence for an ET case by covert tape-recordings infringing the worker's right to privacy, article 8 may clash with the right to have all the evidence heard so as to have a fair trial under article 6. Similar issues arise where the worker does not want to disclose private medical records. The ET will usually allow the evidence to be used if needed for a fair trial.[44] Considerations under articles 6, 8 and 10, taken together, could have a bearing on whether a tribunal should make a Restricted Reporting Order in a sexual harassment case, where it is desired by one party and not by the other.[45]

3.21   It may be hard to challenge a dress code under article 10, unless it is extremely unreasonable.[46] However, a code which discriminates between men and women in relation to hair length or wearing trousers may breach article 10 taken together with article 14.[47]

3.22   Article 11 is interesting because it covers the right to join trade unions. In one case UNISON unsuccessfully challenged restrictions on the right to strike under UK law.[48] There has been a more successful

---

40 *Smith and Grady v UK* [1999] IRLR 734; 88 EOR 49, ECtHR.

41 *X v Y* [2004] IRLR 625; November 2004 *Legal Action* 21, CA. Activities in a private members club may be considered private in some circumstances: *Pay v United Kingdom* [2009] IRLR 139, ECtHR.

42 *Pay v United Kingdom* [2009] IRLR 139, ECtHR.

43 *Goodwin v UK* [2002] IRLR 664, ECtHR.

44 See *De Keyser Ltd v Wilson* [2001] IRLR 324, EAT; *McGowan v Scottish Water* [2005] IRLR 167, EAT; *XXX v YYY and another* [2004] IRLR 137, EAT; *Jones v University of Warwick* [2003] EWCA Civ 151.

45 See obiter comments in *Tradition Securities & Futures SA and others v Times Newspapers Ltd and others* UKEATPA/1415/08; UKEATPA/1417/08; [2009] IRLR 354, EAT.

46 See *Kara v UK* [1999] EHRLR 232.

47 A case such as *Smith v Safeway plc* may now be decided differently. See para 13.43.

48 *UNISON v UK* [2002] IRLR 497, ECtHR.

case challenging inducements to workers to surrender their right to union representation.[49]

Who can claim under the HRA 1998?

3.23 Under the HRA 1998, it is unlawful for public authorities to behave in a manner contrary to the Convention,[50] except where a public authority is forced to act a certain way because of an Act of Parliament. Workers employed by obvious public authorities such as government departments and local authorities should be able to enforce the Convention rights directly. Workers employed by bodies 'some of whose functions only are of a public nature', eg Railtrack, the BBC or GP practices which have both NHS and private patients, may not be able to claim. This is because only the public functions of such mixed bodies will be covered and the employment relationship may be seen as a private function. A service contracted out by a local authority may no longer be carrying out a public function.[51]

3.24 Workers employed in the private sector alone will be unable to make direct claims. However courts and tribunals must interpret domestic law consistently with the Convention as far as possible. For example, employment tribunals should take account of any relevant Convention rights when deciding unfair dismissal claims. Also, claimants may be able to challenge unfair court or tribunal processes under article 6.[52] ET claimants should mention the HRA 1998 in their claim form if they want to rely on it or have it taken into account.

3.25 A court can award damages against a public authority which will be assessed in accordance with article 41 of the Convention.[53]

---

49 See para 2.2.

50 HRA 1998 s6.

51 *R (on the application of Heather and Callin) v Leonard Cheshire Foundation and HM Attorney General* [2002] EWCA Civ 366; (2002) 5 CCLR 317.

52 See para 3.18 above.

53 HRA 1998 s8(4).

Wages

Pay and protection of wages

continued

Chapter 4: Key points

- Employers are obliged to pay wages to workers who are willing and able to work their contractual hours, even if the workers are not required to do so. Some contracts have an express term allowing the employer to lay off workers when there is no work and without pay, but such a term is unusual and can only be relied on for a short period of time.
- Increasingly, different contract arrangements are made so that employers are not obliged to offer paid hourly work on a regular basis, eg casual work and zero hours contracts.
- Employers are not allowed to make deductions from wages. There are some exceptions, eg where there is a statutory requirement to make deductions (tax and National Insurance), where it is a term of the employment contract, or where the worker has agreed in writing in advance to the deduction.
- Any deduction made without such authority can be recovered by claiming in the employment tribunal under Part II of the Employment Rights Act 1996. This is known as a claim for an 'unlawful' or 'unauthorised' deduction.
- The majority of workers are entitled to the national minimum wage. Failure to pay the minimum wage will entitle the worker to recover the shortfall at current rates. The employer will also be committing a criminal offence and can be fined.
- Under the Working Time Regulations 1998, workers are entitled to limits on the hours worked and rest breaks. They are also entitled to four weeks' paid annual leave plus 1.6 weeks additional annual leave in recognition of bank holidays. Statutory holiday entitlement cannot be substituted by a payment in lieu except on termination of employment.
- When off sick, most workers are entitled to statutory sick pay (SSP). They will not be entitled to full pay unless they have such a right under their contract.
- Workers are entitled to receive itemised pay statements (usually payslips) at or before each pay day.

General guide to useful evidence

- Contract of employment – documents or evidence of verbal or implied terms.
- The payslips, P45, P60.
- The employer's pay and tax records.

Introduction

4.1   The payment of wages, and the intervals at which payments are made, is a matter of agreement between the employer and worker, although there are some statutory restrictions. There must be no discrimination on ground of sex[1] or any other unlawful ground, eg race. There is also a national minimum wage.[2]

4.2   The employer is under a statutory duty to give employees a written statement which includes the scale or the method of calculating wages and the intervals at which wages will be paid, whether weekly or monthly or some other period.[3] The employer is also obliged to give employees written itemised pay statements (usually payslips) at or before the time of payment of wages.[4] The pay statements must set out the gross pay and all deductions made from it. As well as this right to be notified of deductions made, there are restrictions on what kind of deductions employers are allowed to make from wages.[5]

4.3   It is a fundamental term of the employment contract to pay wages and deliberate failure to do so will entitle the employee to claim constructive dismissal.[6] Mere delay in payment due to unexpected events, accounting mistakes or temporary faults in the employer's technology may not be a fundamental breach of contract unless repeated or unexplained.[7] It is also possible to sue for the wages owing, either in the employment tribunal (ET) as an unlawful deduction from pay[8] or as a breach of contract in the civil courts (county court or High Court) or, if the contract has terminated, in the ET.[9]

4.4   Unless the contract explicitly says otherwise, the employee is generally entitled to be paid for his/her contractual hours as long as s/he is ready and willing to work. This is so even if for some reason the employer refuses to allow him/her to come in and work, eg due to work shortage or disciplinary suspension. While the employer's obligation in most work situations is to pay the wages contractually agreed,

1 See chapter 5 for the Equal Pay Act 1970.

2 See paras 4.29–4.45.

3 ERA 1996 s1(4)(a) and (b). See paras 1.24–1.28.

4 ERA 1996 s8. See paras 4.57–4.60 below.

5 See paras 4.5–4.25 below.

6 *Cantor Fitzgerald International v Callaghan* [1999] IRLR 234, CA; and see para 6.35 onwards.

7 *Cantor Fitzgerald International v Callaghan* [1999] IRLR 234, CA.

8 ERA 1996 Pt II.

9 Employment Tribunals Extension of Jurisdiction Orders 1994 SI Nos 1623 and 1624.

there is usually no obligation to supply work.[10] The employee's obligation is to be willing and able to perform his/her contractual duties. The failure to do so entitles the employer to deduct a sum equal to the proportion of the time when the employee was not willing to work.[11] Increasingly, different contract arrangements are made so that employers are not obliged to offer paid hourly work on a regular basis, eg casual work and zero hours contracts.

Deductions from pay

The legal framework

4.5 The Wages Act (WA) 1986 repealed the Truck Acts which gave workers the right to be paid in cash. It also set out certain protection against deductions from wages. The WA 1986 was repealed and re-enacted in the ERA 1996 Pt II.

4.6 Part II of ERA 1996 allows employers, if they satisfy the necessary requirements, to make deductions from the pay of workers. There is no control in respect of the extent of the deduction unless the worker is employed in retailing. Section 13 of ERA 1996 deals with the employer's right to make deductions from a worker's wages. Section 18 of ERA 1996 limits the size of the deduction that can be made from the wages of retail workers for cash shortages and stock deficiencies.[12] However, even the limited protection afforded to retail workers is removed on their final pay day.[13]

Who is covered?

4.7 Part II of ERA 1996 covers most categories of workers and extends the definition of 'worker' beyond the restrictive definition of 'employee' in the unfair dismissal provisions.[14] The definition of 'worker' covers those who have entered into, or work under, a contract of employment and any other contract whereby the individual undertakes to do or perform personally any work or services for another party to the contract whose status is not, by virtue of the contract, that of a client or

---

10 *William Hill Organisation Ltd v Tucker* [1998] IRLR 313; *Collier v Sunday Referee Publishing Co* [1940] 4 All ER 234; [1940] 2 KB 647.
11 *Miles v Wakefield MDC* [1987] IRLR 193, HL.
12 ERA 1996 ss17 and 18.
13 ERA 1996 s22.
14 ERA 1996 s230.

customer of any profession or business undertaking carried on by the individual.[15] A limited power of delegation, eg that the person should arrange a substitute when s/he is ill or on holiday, does not necessarily mean that s/he is not a 'worker'.[16] The definition has included agency workers on the books of an employment agency.[17]

4.8   Part II of ERA 1996 excludes workers who carry on a business or profession where the other party is a client. This would exclude professionals such as solicitors, doctors and dentists, and also sole traders and taxi drivers. Part II also covers Crown employment (civil servants), but not those employed in the armed forces.

Unauthorised deductions from wages

Definition of 'wages'

4.9   For the purpose of ERA 1996 Pt II, 'wages' are given a wide definition, covering 'any sums payable to the worker by his employer in connection with his employment, including any fee, bonus, commission, holiday pay or other emolument referable to his employment',[18] including guarantee payments, statutory sick pay[19] and maternity pay.[20] The courts have held that wages do not include notice pay (unless the worker is working out his/her notice or is treated as doing so).[21] Discretionary and ex gratia payments are wages if there is a reasonable expectation that the worker will receive the payment.[22] The definition includes commission that becomes payable after the termination of the worker's contract, provided that it is in connection with the employment.[23]

4.10   Certain payments are expressly excluded from the definition of wages, eg loans and advances on wages, expenses including a car mileage allowance,[24] pensions, allowances or gratuities in connection with the worker's retirement, redundancy payments and benefits in kind.

---

15 ERA 1996 s230.
16 *James v Redcats (Brands) Ltd* [2007] IRLR 296, EAT.
17 *Allied Medicare Ltd v Westwood* (1996) 568 IRLB 18, EAT.
18 ERA 1996 s27.
19 See para 4.51 for failure to pay SSP.
20 ERA 1996 s27.
21 *Delaney v Staples (t/a Montfort Recruitment)* [1992] IRLR 191, HL.
22 *Kent Management Services Ltd v Butterfield* [1992] IRLR 394, EAT.
23 *Robertson v Blackmore Franks Investment Management Ltd* [1998] IRLR 376, CA.
24 *Southwark LBC v O'Brien* [1996] IRLR 420, EAT.

When deductions can be made

4.11   Part II of ERA 1996 prevents the employer from making any deduction from the wages of workers unless it is:

a) authorised by statute.[25] This enables the employer to deduct from wages the PAYE tax and National Insurance payments as required by law or following an order of a court[26] (maintenance payments, fines, etc);

b) authorised by a 'relevant provision in the contract'. There is no requirement that the term of the contract should be in writing and the term in question can be an implied rather than express term. However, it is necessary for the employer to have notified the worker in writing of the existence of the term before making the deduction;[27] or

c) previously agreed in writing by the worker that the deduction may be made.[28]

4.12   The worker's consent to the contractual agreement or the deduction cannot be retrospective, ie after the worker's conduct or event leading to the deduction.[29] Where the written consent is to make deductions in respect of stock shortages, it must have been given before the shortage arose.[30] Similarly, the employer cannot receive any payment from the worker unless the payment satisfies one of the three conditions above. This prevents the employer recovering payments by demand rather than deduction.

4.13   Even if the above three conditions are absent, the employer is entitled to deduct money:

a) for a statutory purpose to a public authority (eg taxes owing to Her Majesty's Revenue & Customs);

b) as a consequence of a strike or industrial action;[31]

c) for any contractual obligation to pay to a third party (eg union dues);[32]

25 ERA 1996 s13(1)(a).
26 Under the Attachment of Earnings Act 1971.
27 ERA 1996 s13(1)(a) and (2).
28 ERA 1996 s13(1)(b).
29 ERA 1996 s13(5)–(6).
30 *Discount Tobacco and Confectionery Ltd v Williamson* (1993) 475 IRLB 5, EAT.
31 ERA 1996 s14(5).
32 ERA 1996 s14(4).

d) in satisfaction of a court or tribunal order requiring the worker to pay the employer, where the worker has given prior written consent;[33]

e) if the deficiency in payment is attributable to an error of computation. However a conscious decision not to make a payment because the employer believes that there is a contractual right not to make the payment does not amount to an error of computation;[34]

f) in respect of any overpayment of wages and/or expenses.[35]

Overpayments of wages

4.14   Unfortunately, there is a complete bar on bringing a claim for unlawful deductions where the employer's reason for the deduction is to recover an overpayment of wages.[36] This is so even if the employer has miscalculated how much the overpayment is, or is not entitled to the money for other reasons.[37] However, the ET cannot just refuse to hear a claim on the employer's assertion that the deduction is for an overpayment. If the worker disputes there was an overpayment, the ET must listen to the evidence and decide on the facts whether it occurred. This is different from deciding whether the employer was entitled to deduct the pay as a matter of contract,[38] but practically speaking, the ET may end up deciding the whole issue. Assuming the ET refuses to hear the case because ERA 1996 Pt II does not apply, the worker must sue in the civil courts if s/he wants to recover the deducted sum on grounds that the employer was never entitled to it. Alternatively, if the sum is outstanding when his/her employment ends and s/he is an employee, s/he can claim for breach of contract in the employment tribunal.[39] Either way, the worker's claim should be expressed as for his/her unpaid wages and not as for the overpaid sum.

4.15   Very often, the worker accepts the sum was originally overpaid, but has innocently spent the money. Whether the worker will be successful in claiming breach of contract as mentioned above, depends on

---

33 ERA 1996 s14(6).

34 *Yemm v British Steel* [1994] IRLR 117, EAT.

35 ERA 1996 s14(1).

36 ERA 1996 s14(1)(a).

37 *Sunderland Polytechnic v Evans* [1993] IRLR 196, EAT; *SIP Industrial Products Ltd v Swinn* [1994] ICR 473, EAT; both rejecting *Home Office v Ayres* [1992] IRLR 59, EAT.

38 *Gill and others v Ford Motor Company Ltd, Wong and others v BAE Systems Operations Ltd* [2004] IRLR 840, EAT.

39 Watch time limits on this. See also para 4.26.

the following principles. At common law, an employer who overpays a worker by mistake (factual or legal)[40] usually has a good claim to restitution, and is bound to assert this when defending the worker's claim. However, this argument will fail if the worker can prove 'change of position'.[41] The worker must prove that s/he did not realise s/he had been overpaid. To see whether this is credible, it is relevant to look at the size and pattern of the overpayments, how recent they were and whether the payslips were clear. It is also important to show the overpayment was not primarily the worker's fault, eg because s/he gave some misleading information to the employer. Finally, the worker must show s/he has changed his/her position in reliance on the money, eg made purchases s/he would not normally have made. The older but similar argument of estoppel (if still valid) may be more beneficial where the worker changed his/her position only in respect of part of the overpayment. The law in this area is complex and developing fast and the above represents a general summary.

What amounts to a deduction?

4.16 Where the total amount of any wages that are paid by an employer to a worker is less than the total amount of the wages that are properly payable to the worker on that occasion, the amount of the deficiency will be treated as a deduction made by the employer from the worker's wages, even where there is a 100 per cent deduction.[42] Any unauthorised deduction from any of the different types of 'wages' or a non-payment of them,[43] such as the failure to pay statutory sick pay, maternity pay or accrued holiday pay,[44] is recoverable in the ET.

Retail workers

4.17 Those working in retail employment are given additional protection regarding the amount of any deductions on account of cash or stock deficiencies.[45] This assumes the deductions are allowed at all under the general rules above. During the worker's employment, the employer

---

40 *Kleinwort Benson Ltd v Lincoln City Council* [1999] AC 349.

41 *Lipkin Gorman (a firm) v Karpnale Ltd* [1991] 2 AC 548; [1992] 4 All ER 512, HL; *Commerzbank AG v Price* [2003] EWCA Civ 1663; 729 IRLB 5, CA.

42 *Delaney v Staples* [1991] IRLR 112, CA.

43 *Kournavos v J R Masterton and Sons* [1990] IRLR 119, EAT.

44 *Greg May (CF and C) v Dring* [1990] IRLR 19, EAT.

45 ERA 1996 s18.

can deduct no more than 10 per cent of the gross wage due on any given pay day, and can only continue to recover up to 10 per cent in the following weeks until the full sum is recovered. In the final week of employment any amount which remains outstanding can be recovered by the employer.[46] Deductions other than for cash or stock shortages are not subject to this 10 per cent ceiling.

4.18   Also, deductions for cash shortages or stock deficiencies may not be made more than 12 months after the employer discovers, or ought reasonably to have discovered, the shortage.[47] This protection was introduced because of the widespread practice of retail employers of deducting cash and stock deficiencies from wages. The worst employers were garage owners, who would hold workers responsible for unpaid fuel bills which were often in excess of the wages owing, resulting in the worker owing money to the employer for the privilege of working!

4.19   Retail employment means employment which involves the carrying out by the worker of retail transactions directly with members of the public and the collection by the worker of amounts payable in connection with retail transactions such as the sale and supply of goods and services.[48] This definition covers workers in shops, banks, building societies, petrol stations, restaurants (waiters and cashiers), homeworkers, those working on the 'lump' in the building trade, and workers involved in the delivery and sale of produce, such as those who do milk rounds.

Remedies and time limits

4.20   The worker can make a claim to the ET asking for a declaration that the employer has made unauthorised deductions and an order that the employer repay the sums deducted.[49] The ET claim must be made within three months of the date of the deduction or, if the worker has made a payment to the employer, of the date when the payment was made.[50] If a worker leaves and a deduction is made from his/her final pay, the time can be counted from the date of the final payslip or payment, even if that is sent some time after the termination date.[51] Even

46 ERA 1996 s22.

47 See the rule in ERA 1996 s18(2) and (3).

48 ERA 1996 s17.

49 ERA 1996 s23.

50 ERA 1996 s23(2).

51 *Grampian Country Chickens (Rearing) Ltd v David M Paterson* EAT/1358/00; May 2002 *Legal Action* 15, EAT.

so, it is advisable to lodge the claim within three months of the termination date.

4.21 The time limit runs from the latest date on which payment could be made under the contract rather than the actual date of payment.[52] So for example, if commission is due on 1 February but usually paid on 20 January, and the worker wants to claim for an underpayment, the three months runs from 1 February. Again, if given the choice, the worker should play safe and count three months from the earlier date.

4.22 If the employer made a series of deductions, the time limit runs from the last deduction.[53] In this situation, a claim could be made for deductions going back more than three months, eg for an ongoing reduction of wages which has not been agreed.

4.23 The ET can extend the time limit if it was not reasonably practicable for the claim to have been made within the three-month period.[54] The extension provision adopts the same form of words as is used for the unfair dismissal provision and it can be assumed therefore that the worker will experience the same problems with ERA 1996 Pt II claims as with unfair dismissal claims[55] if the time limit is missed.

4.24 Wages owed may be claimed either under ERA 1996 Pt II as a deduction, or as a breach of contract in the county court or High Court or, if the contract has been terminated and the worker is an employee, in the ET. There may be advantages in claiming under Part II even though it seems a more artificial concept, eg as counterclaims may be made against contract claims but not against Part II claims. Also, the employer may have a genuine entitlement to the money, but not to acquire it by helping him/herself out of the pay packet. If that happens and the worker wins his/her Part II claim, the employer loses the right to claim in respect of the same sum in the county court or High Court.[56]

4.25 There is an interesting new power whereby, if the tribunal finds the claim for unlawful deductions is well-founded, it can order the employer to pay financial compensation for any further financial loss attributable to that deduction.[57]

52 *Group 4 NightSpeed Ltd v Gilbert* [1997] IRLR 398, EAT.
53 ERA 1996 s23(3).
54 ERA 1996 s23(4).
55 See paras 20.30–20.32.
56 *Potter v Hunt Contracts Ltd* [1992] IRLR 108, EAT.
57 ERA 1996 s24(2). Applicable to tribunal claims on or after 6 April 2009.

Employment tribunal claim for breach of contract

4.26   Once an employee's employment has ended s/he can bring a claim in the ET for breach of contract, eg for holiday pay, wages owing or notice.[58] The claim must arise or be outstanding on the termination of employment, not a result of later events, eg suing for breach of a compromise agreement made some days after termination.[59] It is not possible to bring contract proceedings in the ET for compensation arising out of personal injury sustained at work, or claims concerning living accommodation or clauses in restraint of trade.[60] There is a three-month time limit from the end of employment for bringing an ET contract claim unless it is not reasonably practicable to do so within that period. Any counterclaim must be made within six weeks of receipt of the claim. There is a maximum ceiling of £25,000 for a claim in the ET.

4.27   Many claims, for example for wages owing (though not for pay in lieu of notice), could alternatively be brought under the ERA 1996 Pt II as an unlawful deduction (see paras 4.20–4.25 regarding time-limits). It is not necessary for the worker to be an employee. Since the employer can counterclaim if an action is commenced for breach of contract in the ET, an unlawful deduction claim will be preferable where there is a choice.

The difference between ET and county or High Court claims

4.28   A contract claim in the county court or High Court differs procedurally from one in an ET in that:

a)   only an employee can bring an ET contract claim and only after his/her employment has ended;

b)   except in Scotland if the criteria are met,[61] there is no entitlement to legal aid or Legal Help for representation in the ET (as opposed to Legal Help for case preparation). But legal aid, subject to means and merits, is available for a claim in the county court or High Court provided it is above the small claims limit (£5,000);

---

58 Employment Tribunals Act 1996 s3; Employment Tribunals (Extension of Jurisdiction) (England and Wales) Order 1994 SI No 1623; SI No 1624 for Scotland.

59 SI No 1623 article 3(c) and *Miller Bros & F P Butler Ltd v Johnston* [2002] IRLR 386, EAT.

60 SI No 1623 articles 3 and 5.

61 Advisers in Scotland should check the exact position.

c) the time limit in the county court or High Court is six years whereas in the ET it must be brought within three months of termination, though in some circumstances the cause of action may have arisen in the previous six years;[62]

d) legal costs will only be awarded against an employee in the ET in limited circumstances,[63] but in the county court or High Court costs will normally be awarded to the party who wins (unless it is a case on the small claims track);

e) interest is payable on an ET award six weeks after the decision. In the county court or High Court interest is assessed as from the date on which the sum was due for payment;

f) if an employee has a claim in excess of £25,000 and makes an ET claim which is capped at £25,000, s/he cannot claim the balance in the county court or High Court because the matter has already been litigated.[64] S/he cannot get round this by expressly 'reserving' his/her right to go to the civil courts afterwards. If the employee realises s/he has made a mistake and withdraws the tribunal claim before it is decided, s/he may be able to start again in the civil courts, as long as the ET does not make an order dismissing the withdrawn claim.[65]

National minimum wage

The legal framework

4.29   The National Minimum Wage Act (NMWA) 1998 introduced for the first time a national minimum wage, although in the past there had been minimum pay for certain vulnerable groups of workers.[66] The law is set out in the NMWA 1998 and the National Minimum Wage Regulations (NMW Regs) 1999.[67] A Low Pay Commission has been established to advise the government on pay rates. Its reports are available on its website.[68] Many commentators feel that the minimum pay rates are set too low and do not do enough to tackle poverty. UNISON

62 SI No 1623 article 7.

63 See para 20.143 onwards.

64 *Fraser v HLMAD Ltd* [2006] IRLR 687, CA.

65 *Verdin v Harrods Ltd* [2006] IRLR 339, EAT; *Sajid v Sussex Muslim Society* [2002] IRLR 113, CA; May 2002 *Legal Action* 14, under the old ET rules of procedure.

66 For example, under the Wages Councils.

67 SI No 584.

68 www.lowpay.gov.uk

has made regular submissions to the Low Pay Commission arguing for a 'living wage'.[69] The TUC has also made submissions.[70] The Department for Business Innovation & Skills (BIS) (formerly BERR) is responsible for guidance about the operation of the regulations and offers useful information and links on its website to Directgov (for employees) and Business Link (for employers).[71] The Directgov guidance includes sample calculations for a variety of scenarios. See also the checklists in appendix A at pp731–733.

Who can claim

4.30   A person qualifies for the minimum wage if s/he is a worker over compulsory school age who works or ordinarily works in the UK.[72] Under the NMWA 1998, 'worker' means anyone working under a contract of employment or any other contract to perform personally any work or services, except to a professional client or business customer.[73] A limited power of delegation, ie allowing someone else to do the work, is not inconsistent with being a worker.[74] Agency workers and homeworkers are included.[75] The definition is the same as that used for several other employment rights, eg under the Working Time Regulations 1998[76] and the Part-time Workers (Prevention of Less Favourable Treatment) Regulations 2000.[77]

4.31   Excluded from an entitlement to a minimum wage are most workers employed on a contract of apprenticeship or participating in certain government training schemes,[78] undergraduates on sandwich courses, those on further education courses interrupted by work experience of

69 Its eleventh submission, 'Crunch time? Why the LPC cannot ignore the 'heat or eat' dilemma': UNISON submission to the Low Pay Commission, October 2008, is at www.unison.org.uk/acrobat/B4521.pdf

70 The TUC has an informative section on its website regarding the minimum wages. Also interesting is iIts evidence to the Low Pay Commission Review 2006 at www.tuc.org.uk/em_research/tuc-12360-f0.pdf

71 www.berr.gov.uk/whatwedo/employment/pay/index.html

72 NMWA 1998 s1.

73 NMWA 1998 s54(3).

74 *James v Redcats (Brands) Ltd* [2007] IRLR 296, EAT. See also cases footnoted to para 4.63.

75 NMWA 1998 ss34 and 35.

76 SI No 1833.

77 SI No 1551.

78 See NMW Regs 1999 reg 12(1)–(7) for details.

no more than one year,[79] au pairs and nannies and companions who are treated as a member of their employer's family with free accommodation and meals,[80] and members of the employer's family who live in his/her home.[81]

Method of calculation and the rates

4.32   The minimum wage is periodically increased, usually every October. Historical rates can be found on the Low Pay Commission's website.[82] For the year starting 1 October 2008, the main adult rate was £5.73 per hour;[83] the hourly rate for those aged 18 to 21 years was £4.77;[84] and the hourly rate for those aged 16 and 17 years (and over compulsory school age[85]) was £3.53.[86] The rates for 16–17 year olds and 18–21 year olds are often referred to as 'development rates'. These are all gross sums. The government has announced that in the year starting 1 October 2009, the adult rate will increase to £5.80, the 18–21 year old rate to £4.83 and the 16–17 year old rate to £3.57.[87] It is intended that from 2010, the adult rate will be extended to include 21 year olds.

4.33   The NMW Regs 1999 are complicated. They set out in detail how to work out whether the minimum wage has been paid. The worker must calculate the hourly rate s/he is actually paid for the relevant pay reference period by dividing the total paid by the number of hours worked.[88] The pay reference period is a calendar month, or if a worker is paid at shorter intervals, that shorter interval.[89] If a worker has earned pay in one reference period, eg for overtime or commission, but it is not paid until the next, for calculation purposes it is taken as paid in the

79 NMW Regs 1999 reg 12(8)–(9A).

80 NMW Regs 1999 reg 2(2)(a).

81 NMW Regs 1999 reg 2(2)(b), (3) and (4).

82 www.lowpay.gov.uk

83 NMW Regs 1999 reg 11; The National Minimum Wage Regulations 1999 (Amendment) Regulations 2008 SI No 1894 reg 3.

84 NMW Regs reg 13(1); The National Minimum Wage Regulations 1999 (Amendment) Regulations 2008 reg 5(a).

85 To work out exact school leaving age, see guidance on the HMRC site at www.hmrc.gov.uk/nmw/

86 NMW Regs 1999 reg 13(1A); The National Minimum Wage Regulations 1999 (Amendment) Regulations 2008 reg 5(b).

87 The National Minimum Wage Regulations 1999 (Amendment) Regulations 2009 – awaiting parliamentary approval at the time of writing.

88 NMW Regs 1999 regs 14 and 30.

89 NMW Regs 1999 reg 10.

initial period. There is an online calculator for the national minimum wage at www.worksmart.org.uk/minwage_calc.php

How much has the worker been paid?

4.34   Unfortunately it is not as simple as looking at the worker's payslip to ascertain the total paid. There are all sorts of payments, bonuses, perks and deductions, which make up a pay packet. The NMW Regs 1999 set out which payments by the employer may and may not be taken into account.[90] For a checklist of the main components and sample calculations, see appendix A pp731–733. For pay periods from 1 October 2009, the total paid cannot include payments by the employer which represents amounts paid by customers by way of service charge, tip, gratuity or cover charge.[91] The total also includes performance allowances, but not other allowances (unless consolidated into pay), eg attendance allowances,[92] or reimbursement of expenses.[93] Benefits in kind, eg free meals or luncheon vouchers, cannot be counted towards the employer's payments.[94] The value of free accommodation including provision of related gas and electricity[95] can only be counted to a limited extent (known as the 'accommodation offset') – £4.46 per day in the year starting 1 October 2008 rising to £4.51 in the first year starting 1 October 2009.[96] If it is a contractual requirement to live in and not a perk of the job, the value of free accommodation may not be set off at all.[97] From 1 October 2007, payments made to or deductions by a local housing authority or registered social landlord in respect of provision

---

90 NMW Regs 1999 regs 30–36.

91 NMW Regs 1999 reg 31(1)(e); *Nerva v R L & G Ltd* [1996] IRLR 461, CA; *Nerva v United Kingdom* [2002] IRLR 815, ECtHR.

92 NMW Regs 1999 reg 31(1)(d)as amended by the National Minimum Wage Regulations 1999 (Amendment) Regulations 2009, awaiting parliamentary approval at the time of writing. Regarding the ownership of service charge, etc see *Laird v A K Stoddart Ltd* (2001) 681 IDS Brief 7; 675 IRLB 15, EAT; *Aviation & Airport Services Ltd v Bellfield and others* (2001) 692 IDS Brief 9, EAT.

93 NMW Regs 1999 reg 32.

94 NMW Regs 1999 reg 9.

95 *Leisure Employment Services Ltd v Commissioners for HM Revenue & Customs* [2007] IRLR 450, CA.

96 NMW Regs 1999 regs 9, 31(1)(i), 36 and 36A; The National Minimum Wage Regulations 1999 (Amendment) Regulations 2009, subject to parliamentary approval.

97 See *Vasquez-Guirado and Vasquez-Howard t/a The Watermeadows Hotel v Wigmore* UKEAT/0033/05, where a hotel worker was required to live in and be on call in the hotel 24 hours a day.

of accommodation are not deducted from the total pay calculation except where the accommodation is provided in connection with the worker's employment with that authority or landlord.[98] Certain deductions made by employers are not counted as deductions in the calculation of the total paid, eg deductions for the repayment of loans or due to an accidental overpayment of wages.[99] Where the worker works overtime hours during the pay reference period, payments above the minimum wage for those hours are not counted.[100]

How many hours have been worked?

4.35 The number of hours which the worker has 'worked' during the pay reference period may not be obvious and it is important that the correct type of work is identified, because it affects the calculation. There are four types of work under the NMW Regs 1999: time work,[101] salaried hours work,[102] output work[103] and unmeasured work.[104] Time work is paid by reference to actual hours worked. Salaried hours work is where a worker is entitled to be paid for an ascertainable number of basic hours in a year by an annual salary which is paid in instalments, usually weekly or monthly; and where there is no entitlement to extra payment except for any performance bonus. Output work is where pay is linked to output but not to time. Unmeasured work means any other work, but particularly work where there are no specified hours and the worker is required to work when needed or when work is available.

4.36 Time on call where a worker must be available at or near the workplace can be counted as hours 'worked' within time work or salaried hours work (except when the worker lives there).[105] For example, a driver is waiting at the employer's premises to start a journey or a worker is called into a factory to help with an urgent order, but there is a delay in the materials being delivered. Both must be paid for their waiting time. But if a duty solicitor is on call at home, awaiting urgent calls from a police station, s/he need not be paid while waiting at

---

98 NMW Regs 1999 regs 33(e) and 35(f).
99 NMW Regs 1999 regs 33 and 35.
100 NMW Regs 1999 reg 31(1)(c).
101 NMW Regs 1999 regs 3 and 15.
102 NMW Regs 1999 regs 4 and 16.
103 NMW Regs 1999 regs 5 and 17.
104 NMW Regs 1999 regs 6 and 18.
105 NMW Regs 1999 regs 15(1) and 16(1).

home. Where a worker is provided with suitable facilities for sleeping at or near the workplace, the time during which s/he is allowed to use those facilities is only counted when s/he is awake for the purpose of working.[106]

4.37　Confusingly, 'on call' time is not the same as normal time work during which a worker is allowed to sleep. In the latter case, a worker must be paid for all the time s/he is at work, whether s/he is asleep or not. It is a question of fact whether a worker is 'on call' waiting to work or actually 'working' throughout. In one case, nurses who operated a telephone answering service from their home at night were considered to be working throughout, even though they could sleep while awaiting calls.[107] In another case, a night-watchman required to be on the employers' premises 14 hours each night to respond to the intruder alarm was working throughout even though he could do what he liked including sleep for most of the time.[108]

4.38　Rest breaks to which the worker is entitled are not counted as time at work.[109] Travelling for work duties, though not to and from work, is usually counted as working hours.[110]

4.39　Output and unmeasured work can cause particular difficulties in assessing the number of hours worked. The rules on calculating output work are particularly complex.[111] Unmeasured work is either paid for as the total number of hours spent by the worker in carrying out his/her contractual duties or by reference to a 'daily average' agreement.[112] This is a written agreement between the worker and the employer made before the pay reference period. It determines the average daily number of hours the worker is likely to spend carrying out his/her contractual duties on days when s/he is available to carry out those duties for the full amount of time contemplated by the contract. It must be a realistic average.

4.40　In some cases it may not be clear whether a worker is doing time work or unmeasured work. This can make a big difference to how many hours should be paid for. Unmeasured work probably covers those such as residential care workers who sleep on the employer's

106 NMW Regs 1999 regs 15(1A) and 16(1A).

107 *British Nursing Association v Inland Revenue (National Minimum Wage Compliance Team)* [2002] IRLR 480, CA.

108 *Scottbridge Construction Ltd v Wright* [2003] IRLR 21, CS.

109 NMW Regs 1999 reg 15(7).

110 NMW Regs 1999 regs 15(2) and (3), 16(2) and (3), 17(1) and 18(1).

111 See NMW Regs 1999 regs 24–26A.

112 NMW Regs 1999 regs 27–29.

premises and are on call around the clock, but may be only actively working for a few hours.[113]

Enforcement

4.41   Employers must keep sufficient records to show whether they are paying the minimum wage.[114] A worker who has reasonable grounds to suspect that s/he may have been underpaid has the right to inspect and copy his/her own records.[115] S/he must give his/her employer a 'production notice' requesting production of the relevant records for a specified period and stating whether s/he intends to bring someone with him/her. The employer must then produce the records on reasonable notice at the workplace or at another reasonable location within 14 days.

4.42   A worker who is paid less than the minimum wage can claim an unlawful deduction in the ET[116] or breach of contract of employment in the county court or High Court. The worker can claim arrears calculated at the current minimum wage rates if these are higher than those applicable at the time the underpayment occurred.[117] Some employers try to reduce one part of a worker's contractual pay package, eg attendance allowances, to subsidise an increase in the basic hourly rate. This would be an unlawful deduction from pay even if the overall pay package remained the same.[118]

4.43   As well as individuals taking cases, enforcement can be carried out by Her Majesty's Revenue & Customs (HMRC). HMRC officers have power to enter premises, inspect records, interview employers and pass information onto workers. They can issue a 'notice of underpayment' if they find underpayment, requiring the employer to pay the arrears within 28 days.[119] Officers must at the same time also serve a penalty notice imposing a fine of 50 per cent of the total due subject to a minimum of £100 and maximum of £5000.[120] The penalty is halved

---

113 For some different examples, see *Walton v Independent Living Organisation Ltd* (2003) 731 IDS Brief 9, CA, and *MacCartney v Oversley House Management* [2006] IRLR 514, EAT.

114 NMW Regs 1999 reg 38.

115 NMWA 1998 s10.

116 See para 4.5 onwards.

117 NMWA s17. This also applies to arrears prior to the amendments to s17 coming into force – Employment Act 2008, s8(8).

18   *Laird v A K Stoddart Ltd* (2001) 681 IDS Brief 7; 675 IRLB 15, EAT and *Aviation & Airport Services Ltd v Bellfield* (2001) 692 IDS Brief 9, EAT.

119 NMWA 1998 s19.

120 NMWA 1998 s19A.

if the employer pays the arrears within 14 days. Employers can appeal against the notice of underpayment or the penalty notice to an ET.[121] If the employer does not comply with a valid notice, the officer may on behalf of the worker present an ET claim for unlawful deductions or a claim for breach of contract in the civil courts.[122] HMRC has a dedicated helpline where workers can register complaints anonymously if they wish.[123] HMRC's policy on enforcement and prosecutions (April 2009) is set out on the BIS (formerly BERR) website.[124]

4.44   It is also a criminal offence not to pay the national minimum wage or not to keep or preserve the prescribed records or to make false records.[125]

4.45   A worker must not be subjected to a detriment including dismissal because s/he is about to qualify for the minimum wage or because s/he takes any action or any action is taken on his/her behalf to secure the minimum wage.[126] If an employee is dismissed, it will be treated as automatically unfair dismissal regardless of his/her length of service.[127] HMRC has no power to assist workers with this type of claim.

Holiday pay

4.46   The Working Time Regulations (WTR) 1998[128] set minimum holiday entitlements for most workers,[129] but it is possible for workers to agree greater holiday entitlements with their employers and these become a contractual right. The worker can take whichever is more favourable in each respect of his/her holiday rights under the contract or WTR.[130] The worker's holiday entitlement must be set out in writing in his/her contract or statement of particulars.[131] See para 4.78 onwards for the general position on holidays including under the WTR 1998.

---

121 NMWA 1998 s19C.
122 NMWA 1998 s19D.
123 Telephone 0845 6000 678, Monday to Friday 9 am to 5 pm.
124 At www.berr.gov.uk/files/file50812.pdf
125 NMWA 1998 s31.
126 NMWA 1998 ss23 and 24.
127 ERA 1996 ss104A and 108(1)(gg).
128 SI No 1833.
129 WTR 1998 reg 13.
130 WTR 1998, reg 17.
131 ERA 1996 s1 and see para 1.24 above.

Sick pay

4.47   The position regarding sick pay entitlement should be in writing, as it is one of the terms and conditions which must be provided in a written contract or statement of particulars.[132] Regardless of the contractual position, if an employee is leaving and off sick during his/her statutory notice period, s/he must usually be paid full pay for that period.[133]

Statutory sick pay

4.48   Employees[134] are entitled to statutory sick pay (SSP) from their employers for a period of up to 28 weeks' sickness absence. Employees on fixed-term contracts are included. Some employees are specifically excluded, including those earning below the lower earnings limit, ie normal (average) gross earnings below £95 per week (in the year beginning 6 April 2009).

4.49   The employee must be incapable of doing his/her work due to a specific disease or bodily or mental disablement, or certified as a carrier of an infectious disease.[135] S/he must have been incapable of work for at least four consecutive days (including days s/he does not normally work). Two periods can be linked together if separated by no more than eight weeks. S/he should be paid for each qualifying day, ie a day on which s/he is contractually required to work but is off sick. However, the first three qualifying days (known as 'waiting days') are unpaid. If s/he is off sick within eight weeks of an earlier period, s/he need not serve the three waiting days again. The entitlement ceases if his/her job comes to an end, although not if the employer dismissed him/her to avoid paying SSP.

4.50   Statutory sick pay is paid at a flat weekly rate – £79.15 is the standard rate in the year beginning 6 April 2009. The daily rate is calculated by dividing the weekly rate by the number of qualifying days in a week.[136] SSP is usually paid through the pay packet in the same way as normal wages.

4.51   Employers can decide how and when they want their employees to notify them of sickness. For entitlement to contractual sick pay, the

132 ERA 1996 s1(4)(d)(ii); and see para 1.24 above.
133 See para 1.39 for the precise rule.
134 As defined by the Social Security Contributions and Benefits Act (SSCBA) 1992 and the Statutory Sick Pay (General) Regulations 1982 SI No 894.
135 SSCBA 1992 s151.
136 The HMRC site has the latest SSP rates and an on-line calculator at www.hmrc.gov.uk/calcs/ssp.htm

employers can, within reason, impose any rule they like. For the SSP element, however, they cannot insist that they are notified personally by the employee, as opposed to by a friend or relative. They cannot insist on being contacted more than once a week. Nor can they insist on a medical certificate for the first seven days. For the initial seven-day period, employees must be allowed to self-certify.

4.52   If employers refuse SSP or intend to stop paying it, they should give a written statement (usually on an SSP1 form) explaining why. Workers who are ineligible for SSP or whose SSP runs out may be able to claim incapacity benefit or income support, depending on a different set of rules. They may also have an independent entitlement to contractual sick pay. Employees can claim unpaid SSP as an unlawful deduction under Part II of the ERA 1996.[137] If the employer disputes the employee's entitlement to SSP or its amount, a ruling should first be obtained from HMRC.[138]

4.53   Statutory sick pay and other benefits are not within the scope of this book and the above is only a broad outline. Where the issue arises, specialist advice should be sought. There are full details of the SSP rates, the entitlement provisions and the remedies available for non-payment in the excellent Welfare Benefits and Tax Credits Handbook, which is published annually by the Child Poverty Action Group. HMRC has useful guidance on its website.[139]

Contractual sick pay

4.54   The SSP provisions are a minimum entitlement when away from work on account of sickness. Many employees are covered by a contractual sick pay scheme which generally makes up the difference between the SSP figure and normal wages for a fixed period of time in any given year. The first three days of sickness are usually also covered. A contractual scheme may have various notification requirements which it is important for the employee to follow, even if some of these will not be valid for the SSP element (see above).

4.55   A contractual sickness procedure is normally set out in writing in the contract of employment. If it is not in writing and was never expressly agreed, it may still be possible to imply a term that the employee is entitled to normal pay for a certain amount of time, eg if

---

137 See para 4.5 onwards.
138 *Taylor Gordon and Co Ltd v Timmons* [2004] IRLR 180, EAT.
139 Guidance for employers at www.hmrc.gov.uk/paye/employees/statutory-pay/ssp-overview.htm

the employee has been fully paid in previous years or if all other staff are paid normally when off sick.[140] In the absence of any express term or this kind of implied term, there is no presumption that employees are entitled to the normal rate of pay when off sick.[141]

4.56   If an employee's contract says payment for sickness absence is conditional on management being satisfied the sickness absence is genuine, it is for the employer to make the decision as long as it is in good faith and not perverse. The employer cannot just decide the absence is not genuine without any specific evidence to that effect and merely because the employer's occupational health service disagrees with the employee's GP as to when the employee will be fit to return.[142] On the other hand, if an employer refuses to allow an employee to return to work once the employee is certified as fit by his/her own doctor, s/he must be paid full wages while remaining at home unless the contract says otherwise.[143]

Itemised pay statements

4.57   Employers are obliged to provide employees with an itemised pay statement at or before each pay day.[144] There is no requirement on the employee to request an itemised pay statement. It is an absolute right.[145] Itemised pay statements must include the gross pay, details of all deductions from the gross pay, and the net pay. If the net pay is paid in different ways, the amount and method of payment of each part of the net pay must also be itemised.[146] If the employer supplies the employee with a written statement of a fixed deduction to be made each pay day (such as the repayment of a season ticket loan), the employer need detail the nature of this deduction only once every 12 months.[147]

4.58   If the employer fails to give an employee an itemised pay statement, or deductions are made which were not notified, the employee can apply to the ET for a declaration to this effect,[148] and ask the ET to

140 See paras 1.3–1.6.
141 *Mears v Safecar Security* [1982] IRLR 183, CA.
142 *Scottish Courage Ltd v Guthrie* UKEAT/0788/03.
143 *Beveridge v KLM UK Ltd* [2000] IRLR 765, EAT.
144 ERA 1996 s8.
145 *Coales v John Woods and Co (Solicitors)* [1986] IRLR 129, EAT.
146 ERA 1996 s8.
147 ERA 1996 s9.
148 ERA 1996 s11.

exercise its discretion to make a compensatory award. The declaration is mandatory, but the compensation award is discretionary. The maximum amount of compensation that can be awarded is calculated by taking the date of application to the ET and determining the amount of the unnotified deductions (tax, National Insurance, union subscriptions, etc) on each of the pay days in the 13 weeks prior to the ET application.[149]

4.59   As ignorance of the law is no defence, employers should be made to pay a compensatory award somewhere near the maximum figure. If the reason why the employer has failed to provide itemised pay statements is due to fraud or dishonest conduct, it is likely that the ET will be more willing to make a high award. The compensation is intended to act as a penalty on the employer for non-compliance and it does not matter whether the employer has accounted for the sums deducted to HMRC and therefore ends up paying twice.[150] The Employment Appeal Tribunal (EAT), in a decision in 1979, allowed a low ET award because the provisions had come into effect only recently and the employer was a busy professional person in sole practice.[151] Twenty years later, the EAT took a stronger position[152] and it is now unusual for employers to get away with such leniency. It is important to stress to the ET that the failure to supply these statements is often indicative of some unlawful practice by the employer: usually the failure to make the appropriate tax and National Insurance returns. It can also cause the employee practical inconvenience.

4.60   Employees who do not get itemised pay statements should check with HMRC to discover whether the employer has been committing a fraud by not paying the requisite tax or National Insurance. If the employer deducted National Insurance contributions but did not pass these on to HMRC, the employee is treated as if the contributions have been paid unless the employee agreed or was negligent.[153]

149 ERA 1996 s12(4).
150 *Cambiero v Aldo Zilli & Sheenwalk Ltd t/a Signor Zilli's Bar* EAT/273/96; May 1998 *Legal Action* 21.
151 *Scott v Creager* [1979] IRLR 162, EAT.
152 *Cambiero v Aldo Zilli & Sheenwalk Ltd t/a Signor Zilli's Bar* EAT/273/96; May 1998 *Legal Action* 21.
153 Social Security (Contributions) Regulations 2001 SI No 1004 reg 60.

Working Time Regulations 1998

The legal framework

4.61   The Working Time Regulations (WTR) 1998[154] came into force on 1 October 1998 in order to implement EC Directives on the organisation of working time[155] and protection of young workers.[156] Directgov has some useful guidance for employees including links to the specialist regulations for air, road and sea workers.[157] This has no legal status and simply represents Directgov's interpretation of the law.

4.62   Apart from opting out of the 48-hour week (see below), it is not possible for individuals to contract out of WTR 1998 rights.[158] However, collective or workforce agreements can modify or exclude certain entitlements as set out below. Schedule 1 to the WTR 1998 sets out specific requirements for an agreement to become a workforce agreement.

4.63   'Working time' under the WTR 1998 means any period during which the worker is working, at his/her employer's disposal and carrying out his/her duties plus any period during which s/he is receiving relevant training.[159] It includes overtime, working lunches and travel on the job, but not to and from work. Time while the worker is on call at or near the workplace, although not at home, is all working time even if the worker can sleep during periods of inactivity; but if the worker need not attend the workplace and merely needs to be contactable at all times, then working time is only for the periods when the worker is actually doing work for the employer.[160]

Who is covered?

4.64   The WTR 1998 give rights to workers. Under the WTR 1998, 'worker' means anyone working under a contract of employment or any other

154 SI No 1833.
155 Directives 93/104/EC and 2000/43/EC.
156 Directives 93/104/EC and 94/33/EC.
157 Available at www.direct.gov.uk/en/Employment/Employees/Working HoursAndTimeOff/index.htm
158 WTR 1998 reg 35.
159 WTR 1998 reg 2.
160 *Sindicato de Médicos de Asistencia Pública (Simap) v Conselleria de Sanidad y Consumo de la Generalidad Valenciana* C-303/98 [2000] IRLR 845, ECJ; *Landeshauptstadt Kiel v Jaeger* (C-151/02) [2003] IRLR 804, ECJ. For an example concerning a residential careworker, see *MacCartney v Oversley House Management* [2006] IRLR 514, EAT.

contract to perform personally any work or services, except to a professional client or business customer.[161] A contractual obligation on a worker to undertake the work him/herself or to find someone else to do so can amount to a contract to 'perform personally'.[162] The definition of a worker is the same as that used for several other employment rights, eg under the National Minimum Wage Act 1998 and the Part-time Workers (Prevention of Less Favourable Treatment) Regulations 2000.[163] Temporary and agency workers are covered by the WTR 1998.[164] 'Young workers', ie those over compulsory school age[165] but under 18, are also covered, sometimes with greater protections.

4.65   Certain categories of seafarers, sea fishermen and workers on vessels in inland waterways are excluded from the WTR 1998.[166] Mobile staff in civil aviation are excluded from virtually all the rights except young worker protection.[167] Workers performing mobile road transport activities are excluded from the limits on working hours and night work and from the entitlements to daily and weekly rest periods and daily rest breaks.[168] However, the Road Transport (Working Time) Regulations 2005[169] lay down a 60-hour maximum working week with an average 48 hours over the reference period, plus minimum breaks and rest periods, for certain mobile road workers, including drivers and crew. The rules for who are covered are complex and the Department of Transport has produced 'Road Transport (Working Time) Guidance'.[170] For any other mobile workers than those described above, there are exclusions on the rest periods and breaks and regarding the length of night working.[171] 'Mobile workers' for these purposes are

---

161 WTR 1998 reg 2(1); *Redrow Homes (Yorkshire) Ltd v Wright; Redrow Homes (North West) Ltd v Roberts and another* EAT/337/02 and 1232/02; *Torith Ltd v Flynn* (2003) 728 IDS Brief 10, EAT; *Byrne Brothers (Formwork) Ltd v Baird and others* [2002] IRLR 96, EAT; *Bacica v Muir* [2006] IRLR 35, EAT; *James v Redcats (Brands) Ltd* [2007] IRLR 296, EAT.

162 *Redrow Homes (Yorkshire) Ltd v Buckborough and Sewell* UKEAT/0528/07; [2009] IRLR 34, EAT.

163 SI No 1551.

164 WTR 1998 reg 36.

165 Broadly, 16 years old, but a little more complicated.

166 WTR 1998 reg 18.

167 WTR 1998 reg 18(2).

168 WTR 1998 reg 18(3).

169 SI No 639.

170 On its website at www.dft.gov.uk/pgr/freight/road/workingtime/ rdtransportworkingtimeguidance?page=3#1004

171 WTR 1998 reg 24A.

defined under reg 2 as members of travelling or flying personnel by an undertaking which operates transport services for passengers or goods by road or air. Rail workers are not covered by these general exclusions, but they are excluded in certain specific circumstances under reg 21 as mentioned below. Non-mobile transport workers are now generally covered. The reason for these various exclusions is that in most cases they are covered by sector-specific EU Directives and have their own domestic legislation, which is similar. For further detail, see WTR 1998 reg 18 and links in the Directgov guidance.[172]

4.66   Domestic servants in private households are excluded from much of the protection, although the entitlement to holidays and rest breaks remains.[173]

4.67   Almost all the protections in the WTR 1998, except for annual leave, do not apply where the worker works on 'unmeasured working time'.[174] It is unclear exactly what 'unmeasured time' means. The exception is intended to apply where, due to the specific nature of the work done, the duration of the worker's working time is not measured or pre-determined, or it can be determined by the worker him/herself. The regulations give examples as managing executives or other persons with autonomous decision-making powers; family workers; or workers officiating in religious ceremonies. The problem is that in many workplaces, there are unspoken expectations or hidden pressures to work extra hours. The exception should not apply if someone works extra hours because of an excessive workload and unrealistic deadlines, or because his/her colleagues habitually work long hours and s/he feels this is what the employer expects. Some employers have attempted to interpret this exception widely but advisers should resist this. High-powered, self-regulating managing directors should probably be covered, but not junior workers who are pressurised by higher management to work limitless unpaid overtime.

The 48-hour week

4.68   Regulation 4(1) of the WTR 1998 imposes a contractual obligation on the employer not to require a worker to work more than an average of 48 hours per week including overtime.[175] The employer also has a duty

---

172 N157 above. Also see the useful feature at (2003) IDS Brief 14. For airline pilots holiday pay, see *British Airways plc v Williams & ors* [2008] ICR 779, EAT.

173 WTR 1998 reg 19.

174 WTR 1998 reg 20(1).

175 *Barber v RJB Mining (UK) Ltd* [1999] IRLR 308, HC.

subject to criminal sanctions to take all reasonable steps to ensure no more than 48 hours per week are worked unless the worker has opted out (see below).[176] The 48 hours is usually averaged over 17 weeks, although for some workers it will be 26 weeks.[177] The 26-week period applies to those workers who are partially excepted from the rest break provisions under WTR 1998 reg 21.[178] A collective or workforce agreement cannot modify or exclude the 48-hour ceiling, but in certain circumstances it can extend the period over which hours are averaged.[179] A 52-hour limit applies to doctors in training from 1 August 2009 until 31 July 2011.[180] Certain days off are excluded from the calculation of hours worked over the reference period, eg days off sick, on maternity, paternity, adoption or parental leave, or taken as part of the first four weeks' annual leave.[181]

4.69   A worker can make a written agreement with his/her employer to exclude (ie 'opt out' of) the 48-hour limit either for a specified period or indefinitely.[182] The worker is entitled to end the agreement without the employer's consent on seven days' written notice or any longer notice period specified in the agreement, but no longer than three months.[183] If the worker is dismissed or suffers a detriment for refusing to enter into such an opt-out agreement or for bringing one to an end, s/he can bring a claim to the ET.[184] For an opt-out to be valid, the worker must have expressly and freely consented to work longer hours.[185] Given the inequality of bargaining power, it is doubtful whether the common practice of presenting a worker with an opt-out form to sign on his/her induction leads to free consent. The government has blocked the European Parliament's attempt to remove the UK's right to allow opt-outs from the 48-hour week. This issue has been the main stumbling block in the development of a revised Working Time Directive after five years of negotiations. In its campaign to scrap the opt-out, the TUC points out that 3.25 million people in the UK exceed the

---

176 WTR 1998 reg 4(2).

177 WTR 1998 reg 4.

178 See para 4.76 below.

179 WTR 1998 reg 23(b).

180 The Working Time (Amendment) Regulations 2009 SI No 1567, set out precisely who is covered.

181 See WTR 1998 reg 4(7) for how an adjustment is made in these circumstances.

182 WTR 1998 regs 4(1) and 5.

183 WTR 1998 reg 5.

184 ERA 1996 ss45A and 101A. See para 4.91.

185 *Pfeiffer & others v Deutsches Rotes Kreuz, Kreisverband Waldshut eV* [2005] IRLR 137, ECJ.

48-hour week, some by only a few hours, but 9 per cent are working 66–98 hours per week.

4.70   If a worker who has been working more than 48 hours decides to exercise the opt-out and reduce his/her hours to 48, an employer can probably reduce his/her pay proportionally, especially if pay is explicitly linked to hours worked.[186]

4.71   Young workers generally must not work more than eight hours each day and 40 hours per week.[187]

Night workers

4.72   Broadly speaking, a night worker is someone who works at least three hours between 11 pm and 6 am on most working days.[188] Night workers must not work on average more than eight hours in each 24-hour period, averaged over 17 weeks.[189] If the work involves special hazards or heavy mental or physical strain, there is an absolute limit of eight hours in any 24-hour period. There are exceptions to this protection for certain types of job.[190] A collective or workforce agreement can modify or exclude these limits.[191] A worker who is put onto night work must be given the opportunity of a free health assessment before starting such work and at regular intervals thereafter.[192] If a registered medical practitioner advises that a worker is suffering from health problems connected with night work, the employer must transfer the worker to suitable work not at night if that is possible. Young workers must not work between 10 pm and 6 am or 11 pm and 7 am except in certain sectors.[193] Mobile workers, if covered at all[194] are excluded from the night work limits but must have adequate rest.[195]

---

186 See the obiter comments in *Clamp v Aerial Systems* [2005] IRLR 9, EAT.
187 WTR 1998 regs 5A, subject to regs 27A, 19, 25, 26.
188 WTR 1998 reg 2.
189 WTR 1998 reg 6.
190 See para 4.76 below.
191 WTR 1998 regs 23 and 24.
192 WTR 1998 reg 7.
193 WTR 1998 regs 6A, 27A, 19, 25 and 26.
194 See paras 4.64–4.65.
195 WTR 1998 reg 24A.

Rest periods

4.73   Employers must allow workers to take certain breaks during their working hours. Some mobile workers (if covered at all) are excluded from the
normal rest break entitlements but they must be given adequate rest.[196]

4.74   Workers are entitled to a minimum daily rest period of 11 consecutive hours.[197] There are special rules for young workers. Workers are
also entitled to a weekly rest period of at least 24 consecutive hours
in any given week, which may be given as two 24-hour breaks or one
48-hour break over a fortnight.[198] There are special rules for young
workers.

4.75   During the day, workers whose working time is more than six
hours are entitled to a rest break of 20 minutes without any interrup-
tion and away from the work station.[199] This means one rest break in
the working day, not a break every six hours.[200] There are special rules
for young workers. A period of 'downtime', where the worker need
not work but must remain in radio contact and at the employer's disposal, is not a rest break. Nor can it retrospectively be designated a
rest break just because the employer happened not to call on the
worker.[201] There is nothing to say when during the day this break must
be given, although the Directgov guidance says it should be taken
during the day and not tagged on to its start or end. There is no requirement under the WTR 1998 that the break must be paid, but there may
be an entitlement for paid breaks under the worker's own contract.
An employer cannot suddenly insert a break during normal paid working hours and deduct pay for that period. There is also a little tested entitlement to 'adequate' rest breaks where the worker's health and safety
is put at risk because of the working pattern, in particular because the
work is monotonous or the work-rate pre-determined.[202]

---

196 WTR 1998 reg 24A, but see para 4.65 above for mobile road workers.
197 WTR 1998 reg 10(1).
198 WTR 1998 reg 11.
199 WTR 1998 reg 12.
200 *Corps of Commissionaires Management Ltd v Hughes* UKEAT/0196/08; [2009]
    IRLR 122, EAT.
201 *Gallagher & others v Alpha Catering Services Ltd (t/a Alpha Flight Services)* [2005]
    IRLR 102, CA.
202 WTR 1998 reg 8.

Exceptions

4.76   Shift workers or workers engaged in activities involving periods of work split up over the day, eg cleaning staff, do not have the entitlement to daily and weekly rest periods, although they are entitled to a period of compensatory rest where possible.[203] The entitlements to daily and weekly rest periods and rest breaks during the day as well as the restrictions on the length of night working[204] do not apply in special areas where continuity of service or production by the worker (as opposed to the employer) may be necessary,[205] eg work in hospitals, prisons, security guards, caretakers, media, gas, water and electricity, urban transport services or refuse collection; or where there is a foreseeable surge of activity, eg in tourism or postal services.[206] A 'surge' means an exceptional level of activity beyond the fluctuations experienced within a working day or week.[207] Nor do they apply to workers on board trains or whose work affects train traffic or time-tables.[208] They also do not apply where there have been unusual and unforeseeable circumstances or exceptional events whose consequences are unavoidable.[209] In all these circumstances, the worker should be given an equivalent period of compensatory rest. The fact that an employer may need to provide a continuous service, eg provision of a security guard, does not mean that it has to be the same worker who is present throughout – someone else could cover on breaks.[210] In exceptional cases, where it is not possible to provide compensatory rest, the employer must afford sufficient protection to safeguard the worker's health and safety.[211] However, under WTR 1998 reg 24A, mobile workers[212] are entitled only to adequate rest.[213]

203 WTR 1998 reg 24.
204 See para 4.72 above.
205 *Gallagher & others v Alpha Catering Services Ltd (t/a Alpha Flight Services)* [2005] IRLR 102, CA.
206 WTR 1998 reg 21(c) and (d).
207 *Gallagher & others v Alpha Catering Services Ltd (t/a Alpha Flight Services)* [2005] IRLR 102, CA.
208 WTR 1998 reg 21(f).
209 WTR 1998 reg 21(e).
210 *Corps of Commissionaires Management Ltd v Hughes* UKEAT/0196/08; [2009] IRLR 122, EAT.
211 WTR 1998 reg 24.
212 Defined in WTR 1998 reg 2.
213 *First Hampshire and Dorset Ltd v Feist and others* UKEAT/0510/06.

4.77   An individual worker cannot opt out of his/her entitlement to rest periods and breaks. However, a collective or workforce agreement can modify or exclude these entitlements provided an equivalent period of compensatory rest is given.[214]

Annual leave and bank holidays

The basic entitlement

4.78   The WTR 1998 give workers the right to a minimum of four weeks' paid annual leave.[215] For example, a worker who works a five-day week is entitled to 20 days' paid leave per year; a part-timer who works three days each week is entitled to 12 days' paid leave per year. If the worker works irregular hours or shifts, the calculation will probably be based on the average number of hours/days worked each week.[216] There is no longer a provision for rounding up the leave entitlement if it does not work out as exact days. If there is no collective or workforce agreement setting the dates of the holiday year and no written agreement between the employer and worker on this point, the leave year starts, for workers employed before 1 October 1998, on 1 October; and for other workers, on the anniversary of the start of their employment.[217] In the worker's first year, s/he can only take holiday which s/he has accrued, in this case rounded up to the nearest half day.[218] For example, a worker works five days per week, so his/her holiday entitlement is 20 days (four weeks) per year. After 16 weeks, s/he can take 6.5 days' holiday. This is calculated as follows: $16 \div 52 \times 20 = 6.15$, which is then rounded up to 6.5. In subsequent years, the worker need not wait until s/he has accrued leave entitlement.

4.79   Leave must be taken in the leave year in which it is due and this entitlement cannot be substituted by payment in lieu of the holiday except on the termination of employment.[219] Under the WTR 1998, untaken holidays cannot be carried over, although the worker may have a contractual entitlement to do this. Untaken basic leave is therefore lost. There is a danger that a worker will be strung along with the employer continually refusing his/her proposed holiday dates until time runs out.

---

214 WTR 1998 regs 23 and 24.
215 WTR 1998 reg 13.
216 See para 4.85 regarding the calculation of pay.
217 WTR 1998 reg 13(3).
218 WTR 1998 reg 15A.
219 WTR 1998 reg 13(9)(b).

Workers in this position should give formal notice to take leave under the WTR 1998. Unfortunately there is nothing in the WTR 1998 which prevents employers specifying when in the year the leave must or must not be taken, or how many days at a time, although the worker may have greater rights under his/her contract. For example, an employer can insist that holidays are taken at an annual Christmas shutdown unless the contract indicates otherwise. The employer must give sufficient notice specifying when the leave must be taken. The notice need not be given in writing. Such notice must be given at least twice as many days in advance of the earliest leave day as the number of days to which the notice relates,[220] eg an employer requiring a worker to take two weeks' holiday at Christmas must give at least four weeks' notice. One confusing issue is where the employer requires a worker to take 'leave' on days which appear to be normal weekly rest days, eg every Saturday is designated a leave day.[221] It would seem obvious that days off can only be 'leave' if they occur on days when the worker would otherwise be required to work and for which s/he is paid to work, but this may not be correct. In one case, where oil rig workers worked two weeks offshore followed by two weeks onshore without work obligations, the tribunal decided that the employer could not designate part of the two weeks off as annual leave, but on appeal this was overturned by a majority of the Scottish EAT.[222] This may mean that shift workers who have several days off between their shifts can have their holidays designated during such days. Less controversially, a school can probably designate time during school holidays as annual leave under the WTR.[223]

4.80   A worker can take leave by giving the correct notice specifying the proposed leave days.[224] It is safer to give such notice in writing, although this is not required under the WTR 1998. The notice must be given twice as many days in advance of the first day proposed for leave as the number of days proposed in total.[225] If the employer objects to leave being taken on those dates, s/he must give counter-notice as many days in advance of the earliest date as the total number of days to

---

220 WTR 1998 reg 15.

221 *Sumsion v BBC (Scotland)* [2007] IRLR 678, EAT.

222 *Craig and others v Transocean International Resources Ltd and others.*

223 See comments of EAT in *Sumsion* [2007] IRLR 678, EAT; and *Transocean* UKEATS/0029-30/08; [2009] IRLR 519, EAT.

224 WTR 1998 reg 15.

225 WTR 1998 reg 15(1), (3) and (4).

which the worker's notice relates.[226] For example, a worker wanting to take three days' leave must give at least six days' notice. Employers wishing to refuse that leave must give at least three days' counternotice. Note that workers and employers may have agreed a different notification procedure by a relevant agreement under the rules, eg in a collective agreement or the worker's written contract.[227] This can include setting annual holiday dates in the contract or including a contractual term saying an employee who is leaving can be required to take holidays during his/her notice period.[228] Under the WTR 1998, the employer does not need to have a good reason for refusing leave at any particular time.

4.81   A worker does not lose his/her right to take annual leave because s/he has been off sick throughout the holiday year or through the last part of the holiday year, when s/he has not yet taken his/her full leave entitlement. The employer can refuse to allow a worker to take paid annual leave while on sick leave, but the worker must then be allowed to take the leave at some other time (ie carry it over). If s/he cannot ever take the annual leave because s/he leaves the employment in a future holiday year without ever having returned to work, s/he must be paid in lieu for the whole period.[229] Though strictly-speaking it is untested, it is highly probable that a woman accrues her holiday entitlement while she is absent on maternity leave, even if this is throughout the holiday year. Certainly, she is entitled to take any accrued leave under the Working Time Directive during a period other than the period of her maternity leave.[230] If necessary, it can be carried over to the next holiday year, but not paid in lieu (except if she leaves).[231] See paras 11.53–11.55 and 11.58–11.64 regarding the rights of women on maternity leave.

226 WTR 1998 reg 15(2) and (4).

227 WTR 1998 regs 2(1) and 15(5).

228 *Industrial and Commercial Maintenance Ltd v Briffa* UKEAT/0215-6/08.

229 This is based on the ECJ's interpretation of the Directive in *Stringer and others v HM Revenue and Customs sub nom Commissioners of Inland Revenue v Ainsworth and Schultz-Hoff v Deutsche Rentenversicherung Bund* (C-350/06) [2009] IRLR 214, ECJ, contrary to the decision of the CA in *Commissioners of Inland Revenue v Ainsworth and others* [2005] IRLR 465, CA and it is assumed (though strictly-speaking untested) that the WTR 1998 will be applied in this way.

230 *Merino Gómez v Continental Industrias del Caucho SA* C-342/01 [2004] IRLR 407; 129 EOR 27, ECJ.

231 This interpretation seems likely following *Federatie Nederlandse Vakbeweging v Staat der Nederlanden* [2006] IRLR 561, ECJ.

4.82 Employers cannot unilaterally reduce a worker's pay in order to pay for holidays under the WTR 1998.[232] The practice of 'rolled-up' holiday pay is also unlawful, ie simply increasing the basic wage to cover holiday pay, but not making any payment at the time holiday is taken.[233] Having said that, an employer may set off any sums actually paid in advance under transparent and comprehensive arrangements.[234] This effectively allows rolled-up payments by the back door.

4.83 On the termination of employment, a worker is entitled to receive a payment for any untaken holiday in the last holiday year, calculated proportionally to the leave year,[235] even if s/he has been absent on sick leave all year up to the point of leaving.[236] If there is a greater contractual holiday entitlement, pay in lieu of the additional holiday will only be payable on termination if there is an express right to do so under the contract or a clear term implied by custom and practice. Some contracts exclude all payment for untaken holidays if the dismissal is for gross misconduct. This is permissible regarding any additional contractual rights, but probably not under the WTR 1998. To calculate the amount of leave due on termination, there is a formula in the regulations, $(A \times B) - C$[237] where A is the number of days annual leave to which the worker is entitled, B is the proportion of the leave year which has expired at the termination date, and C is the amount of leave already taken that year. For example, a worker who works five days each week has a 20-day per year leave entitlement. If s/he leaves nine months into the final holiday year, having taken six days paid leave that year, s/he is owed $((20 \times 9/12) - 6)$ nine days.

4.84 Under the WTR 1998 there is no requirement that workers repay excess holiday taken in the year of leaving unless there is a 'relevant agreement', eg the worker's contract or a workforce agreement, allowing this to be done.[238] It will be an unlawful deduction under ERA

---

232 *Davies and others v M J Wyatt (Decorators) Ltd* [2000] IRLR 759, EAT.

233 *Robinson-Steele v R D Retail Services Ltd; Clarke v Frank Staddon Ltd; Caulfield and others v Hanson Clay Products Ltd (formerly Marshall's Clay Products Ltd)* [2006] IRLR 386, ECJ.

234 *Robinson-Steele* [2006] IRLR 386, ECJ; *Lyddon v Englefield Brickwork Ltd* [2008] IRLR 198, EAT. WTR 1998 reg 16(5).

235 WTR 1998 reg 14. See para 4.88 regarding untaken additional leave carried over from a previous year.

236 See n256.

237 WTR 1998 reg 14.

238 WTR 1998 regs 14(4) and 2(1).

1996 Pt II if the employer deducts the excess from the worker's wages without such an agreement.[239]

4.85　　The daily rate of holiday pay for a salaried worker is calculated by dividing his/her annual salary by the number of working days in the year – not the number of calendar days.[240] WTR 1998 reg 16 sets out how to calculate a week's pay, though the contract may be more generous. If a worker has no normal working hours, holiday pay is calculated as an average of the previous 12 weeks' pay. But if a worker has normal working hours and frequently works overtime on a purely voluntary basis, the average amount of overtime pay is not included in the calculation of holiday pay. This is so, even if s/he is contractually obliged to work the overtime but the employer is not contractually obliged to provide it.[241] The same applies if the worker earns commission while at work. His/her holiday pay will be based on his/her basic pay, ie without the commission.[242] The WTR 1998 may not properly implement the Working Time Directive in this respect[243] and public sector workers could try claiming under the Directive.

4.86　　The WTR 1998 provide for a minimum entitlement. There is nothing to prevent an employer agreeing to give additional holidays beyond the legal minimum entitlement. It is an obligation on the employer to give employees within two months of starting employment a statement of particulars including details of any terms and conditions relating to holidays, public holidays and holiday pay.[244]

Additional statutory annual leave

4.87　　Originally under the WTR 1998, employers could choose to include bank holidays in the four weeks' statutory annual leave, unless a worker had a separate contractual entitlement. To remedy this, an additional statutory leave entitlement of up to 8 days has been phased in.[245] An additional 0.8 week's leave applies to the period 1 October 2007 – 31 March 2009 and for any leave year beginning on or after 1 April 2009, the total annual leave entitlement is now 5.6 weeks. For someone working 5 days/week, this translates into 28 working days' leave. There

---

239 *Hill v Chappell* [2003] IRLR 19, EAT.
240 *Leisure Leagues UK Ltd v Maconnachie* [2002] IRLR 600, EAT; *Yarrow v Edwards Chartered Accountants* UKEAT/0116/07.
241 *Bamsey and others v Albon Engineering Ltd* [2004] IRLR 457,CA.
242 *Evans v Malley Organisation Ltd t/a 1st Business Support* [2003] IRLR 156, CA.
243 *Bamsey and others v Albon Engineering Ltd* [2003] 736 IDS Brief 3, EAT.
244 ERA 1996 s1(4)(d)(i); and see para 1.24 above.
245 WTR 1998 reg 13A.

is a total overall cap on the statutory entitlement of 28 days,[245] although a worker may have a greater contractual entitlement. The additional eight days are in recognition of the eight public and bank holidays (though there happen to be nine in Scotland). If, as at 1 October 2007, a worker was already entitled under his/her contract to take 1.6 weeks' or 8 days holiday (whichever is less) in addition to four weeks annual leave, s/he gets no extra statutory days under these rules.[247] There is no right to take the extra eight days on the public/bank holidays in question, nor to get paid extra if required to work on those days, unless the worker has such a right (express or implied, eg by custom and practice) under his/her own contract.

4.88   Unlike the main entitlement, some or all of the additional leave can be carried over to the subsequent holiday year if the employer agrees in a relevant agreement, eg in a collective agreement or the worker's written contract.[248] Payment in lieu of the holiday is not generally permitted except on leaving the job for the current holiday year, but it will be allowed in relation to employment from 1 October 2007 to 1 April 2009.[249] Calculations of holiday pay are potentially complicated, especially for the transitional period. For example, if the worker's holiday year is the calendar year, his/her leave entitlement in 2009 will be 5.4 weeks. If you want to avoid the maths, there is an on-line calculator (developed for employers, but useful for all parties).[250]

Enforcement

4.89   The statutory enforcement of the working hours is carried out by the Health and Safety Executive (for schools, hospitals and factories, etc) or the local authority (for retail, catering, offices and leisure, etc).[251] Inspectors have power to enter and inspect workplaces, to issue improvement or prohibition notices and, in England and Wales, to prosecute.[252] Breach of the obligations can result in criminal proceed-

---

246 WTR 1998 reg 13(3).
247 The extra conditions set out in WTR 1998 reg 26A must also apply, including that all the employer's other workers have the same entitlement.
248 WTR 1998 reg 13A(7).
249 WTR 1998 reg 13A(6).
250 www.businesslink.gov.uk/bdotg/action/layer?topicId=1079427399&r.lc= en&r.s=sl
251 And in some respects, the Civil Aviation Authority or Vehicle and Operator Services Agency.
252 WTR 1998 regs 28–29E, Sch 3.

ings punishable by a fine. It is also an offence, punishable by a fine or in some cases, prison, to obstruct an inspector. Where an offence by a company is committed with the consent, connivance or neglect of any director, manager or officer, that individual can also be found guilty of the offence and punished.[253]

4.90   As stated at para 4.68 above, a worker has a contractual entitlement not to be required to work more than 48 hours without his/her agreement. Unfortunately employers have no obligation to require workers to take rest breaks and holidays.

4.91   Individual workers can make an ET claim for any failure to give rest periods and breaks and paid holidays. The ET can award compensation according to what is just and equitable having regard to the employer's default and any attributable loss for the worker.[254] With regard to the statutory holiday entitlement, the position can become complicated, because there are so many factual permutations including whether the claim concerns taken and unpaid, or refused or improperly claimed holiday; whether it is owed only for the part of a year in which the worker leaves; whether holiday owed from previous years carries over eg because the worker was off sick or on maternity leave or had the contractual right to carry over the extra 1.6 weeks. Not all of these permutations can be covered here. The simplest scenario is where the worker is permitted to take holiday, but not paid for it, or where holiday entitlement is owing for the year in which the worker leaves.[255] In these situations, the worker can claim under WTR 1998 reg 30 or ERA 1996 Pt II as an unlawful deduction.[256] The 3 month time-limit is counted from when payment should have been made, subject to any extension if it was not reasonably practicable to get the claim in on time.[257] In other situations, where the employer refuses to allow the worker to take holiday, a claim for compensation under reg 30 must be made within 3 months of the date when the holiday should have started.[258] The main problems in practice arise when holiday has

---

253 WTR 1998 reg 29B.
254 WTR 1998 reg 30(4); *Miles v Linkage Community Trust Ltd* UKEAT/ 0618/07; [2008] IRLR 602, EAT gives guidance.
255 See para 4.83.
256 *Her Majesty's Revenue and Customs v Stringer and others* [2009] UKHL 31; [2009] IRLR 677.
257 WTR 1998 reg 30(2).
258 It is uncertain whether a Pt II claim would be equally suitable, because the HL in *Stringer* [2009] UKHL 31 was only dealing with a case of untaken holidays in the termination year.

been refused for several years. This leads to interacting issues regarding the nature of compensation for untaken holiday entitlement and time-limits. In conclusion, whatever the circumstances, it is probably best to claim under both WTR 1998 reg 30 and/or ERA 1996 Pt II to cover potential difficulties. The advantage of a Pt II claim is that the time-limit continues to run if there is a series of deductions.

4.92   It is unlawful to dismiss or subject a worker to a detriment for insisting on his/her rights under the WTR 1998, eg for insisting on taking breaks or refusing to work more than 48 hours.[259] This protection may be particularly important in the latter case, as it seems a worker cannot claim compensation in an ET for being forced to work more than 48 hours, but can only go to the county court or High Court for a declaration as to breach of contract and, most unlikely, an injunction.[260] This is not a practical remedy and it may be simpler for a worker, having made sure s/he is protected, to inform the employer politely and in writing that in accordance with the WTR 1998 s/he is not willing to work more than 48 hours. Obviously a worker needs to tread carefully and be sure of his/her rights before upsetting an employer in this way.

4.93   The employer must keep up-to-date records of workers who have agreed to work longer than 48 hours per week plus records which are adequate to show that the 48-hour and night work limits are complied with.[261] Records must be kept for two years. It is an offence for an employer not to comply with any of the relevant requirements in the WTR 1998 including the keeping of adequate records.[262]

---

259 See ERA 1996 ss45A and 101A for this and related reasons, and see *McLean v Rainbow Homeloans Ltd* [2007] IRLR 14, EAT. See also para 6.73 on dismissal for asserting statutory rights.

260 See *Barber v RJB Mining (UK) Ltd* [1999] IRLR 308, HC. But see *Sayers v Cambridgeshire County Council* [2007] IRLR 29, HC, which states no civil claim can be brought for breach of statutory duty.

261 WTR 1998 regs 4(2) and 9.

262 WTR 1998 reg 29(1).

CHAPTER 5

Equal pay

continued

Chapter 5: Key points

- Sex discrimination in pay or contract terms is covered by the Equal Pay Act 1970. Race discrimination in pay is covered by the Race Relations Act 1976.
- The woman must compare her pay with that of a man in the same employment employed on like work, work rated as equivalent under a job evaluation scheme or work of equal value.
- Once the woman proves like work or work of equal value, the burden of proof passes to the employer to prove a genuine material factor defence, ie a genuine reason for the pay differential, which is not tainted by direct or indirect sex discrimination.
- If the reason amounts to indirect sex discrimination, the employer must provide objective justification. In other cases, it seems a neutral non-discriminatory reason (however bad) will do.
- Indirect discrimination is the biggest cause of unequal pay. The concept of indirect discrimination under the Equal Pay Act 1970 is wider than under the Sex Discrimination Act 1975.
- Equal value claims are traditionally lengthy and complex. In recent years, there has been a dramatic increase in collective public sector claims.
- The public sector gender equality duty requires authorities to review pay disparities.

The legal framework

The legislation

5.1   The Equal Pay Act (EqPA) 1970 and, in particular, the concept of equal value introduced by the Equal Pay (Amendment) Regulations 1983,[1] is difficult to understand and apply. EU law has been particularly influential in this area, especially the Treaty of Rome article 119, now numbered 141. This book outlines the key issues so that potential cases may be identified. 'Like work' claims can be relatively straightforward to run in the employment tribunal (ET), but complex and lengthy procedures are involved for 'equal value' claims and this book only touches on the necessary evidence and procedural issues. An adviser considering running an equal value claim for the first time should talk to someone who has done it before.

1 SI No 1794.

5.2   The EqPA 1970 and the Sex Discrimination Act (SDA) 1975 cover separate ground. The SDA 1975 covers sex discrimination in employment generally, except where the EqPA 1970 applies. Although the EqPA 1970 most often applies to pay, in fact it also covers discrimination between men and women in relation to other contract terms,[2] eg sick pay entitlement or the right to have a company car. Bonus payments usually arise from the contract, but may on the facts be wholly discretionary and therefore not within the EqPA 1970.[3] If unsure which statute applies, both should be cited in the ET claim. Indeed, due to the difficulty in some situations of knowing which is the appropriate legislation, it is very often safer to claim under article 141, the Equal Pay Directive[4] (EPD) and the Equal Treatment Directive[5] (ETD) as well as the EqPA 1970 and SDA 1975. Note that discrimination in pay or contract terms on grounds of gender reassignment is covered by the SDA 1975. Race discrimination in pay would be covered by the Race Relations Act (RRA) 1976.

5.3   The former Equal Opportunities Commission (EOC) and the European Commission have both issued codes of practice on equal pay, which are admissible in evidence in any ET claim for equal pay.[6] Where relevant, the codes must be taken into account by the ET.

5.4   In 2003, a questionnaire procedure similar to that available for other sex discrimination claims was made available for equal pay claims. This is a vital tool for gathering information to decide whether unequal pay exists.[7]

5.5   In 2008, the gender pay gap on hourly pay for full-timers was an average 17.1 per cent.[8] Little progress is being made. In recent years, there has been a huge increase in the number of claims brought, especially in local government and the health service. Unfortunately, the length and cost of equal value claims is such that low-paid individuals cannot afford them. Increasingly, equal pay cases are collective and

2 EqPA 1970 s1(2).

3 For an example, see *Hoyland v Asda Stores Ltd* [2006] IRLR 468, CS.

4 75/117/EEC.

5 76/207/EEC.

6 The revised EOC Code on equal pay (2003) is available on the EHRC website at www.equalityhumanrights.com/uploaded_files/code_of_practice_equalpay.pdf. The EC Code: Code of Practice on the implementation of equal pay for work of equal value for men and women COM(96)336 is available from The Stationery Office at www.tso.co.uk, tel: 0870 600 5522.

7 See para 5.54 below.

8 Annual Survey of Hours and Earnings 2008 at www.statistics.gov.uk/StatBase/Product.asp?vink=13101

backed by trade unions or run by private solicitors on a no-win no-fee basis. The unions themselves struggle to finance the bigger claims. Thousands of equal pay claims have now been lodged in local government regarding historic pay discrimination. In local government, the 1997 'single status' agreement (also known as the 'Green Book') was intended to put manual and white collar workers onto new single pay scales based on principles of equal pay. Unfortunately, a large number of councils did not meet the agreed deadline for implementation of 31 March 2007. Where job evaluations have taken place, some staff have benefited whereas others have been put on lower grades, although with a level of pay protection to ease the transition. The validity of the pay protection agreements has in turn come under challenge. Similar sweeping changes have occurred in the NHS through 'Agenda for Change', with pay scales based on a new job evaluation system. Most of the complicated equal pay case-law over the last few years has been in these areas. Regrettably, the scope for negotiated equal pay agreements has been weakened as unions become anxious following challenges to collective negotiations brought by some 'no-win no-fee' lawyers. The difficulty facing unions is to balance the interests of different groups of members, while persuading employers to accept new equality deals for the future and make generous settlements of past claims at a time when they are short of money. If the interests of underpaid women in the past are undervalued in this equation, it can lead to indirect sex discrimination claims against the union.[9] But that is not to say that negotiated deals can never be justified.

5.6   As part of the gender equality duty introduced in 2007,[10] public authorities must have due regard to the need to eliminate unlawful pay discrimination. Authorities subject to specific duties must publish and maintain a Gender Equality Scheme. When formulating the objectives for the Scheme, authorities must consider the need to have objectives which address the causes of any gender-related pay differences.[11] In Scotland, authorities with at least 150 staff must also publish an equal pay statement and report on their equal pay policy every three years.[12]

9 *Allen and others v GMB* [2008] IRLR 690, CA. For an overview of the public sector equal pay crisis and the debate about 'no-win no-fee' lawyers, see 'The union perspective on equal pay' (March 2008) 174 EOR 13.

10 See para 13.102 below for details.

11 The Sex Discrimination Act 1975 (Public Authorities) (Statutory Duties) Order 2006 SI No 2930 reg 2 and the Sex Discrimination (Public Authorities) (Statutory Duties) (Scotland) Order 2007 SSI No 32 reg 2.

12 SSI No 32 regs 6–8.

Who is covered?

5.7   The EqPA 1970 has wider scope than the unfair dismissal provisions of the Employment Rights Act (ERA) 1996. It protects workers employed under a contract of service or apprenticeship and the self-employed having contracted to execute work personally.[13] Both men and women can claim under the EqPA 1970. For ease of reference, this chapter presumes a woman is bringing the claim.

Using EU law

5.8   All UK workers can claim under article 141[14] in the ET in relation to discrimination in pay. Article 141 requires that 'men and women should receive equal pay for equal work' and is expanded by the Equal Pay Directive which can also be relied on in national courts against any employer.[15] More recently, the Equal Treatment Directive was amended also to cover sex discrimination in pay. This is echoed in the Recast Directive,[16] which came into force on 15 August 2006, consolidating seven existing Directives on gender discrimination and interpretative case-law. The government says no action was needed to implement this Directive because domestic law was already compliant. In many circumstances EU law is superfluous because it duplicates rights which exist under UK law. However, in respect of pensions and some other limited matters, EU law may be needed because of exclusions and omissions from the UK legislation. There is also the possibility that article 4 of the Recast Directive requires equal pay claims to be permitted where there is no actual comparator (see para 5.11 below).

What does article 141 mean by 'pay'?

5.9   Unlike the EqPA 1970, article 141 does not apply to all terms and conditions, but only to pay. Article 141 defines pay as 'the ordinary basic or minimum wage or salary and any other consideration, whether in cash or in kind, which the worker receives, directly or indirectly, in respect of his employment from his employer'. This wide definition was

---

13 EqPA 1970 s1(6).

14 References to article 141 are to article 141 of the Treaty of Rome throughout.

15 *Pickstone and others v Freemans* [1988] IRLR 357, HL.

16 Directive on equality between men and women in matters of employment and occupation: No 2006/54.

confirmed by the European Court of Justice (ECJ) in *Garland v British Rail Engineering*,[17] which added that the consideration may be 'immediate or future, provided that the worker receives it, albeit indirectly, in respect of his employment from his employer'.

5.10 Both contractual[18] and statutory redundancy pay[19] fall within article 141, although payment by the National Insurance Fund when the employer defaults is not covered.[20] Some payments made by employers under a statutory obligation, eg statutory sick pay,[21] may also be within article 141. Most significantly, article 141 covers contributions towards and benefits paid under contractual pension schemes,[22] whether supplementary to,[23] or contracted-out from,[24] the state pension scheme. Compensation for unfair dismissal constitutes pay within article 141.[25]

The comparable man

Requirement for a comparator

5.11 Under the EqPA 1970 (unlike the SDA 1975) a woman must find an actual man with whom she can compare herself (unless she is complaining of pay discrimination due to pregnancy).[26] She cannot simply ask the ET to infer that her terms and conditions are less favourable than those of a man would have been.[27] Some commentators believe the amendment of the Equal Treatment Directive to include pay[28] means a hypothetical comparison should suffice under EU law, but this is untested.

---

17 [1982] IRLR 111; [1988] ICR 420, ECJ.

18 *Hammersmith and Queen Charlotte's Special Health Authority v Cato* [1987] IRLR 483; [1988] ICR 132, EAT.

19 *Barber v GRE Assurance Group* [1990] IRLR 240, ECJ.

20 *Secretary of State for Employment v Levy* [1989] IRLR 469, EAT.

21 *Rinner-Kühn v FWW Spezial-Gebaüdereinigung GmbH* [1989] IRLR 493, ECJ.

22 See paras 17.42–17.48 on pensions.

23 *Bilka-Kaufhaus GmbH v Weber von Hartz* [1986] IRLR 317, ECJ.

24 *Barber v GRE Assurance Group* [1990] IRLR 240, ECJ.

25 *R v Secretary of State for Employment ex p Seymour-Smith and Perez* [1999] IRLR 253 ECJ.

26 *Alabaster v Barclays Bank plc and the Secretary of State for Social Security* (No 2) [2005] IRLR 576, CA.

27 *Macarthys Ltd v Smith* [1980] IRLR 219, ECJ.

28 See para 5.8.

The same employment

5.12   The male comparator must be employed by the same or an associated employer. Under EqPA 1970 s1(6) an employer is an associated employer where one company owns another or where two companies come under the control of a third person. The comparator must be employed at the same establishment or at another establishment in Great Britain where common terms and conditions[29] of employment apply generally or to workers of the relevant classes. For example, female support staff employed by a local authority in schools could compare their pay with that of male local authority staff who were not employed in schools, since they were employed under the same collective agreement on common terms and conditions.[30] A comparison can also be made with a man at a different establishment who is employed on different terms and conditions, in a situation where women across both establishments are employed on one set of terms and conditions and men across both establishments are employed on another set of terms and conditions. It is not necessary for there actually to be any men employed in the comparator's type of job at the claimant's establishment, but the comparison may not be allowed if it is extremely unlikely that that kind of job would ever be undertaken there.[31]

5.13   However, under article 141 comparisons are not limited to where the man and woman are employed by the same or an associated employer.[32] The test is whether the comparator is employed in the same establishment or service.[33] It is essential that the pay differences can be attributed to a single source, otherwise there is no single body which is responsible for the inequality and can restore equal treatment.[34] Examples where comparisons can be made between different employers are: (1) where statutory rules apply to pay and conditions in more

29 See *Leverton v Clwyd CC* [1989] IRLR 28, HL on the meaning of 'common terms and conditions'. For more detail of the application of this test, see *British Coal Corporation v Smith* [1996] IRLR 404, HL.

30 *South Tyneside Metropolitan Borough Council v Anderson and others* [2007] IRLR 715,CA.

31 *Dumfries and Galloway Council v North and others* UKEATS/0047/08.

32 *Scullard v Knowles and Southern Regional Council for Education and Training* [1996] IRLR 344; (1996) 67 EOR 44, EAT.

33 *Scullard v Knowles and Southern Regional Council for Education and Training* [1996] IRLR 344; (1996) 67 EOR 44, EAT.

34 *Lawrence and others v Regent Office Care Ltd and others* [2002] IRLR 822; (2002) 110 EOR 27, ECJ.

than one undertaking, establishment or service, eg nursing salaries within a national health service; (2) where several undertakings or establishments are covered by a collective works agreement; (3) where terms and conditions are laid down centrally for more than one organisation or business within a holding company or conglomerate.[35]

5.14 Teachers employed by different Scottish Councils have been able to compare their pay because the salary scales of both were set by the Scottish Joint Negotiating Committee, a quasi-autonomous body, and the whole structure of education was regarded as a 'service'.[36] It is not permissible to use comparators from different government departments because, although technically they have the same employer (the Crown), power to negotiate and set most aspects of pay is delegated to the individual government departments without any co-ordination between them.[37] Workers employed by a Direct Services Organisation established to submit an in-house tender in compliance with the requirements of the Local Government Act 1988 may compare themselves with other employees of the same council provided common terms and conditions apply.[38] However, if the work is contracted out to independent contractors, employees transferred to the new employer can no longer compare their pay with that of council staff.[39] Similarly, an agency worker, even if she previously worked for the employer, cannot compare her pay with a directly employed member of staff, assuming there is no single source in control of pay.[40] Note that it is not necessary to establish that there is a 'single source' when making a claim under the EqPA 1970 where the simpler s1(6) test is satisfied.[41]

5.15 A woman may compare herself with a predecessor, even one who left long before she started.[42] She may not compare her pay with that

35 *Lawrence and others v Regent Office Care Ltd and others* [2002] IRLR 822; (2002) 110 EOR 27, ECJ.

36 *South Ayrshire Council v Morton* [2002] IRLR 256; (2002) 103 EOR 25, CS.

37 *Robertson and others v Department for Environment Food and Rural Affairs* [2005] IRLR 363, CA.

38 *Ratcliffe and others v North Yorkshire CC* EAT 501/92; (1993) 496 IDS Brief 2.

39 *Lawrence and others v Regent Office Care Ltd and others* [2002] IRLR 822; (2002) 110 EOR 27, ECJ. But a contractual pay entitlement notionally varied by an equality clause in the past could transfer – *Gutridge v Sodexo Ltd and North Tees and Hartlepool NHS Trust* [2009] EWCA Civ 759.

40 *Allonby v Accrington & Rossendale College and others* C-256/01 [2004] IRLR 224; May 2004 *Legal Action* 33, ECJ.

41 *North Cumbria Acute Hospitals NHS Trust v Potter and others* UKEAT/0121/07; [2009] IRLR 176, EAT.

42 *Macarthy's v Smith (No 2)* [1980] IRLR 209, CA; *Albion Shipping Agency v Arnold* [1981] IRLR 520; *Kells v Pilkington* [2002] IRLR 693; (2002) 112 EOR 26, EAT.

of a successor, because that amounts to making a hypothetical pay comparison, which is not permitted under the EqPA 1970.[43]

5.16   In certain circumstances a man can make a claim contingent on his female comparator's claim against a different man. For example, a male primary school teacher could name as his comparator a female primary school teacher whose pay was the same or less than his, pending resolution of her equal pay claim using a male secondary school teacher who was paid more than them both.[44] Similarly, a male part-timer could make a claim contingent on the success of a female part-timer bringing an equal pay case on grounds of exclusion of part-timers from an occupational pension scheme.[45]

Comparable jobs

The nature of the comparison

5.17   A woman may compare herself with a man in the same employment if:

a) she is doing like work, ie work which is the same or of a broadly similar nature, and where any differences in the work they actually do are relatively unimportant;[46] or

b) she is doing work rated equivalent to his in a study which evaluates their work in terms of the demand made on each worker under various headings, eg effort, skill and decision[47] (such a study is usually known as a job evaluation scheme); or

c) she is doing work of equal value in terms of the demand made on each worker, eg under such headings as effort, skill and decision.[48]

Where the jobs seem fairly similar (but not identical), it is safer to claim at the same time both 'like work' and, in the alternative, 'work of equal

43 *Walton Centre for Neurology and Neurosurgery NHS Trust v Bewley* [2008] IRLR 588; *Legal Action* Nov 2008, EAT overruling *Diocese of Hallam Trustee v Connaughton* 1128/95 (1996) IDS Brief 4, EAT. But see para 5.11 regarding hypothetical comparators under EU law.

44 *South Ayrshire Council v Milligan* [2003] IRLR 153, CS. Confirmed and expanded by the EAT in *Hartlepool Borough Council and others v Llewellyn and others; McAvoy and others v South Tyneside Borough Council and others* UKEAT/0006/08; 0057/08; 0058/08; 0168/08; 0276/08.

45 *Preston v Wolverhampton Healthcare NHS Trust* [1997] IRLR 233, CA.

46 EqPA 1970 s1(2)(a) and (4).

47 EqPA 1970 s1(2)(b) and (5).

48 EqPA 1970 s1(2)(c).

value'.[49] Then if the ET decides that some of the differences between the jobs are significant, it can immediately turn to the equal value claim.

5.18 The following points should be noted:

- A woman can choose which man she wants to compare herself with and may choose more than one. Choosing more than one man as comparator reduces the risk of losing because the particular man chosen is in some way not typical, eg he has been favoured because he is infirm or red-circled for a non-discriminatory reason.
- Even if there is a man in the same employment doing like work or work rated as equivalent under a job evaluation scheme (and getting the same pay), a woman may still compare herself with a different (higher paid) man who is doing work of equal value.[50] This prevents equal pay claims being defeated by the presence of one or two low-paid men in predominantly female areas of work.
- Where there has been a job evaluation scheme which rates the work of the woman as less than that of her comparable man, the woman cannot claim equal value unless there are reasonable grounds for suspecting that the job evaluation scheme was based on a system which discriminates on grounds of sex or is otherwise unsuitable to be relied on.[51]
- Under article 141 a woman in an equal value claim may compare herself with a man whose work turns out to be of less value than hers,[52] although she can claim only pay equal to his. Employment tribunals now commonly accept this under the EqPA 1970 as well.
- A woman may compare her pay with that of a man whose work is rated lower than hers under a job evaluation scheme.[53]

Like work

5.19 In deciding whether a woman is doing 'like work' to her comparator, the ET should consider the matter in two stages.[54]

1) Is the work done by the woman and her comparator the same or of a broadly similar nature? At this stage, the ET should make a

49 This is where no job evaluation scheme (JES) applies.
50 *Pickstone and others v Freemans* [1988] IRLR 357, HL.
51 EqPA 1970 s2A(2).
52 *Murphy and others v Bord Telecom Eireann* [1988] IRLR 267; (1988) 19 EOR 46, ECJ, where a woman's work was in fact found to be of higher value than her male comparator's, even though she was paid less.
53 *Redcar and Cleveland Borough Council v Bainbridge and ors* [2007] IRLR 91, EAT.
54 *Capper Pass Ltd v Lawton* [1976] IRLR 366, EAT.

general consideration of the type of work and the skill and knowledge required to do it. So, eg women cleaners who clean offices and toilets should easily pass the test when compared with male cleaners who clean offices and urinals.

2) Are any differences between the work done by the woman and her comparator of practical importance in relation to the terms and conditions of employment? In other words, if the jobs were both done by members of the same sex, would you expect the differences in their tasks to warrant a difference in pay? Trivial differences or differences which in the real world are unlikely to be reflected by a pay difference should be disregarded. It does not prevent it being 'like work' if the woman is doing more duties than her comparators.[55]

The ET must look at the tasks actually carried out by the woman and her comparator, rather than to a (perhaps artificially inflated or understated) job description.[56]

5.20 In any 'like work' claim, detailed evidence of the work of both the woman and her comparator needs to be presented to the ET. Often it can take an entire day at the ET to draw out all the elements of each job. If there are several women bringing a joint case, it is usually a good idea for each of them to give evidence as to the nature of the job. This reduces the risk of key elements being omitted.

Job evaluation schemes

5.21 A study measuring the relative value of jobs, either solely of the woman and her comparator, or of some or all workers in the same employment, is commonly known as a job evaluation scheme (JES). There are many methods of evaluation, but the principal distinction is between analytic and non-analytic schemes. An analytic JES is one which evaluates jobs according to a breakdown of demands and characteristics. Factors such as responsibility, working conditions, physical and mental requirements are weighted and measured. A non-analytic JES compares jobs on a 'whole-job' basis, eg by ranking and paired comparisons. There are dangers that a JES may itself be directly or indirectly discriminatory, eg because it over-values traditional male skills and attributes, such as physical strength.

5.22 The JES must be thorough in analysis and capable of impartial

---

55 *SITA UK Ltd v Hope* UKEAT/0787/04/MAA.
56 *Shields v E Coombes (Holdings) Ltd* [1978] IRLR 263, CA.

application.[57] Where there is an existing JES which is analytic,[58] non-discriminatory and suitable to be relied on, it can serve two functions:

1) a woman may claim equal pay and other terms and conditions equal to those of a man whose work has been rated as equivalent (or less)[59] under such a JES;[60]
2) where a woman's work has been rated of less value than a man's under such a JES, she will fail in a claim under EqPA 1970 s1(2)(c) that her work is of equal value to his.[61]

Sometimes an employer may commission a JES after an equal value claim has been started in an attempt to block the claim. In order to have any effect, the JES must be completed at the latest by the final hearing, and it is in the ET's discretion whether it is willing to postpone the hearing if the JES is not ready.[62] A 'completed' JES means one which has been accepted by the employers and workers as a valid study, even though it may not yet have been implemented.[63]

5.23   Where the employer uses a JES which bands job points in advance (eg 210–239 points will be put at grade 5; 240–279 points at grade 6), a woman obtaining, for example, 210 points can demand to be paid equally with a man obtaining anything up to 239 points.[64]

Equal value claims

5.24   The hardest type of claim to bring under the EqPA 1970 is one for equal value. It requires imagination to identify possible cases where different jobs can be considered of equal value when broken down into factors such as effort, skill and demand. This is why special experts have traditionally been used on equal value cases, but this has led to expensive and lengthy procedures. For these reasons, the government has increased the power of tribunals to make the equal value assessment themselves. Examples where jobs have been found of equal value are a group personnel and training officer with a divisional sales trainer;

---

57 *Eaton Ltd v Nuttall* [1977] IRLR 71, EAT; *Diageo plc v Thomson* (2004) 744 IRLB 12, EAT.
58 *Bromley and others v H and J Quick* [1988] IRLR 249, CA.
59 *Redcar & Cleveland Borough Council v Bainbridge and others (No.1)* [2007] EWCA Civ 929; [2007] IRLR 984, CA.
60 EqPA 1970 s1(2)(b); and see para 5.17 above.
61 EqPA 1970 s2A.
62 *Avon CC v Foxall and others* [1989] IRLR 435; [1989] ICR 407, EAT.
63 *Arnold v Beecham Group Ltd* [1982] IRLR 307; [1982] ICR 744, EAT.
64 *Springboard Sunderland Trust v Robson* [1992] IRLR 261, EAT.

a speech therapist with a psychologist; a packer with a labourer; a Grade A nurse with a joiner; a cook, clerical officer and switchboard operator in a hospital with a maintenance assistant. Equal value procedures are set out at paras 5.57–5.67 below.

Defences

5.25   Even where there is like work, work rated as equivalent or work of equal value, the employer has a defence under EqPA 1970 s1(3) if s/he proves on a balance of probabilities that the variation between the woman's and the man's pay (or other terms) is due to a genuine material factor other than sex. In claims based on like work or work rated as equivalent under a JES, such a factor must be a material difference between the woman's case and the man's. When the scope of the EqPA 1970 was broadened to introduce equal value claims, employers were given a wider defence, ie in addition to such a material difference, it can also be any other material factor.

The material difference defence

5.26   Originally this defence was limited to personal factors differentiating the woman and her comparator. For example, a man could legitimately receive higher pay because of his longer service or better skills or productivity or because of red-circling.[65] However, the House of Lords decision in *Rainey v Greater Glasgow Health Board*[66] widened the interpretation of the defence to include circumstances other than the personal qualifications or merits of the workers concerned. There is now little practical difference between the defence that can be used on like work and JES cases, and that for equal value cases.

The material factor defence

5.27   The nature of this defence has been greatly influenced by decisions of the European Court of Justice (ECJ), although its interpretation by ETs and the Employment Appeal Tribunal (EAT) has been inconsistent. Once a woman proves she is paid less than a man doing like work or work of equal value, the law presumes the difference in pay is due to

---

65 Red-circling entails individual salary protection, eg when a worker is demoted on re-organisation or due to ill-health. The longer red-circling has lasted, the less it may be an appropriate GMF defence – see F*earnon and others v Smurfit Corrugated Cases Lurgan Ltd* [2009] IRLR 132, NICA.

66 [1987] IRLR 26; [1987] ICR 129, HL.

sex discrimination (whether direct or indirect). The burden of proof then passes to the employer to show the explanation for the variation in pay is not tainted by sex.[67] The employer must prove:

- the proffered explanation is genuine and not a sham or pretence;
- the lesser pay is due to this reason, ie it is a 'material' (which means 'significant and relevant[68]') factor;
- the reason is not the difference of sex, whether direct or indirect discrimination.

Therefore, provided the pay difference is for a genuine reason, which is not tainted by any kind of sex discrimination, the employer has a valid defence.[69] The House of Lords has said that it does not have to be a good reason, since the purpose of the EqPA 1970 is to eliminate sex discrimination in pay, not to achieve fair wages.[70] On this reasoning, a pay difference based on a mistake or a misunderstanding would still be lawful.

5.28   There is some uncertainty as to whether European law requires more than a neutral explanation, and requires the employer to supply an objective justification for the pay variation. The House of Lords says justification is only necessary in cases of indirect sex discrimination. But in the *Brunnhofer* case,[71] the ECJ stated clearly that 'an employer may validly explain the difference in pay ... in so far as they constitute objectively justified reasons unrelated to any discrimination based on sex and in conformity with the principle of proportionality'. The important point about this case is that the ECJ was requiring objective justification in a case which on its facts did not involve indirect discrimination. In all the previous major cases before the ECJ, where it required objective justification for pay differentials, the cases happened to have involved indirect discrimination. Unfortunately, subsequent EAT cases have differed over whether *Brunnhofer* really does require objective justification in cases which do not involve indirect discrimination.[72] The later cases say it does not.

---

67 *Glasgow City Council v Marshall* [2000] IRLR 272, HL.

68 *Rainey v Greater Glasgow Health Board* [1987] IRLR 26, HL.

69 *Strathclyde Regional Council v Wallace* [1998] IRLR 146, HL; *Glasgow City Council v Marshall* [2000] IRLR 272, HL.

70 *Strathclyde Regional Council v Wallace* [1998] IRLR 146, HL.

71 *Brunnhofer v Bank der Österreichischen Postsparkasse* [2001] IRLR 571, ECJ.

72 *Parliamentary Commissioner for Administration v Fernandez* [2004] IRLR 22, EAT; *Sharp v Caledonia Group Services Ltd* [2006] IRLR 4; May 2006 *Legal Action* 21, EAT; *Villalba v Merrill Lynch & Co Inc and others* [2006] IRLR 437; November 2006 *Legal Action* 16, EAT. See also *Armstrong v Newcastle-upon-Tyne Trust* [2006] IRLR 124, CA, but the CA was not referred to the relevant ECJ judgments.

5.29   As well as personal differences between the workers concerned such as experience and qualifications, the following are examples of genuine material factors, although whether the defence is made out will depend on the specific circumstances in each case:

- market forces and other economic considerations;
- administrative efficiency;
- geographical differences, eg London weighting;
- unsocial hours, rotating shift and night working;

Some equal value cases have confused matters relevant to evaluating the relative worth of each job such as skill, responsibility, effort, with material factors which would justify a pay difference. The EAT in *Davies v McCartneys*[73] suggested that the employer could use as a defence the very matters which were relevant in determining whether a job was of equal value. This approach has been criticised and is open to doubt: once two jobs have been evaluated as equal in terms of these separate demands, an employer ought not to be able to justify a pay difference by saying that s/he personally values one job more highly. The employer's defence may be based on several factors. Where an employer can only partially justify a pay differential, an ET may accept the justification to that extent.[74]

Not a sex-based explanation

5.30   If the genuine material factor defence is tainted by sex discrimination, it fails unless, in the case of indirect discrimination, the employer can provide objective justification. A defence which amounts to direct discrimination cannot be justified.[75] It may be quite easy for the employer to prove that no direct discrimination is involved. For example, in the absence of any other evidence, the ET is unlikely to find any direct discrimination where the worker compares herself with a man who is obviously more skilled and where there are also many skilled women who receive the higher pay.

---

73 [1989] IRLR 429, EAT. This may be only obiter given the actual findings in the case.

74 *Enderby v Frenchay Health Authority and Secretary of State for Health* [1993] IRLR 591; (1993) 52 EOR 40, ECJ.

75 *E Coombes (Holdings) Ltd v Shields* [1978] IRLR 263, CA; *Parliamentary Commissioner for Administration v Fernandez* [2004] IRLR 22, EAT, although beware obiter comments made in *Strathclyde Regional Council v Wallace* [1998] IRLR 146, HL.

5.31 The woman may take it upon herself to prove direct sex discrimination, eg by relying on something she was told or has found out about the true reason for her lower pay; for example, she has heard that the employer believes women will work for less pay than men. Alternatively, the factor put forward by the employer may itself contain an element or history of direct sex discrimination, which is readily apparent or becomes clear on examination, eg in one case[76] a material factor defence of red-circling was rejected because it was based upon previous direct sex discrimination, excluding women from male pay and jobs in the 1960s. Bonus schemes may also be discriminatory in that historically they tend to have been negotiated in male job areas and often comprise automatic payments which are not in reality dependent on productivity.[77]

5.32 A market forces defence can be acceptable, provided it is not discriminatory. The employer must prove the exact amount of the pay differential which is due to market forces. It is for the employer to show the market dictated the higher pay, not for the employees to show their comparators' pay was too high.[78] A market forces defence can be discriminatory where there is job segregation, since female-dominated jobs tend to be paid less precisely because they are traditionally carried out mainly by women. For example in *Ratcliffe v North Yorkshire CC*[79] the council's Direct Services Organisation (DSO) reduced the pay of catering assistants (who were almost exclusively female) in order to compete successfully on a compulsory competitive tendering exercise. Three women brought an equal value case comparing themselves with male council workers, such as road sweepers and refuse collectors, whose work had been rated equivalent under a job evaluation scheme. The House of Lords rejected the council's argument that the DSO had to be able to compete on the open market. This defence was based on sex because the council's competitors could pay less on the open market precisely because such work was done mainly by women.[80] With any market forces defence, the employer must also provide evidence

---

76 *Snoxell v Vauxhall Motors Ltd* [1977] IRLR 123; [1977] ICR 700, EAT.

77 *Cumbria County Council v Dow* (No.1) [2008] IRLR 91, EAT; *Hartlepool Borough Council and Housing Hartlepool Ltd v Dolphin and ors* UKEAT/0007-08/08; [2009] IRLR 168, EAT.

78 *Cumbria County Council v Dow (No.1)* [2008] IRLR 91, EAT.

79 [1995] IRLR 439; (1995) 63 EOR 49, HL.

80 For another example, in a collective bargaining context, see *William Bull Ltd v Wood and others* (2002) 711 IDS Brief 7, EAT.

5.33   Agreements negotiated with many local authorities over the last few years for new unified pay scales have included several years' pay protection for those whose pay will be reduced under the new scales. But where a woman has previously been paid less due to historic direct or indirect sex discrimination, it is not necessarily justifiable to deprive her of a sum for pay protection just because her pay is not in reality reduced.[81] Although the purpose of pay protection is to cushion employees against the shock of an actual salary cut, granting it for an extended period to those previously paid higher rates simply perpetuates past inequality. Whether or not it is justifiable in a particular case depends on a variety of factors, eg the extent of the cut, the duration of the protection, the extent to which the employer is trying to eliminate past discrimination, the cost for an employer of equalising up the pay disparities, the industrial relations consequences of imposing pay-cuts and the extent to which the unions insisted on protection as the price for agreeing single status.

5.34   There is no firm demarcation between direct and indirect discrimination under the EqPA 1970 as there is under the SDA 1975.[82] Whereas the SDA 1975 defines direct discrimination and indirect discrimination, the EqPA 1970 does not, so its meaning has been developed by case-law. The concept of indirect discrimination under the EqPA 1970, when read together with European legislation and case-law, has therefore developed in a way which is broader than that under the SDA 1975. The fundamental question is whether there is a causative link between the claimant's sex and the fact that she is paid less than her comparator,[83] but indirect discrimination in an equal pay case can take many forms. The following examples suggest possible indirect discrimination and the burden of proof will probably transfer to the employer to prove an objective justification for the differential, although the case-law is complicated on this:[84]

1) The pay-rate is determined by gender-linked characteristics, eg a lower hourly rate for part-timers.

81 *Redcar & Cleveland Borough Council v Bainbridge and others (No 1), Surtees and others v Middlesbrough Borough Council, Redcar & Cleveland Borough Council v Bainbridge and others (No 2)* [2008] EWCA Civ 885; [2008] IRLR 776, CA.

82 *Strathclyde Regional Council v Wallace* [1998] IRLR 146, HL.

83 *Ministry of Defence v Armstrong* [2004] IRLR 672, EAT.

84 The Court of Appeal in *Redcar and Cleveland Borough Council v Bainbridge and others and EHRC (intervener) (No 1), Surtees and others v Middlesbrough Borough Council and EHRC (intervener; Redcar & Cleveland Borough Council v Bainbridge and others and EHRC (intervener) (No 2)* [2008] EWCA Civ 885; [2008] IRLR 776, CA reviews this issue. See also 'Justifying pay differentials – when is objective justification required?' (2009) 186 EOR 11.

2) The employer applies a provision, criterion or practice to all workers, but which puts women at a particular disadvantage. For example, the employer pays more for previous experience in a
   male-dominated industry. To measure the adverse impact, the
   tribunal can choose to look at the proportion of men and women disadvantaged by the practice or at the proportion of those advantaged
   by the practice – whichever realistically tests the issue. The tribunal
   should consider everyone affected by the relevant practice, whether
   positively or negatively, but there is no single suitable pool for comparison in every case.[85] These first two types of indirect discrimination are equivalent to the concept under the SDA 1975. (See
   paras 13.52–13.84.)

3) A job which is carried out almost exclusively by women, or where a
   significant number are women, is paid less than a job carried out predominantly by men.[86] It does not matter if there are a significant
   number of men in the disadvantaged group (although this may
   indicate that the employer will have a defence unrelated to sex).[87]

4) The employer uses a pay system which is wholly lacking in transparency (see para 5.36 below), but the average pay for women is
   less than the average pay for men.[88]

5) Any other reason where there is a causative link between the
   claimant's sex and the lesser pay. In this last category, no structured approach is needed and the tribunal need not identify any
   provision, criterion or practice or pools of affected people. Nevertheless, looking at the facts as a whole, there is clearly a discriminatory connection. The link may be established, eg as a result of job
   segregation or from pay practices or structures which disadvantage women because they are likely to have shorter service or work
   less hours than men, due to historical discrimination or disadvantage, or because of the traditional social role of women and
   their family responsibilities.[89]

5.35 For further examples of indirectly discriminatory pay practices, see
paras 5.39–5.50 below. Sometimes the true (and indirectly discrimi-

---

85 *Grundy v British Airways PLC* [2008] IRLR 74; May 2008 *Legal Action* 16, CA.

86 *Enderby v Frenchay Health Authority and Secretary of State for Health* [1993] IRLR
591, ECJ; *British Road Services Ltd v Loughran* [1997] IRLR 92, NICA.

87 *Bailey and others v Home Office* [2005] IRLR 369; November 2005 *Legal Action* 13,
CA.

88 *Enderby v Frenchay Health Authority and Secretary of State for Health* [1993] IRLR
591, ECJ; *Handels-og Kontorfunktionaerernes Forbund i Danmark v Dansk Arbejdsgiverforening* [1989] IRLR 532, ECJ.

89 *Ministry of Defence v Armstrong* [2004] IRLR 672, EAT.

natory) reason is hidden or not obvious, eg a woman is really being paid less because she cannot work unsocial hours, whereas the employer contends that the pay differential is because she is less competent at her job.

5.36   It is important that the pay system is clear and easy to understand; this has become known as transparency.[90] A transparent system is one where workers understand not only their rates of pay but the components of their individual pay packets. The ECJ has said that where an employer operates a pay system which is wholly lacking in transparency but appears to operate to the substantial disadvantage of one sex, the onus will be on the employer to explain and justify objectively the differential, even if the individual worker cannot identify why she has been paid less.[91]

5.37   To justify indirect discrimination, the employer must show:

a) there is a real need on the part of the undertaking;

b) the measures chosen by the employer are appropriate for achieving the objective in question; and

c) are necessary to that end.[92] 'Necessary' does not mean it has to be the only course available to the employer: it just means 'reasonably' necessary.[93] The ET must balance the discriminatory effect against the justification put forward.[94] Unfortunately it seems that the justification need not contemporaneously and consciously feature in the employer's decision-making process, and can even be a reason different from that put forward at the time the pay was decided upon.[95] Nevertheless, retrospective justification will be harder to prove.[96] Indirectly discriminatory terms are not justifiable purely because they have been agreed with a trade union – the union negotiators may not have realised their effect.[97]

90 EOC Code on Equal Pay, paras 19–20.

91 *Handels-og Kontorfunktionaerernes Forbund i Danmark v Dansk Arbejdsgiverforening (acting for Danfoss)* [1989] IRLR 532, ECJ.

92 *Rainey v Greater Glasgow Health Board* [1987] IRLR 26, HL.

93 *Cadman v Health and Safety Executive* [2004] IRLR 971; (2004) 135 EOR 5; May 2005 *Legal Action* 15, CA.

94 *Cadman v Health and Safety Executive* [2004] IRLR 971; (2004) 135 EOR 5; May 2005 *Legal Action* 15, CA.

95 *Cadman* [2004] IRLR 971; (2004) 135 EOR 5; May 2005 *Legal Action*, CA. *Schönheit v Stadt Frankfurt Am Main* [2004] IRLR 783, ECJ.

96 *British Airways PLC v Grundy (No 2)* [2008] IRLR 815, CA.

97 *British Airways PLC v Grundy (No 2)* [2008] IRLR 815, CA.

Summary

5.38 In summary, the key principles relating to the defence are as follows:

- the onus is on the employer to prove any defence;
- the material factor must not be discriminatory, either directly or indirectly;
- the material factor must be significant and relevant, and according to the ECJ, objectively justifiable;
- if the factor involves direct discrimination, it (probably) cannot be justified;
- if the factor involves indirect discrimination, the employer must objectively justify it;
- where pay is governed by merit, flexibility, training or seniority, the comments of the ECJ in the *Danfoss* case[98] should be borne in mind (see para 5.42 below);
- for service-related pay, see comments of the ECJ in *Cadman v Health and Safety Executive*[99] (see para 5.45 below);
- where the pay system is wholly lacking in transparency, the onus will be on the employer to justify a pay differential which appears substantially to disadvantage one sex.

Indirectly discriminatory pay practices

5.39 Most discrimination in pay systems takes the form of indirect or hidden discrimination.[100] See paras 5.34–5.37 above for the legal concept of indirect discrimination under the EqPA 1970. Access to bonuses, for example, tends to be available more in jobs done by men. It may be clear that women generally are paid less well than men, but it may not be possible to identify the requirement or practice causing this.[101] In *Enderby*[102] the ECJ said that where the pay of a predominantly female group is significantly lower than the pay of a predominantly male group doing work of equal value, the employer is required to show

---

98 *Handels-og Kontorfunktionærernes Forbund i Danmark v Dansk Arbejdsgiverforening (acting for Danfoss)* [1989] IRLR 532, ECJ.

99 [2006] IRLR 969, ECJ.

100 See the original Equal Pay Code para 24.

101 See para 5.36 above on 'transparency'.

102 *Enderby v Frenchay Health Authority and Secretary of State for Health* [1993] IRLR 591; (1993) 52 EOR 40, ECJ.

objective reasons for the differential.[103] The higher the proportion of women in the lesser paid group, the more likely it is that justification is required. However, it is not necessary for the underpaid group to be almost exclusively women.[104]

5.40   It is a common defence that the different pay rates were arrived at by independent and distinct collective bargaining processes. This is not sufficient where the outcome is a disparity between the mainly female group and the mainly male group, even if no direct or indirect discrimination can be identified within each process.[105] Otherwise an employer could easily circumvent the principle of equal pay by using separate bargaining processes.[106]

5.41   Sometimes an employer tries to defend a case on the basis that s/he cannot afford to pay the worker more. This may amount to indirect discrimination if the worker is in a job which tends to be done by women, and if her comparator is in a job mainly done by men. Budgetary considerations alone cannot justify indirect discrimination in pay.[107]

5.42   The ECJ's most explicit guidance on what may be considered justifiable or not in indirect discrimination is in *Danfoss*.[108] In that case, the employer awarded pay increments on the basis of a number of criteria, ie flexibility, quality of work, vocational training and seniority. It was not apparent to the workers precisely how the level of each person's pay had been arrived at, but the net effect was that women were on the whole paid less than the men. The ECJ said that where a pay system is characterised by a total lack of transparency, that is, where it is impossible

103 Though see S*pecialarbejderforbundet i Danmark v Dansk Industri acting for Royal Copenhagen A/S* [1995] IRLR 648; (1995) 64 EOR 42, ECJ, which seems to qualify Enderby, at least in the context of pieceworking.
104 *Strathclyde Regional Council v Wallace* [1998] IRLR 146; (1998) 78 EOR 5, HL; *Glasgow CC and others v Marshall and others* [2000] IRLR 272, HL.
105 *Enderby v Frenchay Health Authority and Secretary of State for Health* [1993] IRLR 591; (1993) 52 EOR 40, ECJ and *Strathclyde Regional Council v Wallace* [1998] IRLR 146; (1998) 78 EOR 5, HL; *Glasgow CC and others v Marshall and others* [2000] IRLR 272, HL; *Redcar & Cleveland Borough Council v Bainbridge and others (No.1), Surtees and others v Middlesborough Borough Council, Redcar & Cleveland Borough Council v Bainbridge and others (No.2)* [2008] IRLR 776, CA.
106 See also *Nimz v Freie und Hansestadt Hamburg* [1991] IRLR 222, ECJ; *Kowalska v Freie und Hansestadt Hamburg* [1990] IRLR 447, ECJ. See further the possibly contradictory position of the ECJ in *Specialarbejderforbundet i Danmark v Dansk Industri, acting for Royal Copenhagen A/S* [1995] IRLR 648; (1995) 64 EOR 42, ECJ.
107 *Jorgensen v Foreningen AF Speciallaeger* [2000] IRLR 726, ECJ.
108 *Handels-og Kontorfunktionærernes Forbund i Danmark v Dansk Arbejdsgiverforening (acting for Danfoss)* [1989] IRLR 532, ECJ.

to tell precisely how each worker's pay level was reached, and where there is a statistical imbalance between the pay of male and female workers, the onus is on the employer to justify the difference.

5.43 The ECJ then examined each of the criteria. It recognised that proportionally fewer women were likely to score highly on criteria such as flexibility, vocational training and seniority. Therefore, where statistics indicated that women were generally paid less than men on the basis of flexibility or vocational training criteria, the employer must justify the use of each criterion by showing it was 'of importance for the performance of the specific duties entrusted to the worker concerned'.

5.44 The ECJ took a radical position in respect of merit payments. It said that if women were, on the whole, paid less on the basis of 'quality of work', this could not be justified because 'it is inconceivable that the work carried out by female workers would be generally of a lower quality'. In other words, the employer must be directly discriminating.

5.45 In *Danfoss*, the ECJ said the employer need not justify the use of the seniority criterion because that was obviously justifiable. In the subsequent case of *Nimz v Freie und Hansestadt Hamburg*,[109] the ECJ appeared to change its mind. In the most recent case on the issue, *Cadman v Health and Safety Executive*,[110] the ECJ largely returned to its position in *Danfoss*. It said that an employer does not usually have to justify using length of service as a determinant of pay because length of service goes hand in hand with experience, and experience generally enables workers to perform their duties better. However, where a worker can provide evidence raising serious doubts as to whether length of service, in the particular circumstances, would lead to better performance, then the employer must still provide detailed justification. The ECJ did not clarify how difficult it would be to fall within this exception.[111]

Part-time workers

5.46 Many ECJ cases concern lower pay and benefits for part-time workers.[112] There is a general recognition that a far higher proportion of women

---

109 *Nimz v Freie und Hansestadt Hamburg* [1991] IRLR 222, ECJ.

110 [2006] IRLR 969; November 2006 *Legal Action* 15, ECJ.

111 For the first application of this by the higher courts domestically, see *Wilson v Health and Safety Executive* UKEAT/0050/08; [2009] IRLR 282, EAT. See para 17.21 for the effect of this decision on age discrimination.

112 See also the section on part-time working, paras 11.78–11.99 below.

than men are in part-time work and the issue has been whether employers can justify the differential. In the key case of *Bilka-Kaufhaus GmbH v Weber von Hartz*,[113] a German department store (in line with West German state legislation) excluded part-time workers from its occupational pension scheme. The ECJ said that where a pay practice, applied generally, operated to disadvantage more women than men, it would infringe article 141 unless it were objectively justifiable.[114]

5.47   Working full-time is not a justification in itself for receiving greater hourly pay. Nor would the ECJ in *Rinner-Kühn v FWW Spezial-Gebaüdereinigung GmbH*[115] accept as justification an argument that part-timers were less integrated into the business than full-timers. However, it may be justification if an employer can show that for economic or administrative reasons it needs to discourage part-time working.

5.48   In another case, the ECJ has said that a civil service rule whereby job-sharers progress up an incremental pay scale only in accordance with time actually worked and therefore at half the speed of full-timers with equal competence, cannot be justified merely on the grounds of saving costs.[116] Unfortunately it seems that restricting overtime supplements to cases where the normal full-time working hours are exceeded is not unlawful.[117] On the other hand, it can be indirect discrimination (unless justified) to apply a rule that neither part-timers nor full-timers get paid for the first three hours of overtime each month, since this would represent a higher proportion of part-timers' hours.[118] It may also be unlawful, unless justified, to pay a lower hourly rate for overtime than for normal working hours, since part-timers could end up working the same amount of hours as their full-time colleagues for less pay.[119]

5.49   Statutory entitlement to certain payments such as redundancy pay, sick pay and unfair dismissal compensation is often subject to requirements, eg length of service or age, which may have indirectly

---

113 [1986] IRLR 317. See also *Jenkins v Kingsgate (Clothing Productions) (No 2)* [1981] IRLR 388, EAT.

114 See para 5.37 for more detail on the definition of justification.

115 [1989] IRLR 493, ECJ.

116 *Hill and Stapleton v Revenue Commissioners and Department of Finance* [1998] IRLR 466, ECJ.

117 *Stadt Lengerich v Helmig* [1995] IRLR 216; (1995) 60 EOR 45, ECJ.

118 *Elsner-Lakeberg v Land Nordrhein-Westfalen* [2005] IRLR 209, ECJ.

119 *Voss v Land Berlin* C-300/06; 847 IDS Employment Law Brief 12, ECJ.

discriminatory effect. There have been several major cases challenging such requirements.[120]

5.50   In addition to the above, it may be contrary to the Part-time Workers (Prevention of Less Favourable Treatment) Regulations 2000[121] unjustifiably to pay a part-timer less than a comparable full-timer.

The equality clause

5.51   When a claim succeeds, the way the EqPA 1970 operates is to insert an equality clause into the contract of the woman. Each contractual term that is less favourable than the equivalent term in the contract of the comparable man is modified to make it equal. For these purposes, all monetary payments, eg basic pay, fixed bonuses and attendance allowances, should be added together and regarded as a single term.[122] Once the woman's contract is modified, it remains so even if her male comparator leaves or is promoted or demoted.

5.52   It is irrelevant that, looking at the contracts as a whole, the woman may be said to be equally treated. For example, where a woman receives less basic pay, but better holiday and sick pay, she is nevertheless entitled to have her basic pay increased to the male level.[123] Similarly under article 141, the ECJ has said that the principle of equal pay entails equality in each component of remuneration and does not look at whether the total benefits are the same.[124] However, the overall picture may be relevant to the employer's defence.[125]

Gathering information on pay and questionnaires

5.53   Secrecy about pay allows discrimination to continue. Research by the Institute for Employment Studies shows there is widespread secrecy

---

120 *Rinner-Kühn v FWW Spezial-Gebaüdereinigung GmbH* [1989] IRLR 493, ECJ; *R v Secretary of State for Employment ex p EOC* [1994] IRLR 176; (1994) 54 EOR 30, HL; *R v Secretary of State for Employment ex p Seymour-Smith and Perez* [1999] IRLR 253, ECJ; *Rutherford and another v Secretary of State for Trade and Industry (No 2)* [2004] IRLR 892; (2004) 135 EOR 25; May 2005 *Legal Action* 29, CA.

121 SI No 1551 and para 11.92.

122 *Degnan and others v Redcar and Cleveland Borough Council* [2005] IRLR 615, CA.

123 *Hayward v Cammell Laird Shipbuilders* [1988] IRLR 257, HL.

124 *Barber v GRE Assurance Group* [1990] IRLR 240, ECJ; *Jämställdhetsombudsmannen v Örebro Läns Landsting* [2000] IRLR 421, ECJ.

125 *Jämställdhetsombudsmannen v Örebro Läns Landsting* [2000] IRLR 421, ECJ.

about pay[126] with 22 per cent of employers actually prohibiting employees from discussing their pay with colleagues. In a highly publicised case[127] the EAT commented that 'no tribunal should be seen to condone a City bonus culture involving secrecy and/or lack of transparency ... as a reason for avoiding equal pay obligations'.

Questionnaires

5.54　In April 2003, a new equal pay questionnaire procedure was introduced to help workers find out whether they are being underpaid.[128] The procedure works the same way as in other types of discrimination cases.[129] In summary, the worker can write to her employer, before or after a case has started, asking a series of questions[130] about her own pay, the pay of comparators, the reason for any differences, who decides pay levels and by what mechanism, etc. A standard form can be used, though it is not essential.[131]

5.55　Some employers may object to disclosing information regarding the pay of other workers on grounds of confidentiality or breach of the Data Protection Act 1998. The DTI (BIS) guidance at the back of the standard questionnaire form unfortunately encourages such objections. However, it is hard to understand why the exemption in Data Protection Act 1998 s35(2) should not apply. Otherwise, the questionnaire procedure would be fairly useless and discrimination could not be challenged.[132] In *Barton* the EAT emphasised the importance of questionnaires and that ETs can draw adverse inferences from an evasive or equivocal reply.[133]

Trade unions and Freedom of Information

5.56　In a unionised workplace, another way to find out information about pay practices in the workplace is through the collective bargaining

126 *Monitoring progress towards pay equality* – summary available at www.employment-studies.co.uk/pubs/summary.php?id=1514eoc
127 *Barton v Investec Henderson Crosthwaite Securities Ltd* [2003] IRLR 332; (2003) 118 EOR 22, EAT.
128 Equal Pay (Questions and Replies) Order 2003 SI No 722.
129 See para 21.2 onwards for details.
130 EqPA 1970 s7B.
131 Available at www.equalities.gov.uk/Docs/Equalpayquestionnaire.doc
132 See paras 1.66–1.68 and 21.10 on this and the commentary of Michael Rubenstein at (2003) 117 EOR 22.
133 *Barton v Investec Henderson Crosthwaite Securities Ltd* [2003] IRLR 332; (2003) 118 EOR 22, EAT; *Igen Ltd and ors v Wong; Chamberlin Solicitors and another v Emokpae; Brunel University v Webster* [2005] IRLR 258; 757 IRLB 4, CA.

machinery. It is arguable that statistical information regarding pay forms part of the information which an employer must give a recognised union to bargain effectively.[134] In the public sector, a freedom of information request could be made[135] although this may run into problems of confidentiality where precise salaries (rather than bands) of identifiable individuals are sought.

Equal value procedure

5.57 Traditionally, equal value claims have been long and drawn out, often taking two or more years to complete. Expert evidence and legal representation is almost certain to be used by one or both parties and cases tend to be extremely time consuming and expensive. For these reasons, equal value cases are usually brought by more than one worker (and sometimes by hundreds or thousands) or with an agreement with the employer that all similarly circumstanced female workers will get the benefit (including back pay) of any favourable decision in a test case.

5.58 In October 2004, changes were made to the procedural rules, with the clear intention of controlling the length of case preparation. It was hoped that the built-in timetables would make considerable improvements on the past, ideally enabling hearings to take place within six to nine months, depending on whether an expert is appointed. But the evidence suggests that, if anything, procedural changes have slowed things down. Equal value claims remain long, complex and expensive. If the woman has a good like work claim against a different comparator which would lead to the same compensation, it may sometimes be possible to separate the claims and ask the ET to deal with the like work claim first. If it is successful, the equal value claim need not be pursued.

5.59 The procedural steps of an equal value claim are usually as follows, although there may be additional interim hearings if necessary:

- Questionnaire, Claim, Response.
- Stage 1 equal value hearing, mainly to decide whether to appoint an independent expert and make orders for case preparation.
- Stage 2 equal value hearing, only if an independent expert has been appointed, to decide facts on which his/her report should be based.
- The full hearing at which the ET makes its decision.

134 Trade Union and Labour Relations (Consolidation) Act 1992 ss181–185.
135 See para 1.79 onwards.

Stage 1 equal value hearing

5.60   If there is a dispute as to whether the work is of equal value, there will be a stage 1 equal value hearing, which – if the parties were notified before 5 April 2009 that it had been listed – can be heard by an Employment Judge alone.[136] When the ET notifies the parties of the stage 1 hearing date, it will also set out what will be dealt with at the hearing and the standard case management orders. At the hearing, the ET will strike out the claim if the claimant's work was rated less than her comparator's under a suitable and non-discriminatory JES.[137] An ET can also strike out the claim on any of the usual grounds, eg because it has no reasonable prospect of success.

5.61   Assuming the claim is not struck out, the ET will decide whether to determine the question of equal value itself or to appoint an independent expert to prepare a report. If either party requests, the ET can choose to hear evidence at this early stage regarding whether there is a genuine material factor defence, before deciding whether to appoint an expert. If the ET does decide to appoint an expert, it can change its mind or choose a different expert at any time.[138]

5.62   The ET will make standard orders (as appropriate) with time-scales for case preparation. Broadly, these cover naming the comparator and period of comparison (within 14 days), exchanging written job descriptions, identifying relevant facts, granting access to the claimant and her representative to interview any comparator (within 28 days), providing the ET with an agreed statement of relevant and disputed facts (within 56 days), exchanging witness statements (56 days prior to the hearing), providing a final joint statement of agreed and disputed facts with reasons (28 days before the hearing). If an independent expert is to be appointed, the parties will have to copy to him/her all relevant information they have disclosed to each other. The ET can order the employer to grant the independent expert access to interview relevant staff or management on the premises.[139] Finally, the ET will fix a date for the full hearing or, if an expert is to be appointed, for a stage 2 equal value hearing. In the multiple public sector claims, this indicative time-table is not being met with the stage of agreeing facts and job descriptions prior to instructing experts taking a very long time, sometimes years.

136 Rules for content of the hearing are at Employment Tribunals (Constitution and Rules of Procedure) Regulations (ET Regs) 2004 SI No 1861 Sch 6 r4 and r5 as amended by SI 2008/3240.
137 EqPA 1970 s2A(2) and (2A); paras 5.21-5.22.
138 ET Regs 2004 Sch 6 r10(4).
139 ET Regs 2004 Sch 6 r3(1)(d).

Stage 2 equal value hearing

5.63   A stage 2 hearing in front of a full ET is held where an independent expert has been appointed.[140] At the stage 2 hearing, the ET will make a decision as to any facts that have not been agreed between the parties and will require the expert to prepare his/her report on the basis only of those facts agreed by the parties or decided by the ET. The ET will usually order the expert to prepare and send his/her report to the ET and parties by a specified date. It will also fix a date for the full hearing. The ET has power at any stage, on its own initiative or at a party's request, to order the independent expert to help the ET in establishing the facts on which s/he will rely in preparing his/her report.[141] This may be useful if the parties cannot agree facts or a party is not legally represented or is withholding information.

The full hearing

5.64   The expert's report will be used as evidence in the full hearing, unless it is not based on the agreed or determined facts. If the ET does not allow in the report, it can appoint a different expert or decide the matter itself. The ET can refuse to allow in evidence or hear arguments put by either party if not previously disclosed to the other as ordered.[142] At the hearing, the ET will decide whether the job is of equal value and whether the employer can prove a genuine material factor defence. If the employee wins, the ET may go on to decide remedy there and then.

Expert evidence

5.65   If an independent expert is appointed, the ET will use an expert from the panel of independent experts nominated by the Advisory Conciliation and Arbitration Service (ACAS) and make contact after the stage 1 hearing. The ET rules set out the duties and powers of the independent expert.[143] The ET sends the parties its brief to the independent expert. The expert will get copies of all the relevant information (see para 5.62 above) and be available to attend hearings as required. If delays are caused by the conduct of the parties, the expert must inform

140 Rules for conduct of the stage 2 hearing are set out at ET Regs 2004 Sch 6 rr7–8.
141 ET Regs 2004 Sch 6 r6.
142 ET Regs 2004 Sch 6 r9.
143 ET Regs 2004 Sch 6 r10.

the ET, which has power to order costs or even strike out the claim or response. The final report is sent to the parties, who can ask the expert written questions to clarify the factual basis of the report. Unless the ET agrees otherwise, the parties have just one opportunity to ask these questions within 28 days of the report being sent, and must copy their questions to each other.[144] The expert must provide written answers within a further 28 days.

5.66   The independent expert's opinion has no special status[145] but an ET may well find it very convincing simply because it is independent. Nevertheless, the ET should form its own decision as to whether the work is of equal value.

5.67   In large trade union backed cases, the parties tend to instruct their own experts. The ET's permission is needed and the evidence will be restricted to what is reasonably required.[146] If an independent expert has also been instructed, the parties' own experts can only make an assessment based on the same facts. They must disclose their reports in advance of the hearing and answers written questions within set timescales. Although the ET can choose whether to follow the conclusion of the independent expert, in reality the expert's reasoning and conclusions can only be challenged by another expert. This is why parties usually call their own experts at the hearing. However, it is expensive to instruct an expert (the ET pays for the independent expert[147]) and s/he will not have the same rights of access to the employer's premises and to interview the woman or her comparators. These matters will need negotiation between the parties and reciprocal access should be agreed.

Time limits for claiming and remedies

Remedies

5.68   If a woman succeeds in her claim, any less favourable term in her contract is modified so that, for example, she is no longer paid less than the male comparator.[148] She may also be awarded pay arrears, or compensation in relation to any non-pay term. Under article 141, a

144 ET Regs 2004 Sch 6 r12.
145 *Tennant Textile Colours v Todd* [1988] IRLR 3; (1988) 23 EOR 39, NICA.
146 ET Regs 2004 Sch 6 r11.
147 ETA 1996 s5(2).
148 See paras 5.51–5.52.

part-timer suffering indirect discrimination may have her contract modified so that she receives proportionally the same benefits as full-timers.[149]

5.69   In England and Wales, a woman can claim arrears of remuneration or damages for up to six years from the start of ET proceedings; in Scotland it is only five years.[150] There are special rules where the woman was a minor or 'of unsound mind'[151] or where the employer deliberately concealed relevant information, without which the woman could not reasonably have been expected to start a case.[152] Where the woman's claim is based on work rated as equivalent under a JES, she cannot claim pay arrears for a period prior to the date of the Scheme.[153] For any earlier period, she may have to bring an equal value claim.

5.70   ETs have power to award interest on pay arrears[154] and are prepared to do so. This partly counters the effect of the delays in the ET procedure, so advisers should always seek interest on any claim or settlement. Interest runs from a date midway between the initial breach of the EqPA 1970 and the calculation date by the ET.[155] An award for injury to feelings cannot be made under the EqPA 1970.[156]

Time limits

5.71   The time limit for lodging equal pay claims is set out in detail in EqPA 1970 ss2(4) and 2ZA. Claims must be brought by the 'qualifying date'.[157] In a standard case, this means no later than six months after the last day on which the woman was employed in the employment. A woman needs to be careful. If her contract is varied in some minor respect during her employment, eg to reduce hours, but she is issued with and signs new contract documentation at that time, her previous

149 *Kowalska v Freie und Hansestadt Hamburg* [1990] IRLR 447, ECJ.

150 EqPA 1970 s2(5) as amended; ss2ZB and 2C.

151 EqPA 1970 s11(2A).

152 Note also different wording in Scotland.

153 *Redcar & Cleveland Borough Council v Bainbridge and others (No 1), Surtees and others v Middlesborough Council, Redcar & Cleveland Borough Council v Bainbridge and others (No.2)* [2008] EWCA Civ 885; [2008] IRLR 776, CA.

154 Tribunal (Interest on Awards in Discrimination Cases) Regulations 1996 SI No 2803.

155 *Redcar and Cleveland Borough Council and another v Degnan and others* [2005] IRLR 179, EAT; see para 19.42 for interest on discrimination awards.

156 *Council of the City of Newcastle upon Tyne v Allan and others; Degnan and others v Redcar and Cleveland Borough Council* [2005] IRLR 504, EAT.

157 As defined by EqPA 1970 s2ZA.

employment may be taken to have come to an end for the purposes of triggering the equal pay time-limit.[158] It may not be obvious whether a change in contract terms amounts to the imposition of a new contract (thus ending her previous 'employment' and causing time limit problems) or is simply a variation in the existing one. It depends on what the parties intended, which may not be easy to work out. The fact that the change is fundamental may indicate a new contract has been imposed, but on the other hand, an employee can expressly or impliedly agree to vary a contract, even fundamentally.[159]

5.72   A way round the time limit problem may be if the woman's continuing employment, despite new contracts with varied terms, amounts to a 'stable employment relationship'. This is because, where the woman had a stable employment relationship, the six months runs from the end of that relationship.[160] It is not completely clear what a stable employment relationship amounts to, but it could include a situation where the same work is carried out for the same employer over a period of time through a series of successive contracts with no break.[161] Where there are intermittent contracts without a stable employment relationship, time runs from the end of each contract. But where, for example, such contracts are concluded at regular intervals in respect of the same employment and with the same pension scheme, time would run from the end of such a stable employment relationship. The relationship would stop once the short-term contracts are replaced with a permanent contract.[162] If this happens, it becomes a standard case and whether time starts running afresh from the date the permanent contract started depends on whether the permanent contract was simply a variation of the previous contract or an entirely new contract.[163]

5.73   There are special rules where the woman was under a mental disability[164] or where the employer deliberately concealed relevant

158 *Slack and Others v Cumbria County Council, with EHRC Intervening sub nom Cumbria County Council (No.2)* [2009] EWCA Civ 293; [2009] IRLR 463, CA.
159 *Potter and others v North Cumbria Acute Hospitals NHS Trust and The Casson Claimants* UKEAT/0385/08 illustrates this in the context of Agenda for Change.
160 EqPA 1970 s2ZA(4).
161 *Slack* [2009] EWCA Civ 293; [2009] IRLR 463, CA.
162 *Preston v Wolverhampton Healthcare NHS Trust (No 3)* [2004] IRLR 96, EAT; *Council of the City of Newcastle upon Tyne v Allan and others; Degnan and others v Redcar and Cleveland Borough Council* [2005] IRLR 504, EAT. See also *Jeffery and others v (1) Secretary of State for Education (2) Bridgend College* UKEAT/0677/05.
163 *Degnan and others v Redcar and Cleveland Borough Council* [2005] IRLR 504, EAT.
164 As defined in EqPA 1970 s11(2A).

information, without which the woman could not reasonably have been expected to start a case. Where there has been a TUPE transfer,[165] the time-limit for any claim in respect of the period of employment with the transferor should be counted from the transfer date.[166] This is so even if liability for the underpayment transfers to the transferee under the TUPE rules. However, where the transferee continues to act in breach of the EqPA 1970, eg by inheriting a contractual liability to increase pay to that of a male comparator, time runs from the end of the relevant employment with the transferee with regard to underpay in the post transfer period.[167]

5.74   Because equal pay claims are so complex, it does happen in the large claims that the correct comparators are not identified in the original tribunal claim form. The problem with amending to add new comparator jobs later is that this is regarded as adding a new cause of action, even if the existing claim is on the same basis, ie like work or work rated as equivalent or work of equal value.[168]

165 That is, a transfer under the Transfer of Undertakings (Protection of Employment) Regulations 2006 SI No 246 (TUPE).

166 *Powerhouse Retail Ltd and others v Burroughs* [2006] IRLR 381, HL regarding pension entitlement, generally extended by *Gutridge v Sodexo Ltd and North Tees and Hartlepool NHS Trust* [2009] EWCA Civ 729.

167 *Gutridge v Sodexo Ltd and North Tees and Hartlepool NHS Trust* [2009] EWCA Civ 729 [2008] IRLR 752, EAT. See also para 10.31.

168 *Bainbridge and others v Redcar and Cleveland Borough Council (No.2)* [2007] IRLR 494, EAT.

PART II

Unfair dismissal, redundancy and TUPE

Unfair dismissal: eligibility, fairness and automatic dismissal

continued

6.48   What makes a dismissal unfair?

6.64   Automatically unfair dismissals and detriments short of dismissal

6.100   Dismissal during industrial action

Chapter 6: Key points

- Only employees can claim unfair dismissal. To decide whether a worker is an employee, the label and tax position are not conclusive. The key tests are mutual obligation to give and undertake work, and control by the employer.
- Agency workers may or may not be employees of either the agency or the client organisation (end-user). In the latter case, the key test is whether it is necessary to imply a contract between the worker and the end-user to explain their working relationship.
- For ordinary unfair dismissal, employees must have at least one year's service. Certain breaks in service do not in fact break continuity of employment.
- A dismissal may be substantively unfair (why the employee was dismissed) or procedurally unfair (how the employee was dismissed).
- If the statutory dispute resolution procedures still apply, the statutory dismissal and disciplinary procedure (DDP) must be followed. The employer's failure to follow the DDP will make the dismissal automatically unfair under the Employment Rights Act 1996 s98A. One year's minimum service is required.
- The statutory dispute resolution procedures and s98A were abolished in April 2009, but with some transitional application.
- Once the statutory dispute resolution procedures no longer apply, the *Polkey* principle is fully restored, ie it can be an unfair dismissal purely because unfair dismissal procedures were followed (though compensation will be reduced if there is no substantive unfairness – see chapter 18).
- It is not against the law in itself for an employer to fail to follow a relevant part of the ACAS Code of Practice on Disciplinary and Grievance Procedures, but the tribunal can take it into account. Compensation can also be increased or reduced by up to 25 per cent for either parties' unreasonable failure to follow the Code.
- There are special rules where an employee is dismissed during industrial action, depending on whether or not the action was official.
- There are a large and growing number of grounds on which dismissal is automatically unfair. Most but not all of these grounds do not require any minimum service.
- It is also unlawful to subject employees to a detriment other than dismissal on most but not all of these grounds.

- In respect of many of these grounds, it is unlawful to subject a worker (as well as an employee) to a detriment other than or including dismissal. This is usually where the substantive right being protected is given to workers generally.
- Many of the grounds for automatic unfair dismissal or detriment are to ensure employees/workers are not victimised for asserting their rights, eg to a minimum wage, under the working time regulations or for payslips. The law and evidence required is very similar to that for victimisation under the discrimination legislation.[1]
- This chapter should be read in conjunction with chapter 22 on fair disciplinary procedures.

The legal framework

6.1   The statutory right not to be unfairly dismissed was first introduced by the Industrial Relations Act 1971. It is now contained in the Employment Rights Act (ERA) 1996. The right not to be unfairly dismissed is closely linked to the fair handling of disciplinary hearings. Chapter 22 deals with disciplinaries and grievances as well as the statutory disputes resolution procedures introduced in October 2004. These procedures were abolished in April 2009, but with some transitional effect, and have been replaced with a new compensatory regime based on the ACAS Code (see below).

6.2   The ERA 1996 contains many of the most common statutory employment rights belonging to individuals, apart from the discrimination legislation. As well as unfair dismissal, it includes notice, redundancy, the rights to payslips and written particulars, unlawful deductions from wages and some maternity rights. There are separate regulations dealing with such matters as working time, the minimum wage and transfers. Most collective trade union laws and rights of workers to belong to trade unions are contained in the Trade Union and Labour Relations (Consolidation) Act 1992.

6.3   There are a number of codes of practice in employment law issued by various specialist bodies including the Advisory, Conciliation and Arbitration Service (ACAS). Generally speaking, these codes are not legally enforceable in themselves, but provide guidance which the tribunals and courts must take into account. The ACAS Code of

1 See paras 13.85–13.96.

Guidance on Disciplinary and Grievance Procedures sets out good practice guidelines for the handling of disciplinary and grievance issues in employment.[2] This Code is often referred to in unfair dismissal cases, where procedures prior to dismissal are important (see para 6.57 below).

Who can claim unfair dismissal?

Eligible categories

Employees and the self-employed

6.4 In order to claim unfair dismissal, a worker must be employed (ie work under a contract of service). A worker who is self-employed (ie working under a contract for services) is not entitled to bring a claim. The distinction between these two types of worker can be extremely blurred and difficult to distinguish.

6.5 Unfortunately, there is no clear guidance given by the tribunals and courts to distinguish between those who are employed and those who are self-employed. An 'employee' is defined simply as someone who has entered into, or works under, a contract of employment.[3] A 'contract of employment' means 'a contract of service or apprenticeship, whether express or implied, and (if it is express), whether it is oral or in writing'.[4]

6.6 There is no single test which determines whether a worker is employed or self-employed although there have been a large number of cases trying to establish the approach to be adopted to determine this issue. The approach the tribunals and courts usually apply is referred to as the multiple test which requires all aspects of the relationship to be considered and then to ask whether it could be said that the worker was carrying on a business on his/her own account.[5] The multiple test requires the consideration of a number of factors.

6.7 The first factor is whether there is a mutual obligation to supply and perform work, ie contractually the employer is obliged to provide the work and the worker is obliged to carry it out. This is the most important single factor. If no such obligation exists, the employment

2 A new Code from 6th April 2009 is available on the ACAS website, www.acas.org.uk
3 ERA 1996 s230.
4 ERA 1996 s230.
5 *O'Kelly v Trusthouse Forte* [1983] IRLR 369, CA.

tribunal (ET) will conclude that the worker is not an employee.[6] In *O'Kelly v Trusthouse Forte plc*,[7] butlers who worked in a hotel as 'regular casuals' were not employees, even though they were provided with work on a regular basis, since the hotel was not under an obligation to provide such work. In a later case, power station guides were held not to be employees because the employer had no obligation to provide work and the workers were free to accept or refuse any work which was in fact offered.[8] Although it is a difficulty if the worker has signed an agreement which states there is no mutual obligation, the worker may be able to prove that in reality such obligation does exist. The tribunal must look at the true nature of the relationship. The Court of Appeal has said that tribunals must be alive to the concern that armies of lawyers will simply place clauses denying mutual obligation as a matter of form even when such terms do not begin to reflect the relationship.[9] To override such an express clause by proving it is a sham, the tribunal must be convinced that the real agreement was to a different effect, but there does not need to have been any intent to deceive third parties.[10] The same principle applies where employers insert an artificial 'substitution' clause into a contract of employment. If a worker is entitled to send someone else to work in his/her place, this suggests the contract is not a contract of employment. But the reality of what the parties intended to permit under the working relationship may be quite different.

6.8   Sometimes a worker can be an employed under an overarching contract of employment even though s/he is not required to work all the time, but only as and when required on individual engagements. This is often referred to as a 'global' or 'umbrella' contract. However, it is more likely that a tribunal will interpret this arrangement as not amounting to a contract of employment because there is no mutual obligation to offer and accept any of these individual engagements. In such a situation, it is still possible that the individual engagements, once accepted, would amount to individual contracts of employment in themselves. For example, a teacher employed on a series of individual short-term contracts can be an employee for the period of each

---

6 *Carmichael v National Power plc* [2000] IRLR 43, HL.

7 [1983] IRLR 369; [1983] ICR 728, CA.

8 *Carmichael v National Power plc* [2000] IRLR 43, HL.

9 *Protectacoat Firthglow Ltd v Szilagyi* [2009] EWCA Civ 98; [2009] IRLR 365, CA.

10 *Protectacoat Firthglow Ltd v Szilagyi* [2009] EWCA Civ 98; [2009] IRLR 365, CA; *Consistent Group Ltd v Kalwak and others* [2008] IRLR 505, CA; *Redrow Homes (Yorkshire) Ltd v Buckborough & Sewell* UKEAT/0528/07; [2009] IRLR 34, EAT. See also *Fitton v City of Edinburgh Council* UKEATS/0010/07 re secondment.

individual contract, even if there is no obligation to grant him/her each new contract.[11] There is no minimum length of such contracts, which could even come in to effect on a daily basis.[12] However, it is important that there is mutual obligation to see out the engagement once it is agreed.[13]

6.9   It is also essential that the employer has a sufficient framework of 'control' over the worker, although direct supervision and control is absent in many kinds of employment today.[14] If the worker controls when, where and how s/he performs the work, this degree of autonomy would suggest that s/he is self-employed. However, if the employer has the power to tell the worker when, where and how to perform, it would indicate that the worker is an employee.[15]

6.10   The other provisions of the contract must be consistent with its being a contract of service. The ET will also look at the purpose of the contract and what the parties intended when they formed it. It is the nature of the agreement and the actual performance of the contract which counts, not simply the label attached to the relationship by the parties. Just because a worker is told by an employer that s/he is self-employed does not mean that is the true legal position. Nor is it conclusive that a worker is paying tax on a self-employed basis, although that will be one of the relevant factors.[16]

6.11   The method and mode of payment to the worker may be a relevant factor. If pay is referable to a period of time rather than productivity, this suggests that the worker is more likely to be an employee. S/he is also more likely to be an employee if s/he gets paid sick leave and is subject to the usual disciplinary and grievance procedures.

6.12   'Contract workers', 'temps', 'casuals', people working freelance, agency workers or, less likely, volunteers, may or may not meet the definition of an 'employee'. If these workers are 'employees' and meet the other eligibility requirements (see below), they can claim unfair dismissal. With volunteers, the key factor is whether there is a mutual obligation to provide and attend work, not whether the volunteer has obligations and standards to meet while at work.[17]

11 *Cornwall County Council v Prater* [2006] IRLR 362, CA; *Vernon v Event Management Catering Ltd* UKEAT/0161/07.

12 *Augustin v Total Quality Staff Ltd* UKEAT/0343/07. See para 6.13 for the agency worker context.

13 *Little v BMI Chiltern Hospital* UKEAT/0021/09.

14 *Montgomery v Johnson Underwood Ltd* [2001] IRLR 269, CA.

15 *Ready Mixed Concrete (South East) v Minister of Pensions and National Insurance* [1968] 2 QB 497.

16 *Massey v Crown Life Insurance Co* [1978] ICR 590; [1978] IRLR 31, CA.

17 *Melhuish v Redbridge Citizens Advice Bureau* [2005] IRLR 409, EAT.

Agency workers

6.13   Agency workers may in theory be employees of the organisation to which they are assigned (the 'end-user') or of the agency which assigns them[18] (or neither). If in genuine doubt, the employee should bring a case against both.[19] The usual tests of mutual obligation and control apply when deciding whether the worker is an employee of either party.[20] However, when considering whether the worker is an employee of the end-user, the more important question is whether there is any contract between the worker and the end-user at all. Usually there is no express contract between them, so the issue becomes whether a contract can be implied. A contract can only be implied if it is necessary to do so, to give business reality to the fact that the end-user provides work and the worker carries it out. The problem is that in most cases, this arrangement can be explained by the express agreements between the end-user and the agency, and between the worker and the agency – it is not necessary to imply a contract between the end-user and the worker at all.[21] It needs some specific words or action to convince a tribunal that the agency arrangements no longer explain the relationship. The fact that the arrangement has been going on for a long time is not enough on its own as it is explicable by mutual convenience. It may be easiest to imply a contract of employment when agency arrangements are superimposed on an existing direct contractual arrangement.[22] It is useful to look at the written agreements between the agency and the worker, and the agency and the end-user, which are required to be given under the Conduct of Employment Agencies and Employment Businesses Regulations 2003,[23] although it is not enough simply to look at the label applied to the situation in the documents.[24]

18 *McMeechan v Secretary of State for Employment* [1997] IRLR 353, CA.

19 Provided this is reasonable, which it usually will be. *Astbury v Gist Ltd* UKEAT/0446/04. But since this case, the CA in *James* (fn 21 below) has clarified the law and discouraged hopeful litigation.

20 *Montgomery v Johnson Underwood Ltd* [2001] IRLR 269, CA; *Brook Street Bureau v Dacas* [2004] IRLR 358, CA; *Bunce v Postworth Ltd t/a Skyblue* [2005] IRLR 557, CA.

21 *James v London Borough of Greenwich* [2008] IRLR 302, CA; *Wood Group Engineering (North Sea) Ltd v Robertson* UKEATS/0081/06.

22 Comments of EAT in *James v Greenwich Council* [2007] IRLR 168, EAT at paras 53–62.

23 SI No 3319. See also the original Department of Trade and Industry (DTI) Guidance on the Regulations on the BIS website at www.berr.gov.uk/files/file24248.pdf

24 *Franks v Reuters Ltd and another* [2003] IRLR 423, CA.

A contract of employment can be implied between the worker and the end-user even if the contract between the worker and the agency expressly stipulates there is no such contract of employment,[25] but as already explained, it is difficult to imply such contracts.

6.14   A worker can be an employee of an agency in respect of a single assignment or placement, even if s/he is not an employee of the agency overall.[26] If the worker has accepted a series of individual assignments with the same or different end-users, the question then becomes whether s/he can add together the assignments and maintain continuity between any gaps, so that s/he qualifies to claim unfair dismissal. Where a worker has an express contract of employment with an agency, it is unlikely (though not impossible) that s/he is also an employee of the end-user.[27]

Upper age limit

6.15   There is no longer an upper age limit for claiming unfair dismissal. However, an employer who follows the correct procedures can force an employee to retire at or above the age of 65 or any lower, objectively justifiable, normal retirement age.[28]

Working abroad and ship workers

6.16   An employee can claim unfair dismissal provided his/her employment was in Great Britain (GB). This usually means working in GB at the time of the dismissal, but a peripatetic employee, eg a pilot, with a base in GB could be covered, as could an employee living and working effectively in a British enclave abroad, eg a military base.[29] The position is often unclear on the facts. In borderline cases, all the circumstances of the employment must be considered. Special rules apply to employment on a ship.[30]

---

25 *Brook Street Bureau v Dacas* [2004] IRLR 358,CA; *Royal National Lifeboat Institution v Bushaway* (2005) 784 IDS Brief 5, EAT. See also *Cable & Wireless plc v Muscat* [2006] IRLR 354, CA.

26 *McMeechan v Secretary of State for Employment* [1997] IRLR 353, CA. See also *Cornwall County Council v Prater* n9; *Augustin v Total Quality Staff Ltd & Humphries* UKEAT/0343/07. See para 6.8 above.

27 *Cairns v Visteon UK Ltd* [2007] IRLR 175, EAT.

28 For details, see para 17.24 onwards.

29 *Lawson v Serco Ltd; Botham v Ministry of Defence; Crofts and others v Veta Ltd and others* [2006] IRLR 289, HL.

30 ERA 1996 s199(7).

Categories excluded from claiming unfair dismissal

6.17   Employees in Crown employment (eg working for government departments) can generally claim unfair dismissal, though there are some partial exceptions with regard to certain of the grounds for automatic unfair dismissal in relation to members of the armed services or for employment in the Security Service.[31] Members of the police service are generally excluded.[32] There are certain other special categories.[33] Advisers should check the exact wording of the legislation and up-to-date amendments where any of these exclusions may apply. Special rules also apply to employees of foreign and Commonwealth missions.[34] Depending on the facts and nature of their duties and, most importantly, whether there was an intention to create legal relations, it is possible for church ministers to claim unfair dismissal.[35] Under Article 9 of the European Convention on Human Rights (freedom of religion) a tribunal must take it into account if the church in the particular case does not believe in creating legal relations.

Contracting out

6.18   An employee cannot agree to give up his/her right to claim unfair dismissal.[36] The only exception is where his/her claim has been settled through ACAS or in a compromise agreement.[37] It used to be possible for employees on fixed-term contracts to enter waiver clauses to exclude their right to claim unfair dismissal if their contracts were not renewed. These clauses are no longer effective for dismissals after 25 October 1999 provided the contract and waiver were not entered before that date.[38]

Illegal contracts of employment

6.19   Unfair dismissal claims can only be brought where the worker is an employee and they are therefore based on the contract of employment. If the contract of employment is illegal, the employee will be unable to

---

31 For details see ERA 1996 ss191–193.
32 Apart from ERA 1996 s100 dismissals. See ERA 1996 s200.
33 For example, see ERA 1996 s199 regarding mariners.
34 This can be complex. See the State Immunity Act 1978.
35 *New Testament Church of God v Stewart* [2008] IRLR 134, CA.
36 ERA 1996 s203(1).
37 See para 20.161.
38 ERelA 1999 s18(6).

claim unfair dismissal.[39] Note that, although there will be difficulties, the rule may not be quite so strict in the context of discrimination.[40] An employment contract will be illegal in the following circumstances:

- Where, to the employee's knowledge, the contract of employment involves a fraud on HM Revenue & Customs, eg the employer is not paying the appropriate income tax on the employee's wages. A common indication of a fraud is when wages are wholly or partly in cash and payslips are inaccurate or non-existent. The employee must have knowledge of the facts which make the performance of the contract illegal, but it is irrelevant whether s/he realises that what s/he is doing is illegal (ignorance of the law is no excuse). Moreover, the employee must have actively participated in the fraud, not just turned a blind eye.[41] This seems to entail knowingly entering arrangements which s/he knows misrepresent the facts of the employment relationship, eg falsely representing that certain payments were expenses or concealing under-the-counter payments. It does not make a contract illegal to wrongly describe it as self-employed and to pay tax on that basis, if the parties are in good faith and have not misrepresented the facts to HM Revenue & Customs.[42]
- Where the performance of the employment contract is illegal at certain times, the prohibited period will not count towards the required length of continuous employment for an unfair dismissal claim. An employee must be continuously employed for one year after the end of the prohibited period in order to qualify for the general protection against unfair dismissal.[43]
- A contract for an immoral or criminal purpose, eg procuring prostitutes, will not be recognised by the ET. It is necessary for the main purpose of the employment to be the immoral or criminal purpose rather than it being an incidental part of the employment contract.[44] The conduct and relative moral culpability of the parties may be taken into account when deciding whether a contract is illegal.[45]

---

39 *Tomlinson v Dick Evans U Drive* [1978] ICR 639; [1978] IRLR 77, EAT.

40 See para 13.17 for discrimination.

41 *Hall v Woolston Hall Leisure Ltd* [2000] IRLR 578, CA.

42 *Enfield Technical Services Ltd v Payne, BF Components Ltd v Grace* [2008] IRLR 500, CA.

43 See also *Blue Chip Trading Ltd v Helbawi* UKEAT/0397/08; [2009] IRLR 128, EAT regarding a national minimum wage claim where a student worked excessive hours during term-time contrary to the immigration rules.

44 *Coral Leisure Group Ltd v Barrett* [1981] IRLR 204; [1981] ICR 503, EAT.

45 *Newcastle Catering Ltd v Ahmed and Elkamah* [1991] IRLR 473, CA.

Qualifying service

Length of continuous employment

6.20   To claim unfair dismissal, an employee must have been continuously employed for at least one year at the effective date of termination (EDT) of his/her contract of employment.[46] There is no longer a requirement to work a specific number of hours in a week to qualify for the right not to be unfairly dismissed. There is no minimum service requirement for certain automatic unfair dismissals, eg where dismissal is related to pregnancy or maternity.[47]

Weeks which count towards continuous service

6.21   Continuous employment is measured by 'qualifying' weeks.[48] It is broken by a week that does not qualify with the result that the employee will have to start again in accruing the one year continuous service.[49] If during all or part of a week a worker is away on account of holiday or sickness or other recognised absence, that week will nevertheless count if the contract of employment is still running. Equally, if an employee resigns or is dismissed in one week and re-engaged in the subsequent week, each week counts and continuity is not broken.

Continuity if the employee leaves work and returns

6.22   The period of continuous employment must be of unbroken service except in limited circumstances. Where an employee is absent from work but the contract continues, there is no problem and continuity is preserved. In some circumstances, even though the contract is terminated because the employee leaves, when s/he subsequently returns to the job continuity is preserved and the weeks of absence will count towards his/her continuity of employment. Continuity is preserved where the contract of employment is not in existence and the employee is absent from work in any of the following circumstances:

- on account of a temporary cessation of work. This is when the employer lays off employees through lack of work.[50] It can also cover regular breaks between contracts, eg teachers who are

---

46 ERA 1996 s108(1).
47 ERA 1996 s99. See paras 6.64–6.99 for full list of automatic unfair dismissals.
48 ERA 1996 s212(1).
49 ERA 1996 Pt XIV Chapter 1.
50 ERA 1996 s212(3)(b).

contracted from September to July every year but not over the summer.[51] Whether a break can be considered 'temporary' may not be clear;[52]

- because of sickness or injury, subject to a maximum of 26 weeks;[53]
- in such circumstances that, by arrangement or custom, the employee is regarded as continuing in employment for all or any purposes.[54] This can be helpful when, eg an employer agrees that an employee may leave to visit family overseas and return subsequently to the same employment. At the outset, both parties must regard the employee as continuing in employment for the entire period of the absence.[55] Women taking advantage of child-break schemes need to be extremely careful about the terms of the scheme so they do not lose continuity.[56] Ideally they should simply take unpaid extended leave, without terminating their employment at all;
- the employee is reinstated or re-engaged through ACAS conciliation following dismissal, or a compromise agreement, or as a result of bringing an ET claim, eg through a reinstatement or re-engagement order made by the ET, or as a result of a decision taken arising out of the use of the statutory dispute resolution procedures or the duty to consider procedure in regard to age and retirement.[57]

The presumption of continuity

6.23   The period of continuous employment begins on the day the employee starts work[58] and is presumed to continue[59] until the effective date of termination of the contract of employment.[60] The presumption of continuity is very important for employees, since it means that it is for the

---

51 *Ford v Warwickshire CC* [1983] IRLR 126, HL. Note that ERA 1996 s212(3)(c) may also help. See also para 1.45 regarding possible entitlement to permanent status after four years.

52 *Fitzgerald v Hall, Russell & Co Ltd* [1970] AC 984, HL; *Flack v Kodak Ltd* [1986] IRLR 255, CA.

53 ERA 1996 s212(3)(a) and (4).

54 ERA 1996 s212(3)(c).

55 *Curr v Marks & Spencer plc* [2003] IRLR 74, CA.

56 *Curr v Marks & Spencer plc* [2003] IRLR 74, CA; *Bright v Lincolnshire CC* (2003) 707 IRLB 8, EAT.

57 Employment Protection (Continuity of Employment) Regulations 1996 SI No 3147. See chapter 22 regarding the procedures.

58 ERA 1996 s211(1)(a).

59 ERA 1996 s210(5).

60 ERA 1996 s97.

employer to prove there has been a break which is not recognised by the law as preserving continuity.[61]

Identifying the effective date of termination

6.24   The EDT is identified in the same way as for time limit purposes[62] except that, for the purposes of calculating length of continuous service, it is artificially extended when the employer fails to give notice. In those circumstances, the EDT is when the minimum statutory notice period, not the contractual notice period, would have expired.[63] The ETD will not be extended if the employee was dismissed without notice because s/he committed gross misconduct.[64]

Transfer of the business and associated employers

6.25   Continuity of employment is preserved where there has been a transfer of the business.[65] For the general effect of TUPE, see chapter 10. Continuity is also preserved if, at the time the employee starts work for a new employer, the new employer is an 'associated' employer of the original employer. Companies are associated employers if one company directly or indirectly controls the other, or if both companies are under the control of a third person.[66] Any gap in service between the old and new employers may be preserved by the usual rules (para 6.22 above).

'Contract workers, casuals and temps'

6.26   With the deregulation of the labour market, workers are employed on an increasingly insecure basis under a number of labels which have no legal meaning. Whether or not contract workers, casuals and temps can claim unfair dismissal depends on whether they meet the eligibility requirements set out in this chapter. In particular:

- Are they employees? This is a question of fact having regard, in particular, to the issue of mutual obligation (see paras 6.4 and 6.14).

61 ERA 1996 s210(5).
62 See para 20.28.
63 ERA 1996 s97(2); *Fox Maintenance v Jackson* [1977] IRLR 306; [1978] ICR 110, EAT.
64 *Lanton Leisure Ltd v White & Gibson* [1987] IRLR 1919, EAT.
65 ERA 1996 s218(2) and possibly the Transfer of Undertakings (Protection of Employment) Regulations 2006 SI No 246 reg 4 (TUPE).
66 Employment Rights Act 1996, s218(6) and s231. Where one company is in liquidation, see *Da Silva Junior v Composite Mouldings & Design Ltd* UKEAT/0241/08.

- Do they have the requisite length of service? Remember that a series of fixed-term contracts without a break which counts ...... be added together.
- Have they been dismissed? Failure to renew a fixed-term contract is a dismissal in law.
- It is no longer possible to exclude the right to claim unfair dismissal on expiry of fixed-term contracts by written waiver clauses.[67] Whether or not the failure to renew a fixed-term contract is in practice fair or unfair, will be subject to the usual reasonableness test (see below). However, it cannot necessarily be assumed that just because the contract was for a fixed-term period, non-renewal is fair.

What is a dismissal?

6.27   To bring a claim for unfair dismissal, the employee must have been dismissed in a way recognised by the ERA 1996.[68] There are various types of dismissal:

- termination by the employer;
- expiry of a fixed-term contract;
- forced resignation;
- resignation amounting to constructive dismissal.

Termination by the employer

6.28   Usually the employer terminates the employment with or without notice. Notice of dismissal occurs when there is an ascertainable date, not merely advance warning. If an employee resigns simply because s/he has been warned of a future dismissal, s/he cannot claim actual or constructive dismissal.

6.29   Sometimes there is an argument where an employer uses ambiguous words, which the employee may understand as a dismissal, but the employer later denies s/he said at all or that they meant any more than 'Go home for the rest of the day'. If there is a dispute over whether a dismissal has occurred, the onus is on the employee to show on the balance of probabilities that s/he has been dismissed. If the ET cannot decide this issue on the available evidence, the employee's claim will fail.[69] If the employee cannot prove s/he was dismissed, the tribunal will

---

67 ERA 1999 s18(6). See para 6.18.

68 ERA 1996 s95.

69 *Morris v London Iron and Steel Co* [1987] ICR 855; [1987] IRLR 182, CA.

say s/he resigned and has no rights. However, if the employer's behaviour amounted to a fundamental breach of contract, the employee may be able to claim constructive dismissal instead.

6.30   Where the employer's words are ambiguous, the ET will look at the purpose and effect of those words in the light of all the surrounding circumstances and, in particular, the conduct of the parties and what happened before and after the disputed dismissal.[70] The ET must then decide how a 'reasonable' employee would have interpreted the employer's words.[71] If the employer's words clearly indicated a dismissal, and are taken at face value, the dismissal probably stands even if the employer did not mean to dismiss and a reasonable listener would have understood that.[72] The situation is different where the dismissal (or resignation) took place in 'the heat of the moment', for example, as a result of an argument between the employer and employee.[73] If the employer retracts the dismissal soon afterwards, the ET may consider that s/he was entitled to do so and that if the employee refuses to come back, s/he has in fact resigned. The period of time in which a party may retract depends on the circumstances but usually it should be shortly afterwards.

6.31   A similar principle applies where an employee resigns in the heat of the moment and instantly retracts the resignation. If the employer refuses to accept the retraction, the ET may consider the employee to have been dismissed. Similarly, where the employee is immature or of below average intelligence and resigns while under emotional stress, the ET will not necessarily treat those words as constituting a resignation, if the employee never intended it.[74]

6.32   An employee who wants to leave before his/her notice expires, eg to start a new job, must be careful as s/he could lose his/her right to claim unfair dismissal. If his/her employer agrees to the employee leaving early, the dismissal almost certainly still counts as a dismissal in law.[75] If the employer refuses to agree, the employee must give counter-notice in accordance with ERA 1996 s95(2), though it is not completely clear how this works.[76]

---

70 *Tanner v D T Kean Ltd* [1978] IRLR 110.

71 *J & J Stern v Simpson* [1983] IRLR 52, EAT.

72 But the case-law is conflicting on this.

73 *Martin v Yeoman Aggregates Ltd* [1983] IRLR 49, EAT.

74 *Barclay v City of Glasgow District Council* [1983] IRLR 313, EAT.

75 *McAlwane v Boughton Estates Ltd* [1973] ICR 470, NIRC; *CPS Recruitment Ltd v Bowen and the Secretary of State for Employment* [1982] IRLR 54, EAT.

76 In a redundancy case, s/he must comply with ERA 1996 s136(3)(b).

Expiry of a fixed-term contract

6.33 Non-renewal of a fixed-term contract on its expiry is treated as a dismissal.[77] A fixed-term contract is a contract for a specific term and at its commencement the termination date is ascertainable.[78]

Forced resignation

6.34 If the employee resigns as a result of the employer saying that s/he must resign or otherwise be dismissed, this counts as a dismissal.[79] The difficult issue for the ET to decide is whether the resignation was forced. An employee should be wary of resigning in these circumstances, because it may be difficult to prove that s/he was threatened in this way.

Constructive dismissal

6.35 There is much confusion among the public about the meaning of 'constructive dismissal'.[80] Constructive dismissal occurs when an employee resigns (with or without giving notice) because of a 'fundamental' or 'repudiatory' breach of the employment contract by the employer. In order to bring an unfair dismissal case, an employee still needs to meet the other eligibility criteria, eg length of service. S/he will also have to prove the constructive dismissal was unfair. Constructive dismissal is usually difficult to prove with lots of pitfalls and an employee should be very careful about resigning if s/he wants to be able to claim unfair dismissal.

6.36 For constructive dismissal, the employer must have broken the contract and it is not enough that s/he simply acted unreasonably.[81] So, for example, if the employer gives the worker an instruction which is unreasonable but which is allowed by the contract, there is no breach of contract and therefore no constructive dismissal. However, extremely unreasonable behaviour might breach the implied contract term of trust and confidence (see below).

6.37 Before resigning, an employee needs to consider which contract term the employer has broken. This means being sure what the contract

---

77 ERA 1996 s95(1)(b).

78 *BBC v Dixon* [1979] IRLR 114; [1979] ICR 281, CA.

79 *Sheffield v Oxford Controls Company Ltd* [1979] IRLR 133, EAT; *Sandhu v Jan de Rijk Transport Ltd* [2007] IRLR 519, CA.

80 ERA 1996 s95(1)(c).

81 *Western Excavating (ECC) Ltd v Sharp* [1978] IRLR 27, CA.

says on the point in dispute. Contracts consist of express terms (verbal or written), which are sometimes ambiguously worded, and unwritten implied terms, which can be even more uncertain. Many constructive dismissal claims rely on the employer's breach of one of the generally implied terms, for example:

- not to subject the employee to capricious or arbitrary treatment;
- not to break trust and confidence;
- to take reasonable care for the employee's health and safety.[82]

It can be particularly difficult to know when such an implied term has been broken in practice. Examples of breach of the implied term of trust and confidence could be:

- persistent and unwanted amorous advances towards a female employee;[83]
- failure to investigate properly the employee's allegations of sexual harassment;[84]
- undermining a supervisor by reprimanding him/her in the presence of subordinates;[85]
- swearing abusively at the employee, unless such language is commonly used and directed at each other by staff.[86]

It is uncertain whether the band of reasonable responses test (see para 6.55) applies in constructive dismissal cases, when tribunals decide whether the employer has broken the implied term of trust and confidence.[87]

Fundamental breach of contract

6.38   The employee cannot resign unless the breach of contract is 'fundamental'. There are no hard and fast rules on this and it is for the ET to decide what impact the breach has on the contractual relationship of the parties. The working relationship will be relevant and what in one

---

82 For constructive dismissal and stress, see para 17.155.

83 *Western Excavating (ECC) v Sharp* [1978] IRLR 27; [1978] ICR 221, CA.

84 *Bracebridge Engineering Ltd v Darby* [1990] IRLR 3, EAT.

85 *Hilton International Hotels (UK) Ltd v Protopapa* [1990] IRLR 316, EAT.

86 *Ogilvie v Neyrfor-Weir Ltd* (2003) 737 IDS Brief 111, EAT.

87 *Bournemouth University Higher Education Corporation v Buckland* UKEAT/0492/08; *Claridge v Daler Rowney Ltd* [2008] IRLR 672, EAT; *Nationwide Building Society v Niblett* UKEAT/0524/08.

job may amount to a fundamental breach, in another will not. Many constructive dismissal cases arise when an employer tries to vary the employee's contract unilaterally, eg by substantial cuts in pay or changes in hours or shifts. A serious change of contractual job content or demotion can also be fundamental breach. An act of discrimination by the employer may well amount to constructive dismissal, though it is untested whether this applies in all cases. In one case, an unjustifiable refusal to allow a woman to work part-time on her return from maternity leave together with refusal on grounds that she was a woman amounted to a fundamental breach of trust and confidence.[88]

6.39   Sometimes a single breach of contract is enough if it is sufficiently serious. Alternatively the employee can rely on a series of breaches, where each breach in isolation might not constitute a significant and fundamental breach, but taken together they do. The final act by the employer may be relatively insignificant, though it cannot be completely trivial and must add something to the earlier incidents. This is known as the 'last straw' doctrine.[89] It an objective test – an innocuous act by the employer cannot be the last straw even if the employee genuinely interprets it as hurtful.

An anticipatory breach

6.40   When an employer breaks a term of a contract with immediate effect, this constitutes an actual breach. When the employer merely indicates in advance a clear intention to commit a fundamental breach, this is called an 'anticipatory breach'. An employee who resigns as a result of an anticipatory breach may claim constructive dismissal.[90] However, an employee should be careful not to resign prematurely where the employer has not finally decided to commit the fundamental breach. The employer may still be willing to negotiate. For example, an invitation to use the grievance procedure in response to a proposed step will indicate that the employer has made no final decision. Equally, an employer's statement that, 'I expect you to co-operate in the manner asked of you', is only a forceful request, falling short of an actual breach of contract.

---

88 *Shaw v CCL Ltd* UKEAT/0512/06; [2008] IRLR 284, EAT.
89 *Omilaju v L B C Waltham Forest* [2005] EWCA Civ 1493; [2005] ICR 481, CA; *Lewis v Motorworld Garages Ltd* [1985] IRLR 465, CA.
90 *Harrison v Norwest Group Administration Ltd* [1985] IRLR 240, CA.

When to resign

6.41   Once the employee is sure that the employer has committed an actual or anticipatory breach, s/he must resign fairly promptly, since any delay may be taken by the ET as acceptance of the employer's conduct. This is known as 'affirming' the contract or 'waiving' the breach. An employee is often reluctant to resign before s/he has found another job and this can cause problems. If the conduct of the employer is the effective but not the sole cause for the resignation this is sufficient. Therefore if an employee resigns as a consequence of securing another job, but the seeking of alternative employment was driven by the fundamental breach, s/he probably can still claim constructive dismissal.[91] Nevertheless it is safest not to wait too long.

6.42   How long an employee can afford to delay depends on the facts of each case. A written objection or statement that the employee is 'working under protest' is not enough to keep his/her position open indefinitely. An employee's actions, by staying in the job, and even changing his/her behaviour, speak louder than words. Delay is very risky where the employer's breach has immediate impact on the employee, eg a pay cut, and particularly where the employee has to behave differently to comply with the breach, eg new duties or location. It may be legitimate to object in writing and request a short trial period before resigning.[92] There is less urgency where the breach has no immediate impact, eg a change in retirement age or sick pay entitlement, provided a written protest is made immediately.

6.43   An employee can probably delay long enough to establish the nature of the breach and give the employer an opportunity to change his/her mind, eg by negotiating or taking out a grievance. However, s/he needs to be careful to object in writing from the outset, not to be strung along for too long in pointless negotiations, and if s/he gives an ultimatum, to stick to it.[93] Equally, if s/he has waited the outcome of a lengthy grievance which is decided against him/her, s/he needs to make up his/her mind very quickly afterwards. It is not necessarily problematic to delay while off sick as a result of the employer's behaviour, but this depends on the general circumstances.[94]

---

91 *Jones v F Sirl & Son (Furnishers) Ltd* [1997] IRLR 493.

92 See, eg *Bevan v CTC Coaches* (1989) 373 IRLIB 10, EAT.

93 *W E Cox Toner (International) Ltd v Crook* [1981] IRLR 443, CA.

94 *El-Hoshi v Pizza Express Restaurants Ltd* (2004) UKEAT/0857/03; November 2004 *Legal Action* 20, EAT.

6.44   When the employee does resign, s/he should make it clear in writing that it is in response to the employer's fundamental breach and not for any other reason. An employee is not precluded from bringing a claim for constructive dismissal because no mention is made at the time of resignation that it is a constructive dismissal, but it may be harder to prove why s/he left.[95]

Situations where there is no dismissal

6.45   Where an unforeseen event occurs which makes future performance of the employment contract impossible or radically different, eg terminal sickness or imprisonment, the contract is frustrated and the employee cannot claim s/he has been unfairly dismissed. This is, however, very rare. Employers sometimes try to claim frustration inappropriately, eg in cases of ordinary long-term sickness. Given the change in emphasis towards the treatment of lengthy sickness arising from the Disability Discrimination Act 1995, frustration in these circumstances should apply less readily.

6.46   Termination by mutual agreement means the employee cannot claim unfair dismissal or other rights dependent on a dismissal having taken place. It is not always obvious whether a mutual termination has taken place. Voluntary redundancy depends on the facts; it may be a dismissal, although it is likely to be fair.[96] Similarly, early retirement, unless involuntary, is usually a mutually agreed termination. Employees need to be careful. A dismissal accompanied by a settlement package, however small, may appear later to an ET to indicate a mutually agreed termination.

6.47   An employer cannot deprive an employee of the right to claim unfair dismissal by agreeing in advance that the contract will automatically terminate on the happening of a certain event, eg the worker's late return from holiday. This would effectively circumvent the ET's jurisdiction and is invalid.[97]

---

95 *Weathersfield Ltd v Sargent* [1999] IRLR 94, CA.
96 *Burton, Allton and Johnson v Peck* [1975] IRLR 87, QBD; *Birch and Humber v University of Liverpool* [1985] IRLR 165, CA; *Optare Group Ltd v Transport and General Workers Union* UKEAT/0143/07; [2007] IRLR 931, EAT.
97 ERA 1996 s203 and *Igbo v Johnson Matthey Chemicals* [1986] ICR 505; [1986] IRLR 215, CA.

What makes a dismissal unfair?

The two stages

6.48 ERA 1996 s98 sets out how an ET should decide whether a dismissal is unfair. There are two basic stages.

1) The employer must show what was the reason, or if more than one, the principal reason, for the dismissal.[98] The reason must be one of the five potentially fair reasons set out in ERA 1996 s98(2) or some other substantial reason of a kind such as to justify dismissal.
2) The ET must then decide in accordance with ERA 1996 s98(4) whether it was fair to dismiss the employee for that reason.

The reason for the dismissal

6.49 The potentially fair reasons are the following:

- a reason relating to the employee's capability or qualification for performing work of the kind s/he was employed to do;[99]
- a reason relating to the conduct of the employee;[100]
- retirement of the employee;[101]
- the employee is redundant;[102]
- the employee could not continue to work in the position s/he held without contravention of a duty or restriction imposed by or under an enactment;[103]
- for some other substantial reason of a kind such as to justify the dismissal of an employee holding the position which the employee held.[104]

If the employer cannot show the reason for dismissal, the dismissal will be unfair. If there are several reasons, the employer must establish the principal reason. The dismissal will be unfair if the reason shown is insignificant, trivial or unworthy.[105]

---

98 ERA 1996 s98(1).
99 ERA 1996 s98(2)(a).
100 ERA 1996 s98(2)(b).
101 ERA 1996 s98(2)(ba).
102 ERA 1996 s98(2)(c).
103 ERA 1996 s98(2)(d).
104 ERA 1996 s98(1)(b).
105 *Gilham and Others v Kent CC* (No 2) [1985] ICR 233; [1985] IRLR 18, CA.

6.50   The reason for dismissal will be the set of facts known to the employer at the time of dismissal or a genuine belief held on reasonable grounds by the employer which led to the dismissal.[106] An employer is not prohibited from giving one reason for dismissal at the time or immediately afterwards and another once ET proceedings have started, although the change may affect the employer's credibility. It is the true reason for the dismissal at the time of the dismissal which is relevant. The ET will be reluctant to accept a change of reason if raised at the hearing for the first time, particularly if it will cause prejudice to the employee and the employee will not have had the fullest opportunity to answer the allegations made.[107]

Was it fair to dismiss for that reason?

6.51   ERA 1996 s98(4) sets out the statutory test of fairness:

> ... the determination of the question whether the dismissal is fair or unfair (having regard to the reason shown by the employer) –
> (a) depends on whether in the circumstances (including the size and administrative resources of the employer's undertaking) the employer acted reasonably or unreasonably in treating it as a sufficient reason for dismissing the employee, and
> (b) shall be determined in accordance with equity and the substantial merits of the case.

The ET must take into account a number of considerations in deciding the fairness of a dismissal under ERA 1996 s98(4). The relevant factors vary according to the reason for the dismissal.[108] However, there are also broad considerations which apply to all section 98(4) dismissals. See also chapter 22 regarding fair disciplinary procedures.

Employer's size and administrative resources

6.52   In deciding whether a dismissal is fair, an ET must have in mind the size and administrative resources of the employer. This is particularly relevant when considering the actions taken by an employer prior to dismissal. The larger the employer, the greater the obligation to operate proper disciplinary, grievance and consultative procedures. This does not mean small employers can get away with poor employment practices, but they may be able to take a more informal approach.

106 *Abernethy v Mott, Hay and Anderson* [1974] ICR 323; [1974] IRLR 213, CA.
107 *Hotson v Wisbech Conservative Club* [1984] ICR 859; [1984] IRLR 422, EAT.
108 See chapter 7.

Equity and the substantial merits of the case

6.53   Equity requires that an employer treats employees consistently; an arbitrary or capricious dismissal will be inequitable. If, on a different occasion, the employer failed to dismiss another employee for a similar offence, the dismissal may well be inequitable and therefore unfair.[109]

Human rights

6.54   If the Human Rights Act 1998 applies because a right under the European Convention on Human Rights is involved in the facts surrounding the dismissal, the ET must consider whether the dismissal was fair having regard to that Convention right.[110] This applies whether the employee was employed in the private or public sector.

The band of reasonable responses

6.55   The real question is not whether the ET would itself have chosen to dismiss the employee in the circumstances, but whether the decision to dismiss fell within 'the band of reasonable responses' open to a reasonable employer. The ET must not substitute its own opinion for that of the employer. The ET may think that the dismissal was harsh, but nevertheless within the band of reasonable responses. Within such a band, one employer might reasonably retain the employee whereas another employer might reasonably dismiss him/her. If so, then it is not unfair dismissal, even if the ET would not itself have chosen to dismiss.[111]

6.56   This is a very important concept which results in many claims of unfair dismissal being rejected. It is to be noted that ERA 1996 s98(4) gives no scope or support for this approach. It is a judicial creation which benefits only the employer and removes any meaningful role for the ET members, who are appointed for their industrial experience and common sense. Unfortunately, the case-law is very firmly established on the point and legal challenges have failed.[112]

---

109 But see para 7.34.
110 See the guidelines in *X v Y* [2004] IRLR 625, CA and para 3.13 onwards.
111 *British Leyland (UK) v Swift* [1981] IRLR 91, CA; *Iceland Frozen Foods v Jones* [1982] IRLR 439, EAT.
112 *Post Office v Foley; HSBC Bank plc v Madden* [2000] IRLR 827, CA.

The ACAS Code

6.57   Although it is not against the law in itself to fail to follow any relevant part of the ACAS Code on Disciplinary and Grievance Procedures, the Code sets standards of sound industrial practice and a tribunal must take it into account.[113] The latest edition of the Code (6th April 2009) is disappointingly short and basic, setting out minimal standards of good practice. This may be because a tribunal is now able to increase or reduce compensation by up to 25 per cent for any unreasonable failure by the employer or employee respectively to follow the Code's guidance.[114] ACAS has also produced a guidance booklet, 'Discipline and Grievances at Work: The ACAS Guide', but this has no formal legal status, and it is hard to know whether tribunals will find it persuasive. For more detail of the Code and guidance booklet, see chapter 22.

Procedural unfairness

6.58   The key case of *Polkey v AE Dayton Services*[115] established that a dismissal may be unfair purely because the employer failed to follow fair procedures in carrying out the dismissal. This case overturned the previous 'no difference' rule, so that it is now unfair to omit fair procedures even if following them is unlikely to have altered the decision to dismiss. However, compensation will often be reduced if the dismissal was substantively fair, ie for a fair reason.[116] The only exception to *Polkey* is if the employer was reasonable to consider at the time that carrying out such procedures would have been utterly futile. It is very rare that consultation, for example, would be utterly futile. The exception probably envisages circumstances such as making unexpected redundancies following a sudden and unforeseen financial crisis.[117] But even the appointment of a receiver is something which has usually been foreseen and may not involve closure, so would not usually excuse consultation.

6.59   The House of Lords in *Polkey* gave some guidance on what it considered to be fair procedures. It would not normally be fair to dismiss an employee for incapacity without giving him/her fair warning and an opportunity to improve; in a conduct case, a dismissal would not

---

113 *Lock v Cardiff Railway Company Ltd* [1998] IRLR 358, EAT.
114 See para 18.53.
115 [1987] IRLR 503, HL.
116 See para 18.54.
117 *Spink v Express Foods Group Ltd* [1990] IRLR 320, EAT.

normally be fair unless the employer fully investigated and listened to what the employee had to say; in a redundancy case, it would not normally be fair unless the employer warned and consulted any affected employees or their representatives, adopted a fair basis for redundancy selection and took reasonable steps to find redeployment.[118] The *Polkey* principle is unlikely to apply to very trivial procedural failings.

6.60   Failure to hear an appeal would almost always make a dismissal unfair, as would procedural defects in the appeal, unless these were very minor.[119] On the other hand, a comprehensive appeal process can cure procedural defects in the original dismissal. It is not relevant whether the appeal is by way of rehearing or review, but what is important is whether the disciplinary process as a whole is fair.[120]

6.61   When the statutory dispute resolution procedures were introduced in October 2004, *Polkey* was partially reversed (as explained below). With the abolition of the dispute resolution procedures, *Polkey* has been fully restored.

The statutory dispute resolution procedures

6.62   Although the statutory dispute resolution procedures were abolished in April 2009, it is still necessary to know the rules. This is partly because of the transitional provisions, in that the procedures still apply where steps 1 or 2 of the statutory minimum disciplinary and dismissal procedure (DDP) were followed prior to 6 April 2009, even though the dismissal took place subsequently.[121] Quite apart from that, advisers will be running cases concerning pre-April 2009 dismissals for some time yet.

6.63   Under the procedures, if the employer dismisses an employee, having failed to follow any step of an applicable DDP, the dismissal will be automatically unfair under ERA 1996 s98A(1). On the other hand, if the employer correctly follows the DDP, this does not necessarily mean the dismissal is fair. It may be unfair because it was not reasonable to dismiss for the particular reason (known as 'substantive' unfairness) or it may be unfair under s98A(2) because the employer

---

118 *Polkey* [1987] IRLR 503, HL.

119 *West Midlands Co-operative Society v Tipton* [1986] IRLR 112, HL; *Whitbread & Co PLC v Mills* [1988] IRLR 501, EAT.

120 *Taylor v OCS Group Ltd* [2006] EWCA Civ 702; [2006] IRLR 613, CA; *Whitbread & Co PLC v Mills* [1988] IRLR 501, EAT.

121 See para 22.67.

failed to follow other fair procedures, eg as set out in the ACAS Code or the employer's own disciplinary procedure. The DDP only sets very minimum standards of procedural fairness. However, failure to follow additional fair procedures (whether the employer's own internal procedures or simply good procedural practice)[122] will not in itself make the dismissal unfair under ERA 1996 s98A(2), if the employer shows s/he would have decided to dismiss the employee even if s/he had followed such other procedures. This is often referred to as 'the partial reversal of *Polkey*'. Note that where a dismissal is automatically unfair under ERA 1996 s98A(1), it is irrelevant that the employer would have dismissed the employee in any event,[123] although the compensatory award may be reduced under *Polkey* principles if the dismissal was otherwise for a good reason.

Automatically unfair dismissals and detriments short of dismissal

6.64　Certain dismissals are not subject to the reasonableness test and are treated as automatically unfair. In most of these cases, there is no minimum service requirement. It is also unlawful to subject an employee to a detriment other than dismissal for most of the automatically unfair reasons. The most common reasons are set out below. The list is constantly added to as employees or workers are given new rights which they must be allowed to assert without fear of dismissal or detriment. Several of the listed reasons apply to workers generally as well as to employees. This is where the substantive right is given to workers. In such cases, the worker can claim for dismissal as well as action other than dismissal under the general heading of 'detriment'. The law of unfair dismissal does not apply to non-employees and this is why dismissal of a worker is treated within the word 'detriment'. Detrimental action after the worker has left, eg by providing a poor reference, is probably also unlawful.[124]

---

122 *Kelly-Madden v Manor Surgery* [2007] IRLR 17, EAT, confirming EAT's obiter view in *Alexander and anor v Brigden Enterprises Ltd* [2006] IRLR 422, EAT, but disagreeing with the obiter views of another division of the EAT in *Pudsey v Network Rail* EAT 0707/05 and *Mason v Governing Body of Ward End Primary School* [2006] IRLR 432, EAT.

123 *Wareing v Stone Cladding International Ltd* EAT/0498/06.

124 *Woodward v Abbey National plc* [2006] IRLR 677, CA.

Failure to follow the statutory DDP

6.65　It is automatic unfair dismissal to dismiss an employee with at least one year's service without following the minimum steps of the DDP under the statutory dispute resolution procedures (where these still apply).[125]

Pregnancy and maternity

6.66　It is automatically unfair to dismiss a female employee or select her for redundancy due to pregnancy or maternity.[126] There is no minimum qualifying service.[127] A woman who is dismissed while pregnant but for non-related reasons can claim ordinary unfair dismissal but only if she has the usual qualifying service. It is also unlawful to subject a female employee to a detriment other than dismissal.[128] The prohibited reasons are those connected with any of the following:[129]

a) the employee's pregnancy or the fact that she has given birth (in the case of dismissal), where it ends the ordinary or additional maternity leave period;[130]

b) the fact that she took or sought to take the benefits of ordinary or additional maternity leave;[131]

c) the fact that she failed to return after maternity leave when the employer had not notified her of her return date (see para 11.25) or because she undertook or refused to work on the keeping-in-touch days (see paras 11.61–11.62);[132]

d) a requirement or recommendation for a health and safety suspension (see para 11.71 below);[133]

e) if she is made redundant during the ordinary or additional maternity leave period and not offered any existing suitable alternative vacancy.[134]

---

125 See chapter 22.

126 ERA 1996 s99. The Sex Discrimination Act 1975 will also apply, see paras 11.1–11.11.

127 ERA 1996 ss108(3)(b).

128 ERA 1996 s47C.

129 Maternity and Parental Leave etc Regulations (MPL Regs) 1999 SI No 3312 regs 19 and 20.

130 MPL Regs 1999 regs 19(2)(a), (b) and 20(3)(a), (b) and (4).

131 MPL Regs 1999 regs 19(2)(d) and (e) and 20(3)(d) and (e).

132 MPL Regs 1999 regs 19(2)(ee) and (eee) and 20(3)(ee) and (eee).

133 MPL Regs 1999 regs 19(2)(c) and 20(3)(c).

134 MPL Regs 1999 reg 20(1)(b).

6.67   It is not automatic unfair dismissal to dismiss for the above reasons where the employer proves it is not reasonably practicable, for reasons other than redundancy, to allow the woman to return to a suitable and appropriate alternative job, and an associated employer offers such a job, which the woman accepts or unreasonably refuses.[135] The woman may be able to claim unfair dismissal on ordinary principles, but she will need one year's minimum service.

6.68   If a woman is dismissed while pregnant or at the end of her maternity leave, she is entitled to written reasons for her dismissal, whether or not she asks for them, and regardless of her length of service.[136] For more details of pregnancy and maternity rights, see chapter 11.

Other family and domestic entitlements

6.69   It is automatically unfair to dismiss an employee or subject him/her to a detriment other than dismissal for any of the following reasons:

- because s/he took or sought to take parental leave or time off for care of dependants under ERA 1996 s57A;[137]
- because s/he refused to sign a workforce agreement related to parental leave or because s/he is a workforce representative or candidate;[138]
- because s/he took or sought to take adoption or paternity leave or returned late from additional adoption leave because the employer did not correctly notify the end date;[139] similar exceptions apply as for maternity leave.[140]

There is no minimum service requirement to make these claims.[141] It is not automatic unfair dismissal to dismiss for the above reasons where the employer proves it is not reasonably practicable, for reasons other than redundancy, to allow the employee to return to a suitable and appropriate alternative job, and an associated employer offers such a job, which she accepts or unreasonably refuses.[142]

135 MPL Regs 1999 reg 20(7) and (8).
136 ERA 1996 s92(4).
137 ERA 1996 s99; MPL Regs 1999 regs 20(3)(e) and 19(2)(e).
138 ERA 1996 s99; MPL Regs 1999 regs 20(3)(f)(g) and 19(2)(f)(g).
139 ERA 1996 s99; Paternity and Adoption Leave Regulations 2002 SI No 2788 regs 29 and 28.
140 Paternity and Adoption Leave Regulations 2002 reg 29(4).
141 ERA 1996 s108(3)(b).
142 MPL Regs 1999 reg 20(7)-(8) and Paternity and Adoption Leave Regulations 2002 reg 29(5)–(6).

Flexible working

6.70   The right to request flexible working is set out at paras 11.100–11.115. It is automatic unfair dismissal to dismiss an employee because s/he has applied for flexible working under the statutory scheme, exercised the right to be accompanied, accompanied someone else or brought an ET claim.[143] There is no minimum service requirement.[144] It is unlawful to subject an employee to a detriment other than dismissal for the same reasons.[145]

Part-time working

6.71   Paragraphs 11.92–11.99 set out workers' rights under the Part-time Workers (Prevention of Less Favourable Treatment) Regulations (PTW Regs) 2000.[146] It is automatic unfair dismissal to dismiss an employee because s/he has done anything in relation to the PTW Regs 2000 including alleging that the employer has broken the regulations (unless a false allegation in bad faith), refusing to forgo a right under the regulations, bringing a case or giving evidence for a colleague, or requesting a written statement of reasons why the employer has broken the regulations.[147] It is also automatic unfair dismissal to dismiss an employee because the employer believes or suspects s/he has done or intends to do any of those things. There is no minimum service requirement.[148] A worker who is not an employee also must not be dismissed for those reasons. It is unlawful to subject both employees and workers generally to a detriment other than dismissal for those reasons.[149]

Fixed-term employees

6.72   The rights of fixed-term employees are set out at paras 1.41–1.49. It is automatic unfair dismissal to dismiss an employee because s/he has done anything in relation to the Fixed-term Employees (Prevention of Less Favourable Treatment) Regulations (FTE Regs) 2002[150] including

143 ERA 1996 s104C; Flexible Working (Procedural Requirements) Regulations 2002 SI No 3207 reg 16.
144 ERA 1996 s108(3)(gi).
145 ERA 1996 s47D; SI No 3207 reg 16.
146 SI No 1551.
147 PTW Regs 2003 reg 7.
148 ERA 1996 ss108(3)(i).
149 PTW Regs 2003 reg 7(4).
150 SI No 2034.

alleging that the employer has broken the regulations (unless a false allegation in bad faith), refusing to forgo a right under the regulations, bringing a case or giving evidence for a colleague, or requesting a written statement of reasons why s/he has been treated contrary to the regulations.[151] It is also automatic unfair dismissal to dismiss an employee because the employer believes or suspects s/he has done or intends to do any of those things. There is no minimum service requirement.[152] It is also unlawful to subject an employee to a detriment other than dismissal for those reasons.[153]

Dismissal for asserting a statutory right

6.73 It is automatically unfair to dismiss an employee or select him/her for redundancy for alleging that the employer has infringed a statutory right or for bringing proceedings to enforce such a right.[154] Employees qualify for this protection regardless of their length of service.[155]

6.74 The statutory rights covered include: minimum notice; any right conferred by the ERA 1996 and various rights under TULR(C)A 1992 which can be enforced in an ET, eg rights to ante-natal care, itemised payslips, statements of terms and conditions; the right not to have unlawful deductions from wages; the right to time off for trade union activities and the right not to suffer action short of dismissal which prevents, deters, penalises or compels union membership; rights conferred by the WTR 1998 and by TUPE 2006.

6.75 As long as the employee's allegation is made in good faith, it does not matter whether s/he is correct in thinking s/he has the right or that it has been infringed. It is also unnecessary for the employee to specify the right, as long as s/he has made it reasonably clear to the employer what the right was.

6.76 This concept is similar to the law prohibiting victimisation for taking up issues of race or sex discrimination and there are likely to be similar difficulties of proving the link between a dismissal and the assertion of a statutory right. It is therefore wise to make any request, eg for payslips or clarification of terms and conditions, in a reasonable manner and in writing.

151 FTE Regs 2002 reg 6(1) and (3).
152 ERA 1996 ss108(3)(j).
153 FTE Regs 2002 reg 6(2) and (3).
154 ERA 1996 ss104 and 105(7).
155 ERA 1996 s108(3)(g).

Health and safety

6.77   It is automatically unfair to dismiss or select for redundancy an employee because, in circumstances of danger which s/he reasonably believes to be serious and imminent:

- s/he refuses to work in the place of work, when s/he cannot reasonably be expected to avert the danger;[156] or
- s/he takes appropriate steps for self-protection or to protect others and does not act negligently in doing so.[157] The reasonableness of the employee's actions will be judged by reference to all the circumstances, including the employee's knowledge and the facilities and advice available to him/her at the time.[158]

6.78   There have been few cases on the meaning and scope of this protection.[159] However, successful ET cases have included dismissals for refusal to drive defective vehicles and a dismissal of a young female employee who refused to take rubbish alone at night to a deserted dump.[160] The Employment Appeal Tribunal (EAT) has confirmed that steps taken to protect members of the public are also covered, eg a chef who was dismissed for refusing to cook food which he considered unfit for human consumption.[161] 'Circumstances of danger' have a wide meaning and can include danger of violence from other employees.[162]

6.79   Where there is no health and safety representative at the workplace or it is impracticable for the employee to raise the particular issue through the representative, it is also automatically unfair to dismiss an employee because s/he brings to the employer's attention by reasonable means conditions of work which s/he reasonably believes are harmful or potentially harmful to health and safety.[163] It is also unlawful to subject the employee to any detriment other than dismissal on any of these grounds.[164]

---

156 ERA 1996 s100(1)(d).
157 ERA 1996 s100(1)(e) and (3).
158 ERA 1996 s100(2).
159 For a useful round-up as at January 2001, see (2001) 656 IRLB 9.
160 See (1996) 544 IDS Brief 4 for a round-up and *Kerr v Nathan's Wastesavers* at p27 of the article.
161 *Masiak v City Restaurants (UK) Ltd* [1999] IRLR 780, EAT.
162 *Harvest Press Ltd v McCaffrey* [1999] IRLR 778, EAT.
163 ERA 1996 s100(1)(c).
164 ERA 1996 s44.

6.80   Employees designated with a specific health and safety duty under statute or by agreement with the employer have a similar right not to be dismissed or subjected to detrimental treatment because they carry out or propose to carry out their health and safety duties.[165] The way in which the designated employee carries out his/her health and safety activities is also protected, as long as the representative is not acting maliciously or irrelevantly.[166]

6.81   There is no minimum service requirement to claim unfair dismissal for the above reasons.[167] As with trade union dismissals, a health and safety representative who has been dismissed may be entitled to interim relief and enhanced compensation. There is also enhanced compensation for ordinary employees taking up health and safety issues as above.

6.82   Note that the Public Interest Disclosure Act 1998 can also be invoked in some circumstances where a worker is victimised for taking up health and safety issues. Whistleblowing law protects workers (not just employees) who raise concerns about health and safety through the proper channels.[168]

Trade unions and employee representatives

6.83   It is unlawful for an employer to subject a worker to a detriment including dismissal in order to prevent, deter or penalise him/her for joining or not joining a trade union, taking part in its activities, using its services, or refusing to accept an inducement.[169] Where the worker is an employee, it is automatically unfair to dismiss him/her or select him/her for redundancy for any of those reasons.[170] An employee can claim unfair dismissal for these reasons regardless of his/her length of service.[171] Employee representatives are also protected.[172]

---

165 ERA 1996 ss100(1)(a)(b) and 47(1)(a)(b).
166 *Goodwin v Cabletel UK Ltd* [1997] IRLR 665, EAT.
167 ERA 1996 ss108(3)(c).
168 See paras 6.91–6.97 for details. See also paras 17.149–17.155 on health and safety and stress.
169 TULR(C)A 1992 s146; paras 2.1–2.6 above.
170 TULR(C)A 1992 s152.
171 TULR(C)A 1992 s154.
172 ERA 1996 ss47 and 103.

The right to be accompanied in disciplinaries and grievances

6.84   The statutory right to be accompanied to disciplinaries and grievances is set out at para 22.80. It is unlawful to subject a worker to a detriment either because s/he has exercised the right to be accompanied or because s/he has accompanied or sought to accompany another worker.[173] It is also automatic unfair dismissal to dismiss an employee for those reasons. No minimum service requirement applies.[174]

Not declaring spent convictions

6.85   The Rehabilitation of Offenders Act 1974 gives certain workers the right not to disclose previous convictions which are 'spent' as a result of the passage of a specified length of time. The length of time depends on the nature of the conviction and the rehabilitation period ranges from six months to ten years. It is thought to be automatically unfair to dismiss an employee for failing to disclose a 'spent' conviction.[175] There is still the need to satisfy the qualifying requirements as with ordinary unfair dismissal claims. It is to be noted that exception orders can be made to exclude the protection of the 1974 Act.[176]

Jury service

6.86   It is automatically unfair to dismiss an employee or select him/her for redundancy because of jury service unless the employer told him/her that his/her absence was likely to cause substantial injury to the employer's undertaking and the employee unreasonably refused to apply to be excused from the service.[177] There is no minimum service requirement.[178] It is also unlawful to subject an employee to a detriment other than dismissal for this reason.[179]

---

173 ERelA 1999 s12.
174 ERelA 1999 s12(4).
175 Rehabilitation of Offenders Act 1974 s4(3)(b).
176 Rehabilitation of Offenders Act 1974 s4(3)(b); *Wood v Coverage Care Ltd* [1996] IRLR 264.
177 ERA 1996 s98B.
178 ERA 1996 ss108(3)(aa).
179 ERA 1996 s43M.

Minimum wage, working time and tax credits

6.87 Paragraphs 4.61–4.93 deal with the Working Time Regulations 1998[180] and paragraphs 4.29–4.45 set out the law on the minimum wage. It is automatic unfair dismissal to dismiss an employee or select him/her for redundancy for any of the following reasons, regardless of length of service.[181] It is also unlawful to dismiss a worker or subject a worker (including an employee) to a detriment other than dismissal:

a) in connection with rights under the Working Time Regulations 1998;[182]

b) because of qualifying for a minimum wage rate or seeking to enforce the minimum wage, etc;[183]

c) because the worker took action to secure the benefit of a tax credit and certain related reasons.[184]

Sunday trading

6.88 Shop workers[185] and betting workers need not work Sundays unless they give their employer a written opting-in notice and expressly agree to work Sundays or on a particular Sunday.[186] An employee who is a protected shop worker or betting worker will be treated as automatically unfairly dismissed if the reason, or where there is more than one reason the principal reason, for dismissal is the refusal to do shop work or betting work on a Sunday.[187] No minimum service is required.[188] S/he also has the right not to be subjected to a detriment.[189]

Trustees of occupational pension schemes

6.89 The dismissal of an employee is treated as automatically unfair if the reason relates to any function discharged as a trustee of an occupational pension scheme.[190] No minimum service qualification is

180 SI No 1833.
181 ERA 1996 ss108(3).
182 ERA 1996 ss101A and 45A.
183 ERA 1996 s104A; National Minimum Wages Act 1998 s23.
184 ERA 1996 s104B; Tax Credits Act 1999 Sch 3 para 1.
185 Defined by ERA 1996 s232.
186 See ERA 1996 s36 for full details.
187 ERA 1996 s101.
188 ERA 1996 s108(3).
189 ERA 1996 s45.
190 ERA 1996 s102.

required.[191] The employee also has the right not to be subjected to a detriment other than dismissal.[192]

Dismissal because of the transfer of an undertaking

6.90   It is automatically unfair to dismiss an employee due to the transfer of an undertaking unless the dismissal is for an economic, technical or organisational reason entailing changes in the workforce. It is necessary to have at least one year's qualifying service. For more details, see chapter 10 on the Transfer of Undertakings Regulations.

Protection for whistleblowers

6.91   Public inquiries found that in many of the major disasters of the 1990s, workers were aware of the danger but were afraid to speak out. Partially as a response to this, the Public Interest Disclosure Act (PIDA) 1998 introduced a new Part IVA into the ERA 1996 to provide public interest whistleblowers with protection against victimisation. The provisions are complex and should be read closely before taking any action. There is a short checklist on p734 which must be read together with this text if a worker is considering blowing the whistle. There have been a surprisingly large number of whistleblowing cases brought so far. There is a tendency for this type of case to settle, but where they are fought, they can be long, expensive and confrontational. Much of the case-law interpretation has been disappointing, offering less protection than must have been originally intended. The charity Public Concern at Work provides expert advice and has a very practical website.[193]

6.92   The law covers workers[194] (not just employees), contractors, agency workers, homeworkers, NHS professionals (even if self-employed) and trainees.[195] It is automatic unfair dismissal to dismiss an employee because s/he has made a 'protected disclosure' of information.[196] No minimum service is required.[197] It is also unlawful to dismiss a worker for making a protected disclosure. In addition, a worker (including an employee) has a right not to be subjected to a detriment other than

191 ERA 1996 ss108(3).
192 ERA 1996 s46.
193 At www.pcaw.co.uk, tel: 020 7404 6609.
194 As defined by ERA 1996 ss230(3) and 43K.
195 See ERA 1996 ss 43K, 191, 193, 196 and 200 for who is covered and exceptions. Also *Croke v Hydro Aluminium Worcester Ltd* UKEAT/0238/05.
196 ERA 1996 s103A.
197 ERA 1996 ss108(3)(ff).

dismissal,[198] eg disciplinary action, lack of promotion or a poor reference after s/he has left.[199] A threat could also amount to a detriment. An employer can be vicariously liable for a detriment inflicted on the worker by a co-worker.[200] For example, in one case a support worker in a residential home was harassed by another support worker because she had reported to management a resident's complaint about the latter.[201]

6.93   The worker is only protected if s/he discloses certain categories of information ('a qualifying disclosure') and makes the disclosure to the correct person and in the correct way.[202] A 'qualifying disclosure' means any disclosure of information which the worker reasonably believes tends to show one or more of the following:[203]

- that a criminal offence has been, is being or is likely to be committed, eg fraud or assault;
- that a person has failed, is failing or is likely to fail to comply with a legal obligation. This includes a legal obligation contained in the worker's contract of employment and could also include any statutory requirement or common law obligation, eg negligence, nuisance or defamation.[204] In theory, a complaint about an employer's breach of contractual obligations could have very wide application. The scope for using the whistleblowing protection in this context has not been fully explored. The disclosure need not necessarily concern wrongdoing by the worker's employer; it can include wrongdoing by a third party, eg fraud or breach of health and safety obligations by a client of the employer;[205]
- that a miscarriage of justice has occurred, is occurring or is likely to occur;
- that the health and safety of any individual has been, is being or is likely to be endangered, eg risks to hospital patients, train passengers or consumers as well as to work colleagues and the worker him/herself;[206]

198 ERA 1996 s47B.
199 *Woodward v Abbey National plc* [2006] IRLR 677, CA.
200 *Cumbria County Council v Carlisle-Morgan* UKEAT/0323/06; [2007] IRLR 314, EAT; *Majrowski v Guy's and St Thomas's NHS Trust* [2006] IRLR 695, HL.
201 *Cumbria County Council v Carlisle-Morgan* UKEAT/0323/06; [2007] IRLR 314, EAT.
202 ERA 1996 ss43A and 43B.
203 ERA 1996 s43A.
204 *Parkins v Sodexho Ltd* [2002] IRLR 109, EAT.
205 *Hibbins v Hesters Way Neighbourhood Project* UKEAT/0275/08; [2009] IRLR 198, EAT.
206 See also paras 17.144–17.155 on health and safety and stress.

- that the environment has been, is being or is likely to be damaged;
- that information tending to show any of the above has been, is being or is likely to be concealed.

The worker's allegations need not be factually correct, but it must have been reasonable for the worker to believe that the factual basis of what was disclosed was true and that it tends to show one of the above-listed matters.[207] It does not matter that the information is confidential, but the worker must not commit an offence by making the disclosure, eg by breaching the Official Secrets Act 1989. The worker is protected even if the particular malpractice is not occurring, as long as s/he reasonably believed that it was.

6.94   Sections 43C–43H of ERA 1996 set out to whom qualifying disclosures may be made and in what circumstances. It is important to read these carefully, but in general, internal disclosures[208] are more readily protected. For example, a worker who makes disclosure to someone with managerial responsibility only needs a reasonable belief about the malpractice and to make the disclosure in good faith. The same applies to disclosure made to someone authorised by an employer under a procedure,[209] eg an internal whistleblowing procedure, which allows the matter to be raised with a trade union or health and safety representative, an external auditor, a retired director or the employer's lawyers. There is no requirement to have such an internal procedure, but employers may find that it encourages internal disclosure first. During parliamentary debate, the government and the sponsors of the bill consistently expressed the view that trade unions would have a valuable role both in framing such procedures and in being authorised to receive disclosures. In 2003, UNISON together with Public Concern at Work carried out a survey into whistleblowing in the NHS.[210]

6.95   Disclosures can also be made in certain circumstances to a person prescribed by the secretary of state,[211] eg in the Public Interest Disclosure (Prescribed Persons) Order 1999.[212] The prescribed bodies include

---

207 *Darnton v University of Surrey* [2003] IRLR 133, EAT. See also *Babula v Waltham Forest College* [2007] IRLR 346, CA.

208 ERA 1996 ss43C and 43E.

209 ERA 1996 s43C(2).

210 'Is whistleblowing working in the NHS: The Evidence', May 2003 survey, available at www.pcaw.co.uk/policy/wbworkinginnhs.htm

211 ERA 1996 s43F.

212 SI No 1549, as amended by SI 2003 No 1993. A list of prescribed bodies can be found by clicking the link at www.direct.gov.uk/en/Employment/Resolving-WorkplaceDisputes/Whistleblowingintheworkplace/DG_175821

(as appropriate) the Charity Commissioners, the HM Revenue & Customs Commissioners, the Data Protection Registrar, the Director General of Electricity Supply or Gas Supply or Water Services, the Director of the Serious Fraud Office, the Health and Safety Executive, the Environment Agency, the Rail Regulator, the Civil Aviation Authority, and local authorities responsible for health and safety or consumer protection. Disclosure can be made to these bodies even if the matter has not been raised internally first, provided that the worker makes the disclosure in good faith and reasonably believes that the relevant failure falls within a matter for which that body is prescribed and that the information disclosed and any allegation made is substantially true.

6.96   The requirement that disclosures be made in good faith is extremely important. If the worker has an ulterior motive, eg personal antagonism towards his/her manager, s/he will not be protected, even if s/he reasonably believes the information is true.[213] It is for the employer to prove that a disclosure is not in good faith, and this will require strong evidence.[214] It is common for workers to be fiercely cross-examined on this aspect and, as people tend to have mixed motives, it is often problematic. Disclosures can be made in the course of obtaining legal advice[215] even if not in good faith. However, if the lawyer is authorised to pass on the disclosure, eg by communicating with the employer, then the worker's good faith is necessary in the usual way. Disclosures to trade union lawyers would also be covered, but it is less certain whether disclosure to a lay trade union official for the purpose of getting legal advice is covered. Trade unions may be best advised to set up specific advice lines to cover this situation. Disclosure to a trade union official for other purposes must otherwise fit one of the other categories of protected disclosure, eg as part of an authorised internal procedure (see above).

6.97   Wider disclosures, eg to the media, MPs or police, are protected only in more limited circumstances, including that they are in good faith and not made for personal gain.[216] It must be reasonable in all the circumstances to make the disclosure, taking account in particular of the identity of the person to whom disclosure is made, and also

213 *Street v Derbyshire Unemployed Workers' Centre* [2004] IRLR 687; November 2004 *Legal Action* 20, CA.

214 *Lucas v Chichester Diocesan Housing Association Ltd* EAT 0713/04; 779 IDS Brief 10; *Bachnak v Emerging Markets Partnership (Europe) Ltd* (2006) 801 IDS Brief 9, EAT.

215 ERA 1996 s43D.

216 ERA 1996 s43G.

the seriousness of the matter, the likelihood of recurrence and the employer's reaction if the matter was previously raised internally.[217] Except where the disclosure relates to a failure of an exceptionally serious nature,[218] the worker must already have made disclosure to his/her employer or reasonably fear a detriment if s/he raises it with his/her employer or a prescribed body, or if there is no prescribed body, s/he must reasonably fear that the evidence will be concealed or destroyed by the employer.[219] Any term in an agreement or contract of employment which tries to gag a worker by imposing confidentiality will be void, provided the disclosure is otherwise within the ERA 1996.[220]

6.98   When bringing a case, workers should be careful to address each stage of the legal requirements in the tribunal claim and in the evidence.[221] There are no complex rules about who has the burden of proof in whistleblowing cases – the tribunal will just listen to the evidence as a whole.[222] The worker needs to show that the employer has subjected him/her to a detriment on the ground that s/he made the initial disclosure.[223] It is not enough that the worker becomes distressed because the employer fails to do anything about the allegations, eg out of laziness or inefficiency, as opposed to a deliberate decision to ignore or persecute the worker precisely because s/he made the disclosure. A worker may also be unprotected if the true reason s/he is disciplined is not for making a disclosure, but for taking unauthorised actions to prove the risk s/he is complaining about, eg hacking into a computer to prove data protection may be inadequate.[224] Remedies are similar to those for ordinary unfair dismissal except that there is no ceiling on the compensatory award.[225] In detriment cases, awards can be made for injury to feelings along the lines of discrimination cases.[226] Interim relief may also be claimed if the ET application is lodged within seven days from the effective date of termination.[227]

217 ERA 1996 ss43H(2) and 43G(3).
218 ERA 1996 s43H.
219 ERA 1996 s43G.
220 ERA 1996 s43J(2).
221 *ALM Medical Services Ltd v Bladon* [2002] IRLR 807, CA.
222 *Kuzel v Roche Products Ltd* [2008] IRLR 530, CA.
223 *Harrow LBC v Knight* [2003] IRLR 140, EAT.
224 *Bolton School v Evans* [2007] IRLR 140, CA.
225 ERA 1996 s124(1A).
226 See para 19.13 onwards.
227 ERA 1996 ss128 and 129.

Retirement

6.99   The rules regarding unfair dismissal and retirement are complicated and are set out in more detail at paras 17.24–17.40. In brief, it is automatically unfair to dismiss an employee for retirement:

- before the age of 65 or any earlier objectively justifiable normal retirement age;
- at retirement age, but without having followed the statutory procedures to notify impending retirement and consider any request to continue working.

Dismissal during industrial action

6.100   It is automatically unfair to dismiss an employee within the protected period – generally the first 12 weeks of industrial action (with some extensions) because s/he took protected industrial action.[228] This includes later dismissals, where the employee had stopped taking industrial action within the 12 weeks.[229] No minimum service is required.

6.101   After the first 12 weeks, the position is less straightforward. An ET will have no jurisdiction to hear the employee's unfair dismissal claim if all those taking part in the action or affected by the lock-out were also dismissed and none were re-engaged within three months.[230] This is designed to protect employees against selective or targeted dismissals. The only exception is if the employee is dismissed for specific reasons related to family, dependant leave, health and safety, working time, employee representatives or whistleblowing.[231]

6.102   An employee dismissed while taking part in unofficial industrial action cannot claim unfair dismissal.[232] Broadly speaking, industrial action is unofficial unless some or all of its participants are members of a trade union which has authorised or endorsed the action.[233] There are complicated rules on this. There are the same exceptions as for dismissals on official action.[234]

---

228 See TULR(C)A 1992 s238A(2) for details.
229 TULR(C)A 1992 s239(1).
230 TULR(C)A 1992 s238.
231 TULR(C)A 1992 s238(2A).
232 TULR(C)A 1992 s237(1).
233 TULR(C)A 1992 s237(2).
234 TULR(C)A 1992 s237(1A).

Types of unfair dismissal

continued

Chapter 7: Key points

Capability or qualification dismissals

- Capability dismissals cover sickness, injury and qualification dismissals as well as dismissals relating to ability to do a job.
- Sickness and injury dismissals fall into two categories, long-term sickness/injury and intermittent absence from work. The employer has to satisfy different requirements depending on the category.
- With long-term sickness/injury dismissals, the employer should obtain a medical report (to find out the nature and likely duration of the illness/injury) and discuss this report with the employee before dismissing. See also the adjustments suggested under the Disability Discrimination Act 1995.
- How long the employer should wait depends on the difficulty of covering the employee's absence, and the prognosis. There should be no rigid rule.
- With a competence dismissal, the test is not whether the employee was actually incompetent, but whether the employer genuinely believed s/he was incompetent, on reasonable grounds, having carried out a proper investigation.
- Only in exceptional cases will a dismissal for a first act of incompetence be fair. The exceptions concern employees who are responsible for the safety of the public, eg as airline pilots or bus drivers. Otherwise, employers should give an opportunity to improve, and offer guidance and support if appropriate.

General guide to useful evidence

- With sickness dismissals, get a copy of all the medical reports. If the employer did not rely on a medical report, get a report from the employee's GP for use at the employment tribunal (ET) hearing.
- If other employees have had more time off and there is any suggestion of inequitable treatment or discrimination, get details of their sickness records. This might be evidenced by the statutory sick pay (SSP) records or in a discrimination case, by a questionnaire.
- If the dismissal is due to incompetence, get information on the nature and consequences of the incompetence; check past appraisals. Try to discover whether any other employees have committed similar acts and whether they were dismissed.

- Obtain any written sickness and capability procedures.

Conduct dismissals

- It is usually only with acts of gross misconduct that an employer can fairly dismiss for a first offence. Acts of gross misconduct are normally set out in the disciplinary procedure.
- The ET's function is not to determine whether the employee was guilty of the offence. The ET has to determine whether the employer acted reasonably in dismissing the employee. If the employee was not guilty, then it may well be an unfair dismissal, but this is not always the case.
- The test is not whether the employer genuinely believed the employee was guilty, on reasonable grounds, having carried out a proper investigation.
- The ET cannot decide what investigation and decision it would have conducted and reached itself. It can only measure what the employer did by the objective standard of any reasonable employer.

General guide to useful evidence

- It is important to get a copy of the disciplinary procedure and check whether the employer followed it.
- Obtain notes of the disciplinary hearing and ask the worker for his/her version. Decide whether it was fairly and properly conducted. Had the decision already been made to dismiss?
- Ascertain the evidence relied on by the employer in deciding to dismiss. Obtain copies of earlier warnings.
- Find out whether any other employees have committed similar acts of misconduct and not been dismissed.

'Some other substantial reason' dismissals

- The most common types of 'some other substantial reason' dismissal are where the dismissal arises out of a reorganisation at the workplace or refusal to agree a variation of contract terms.
- It is necessary for the dismissal to be for a substantial reason. Where the two cannot be reconciled, the tribunals treat the interests of the employer as being more important than those of the employee.
- Dismissals due to incompatibility with other employees will be for some other substantial reason.

General guide to useful evidence
- Any evidence to show that it was not prejudicial to the employer to continue to employ the employee will be valuable.
- Find out if any other employees in a similar situation were dismissed.

Capability or qualification dismissals

7.1 An employer may claim that a dismissal relates to the capability or qualifications of the employee for performing work of the kind s/he was employed to do.[1] The statutory definition of 'capability' is 'capability assessed by reference to skill, aptitude, health or any other physical or mental quality'.[2] 'Qualification' means 'any degree, diploma or other academic, technical or professional qualification relevant to the position which the employee held'.[3]

Incompetence dismissals

7.2 An incompetence dismissal is one that is due to the employee's inability to perform the job to the standard expected by the employer. It includes situations where that standard is higher than the norm in the industry.[4]

The reasonableness test: ERA 1996 s98(4)

7.3 It is important to note that the employer need not prove in the ET that the employee actually was incompetent. The employer need show only that s/he genuinely and reasonably believed that the employee was incompetent. The test is as follows:
Did the employer honestly believe that the employee was incompetent or unsuitable for the job?

- If so, was such belief held on reasonable grounds?
- In forming such a belief, did the employer carry out a proper and adequate investigation? In most cases, this would include giving the employee an opportunity to answer the criticisms.[5]

1 Employment Rights Act (ERA) 1996 s98(2)(a).
2 ERA 1996 s98(3)(a).
3 ERA 1996 s98(3)(b).
4 *Brown v Hall Advertising* [1978] IRLR 246, EAT.
5 *McPhie and McDermott v Wimpey Waste Management* [1981] IRLR 316, EAT.

To show that the employer's belief was reasonable, the ET may accept evidence of the honest views of the employee's managers. Other evidence against the employee may include complaints by customers or other staff, or a drop in sales figures. On the other hand, the employee may be able to prove the employer's belief was unreasonable, eg by showing s/he had above-average sales figures or s/he was under-staffed or over-worked, or that s/he recently had a good appraisal or a merit pay rise. Remember that since the ET cannot make its own judgment on the level of the employee's competence, the employer only needs enough evidence to show his/her belief was reasonable.

7.4   Other factors are relevant to the fairness of the dismissal. The employer should previously have made the employee aware of his/her dissatisfaction, given reasonable time to improve and warned of the consequences if s/he did not. The amount of time which should be allowed for improvement depends on the facts including the type of job, the level of incompetence, length of service and seniority. An ET usually expects the employer to have taken steps to try to improve the situation, eg by offering support and/or supervision, or retraining, setting targets and monitoring progress. The extent of assistance that should have been offered depends on the employer's size and administrative resources.

7.5   It is rarely fair to dismiss an employee on the basis of one act of incompetence. The exception is where the consequences are so serious that to continue to employ the employee would be too risky and dangerous, eg when a mistake is made by an airline pilot or a coach driver.[6] In this type of situation, dismissal without retraining or being given the chance to improve would usually be fair.

7.6   The ET may also take into account whether the employer had any alternative vacancy which could have been offered to the employee prior to dismissal. An employer will not be expected to create a vacancy or new job for the employee. The failure to offer alternative employment is not an overriding factor in capability dismissals but it is a relevant consideration, particularly where a large employer had appropriate vacancies which were not offered to the employee.

Aptitude and mental quality dismissals

7.7   An 'aptitude' dismissal may be because an employee is inflexible at work or is difficult or disruptive or not prepared to adapt.[7] 'Mental

---

6 *Alidair Ltd v Taylor* [1978] IRLR 82; [1978] ICR 455, CA.

7 *Abernethy v Mott, Hay and Anderson* [1974] ICR 323; [1974] IRLR 213, CA.

quality' would include an employee's lack of drive or having a personality which has a detrimental effect on colleagues' work or on customers.[8] If an employee has not satisfied the necessary standards required by the employer due to carelessness, negligence or idleness, this is more appropriately dealt with as misconduct rather than incapability.[9]

The reasonableness test: ERA 1996 s98(4)

7.8 The employer must show that the employee's inflexibility or other mental quality was detrimental to the business. Prior to dismissal, the employer should have given sufficient and adequate warnings detailing the alleged shortcomings and the employee ought to have been provided with a reasonable opportunity to improve. As usual, the employer's size and administrative resources will be relevant in judging the adequacy of the procedures followed.

Sickness, injury and other health dismissals

7.9 An employer who dismisses an employee for ill-health or sickness absences may be dismissing on grounds of capability or conduct.[10] It will be a dismissal for conduct if the employer believes that the employee is not ill but is using sickness as an excuse not to work. Since different considerations will be relevant to the fairness of dismissing for conduct, it needs to be established what was the principal reason for dismissal. This section deals with capability dismissals. Note that in some circumstances, an employee may gain protection from the Disability Discrimination Act 1995 (see chapter 15).

The reasonableness test: ERA 1996 s98(4)

7.10 There are two distinct forms of absence from work as a result of ill-health:

1) several intermittent absences, not necessarily for the same reason; and
2) a prolonged continuous absence due to a single medical condition.

The proper steps for an employer to take, prior to dismissing an employee, depend on whether the ill-health was intermittent or

---

8 *Bristow v ILEA* (1979) EAT 602/79.
9 *Sutton and Gates Ltd v Boxall* [1978] IRLR 486.
10 See para 7.50.

continuous. In respect of both situations, it is necessary for the employer to have regard to the whole history of employment and take into account a range of factors such as the nature of the illness, the length of absences, the likelihood of the illness recurring, the need of the employer to have the employee's work done, and the impact on others of the employee's absence.

(1) Intermittent absences

7.11   Before dismissing, the employer must have made it clear to the employee what level of attendance was expected. If the employer is dissatisfied with the employee's attendance record, s/he should conduct a fair review of the record and give the employee an opportunity to explain the reason for the various absences.[11] Any warning after the review should make it clear that the employee may be dismissed if there is no improvement. If there is no satisfactory improvement following a warning, dismissal will usually be fair.[12]

7.12   An employer also ought to take into account the following factors:

- the length of absences and periods of good health;
- the likelihood of future absences;
- the nature of the employee's job and the effect of absences;
- the consistent application of the employer's absenteeism policy.[13]

Employees should be gently warned that their absence may lead to dismissal, but genuine illness should not be treated as a disciplinary matter. The employer should handle each case individually in a sympathetic, understanding and compassionate manner.[14]

7.13   If there is an underlying medical condition, the employer should usually take medical advice and follow the steps appropriate in cases of long-term sickness (see below).

(2) A single period of prolonged absence

7.14   The basic question is whether in all the circumstances the employer could be expected to wait any longer and, if so, how much longer.[15] Each case must be considered on its own facts and an employer cannot

---

11 *Rolls-Royce v Walpole* [1980] IRLR 343, EAT.
12 *International Sports Co v Thompson* [1980] IRLR 340, EAT.
13 *Lyncock v Cereal Packaging* [1988] IRLR 510, EAT. Inconsistency may also indicate discrimination.
14 *Lyncock v Cereal Packaging* [1988] IRLR 510, EAT.
15 *Spencer v Paragon Wallpapers* [1976] IRLR 373, EAT.

hold rigidly to a predetermined period of sickness after which any employee may be dismissed.

7.15 An ET would expect the employer to have found out the true medical position and to have consulted with the employee before making a decision. A medical report on the implications and likely length of illness should generally be obtained from the employee's GP or a company doctor or independent consultant. Where the employer gets a report from a company doctor, the employer should also be willing to consider a report from the employee's own GP or specialist. Whereas the former may be more familiar with working conditions, the latter may be better placed to judge the employee's health.

7.16 The Access to Medical Reports Act 1988 covers workers' access to reports prepared by a medical practitioner who has responsibility for their clinical care.[16] An employer must not apply to a worker's doctor for a report without first getting the worker's written consent, having notified the worker in writing of his/her rights under the Act.[17] Most employers have a standard notification and consent form for this. The worker is entitled to see the report before it is sent to the employer if s/he so requests and to make amendments with the doctor's agreement.[18] The worker must be told of these rights at the time s/he is asked for his/her consent to the obtaining of the report. The employer is supposed to tell the medical practitioner that the worker wants access to the report before it is supplied, but it is advisable for the worker also to remind the doctor of this. If the doctor does not consent to any requested amendments, the worker has the right to attach a personal statement to the report.[19] The doctor must give the worker a copy of the report if requested, except in certain excepted circumstances.[20] A worker may also have rights under the Data Protection Act 1998 or the Access to Health Records Act 1990 to health records held on him/her by the employer or any external doctor working for the employer.

7.17 If an employee refuses to see a company doctor or allow any medical report, s/he increases the risk of being fairly dismissed.

7.18 Once the employer has the report, a meeting should be arranged to discuss its contents with the employee. In general, the employer must take such steps as are sensible in the circumstances to discuss the

16 Access to Medical Reports Act 1988 ss1 and 2.
17 Access to Medical Reports Act 1988 s3.
18 Access to Medical Reports Act 1988 ss4(1) and 5(2).
19 Access to Medical Reports Act 1988 s4.
20 Access to Medical Reports Act 1988 s6(2) and 7.

matter and become informed of the true medical position.[21] Consultation will often throw new light on the problem, bringing up facts and circumstances of which the employer was unaware.[22]

7.19　　Unless the medical advice is obviously inaccurate, based on inadequate information or lack of proper examination, the employer is allowed to rely on what the doctor says, as long as the employee gets a chance to comment. If the employee's GP report is more favourable than the employer's own medical report (often from occupational health practitioners), the employer can choose which report to follow if s/he has a good reason for the choice. Obviously the GP knows the employee better, whereas an occupational health doctor will be more familiar with the work environment. In some cases, the difference could only reasonably be resolved by getting a third opinion from a specialist.

7.20　　The employer's decision ought to be based on the following factors:

- the nature and likely duration of the illness;
- the need for the employee to do the job for which s/he was employed and the difficulty of covering his/her absence. The more skilful and specialist the employee, the more vulnerable s/he is to being fairly dismissed after a relatively short absence;
- the possibility of varying the employee's contractual duties. An employer will not be expected to create an alternative position that does not already exist nor to go to great lengths to accommodate the employee.[23] However, a large employer may be expected to offer any available vacancy which would suit the employee. What is reasonable very much depends on the facts.
- whether or not contractual sick pay has run out is just one factor either way.[24]

There is rarely any useful purpose served by issuing a disciplinary warning to an employee who is long-term sick. What is needed is simply a discussion about the position. The issue relates to the employee's capability, not conduct, and the consequence of a warning may be counter-productive.[25]

---

21 *East Lindsey DC v Daubney* [1977] IRLR 181; ICR 566, EAT.
22 *East Lindsey DC v Daubney* [1977] IRLR 181; ICR 566, EAT.
23 *Garricks (Caterers) v Nolan* [1980] IRLR 259, EAT.
24 *Hardwick v Leeds Area Health Authority* [1975] IRLR 319, EAT; *Coulson v Felixstowe Dock & Railway Co* [1975] IRLR 11, EAT.
25 *Spencer v Paragon Wallpapers* [1976] IRLR 373, EAT.

7.21 Sometimes the nature of the illness or injury is such that an employee may never be able to perform his/her contractual duties again or any performance would be radically different from what s/he and the employer envisaged at the outset. If this happens, the contract of employment may be 'frustrated' and just come to an end (see para 6.45). Since the employer will not have actually dismissed the employee, the employee will be unable to claim unfair dismissal or notice.[26] The courts and tribunals are extremely reluctant to say that an employment contract has ended in this way because of the dire consequences for the employee.

7.22 An employee suffering from long-term ill-health may succeed in a claim under the Disability Discrimination Act (DDA) 1995, where s/he would have failed in an unfair dismissal claim. The DDA 1995 places greater obligations on the employer, eg to modify the employee's duties or actively find alternative employment.

Ill-health or stress caused by the employer

7.23 If the employee is unable to do the job because of injury or ill-health originally caused by the employer, this does not necessarily mean the dismissal is unfair. The ET can take it into account when considering whether it is reasonable to dismiss in the circumstances, but it is unlikely to be a big factor.[27] The employee may have claims against the employer outside the employment law field, eg for personal or industrial injuries. For an introduction to employers' duties to do risk assessments and personal injuries claims for stress, see paras 17.144–17.155.

The NHS Injury Benefits Scheme

7.24 The NHS Injury Benefits Scheme provides benefits for any NHS employee who loses pay because s/he is on certified sick leave or permanently disabled. It applies where an injury, disease or condition developed as a result of work in the NHS, eg RSI or severe stress. It does not matter if it is an injury which is due to the employee's own fault. There is a temporary injury allowance while the worker is off sick and a permanent injury benefit if s/he retires or moves to a lower paid job outside the NHS. Usually the employer decides on entitlement to the temporary allowance, but the claim can be referred to the NHS Pension Agency. Entitlement to permanent benefit is always

26 See paras 6.27–6.47 above on types of dismissal under the ERA 1996.
27 See *McAdie v Royal Bank of Scotland plc* [2007] IRLR 895, CA.

determined by the Agency. For more details, employees should consult their trade union representative, the NHS Pensions Agency[28] or the Pensions Officer of the employing NHS Trust. The scheme is set out at www.injurybenefit.nhsbsa.nhs.uk/index.htm#content. There is an NHS Pensions' Agency Guide at www.nhspa.gov.uk/booklets_new/ sdib_new.pdf. The Scottish Public Pensions Agency administers an injury benefits scheme under a different set of rules, and has published an Injury Benefits Scheme Booklet at www.sppa.gov.uk/nhs/ documents/SPPANHSInjuryBenefitsSchemeGuide_000.pdf.

Going on holiday while on sick leave

7.25   Employees may legitimately not be at home during sickness leave. They may be out visiting the doctor or staying with relatives. As long as they keep in touch in the way required by their contract or sickness procedure, they need not be available to answer every telephone call. Occasionally employees are dismissed for going on holiday or attending college while off sick. This is not necessarily contradictory, as the employee may be absent due to work-related stress, and a holiday may in fact help.[29] Nevertheless, it is advisable for an employee ask his/her GP whether it is a good idea to go, and then to check with the employer.

Dismissals due to other physical quality

7.26   An 'other physical quality' would include an injury or loss of faculty which affected the employee's ability to perform the job. Employees may also gain protection from the DDA 1995.[30] Although outside the scope of this book, note that an injury sustained at work may give rise to a personal injury claim against the employer, including compensation for loss of earnings.

The reasonableness test: ERA 1996 s98(4)

7.27   The employer will usually be able to justify dismissal if the injury is such that it is impossible or dangerous for the employee to perform his/her job. Before dismissal, the employer should consult the employee concerning the injury and its consequences for future employment. It may be possible for the employee to retrain or use

28 Telephone: 01253 774 547.
29 For example, *McMaster v Manchester Airport plc* (1997) EAT 149/97.
30 See chapter 15.

aids to overcome the loss of faculty. An employer should offer any suitable alternative vacancy.

Qualification dismissals

7.28 A qualification dismissal is one where an employee loses a qualification or fails to obtain a qualification which was a condition of his/her employment. A common example is disqualification from driving when having a licence is a necessary requirement of the job. This requirement need not be expressly stated in the contract where the job clearly entails driving duties.[31] An employer may also require a qualification during the employee's employment which the employee does not possess and is unable or unlikely to acquire.

The reasonableness test: ERA 1996 s98(4)

7.29 Where an employee loses a qualification which s/he is required to have under his/her contract or which is necessary for the job, it may be fair to dismiss. The employer would not usually be expected to create an alternative job, but s/he should make an effort appropriate to the size and administrative resources of the enterprise and the availability of vacancies.

7.30 An employer may require new qualifications because of the introduction of new technology or a different mode of operation. It may be fair to dismiss an employee who fails to acquire the new qualification if the employer can justify the need for it. The employer must also act reasonably in the introduction of the requirement, eg by offering retraining. Failure to give an employee a fair and proper opportunity to satisfy the new requirement will make the dismissal unfair.[32] An employer's insistence on certain qualifications may be indirect discrimination contrary to the Race Relations Act 1976 or Sex Discrimination Act 1975.[33]

Conduct dismissals

7.31 Unlike with capability and qualification dismissals, there is no statutory definition of conduct dismissals. Nevertheless, there are a number of activities which are recognised as potential misconduct and are

31 *Tayside RC v McIntosh* [1982] IRLR 272, EAT.
32 *Evans v Bury Football Club* (1981) EAT 185/81.
33 See para 13.52 onwards.

usually listed in the disciplinary procedure if there is a written contract of employment, eg:

- theft or other dishonesty;
- violence and fighting;
- unauthorised absenteeism[34] or lateness;
- disobedience;
- being under the influence of alcohol or drugs;[35]
- threatening or abusive language;
- misuse of telephone, e-mail or internet;
- behaviour undermining the implied term of fidelity and good faith.

Some acts of misconduct amount to 'gross misconduct'. The main relevance of this concept is that an employer dismissing for gross misconduct need not give notice under the contract.[36] Unfair dismissal is a separate issue. It may be fair or unfair to dismiss an employee for gross misconduct. However, as gross misconduct involves more serious forms of misconduct, it is more likely to be fair to dismiss for a single act, with no previous warnings.

7.32   Conduct outside working hours might lead to a fair dismissal in some circumstances, where it has relevance for the work situation. Whether a dismissal is fair will depend on a number of factors, such as adverse publicity, implications for the workplace, relevance to the job and whether the conduct outside work could be said to breach the implied term of trust and confidence. Where relevant, an ET should bear in mind the employee's right to respect for his/her private life under the European Convention on Human Rights, but this can be outweighed by the impact on the employer.[37]

Issues of fairness common to many conduct dismissals

7.33   For general principles of fairness in any unfair dismissal case, see paras 6.48–6.61 and chapter 22 regarding disciplinary procedures. An employer should take account of the explanation given by the employee, actions taken in previous similar cases, the employee's disciplinary and general record, length of service and whether the intended

---

34 Though this may be a capability issue; see para 7.9 on health.

35 This may also be a capability issue.

36 See wrongful dismissal, summary dismissal and gross misconduct, paras 1.29–1.30.

37 For an interesting example, see *Pay v United Kingdom* [2009] IRLR 139, ECtHR. See also para 3.20 above.

disciplinary action is reasonable under the circumstances. The following issues frequently arise in conduct dismissals, although some of the principles may be transferable to other types of dismissal:

- inconsistency in the treatment of different employees;
- taking account of previous warnings;
- the importance of the disciplinary rules
- cross-examination of witnesses at the disciplinary hearing.

Inconsistency

7.34 The ACAS Code says employers should act consistently. It may be unfair[38] for the employer to dismiss an employee for a particular offence, when other employees have been treated more leniently for the same offence.[39] It is also unfair suddenly to clamp down on a particular offence which has been treated lightly in the past, without any prior warning. Any argument about inconsistency only works if the comparable situations really are similar. In reality, few cases are identical. An employer may also be able to give a good reason for making a distinction, though it is not a good reason that different managers dealt with the two incidents.[40] An employee cannot complain of inconsistency in failing to discipline a colleague, if the employer was unaware of the other person's misconduct. Lack of consistency by an employer is not regarded by tribunals to be as significant as it once was. It is more important for the tribunal to consider the individual facts of the particular case and to decide on the usual section 98(4) test whether the dismissal fell within the band of reasonable responses.[41]

Disciplinary rules

7.35 Many written disciplinary procedures contain a set of rules specifying disciplinary offences as well as those which are regarded as gross misconduct. The ACAS Code[42] says rules and procedures should be clear, specific and in writing; employees and where appropriate, their representatives, should be involved in the development of rules and procedures; and it is important to help employees and managers understand what the rules and procedures are, where they can be found

---

38 And possibly unlawful discrimination.
39 *Post Office v Fennell* [1981] IRLR 221, CA, but see *Levenes Solicitors v Dalley* UKEAT/0330/06.
40 But this may defeat a discrimination claim.
41 *Levenes Solicitors v Dalley* UKEAT/0330/06.
42 Code, para 2.

and how they are to be used. Unless an offence is very obviously gross misconduct, it will be relevant to consider whether it is mentioned in the rules (though not conclusive). A written rule effectively operates as a warning. On the other hand, it will be unfair for an employer auto-matically to dismiss for any offence listed as dismissable within the rules, without considering the circumstances of the individual case.

Taking account of previous warnings

7.36   The ACAS Code recommends that an employee is told how long a warning will remain current. Previous live warnings can be taken into account in a decision to dismiss, even if they concern different offences, although this may affect how much significance should be attributed to them. It is a question of overall fairness, taking account of the number of previous warnings, the time periods between them, and the nature of the offence each time.[43] If a warning is subject to an appeal at the time of the later offence, an employer can rely on its exis-tence provided it is also taken into account that an appeal is pending.[44] If the appeal on the previous warning is due to be heard very soon, arguably the employer should wait and deal with the appeal before moving onto the subsequent offence.

7.37   It is recognised good practice that warnings are disregarded for disciplinary purposes after a specified period, eg six months for a first written warning and 12 months for a final written warning. Many dis-ciplinary procedures also recommend that warnings are disregarded or removed from the file after a period. If the employer has chosen to state the warning will lapse after a specified period, it is unfair subse-quently to rely overtly on the lapsed warning in deciding to dismiss, especially where the final offence would not otherwise justify dismissal on its own.[45] On the other hand, there are circumstances where the existence of previous warnings can help to make the employer's deci-sion to dismiss reasonable. This sounds contradictory, but the case of *Airbus UK Ltd v Webb*[46] provides a good example. In that case, the com-pany decided it would be reasonable to dismiss five employees for watching TV while on night duty, but if there was a good reason not to dismiss anyone, s/he would be given a lesser penalty. Four employees with good disciplinary records were therefore given warnings, but

43 *Auguste Noel Ltd v Curtis* [1990] IRLR 326, EAT.
44 *Tower Hamlets Health Authority v Anthony* [1989] IRLR 394, CA.
45 *Diosynth Ltd v Morris Thompson* [2006] IRLR 284, CS. But this is weakened by *Airbus UK Ltd v Webb*, see note 46.
46 [2008] EWCA Civ 49; [2008] IRLR 309, CA.

Mr Webb was dismissed because he had previously been disciplined for doing other things when he should have been working. In fact, he had a final written warning which had expired only 3 weeks before this further offence. The Court of Appeal said the fact that the employer took account of an expired warning in this way did not mean the dismissal had to be unfair. Presumably this principle also means that if offences are continually repeated just after warnings have lapsed, there may come a point where an employer could reasonably take them into account.

Cross-examination at the disciplinary hearing

7.38   Some disciplinary procedures give employees the right to cross-examine witnesses against them at disciplinary hearings. Otherwise, it all depends on the facts whether an employer can act reasonably without allowing the employee to cross-examine witnesses against him/her.[47] It is always important that employees should know the evidence against them but it may be enough if they have been shown witness statements. If the employer is relying on information from an informant who wishes to remain anonymous, it is important that:

- a full statement is taken and shown to the employee;
- the hearing officer interviews the informant and takes careful notes;
- the employer considers whether the informant has any reason to fabricate information against the employee.[48]

Theft and other dishonesty

7.39   An employee may be dismissed for an act of dishonesty, whether at work or outside work,[49] and whether against the employer, a fellow employee or the public. Dishonesty dismissals often relate to offences peculiar to the working environment such as borrowing money without authorisation, fraudulent expense claims,[50] unauthorised use of the employer's property and clocking offences.[51]

---

47 *Santamera v Express Cargo Forwarding t/a IEC Ltd* (2003) 711 IRLB 14, EAT, clarifying *Ulsterbus Ltd v Henderson* [1989] IRLR 251, NICA.

48 See *Linfood Cash & Carry Ltd v Thomson and another* [1989] IRLR 235, EAT for full guidelines.

49 *Singh v London Country Bus Services* [1976] IRLR 176, EAT.

50 *John Lewis and Co v Smith* (1981) EAT 289/81.

51 *Engineering Services v Harrison* (1977) EAT 735/77.

The reasonableness test: ERA 1996 s98(4)

7.40   It is imperative to understand the difference between the criminal law and unfair dismissal law. Many employees feel that the ET is the arena for them to clear their name. Unfortunately the real issue is not whether the employee actually committed the offence but whether, in the circumstances, it was reasonable for the employer to dismiss. An ET may well find that an employee was fairly dismissed for suspected theft, even though by the time of the ET hearing s/he has been acquitted by a criminal court. The employer need not await the outcome of any criminal trial. What counts is whether the employer, at the time of dismissal and having carried out reasonable investigations, genuinely and reasonably believed that the employee committed the theft.[52] Equally, it does not automatically justify a dismissal that an employee has been charged with a criminal offence.

7.41   In order to dismiss fairly for dishonesty, the employer must:

- genuinely believe that the employee was dishonest;
- hold that belief on reasonable grounds; and
- have carried out proper and adequate investigations.[53]

The final question is whether dismissal is a fair sanction and in proportion to the offence. The ET cannot substitute itself for the employer and decide whether it would itself have dismissed or carried out a fuller investigation.[54] It is irrelevant whether the evidence against the employee is insufficient to satisfy an ET of his/her guilt, if by the objective standards of a reasonable employer, the investigation and conclusion was reasonable.[55] It therefore does not help to put evidence of the employee's innocence to the ET if the employee chose not to produce that evidence to his/her employer at the time (unless that was due to the employer's failure properly to investigate).

7.42   If the employer is unable to ascertain which of a group of employees was guilty of the dishonesty, the employer may fairly dismiss all of them solely on reasonable suspicion, provided that:

- after proper investigation, the employer tries and is unable to identify which employee is guilty;

---

52 *British Home Stores v Burchell* [1978] IRLR 379; [1980] ICR 303, EAT.

53 *British Home Stores v Burchell* [1978] IRLR 379; [1980] ICR 303, EAT; *Weddel and Co v Tepper* [1980] ICR 286; [1980] IRLR 96, CA.

54 *Iceland Frozen Foods Ltd v Jones* [1982] IRLR 439, EAT; *Post Office v Foley; HSBC Bank plc v Madden* [2000] IRLR 827, CA; *Sainsbury's Supermarkets Ltd v Hitt* [2003] IRLR 23, CA.

55 *Post Office v Foley; HSBC Bank plc v Madden* [2000] IRLR 827, CA.

- the employer genuinely believes, on reasonable grounds, that one or more of the group is guilty; and
- any member of the group was capable of having carried out the dishonest act.[56]

It will be inequitable and unfair to dismiss only some members of the group to which the employer has narrowed things down. However, the more 'suspects' the employer dismisses, the stronger business reasons s/he will need for taking such drastic action.

7.43   It is very important that the employer follows a fair procedure and investigates properly. The degree of appropriate investigation depends on a number of factors including the complexity of the case,[57] the nature of the offence, the size and administrative resources of the employer[58] and whether the employee confessed to the misconduct or was caught red-handed.

7.44   The employer's disciplinary procedure should be followed in conducting the investigation, or in the absence of a procedure, whatever steps the ET deems fair in order to ensure justice.[59] A failure to follow a contractual disciplinary procedure will often, but not necessarily, result in a finding of unfair dismissal.[60] Regard will be had to the ACAS Code of Practice, especially if there is no contractual procedure. Any contractual procedure should state what acts of misconduct are considered by the employer to be gross misconduct, the various stages of the procedure itself, the right to be represented and the right of appeal against any decision reached.

7.45   An investigatory officer may go on to hold the disciplinary hearing as long as s/he has not become so involved that s/he cannot be impartial.[61] A person who has been a witness, should not normally hold the disciplinary inquiry, but there are certain exceptions.[62] Furthermore, it is a requirement of the rules of natural justice that an employee knows the allegations made against him/her, that s/he has

---

56 *Monie v Coral Racing* [1980] IRLR 464; [1981] ICR 109, CA; *Whitbread and Co v Thomas* [1988] IRLR 43; [1988] ICR 135, EAT.

57 *British Home Stores v Burchell* [1978] IRLR 379; [1980] ICR 303, EAT.

58 ERA 1996 s98(4).

59 The statutory disputes resolution procedures only set minimum standards. See para 22.71 for the stages of the statutory dismissal and disciplinary procedure (DDP).

60 *Stoker v Lancashire CC* [1992] IRLR 75; *Westminster CC v Cabaj* [1996] IRLR 399, CA.

61 *Slater v Leicestershire Health Authority* [1989] IRLR 16, CA.

62 *Slater v Leicestershire Health Authority* [1989] IRLR 16, CA.

an opportunity to answer those allegations fully and that the conduct of the investigation and internal hearings is in good faith.[63] The allegations must be clearly put to the employee. It would be unfair, for example, to tell the employee that s/he is facing an allegation of breach of procedures, but to dismiss him/her for dishonesty. Delays in the investigation can make a dismissal unfair if the result is inability to speak to certain witnesses or faded memories.[64]

7.46   As for whether dismissal was a fair sanction, the ET cannot substitute its own view. As always, the test is that of a reasonable employer. Relevant factors which an employer should take into account are the employee's length of service and past conduct.[65] An employer may also consider the conduct of an employee after an offence is discovered. For example, if the employee persistently lies, that would influence the decision to dismiss.[66]

7.47   Since dishonesty is gross misconduct, dismissal for a single act is usually justified and warnings are not normally appropriate. It is important to emphasise long service and, if relevant, the minor extent of the dishonesty, on the employee's behalf.

Violence or fighting dismissals

7.48   Violence or fighting usually constitutes gross misconduct even if the employer's disciplinary procedure does not explicitly describe it as such.[67] Nevertheless, this does not mean that a dismissal for violence is always fair. An employer must carry out an investigation and take into account all relevant matters,[68] eg the nature and circumstances of the violence, whether it was in public view, the proximity to machinery or dangerous objects,[69] the status of the employees, the length of service[70] and the nature of any provocation. If the fight is between employees with different racial backgrounds, it is also worth checking whether there was any racial harassment provoking the fight.[71]

63 *Khanum v Mid-Glamorgan Area Health Authority* [1978] IRLR 215; [1979] ICR 40, EAT.

64 *A v B* [2003] IRLR 405, EAT.

65 *Trusthouse Forte (Catering) Ltd v Adonis* [1984] IRLR 382, EAT; *Strouthos v London Underground Ltd* [2004] IRLR 636, CA.

66 *British Leyland (UK) Ltd v Swift* [1981] IRLR 91, CA.

67 *CA Parsons and Co v McLoughlin* [1978] IRLR 65, EAT.

68 *Taylor v Parsons Peebles* [1981] IRLR 119, EAT.

69 *Greenwood v HJ Heinz and Co* (1977) EAT 199/77.

70 *Ealing LBC v Goodwin* (1979) EAT 121/79.

71 See chapters 13 and 16 on race discrimination.

7.49 The employer should speak to the parties involved and any witnesses. If the employer cannot ascertain who was responsible for the violence, the employer may dismiss all concerned if it was serious.[72] It will not usually help an employee who participated in fighting to say that another employee initiated it.

Dismissals for unauthorised absences or lateness

7.50 Dismissals for absenteeism may relate to capability and ill-health.[73] Conduct absenteeism is where an employee is absent without authority and it is usually a form of bad time-keeping. There may also be issues regarding not properly notifying absence under the employer's sickness procedure (see also para 7.25 above). A common form of unauthorised absenteeism is where an employee returns late from a holiday.

General absenteeism or lateness

7.51 An employer is rarely entitled to dismiss for a single occasion of lateness or absenteeism. The usual situation is when an employee is frequently late or absent from work. Some large employers set out in the contract of employment an 'expected level of attendance' below which an employee will be dismissed. However, it is not necessarily fair to dismiss an employee who falls below this level. The employer should fairly review the employee's attendance record and the reasons for the absences. Appropriate warnings should be given after the employee has had the opportunity to explain. If there is no improvement, the employee's subsequent dismissal is likely to be fair.[74]

7.52 As well as fairness in procedures, the ET will take into account:

- the employee's age, length of service and performance;
- the likelihood of an improvement in attendance;
- the effect of absences on the business;
- the known circumstances of each absence, eg a temporary domestic problem.[75]

If lateness or absences are caused by a health condition, eg depression or tiredness in the morning, this may be a matter requiring reasonable adjustments under the DDA 1995.[76]

72 *Monie v Coral Racing* [1980] IRLR 464, CA.
73 See para 7.9.
74 *International Sports Co v Thompson* [1980] IRLR 340, EAT.
75 *Post Office v Stones* (1980) EAT 390/80.
76 See chapter 15.

Late return from holiday

7.53   Where an employer has warned the employee in advance that failure to return from holiday on the due date will be treated as gross misconduct, it will be easier to justify a dismissal. Unless the employee can put forward compelling reasons why s/he should not be dismissed, dismissal will be fair.[77] It may well be discriminatory if the employer disregards medical certificates just because they are from abroad. Usually the employer should wait until the employee comes back to work or invite an explanation by post.

7.54   Sometimes an employer informs the employee that if s/he returns late from holiday, s/he will be taken to have dismissed him/herself. Legally this is not recognised as a resignation or mutual termination. The employee cannot be deprived of the right to claim unfair dismissal in this way.[78]

Disobedience

7.55   This type of dismissal usually arises when an employee refuses to obey an order or instruction of the employer. The instruction may or may not be one with which the employee is required to comply under the contract of employment.

The reasonableness test: ERA 1996 s98(4)

7.56   The two key considerations are: (a) the nature of the employer's instruction, and (b) the employee's reason for refusal to comply.

7.57   An employee is entitled to refuse any unlawful,[79] unreasonable or dangerous instruction. Although the starting point is whether the employee is obliged to comply with the instruction under the employment contract, this does not necessarily determine whether a refusal is reasonable.[80] It may be unfair to dismiss an employee who refuses to obey a contractual instruction or fair to dismiss an employee who refuses to obey a non-contractual order. An employee who fails to co-operate with an employer's request to do non-contractual overtime,[81] to adapt to new

---

77 *Rampart Engineering v Henderson* (1981) EAT 235/81.
78 See paras 6.27–6.47 on what constitutes dismissal under the ERA 1996.
79 *Morrish v Henlys (Folkestone)* [1973] 2 All ER 137; [1973] ICR 482, NIRC.
80 *Redbridge LBC v Fishman* [1978] IRLR 69; [1978] ICR 569, EAT.
81 *Horrigan v Lewisham LBC* [1978] ICR 15, EAT.

technology[82] or otherwise go along with a reorganisation[83] will often be found to have acted unreasonably and to be fairly dismissed.

7.58 Where an employee is required to comply with a contractual term which has not previously been operated and which will cause inconvenience or hardship, the employer must give reasonable advance notice. If no notice is given, an employee may be entitled to refuse to comply with the instruction in the short term[84] on this ground alone.

7.59 The ET must consider also the employee's reason for refusing to obey the instruction and it should weigh up the competing interests and take into consideration the nature of the contractual relationship between the employer and employee generally. There may be good reason for the employee's refusal, eg a pregnant woman refusing to work close to a VDU screen, a risk to the employee's safety in handling money or a risk of civil liability.[85]

7.60 It can be automatic unfair dismissal to dismiss an employee because s/he refuses to work in a situation of serious and imminent danger.[86]

Dependency on drugs or alcohol or possession of drugs

7.61 Taking or possessing drugs at work, and sometimes out of work, tends to be treated as gross misconduct. Drinking at work may be treated as misconduct depending on the circumstances and what the contract says. Dependency on drugs or alcohol is now more likely to be treated by an enlightened employer as a medical condition[87] and will not be referred to as an act of misconduct in the disciplinary procedure. The advantage of treating this as a health issue is that the requirements relating to capability dismissals apply. These are more conducive to helping the employee, as medical reports will be obtained and appropriate treatment will be encouraged.

Dependency on alcohol or drugs

7.62 The employer must have a genuine and reasonable belief, based on proper and adequate investigation, that the employee is dependent. The employee should be given the chance to answer the allegations and

---

82 *Cresswell v Board of Inland Revenue* [1984] 2 All ER 713; [1984] IRLR 190, Ch D.

83 *Ellis v Brighton Co-operative Society* [1976] IRLR 419, EAT.

84 *McAndrew v Prestwick Circuits* [1988] IRLR 514, EAT.

85 *UCATT v Brain* [1981] IRLR 224, CA.

86 See paras 6.77–6.78 for details.

87 See para 7.9 onwards for capability/health dismissals and *Strathclyde RC v Syme* (1979) EAT 233/79.

to obtain a medical or specialist report if s/he wishes, particularly if the employer treats it as a sickness issue.

7.63   In deciding whether to dismiss, the following factors will be relevant:

- whether the contract of employment or disciplinary procedure treats alcohol/drug dependency as a matter of conduct or capability;
- whether the employee is responsible for the safety of others, eg a coach driver or operator of dangerous machinery. If so, the employee should not be permitted to continue on the job. The employer may dismiss or transfer the employee to safer duties;
- whether the employee works in an environment which is potentially dangerous to others or him/herself, eg an electrician. Similar considerations apply; and
- whether there is a risk of adverse publicity or harm to customer relations (which would be a dismissal for 'some other substantial reason').

Taking or possessing drugs in or out of work

7.64   Most employers are uninformed about the different types of drugs and their effect, so summary dismissal is common for using or possessing drugs, particularly when at work. Many ETs take a hard line on any drug-related dismissal.

7.65   It will usually be fair to dismiss an employee for using or possessing drugs in or out of work, when there is a risk of adverse publicity, harm to customer relations or other harm to the employer's business interests.[88] However, if the possession or use of drugs is outside the work environment, not a matter of public knowledge and could not harm the business, the employee may be able to show that dismissal is unfair.[89]

Drinking at work

7.66   This may not be a matter of alcohol dependency at all and it will not necessarily be misconduct to drink at work. This will depend on whether the contract or disciplinary procedure expressly lists drinking as misconduct or, if not, whether the employee and employer clearly contemplated that it would be misconduct. In certain jobs there is a zero-tolerance policy. This depends on the nature of the job, factors such as proximity to dangerous equipment and custom and practice.

---

88 This would be a dismissal for 'some other substantial reason'.
89 *Norfolk CC v Bernard* [1979] IRLR 220, EAT.

Misuse of telephone, e-mail, internet or social networking sites

7.67   This is increasingly becoming a source of dismissal. An employee is entitled to be informed clearly in advance as to what his/her employer's policy is on private use of the telephone, e-mail, internet and social networking sites.[90] There is an issue both as to use of working time and of inappropriate content. If the policy allows 'reasonable' personal use, it should be clear what amounts to 'reasonable' and it should be applied consistently by different managers. An employer could reasonably dismiss for gross misconduct a lead personnel officer who downloaded pornography from the internet on his computer.[91] Downloading, and certainly circulating, pornography may also lead to sexual harassment claims.[92] If an employee uses an unauthorised password to enter a computer known to contain information to which s/he is not entitled, it is gross misconduct regardless of whether s/he has some illegitimate purpose or simply idle curiosity. Having said that, the employer should have clearly notified rules regarding unauthorised access.[93] On social networking sites, it may be reasonable to discipline or dismiss employees for making comments which are defamatory or which breach confidentiality or bring the business into disrepute. On the other hand, there is a right to freedom of expression under article 10 of the European Convention on Human Rights and it is strongly arguable that employees should be allowed to make negative comments as long as they are not damaging.

Redundancy dismissals

7.68   See chapter 8 for all aspects of redundancy including unfair redundancy dismissals.

Statutory restriction dismissals

7.69   There are very few cases where the employer relies on a statutory restriction as the reason for dismissal. The most common example is

90 See paras 1.75–1.78 on this and on employer monitoring.
91 *Thomas v London Borough of Hillingdon* EAT/1317/01.
92 See para 17.91 onwards regarding harassment.
93 *Denco Ltd v Joinson* [1991] IRLR 63, EAT.

the loss of a necessary qualification for a job, eg a van driver losing his/her driving licence. The employer must show that the statutory restriction affected the work that the person was employed to perform and that no alternative employment was available. The larger the employer, the greater the duty to try to find an alternative to dismissal.

7.70 Consultation on the consequences of the ban and possible alternatives is very important.[94] Where a restriction does not prevent the employee from doing his/her job but makes it difficult, eg a salesperson losing a driving licence, the employer should consult on what assistance may be possible. Even where continued employment of the employee would be unlawful, eg where a GP has been struck off the medical register, the employer should still consult on the likelihood of the decision being reversed.

Dismissals for some other substantial reason (SOSR)

7.71 A dismissal which is not for one of the four potentially fair reasons may still be fair if it is for 'some other substantial reason of a kind such as to justify the dismissal'.[95] The most common SOSR dismissals are for reorganisation including variation of the contract of employment, in order to protect the employer's business interests or as a consequence of the transfer of a business. Other situations where a dismissal might be deemed to be for SOSR are where the interests of the business might suffer as a result of friction at work between two colleagues, or an employee is incompatible and does not fit in, or due to adverse publicity on any matter, eg relating to an employee taking drugs or having a criminal conviction. Note that a substantial reason is one which is not trivial or unworthy but one which would justify the dismissal.[96]

Dismissals due to reorganisation or variation of contract

7.72 It is sometimes hard to differentiate between a reorganisation and a redundancy situation. Employers usually try to claim that the dismissal is because of reorganisation, in order to avoid making a redundancy payment.

---

94 *Sutcliffe and Eaton v Pinney* [1977] IRLR 349, EAT.
95 ERA 1996 s98(1).
96 *Gilham v Kent CC (No 1)* [1985] IRLR 16, CA.

7.73   An employee may be dismissed because s/he cannot or will not accept a change in terms and conditions resulting from the reorganisation. The employer first needs to prove that the reorganisation or the employee's refusal or inability to fit in with it was a substantial reason such as could justify dismissal, otherwise the dismissal will be unfair.[97] In practice, it is fairly easy for the employer to meet this initial requirement.

7.74   An employer is entitled to reorganise the workforce and terms and conditions of employment to improve efficiency and to dismiss an employee who does not co-operate with the changes.[98] It is sufficient to amount to a potentially fair reason for dismissal for the employer to show that the reorganisation is for sound business reasons requiring a change in the employee's terms and conditions.[99] The reorganisation need not be essential.

7.75   It is very hard for an employee at the ET to challenge the employer's reasons as not being sound and good. The employer needs only to demonstrate the benefits to the business of the reorganisation, perceived at the time of dismissal. If the employer cannot demonstrate these benefits existed and their importance at the time of dismissal, the dismissal will be unfair as the employer will not have established a 'substantial' reason for dismissal.[100]

The reasonableness test: ERA 1996 s98(4)

7.76   Although the ET should consider a number of factors when deciding whether it was fair to dismiss, it primarily looks at the situation from the employer's point of view, ie whether a reasonable employer would make those changes to the employee's terms of employment.[101] The ET considers the competing advantages and disadvantages to the employer and the employee, but the main emphasis in reorganisation dismissals is on the employer's interests which are paramount. Nevertheless, there have been some ET decisions, endorsed by the Employment Appeal Tribunal (EAT), indicating that an employer does not have a completely free hand.[102] It is unlikely that an ET would think it fair to

---

97 ERA 1996 s98(1).
98 *Lesney Products and Co v Nolan* [1977] IRLR 77, CA.
99 *Hollister v National Farmers Union* [1979] ICR 542; [1979] IRLR 238, CA.
100 *Banerjee v City and East London Area Health Authority* [1979] IRLR 147, EAT.
101 *Chubb Fire Security v Harper* [1983] IRLR 311, EAT.
102 *Interconnections Systems v Gibson* (1994) 508 IRLB 8, EAT; *Selfridges Ltd v Wayne and others* (1995) 535 IRLB 13, EAT.

cut pay or reduce terms and conditions merely to increase profitability of an already successful business. However, it goes too far to say that significant changes can be made only if the survival of the business is at stake. Whether or not the majority of the workforce have agreed to changes to their terms and conditions will also be a factor.[103] A change in terms and conditions may also lead to a successful discrimination claim, eg for indirect sex discrimination on an introduction of flexi-shifts.

7.77   Consultation plays an important part in all types of dismissal including reorganisation. For options when an employer tries to vary terms and conditions, see paras 1.20–1.23.

Dismissals to protect employers' business interests

7.78   There is an implied term of fidelity and good faith in every employment contract which lasts as long as the employee is employed. Some employees also agree to express terms which restrict their future employment in the same industry for a given period. These terms are known as 'restrictive covenants'.

7.79   An employee dismissed for breaking the implied term of good faith and fidelity will be dismissed for SOSR and perhaps also misconduct. In addition, there may be a substantial reason potentially justifying dismissal if:

- an employee refuses to sign a restrictive covenant and the employer is genuinely seeking to protect the business interests;[104] or
- there is a genuine risk arising from an employee's relationship with a competitor.[105]

The reasonableness test: ERA 1996 s98(4)

7.80   Where dismissal is for refusing to sign a restrictive covenant, the ET will take into account the necessity of applying it, whether the industry usually requires employers to take this precaution and whether the employee's job was of sufficient importance. The ET will also consider the manner and method of the introduction of the clause and whether it was consistently introduced among other employees.

---

103 See appendix A, p728, for a checklist on variation of terms and conditions.
104 *RS Components v Irwin* [1973] ICR 535; [1973] IRLR 239, NIRC.
105 *Skyrail Oceanic v Coleman* [1981] ICR 864, CA.

Other SOSR dismissals

7.81   Where dismissal is due to a personal relationship with a competitor, the ET should take into account the nature of the relationship and its bearing on the work situation. The manner of the employee's dismissal and the degree of notice or warning of impending dismissal are also relevant.[106] If dismissal is due to a personality clash with colleagues, the employer should do all that is reasonable to try to remedy the problem, which might involve transferring the employee.[107]

Dismissals on transfer of an undertaking

7.82   Depending on the facts, a dismissal of an employee on or after the transfer of an undertaking for an economic, technical or organisational reason entailing changes in the workforce of either the transferor or transferee is treated either as a redundancy dismissal or as dismissal for a substantial reason of a kind that can justify dismissal.[108]

7.83   Dismissals at the time of a transfer usually arise out of the desire of the buyer or seller or both to reduce the workforce or their terms and conditions so as to make the business a more valuable asset.

The reasonableness test: ERA 1996 s98(4)

7.84   Dismissals connected with a transfer are automatically unfair unless for an economic, technical or organisational reason entailing a change in the workforce. If they are for such a reason, they may be fair or unfair, depending on the facts in the usual way. For more detail, see chapter 10.

106 *Skyrail Oceanic v Coleman* [1981] ICR 864, CA.
107 *Turner v Vestric Ltd* [1981] IRLR 23, EAT.
108 Transfer of Undertakings (Protection of Employment) Regulations 2006 SI No 246 reg 7(3).

CHAPTER 8

Redundancy

continued

Chapter 8: Key points

- Redundant employees have a right to reasonable time off to look for work during the notice period.
- An employee who is dismissed for redundancy may be entitled to statutory redundancy pay.
- An employee who is put on short-time working or laid off without pay may resign and claim statutory redundancy pay if s/he follows the correct procedure.
- Even where there is a genuine redundancy situation the employee may have been unfairly dismissed.
- A redundancy dismissal may be unfair if there has been inadequate consultation by the employer or unfair selection for dismissal. Larger employers will be expected to have more sophisticated selection criteria than small enterprises. Criteria should be possible to measure objectively.
- Length of service is a fairly common selection criterion but can be discriminatory.
- The employer is expected to offer any available alternative employment which the employee is capable of doing.
- Watch out for direct and indirect discrimination against black and minority ethnic workers, women and pregnant women, or discrimination related to disability, sexual orientation, religion or age.
- Until the transitional arrangements have passed, the statutory dispute resolution procedures may still apply (see Chapter 22). If so, an employer should follow the dismissal and disciplinary procedure (DDP) before dismissing the employee. Note that the DDP does not apply where the dismissal is one of 20 or more redundancies. If claiming redundancy pay, an employee must send a step 1 grievance letter and wait 28 days before lodging a tribunal claim.
- See interview checklist at p694.

General guide to useful evidence

- Get copies of all minutes, notes and memoranda of meetings at which the redundancy dismissal was discussed.
- Get a list of all workers who could have been selected for redundancy; ascertain who was retained; try to discover when they started their employment, why they have been kept on, and how they met the selection criteria.

> - Find out all vacancies available shortly before and after the dismissal (including the whole of the notice period) to see whether the worker could have done any of them.
> - Find out from those workers who are still employed, what happened to the worker's job after the dismissal. Was the worker simply replaced? If so, find out who the new worker is, and get a copy of the job advert and the letter of appointment.

8.1   An employee who is made redundant may claim statutory redundancy pay. Some employees have a greater contractual entitlement and much of the public sector has its own schemes. An employee may be able to get additional compensation if s/he has a claim for unfair dismissal and/or discrimination on grounds of race, religion, sex, sexual orientation, disability or age. An adviser must be careful because the time limits are different for each of these claims. The time limit to claim redundancy pay from the employment tribunal (ET) is fairly relaxed. Within six months of the termination date, the employee must either claim the pay in the ET or make a written claim to the employer or lodge an unfair dismissal claim.[1] But if the employee wants to claim unfair dismissal or discrimination at the same time, s/he must meet the three-month time limit for these latter claims. These time limits are all subject to extension if the statutory dispute resolution procedures still apply, although these have been abolished apart from transitional arrangements.[2] See p694 for an interview checklist applicable to a redundant employee. For a detailed guide on law and evidence in discrimination situations, see *Redundancy Discrimination: Law and evidence for tribunal cases* by Tamara Lewis.[3]

The definition of 'redundancy'

8.2   In broad terms, there are three main redundancy situations:

1) closure of the business as a whole;
2) closure of the particular workplace where the employee was employed; and

---

1 Employment Rights Act (ERA) 1996 ss164 and 145.
2 See Chapter 22 onwards for details.
3 See bibliography, Appendix F, for availability.

3) reduction in the size of the workforce.

The statutory definitions are a little more complex.[4]

Closure of the business

8.3 ERA 1996 s 139(1) states:

> ... an employee who is dismissed shall be taken to be dismissed by reason of redundancy if the dismissal is wholly or mainly attributable to –
> (a) the fact that his employer has ceased or intends to cease –
>   (i) to carry on the business for the purposes of which the employee was employed ...

The closure may be permanent or temporary,[5] eg, closure of a restaurant for refurbishment.

Closure of the workplace

8.4 A dismissal is deemed to be for redundancy if it is attributable wholly or mainly to the fact that the employer 'has ceased or intends to cease ... to carry on that business in the place where the employee was so employed'.[6] The employee is dismissed for redundancy if dismissed when his/her own workplace closes, even if under the contract s/he could be required to work elsewhere.[7] For example, an employee working in one branch of a restaurant or retail chain is dismissed when his/her branch closes, even though there is a mobility clause in his/her contract.

8.5 The employee needs to be careful if, instead of being made redundant, s/he is instructed to work at a different location or branch. If the employee refuses, s/he may lose his/her redundancy pay because s/he has refused an offer of suitable alternative employment (below). Also, if the employee refuses a move when there is a mobility clause, s/he may be dismissed for misconduct rather than redundancy. There is nothing to stop an employer invoking a mobility clause to avoid redundancy payments.[8] A mobility clause is one which means the worker can be contractually required to move workplace, eg: 'Your place of work is at (*address*). However, you may also be required to

---

4 Note there is a different definition of redundancy for the purposes of collective consultation, see para 2.17.

5 ERA 1996 s139(6).

6 ERA 1996 s139(1)(a).

7 *Bass Leisure Ltd v Thomas* [1994] IRLR 104, EAT; *High Table Ltd v Horst and others* [1997] IRLR 513, CA.

8 *Home Office v Evans* [2008] IRLR 59, CA.

work at any other company premises within reasonable travelling distance of your home.'

Reduction of the workforce

8.6   It is a dismissal for redundancy where it is:

> ... wholly or mainly attributable to ...
> (b) the fact that the requirements of that business –
>   (i) for employees to carry out work of a particular kind, or
>   (ii) ... to carry out work of a particular kind in the place where the employee was employed by the employer,
> have ceased or diminished or are expected to cease or diminish.[9]

This is where, for whatever reason, the employer wants fewer employees doing a particular kind of work. There need not necessarily be less work to be done.[10] The employer may just have decided to cut costs by reducing staff and making those remaining do more work. As long as the employee is dismissed as a result of the employer's diminished requirements, s/he is dismissed for redundancy, regardless of what kind of work s/he actually did or could be required to do under his/her contract.[11]

8.7   It is obviously a redundancy situation where the employer wants fewer employees overall. It is less clear where the employer retains the same number of employees, but on different work from before. It is redundancy if a particular type of job has disappeared altogether, but if it has simply been altered or modernised, eg, by technology, this may not be the case. The test is whether the changed job requires different aptitudes, skill or knowledge.[12]

8.8   Finally, an employer may offer a redundant employee another employee's job. The other employee is then treated as dismissed for redundancy.[13] This process is known as 'bumping' and usually occurs in recognition of long service, though it occurs only rarely now.[14]

---

9 ERA 1996 s139(1)(b).

10 *McRea v Cullen & Davison Ltd* [1988] IRLR 30, NICA.

11 *Safeway Stores plc v Burrell* [1997] IRLR 200, EAT; *Murray and another v Foyle Meats Ltd* [1999] IRLR 562, HL.

12 *Amos and others v Max-Arc Ltd* [1973] IRLR 285, NIRC.

13 *Gimber and Sons v Spurrett* [1967] ITR 308.

14 Whether the 'bumped' employee has been unfairly dismissed (see para 8.29) or discriminated against is a separate question.

Redundancy payments

8.9   An employee dismissed on the ground of redundancy is entitled to statutory redundancy pay if s/he meets the necessary eligibility requirements, ie, s/he is an employee; s/he has at least two years' continuous service; and s/he has been dismissed for redundancy.[15] There is a presumption for these purposes that a dismissal is for redundancy unless the employer proves otherwise.[16] The calculation of statutory redundancy pay is set out at para 18.21 below. There is also a new right whereby a tribunal can order an employer to pay an employee an appropriate amount as compensation if the employee suffers any financial loss as a result of non-payment of his/her redundancy entitlement.[17]

Suitable alternative employment

8.10   The employee will lose his/her statutory redundancy pay if s/he unreasonably refuses an offer of suitable alternative employment.[18]

What constitutes a valid offer?

8.11   The offer of alternative employment must be made before the old job ends and the new job must start immediately or within four weeks of the end of the previous employment. The offer need not be in writing, but it will be for the employer to prove that a suitable offer was made.[19] If the employee says s/he is not interested in receiving any alternative offer and the employer therefore does not make one, the employee will not be taken to have unreasonably refused a suitable offer and will be entitled to a redundancy payment.[20] The offer must set out the main terms of the new job in enough detail to show how it differs from the old one[21] and the starting date should be clear.

8.12   If the employee accepts the offer, s/he is treated for redundancy purposes as never having been dismissed.[22] However, s/he can still

---

15 If relevant, see para 17.24 onwards regarding retirement dismissals.
16 ERA 1996 s163(2).
17 ERA 1996 s163(5). Applicable to tribunal claims on or after 6 April 2009.
18 ERA 1996 s141.
19 *Kitching v Ward* [1967] ITR 464; (1967) 3 KIR 322, DC.
20 *Simpson v Dickinson* [1972] ICR 474, NIRC. Although different rules may apply to collectively agreed and other contractual redundancy schemes.
21 *Havenhand v Thomas Black Ltd* [1968] 2 All ER 1037; [1968] ITR 271, DC.
22 ERA 1996 s138(1).

claim unfair dismissal from the original job.[23] S/he may want to do this if, eg, his/her pay in the new job is lower.

The statutory trial period

8.13 Where the employee is dismissed for redundancy and offered an alternative job as above, s/he can try out the new job, where it differs from the old one, for a trial period of up to four weeks.[24] If s/he leaves or gives notice to leave within this period, the original redundancy dismissal stands and s/he can still claim redundancy pay.[25] The trial period starts on the date the employee begins the new job and ends four calendar weeks later, by which time the employee must have decided whether to accept the new job permanently. If the employee works beyond the four-week period, s/he will lose the right to claim redundancy pay. It is irrelevant whether the employee is unable to work the four weeks, eg, because s/he is off sick or the workplace is closed for Christmas.[26] However, an offer of a different alternative job will attract another four-week trial period. The four-week trial period is a strict time limit and can be extended only by agreement for the purpose of retraining the employee; such agreement must be in writing and specify a new date when the trial period will end.[27]

Unreasonable refusal of a suitable offer

8.14 The employer must prove both that the offer was suitable and that the employee's refusal was unreasonable. There is very little case-law guidance on what an employee may refuse and it depends on the particular situation. 'Suitability' tends to mean objective job-related factors such as pay, status, hours and location. The reasonableness of a refusal depends more on the employee's individual circumstances, eg, domestic factors and health. A very common form of alternative offer is of the same job but in a different location. Whether this is a suitable offer which the employee cannot reasonably refuse depends on a combination of factors such as extra travelling time and expense, childcare responsibilities, health, and status of the job (the higher the status, the more an ET would expect an employee to travel). If an employee is

---

23 *Hempell v W H Smith & Sons Ltd* [1986] IRLR 95, EAT; *Jones v Governing Body of Burdett Coutts School* [1998] IRLR 521, CA.
24 ERA 1996 s138.
25 ERA 1996 s138(2)(b).
26 *Benton v Sanderson Kayser Ltd* [1989] IRLR 19, CA.
27 ERA 1996 s138(3).

going to refuse a job because of travel difficulties, it is important that s/he knows precisely what the travel would entail. It may also be helpful at least to try it out.

The common law trial period

8.15 The above rules apply where the employer has actually dismissed the employee for redundancy and then made an offer of alternative employment. Quite often an employer starts discussing alternative jobs before dismissing the employee. If the employer offers or imposes a new job without dismissing the employee, the situation is similar to where an employer tries to vary the contract of employment unilaterally.[28] The employee needs to decide whether to accept or refuse the new job. If s/he refuses and resigns, s/he can claim constructive dismissal[29] and redundancy pay as long as s/he does not affirm by waiting too long.[30] S/he can ask to try the job for a short while, as long as s/he makes it clear this is not an acceptance of the change, and as long as s/he does not leave it too long. This is sometimes known as a 'common law' trial period. It need not be the strict four weeks of the statutory trial period, but since it can sometimes be ambiguous as to whether there has been a dismissal and therefore whether the statutory period applies, it is usually safer to stick to four weeks anyway.

Lay-off and short-time

8.16 Normally an employee can claim statutory redundancy pay only if s/he is dismissed for redundancy. This includes constructive dismissal, for example if s/he resigns due to a fundamental breach of contract, such as being sent home without pay, when under his/her contract this is not permitted. But there is a problem if an employee has a contract which allows him/her to be temporarily laid off without pay or put on short-time working (ie fewer hours), with a consequent cut in pay. This situation could carry on indefinitely, without the employee being able to sue for his/her lost wages or resign and claim redundancy pay. There are therefore special statutory rules which cover this situation once the employee has been laid off or put on short-time for at least four consecutive weeks or six weeks in a 13-week period. There is a specified

28 See paras 1.20–1.23.
29 See paras 6.35–6.44.
30 *Air Canada v Lee* [1978] IRLR 392, EAT.

procedure involving notices and counter-notices which enables the employee to resign and claim redundancy pay.[31] If the employer has no money to pay the redundancy pay, this can be recovered from the National Insurance Fund.[32]

Guarantee pay

8.17   Where an employee is not provided with work on any day when s/he would normally be required to work under his/her contract because of lesser requirements of the employer's business for the employee's type of work, s/he may be entitled to a small guarantee payment from his/her employer. The rules are set out in ERA 1996 ss28–35. This sum is a minimum and is set off against any contractual wages to which the employee is entitled.[33] The maximum amount of guarantee pay for any one day is currently £21.50.[34]

Unfair redundancy dismissal

8.18   A dismissal for redundancy may be automatically unfair for failure to follow the statutory minimum disciplinary procedure (if it still applies) or on one of the specified grounds, eg selecting a woman for redundancy because she is pregnant.[35] Alternatively, it may be unfair on general principles for one or more of the following reasons:

a) there was no genuine redundancy situation;
b) the employer failed to consult;
c) the employee was unfairly selected; or
d) the employer failed to offer alternative employment.

The Employment Appeal Tribunal (EAT) in *Williams v Compair Maxam Ltd*[36] set out guidelines for the fair handling of redundancy dismissals. It is not necessarily unfair to fail to follow the guidelines in every case,

31 ERA 1996 ss147–150.

32 See para 18.69.

33 ERA 1996 s32.

34 See Directgov site for guidance and the latest amount at www.direct.gov.uk/en/Employment/Understandingyourworkstatus/Temporarylayoff/DG_177591

35 See para 6.66 onwards.

36 [1982] IRLR 83, EAT; approved by *Robinson v Carrickfergus Borough Council* [1983] IRLR 122, NICA.

but they do provide a useful standard. For general principles on unfair dismissal, including unfair dismissal on grounds of redundancy, see chapter 6.

No genuine redundancy situation

8.19 An employee cannot challenge whether the employer acted reasonably in creating the redundancy situation. The ET cannot investigate the commercial and economic reasons which prompted a closure or look into the rights and wrongs of the employer's decision.[37] However, an ET is entitled to investigate whether the redundancy situation is in fact genuine.[38]

Failure to consult

8.20 The employer should give as much warning as possible of impending redundancies to enable the union and affected employees to consider possible alternative solutions and if necessary, find alternative employment.[39]

8.21 Consultation is very important in redundancy situations and can take many forms. At one end of the spectrum it involves collective discussions and meetings with the union; at the other end it will entail discussions with individual employees who are likely to be made redundant. Failure to consult individually may well make a dismissal unfair, although compensation may be limited if consultation would not have made any difference to the outcome.[40] If the statutory dispute resolution procedures applied and there were less than 20 redundancies, employers contemplating dismissing for redundancy should have written to the employee setting out the circumstances making redundancy likely, and inviting him/her to a meeting to discuss the situation.[41]

8.22 Consultation requires the employer to consider options which would not involve making the employee redundant, including early retirement, seeking volunteers, alternative employment, lay-off and short-time working. The employees and their representatives should be involved in this process. Consultation means more than

---

37 *James W Cook & Co (Wivenhoe) Ltd v Tipper and others* [1990] IRLR 386, CA; *Moon v Homeworthy Furniture (Northern) Ltd* [1976] IRLR 298, EAT.

38 *James W Cook & Co (Wivenhoe) Ltd v Tipper and others* [1990] IRLR 386, CA.

39 *Williams v Compare Maxam Ltd* [1982] IRLR 83, EAT.

40 See para 18.54.

41 See chapter 22 for details.

communicating a decision already made. The Industrial Relations Code of Practice,[42] which has been repealed, provided a good definition of consultation. It defined consultation as jointly examining and discussing problems of concern to both management and employees. It involves seeking mutually acceptable solutions through a genuine exchange of views and information.[43] Furthermore, the courts have held that fair consultation involves consultation when the proposals are still at a formative stage, there is adequate information on which to respond, adequate time in which to respond, and conscientious consideration by an authority of the response to consultation.[44]

8.23   There are special rules requiring collective consultation with trade union or employee representatives on mass redundancies.[45] Failure to follow these rules enables a trade union or employee representative to claim a protective award for each affected employee. This is a separate matter from the obligation to consult in unfair dismissal cases.

8.24   Although failure to follow the rules on collective consultation will not necessarily make the dismissal of an individual employee unfair, it is one factor in assessing the reasonableness of the dismissal.[46] On the other hand, even if there has been union consultation, it is normally important that the employer has also consulted the individual employees. Collective consultation tends to concentrate on matters such as choice of selection criteria and how the process will take effect, whereas individuals want the opportunity to make representations on their own position,[47] eg how they should be assessed against the criteria and suggestions for alternative employment.

Unfair selection

8.25   As a first stage, the employer must choose a fair pool from which to select the redundant employees. Employers have a lot of flexibility in deciding on a pool, provided they apply their mind to it and act from genuine motives.[48] However, it could be unreasonable to restrict the pool artificially, eg, by not including all those doing similar work.

---

42 1972 para 46.

43 *Heron v Nottingham City Link* [1993] IRLR 372, EAT.

44 *R v British Coal Corporation ex p Price* [1994] IRLR 72, HC; *Rowell v Hubbard Group Services Ltd* [1995] IRLR 195, EAT.

45 See paras 2.17–2.26 and 2.32–2.33.

46 *Williams v Compair Maxam Ltd* [1982] IRLR 83.

47 *Mugford v Midland Bank plc* [1997] IRLR 208, EAT.

48 *Thomas & Betts Manufacturing Ltd v Harding* [1980] IRLR 255, CA.

8.26   Once a reasonable pool is chosen, the employer can choose any reasonable selection criteria, provided these can be objectively measured and are not discriminatory. Ideally the employer should try to agree the criteria with the union, if there is one.[49] It is common these days to use multiple selection criteria, which often include length of service,[50] productivity (if it can be objectively assessed), time-keeping, the employee's adaptability and the employer's future needs. Length of service is less popular nowadays, especially if it has discriminatory effect. If attendance is one of the criteria, it should be judged over a substantial period, particularly for long-standing employees. It may be unreasonable not to look at the reasons behind each employee's absence.[51] Vague criteria such as 'attitude to work' could be unreasonable.[52] Certain criteria may also be discriminatory.[53]

8.27   Having chosen fair selection criteria, the employer must apply these fairly and objectively. A reasonable criterion such as 'merit' can be challenged if it is not judged in an objective manner. Unfortunately it is hard to challenge the employer's assessment of the employees against the various criteria. The ET will not order disclosure of the assessment forms of all employees in the selection pool unless it is clear from the tribunal claim why these are relevant and why the redundancy is unfair.[54] Nevertheless, the ET does not simply have to accept the employer's assertion that it has applied its selection criteria fairly.[55] An ET does need to know how the claimant's markings compare with those of the retained employees in deciding whether the employer acted reasonably. Disclosure or additional information regarding all the employees in the redundancy selection pool can therefore be relevant.[56] In discrimination cases, however, an employee should be able to get more detailed comparable information, eg, through the questionnaire procedure.[57]

49 *Williams v Compair Maxam Ltd* [1982] IRLR 83, EAT.

50 *Bessenden Properties v Corness* [1974] IRLR 338 [1977] ICR 142, HL. See also para 8.37 below.

51 *Paine and Moore v Grundy (Teddington) Ltd* [1981] IRLR 267, EAT.

52 *Graham v ABF Ltd* [1986] IRLR 90, EAT.

53 See para 8.36 below.

54 *British Aerospace plc v Green and others* [1995] IRLR 433, CA. See paras 20.62–20.66 on principles for disclosure.

55 *FDR Ltd v Holloway* [1995] IRLR 400, EAT.

56 *FDR Ltd v Holloway* [1995] IRLR 400, EAT, stating *British Aerospace plc v Green and others* [1995] IRLR 433, CA should not be taken too literally.

57 See para 21.2.

8.28   The lengths to which the ET expects an employer to go in drawing up and applying criteria will depend on the employer's size and
administrative resources.[58] Usually the ET expects the medium or
large employer to have adopted a methodical approach, awarding each
potentially redundant employee with points against various criteria
and dismissing those who score least.[59] This selection process, provided it is consistent and measured objectively, will in most cases justify the dismissal. However, even small employers must show that
they used a fair selection method.

8.29   In some circumstances, a tribunal may expect an employer to consider dismissing an employee with shorter service who works in a
non-redundant post to make way for an employee of longer service, or
otherwise greater suitability, who works in a redundant post.[60] This is
called 'bumping'. Whether it is unfair to fail to consider bumping very
much depends on the facts,[61] and the employee would have to show, not
only that there were powerful reasons to prefer him/her over the
bumped employee, but that s/he could easily slot in and undertake
the bumped employee's work. Bumping may be expected if it has happened regularly in the past.[62] Moreover, the bumped employee may
be able to claim that s/he has him/herself been unfairly dismissed,
again depending on the facts.[63]

Failure to offer alternative employment

8.30   The employer must at least look for alternative employment and should
offer any suitable available vacancies. The employer's duty is not limited to offering similar positions or positions in the same workplace and
s/he should consider the availability of any vacancies with associated
employers.[64]

8.31   When offering alternative employment, the employer must give
sufficient detail of the vacancy and, unless the job functions are obvious, allow a trial period. Failure to do so is likely to make the dismissal

---

58 ERA 1996 s98(4).
59 *Williams v Compair Maxam* [1982] IRLR 83; [1982] ICR 156, EAT.
60 *Thomas and Betts Manufacturing Co Ltd v Harding* [1980] IRLR 255, CA.
61 *Green v A & I Fraser (Wholesale Fish Merchants) Ltd* [1985] IRLR 55, EAT.
62 *Thomas and Betts Manufacturing Co v Harding* [1980] IRLR 255, CA and para 8.8
   above.
63 *Barbar Indian Restaurant v Rawat* [1985] IRLR 57, EAT.
64 *Vokes Ltd v Bear* [1973] IRLR 363, NIRC, though later cases have suggested the
   duty in *Vokes* is too onerous.

unfair.[65] It is up to the employee whether to accept the alternative employment, which might even involve demotion or a reduction in pay.[66] Employers should consult about possibilities and not make assumptions about what jobs an employee would find acceptable.

8.32 Employees who unreasonably refuse a suitable alternative offer will reduce their chances of winning an unfair dismissal case or receiving full compensation if they do win. They will also lose their entitlement to statutory redundancy pay (see above).

8.33 One of the main purposes of consultation is to consider other employment, eg, transfer to another workplace, as an alternative to dismissal. The ET will look at vacancies existing during the consultation period (regardless of whether there was actual consultation) and during the employee's notice period as well as at the time of dismissal itself. For relevant evidence in an unfair redundancy dismissal, see para 9.17.

Redundancy and discrimination

Pregnancy/maternity dismissals

8.34 Selection for redundancy dismissal due to pregnancy, maternity or a related reason is automatically unfair and no minimum qualifying service is required to make a claim. Where a woman is made redundant while pregnant or on maternity leave, but not due to that fact, the normal test of fairness applies. However, a woman made redundant on maternity leave must be offered any suitable available vacancy, however inconvenient for the employer. Failure to do this is automatically unfair dismissal. Redundancy selection due to pregnancy or maternity may also be sex discrimination. See paras 11.1–11.11 regarding pregnancy dismissals.

Race discrimination – direct

8.35 In any case where a black, Asian or other minority ethnic worker, or someone born abroad, has been selected for redundancy, it is worth checking that there has been no direct discrimination. Indications may be the racial composition of those made redundant as compared with those retained. It is essential to ascertain why the employer says

---

65 *Elliott v Richard Stump Ltd* [1987] ICR 579; [1987] IRLR 215, EAT.
66 *Avonmouth Construction Co v Shipway* [1979] IRLR 14, EAT.

the worker has been selected. A common indicator of direct race discrimination is where retained white workers score equally badly or worse on the selection criteria. A questionnaire should be used to establish the selection criteria and whether they were consistently applied between black and white workers.[67] Direct discrimination may also occur on other grounds, eg religion, age, sex or sexual orientation. For evidence to prove direct discrimination, see paras 16.11–16.35.

Indirectly discriminatory selection criteria

8.36   Criteria for selecting which workers are made redundant are frequently indirectly discriminatory.[68] Criteria such as hours worked, flexibility, mobility, or attendance records could adversely affect women. Black workers may suffer from criteria based on conduct records, internal appraisals or customer complaints, if they have been subjected to direct discrimination in those areas. Unjustifiable selection of a part-time worker would be a breach of the Part-time Workers (Prevention of Less Favourable Treatment) Regulations 2000.[69] The selection first of workers on temporary or short fixed-term contracts may be unjustifiable indirect race or sex discrimination.[70]

Last in, first out (LIFO)

8.37   Length of service is still sometimes applied as a means of redundancy selection. Although in many workplaces this requirement clearly disadvantages women, young people and black and other minority ethnic workers, it is a traditional selection method which has often been found justifiable in the past. Where LIFO has an obvious adverse impact, the following approach should be taken to challenge its justifiability:

- The higher the proportion of black and women workers made redundant due to the application of this criterion, the stronger the necessary justification from the employer.[71]

---

67 See *RRA Questionnaires: How to use the Questionnaire procedure*, by Tamara Lewis. Details of availability in bibliography at pp784–785 below.

68 See para 13.52 onwards.

69 SI No 1551. See paras 11.92–11.99.

70 For example, as in *Whiffen v Milham Ford Girls' School* [2001] IRLR 468, CA; it may also be a breach of the Fixed-term Employees (Prevention of Less Favourable Treatment) Regulations 2002; see paras 1.41–1.49. See also list of indirectly discriminatory criteria in appendix B.

71 *Hampson v Department of Education and Science* [1990] IRLR 302, HL.

- The employer must show that the use of LIFO serves a real business need. Nowadays employers' main concern is to retain a balanced and flexible workforce.[72] This need is unlikely to be served by over-emphasis on length of service.
- Current working practices show that workers are employed increasingly on short-term and temporary contracts and little premium is placed on long service by employers.
- The mere fact that a particular requirement has been widely used in the past does not make it justifiable now. Nor should it be an objective justification that LIFO is or was preferred by certain trade union negotiators.

Use of the criterion may be hard to challenge as indirect age discrimination if it is simply one of several selection criteria, especially as redundancy selection criteria may be considered a 'benefit' which under the Employment Equality (Age) Regulations 2006 requires a lower level of justification by the employer.[73]

Redundancy and disability

8.38   A disabled worker may be selected for redundancy because of failure to make reasonable adjustments to allow for his/her disability. For example, s/he may not score well on selection criteria such as hours worked, flexibility, mobility, or sickness record. S/he may be unable to fulfil new flexible working practices or multiple duties. The employer needs to make appropriate reasonable adjustments by modifying selection criteria, eg by being careful not to hold it against a disabled worker that s/he has refused to work overtime in the past.

8.39   The employer may be expected to take a more active role in seeking appropriate alternative employment than may be an employer's duties under ordinary unfair dismissal law. The duty to make reasonable adjustments applies to any suitable vacancies, eg modifications to equipment or provision of training. Chapter 15 deals with disability discrimination generally.

Preventing discriminatory dismissals

8.40   In rare cases, it may be possible to prevent a public employer embarking on a discriminatory redundancy selection policy by means of an

---

72 IRS Employment Trends 504.
73 *Rolls Royce PLC v UNITE the Union* [2009] EWCA Civ 387; [2009] IRLR 576, CA.

application for judicial review in the High Court; it will be necessary clearly to establish that the policy definitely has discriminatory effect and on a fairly widespread basis.[74] With public authorities, it is arguable that they should carry out an equality impact assessment before deciding what criteria to choose.[75]

Time off to look for work

8.41   An employee who has been continuously employed for at least two years has the right to reasonable time off during the notice period (where s/he is being made redundant) to look for a new job or make training arrangements for future employment.[76] It is irrelevant whether the employee has turned down an offer of suitable alternative employment.[77] It is not necessary to have concrete job interviews; the time can be used going into job centres for example. There is no statutory requirement to give the employer proof of where s/he has been, though this may be relevant to whether the time was 'reasonable'.

8.42   There is no set amount of time which the employee can have off. It is a question of what is reasonable, balancing the employer's needs against the employee's. However, the employee is only entitled to be paid for a maximum of ⅖ week's pay for time off taken during the whole notice period. The employer must give the time off during working hours and cannot ask the employee to rearrange his/her hours or make up the time.[78]

---

74 *R v Hammersmith & Fulham LBC ex p NALGO* [1991] IRLR 249, HC.

75 See paragraphs 13.97–13.104 and 15.50–15.52 regarding the public sector duties.

76 ERA 1996 s52. There are a few excepted professions. See ERA 1996 ss192, 199 and 200.

77 *Dutton v Hawker Siddley Aviation Ltd* [1978] IRLR 390, EAT.

78 *Ratcliffe v Dorset CC* [1978] IRLR 191, EAT.

Evidence in ordinary unfair dismissal cases

Burden of proof

9.1   If dismissal is disputed, the burden is on the employee to prove that it occurred. Once dismissal is proved, the employer must show the reason (or if there is more than one reason, the principal reason) for the dismissal and that it was one of the potentially fair reasons set out in the Employment Rights Act (ERA) 1996 s98. In cases where the employee claims automatic unfair dismissal, s/he will need to provide evidence which helps prove that the dismissal was for the automatically unfair reason.[1]

What kind of evidence is helpful?

Proving a disputed dismissal

9.2   If the employee seeks advice shortly after dismissal, it is essential to see any letter of dismissal. In any event the employer should be asked under ERA 1996 s92 for confirmation of the dismissal and the written reasons for it.[2] Where dismissal is during pregnancy, the employers should automatically supply such a statement, whether requested or not, but it is worth asking if they do not.[3]

9.3   If there is a dispute whether the employee was actually dismissed, supporting documents and witnesses will be needed. As early as possible, try to obtain a signed statement plus the name and address of any witnesses to the dismissal. If the employer decided to dismiss before the employee knew about it, any documentary proof will be helpful, eg a copy of job advertisements which had already appeared for the employee's job.

9.4   If advising on a potential constructive dismissal claim, where the employee must show a fundamental breach of contract, all contractual documents must be obtained. These may comprise a letter of appointment, statement of main terms and conditions under ERA 1996 s1, notices of variation of contract[4] and staff handbook. Also obtain the employee's resignation letter. If s/he resigned without

---

1 See para 6.98 regarding the burden of proof on whistleblowing dismissals.
2 ERA 1996 s92. Note that to found a claim for compensation for supplying false reasons, those reasons must have been supplied in response to a formal written request: *Catherine Haigh Harlequin Hair Design v Seed* [1990] IRLR 175, EAT. See para 20.11 for details.
3 ERA 1996 s92(4).
4 Under ERA 1996 s4.

putting anything in writing, it is important to write a letter as soon as possible, setting out what happened, unless it is now so long since the resignation that it would look very odd.

Conduct and capability dismissals

9.5   Find out whether the employee has received any written or verbal warnings in the past, particularly concerning the matter for which s/he was dismissed. Copies of the written warnings should be obtained. With verbal warnings, check when they were given, by whom and roughly what was said. Under some procedures, verbal warnings are recorded in writing.

9.6   The relevant provisions of the contract of employment or staff handbook must be examined, in particular check the notice provisions, the disciplinary procedure and, if relevant, which offences are listed as disciplinary matters and what amounts to gross misconduct. Ascertain whether the contractual procedures were in fact followed.

9.7   The employee should be asked what investigative and disciplinary hearings took place, who was present, whether s/he was advised s/he could bring a representative, how much warning s/he was given of the hearing and whether s/he knew what it would be about in advance. Obtain the letter inviting the employee to the disciplinary hearing and copies of any evidence, eg statements which s/he was given in advance or during the hearing. Ask the employee at what point in the meeting s/he was told that s/he was dismissed. If the employer said something at the start of the hearing to indicate that the decision to dismiss had already been taken, this would be unfair. It is surprising how often the letter of dismissal has been typed prior to the disciplinary meeting, which is a strong indication that the hearing was a sham! In general, what is important is what the employer knew or ought to have known, had s/he properly investigated or consulted at the time of dismissal. Therefore establish what the employee told the employer, or would have told the employer if s/he had had the chance.

9.8   Ascertain who took notes at the hearing and whether the employee has a copy of his/her own notes. Ask the employer immediately for a copy of his of her notes so they can be agreed as an accurate record while memories are fresh. Also try to get the employee's best recollection of the detail of the meeting and, in particular, what each person said as soon as possible, as important matters may be forgotten if there is a delay. See para 9.18 regarding tape recordings of the hearing.

9.9   If relevant (eg with fighting, alcohol or lateness dismissals), establish how the employer treated similar offences or problems in the past. For capability dismissals, seek documents and information to establish the nature of the criticisms by the employer, whether and when these were taken up with the employee, and obtain relevant letters of complaint or criticism and appraisals. Find out about any training and support offered. Also obtain any evidence proving the employee did carry out good work, eg performance-related bonuses or thank you letters from customers. With sickness, injury, incapability or qualification dismissals, find out what other jobs the employer had available at the relevant time.

Absenteeism and lateness

9.10   If the employee believes other employees with worse records were retained, seek disclosure of their attendance records.[5] The names of the other employees will be needed so that their statutory sick pay (SSP) or attendance records can be obtained from the employer to make this comparison. It will be for the employer to show the reason for the differential treatment.

9.11   Ascertain to what extent the employee was made aware of the employer's dissatisfaction with his/her attendance and whether it was made clear that dismissal would follow a failure to improve. If there was only a general verbal warning, given to a group of employees, clarify from another of those employees what was said and whether it was clear that dismissal might ensue. Get copies of any written individual or collective warnings which the employee mentions.

9.12   Check whether the employer properly reviewed the employee's attendance record prior to giving any warning or dismissal. The employer should have consulted the employee as to the reasons for the absences or lateness. In general, consider whether the employer approached the dismissal of the employee with sympathy and understanding.

Prolonged sickness absence

9.13   If the employer obtained a medical opinion on the employee's state of health, obtain a copy of the report. It is often important also to get a copy of the employer's letter instructing the doctors. Was the employee consulted in respect of the employer's medical report? If so, copies of notes taken of the meeting and a statement from the employee on what was said should be obtained. Ask the employee whether s/he was offered the opportunity of getting his/her own medical report. Get copies of any correspondence with the employee about this.

5 See para 20.62 regarding the disclosure process while running a case.

9.14   Consider the importance of the employee's job and whether the employer could be expected to hold it open any longer. What arrangements were made during the employee's absence? What other short-term solutions were possible?[6] How soon after the dismissal was the vacancy filled?

Injury

9.15   Clarify whether the injury was such as to make the performance of the job impossible. Could the employee, through retraining or the use of aids, have continued to do the job?[7] Was there any consultation with the employee on the medical prognosis and what s/he could do? Was the employee warned s/he may be dismissed? Get copies of any correspondence. If the employee seeks advice while still employed, the employer may have a beneficial sickness retirement scheme or medical insurance covering sick pay from which the employee can claim. Also consider whether the employee should take advice in respect of a personal/industrial injury claim if the injury occurred at work.

Qualifications

9.16   Establish whether the qualification was a term of the contract or otherwise a genuine requirement of the job. If not, the employer will find it hard to justify dismissal. If the employer has changed the requirement, why was the change necessary? Are there any other employees doing the same job who do not have the qualifications, and are new employees expected to be qualified? Also, find out whether other jobs were available which the employee was qualified to do at the time of dismissal. Get copies of all correspondence. Finally, consider whether the requirement had a discriminatory effect on the employee (see para 13.52 regarding indirect discrimination).

Redundancy dismissals

9.17   If relevant, find out what selection criteria were adopted by the employer and how the employee was measured and scored. Were there other employees in similar jobs who were not made redundant, particularly any who had shorter service? To check whether it was a genuine redundancy, find out whether a new employee has simply replaced the

---

6 See chapter 15 if the employee's sickness may amount to a disability.

7 See chapter 15 for any protection an employee may have if the injury causes a disability.

employee in the same job. It is important to obtain all internal and external advertisements and vacancy lists relating to suitable vacancies at the time of dismissal and for a short period before and after. These are relevant both to the genuineness of the redundancy (advertisements for the same job) and to the availability of alternative jobs which should have been offered. The employee should be asked what other jobs s/he could and would have done for the employer and whether s/he was consulted about vacancies or doing any other work. Get copies of all correspondence related to the redundancy. See also para 8.27 regarding documents and information relevant to other employees in the selection pool where the employee is claiming unfair selection.

Admissibility of recorded evidence

9.18   Sometimes employees secretly record conversations, meetings or disciplinary hearings with their employer. This is a risky strategy as, if they are found out, it may be a ground for dismissal. There is no public policy reason why a secret recording of a disciplinary hearing should not be heard by a tribunal, since the employer has usually intended that there is a public record of such a meeting in the form of minutes.[8] On the other hand, recordings of the disciplinary panel's private deliberations would not usually be allowed as evidence, except perhaps where they contained the only, or incontrovertible, proof of discrimination.[9] Covert recordings by the employee or the employer may in rare cases breach the other's privacy contrary to the Human Rights Act 1998,[10] but the tribunal will probably allow in the evidence if it is necessary for a fair hearing.[11] In practical terms, employees need to decide whether it is worth using any secret recordings they have obtained. Usually the tribunal will disapprove of the fact that the employee acted in an underhand manner and the value of the content needs to outweigh the bad impression it makes. In the context of a disciplinary hearing, where the employee's main concern is that minutes will not be accurate, it is better openly to ask the employer to make a recording, which can be available to both sides. Bear in mind

---

8 *Chairman and Governors of Amwell View School v Dogherty* (2006) 815 IDS Brief 9, EAT.

9 *Chairman and Governors of Amwell View School v Dogherty* (2006) 815 IDS Brief 9, EAT.

10 See para 3.20.

11 *Jones v University of Warwick* [2003] All ER 760, CA; *XXX v YYY and another* [2004] IRLR 471, CA.

that recordings can be long, boring and inconclusive. Moreover, the employee does not always perform well in the hearing. If a recording is to be used, the employee should prepare a transcript well in advance of the tribunal hearing and agree it is accurate with the employer.

Without prejudice and privilege

Without prejudice

9.19   Statements and offers made during negotiations, whether in writing or verbally, are not generally admissible as evidence in tribunals or courts if they were genuinely aimed at settling a dispute. If an adviser or employee wants to ensure the content of settlement discussions cannot be referred to in the tribunal, s/he should write the phrase 'without prejudice' at the top of any settlement letter or say it at the start of any settlement conversation. Even if s/he omits to use the actual words, it is possible that without prejudice privilege may still apply. On the other hand, writing the phrase 'without prejudice' at the top of a letter which is not conducting a negotiation will not have the effect of keeping it off the record. Settlement negotiations through ACAS are also kept private from the tribunal.

9.20   The reason for the without prejudice rule is public policy in encouraging settlement negotiations without parties being inhibited in case the negotiations fall through and they are quoted in the tribunal. It therefore only applies if there is a genuine dispute. There is obviously a dispute if a tribunal case has started, but the mere fact that a worker has brought a grievance may not amount to a dispute because it could in theory be upheld by the employer.[12] Without prejudice privilege can apply before litigation has started provided the parties have contemplated – or might reasonably have contemplated – that litigation will occur if they cannot agree.[13] In rare circumstances, the without prejudice protection will not apply, eg because it would hide an unambiguous impropriety (see para 16.32 for an example) or because both parties have waived privilege. The case-law regarding these exceptions can be complicated and is beyond the scope of this book. The problem with the without prejudice rule is that employees may need to refer to something said to them in without prejudice discussions in order to prove their tribunal case. For example, employees needs to be careful about resigning because of something said during without prejudice discussions,

12 *BNP Paribas v Mezzotero* [2004] IRLR 508; November 2004 *Legal Action* 16, EAT.
13 *Framlington Group Ltd and Axa Framlington Group Ltd v Barnetson* [2007] EWCA Civ 502; [2007] IRLR 598, CA.

because they may find they are unable to refer to this in their constructive dismissal claim.[14]

Privilege

9.21   The law of privilege is important because it keeps certain communications private. It can get very complicated, but here are a few key points. 'Legal advice privilege' protects confidential communications between a client and his/her professional adviser made for the purpose of giving or seeking legal advice, regardless of whether litigation is envisaged. It applies to the advice of solicitors, barristers or other lawyers acting in that capacity and not, for example, to advice given as a friend. It does not apply to non-qualified employment consultants. 'Litigation privilege' protects confidential communications between a client, his/her legal adviser (whether or not a qualified lawyer) and a third party, eg a medical expert or witness, where such communication comes into existence for the dominant purpose of use in connection with actual or contemplated litigation. It is not enough that it is created for another purpose, eg resolving a grievance, where litigation is only vaguely in mind.[15] A party can lose privilege by 'waiving' it, eg by referring too explicitly to parts of confidential documents or advice. Again, the rules around this are complex and it is best to be careful.

---

14 *Broie v Nicola Ward t/a First Steps Nursery* UKEAT/0526/07.] For correspondence headed 'without prejudice save as to costs', see para 20.151.
15 *Howes v Hinckley & Bosworth Borough Council* UKEAT/0213/08.

TUPE

Chapter 10: Key points

- The TUPE Regs 2006 replaced the TUPE Regs 1981 from 6 April 2006.
- The TUPE Regs protect employees on transfer of the business in which they are employed.
- Many situations are now covered by the TUPE Regs and a purposive approach should be adopted. The mechanism of the transfer does not matter, provided there is a change of legal person responsible for running the undertaking who acts as employer.
- The TUPE Regs cover business transfers, ie a transfer of an economic entity (ie an organised grouping of resources) which retains its identity after transfer.
- The TUPE Regs also now explicitly cover service provision changes, ie contracting out of services; services reverting in-house; and the transfer of the service between two successive contractors.
- Protected employees are those who are employed immediately before the transfer or who are dismissed in advance but in connection with the transfer, unless their dismissal was for an economic, technical or organisational (ETO) reason entailing changes in the workforce.
- Where part of an undertaking is transferred, an employee must have been assigned to that part, even if s/he has carried out some duties for non-transferred parts.
- It is automatically unfair to dismiss (or constructively dismiss) an employee in connection with the transfer except for an ETO reason entailing changes in the workforce, in which case the ordinary test of fairness will apply. The normal eligibility rules for claiming unfair dismissal apply to both situations.
- Where an employee is covered, rights, liabilities and contractual terms transfer, eg wages owed, liability for previous discriminatory acts and continuous service, but the pension situation is complex.
- There are special requirements and guidance for parts of the public sector under the Cabinet Office Statement of Practice and various Codes of Practice.
- For collective consultation on transfers, see paras 2.27–2.34.
- Discrimination law (with no minimum service requirement) will apply if the new employer refuses to take on employees or treats them less favourably, eg on grounds of race or disability.

- Contracting out plays havoc with equal pay protection, since contracted-out employees cannot compare their pay with employees retained in-house (see para 5.14).

General guide to useful evidence

- Evidence comparing the nature of the undertaking before and after the transfer by reference to factors such as location, staff, customers, product and service.
- Legal and other documents relating to the transfer and any related transfers of assets and staff. Consultation documents with the trade union/employee representatives. Letters to employees.

The Transfer of Undertakings Regulations

10.1   The Transfer of Undertakings (Protection of Employment) Regulations 2006 (the TUPE Regs)[1] protect employees' rights on transfer of the business in which they are employed. Where there is a transfer to which the TUPE Regs apply, the new employer effectively stands in the shoes of the old employer, and employees maintain continuous service for the purpose of all statutory rights. The TUPE Regs also transfer the existing contractual terms and conditions, as well as any outstanding liabilities and rights.[2] In practice, the most important protection is against unfair dismissal because of the transfer, but this only helps employees with at least one year's service.[3] The TUPE Regs potentially apply to a transfer from the UK to a business which is based outside the UK and even outside the EU.[4]

10.2   The TUPE Regs were brought in to implement the European Acquired Rights Directive, also known as the Business Transfers Directive.[5] This means they should be interpreted as far as possible in line with decisions of the European Court of Justice (ECJ) under the Directive.[6] The law is difficult and constantly developing through decisions

---

1 SI No 246.

2 TUPE Regs reg 4.

3 The usual qualifying requirements for claiming unfair dismissal apply.

4 *Holis Metal Industries Ltd v GMB and another* [2008] IRLR 187, EAT.

5 2001/23/EC, which updates and consolidates previous directives.

6 Where there is a conflict between the TUPE Regs and the Directive, similar rules apply as to when UK legislation has not fully implemented EU discrimination law. See chapter 3.

of the ECJ and UK courts. Developments need to be monitored. The TUPE Regs 2006 replaced the earlier 1981 Regs with effect from 6 April 2006. BERR (now BIS) has issued a guide to the 2006 TUPE Regs for employees, employers and representatives.[7] This is helpful, but it has no legal status.

What is the method of transfer?

10.3   Much of the case-law has concerned when the TUPE Regs apply. This means looking at what form of transfer, as well as what kind of undertaking, is covered. A transfer may occur in many different ways, although the most common means is by a straightforward sale of a business, eg a restaurant chain under a brand name is sold by one company to another with little visible change. It may also take place by some other form of disposition such as granting a lease, franchise, contract or gift, even if ownership of physical property has not been transferred. Note that a share take-over is not in itself a transfer, since ownership remains in the same legal person, ie the company.[8] However, a share sale could be accompanied or followed by a transfer.[9]

10.4   A transfer may take place as a result of a series of transactions[10] provided the business retains its identity, for example:

- a factory is transferred back from a lessee to the owner, who then sells it on to another company;[11]
- an NHS Trust cleaning contract can transfer between two successive contractors (the first contractor hands back the cleaning services at the end of its contract, which are immediately transferred on to the second contractor);

There will be a particular date at which the transfer is considered to take place and the employees' contract rights transfer.[12]

---

7 Available on its website at www.berr.gov.uk/files/file20761.pdf

8 *Brookes and others v Borough Care Services and another* [1998] ICR 1198, EAT.

9 *Millam v Print Factory (London) 1991 Ltd* [2007] IRLR 526, CA, though this very much depends on the facts.

10 TUPE Regs reg 3(6)(a).

11 *P Bork International A/S v Foreningenaf Arbedjsledere i Danmark* [1989] IRLR 41, ECJ.

12 *Celtec Ltd v Astley and others* [2005] IRLR 647, ECJ.

What is a relevant transfer?

10.5   There are two forms of transfer under the TUPE Regs. The first type follows the old definition and case-law under the 1981 TUPE Regs and is set out from para 10.6 below. The DTI (BIS) guide refers to it as a 'business transfer'. The second type, introduced in the 2006 TUPE Regs, is referred to as a 'service provision change', and is set out from para 10.12 below. Some situations may fall under both definitions.

Business transfers

10.6   Under TUPE Regs reg 3(1)(a), a transfer of an undertaking or business occurs when there is a transfer of an economic entity which retains its identity. An economic entity means an organised grouping of resources which has the objective of pursuing an economic activity, whether that activity is central or ancillary.[13] This newly worded definition in the 2006 TUPE Regs essentially reflects the case-law which had already developed under the 1981 TUPE Regs. There are two stages which must be proved:[14]

1) That the undertaking was a stable economic entity prior to transfer.
2) That the entity was transferred in a recognisable form.

The following are broad guidelines taken from the case-law as to when TUPE will apply, but the particular facts of every case will be important. It should also be remembered that most of the case-law developed before the 2006 TUPE Regs came into force.

Stage 1: stable economic entity

10.7   The undertaking transferred must be a stable economic entity, but it need not own any tangible assets. For example, it could be a labour-only contract such as the provision of cleaning services or management of a shopping centre. It is not necessary for property to be transferred by the transferee to the transferor.[15] An organised grouping of wage-earners who are specifically and permanently assigned to a common

---

13 TUPE Regs reg 3(2).
14 *Whitewater Leisure Management Ltd v Barnes and others* [2000] IRLR 456, EAT; and see *Cheesman and others v R Brewer Contracts Ltd* [2001] IRLR 145, EAT for a useful summary of the principles.
15 TUPE Regs reg 3(6)(b).

task may amount to an economic entity.[16] Relevant factors to consider are the entity's workforce, management staff, the way work is organised, its operating methods and where appropriate, the operational resources available to it.[17] A single employee such as a cleaner can amount to an entity depending on the facts, eg if the task to be performed is complex and sophisticated and requires careful planning, specification and costings.[18]

10.8   Either the whole undertaking or a severable part of it must be transferred, eg the transfer of one shop in a chain or contracting out a cleaning or catering service. Non-commercial ventures are covered,[19] eg non-profit enterprises, voluntary organisations, free advice centres, charities, NHS trusts[20] and local education services.[21] It can include transfers between subsidiary companies within a corporate group.[22] An administrative reorganisation or transfer of administrative functions between public administrative authorities is not covered.[23] The scope of this exclusion is not entirely clear, but certain intra-governmental transfers may not be covered by TUPE. The rights of public sector employees in these instances are intended to be covered by other means, ie certain case-specific specialist legislation, and the government also expects the TUPE principles to be applied as a matter of good practice.[24]

Stage 2: transferred in a recognisable form

10.9   The undertaking must be transferred in a recognisable form from one employer to another. The overall test is whether the business in question retains its identity, this being indicated in particular by the continuation or resumption of its operation by the new employer.[25] The

---

16 *Sánchez Hidalgo v Asociación de Servicios Aser* [1999] IRLR 136, ECJ; *Francisco Hernández Vidal SA v Gomez Pérez* C-127/96 [1999] IRLR 132, ECJ; *Cheesman and others v R Brewer Contracts Ltd* [2001] IRLR 145, EAT.

17 *Sánchez Hidalgo v Asociación de Servicios Aser* [1999] IRLR 136, ECJ; *Francisco Hernández Vidal SA v Gomez Pérez* C-127/96 [1999] IRLR 132, ECJ; *Cheesman and others v R Brewer Contracts Ltd* [2001] IRLR 145, EAT.

18 *Dudley Bower Building Services Ltd v Lowe* [2003] IRLR 260, EAT.

19 *Dr Sophie Redmond Stichting v Bartol and others* [1992] IRLR 366, ECJ.

20 *Porter and Nanayakkara v Queen's Medical Centre (Nottingham University Hospital)* [1993] IRLR 486, HC.

21 *Kenny and others v South Manchester College* [1993] IRLR 265, HC.

22 *Allen and others v Amalgamated Construction Co Ltd* [2000] IRLR 119, ECJ.

23 *Henke v Gemeinde Schierke and Verwaltungsgemeinschaft 'Brocken'* [1996] IRLR 701, ECJ; TUPE Regs reg 3(5).

24 See Statement of Practice para 10.19 onwards.

25 *Spijkers v Gebroeders Benedik Abbatoir CV* [1986] CMLR 296, ECJ.

greater the similarity between the business run before and after the transfer, the more likely it is to satisfy this test. So, for example, a chocolate factory which is sold to be converted into a nightclub, would be a mere sale of assets and not of an undertaking. However, the business need not be identical before and afterwards in the way that it is run.

10.10   Case-law has suggested certain guidelines in deciding whether a business has retained enough of its identity on transfer to be covered by the TUPE Regs, although no single factor needs to be present in every case and an overall assessment must be made. In weighting factors, the type of undertaking must also be taken into account.[26] Employment tribunals must take a purposive approach, ie remember that the purpose of the TUPE Regs and the Directive is to protect employees. Relevant factors[27] will be:

- the type of business or undertaking concerned. Its size is irrelevant;
- whether the business's tangible assets, such as buildings and equipment, are transferred. Catering is an activity essentially based on equipment. It is therefore important whether the equipment is transferred.[28] It is not essential that ownership (as opposed to use) of assets is transferred.[29] For example, if a hospital provides a kitchen and equipment for its contract caterers, it is enough if both transferor and transferee use that same equipment.[30] If the business solely comprises services, transfer of assets will be particularly unimportant;
- the value of the intangible assets, eg goodwill, at the time of transfer and whether they are transferred;
- in a labour-intensive undertaking, whether or not the majority of employees are taken over by the new employer;[31] in an undertaking based significantly on tangible assets, whether these have transferred;[32] However, these are just factors. The fact that no assets are transferred in an 'asset-reliant' undertaking, does not necessarily

26 *Allen and others v Amalgamated Construction Co Ltd* [2000] IRLR 119, ECJ.
27 Sometimes referred to as the *Spijkers* factors. Set out by the ECJ in *Spijkers v Gebroeders Benedik Abbatoir CV* [1986] CMLR 296, ECJ and confirmed in numerous cases including *Dr Sophie Redmond Stichting v Bartol and others* [1992] IRLR 366, ECJ.
28 *Abler and others v Sodexho MM Catering Gesellschaft mbH and Sanrest Großküchen Betriebsgesellschaft mbH (intervener)* [2004] IRLR 168, ECJ.
29 *Allen and others v Amalgamated Construction Co Ltd* [2000] IRLR 119, ECJ.
30 *Abler and others v Sodexho MM Catering Gesellschaft mbH and Sanrest Großküchen Betriebsgesellschaft mbH (intervener)* [2004] IRLR 168, ECJ.
31 See comments below at para 10.13 regarding *Süzen* and contracting out.
32 *Oy Liikenne AB v Liskojärui and Juntunen* [2001] IRLR 171, ECJ.

mean there is no TUPE transfer.[33] Indeed, it is not always possible or necessary to characterise a business exclusively as 'labour-intensive' or 'asset-reliant'.[34]

- whether customers are transferred;
- the degree of similarity between the activities carried on before and after the transfer;
- the period, if any, during which those activities are suspended.

It does not matter if the new employer intends to integrate the transferred undertaking into his/her own business, provided that immediately after transfer the entity carries on the same activities as before and so retains its identity.[35] To say otherwise would make the TUPE Regs largely ineffective as every business is likely to wish to integrate any new business it has acquired. However, the ECJ has stated, rather unintelligibly, that if there are organisational changes post transfer, there must still be a 'functional link of interdependence and complementarity between the various elements of production transferred'.[36] It is also possible that an identifiable economic entity is divided into two parts, both of which are transferred. For example, a service providing refuse collection to a whole borough may be divided geographically into the north and south of the borough on transfer to two new contractors. Depending on the facts, this does not necessarily prevent there being a transfer.[37]

10.11   Applying these guidelines tends to be difficult. For example, in one case[38] there was a transfer of an undertaking to provide medical services, but the method of provision would change. The object of the undertaking remained the same, even though the method of achieving that object changed as medical science developed. By contrast, there was no transfer where an NHS Trust hospital shop selling newspapers, magazines, confectionery and flowers was changed on transfer to a major chain convenience store with a much wider range of goods, longer opening hours and a more commercial outlook. The ET considered that the identity of the original shop had been replaced by an entirely new and different concept.[39] These examples are simply illustrative. It is essential to give detailed examination to all the facts.

---

33 *Balfour Beatty Power Networks Ltd and another v Wilcox* [2007] IRLR 63, CA.
34 *Balfour Beatty Power Networks Ltd and another v Wilcox* [2007] IRLR 63, CA.
35 *Farmer v Danzas (UK) Ltd* (1995) 518 IRLB 14, EAT.
36 *Klarenberg v Ferrotron Technologies GmbH* [2009] IRLR 301, ECJ.
37 *Fairhurst Ward Abbotts Ltd v Botes Building Ltd* [2004] IRLR 304, CA.
38 *Porter and Nanayakkara v Queen's Medical Centre (Nottingham University Hospital)* [1993] IRLR 486, HC.
39 *(1) Matthieson (2) Cheyne v United News Shops Ltd* EAT 554/94.

Contracting out – service provision changes

Applying the business transfers definition

10.12 The principle that the TUPE Regs can cover the contracting out of services, often as a result of a compulsory competitive tendering exercise in the public sector, was well-established prior to the 2006 TUPE Regs.[40] Contracting-out situations can therefore still be covered under the 'business transfers' definition, which reflects the older law. However, the wording of the EU Directive and the definition of business transfers is not always adequate to cover the situations which arise. Many problems arose under the 1981 TUPE Regs.

10.13 Following the business transfers definition, the ECJ in *Süzen* said that an 'entity' cannot be reduced to the activity it is carrying out. An entity's identity also emerges from other factors, eg workforce, management structure, operating methods and resources. Therefore, in a labour-intensive sector, where there is no transfer of significant tangible or intangible assets, there may be no transfer unless the new employer takes over a major part of the employees (in terms of numbers and skills).[41] However, the Court of Appeal has said repeatedly that the importance of Süzen has been overstated. It is still necessary to consider all the facts characterising the transaction in question. The failure to appoint any of the former employees does not point conclusively against a transfer. It is relevant to consider why the employees were not taken on, eg whether it was a deliberate attempt to avoid the TUPE Regs.[42] The intention of the parties and the fact that the transferee tendered on the basis that TUPE applied would also be helpful.[43]

10.14 The undertaking must be a stable economic entity and not one where the contracted service is itself of limited duration, whoever is running it. For example, in one case the transfer of part of a building contract for the construction of a canteen was not covered by the

---

40 *Rask and Christensen v ISS Kantineservice A/S* [1993] IRLR 133, ECJ; *Dines and others v (1) Initial Health Care Services Ltd (2) Pall Mall Services Group Ltd* [1994] IRLR 336; [1995] ICR 11, CA.

41 *Süzen v Zehnacker Gebaudereinigung GmbH Krankenhausservice* [1997] IRLR 255, ECJ; *Allen and others v Amalgamated Construction Co Ltd* [2000] IRLR 119, ECJ.

42 *ECM (Vehicle Delivery Service) v Cox* [1999] IRLR 559, CA; *ADI (UK) Ltd v Willer and others* [2001] IRLR 542, CA; *RCO Support Services Ltd v UNISON* [2002] IRLR 401, CA.

43 *Lightways (Contractors) Ltd v Associated Holdings Ltd* [2000] IRLR 247, CS.

TUPE Regs.[44] It is different where complete works projects are transferred.[45]

10.15 Examples where the original TUPE Regs applied include:

- the contracting out of cleaning services by a bank which had previously employed one cleaner to do the work;[46]
- the transfer of hospital cleaning services from one contractor at the end of its contract to another;[47]
- a college's termination of a catering contract in order to provide its own catering service;[48]
- the contracting out to a college of prison education previously provided by the local education authority;[49]
- the transfer of a subsidy or grant by a public body, eg a local authority, from one advice agency to another with similar aims.[50]

Service provision changes – the new definition

10.16 Subject to specified exceptions, the government wanted the TUPE Regs to apply to all contracting-out situations, without the legal complications and uncertainties set out above. It therefore introduced an additional definition of a transfer into the 2006 TUPE Regs. Under 2006 TUPE Regs reg 3(1)(b), service provision changes are explicitly covered.

10.17 Service provision changes cover any stage of the contracting-out or outsourcing process, ie the original grant of a contract, reassignment of the contract to a different contractor, and taking the service back in-house. The definition applies where:

(i) immediately before the change, there is an organised grouping of employees, which has as its principal purpose the carrying out of the activities concerned on behalf of the client (the contracting body); and

---

44 *Ledernes Hovedorganisation, acting on behalf of Ole Rygaard v Dansk Arbejdsgiver-forening, acting on behalf of Stro Molle Akustik A/S* [1996] IRLR 51, ECJ. This principle should not be applied too widely: *BSG Property Services v Tuck* [1996] IRLR 134, EAT.

45 *Allen and others v Amalgamated Construction Co Ltd* [2000] IRLR 119, ECJ.

46 *Schmidt v Spar-und Leihkasse der fruheren Amter Bordesholm, Kiel und Kronshagen* [1994] IRLR 302, ECJ.

47 *Dines and others v (1) Initial Health Care Services Ltd (2) Pall Mall Services Group Ltd* [1994] IRLR 336; [1995] ICR 11, CA.

48 *Campion-Hall v (1) Wain (2) Gardner Merchant Ltd* (1996) 561 IDS Brief 5, EAT.

49 *Kenny and another v South Manchester College* [1993] ICR 934; [1993] IRLR 265, HC.

50 *Dr Sophie Redmond Stichting v Bartol and others* [1992] IRLR 366, ECJ.

(ii) the client intends that, following the service provision change, the activities will be carried out by the transferee.[51]

The advantage of this wording is that it focuses on whether the activities are intended by the client to remain the same, as opposed to whether employees or assets transfer. Minor changes in the way activities will be carried out by the transferee are within the definition.[52] It does not matter if the service is split in two after the transfer, but if the service becomes completely fragmented, there may be no service provision change.[53]

10.18   An 'organised grouping of employees' can comprise one employee.[54] But the definition does not apply if there is no identifiable group of employees in the first place, eg the client grants a contract for courier services, but prior to this, courier services were carried out by various different couriers on an ad hoc basis, as opposed to a permanent dedicated team. Difficulties may arise where a group of employees spend part of their time carrying out the relevant activities, but spend the rest of their time on other activities. Contracts for single specific events or short-term tasks (eg organising a conference), or wholly or mainly for the supply of goods as opposed to services (eg supplying sandwiches to a staff canteen to sell on, as opposed to running the canteen) are also excluded.[55] The government says it does not prevent the definition applying if the transferor carries out the activities in a new or innovative manner, eg by computerisation.[56]

Public sector transfers

10.19   The government has said it is committed to ensuring that transferred workers are treated fairly and it has issued these important documents:

1) A Code of Practice on workforce matters in local authority service contracts. This applies to local authority contracts in England advertised on or after 13 March 2003. Also on 13 March 2003, statutory guidance was issued in the form of a Best Value Performance

51 TUPE Regs reg 3(3)(a).
52 *Metropolitan Resources Ltd v (1) Churchill Dulwich Ltd – in liquidation (2) Martin Lambridge and others* UKEAT/0286/08.
53 *Kimberley Group Housing Ltd v Hambley and others; Angel Services (UK) Ltd v Hambley and others* [2008] IRLR 682, EAT; *Clearsprings Management Ltd v Ankers and others* UKEAT/0054/08.
54 TUPE Regs reg 2(1).
55 TUPE Regs reg 3(3).

Improvement Circular. The code appears at Annex D.[57] A similar code appears to have been promulgated by the Welsh Assembly in March 2005. In Scotland, the Scottish Executive and Scottish TUC have agreed on a protocol which is similar to the code.[58] The Code is applied to Fire and Rescue Authorities by ODPM 09/2004, see Annex E.[59] There is a parallel Code for Police Authority Service Contracts – see Appendix F to the Best Value and Planning Guidance for Police Authorities and Forces.[60]

2) A Code of Practice on Workforce Matters in Public Sector Service Contracts (March 2005).[61] This applies to the public sector generally, including the civil service, NHS and maintained schools, but does not apply where the Local Authority Code applies and is subject to certain exemptions, eg higher and further education institutions, Academies, and where the ROE model applies in NHS PFI contracts.

3) The Cabinet Office Statement of Practice on Staff Transfers in the Public Sector plus its annex, A fair deal for Staff Pensions (Jan 2000, revised Nov 2007).[62]

10.20   Under the Local Government Act 2003, authorities are required to monitor compliance with the Local Authority Code and to confirm in their annual Best Value Performance Plans that individual contracts comply with the requirements in the Code. The Audit Commission oversees this process. The enforcement of the Code is by way of a clause in the contract between the contracting authority and the contractor. The effectiveness of this mode of enforcement is uncertain. Paragraphs 13–16 of the Code set out the expected steps of enforcement.

---

56 See paras 27-29 of the Public Consultation Document with the draft revised regulations, URN 05/926, at www.berr.gov.uk/files/file16389.pdf

57 ODPM Circular 03/2003 is available at www.communities.gov.uk/publications/localgovernment/odpmcircularbest

58 Public Private Partnerships in Scotland – Protocol and Guidance concerning Employment Issues, 2002.

59 At www.communities.gov.uk/archived/publications/fire/guidancebest

60 At http://police.homeoffice.gov.uk/news-and-publications/publication/finance-and-business-planning/bestvalueplanguidjuly03.pdf?view=Binary

61 Available at www.ogc.gov.uk/documents/Code_of_Practice_on_workforce_matters.pdf

62 This is available at www.hm-treasury.gov.uk/d/staff_transfers_145.pdf See also The Best Value Authorities Staff Transfers (Pensions) Direction 2007 available at www.communities.gov.uk/publications/localgovernment/authorities-staff-transfers

UNISON has produced an excellent negotiators' guides[63] which make suggestions on how trade union branches can get involved and monitor implementation of the Code.

10.21 The Cabinet Office Statement of Practice applies to the NHS and central government as well as local authorities. However, it is only a policy statement and is not enforceable in itself except in respect of local and other authorities covered by the Code of Practice, which are required to apply the principles set out in the Statement of Practice. With other employers, it is still a useful document for trade union negotiators because it puts pressure on employers and contractors to take steps which ensure the TUPE Regs apply.

10.22 The rest of this chapter sets out the general law under the TUPE Regs and, if relevant, indicates what the Codes of Practice, Statement of Practice or Scottish Protocol say on the matter. If advising or negotiating on a public sector transfer, it is important to read those documents, although they are less crucial than they were before the specific definition of service provision changes was introduced with the 2006 TUPE Regs.

10.23 The National Health Service and Community Care Act 1990 governs transfers from local health authorities to NHS Trusts.[64] The Education Reform Act 1988 covers transfers to grant-maintained or opted-out schools.

Which workers are protected?

10.24 The TUPE Regs protect employees who are employed by the transferor and assigned to the organised grouping of resources or employees immediately before,[65] ie at the moment of,[66] the transfer. It is irrelevant if the employee is off work at the time of the transfer due to sickness, holidays, maternity leave, etc.[67] Employees dismissed in

---

63 'Organising Guide to Transfers of Employment 2008' available at www.unison.org.uk/acrobat/PCU_Organising_guide.pdf and 'UNISON Guide: Best Value Code of Practice on Workforce Matters in Local Authority Service Contracts in England and Police Authority Contracts in England and Wales', July 2003. Available at www.unison.org.uk/acrobat/13612.pdf From the legal viewpoint, remember the latter was written prior to the 2006 TUPE Regs.

64 See also *Gale v Northern General Hospital NHS Trust* [1994] IRLR 292, CA.

65 TUPE Regs reg 4(1) and (3).

66 *Secretary of State for Employment v Spence and others* [1986] ICR 651; [1986] IRLR 248, CA.

67 *Fairhurst Ward Abbotts Ltd v Botes Building Ltd* [2004] IRLR 304, CA.

advance of the transfer, but for a connected reason which is not an economic, technical or organisational (ETO) reason entailing a change in the workforce, are deemed to be employed immediately before the transfer.[68]

10.25   Where part of an undertaking is transferred, the TUPE Regs protect only those employees 'assigned' to that part.[69] An employee may be assigned to the transferred part even though s/he carried out duties for other parts of the original employer's business.[70] An ET must look at all the facts, such as time spent in each part, value given, and allocation of costs and contractual terms. Employers may try to shift employees around immediately before a transfer so as to get rid of unpopular staff. However, the ET will look at the reality of the situation, and if the employee was assigned only temporarily to the part transferred, s/he will not be part of the transfer.[71] In the absence of other factors, where employees were previously assigned to the whole of an undertaking, which is subsequently split and transferred to two different transferees, their contracts will transfer to the transferee which takes over the greater part of the transferor's activities.[72]

Dismissal due to the transfer

10.26   It is automatically unfair for the transferor or transferee to dismiss an employee if the sole or principal reason is the transfer itself, or for a reason connected with the transfer unless that reason is an ETO reason entailing changes in the workforce.[73] This can include dismissals by the transferor in advance of the transfer, even at a very early stage where a number of potential transferees are interested, but no concrete decision has been made.[74] There is no statutory definition of

---

68 *Litster v Forth Dry Dock and Engineering Co Ltd* [1989] ICR 341; [1989] IRLR 161, HL; TUPE Regs reg 4(3). See para 10.26 for meaning of ETO.

69 *Botzen and others v Rotterdamsche Droogdok Maatschappij BV* [1986] 2 CMLR 50, ECJ.

70 *Duncan Webb Offset (Maidstone) Ltd v Cooper and others* [1995] IRLR 633, EAT; *Buchanan-Smith v Schleicher and Co International Ltd* [1996] IRLR 547, EAT; *CPL Distribution Ltd v Todd* [2003] IRLR 28, CA.

71 *Securiplan v Bademost* EAT; (2003) 746 IDS Brief 6, EAT; TUPE Regs reg 2(1).

72 *Kimberley Group Housing Ltd v Hambley and others; Angel Services (UK) Ltd v Hambley and others* [2008] IRLR 682, EAT.

73 TUPE Regs reg 7(1).

74 *CAB Automotive Ltd v Blake and others* UKEAT/0298/07; *Morris v John Grose Group Ltd* [1998] IRLR 499, EAT; though beware *Ibex Trading Co Ltd (In administration) v Walton and others* [1994] IRLR 564, EAT.

'ETO' but the DTI (BIS) guide suggests that economic reasons could relate to the profitability or market performance of the business; technical reasons could relate to equipment or production processes; and organisational reasons could relate to management or organisational structure.

10.27   It is a question of fact whether a dismissal is connected with a transfer. There is a rebuttable presumption that dismissals at the time of a transfer are connected with it, but a dismissal may also be connected with it if it takes place in advance or some time afterwards. There is no fixed time period afterwards within which a dismissal will be deemed 'connected', and it can be years later if the evidence still suggests a connection.[75]

10.28   To avoid an automatically unfair dismissal, any 'economic' reason must relate to the conduct of the business itself and not just be to secure an enhanced sale price.[76] A contracting-out situation can be ambiguous and will depend on the facts of the case. For example, where it is a condition of the contract that a new contractor reduces the contract price by reducing staff, what is the reason for the dismissals of the redundant staff? Is it a cost saving relating to the conduct of the business which would have happened whether or not there was a transfer, or is it just a way to reduce the cost of the contract to prospective bidders?[77] The main restriction on the ETO exception is that it must entail changes in the workforce. This means the employer cannot simply alter an employee's contractual terms, eg to harmonise with the existing workforce, but there must be a change in the overall numbers of the workforce or a change in job functions.[78] Such a change must be the objective of the employer's plan, not just a possible consequence. If the dismissal is by the transferor, the ETO reason must relate to the future conduct of the transferor's business, as opposed to changes in the transferee's workforce.[79]

10.29   If the ETO exception does apply, it does not mean the dismissal is fair. The ordinary principles to determine unfair dismissal claims will

---

75 See also paragraph 10.38 for 'connected' reasons in the context of variation of terms.

76 *Wheeler v (1) Patel (2) J Golding Group of Companies* [1987] IRLR 211; [1987] ICR 631, EAT; *Gateway Hotels Ltd v Stewart and others* [1988] IRLR 287, EAT. Although see *Whitehouse v Chas A Blatchford and Sons Ltd* [1999] IRLR 493, CA and *Kerry Foods Ltd v Creber and others* [2000] IRLR 10, EAT.

77 See *Whitehouse v Chas A Blatchford & Sons Ltd* [1999] IRLR 493, CA, which is a strange interpretation of a factual situation – see IRLR commentary at p450.

78 *Delabole Slate Ltd v Berriman* [1985] IRLR 305, CA.

79 *Hynd v Armstrong and others* (2007) 828 *IDS Brief* 14, CS; 2007 CSIH 16.

apply, as the reason for dismissal is treated as a dismissal for redundancy or some other substantial reason.[80] To claim ordinary or automatic unfair dismissal, the worker must be an employee with at least one year's service[81] and have been dismissed in law. This includes constructive dismissal and failure to renew a fixed-term contract.[82]

10.30   An employee may resign and claim constructive dismissal in the usual way if his/her employer is in fundamental breach of contract.[83] Even where the employer has not broken the contract, the employee may claim s/he has been dismissed if the transfer involves, or would involve, a substantial change in working conditions to his/her material detriment.[84] What this means is untested, but it probably covers substantial changes in location or hours, even though such changes are allowed under the contract. Although the employee can claim s/he has been dismissed in these situations, the dismissal will not necessarily be unfair, as explained above. Note that notice pay cannot be claimed in respect of a 'material detriment' resignation.[85]

The effect of a transfer

10.31   Where the TUPE Regs apply, the new employer stands in the shoes of the old employer for most purposes. The contractual terms and conditions are transferred[86] as are all the transferor's rights, powers, duties and liabilities under or in connection with the contract.[87] This would include wages owed, liability for discrimination by the former employer[88] and tortious liability,[89] eg for negligence leading to personal injury. If the transferor had an employers' liability insurance policy, the transferor's right to an indemnity under the policy for any such liability

---

80 TUPE Regs reg 7(3)(b).

81 Collective Redundancies and Transfer of Undertakings (Protection of Employment) (Amendment) Regulations 1995 SI No 2587. See also *MRS Environmental Services Ltd v Marsh and another* (1996) 571 IDS Brief 2, EAT.

82 See para 6.26 for the rights of employees on temporary contracts.

83 TUPE Regs, reg 4(11).

84 TUPE Regs, reg 4(9).

85 TUPE Regs, reg 4(10).

86 TUPE Regs reg 4(1).

87 TUPE Regs reg 4(2).

88 *DJM International Ltd v Nicholas* [1996] IRLR 76, EAT.

89 *Bernadone v Pall Mall Services Group and others; Martin v Lancashire CC* [2000] IRLR 487, CA.

would also transfer.[90] It may also include liability for higher pay arising from an EqPA 1970 comparison, even though the employee's comparator has not transferred and no equal pay case was brought prior to the transfer.[91] A contractual right to have pay rates set by reference to a collective agreement also transfers, even if the transferee will have no access to the collective bargaining machinery.[92] The TUPE Regs probably also transfer acquired continuous service for statutory employment rights.[93] It is impossible to transfer an employee's entitlement to participate in the original employer's profit-share scheme, so what transfers is an entitlement to participate in a scheme of substantial equivalence.[94] The transferor and transferee are jointly and severally liable for any compensation due to failure collectively to consult the trade union or employee representatives about the transfer.[95]

10.32   To ensure the transferee is well placed to honour obligations towards the employees, the transferor must give the transferee written 'employee liability information' at least 14 days before the transfer.[96] This comprises, in respect of each employee subject to the transfer, the employee's identity and age; the particulars required under ERA 1996 s1;[97] information regarding any disciplinary action or grievance taken within the previous two years in circumstances where the ACAS Code on Disciplinary and Grievance procedures applies;[98] information regarding any court or tribunal case brought by the employee within the previous two years or which is likely to be brought; and applicable collective agreements. The Information Commissioner has issued guidance regarding protection of data regarding employees on transfe[99]

10.33   The precise legal position regarding transfer of pensions is beyond the scope of this book. The law is complex and developments in leg-

---

90 *Bernadone v Pall Mall Services Group and others; Martin v Lancashire CC* [2000] IRLR 487, CA. See TUPE Regs reg 17 regarding liability where the transferor was not required to hold employers' liability insurance.

91 *Gutridge v Sodexo Ltd and North Tees & Hartlepool NHS Foundation* [2009] EWCA Civ 759.

92 *Alemo-Herron and others v Parkwood Leisure Ltd* UKEAT/0456/08; [2009] IRLR 322, EAT.

93 Although this is usually preserved in any event by ERA 1996 s218(2).

94 *Mitie Managed Services Ltd v French* [2002] IRLR 512, EAT.

95 See para 2.27. TUPE Regs reg 15(9).

96 TUPE Regs reg 11.

97 See para 1.24.

98 This is the practical meaning of the section at the moment, though it is worded more widely. See para 22.3 regarding the ACAS Code.

99 Available on his site: www.ico.gov.uk

islation and case-law should be watched. The following is only a broad guide. Occupational pension schemes are excluded from the TUPE Regs in so far as they cover old age, invalidity or survivors' benefits.[100] Early retirement benefits paid on dismissal to employees who have reached a certain age do not fall within this category and should transfer.[101] Accrued pension rights should be preserved,[102] but there is probably no entitlement to continued membership or contributions.[103] Although, with these exceptions, occupational pension schemes do not transfer, the Pensions Act 2004 and the Transfer of Employment (Pension Protection) Regulations 2005[104] have introduced a minimum occupational pension entitlement to transferred employees who had such an entitlement with their employers before the transfer. Unfortunately there is no requirement that the post-transfer pension is equivalent to the original scheme. In the public sector, the government has said it will continue to follow the more generous policy set out in Annex A to the Cabinet Office Statement of Practice (above). Annex A is clarified by an HM Treasury Guidance Note, 'Fair Deal for Staff Pensions; Procurement of Bulk Transfer Arrangements and Related Issues' (June 2004).

10.34   If the TUPE Regs apply to a particular employee, s/he should usually claim for any transferred rights or unfair dismissal against the transferee, even if s/he never started work for the new employer and was dismissed in advance of the transfer, provided that it was for a connected reason.[105] However, if dismissal by the transferor was for an ETO reason or unconnected with the transfer, the employee may have to sue the transferor. If in doubt as to who to sue, eg due to uncertainty whether the TUPE Regs apply or the transferor's reason for dismissal or any other complication, it is probably safest to claim in the alternative against the old employer and the apparent transferee. Where the transferor is subject to insolvency proceedings, certain debts will be paid to the extent that they are covered by the National Insurance

---

100 TUPE Regs reg 10. See also Council Directive 2001/23/EC article 3(4).
101 *Beckmann v Dynamco Whicheloe Macfarlane Ltd* C-164/00 [2002] IRLR 578, ECJ; *Martin v South Bank University* [2004] IRLR 75, ECJ.
102 Article 3(4)(b) of 2001/23/EC.
103 *Walden Engineering Co Ltd v Warrener* [1993] IRLR 420, EAT; *Adams and others v Lancashire CC and BET Catering Services Ltd* [1997] IRLR 436, CA.
104 SI No 649.
105 *Stirling DC v Allan and others* [1995] IRLR 301, CS.

Fund rather than transfer to the transferee.[106] Also, the rules regarding automatic unfair dismissal for a reason connected with the transfer (see above) do not apply in relevant insolvency situations. The DTI (BIS) guide suggests these insolvency exceptions apply where the business is transferred as a going concern, rather than being wound up, but it is a bit more technical than that. The idea is to help rescue failing businesses. There is an additional DTI (BIS) guidance note regarding the effect of insolvency under the TUPE Regs: 'Redundancy and insolvency payments'.[107]

10.35   An employee's contract of employment and all the rights, powers, duties and liabilities in connection with it, will not transfer if the employee tells the transferor or the transferee that s/he objects to becoming employed by the transferee. His/her employment will simply terminate on the transfer, but s/he will not be treated as having been dismissed and s/he will not be able to claim unfair dismissal or redundancy pay.[108] If the employee agrees to stay on with the transferor, s/he may have to negotiate new terms and conditions, as her old contract of employment will probably no longer apply.[109]

10.36   An employee, who is employed in the undertaking to be transferred, cannot be forced to stay with the transferor because the TUPE Regs will automatically apply. For example, the transferor cannot prevent employees against their will from transferring by insisting they remain with the transferor and redeploying them at the moment of transfer under contractual mobility clauses.[110] It sometimes happens that employees employed in the business to be transferred choose to remain with their original employer, but to work for the transferee on secondment. In such situations, despite what everyone agrees and believes, it is very likely that the employee's employment will have transferred to the transferee at the date of transfer of the business.[111] If the employee then returns to work for the transferor at the end of the

106 TUPE Regs reg 8. The rules are complicated regarding what kind of insolvency proceedings are covered – see *Secretary of State for Trade and Industry v Slater and ors* UKEAT/0119/07; [2007] IRLR 928, EAT and *Oakland v Wellswood (Yorkshire) Ltd* UKEAT/395/08; [2009] IRLR 250, EAT.

107 Available at www.berr.gov.uk/files/file30031.pdf

108 TUPE Regs reg 4(7)–(8), unless reg 4(9) applies – see para 10.30.

109 See, eg, *Sunley Turriff Holdings Ltd v Thomson and others* [1995] IRLR 184, EAT.

110 *Royal Mail Group Ltd v Communication Workers Union* UKEAT/0338/08; [2009] IRLR 108, EAT. It may be different if such redeployment takes place prior to transfer.

111 *Celtec Ltd v Astley* [2006] IRLR 635, HL; *Capita Health Solutions Ltd v McLean* [2008] IRLR 595, EAT.

secondment period, this will probably be deemed a new contract of employment between the employee and the transferor, which means the employee will lose his/her continuous service (unless that is preserved by 'custom or arrangement' – see para 6.22.)

10.37   A difficulty can arise regarding the transfer of migrant workers who require sponsorship under the new points-based immigration system. An employer needs to be licensed to sponsor migrant workers. If the transferor was licensed but the transferee is not, the latter must apply for a licence within 28 days. If it chooses not to, its employees who are sponsored migrants will have a limited amount of time to find a new sponsor. Quite apart from this, transferees must check the documents of all their employees within 28 days of the transfer to check no illegal workers have transferred contrary to the rules in the Immigration, Asylum and Nationality Act 2006 (see para 13.18).

Changing the terms and conditions

10.38   The TUPE Regs preserve contractual terms and conditions and prohibit changes due to the transfer alone. An employer's attempt to impose new terms and conditions, even if s/he has secured the employee's agreement (expressly or by affirmation) will be ineffective if the change is due to the transfer, eg to harmonise terms and conditions.[112] So, for example, an employee retained by the new employer ostensibly on changed terms and conditions could subsequently insist on the previous terms still applying.[113] A variation to the contract can be agreed if it is unconnected with the transfer. In addition, the TUPE Regs permit an agreed variation connected to the transfer, if it is for an ETO reason entailing a change in the workforce.[114] However, this seems contrary to EU law and the *Daddy's Dance Hall* case, and it remains to be tested in the courts. Unlike an employee, an employer cannot rely on the TUPE Regs to contend that a variation agreed on a transfer is void. There is nothing to stop an employee agreeing additional rights.[115] The employee has less protection if s/he is dismissed by the transferor and offered new terms and conditions by the transferee. If s/he

112 TUPE Regs reg 4(4)(a).
113 *Foreningen A F Arbejdsledere i Danmark v Daddy's Dance Hall A/S* [1988] IRLR 315, ECJ; *Credit Suisse First Boston (Europe) Ltd v Lister* [1998] IRLR 700, CA; *Martin v South Bank University* [2004] IRLR 75, ECJ.
114 TUPE Regs regs 4(4)(b) and 5.
115 *Regent Security Services Ltd v Power* [2008] IRLR 66, CA.

accepts these, the new terms and conditions will apply, and his/her only remedy will be any claim regarding the dismissal (see paras 10.26–10.30).

10.39 It depends on the facts whether the reason for changing terms and conditions is connected with the transfer. A connection may be indicated if the change is to bring terms and conditions into line with those of existing staff of the transferor, or if the change occurs at the time of the transfer as opposed to much later.[116] On the other hand, if the business was already in financial trouble and the transferee was trying to save money by cutting pay prior to the transfer, the fact that the transferee cuts salaries for the same reason suggests the contract change is not connected with the transfer.[117]

10.40 There is an exception for insolvency situations, where the business is transferred as a going concern. The transferor, transferee or insolvency practitioner is permitted to make a written agreement with trade union or employee representatives to change terms and conditions, even if this is for reasons connected with the transfer which are not an ETO reason, provided the changes are designed to safeguard employment opportunities by ensuring the survival of the undertaking.[118]

Public sector transfers

10.41 For employees covered by the Codes of Practice, the Code requires contractors to confirm their obligations to protect employees' terms and conditions when they transfer. Even then, the protection may be inadequate in the long term. To win contracts, companies may tender on an unsustainable economic basis without making future redundancies or cutting pay. In an attempt to avoid this, the Statement of Practice says the contracting authority should ensure it is satisfied that bidders' proposals fully meet the requirements of the TUPE Regs.

New employees

10.42 One problem is that new employees get taken on with less favourable terms and conditions than those of transferred staff, making the former

---

116 Though in *Taylor v Connex South Eastern Ltd* (2001) 662 IRLB 13; 670 IDS Brief 10, EAT and *London Metropolitan University v Sackur* UKEAT/0286/06, a change made two years later was found to be connected.

117 See eg *Carlton Care Ltd v Rooney and others* EAT/112/00, although under the 1981 TUPE Regs.

118 TUPE Regs reg 9; and see BIS Guidance Note, n7 above.

less desirable to retain in the long term. UNISON and other unions lobbied hard for legislation to help prevent such a two-tier system after contracting out. As a result, the government states in the Codes of Practice that the transferee will consult representatives of the recognised trade union on the terms and conditions to be offered to new joiners. This should be a genuine dialogue. The intention is that contractors and trade unions should be able to agree on a particular package of terms and conditions, in keeping with the terms of the Codes.

10.43   The Codes say that overall, new employees must be employed on fair and reasonable terms and conditions which are no less favourable (apart from pensions) than those of transferred employees. Unfortunately this does mean that they can have different terms and conditions, some being more favourable and some being less favourable. New joiners must also be offered pension provision, which may be either membership of the local government pension scheme, membership of a good quality employer pension scheme or membership of a stakeholder pension scheme with an employer contribution. It is a pity that stakeholder pensions are one of the options because they may offer lower pension benefits. These rules regarding new joiners only apply in sectors covered by the Codes.[119]

119 Paras 10.19 onwards.

PART III

Equality and discrimination

CHAPTER 11

Work and family life

continued

Chapter 11: Key points
Pregnancy-related dismissals and discrimination

- Dismissals for reasons connected with pregnancy or maternity leave are automatically unfair. Other detrimental treatment is also unlawful. There is no minimum qualifying service.
- Dismissal or other discrimination due to pregnancy and related reasons such as pregnancy-related sickness is unlawful sex discrimination in itself if it occurs during pregnancy or maternity leave.
- In limited circumstances, eg pregnancy-related sickness occurring after maternity leave, a comparison with a man in equivalent circumstances may be necessary to prove sex discrimination.
- A woman cannot claim full pay while on maternity leave purely because her absence is pregnancy-related.

General guide to useful evidence

- Evidence proving that the detriment or dismissal was for pregnancy or a related reason as opposed to the reason put forward by the employer.
- If comparison with a man is necessary, evidence showing how a man would have been treated in comparable circumstances, eg if he required sick leave.

Maternity rights and family related leave

- Pregnant women are entitled to risk assessments and paid time off if specified risks exist. They are also entitled to reasonable time off for antenatal care.
- Every employee is entitled to 26 weeks' ordinary maternity leave (OML) followed by 26 weeks' additional maternity leave (AML).
- There are two weeks' compulsory maternity leave (CML) for all women following childbirth.
- The correct notifications must be given before starting leave and if wanting to come back early.
- Maternity leave is automatically triggered by any pregnancy-related absence in the last four weeks before the expected week of childbirth (EWC).
- There are similar rights for adoption leave for employees with at least 26 weeks' service.
- There is a right to two weeks' paternity leave.

- During statutory maternity leave, women are entitled to their normal terms and conditions other than pay.
- Statutory maternity, paternity and adoption leave pay are available for those who qualify.
- Employees with one year's service are entitled to a total of 13 weeks' unpaid parental leave to take care of children under five years old (18 if disabled).
- Employees are entitled to reasonable unpaid time off as dependant leave to make arrangements when certain emergencies arise with children or other dependants.
- It is automatic unfair dismissal to dismiss an employee and unlawful to subject him/her to a detriment for reasons connected with maternity, parental or dependant leave (see paras 6.66–6.69). It is also automatic unfair dismissal to dismiss her for asserting a statutory right, eg the right to time off for antenatal care.

Part-time and flexible working

- Eligible employees can formally request flexible working under the Flexible Working Regulations 2002 in order to care for children under 17 (18 if disabled) or certain adults. Employers can refuse to give permission, but must give reasons why not.
- Refusal to permit a woman or married person to work part-time or arrive or leave at certain hours may be unlawful indirect sex discrimination under the Sex Discrimination Act 1975.
- It may also be indirect sex discrimination unjustifiably to treat part-time workers less well than full-timers.
- Where part-timers are given less favourable contractual terms and conditions, including pay rates, the Equal Pay Act 1970 applies.
- Under the Part-time Workers Regulations 2000, a part-timer (male or female) should be treated equally with a comparable full-timer (on a pro rata basis), unless an employer can justify not doing so.
- The main issue on part-time working will usually be whether the employer can justify insisting on full-time working.

General guide to useful evidence

- Find out the employer's justification.
- Evidence to show why part-time working in the job will be satisfactory or even beneficial.

> *To claim sex discrimination:*
> - Evidence generally and within the appropriate pool showing that women more often work part-time and are less able to work full-time than men.
> - Evidence showing that the particular worker has difficulty working full-time.
>
> *To claim under the Equal Pay Act 1970 or Part-time Workers Regulations 2000:*
> - Evidence regarding the chosen comparator.

Pregnancy-related dismissals and discrimination

11.1   In September 2003, the former Equal Opportunities Commission (EOC) launched a formal investigation into pregnancy discrimination, including discrimination while on maternity leave and on return to work. In June 2005, it published its final report: 'Greater Expectations: Final Report of the EOC's Investigation into New and Expectant Mothers in the Workplace'.[1] The report says the data it has collected shows that the level of pregnancy discrimination in the workplace is 'appalling'. The EOC was stunned at the number of women who said they had been dismissed, demoted, denied training or promotion, or bullied into quitting, just because of their pregnancy. It estimated that each year, almost half of the 440,000 pregnant women in Great Britain experience some form of disadvantage at work as a result, and 30,000 are forced out of their jobs. But fewer than 1 in 20 will seek advice and only three per cent who lose their job will bring an employment tribunal (ET) case. In 2005/06 only 1,504 cases were registered in the ET regarding dismissal or detriment linked to pregnancy. For evidence to prove pregnancy discrimination, see para 16.35 below.

11.2   Under the Employment Rights Act (ERA) 1996 s99, it is automatically unfair to dismiss a female employee for a number of reasons related to her pregnancy, maternity or maternity leave (see paras 6.66–6.68 above). There is no minimum service requirement to claim unfair dismissal for these reasons. A woman is entitled to written reasons if she is dismissed while pregnant or on maternity leave, again regardless of her length of service.[2]

---

1 The Summary Final Report is currently available at
   http://83.137.212.42/sitearchive/eoc/PDF/suffer_summary.pdf
2 ERA 1996 s92(4); see paras 20.12–20.16.

11.3   Women may also claim that dismissal in such circumstances is unlawful sex discrimination contrary to the Sex Discrimination Act (SDA) 1975.[3] Where possible, women should usually claim under both statutes, since a successful sex discrimination claim would lead to additional compensation. Claiming under the SDA 1975 also enables a woman to use the useful SDA questionnaire procedure to gather evidence. Sometimes making a claim under the SDA 1975 will be the only legal option, eg because the woman does not meet the other qualifying requirements for claiming unfair dismissal under the ERA 1996, for instance, because she is a contract worker and not an employee. Discrimination in pay and contract terms would be covered by the Equal Pay Act 1970.

11.4   Less favourable treatment of a woman due to pregnancy or maternity is also prohibited by EU law. It is covered by the general provisions of Article 141 and the Equal Treatment Directive[4] (ETD) as well as the Pregnant Workers Directive[5] (PWD). Until October 2005, pregnancy-related discrimination was covered by the standard definition of sex discrimination in the SDA 1975, as expanded by national and EU case-law. From 1 October 2005, the SDA 1975 was amended to introduce explicit prohibitions on pregnancy and maternity discrimination. Ostensibly this was to implement the amended ETD and to reflect EU case-law, but the new sections were more restrictive than the law as it has developed and had to be amended again on 6 April 2008.[6]

11.5   Under SDA 1975 s3A, it is unlawful to discriminate against a woman on the ground of her pregnancy, including any illness caused by the pregnancy,[7] or because she seeks to exercise or has exercised a statutory right to maternity leave. No comparison is required with how a man in an equivalent situation would be treated. Section 3A(1) now states:

> A person discriminates against a woman if –
> (a) at a time in a protected period, and on the ground of the woman's pregnancy, the person treats her less favourably ...;

Following a judicial review by the EOC,[8] the 2008 amendment removed the need to make any comparison with how the woman would have

---

3 Unlike unfair dismissal, discrimination law does not apply only to employees.
4 76/207/EEC.
5 92/85/EEC.
6 By SI 2008/656.
7 SDA 1975 s3A(3)(b).
8 *Equal Opportunities Commission v Secretary of State for Trade and Industry* [2007] EWHC 483 (Admin).

been treated if she was not pregnant. It is well-established in the case-law that no comparison is required either with a man or with a non-pregnant woman. It need only be shown that the discrimination is 'related to' the woman's pregnancy.[9] Although in many situations, for instance, a failed promotion, it is useful as a matter of evidence to compare the way a pregnant woman is treated with the treatment of a non-pregnant comparator, such a comparison does not always work. For example, an employer who refuses a woman permission to take the additional toilet breaks she needs as a result of her pregnancy, would presumably equally refuse a non-pregnant worker permission to take so many breaks. However, the employer's behaviour would clearly be pregnancy-related discrimination.

11.6   There is no justifiability defence available to the employer for pregnancy-related discrimination. The European Court of Justice (ECJ) has consistently taken a very firm line on this principle, even when the results seem unfair to the employer. In the leading case of *Webb*,[10] Mrs Webb was taken on for a permanent job, but initially to cover another worker's maternity leave. She was dismissed when the employer discovered she could not cover the leave, due to her own maternity leave. Nevertheless, this was unlawful discrimination. In another case[11] a temporary nurse in a heart clinic applied for a permanent post which was to start immediately. She was eight weeks pregnant at the time. Under German law, pregnant women could not work in an operating theatre for health and safety reasons. Her application was therefore rejected. The ECJ said this was unlawful sex discrimination.

11.7   It is the same if the woman was only employed on a short fixed-term contract,[12] although this may mean she does not get much compensation. Mrs Brandt-Nielsen was employed for a six-month fixed-term contract starting 1 July 1995. In August 1995 she told her employer that she was pregnant with a due date of early November. She was dismissed on the grounds that she had not said she was pregnant when she was recruited. The ECJ said that dismissal of a worker on account of pregnancy was direct sex discrimination whatever the nature and extent of the economic loss incurred by her employer as a result of her pregnancy. This was so even though she had knowingly failed to

9 See also the wording in the ETD article 7.

10 *Webb v EMO Air Cargo (UK) Ltd (No 2)* [1995] IRLR 645, HL; *Webb v EMO Air Cargo (UK) Ltd* [1994] IRLR 482, ECJ.

11 *Mahlburg v Land Mecklenburg-Vorpommern* [2000] IRLR 276, ECJ.

12 *Jimenez Melgar v Ayuntamiento de los Barrios* [2001] IRLR 848; (2001) 100 EOR 46, ECJ; *Tele Danmark A/S v Handels-og Kontorfunktionærernes Forbund i Danmark acting on behalf of Brandt-Nielsen* [2001] IRLR 853; (2002) 101 EOR 32, ECJ.

inform her employer of her pregnancy on recruitment and even though she was unable to work a substantial part of the term of a fixed-term contract.[13] As an employee's pregnancy is not a factor which an employer can lawfully be influenced by, the woman is not obliged to tell her employer that she is pregnant.[14]

11.8   It is pregnancy discrimination for a sick pay scheme to exclude pregnancy-related illness.[15] A woman absent due to a pregnancy-related illness must be paid the same sick pay as anyone else, but she is not entitled to full pay just because she is pregnant, if there is no such entitlement under her contract.[16]

11.9   The period from when a woman becomes pregnant until the end of her maternity leave is known as the 'protected period'.[17] It is pregnancy discrimination (without needing a male comparison) to treat a woman less favourably due to her pregnancy at any time through this protected period. However, where the unfavourable treatment occurs after the end of her maternity leave, a comparison with a man in a similar position is still necessary to prove sex discrimination, eg where a woman is dismissed due to a pregnancy-related illness occurring after her maternity leave period.[18] In such a case, a woman is entitled to be treated no worse than a man would be treated if sick for a similar period disregarding the earlier period of absence during pregnancy and maternity leave.[19]

11.10   For discrimination during maternity leave, see paras 11.58–11.60 below. A woman who is dismissed because her replacement, while she is on maternity leave, is more efficient may claim pregnancy discrimination because, had she not been absent the unfavourable comparison would not have arisen.[20]

---

13 *Tele Danmark A/S v Handels-og Kontorfunktionærernes Forbund i Danmark acting on behalf of Brandt-Nielsen* [2001] IRLR 853; (2002) 101 EOR 32, ECJ.

14 *Busch v Klinikum Neustadt GmbH & Co Betriebs-KG* C-320/01 [2003] IRLR 625, ECJ.

15 *Handels-og Kontorfunktionærernes Forbund i Danmark acting on behalf of Hoj Pedersen v Faellesforeningen for Danmarks Brugsforeninger acting on behalf of Kvickly Skive* C-66/96 [1999] IRLR 55; (1999) 83 EOR 43, ECJ.

16 *North-Western Health Board v McKenna* [2005] IRLR 895, ECJ; see para 11.59 below.

17 SDA 1975 s3A(1).

18 *Handels og-Kontorfuntionærernes Forbund i Danmark (acting for Hertz) v Dansk Arbejdsgiverforening* [1991] IRLR 31, ECJ; *Brown v Rentokil Ltd* [1998] IRLR 445; (1998) 81 EOR 45, ECJ.

19 *Brown v Rentokil Ltd* [1998] IRLR 445; (1998) 81 EOR 45, ECJ; *Healy v William B Morrison & Sons Ltd* (2000) 642 IRLB 6, EAT.

20 *Rees v Apollo Watch Repairs plc* (1996) 563 IDS Brief 6, EAT.

11.11   Dismissal of a female worker because she is undergoing an advanced stage of IVF treatment, ie between the follicular puncture and the immediate transfer of the fertilised ova into the uterus, constitutes direct sex discrimination under the ETD and presumably also under the SDA 1975, without needing to make any comparisons with how a man would be treated. It will not be 'pregnancy discrimination' until after the transfer of the egg, but either way, the woman will be legally protected.[21]

11.12   Note that men cannot claim sex discrimination if an employer chooses to give special treatment to women in connection with pregnancy or childbirth.[22]

Maternity leave

11.13   The rules regarding maternity leave have always been complex. The law is set out in the ERA 1996 and the Maternity and Parental Leave etc Regulations 1999.[23] Although the rules are now simpler than in the past, the law is still complex and uncertain in some areas. The following is therefore only a general introduction.

11.14   Historically, a woman risked losing all her rights if she failed to take the correct steps before and after maternity leave. Although there are more safeguards now, even under the current law, there are important rules to comply with. If a woman is refused maternity leave or not allowed to return for a reason related to pregnancy or maternity leave,[24] she may be able to claim unlawful detriment or unfair dismissal under the ERA 1996 as well as sex discrimination under the SDA 1975.[25] If the woman is dismissed for an unconnected reason, she can claim ordinary unfair dismissal, provided she has one year's service. There are advantages in claiming jointly under the ERA 1996 and the SDA 1975 where both apply, since the SDA 1975 can attract additional compensation and also enables use of the questionnaire procedure. In some cases, the woman may only be able to use the

---

21 *Mayr v Bäckerei und Konditorei Gerhard Flöckner OHG* [2008] IRLR 387, ECJ concerning the definition of 'pregnancy' for the purposes of the Pregnancy Workers Directive.

22 SDA 1975 s2(2).

23 SI No 3312 as amended by the Maternity and Parental Leave etc and the Paternity and Adoption Leave (Amendment) Regulations 2006 SI No 2014.

24 See paras 6.66–6.67 for full list.

25 For discrimination on grounds of maternity leave, see also SDA 1975 ss3A and 6A.

SDA 1975, eg because she has not followed the procedural require-ments to obtain her rights under the ERA 1996 or she is not an employee. There are other possible claims which may apply, eg it would be automatic unfair dismissal to dismiss the woman for assert-ing a statutory right such as the right to maternity leave or to time off for antenatal care.[26]

11.15 All employees, regardless of length of service, are entitled to 12 months' statutory maternity leave, comprising 26 weeks' ordinary maternity leave (OML) and a further 26 weeks' additional maternity leave (AML). There is also a short period of two weeks' compulsory maternity leave (CML) available for all workers.

Ordinary maternity leave (OML)

11.16 The first 26 weeks of statutory maternity leave are OML.[27] There is a com-pulsory leave period of two weeks after childbirth (and any period where there is a relevant statutory prohibition on the woman working).

11.17 Ordinary maternity leave starts on a date notified by the woman, which she can subsequently vary. It can start earlier, eg if childbirth occurs, or on the first day after the start of the fourth week before the expected week of childbirth (EWC) when she is absent from work wholly or partly because of pregnancy.[28] This means that maternity leave could start automatically, even though the woman does not want it to, just because she is off work through pregnancy-related sickness for an isolated day. However, her employer may be prepared to make an agreement that her leave is not automatically triggered in this way.

The required notifications

11.18 The woman must give notice no later than the end of the fifteenth week before her EWC (or if that is not reasonably practicable, as soon as reasonably practicable afterwards) of:

- her pregnancy;
- the expected week of childbirth (EWC);
- (in writing if her employer so requests) the date she intends her OML to start.[29] This cannot be earlier than the eleventh week before the EWC.

26 See paras 6.73 and 11.77.
27 Maternity and Parental Leave etc Regulations (MPL Regs) 1999 SI No 3312 as amended reg 7.
28 MPL Regs 1999 reg 6.
29 MPL Regs 1999 reg 4.

Advisers may find it useful to obtain the annual statutory maternity pay tables from HM Revenue & Customs. These set out the dates of the fourth, eleventh and fifteenth weeks before any EWC.[30]

11.19 The woman can change her mind about the date she wants her leave to start, as long as she gives her employer at least 28 days' notice before the date varied or the new date (whichever is earlier), or if that is not reasonably practicable, as soon as is reasonably practicable.[31]

11.20 Where the woman's OML is automatically triggered by a pregnancy-related absence in the last four weeks before the EWC (see above), she must notify the employer (in writing if requested) as soon as reasonably practicable that she is absent due to pregnancy and the date her absence began for that reason. Similarly, if her leave is triggered by giving birth, she must notify her employer (in writing if requested) as soon as is reasonably practicable after the birth that she has given birth and the date on which it occurred. Otherwise she will lose her right to OML.[32]

11.21 If requested by her employer, the woman must produce a certificate from a registered medical practitioner or midwife stating the EWC.[33] The EWC means the week, beginning with midnight between Saturday and Sunday, in which it is expected that childbirth will occur.[34]

11.22 If a woman has a premature birth, her maternity leave will start on the day after the baby is born (regardless of any date she has formally noted for maternity leave).[35] The woman is entitled to her full leave if she has given birth to a live baby, even if the baby does not survive very long, or if she has a stillbirth after 24 weeks of pregnancy.[36]

Additional maternity leave (AML)

11.23 The right to AML used to be available only to women who had been employed for at least 26 weeks at the start of the fourteenth week before the expected week of childbirth. However, women no longer

---

30 A complete set of tables showing important dates for statutory maternity pay (SMP) and statutory paternity pay (SPP) and maternity/paternity leave are at pp35–36 of *Employer Help Book for Statutory Maternity Pay E15 (2009)* at www.hmrc.gov.uk/helpsheets/e15.pdf

31 MPL Regs 1999 reg 4(1A).

32 MPL Regs 1999 reg 4(3) and (4).

33 MPL Regs 1999 reg 4(1).

34 MPL Regs 1999 reg 2(1).

35 MPL Regs 1999 reg 6(2).

36 MPL Regs 1999 reg 2(1).

need any qualifying service.[37] Additional maternity leave starts on the day after the expiry of OML and continues for 26 weeks.[38]

The required notifications

11.24   The woman must make the same notifications as for OML. She need not state explicitly that she will be taking AML as it is presumed that she will do so.

Returning from ordinary or additional maternity leave

The return date

11.25   Within 28 days of receiving the woman's notification of when she intends to take her leave (see paras 11.17–11.18 above), the employer must notify her of the date when her maternity leave period will end.[39] If the woman has notified the employer of a variation in the start date, the employer must notify her within 28 days of the start of her OML of when the maternity leave period will end.[40]

11.26   It is then assumed that the woman will return at the end of her 12 months' leave. If she wants to return early, she must give at least eight weeks' notice. Otherwise her employer can postpone her return for up to eight weeks (though not beyond the end of the relevant maternity leave period).[41] The woman can change her mind about her return date as long as she gives at least eight weeks' notice before her original date or her new date, whichever is earlier.[42]

11.27   If a woman is unable to return after her leave due to sickness, the normal sick-leave procedures at her workplace will apply. If the woman is dismissed during her statutory maternity leave, but before its expiry, the leave period ends at the time of the dismissal.

11.28   Paragraphs 11.53–11.66 below set out the woman's rights during her maternity leave and the nature of the job to which she is entitled to return.

---

37 MPL Regs 1999 reg 4(1).

38 MPL Regs 1999 reg 7(4).

39 MPL Regs 1999 reg 7(6) and (7). See para 6.66 if the woman is dismissed for returning late when she did not receive this notification.

40 MPL Regs 1999 reg 7(6) and (7).

41 MPL Regs 1999 reg 11.

42 MPL Regs 1999 reg 11.

Adoption leave

11.29 ERA 1996 ss75A and 75B give employees a right to adoption leave which is similar to the right to maternity leave, but does differ in a few important respects. The law is set out in the Paternity and Adoption Leave Regulations (PAL Regs) 2002.[43] The following is only a very brief summary and advisers need to check the Regulations. Government websites have separate guidance for employers and employees, though this has no formal legal status.[44]

11.30 To be entitled to any adoption leave, an employee must have been continuously employed for 26 weeks at the time s/he is notified of having been matched with the child.[45] This differs from the entitlement to statutory maternity leave, where no minimum service is required. Either adoptive parent can take the leave but not both. However, the other parent may be able to take paternity leave.[46]

11.31 No later than seven days after the date the employee is notified of having been matched with the child, the employee must give the employer notice of the date when the child is expected to be placed with him/her and the date when s/he wishes the leave to begin. The employee can give notice to vary the date once given.[47] Within 28 days of this notification, the employer must write to the employee setting out the date s/he is due to return.[48] If the employer requests, the employee must also provide the employer with documents issued by the adoption agency confirming certain details.[49]

11.32 Ordinary adoption leave starts either when the child is placed with the employee or on a date up to two weeks earlier which the employee has notified to the employer.[50] The employee will usually be entitled to 26 weeks of ordinary adoption leave and a further 26 consecutive weeks of additional adoption leave.[51] If the employee wishes to return earlier, s/he must give at least eight weeks' notice.[52] If the placement is

43 SI No 2788 as amended by the Maternity and Parental Leave etc and the Paternity and Adoption Leave (Amendment) Regulations 2006 SI No 2014.

44 Access via www.berr.gov.uk/employment/employment-legislation/employment-guidance/page34281.html

45 PAL Regs 2002 reg 15(2).

46 PAL Regs 2002 reg 8 and para 11.34 below.

47 PAL Regs 2002 reg 16(4)–(5).

48 PAL Regs 2002 reg 16(7) and (8).

49 PAL Regs 2002 reg 17(3).

50 PAL Regs 2002 reg 16.

51 PAL Regs 2002 reg 20.

52 PAL Regs 2002 reg 25.

disrupted during adoption leave, eg because it will not take place or because the child dies, the employee will be entitled to eight weeks' leave from the disruption or death, although not beyond the end of the additional adoption leave period.[53]

11.33   An employee's rights during ordinary and additional adoption leave and on return are virtually identical to those for ordinary and additional maternity leave (see paras 11.53–11.62 below).[54]

11.34   Statutory adoption pay is available for employees who meet the necessary criteria. It is payable during adoption leave for a maximum of 39 weeks at 90 per cent weekly pay or £123.06,[55] whichever is less.

Paternity leave

11.35   The right to paternity leave is set out in ERA 1996 ss80A–80E and the PAL Regs 2002.[56] As with the rights to maternity and adoption leaves, the rules are detailed and the following is only a summary.

11.36   An employee who is the father of the child or married to or the partner of the child's mother is entitled to paternity leave if he has responsibility for the child's upbringing.[57] Same-sex partners are included.[58] The employee must have been continuously employed for at least 26 weeks ending with the week immediately preceding the 14th week before the expected week of childbirth (EWC).[59] There is a right to paternity leave even if the child has died or was stillborn after 24 weeks of pregnancy.

11.37   The employee can take either one week's leave or two consecutive weeks, but not two separate weeks and not individual days.[60] The leave must be taken within 56 days of the child's birth or, if the child is born prematurely, of the EWC.[61]

11.38   In or before the fifteenth week before the EWC, the employee must give the employer notice of his intention to take paternity leave, specifying the EWC, the length of leave he wishes to take and the start

---

53 PAL Regs 2002 reg 22.
54 PAL Regs 2002 regs 19–21, 23–24, 26–27.
55 From 5 April 2009. Rates may increase annually.
56 SI No 2788.
57 PAL Regs 2002 reg 4.
58 PAL Regs 2002 reg 2.
59 PAL Regs 2002 reg 4.
60 PAL Regs 2002 reg 5.
61 PAL Regs 2002 reg 5.

date.[62] He can vary the date by giving 28 days' notification.[63] If it is not reasonably practicable to give these notifications, the employee must give them as soon as reasonably practicable afterwards.

11.39 The employee is also entitled to take paternity leave where he is married to or the partner of the child's adopter.[64]

11.40 The employee is entitled to return to the job in which he was employed previously. If he has added the paternity leave onto other statutory absences, eg additional adoption leave or parental leave of more than four weeks, then if it is not reasonably practicable to let him return to the same job, he is entitled to return to another job which is suitable and appropriate for him.[65]

11.41 During paternity leave, the employee is entitled to the benefit of all his terms and conditions of employment as if he had not been absent, apart from wages or salary.[66] Employees who meet the necessary criteria can claim statutory paternity pay at 90 per cent weekly pay or £123.06,[67] whichever is less.

Proposed additional paternity leave and pay

11.42 The government is reconsidering its proposal to pass regulations to grant additional paternity leave, so that up to 26 weeks' leave for the purpose of caring for the child can be taken before the child's first birthday.[68] The idea was that such leave would be available only when the mother has returned to work before the end of her maternity leave period.

Parental leave

11.43 Employees have a limited right to have unpaid leave for the purpose of caring for a child.[69] There is government guidance for employees on the Directgov site and employers on the Business Link site, though this has

62 PAL Regs 2002 reg 6(1).
63 PAL Regs 2002 reg 6(4) and (5) for details.
64 See PAL Regs 2002 regs 8–11 for details.
65 PAL Regs 2002 reg 13(2).
66 PAL Regs 2002 reg 12.
67 From 5 April 2009, rates may increase annually.
68 ERA 1996 s80AA introduced by the Work and Families Act 2006.
69 MPL Regs 1999 reg 13.

no formal legal status.[70] There is no definition in the MPL Regs 1999 of what 'caring for a child' means, but the Directgov guidance defines it as leave taken to look after a child's welfare or make arrangements for the good of your child. Reasons for the leave need not be connected with the child's health. Directgov and Business Link suggest it could cover settling a child into new childcare arrangements; accompanying a child to hospital; spending more time with a child in early years; checking out new schools, and enabling a family to spend more time together, eg by taking a child to stay with grandparents. But employees need to be careful because these suggestions have not all been legally tested. Leave is unpaid, although income support may be available.

Who is entitled?

11.44   Employees who have been continuously employed for at least one year and who have or expect to have parental responsibility for a child are entitled to parental leave. Generally there is no entitlement to leave requested after a child's fifth birthday, but there are exceptions:[71]

- up to but not including the child's eighteenth birthday where s/he is entitled to a disability living allowance;
- where a child is placed with the employee for adoption by the employee, up to but not including the fifth anniversary of the date placement began or the child's eighteenth birthday, whichever is earlier;
- where the default scheme applies and the employer postponed the requested leave, up to the end of the period to which it was postponed.

Overall scheme: how the entitlement works

11.45   An employee is entitled to a total of 13 weeks' leave in respect of each child and 18 weeks' for a disabled child.[72] A part-time employee's entitlement is pro rata.[73] Both parents are entitled to parental leave. The mother can take parental leave immediately after her statutory maternity leave if she wishes.

11.46   During parental leave, an employee is entitled to the benefit of the

70 Both available via links at www.berr.gov.uk/whatwedo/employment/workand-families/paremtal-leave/index.html
71 MPL Regs 1999 reg 15.
72 MPL Regs 1999 reg 14.
73 MPL Regs 1999 reg 14.

employer's implied obligation of trust and confidence and any terms and conditions relating to notice pay on termination; compensation in the case of redundancy; and disciplinary or grievance procedures. The employee is bound by the implied term of trust and confidence; the obligation to give notice of termination; the obligation not to disclose confidential information and not to participate in any other business; and obligations regarding acceptance of gifts and benefits.[74]

11.47 The government had wanted collective or workforce agreements to be made, setting out detailed rules regarding how a parental leave scheme would work, and that such schemes would be incorporated into individual employees' contracts. A collective agreement or workforce agreement cannot agree less than the minimum entitlements, but can be more generous. It can also work out the precise rules as to how and when leave is taken.

11.48 If there is no such collective agreed scheme, a default scheme applies (see below).[75] The default scheme may be less generous than a scheme which could be negotiated by collective agreement. For example, a collective agreement could negotiate more flexible notice requirements than appear in the default scheme. Other examples of more generous terms could include allowing more than 13 weeks in total, allowing paid leave, allowing leave for children older than 5 years, or allowing leave to be taken in single days or in the form of reduced hours working.[76]

The default scheme

11.49 The default scheme is set out in Schedule 2 to the MPL Regs 1999.[77] Better terms may be collectively agreed. The key elements of the scheme are as follows, though for exact details the Regulations should be checked. Under the scheme, an employee cannot take more than four weeks in respect of an individual child during a particular year. The employee can only take the leave in one-week blocks (or part-time equivalent), but not in single days.[78] The exception is for a child entitled to a disability living allowance. An employee is not entitled to the leave unless s/he produces, if requested, any evidence to the employer which is reasonably required to establish the employee's responsibil-

---

74 MPL Regs 1999 reg 17.
75 MPL Regs 1999 reg 16.
76 Without such agreement, the restricted default scheme will apply to this, eg as in the *Rodway* case, see para 11.49, n78.
77 SI No 3312.
78 *Rodway v South Central Trains Ltd* [2005] IRLR 583, CA.

ity for the child, the child's date of birth or adoption date, or the child's entitlement to a disability living allowance.

11.50   The employee must give the correct notice. Except where a baby is yet to be born or adopted, the required notice must specify the dates the leave period will start and end, and give the employer at least 21 days' notice of the start. The employer can postpone this leave if the operation of the business would be unduly disrupted, provided the employer agrees a period of leave of equivalent length may be taken within six months, starting on a date determined by the employer after consulting the worker. The employer must give the employee written notice of such postponement, stating the reason for it and specifying the new dates. The notice must be given to the employee no more than seven days after the employee's notice was given to the employer.

11.51   If the employee is an expectant father, he need only specify the EWC and the duration of the leave period. He must give the notice at least 21 days in advance of the EWC. If the child is to be adopted, the employee need only notify the expected week of placement, the duration of the required leave, and again must give notice at least 21 days in advance.

11.52   An employee can bring an ET claim if his/her employer unreasonably postpones or prevents him/her taking parental leave.[79] The claim must be made within three months of the matters complained of, and the ET can award compensation which it considers just and equitable, having regard to the employer's behaviour and any resultant loss suffered by the employee.[80]

The right to return after maternity or parental leave

Ordinary maternity leave

11.53   A woman is entitled to return to the job in which she was employed before her absence on no less favourable terms and conditions than had she not been absent.[81] Her seniority, pension rights and similar rights must be as if she had not been absent.[82] The 'same job' does not mean the woman has to be allowed to return to literally the same position as

---

79 ERA 1996 s80(1).
80 ERA 1996 s80(2) and (4).
81 MPL Regs 1999 regs 18(1), 18A(1)(a)(ii) and (b).
82 MPL Regs 1999 reg 18A(1)(a)(ii).

before she went onto leave. On the other hand, the employer cannot change her duties or workplace just because that is allowed by the woman's contract. Basically, the tribunal will take account of the normal range of variation in duties and location which occurred before the woman went onto leave. The legislation seeks to ensure there is as little dislocation as reasonably possible in her working life, so as to avoid adding to the burdens which will inevitably exist in her family or private life simply because she has a very young infant making new demands upon her.[83]

Additional maternity leave and/or parental leave

11.54 An employee who takes parental leave for four weeks or less either as an isolated period or preceded by other statutory leaves (excluding AML or additional adoption leave) is entitled to return to the job in which s/he was employed before his/her absence.[84] In any other case, eg if s/he takes AML or more than four weeks' parental leave or adds less than four weeks' parental leave onto AML, the same applies, except that if it is not reasonably practicable to return to the same job, the right is to return to another job which is suitable and appropriate for the employee in the circumstances.[85] The position is different where a redundancy situation arises during maternity leave (see para 11.56 below).[86]

11.55 The employee is entitled to return on terms and conditions (including remuneration) not less favourable than those which would have applied had s/he not taken any maternity or parental leave and with seniority, pension and similar rights treated as if s/he had not been away.[87] On return, the employee should therefore get any pay-rise awarded during his/her leave. Also see the requirements of Social Security Act 1989 Sch 5 regarding pensions.[88] See para 4.81 regarding accrual of statutory annual leave

83 *Blundell v (1) The Governing Body of St Andrew's Catholic Primary School (2) Assid* UKEAT/0329/06; [2007] IRLR 652, EAT.
84 MPL Regs 1999 reg 18(1).
85 MPL Regs 1999 reg 18(2).
86 MPL Regs 1999 reg 18(4).
87 MPL Regs 1999 reg 18A(1). Women returning from AML protected by SI 2008/1966 where the EWC was on or after 5 October 2008.
88 MPL Regs 1999 reg 18A(2).

Redundancy during maternity leave

11.56   Where, during OML or AML, it is not practicable due to redundancy for the woman's employer to continue to employ her under her existing contract of employment, the woman must be offered any suitable available vacancy with her employer or an associated employer.[89] The terms and conditions (including capacity and place) must not be substantially less favourable than had she continued under the previous contract.[90]

11.57   The offer must be made before the end of her existing contract of employment and must start immediately on the ending of her existing contract of employment.

Rights during leave

11.58   Less favourable treatment of a woman because she is absent on maternity leave is unlawful sex discrimination under SDA 1975 s3A(1)(b) and the previous domestic and EU case-law.[91] A woman should be told of any job vacancies arising while she is on leave in which she may be interested. Failure to do so could amount to a fundamental breach of trust and confidence entitling her to resign[92] and may also be sex discrimination. It is discriminatory to fail to give a woman a performance-related pay assessment because she has been absent on maternity leave.[93] Similarly, a woman must be given the benefit of any pay rise awarded before or during maternity leave.[94]

11.59   Despite these cases, a woman cannot argue that she should be paid full wages during maternity leave purely because her absence is pregnancy-related.[95] This is because women on maternity leave are in a special position that affords them special protection, but which is not comparable with the position of other workers. The only requirement under EU law is that maternity pay must not fall below an

---

89 MPL Regs 1999 reg 10.

90 MPL Regs 1999 reg 10(3).

91 *Land Brandenburg v Sass* [2005] IRLR 147, ECJ; *Sarkatzis Herrero v Instituto Madrileno de la Salud* [2006] IRLR 296, ECJ.

92 *Visa International Service Association v Paul* [2004] IRLR 42, EAT.

93 *Caisse Nationale D'Assurance Vieillesse des Travailleurs Salaries (CNAVTS) v Thibault* [1998] IRLR 399, ECJ.

94 *Gillespie v Northern Health and Social Services Board* [1996] IRLR 214, ECJ.

95 *Gillespie v Northern Health and Social Services Board* [1996] IRLR 214, ECJ; SDA1975 s6A.

adequate level, ie that of statutory sick benefits.[96] This requirement is normally satisfied by the level of statutory maternity pay.[97] Even where the contract gives contractual sick pay, but not contractual maternity pay, this is not sex or pregnancy discrimination.[98] The same applies if there is contractual pay for both sickness and maternity leave, but only the maternity pay must be repaid if the woman fails to return to work for a specified time after her absence.[99]

11.60   A woman on maternity leave is entitled to the benefit of her terms and conditions except for remuneration (and is also bound by obligations) which would apply if she was not absent.[100] This includes non-contractual matters which are connected with her employment.[101] 'Remuneration' refers only to sums payable as wages or salary.[102] This suggests that the woman will still be entitled to benefits in kind, eg health insurance and company cars. The position regarding occupational pension contributions is complex and not dealt with in this book. It is discriminatory to deprive a woman of a bonus (whether contractual or discretionary), payable in respect of a period before or after her maternity leave or in respect of the compulsory leave period (usually two weeks).[103] It seems it is not discriminatory to reduce a woman's contractual bonus in respect of any other period when she was absent on maternity leave.[104] For the position regarding annual leave entitlement, see para 4.81 above.

---

96 *Gillespie v Northern Health and Social Services Board* [1996] IRLR 214, ECJ; *Gillespie v Northern Health and Social Services Board (No 2)*; *Todd v Eastern Health and Social Services Board and Department of Health and Social Services* [1997] IRLR 410, NICA.

97 But see *Banks v (1) Tesco Stores Ltd (2) Secretary of State for Social Security* (1999) 648 IDS Brief 9, EAT, where the woman was ineligible even for statutory maternity pay (SMP).

98 *Gillespie v Northern Health and Social Services Board (No 2)*; *Todd v Eastern Health and Social Services Board and Department of Health and Social Services* [1997] IRLR 410, NICA.

99 *Boyle v Equal Opportunities Commission* [1998] IRLR 717, ECJ.

100 MPL Regs 1999 reg 9. The exclusion of remuneration is mirrored by SDA s6A where it is non-contractual and s6(6) where it is contractual.

101 ERA 1996 s71(5)(a).

102 MPL Regs 1999 reg 9.

103 Equal Pay Act (EqPA) 1970 s1(2)(e) if contractual; if discretionary: *Lewin v Denda* [2000] IRLR 67, ECJ and SDA 1975 s6A(2) for women whose EWC was on or after 5 October 2008.

104 *Hoyland v Asda Stores Ltd* [2006] IRLR 468, CtS, though this is untested by the ECJ and Hoyland did not concern discretionary bonuses. See also SDA 1975 s6A regarding non-contractual bonuses.

Keeping in touch

11.61   An employee can carry out up to ten days' work or training for her employer during her statutory maternity leave without bringing the leave to an end or losing her maternity pay.[105] It is for the employer and employee to agree any additional payments for working those days. The days can be worked singly or in blocks. Any work carried out on a particular day counts as a day's work. The maternity leave period does not get extended if the employee does choose to work any of these days. In addition, reasonable contact can be made from time to time by the woman or her employer, eg to discuss arrangements for the woman's return to work. Contact can be made in any way, eg by telephone, e-mail, letter or in person. What amounts to 'reasonable' presumably depends on all the circumstances – the type of work, any agreement between the woman and the employer before her leave, whether there is important information to communicate, and what the woman feels happy with.

11.62   Neither the employer nor the employee can insist on work being carried out during maternity leave. If a woman is dismissed or otherwise penalised for refusing to do such work, she can claim automatic unfair dismissal or unlawful detriment.[106] No work must be carried out in the two week compulsory leave period following childbirth.

Statutory maternity pay

11.63   Women who meet the service and earnings qualifying conditions can claim statutory maternity pay (SMP) for 39 weeks of their leave period. The government's plan to increase SMP to 52 weeks by the end of this Parliament is under reconsideration. A woman must have been continuously employed for at least 26 weeks into the 15th week before her expected week of confinement (EWC). A woman should give 28 days' notice of when she wants her SMP to begin, in writing if the employer requests. Normally she cannot start receiving SMP until she has reached the 11th week before her EWC (although she need not still be employed by then). She also cannot receive SMP until she has stopped work entirely for the employer (except for keeping in touch days, which are exempt – see para 11.61). Subject to the above, it does not matter if the woman is made redundant or otherwise leaves the employment before or after her maternity pay period begins.

105 MPL Regs 1999 reg 12A.
106 MPL Regs 1999, regs 20(3)(eee) and 19(2)(eee).

Moreover, if the employer dismisses her before she reaches 26 weeks' service or before the 15th week before her EWC, and she can prove this was to avoid liability for SMP, she can still claim, provided she had been employed for at least 8 weeks at the time of dismissal. A woman's right to receive SMP is not dependent on whether she intends to return to work after the child is born and an employer cannot try to recover SMP if she does not return. However, a woman can be required to return the amount of any higher contractual maternity pay if she does not return to work afterwards, if there is a contractual agreement to that effect.[107] SMP is paid at 90 per cent of the woman's average pay, but subject to a weekly maximum of £123.06[108] after the first six weeks. Women who do not qualify for SMP may be able to claim Maternity Allowance. The calculation of SMP must take account of any pay rises between the start of the period over which maternity pay is calculated and the end of maternity leave.[109] The above is a loose overview, without all the detailed rules, and should not be relied on for giving advice in individual cases. Social security benefits are not within the scope of this book and specialist advice must be obtained in this area.

Contractual rights to maternity or parental leave

11.64　Where an employee is entitled to maternity or parental leave and also has a right under his/her contract of employment, s/he cannot exercise each right separately, but may take advantage of whichever right is in any particular respect the more favourable.[110]

Dependant leave

11.65　An employee is entitled to reasonable unpaid[111] time off to take action necessary for any of the following purposes:[112]

107 *Boyle v Equal Opportunities Commission* [1998] IRLR 717, ECJ.
108 From 5 April 2009. Rates may increase annually. More detail of eligibility can be found at www.direct.gov.uk/en/MoneyTaxAndBenefits/BenefitsTaxCreditsAndOtherSupport/Expectingorbringingupchildren/DG_10018741
109 The Statutory Maternity Pay (General) (Amendment) Regulations 2005 SI No 729, putting into effect *Alabaster v Woolwich plc* [2004] IRLR 486; November 2004 *Legal Action* 18, ECJ.
110 MPL Regs 1999 reg 21.
111 Unless the contract of employment gives a right to paid leave.
112 ERA 1996 s57A(1).

(a) to provide assistance on an occasion when a dependant is injured
   or assaulted, falls ill or gives birth;
(b) to make care arrangements for a dependant who is ill or injured;
(c) in consequence of the death of a dependant;
(d) because of the unexpected disruption or termination of arrangements for the care of a dependant;
(e) to deal with an incident involving the employee's child which occurs
   unexpectedly while the child is at an educational establishment.

11.66   The employee may not have time off to allow him/her personally to
provide care beyond the reasonable amount necessary to deal with
the immediate crisis.[113] If the dependant has an underlying medical
condition which is likely to cause regular relapses, the situation is
no longer covered.[114] Time off due to an 'unexpected disruption' to
care arrangements is not confined to sudden emergencies, although the
time lapse between the employee becoming aware of the future
disruption and the date of that disruption may affect whether it is
'necessary' for the employee to take the time.[115] For example, it may be
necessary to take the leave if an employee has received only two
weeks' notice of the unavailability of a childminder, but it is unlikely to
be necessary if s/he has had 6 months' forewarning. The employee's
time off in consequence of the death of a dependant includes such
matters as making arrangements for and attending the funeral, applying for probate and being interviewed by the probate office, but it does
not extend to time off for a bereavement reaction by way of compassionate leave.[116]

11.67   To have the right to dependant leave, the worker must tell the
employer, as soon as reasonably practicable, how long s/he expects to
be absent and the reason.[117] S/he needs to say enough to indicate the
nature of the problem and that something has happened which makes
it urgent to leave work, but s/he does not need formally to spell out all
the circumstances.[118] The amount of time off which is 'reasonable'
depends on the individual circumstances. The employer can take
account of the number, length and dates of previous absences, but

113 *Qua v John Ford Morrison Solicitors* [2003] IRLR 184; 116 EOR 26, EAT.
114 *Qua v John Ford Morrison Solicitors* [2003] IRLR 184; 116 EOR 26, EAT.
115 *The Royal Bank of Scotland PLC v Harrison* UKEAT/0093/08; [2009] IRLR 28,
   EAT.
116 *Forster v Cartwright Black* [2004] IRLR 781, EAT.
117 ERA 1996 s57A(2).
118 *Truelove v Safeway Stores plc* UKEAT/0295/04; (2005) 774 IDS Brief 7; (2005) 139
   EOR 27; May 2005 *Legal Action* 28, EAT.

cannot take account of any disruption or inconvenience caused to the business.[119]

11.68　　A 'dependant' means a spouse, civil partner, child, parent or person (other than a tenant, lodger or employee) who lives in the employee's household, eg a grandparent or cohabitee. In relation to the right to time off in categories (a), (b) or (d) above, it also includes anyone who reasonably relies on the employee for assistance or to make arrangements in those circumstances.[120]

11.69　　An employee can complain to an ET within three months of any refusal of such time off. The ET can award compensation which it considers just and equitable including for resulting loss.[121]

Detriments and automatic unfair dismissal

11.70　It is automatically unfair dismissal to dismiss an employee for a number of reasons related to the fact that s/he has taken maternity, paternity, adoption, parental or dependant leave. No minimum qualifying service is required. It is also unlawful to subject an employee to a detriment other than dismissal for any of those reasons. See paras 6.66–6.69 for the reasons and exceptions.

Suspension from work on maternity grounds

11.71　The Management of Health and Safety at Work (Amendment) Regulations 1999[122] implement the health and safety provisions of the EU Pregnant Workers' Directive.[123] The Health and Safety Executive has issued guidance to employers on the known risks and what action should be taken.[124]

11.72　　As part of their general duty to carry out risk assessment in the workplace,[125] where employees include women of child-bearing age and the work could involve a risk to the mother or baby, employers must include any risk which might be posed to a new or expectant

119 *Qua v John Ford Morrison Solicitors* [2003] IRLR 184; 116 EOR 26, EAT.
120 ERA 1996 s57A(3) and (4).
121 ERA 1996 s57A(4).
122 SI No 3242.
123 92/85/EEC.
124 See www.hse.gov.uk
125 See paras 17.146–17.148.

mother.[126] Once the woman has notified her employer in writing that she is pregnant, has given birth in the previous six months or is breast-feeding, the employer must carry out a specific risk assessment in relation to her. The assessment need not be in writing. Where the risk cannot otherwise be avoided, the employer must alter the woman's working conditions or hours of work.[127] If it is not reasonable to do this or it would not avoid the risk, the employer should suspend the woman from work for as long as necessary.[128] This is the woman's entitlement to a health and safety suspension.[129] However, the woman is entitled to be offered any available suitable alternative work before being suspended.[130] It would be sex discrimination for an employer to impose a change of duties or suspension on an unwilling woman, where it is not necessary because of a low level of risk.[131] In most situations, however, it is the woman who wants an adjustment to be made and the employer who is unsympathetic.

11.73　The woman is entitled to be paid during her suspension, unless she has turned down an offer of suitable alternative work for the relevant period.[132] The work must be of a kind which is both suitable in relation to the woman and appropriate for her to do in the circumstances, and on terms and conditions not substantially less favourable than her normal terms and conditions.[133] The woman must produce a medical certificate confirming her pregnancy within a reasonable time of any written request to do so by her employer.[134]

11.74　The risks covered may include night-working[135] and any physical, biological or chemical agent which carries risk to the health and safety of a new or expectant mother, including the risks specified in Annexes I and II to the Pregnant Workers Directive.[136] Physical risks include

126 SI No 3242 reg 16(1).
127 SI No 3242 regs 16(2) and 18.
128 SI No 3242 reg 16(3).
129 ERA 1996 s66.
130 ERA 1996 s67(1).
131 *New Southern Railway Ltd v Quinn* [2006] IRLR 266, EAT.
132 ERA 1996 s68.
133 ERA 1996 s67(2).
134 SI No 3242 reg 18(2).
135 SI No 3242 reg 17.
136 Guidance on the annexed risks and ways to avoid them is available in an EU Commission Communication at http://europa.eu.int/eur-lex/en/com/cnc/2000/com2000_0466en02.pdf and also set out in (1995) 60 EOR 35. The Health and Safety Executive provides guidance regarding risk assessments for expectant mothers at www.hse.gov.uk/mothers/.

extremes of heat and cold, prolonged exposure to loud noise, manual handling of loads, regular exposure to shocks and low-frequency vibration, working in tightly fitted workstations, excessive physical or mental pressure causing stress and anxiety, fatigue from standing and other physical work, travelling inside or outside the establishment. Steps to avoid risks could include ensuring available seating, granting longer and more frequent rest breaks, adjusting workstations, ensuring that hours and volume of work are not excessive and that, where possible, the woman has some control over how her work is organised.

11.75   The provisions regarding fatigue are particularly important, but their scope in practice is untested. An example would seem to be as follows: a woman may find that due to pregnancy-related fatigue, she is unable to work her full hours. Her employer must allow her to work reduced hours on full pay (or, if it sufficed, alter her duties so they were less tiring). If the woman became unable to work at all, she must be suspended on full pay. It would be automatically unfair to dismiss her for these reasons.

11.76   Where a woman is suspended without pay, she may claim her pay from an ET. Where she is on paid suspension but the employer has failed to offer some available suitable alternative work, an ET may award any sum it considers just and equitable, with no ceiling.[137] The time limit for these claims is three months from the date the suspension started.[138] It is automatically unfair to dismiss a woman because of her entitlement to a medical suspension and it is unlawful to subject her to a detriment for that reason.[139] It is also automatic unfair dismissal to dismiss a woman who refuses to work in a situation which she reasonably believes may entail serious and imminent danger and unlawful to subject her to a detriment for that reason.[140] If a woman is injured as a result of the employer's failure to comply with the Management of Health and Safety at Work Regulations, she may sue for damages.[141] Failure to carry out a proper risk assessment when there is a pregnant employee may also be sex discrimination[142] and, if the woman resigns as a result, constructive dismissal.[143] In some

---

137 ERA 1996 s70.

138 ERA 1996 s70(2).

139 See para 6.66.

140 See paras 6.77–6.79.

141 SI No 3242 reg 22.

142 *Hardman v Mallon t/a Orchard Lodge Nursing Home* [2002] IRLR 516; (2002) 107 EOR 25, EAT.

143 *Bunning v G T Bunning & Sons Ltd* [2005] EWCA Civ 983; 771 IRLB 15, CA.

circumstances, an employment agency will have a duty to carry out the risk assessment and will be guilty of sex discrimination if it fails to do so.[144]

Time off for antenatal care

11.77   A pregnant employee must not be unreasonably refused time off during her working hours to attend an appointment for antenatal care, which has been made on the advice of a medical practitioner, registered midwife or registered health visitor.[145] Apart from on the first appointment, if her employer so requests, the woman must produce a certificate from one of the latter, confirming her pregnancy and a document proving the appointment has been made.[146] Antenatal care probably includes relaxation classes attended on medical advice.[147] If the woman is allowed the time off, she is entitled to be paid for it.[148] If the employer unreasonably refuses the time off or allows it, but fails to pay, the woman can claim the pay for the time she should have been allowed. She must bring her ET claim within three months of the date of the appointment.[149] There is no equivalent entitlement for the woman's partner, but the government is keen to encourage employers to adopt a flexible approach. The DTI's (BIS's) 'Fathers-to-be and antenatal appointments: a good practice guide' can be downloaded from the BIS website.[150]

Part-time working and job-shares

11.78   There is no absolute right to work part-time though unjustifiable refusal of a request may amount to indirect sex discrimination under the SDA 1975. It may also be indirect sex discrimination under the SDA 1975 or EqPA 1970 unjustifiably to treat a part-timer less favourably than a full-timer, eg in relation to her terms and conditions.[151] The Part-time Workers (Prevention of Less Favourable

---

144 *Brocklebank v Silveira* UKEAT/0571/05.
145 ERA 1996 s55(1).
146 ERA 1996 s55(2)–(3).
147 As accepted by an ET in *Gregory v Tudsbury Ltd* [1982] IRLR 267.
148 ERA 1996 s56 sets out how the pay should be calculated.
149 ERA 1996 s57.
150 At www.berr.gov.uk/files/file20795.pdf
151 The EqPA 1970 governs sex discrimination in pay and other contractual terms.

Treatment) Regulations (PTW Regs) 2000[152] also protect part-timers' terms and conditions. The key differences between the PTW Regs 2000 and the SDA 1975 or EqPA 1970 regarding part-timers are:

- because of the way the definition of indirect sex discrimination works, the SDA 1975 will mainly protect women or married workers, but is unlikely to help single men;
- under the SDA 1975, the worker needs to prove it is a particular disadvantage for women generally as well as herself (or for married people) to work full-time. This is irrelevant under the PTW Regs 2000;
- the EqPA 1970, SDA 1975 and the PTW Regs 2000 all cover discrimination in terms and conditions, but in most situations only the SDA 1975 allows a worker to challenge a refusal to allow him/her to work part-time. However, dismissing a worker for refusing to change from part-time to full-time work would potentially be unlawful under the PTW Regs 2000;
- the PTW Regs 2000 require a comparator;
- the SDA 1975 enables workers to challenge other types of requirement which do not fit in with childcare, eg start or finish times. The PTW Regs 2000 only deal with part-time working.

11.79 In many ways, the PTW Regs 2000 are simpler to use than the SDA 1975. But where possible, a worker should claim both under the PTW Regs 2000 and the SDA 1975 or EqPA 1970. Although more difficult to prove, the advantage of a sex discrimination or equal pay claim is that the questionnaire procedure can be used in running a case. It may also attract additional compensation, eg for injury to feelings under the SDA 1975.[153]

Part-time working and sex discrimination

Is there a right to work part-time?

11.80 There is no absolute right in sex discrimination law to work part-time or to job-share. However, a number of cases have accepted that women are adversely affected due to childcare responsibilities when only full-time work is available, and this can be unlawful as indirect sex discrimination. It may also be indirect sex discrimination against married workers, which could give protection to a married man with childcare

152 SI No 1551.
153 Not available under the PTW Regs 2000 reg 8(11).

responsibilities. More recently, there has been recognition that workers may need time off to care for adult relatives. The evidence indicates that women are more likely to be carers for adults than men,[154] but there have been few cases on this specific point.

11.81   The main case establishing that refusal to let women work part-time may be unlawful indirect sex discrimination was *Home Office v Holmes*[155] in 1984. The stages of proving indirect discrimination are dealt with at para 13.52 onwards. Most of the case-law on part-time working was established under the old definition of indirect sex discrimination, prior to its amendment in 2001 and again in 2005. Under the current definition, certain legal difficulties in the past should become less problematic. The following stages apply.

Is full-time working a provision, criterion or practice?

11.82   There should be no difficulty in proving that an employer who requires a woman to work full-time is imposing a provision, criterion or practice that she do so.[156]

Is full-time working a disadvantage?

11.83   The woman no longer needs to prove that she 'cannot comply'[157] with the full-time work requirement. She only needs to show it is a disadvantage. Many of the cases under the pre-2001 definition insisted the woman must prove she was completely unable to work full-time, eg because she could not afford or find suitable childcare. These cases ignored the reality that many women wish to work part-time because they feel it makes their children happier or easier to deal with, or because it is a physical and emotional strain to work full-time while bringing up children, or to keep rearranging childcare.

11.84   A few of the very early cases did recognise this. In *Holmes* the ET noted that attempting to fulfil parental responsibilities and work full-time entailed excessive demands on Ms Holmes' time and energy. In *Price*, another early case, the Employment Appeal Tribunal (EAT) stated quite clearly that although a woman 'is not obliged to marry, or to have children, or to mind children; she may find somebody to look after

---

154 See para 16.40.

155 [1984] IRLR 299; [1984] ICR 678, EAT.

156 See *Home Office v Holmes* [1984] IRLR 299, EAT and *Briggs v North Eastern Education and Library Board* [1990] IRLR 181, NICA, on the wording 'requirement or condition' which is encompassed within 'provision, criterion or practice'.

157 As in the pre-2001 definition.

them ...' but to say that for those reasons she can comply with a requirement to work full-time would be 'wholly out of sympathy with the spirit and intent of the Act'.[158]

11.85　　Under the current definition of indirect discrimination, a woman should only have to show that full-time working puts her at a disadvantage. The disadvantage need not be economic, but could for example, include the stress of maintaining practical childcare arrangements or physical tiredness. It is not quite clear whether it is enough that a woman simply wants to spend more time with her child, though *Price* (see above), suggested that it should be. If an ET takes an unsympathetic approach, a woman will be in difficulty if she has demonstrated that, pending the tribunal hearing, she can in fact work full-time without undue difficulty. On the other hand, she will not want to resign if there is a chance that the ET can help her. This is a good reason for asking the ET for an early hearing date on the ground that the woman's job is in jeopardy because she cannot continue working. Sometimes an employer may agree that she works part-time pending the result. If not, she may have to show the ET that her childcare arrangements could only be sustained in the short term and were causing great stress, expense or inconvenience. A woman could try to avoid this trap by using up her days off to work part-time in practice. Ms Holmes took six months' sick leave. Having said that, maybe this approach is unnecessarily cautious. The former President of the EAT made a useful observation recently in one of the first cases to look closely at the current definition of indirect discrimination (albeit an age discrimination case).[159] He said that a woman who wished to work part-time for childcare reasons but was forced to work full-time because she would otherwise lose her job, may well be considered at a 'disadvantage' for the purpose of the current definition.

Would it put women at a particular disadvantage?

11.86　The worker needs to show that full-time working would put women at a particular disadvantage compared with men (or married people compared with unmarried people). Many tribunals are prepared to accept this fact and not require proof, but the worker must be prepared with the evidence.[160]

---

158 *Price v Civil Service Commission* [1977] IRLR 291, EAT.
159 *Eweida v British Airways PLC* UKEAT/0123/08; [2009] IRLR 78, EAT.
160 See paras 16.36–16.41.

Is the requirement justifiable?

11.87   To be justifiable, employers must prove that insisting on full-time working is a proportionate means of achieving a legitimate aim. This depends very much on the facts and practicalities of the particular case. In one old case,[161] for example, a health visitor was permitted to work part-time after maternity leave, provided her hours were spread over five days. The worker objected that this involved her in greater expenses for the same wage. Nevertheless, the EAT found the requirement justified because patients needed regular personal contact and health visitors should be available five days a week for consultation with doctors or social workers. On the other hand, there have been many similar cases where tribunals have found employers unjustified in refusing job-share or part-time working in a whole variety of jobs. The crucial point is that a tribunal must not simply consider whether the employer has a good reason for requiring the woman to work full-time; it must balance the employer's reasons against the discriminatory effect on the woman.[162]

11.88   The increasing move towards part-time and flexible working, backed by enabling legislation, means it is harder for employers than in the past to justify insisting on full-time working or treating part-timers less favourably. In negotiating with her employer or running a case, a woman could point to the Best Practice Guidelines accompanying the PTW Regs 2000.[163]

Common forms of discrimination against part-timers

11.89   The application of the redundancy selection criterion of part-timers first may well be unlawful sex discrimination.[164] Most difficulties facing part-time workers, however, concern less favourable terms and conditions, particularly indirect discrimination in 'pay' in its broadest sense. Because article 141 of the Treaty of Rome is binding on all employers, EU law has been very helpful in securing equality of pay, pension contributions,[165] sick pay, etc. Examples of indirect discrimination against part-timers or job-sharers include (subject to justification):

---

161 *Greater Glasgow Health Board v Carey* [1987] IRLR 484, EAT.

162 For a robust expression of this principle, see *Craddock v Cornwall County Council & another* UKEAT/0367/05.

163 See para 11.101.

164 *Clarke v Eley* (IMI) Kynoch [1982] IRLR 482; [1983] ICR 165, EAT.

165 See para 17.42 regarding pensions.

- requiring a longer period of part-time service than full-time service in order to be eligible for promotion;[166]
- on a job-sharer converting to full-time working, placing her on the incremental scale according to actual hours worked in the post in the past, so that she is lower in the scale than had she worked the same number of years full-time.[167]

It may be direct sex discrimination if the employer is willing to allow a man to work part-time or to be flexible with his hours, but not a woman (or vice versa).

Shifts, flexible hours and mobility: sex discrimination

11.90   A requirement that an employee work shifts or flexible hours may indirectly discriminate against a woman because of childcare commitments. Similarly, an employer's attempt to alter a woman's hours (whether or not permitted to do so by her contract), even in a minor way, may be indirect discrimination if, for example, it interferes with her arrangements for collecting her children from school. Conversely, an employer's refusal to allow a woman to arrive or leave half an hour late or early in order to transport her children to and from school, may be discriminatory. In all cases, the main issue is likely to be whether the change or refusal is justifiable. Similar considerations apply with mobility requirements. In one case, where a lone parent was unable to comply with new flexi-rotas due to childcare, the EAT said that employers should consider carefully the impact which a new roster might have on a section of their workforce and take a reasonably flexible attitude towards accommodating a worker's particular needs.[168]

11.91   On the other hand, any assumption made by an employer that women will be less mobile or flexible is directly discriminatory. Interview questions concerning mobility or flexibility, if asked only of female candidates, are likely to lead to poorer interview performance and constitute direct discrimination in the arrangements made for determining who should be offered employment.[169]

---

166 For example, see *Gerster v Freistaat Bayern* [1997] IRLR 699, ECJ.
167 *Hill and Stapleton v Revenue Commissioners and Department of Finance* [1998] IRLR 466, ECJ.
168 *London Underground Ltd v Edwards (No 2)* [1997] IRLR 157; (1997) 72 EOR 46, EAT. Note that this case went to the Court of Appeal on a number of different points.
169 SDA 1975 s6(1)(a).

The Part-time Workers Regulations

11.92   The Part-time Workers (Prevention of Less Favourable Treatment) Regulations (PTW Regs) 2000[170] were brought in to implement the EU Part-Time Work Directive.[171] There are currently approximately six million part-time workers in Great Britain. In introducing the Regulations, the government said it believes the economy and society will gain as a whole if people are able to achieve a better balance between work and family responsibilities.

11.93   The PTW Regs 2000 are not confined to employees, and cover any individual working under an oral or written contract whereby s/he undertakes to perform work or services personally. It excludes situations where the employer is a client or customer of a business carried out by the individual.[172]

11.94   A part-time worker must not be treated less favourably than a comparable full-time worker on the ground that s/he is a part-timer as regards his/her contract terms or by being subjected to any other detriment.[173] The worker cannot rely on a hypothetical comparator.[174] A comparable full-time worker means someone who, at the time of the less favourable treatment, is employed by the same employer, under the same type of contract and engaged in the same or broadly similar work.[175] The work need not be identical as long as a large amount of it is the same. Comparison must be made with a worker at the same establishment, unless the only comparable worker is at a different establishment. Also, if the worker changes from full-time to part-time working, s/he must not be treated less favourably than beforehand.[176]

11.95   The worker need not show that his/her part-time status is the only reason that s/he has been treated less favourably.[177] Once a worker proves less favourable treatment on grounds of being a part-timer,[178] a 'pro rata principle' applies, ie a part-timer must not receive a lesser proportion of a full-timer's pay or other benefit, than the proportion that

---

170 SI No 1551.
171 97/81/EC and 98/23/EC.
172 PTW Regs 2000 reg 1(2).
173 PTW Regs 2000 reg 5(1) and (2).
174 *Carl v The University of Sheffield* UKEAT/0261/08.
175 PTW Regs 2000 reg 2. For an analysis of who is a comparable worker, see *Matthews v Kent & Medway Towns Fire Authority* [2006] IRLR 367, HL.
176 PTW Regs 2000 regs 3.
177 *Sharma and others v Manchester City Council* UKEAT/0561/07; [2008] IRLR 336, EAT; *Carl v The University of Sheffield* UKEAT/0261/08.
178 *McMenemy v Capita Business Services Ltd* [2006] IRLR 761, EAT.

the number of his/her weekly hours bears to the number of weekly hours of the full-timer.[179] As with the SDA 1975, there is an exception if the employer can objectively justify less favourable treatment.[180] In addition, a part-timer cannot claim equivalent overtime rates until s/he has worked more hours than the comparable full-timer in the relevant period.[181]

11.96　The part-timer can request a written statement detailing reasons for any treatment s/he considers less favourable,[182] though on dismissal she must request written reasons under ERA 1996 s92.[183] It is automatic unfair dismissal to dismiss an employee for requesting such a statement or for claiming any rights under these regulations in good faith.[184] It is also unlawful to subject a worker to a detriment including dismissal.

11.97　A worker can claim compensation from an ET if his/her employer breaches the Regulations, but s/he cannot claim for injury to feelings.[185]

11.98　Some examples of the effect of the Regulations are that, unless the employer can objectively justify otherwise:

- Current or past part-time status should not constitute a barrier to promotion.
- Part-time workers should receive the same hourly rate as comparable full-time workers.
- Part-timers should not be less favourably treated than full-timers in calculating the rate of sick pay, how long it is paid, or the length of service required to qualify for payment.
- Employers should not discriminate against part-timers over access to pension schemes.
- Part-timers should not be excluded from training.
- Part-timers should not be targeted for redundancy selection.

11.99　The government has issued guidelines for compliance with the Regulations and for best practice. These are available on the BIS website.[186] Although the PTW Regs 2000 give no right to work part-time, the

179 PTW Regs 2000 regs 1(2) and 5(3).
180 PTW Regs 2000 reg 5(2).
181 PTW Regs 2000 reg 5(4).
182 PTW Regs 2000 reg 6.
183 See para 20.12.
184 PTW Regs 2000 reg 7.
185 PTW Regs 2000 reg 8.
186 'Part-time workers. The law and best practice – a detailed guide for employers and part-timers' URN No 02/1710 at www.berr.gov.uk/employment/employment-legislation/employment-guidance/page19479.html

Best Practice Guidelines make useful recommendations which can be used in indirect sex discrimination cases:

- At all levels of an organisation including skilled and managerial positions, employers should seek to maximise the range of posts designated as suitable for part-time working or job-share.
- Larger organisations should keep a database of those interested in job-share.
- Employers should actively consider whether it would be appropriate to introduce flexible forms of working, eg term-time working, lunch-time working, flexi-time, home-working, a parental leave scheme and reduced-hours working.
- Larger organisations should consider whether to provide childcare facilities on site or offer a contribution towards childcare costs.

Flexible working

11.100   In April 2003, new legislation to encourage flexible working for childcare purposes took effect. This was expanded from April 2007 to include carers for certain adults and from 6th April 2009 to extend to children over 5 and under 17.[187] The law is contained in the ERA 1996 ss80F–80I and expanded in the Flexible Working (Eligibility, Complaints and Remedies) Regulations 2002[188] and the Flexible Working (Procedural Requirements) Regulations 2002.[189] There is useful government guidance on the Directgov and Business link sites,[190] although it has no legal status.

11.101   The Regulations do not give any right to work flexibly, but they make it easier for an employee to make the request and have it properly considered. Of course any worker can ask his/her employer for changes in hours or other flexible arrangements. However, to have the specific statutory right to consideration, there are certain conditions.

11.102   An eligible employee may apply to his/her employer for a change in his/her terms and conditions of employment regarding hours, time

187 The Flexible Working (Eligibility, Complaints and Remedies) (Amendment) Regulations 2009 SI No 595.
188 SI No 3236, as amended by the Flexible Working (Eligibility, Complaints and Remedies)(Amendment) Regulations 2006 SI No 3314.
189 SI No 3207.
190 Access via links at www.berr.gov.uk/whatwedo/employment/employment-legislation/employment-guidance/page35662.html

of work or working partly or wholly from home.[191] Any permitted change will be permanent (unless agreed otherwise) and the employee will have no right to revert back to his/her former hours of work. If either the employer or employee is unsure about whether the change would work, they could agree a trial period.

11.103   In respect of childcare, the purpose of the change must be to enable the employee to care for a child. The application must be made before the child's seventeenth birthday or, if the child is disabled, his/her eighteenth birthday.[192] The employee must have at least 26 weeks' continuous service, and be either the parent (including adopted or foster parents) or guardian of the child, or their partner or spouse, with responsibility for the child's upbringing.[193] Agency workers are not covered.[194]

11.104   Caring for a child can include collecting the child from school or simply spending more time with him/her. The government guidance, especially on the Business Link site, gives a large number of examples of different types of flexible working including part-time working and job-share, different shift-patterns, homeworking, shift-swapping, self-rostering, term-time working, annual hours, compressed hours (working the same number of hours over a shorter period) and reduced hours (eg starting an hour later each day). Working fewer hours will of course usually mean less pay.

11.105   In respect of carers for adults, again an employee must have at least 26 weeks' continuous service to be eligible for this right. The employee must be – or expect to be – caring for a person aged 18 or over who is in need of care and is either married to or the partner or civil partner of the employee; a relative of the employee; or someone living at the same address as the employee.[195] The relatives who are covered are parents, adopters, guardians, special guardians, parents-in-law, step-parents, children or stepchildren, children-in-law, siblings, step-siblings, siblings-in-law, aunts, uncles and grandparents. Adoptive relationships and relationships of the full blood or half blood are included. There is no definition of what caring for an adult must entail, but the government's original guidance envisaged it can involve a wide variety of

---

191 ERA 1996 s80F(1).
192 Flexible Working (Eligibility, Complaints and Remedies) Regulations 2002 reg 3A.
193 Flexible Working (Eligibility, Complaints and Remedies) Regulations 2002 reg 3(1).
194 ERA 1996 s80F(8).
195 Flexible Working (Eligibility, Complaints and Remedies) Regulations 2002 reg 3B.

activities, eg nursing tasks; help with personal care or mobility; practical household tasks; helping with financial matters; escorting to appointments; emotional support and keeping the person company.

The procedure

11.106   The application must be in writing.[196] There is a standard application form on the BIS website,[197] but this need not be used and a letter, e-mail or fax will suffice, as long as it contains the required information,[198] ie:

- the date of the current application;
- the date of any previous application or confirmation that there has been none;
- a statement that the application is being made under the statutory right to request a flexible working pattern;
- confirmation that the employee has the relevant relationship to the child or adult to be cared for;
- the flexible working pattern applied for and the date it should come into effect;
- an explanation of what effect, if any, the employee thinks the proposed change will have on the employer and suggestions as to how the effect may be dealt with.

The employee is not expected to know exactly what the effect on the employer may be, but this is just to show s/he has considered the likely impact of the proposed change. A well-thought out application also makes it more likely the employer will agree.

11.107   Within 28 days of the application, the employer must either write to the employee agreeing to the requested variation and specifying a start date, or hold a meeting to discuss it.[199] The employer must give the employee a written decision within 14 days after the meeting. If the employer agrees with the employee's request, the decision must specify the contract variation agreed to and the date when it will take effect. If the request is refused, the employer must specify the grounds of refusal and sufficient explanation why those grounds apply (see para 11.111 below). The refusal must also be dated and set out the appeal procedure.[200]

---

196 Flexible Working (Eligibility, Complaints and Remedies) Regulations 2002 reg 4.
197 At www.berr.gov.uk/files/file37031.doc
198 ERA 1996 s80F.
199 Flexible Working (Procedural Requirements) Regulations 2002 reg 3.
200 Flexible Working (Procedural Requirements) Regulations 2002 regs 4–5.

11.108 The employee can make a written appeal within 14 days of the employer's written refusal. The appeal must be dated and set out the grounds of appeal. An appeal meeting should be held within a further 14 days, unless the employer has notified the employee that the appeal is upheld and the variation agreed. Where an appeal meeting is held, the employer must give a written decision within 14 days, either upholding the appeal or specifying the grounds of refusal with sufficient explanation why those grounds apply.[201]

11.109 Any of these timescales can be extended by written agreement and there are also special rules if the employee is on holiday or off sick.[202] The time and place of the original and appeal meetings must be convenient to both sides.[203] The employee has the right to be accompanied by a companion, ie a worker employed by the same employer, who can address the meeting and confer with the employee but cannot answer questions on the employee's behalf. The employer must allow this companion time off to accompany the employee, and if necessary, must postpone the meeting to a mutually convenient time.[204]

The employer's grounds for refusal

11.110 An employee cannot make more than one application to the same employer in 12 months.[205] S/he should therefore choose a good time to make the request.

11.111 The employer may only refuse the application on one of the specified grounds,[206] ie:

- additional costs;
- detrimental effect on ability to meet customer demand;
- inability to recruit additional staff or re-organise work amongst existing staff;
- detrimental impact on quality or performance;
- insufficient work during the periods the employee proposes to work;
- planned structural changes.

The grounds must include a sufficient explanation as to why those grounds apply.

201 Flexible Working (Procedural Requirements) Regulations 2002 regs 6–10.
202 Flexible Working (Procedural Requirements) Regulations 2002 regs 12–13.
203 Flexible Working (Procedural Requirements) Regulations 2002 reg 11.
204 Flexible Working (Procedural Requirements) Regulations 2002 reg 14.
205 ERA 1996 s80F(4).
206 ERA 1996 s80G.

11.112   As long as the employer's refusal falls under one of the specified grounds and gives a sufficient explanation based on correct facts as to why those grounds apply, the employee cannot challenge the refusal under this procedure. However, a tribunal is entitled to examine evidence as to the circumstances leading to the refusal in case this indicates the employer was relying on incorrect facts.[207] As the grounds cover almost every situation, the employee's best chance of success will be to persuade the employer to agree the request. S/he should present a well thought-out application, showing how the change will not harm the business and may in fact benefit the employer. It may be helpful to cite some of the positive case studies set out in the guidance for employers mentioned at para 11.100 above.

11.113   It is also important to consider whether the employee has other rights, eg under his/her contract or under discrimination law. For example, it may be direct discrimination if the employer refuses a request from a black worker to adjust hours when s/he has agreed a similar request by a comparable white worker. Or it may be indirect sex discrimination if the employer unjustifiably refuses a woman's request to change her hours for childcare reasons.[208] A worker may also have a right to reduce or adjust hours for reasons related to his/her disability.[209]

Enforcement

11.114   An employee can bring an ET case within three months if the employer fails to hold the meetings or notify the decision, or if a decision to reject the application is based on incorrect facts or an impermissible ground.[210] No claim can be brought if the application has been agreed or withdrawn.[211] If the ET finds the claim well-founded, it can order reconsideration of the application and award such compensation as is just and equitable up to eight weeks' pay. An employee can also make an ET claim if the employer refuses to allow him/her to be accompanied.[212] The ET can order compensation of two weeks' pay. In each

---

207 *Commotion Ltd v Rutty* [2006] IRLR 171, EAT.

208 See paras 11.80–11.88.

209 See para 15.34.

210 ERA 1996 s80H(1); Flexible Working (Eligibility, Complaints and Remedies) Regulations 2002 reg 6.

211 ERA 1996 s80H(2).

212 Flexible Working (Procedural Requirements) Regulations 2002 reg 15.

case, a week's pay is subject to the same maximum as applicable to redundancy payments.[213]

11.115　It is unlawful to subject someone to a detriment because s/he has made an application for flexible working under this procedure, exercised the right to be accompanied, accompanied someone else or brought an ET claim, and it is automatic unfair dismissal to dismiss someone for the same reasons.[214]

---

213 Flexible Working (Procedural Requirements) Regulations 2002 reg 15. And see para 18.17.
214 ERA 1996 ss47E and 104C; Flexible Working (Procedural Requirements) Regulations 2002 reg 16.

Overview of discrimination law

Chapter 12: Key points

- The Sex Discrimination Act 1975 covers discrimination related to sex, married workers, civil partners, pregnancy and gender re-assignment. The Equal Pay Act 1970 applies to sex discrimination in pay or contract terms.
- The Race Relations Act 1976 covers discrimination related to race, colour, nationality, ethnic or national origins. There is wider protection in some respects for race, ethnic or national origins, but these categories probably incorporate 'colour'.
- The Disability Discrimination Act 1995 covers disability discrimination.
- The Employment Equality (Religion or Belief) Regulations 2003 cover discrimination related to religion, religious or philosophical belief.
- The Employment Equality (Sexual Orientation) Regulations 2003 cover discrimination on grounds of sexual orientation.
- The Employment Equality (Age) Regulations 2006 cover age discrimination.
- Except for the Equal Pay Act 1970, all the discrimination legislation is very similar in structure, but with confusing differences in the detail.
- In October 2007, a new Equality and Human Rights Commission started up with a remit for all forms of discrimination and replaced the legacy commissions: Equal Opportunities Commission (previous remit over the Sex Discrimination Act 1975 and the Equal Pay Act 1970), Commission for Racial Equality (previous remit over the Race Relations Act 1976) and Disability Rights Commission (previous remit over the Disability Discrimination Act 1995).
- There are EU Directives underpinning discrimination law. When implementing an EU Directive, the government must not reduce pre-existing discrimination rights.
- There is a duty on public authorities under the Race Relations Act 1976, Sex Discrimination Act 1975 and the Disability Discrimination Act 1995, to promote equality of opportunity.
- A single Equality Bill is making its way through parliament, with a view to making discrimination law simpler and more effective in a unified Act.

Introduction

12.1   In recent years, discrimination law has undergone huge change and expansion, largely driven by Europe. This chapter provides an overview, although each area is dealt with separately in fuller detail. Under the European Communities Act 1972 s2, regulations implementing directives can go no further than the directive which is being put into effect. The result of the government choosing this mode of implementation (as opposed to primary legislation) is fragmented law and particular problems under the Race Relations Act (RRA) 1976 (see below). Note that the regulations referred to below do not apply to Northern Ireland where there is separate legislation.

12.2   The relationship between European directives and national rights is explained at paras 3.1–3.12. There is an important 'non-regression' principle in the directives, which means that implementation of the directives cannot result in a diminution of rights already established in UK law.[1]

12.3   Member states must ensure that judicial procedures 'are available' to those whose rights under the directives are infringed.[2] Sanctions must also be effective.[3] As with the Human Rights Act (HRA) 1998 and the right to a fair trial under article 6 of the European Convention on Human Rights,[4] these requirements in the directives may have implications regarding how hearings are conducted and what remedies are awarded.[5]

Sex discrimination[6]

12.4   The Sex Discrimination Act (SDA) 1975 prohibits discrimination based on sex (ie gender), marital status (ie being married) or civil partnership status. It also forbids discrimination against workers undergoing

---

1 This was part of the reason for the successful judicial review in *Equal Opportunities Commission v Secretary of State for Trade and Industry* [2007] IRLR 327, HC; see para 11.05 above.

2 General Framework Directive 2000/78/EC article 9; Race Discrimination Directive 2000/43/EC article 7; Equal Treatment Directive (ETD) 76/207/EEC article 6.

3 General Framework Directive article 17; Race Discrimination Directive article 15; ETD article 6.

4 See paras 3.18–3.19.

5 See para 21.54 regarding Restricted Reporting Orders.

6 See also chapters 13 and 14.

gender re-assignment. It does not cover discrimination on grounds of sexual orientation. Sex discrimination in pay and contract terms is dealt with by the Equal Pay Act (EqPA) 1970. The EqPA 1970 is structured quite differently from the SDA 1975 and other discrimination legislation and is not dealt with in the remainder of this chapter.[7]

12.5   Until replaced by the Equality and Human Rights Commission (EHRC), the body with a remit to oversee the operation of the SDA 1975 and the EqPA 1970 was the Equal Opportunities Commission (EOC). There is a Code of Practice under the SDA 1975 issued by the EOC. In April 2007, a new duty on public authorities in respect of gender, similar to the duty under RRA s71 (see para 12.11 below) came into effect, supported by specialist Codes.

12.6   In Europe, sex discrimination in pay is covered by article 141 (formerly 119) of the Treaty of Rome and the Equal Pay Directive. The Equal Treatment Directive,[8] which covers all other forms of sex discrimination, was amended by the Equal Treatment Amendment Directive[9] to include pay. The practical significance of this change is untested. On 15 August 2006, a Directive on equality between men and women in matters of employment and occupation[10] came into force, which was required to be implemented by 15 August 2008. Known as the Recast Directive, this consolidates the seven existing directives dealing with equality between men and women in employment plus the interpretative case-law. The existing Directives are repealed with effect from 15 August 2009.

Race discrimination[11]

12.7   The RRA 1976 was modelled on the SDA 1975 when it was introduced, although over the years there have been some changes to sex discrimination law alone due to European requirements. The RRA 1976 covers all forms of race discrimination including race discrimination in pay and contract terms.

12.8   The first Race Relations Act was passed in 1965, after Lord Brockway had unsuccessfully presented a race relations bill to Parliament on nine occasions. However, race discrimination in employment was not

---

7 See chapter 5.
8 76/207/EC.
9 2002/73/EC.
10 2006/54/EC.
11 See also chapters 13 and 14.

covered until the 1968 Act, and even then, individuals could not bring their own cases in tribunals. They had to go through what was then the Race Relations Board. The first time individuals could directly claim in tribunals was with the 1976 Act.

12.9   The RRA 1976 forbids discrimination on grounds of race, colour, nationality, ethnic or national origins. It does not cover discrimination purely on religious grounds, though there is some overlap.[12] The RRA 1976 is even-handed in that it forbids discrimination on grounds of colour, whether that is being white or being black. But it is important to remember that the reason for the introduction of the Act was the statistical evidence of the high level of discrimination against black workers.

12.10   The Commission for Racial Equality (CRE) was established in 1976, with similar powers to the EOC. The Equality and Human Rights Commission (EHRC) has taken over its remit. There is a Code of Practice on Employment which the CRE revised in April 2006.

12.11   As a result of the MacPherson report following the Stephen Lawrence inquiry, the government introduced a new duty on public authorities under RRA 1976 s71.[13] The CRE issued a series of specialist Codes in support of this duty.

12.12   In 2000, the European Council issued a Directive on Equal Treatment Between Persons Irrespective of Racial or Ethnic Origins.[14] This is known as the 'Race Directive', 'Race Discrimination Directive' or the 'Race Equal Treatment Directive'. This had to be implemented by 19 July 2003. Although most of its requirements were already in the RRA 1976, there were a few areas – particularly in relation to the definitions – where the existing wording of the RRA 1976 had to be changed.

12.13   The government issued the Race Relations Act 1976 (Amendment) Regulations 2003[15] to make these changes from 19 July 2003. Unfortunately, by choosing to implement the Directive by regulations rather than primary legislation, the government was unable to go beyond what the Directive required. The result is that the changes only apply explicitly to discrimination on grounds of race, or ethnic or national origins, but apparently not to discrimination on grounds of colour or nationality. This not only creates two-tier rights, but it makes things

---

12 See paras 13.27–13.29.

13 Introduced by the Race Relations (Amendment) Act 2000 to promote equality of opportunity.

14 2000/43/EC.

15 SI No 1626.

extremely complicated. It may lead to undesirable debates about what 'race' means – something which the wording of the RRA 1976 was able to by-pass. Fortunately the EAT has expressed the view that the Directive must have been intended to include colour and the RRA 1976 should be interpreted accordingly.[16]

12.14   Article 39, formerly article 48, of the Treaty of Rome requires freedom of movement for workers within the EU, ie no discrimination based on nationality between workers of the member states.

Discrimination on grounds of sexual orientation[17]

12.15   In 2000, the European Council issued a Directive Establishing a General Framework for Equal Treatment in Employment and Occupation.[18] This is known as the 'General Framework Directive' or sometimes the 'Framework Employment Directive' or the 'Equal Treatment Framework Directive'. The Directive forbids discrimination in employment on grounds of sexual orientation, religion, disability and age. In order to implement the Directive in respect of sexual orientation, the Employment Equality (Sexual Orientation) Regulations 2003[19] came into force on 1 December 2003.

12.16   Sexual orientation means orientation towards persons of the same sex or persons of the opposite sex or both. The general structure of the Regulations is the same as for the SDA 1975, RRA 1976 and regulations regarding religious discrimination. Until the EHRC, there was no specialist body equivalent to the EOC and CRE.

Religious discrimination[20]

12.17   In order to implement the General Framework Directive in respect of religion, the Employment Equality (Religion or Belief) Regulations 2003[21] came into force on 2 December 2003. It is unlawful to discriminate on grounds of religious or philosophical belief including lack of such belief. There is no further definition. Unlike the Fair

16 See paras 13.10–13.12.
17 See also paras 17.74–17.90.
18 2000/78/EC.
19 SI No 1661.
20 See also paras 17.49–17.73.
21 SI No 1660.

Employment and Treatment (Northern Ireland) Order 1998 in Northern Ireland, political belief is not explicitly covered. However, the removal in 2007 of the word 'similar' from the definition 'similar philosophical belief' in the original Regulations leaves open the question as to what kinds of beliefs may be protected and whether this would extend to fundamental political beliefs. The general structure of the Regulations is the same as for the SDA 1975, RRA 1976 and regulations regarding discrimination related to sexual orientation. Until the EHRC, there was no specialist body equivalent to the EOC and CRE.

Disability discrimination[22]

12.18   After several attempts at private members bills, disability discrimination was finally made unlawful by the Disability Discrimination Act (DDA) 1995. The employment provisions did not come into force until December 1996. The DDA 1995 forbids unjustifiable discrimination against workers with a disability. There is a complex definition of 'disability'. Far more workers are covered by the definition in the DDA 1995 than by the measures used in social security legislation.

12.19   Until replaced by the EHRC, the body with overall responsibility for the workings of the DDA 1995 was the Disability Rights Commission (DRC). There is a Code of Practice and official Guidance on the definition of disability, both of which have been revised. The General Framework Directive forbids disability discrimination and the DDA 1995 therefore needs to be interpreted consistently with that Directive where possible. There have been very few European cases on disability discrimination to date.

12.20   The DDA 1995 is similar in structure to other discrimination law, but it has certain unique aspects in its definitions, which must not be confused with the other areas. In December 2005, a disability-equality duty on public authorities was introduced. It is similar to that under RRA 1976 s71 (see para 12.11 above).

22 See also chapter 15.

Age discrimination[23]

12.21   The General Framework Directive forbids age discrimination and was implemented by the Employment Equality (Age) Regulations 2006,[24] with effect from 1 October 2006. The Regulations protect against discrimination on grounds of any age, so older and -younger workers are equally protected. However, the protection for older workers is undermined by the default retirement age for employees of 65. The ECJ has asked the High Court to decide whether the government can justify having a default retirement age of 65 beyond which an employee cannot claim unfair dismissal or age discrimination if the employer follows correct procedures. The general structure of the Regulations is otherwise similar to that of the other discrimination strands except that there is uniquely a justification defence available for direct age discrimination.

Fair employment in Northern Ireland

12.22   In Northern Ireland alone, the Fair Employment and Treatment (Northern Ireland) Order 1998 makes it unlawful to discriminate on grounds of religious belief or political opinion. The overall structure of the legislation is very similar to that of the RRA 1976, but with specific duties to monitor and take action where monitoring reveals discrimination. Although it is very interesting and important, unfortunately it is a specialist area which is beyond the scope of this book.

Overview

12.23   Generally similar wording is used in the various statutes and regulations for all the main concepts, eg direct discrimination, indirect discrimination, victimisation and harassment (with the addition of reasonable adjustment instead of indirect discrimination in the case of disability). There are also similarities in other areas, eg the concept of vicarious liability; the definition of employee; the inclusion of contract workers; the burden of proof; and coverage of post-dismissal discrimination. However, small but important differences in wording together with the multiplicity of Acts and Regulations, not to men-

23 See also paras 17.01–17.48.
24 SI No 1031.

tion the two-tier law under the RRA 1976, means the legislation is not at all coherent and easy to use.

12.24   In Spring 2005, the government announced two separate reviews, an Equality Review and a Discrimination Law Review. The Equality Review, chaired by Trevor Phillips, investigated causes of persistent discrimination and inequality in British society. A report – *Fairness and Freedom: The Final Report of the Equalities Review* – was published in February 2007.[25] The parallel Discrimination Law Review was to assess how anti-discrimination legislation can be modernised, with a view to developing a single Equality Act, which would cover all strands of discrimination in a new and hopefully effective way. Consultation and developments on the proposed new Act have been endlessly delayed, with the government showing a disappointing conservatism in its approach. An Equality Bill was finally introduced to Parliament on 24 April 2009. The Bill consolidates all the current discrimination legislation, irons out most of the inconsistencies and introduces a few new features, most notably a single public sector duty to promote equality of opportunity across all the discrimination strands. It is hoped that the Bill will reach the House of Lords by October 2009 and receive Royal Assent by Spring 2010, coming into force October 2010. But with the possibility of a General Election, it remains to be seen whether the Act will be passed before the end of this government and in what form.

12.25   A new Equality and Human Rights Commission (EHRC) started up in October 2007. The EHRC replaced the CRE, DRC and EOC (now sometimes referred to as the 'legacy commissions'), and it has additional responsibility for religion, sexual orientation and age discrimination and for human rights. The EHRC cannot give legal assistance to individuals on human rights cases unless there is also an equality dimension, but it does have power to hold formal inquiries or take judicial proceedings to prevent breaches of the Human Rights Act 1998.

---

25 Available at www.theequalitiesreview.org.uk/publications.aspx

Discrimination on grounds of race and sex

continued

13.97   Duty of public authorities

Chapter 13: Key points

- The Race Relations Act 1976 and Sex Discrimination Act 1975 cover race and sex discrimination in employment. In certain respects, the Race Relations Act 1976 gives greater rights to those discriminated against on grounds of race, ethnic or national origins as opposed to colour (although 'race' probably incorporates this) or nationality.
- The Race Relations Act 1976 and Sex Discrimination Act 1975 are very similar, except the Equal Pay Act 1970 covers sex discrimination in pay and contract terms. The legislation does not only protect employees.
- There are three types of unlawful discrimination: direct discrimination, indirect discrimination and victimisation. They have very precise legal meanings. Harassment is also unlawful.
- Direct discrimination means less favourable (different) treatment. There is no defence but there are some exceptions for genuine occupational qualifications or requirements and positive action.
- Indirect discrimination is where a requirement, condition, provision, criterion or practice disadvantages the worker and others of his/her racial group or sex. There is a defence if the employer objectively justifies the requirement's application.
- Victimisation is where the worker is punished for complaining about discrimination.
- Public authorities have special duties to monitor and eliminate discrimination under Race Relations Act 1976 s71 and under the Sex Discrimination Act 1975 s76A.

General guide to useful evidence

- Direct discrimination: an actual comparator of a different race or sex who has been treated better in similar circumstances.
- Evidence discrediting the employer's likely explanation of events.
- Indications of prejudice by the relevant decision-makers (not legally essential but can strengthen the case).
- Statistics as to the position and treatment of workers generally within the workplace by reference to race or sex.
- Indirect discrimination: statistics or other evidence showing people of the worker's race or sex would tend to be disadvantaged by the particular requirement, condition, provision, criterion or practice.
- Evidence showing the worker is disadvantaged by the requirement, condition, provision, criterion or practice.

The legal framework

13.1   The principal statute prohibiting race discrimination in employment is the Race Relations Act (RRA) 1976. The legislation prohibiting discrimination on grounds of sex, marital or civil partnership status is contained in the Sex Discrimination Act (SDA) 1975. The SDA 1975 is structured in a similar way to the RRA 1976 except that sex discrimination in pay and other contractual terms is dealt with separately[1] under the Equal Pay Act (EqPA) 1970. More recently, other areas of discrimination law have followed the wording and structure of the RRA 1976 and SDA 1975. See chapter 12 for an overview.

13.2   A revised 'Code of Practice on racial equality in employment' came into effect on 6 April 2006. The Code of Practice was produced by the Commission for Racial Equality (CRE) under RRA 1976 s47. The Equal Opportunities Commission (EOC) issued a similar 'Code of Practice for the elimination of discrimination on the grounds of sex and marriage and the promotion of equality of opportunity in employment' under SDA 1975 s56A, which was brought into effect on 30 April 1985. The Codes are available on the website for the Equality and Human Rights Commission (EHRC).[2]

13.3   The Codes of Practice lay down guidelines for good employment practice, but they are not legally actionable in themselves.[3] However, the Codes are admissible in evidence at a hearing and the employment tribunal (ET) should 'take into account' any relevant provision in reaching its decision. In 1988 the Court of Appeal endorsed the importance of the Race Relations Code of Practice.[4]

13.4   The Race Relations (Amendment) Act 2000 amended section 71 of the RRA 1976 to introduce new duties on public authorities to eliminate discrimination and promote equality of opportunity.[5] The CRE has issued Codes and Guidance to accompany this duty. A similar duty, supported by EOC Codes, was introduced as section 76A of the SDA 1975 by the Equality Act 2006 with effect from 6 April 2007.[6]

---

1   Except where it is against transsexuals. See para 5.2 above for the ambit of the Equal Pay Act (EqPA) 1970. Also note SDA 1975 s8.
2   www.equalityhumanrights.com, search 'codes'.
3   RRA 1976 s47(10); SDA 1975 s56A(10).
4   See paras 16.27–16.29.
5   See para 13.97.
6   See para 13.102.

EU legislation: sex discrimination

13.5   In some circumstances EU legislation applies to discrimination on grounds of sex and marital or family status. The key legislation is:

a) article 141 (formerly article 119) of the Treaty of Rome, which lays down the principle of equal pay for equal work;

b) the Equal Pay Directive[7] (EPD), which expands the principle set out in article 141;

c) the Equal Treatment Directive[8] (ETD), which provides for equal treatment between men and women in their access to employment, training, promotion, working conditions and dismissal. This was amended by the Equal Treatment Amendment Directive and now also covers pay;[9] and

d) the Directive on Equality between Men and Women in matters of Employment and Occupation,[10] known as the Recast Directive, consolidates the seven existing directives dealing with equality between men and women in employment, including the ETD and EPD, together with interpretative case-law. It was required to be implemented by 15 August 2008 and the individual directives which it replaces to be repealed with effect from 15 August 2009. The following text still refers to the individual directives.

13.6   The general position regarding the interaction between EU and national law is set out at para 3.1 onwards, where it is explained when EU legislation and case-law can be relied on by individual workers in the UK. Broadly speaking, the sex discrimination position is as follows.

Equal pay

13.7   In almost all equal pay cases, a worker can claim the benefit of article 141 directly against private as well as state employers.[11] This is because of the status of the Treaty of Rome. In so far as the EPD merely interprets article 141, it can also be used directly against a non-state employer, but it cannot be used in so far as it establishes rights additional to those contained in article 141. Article 141(1) states:

> Each member state shall ensure that the principle of equal pay for male and female workers for equal work or work of equal value is applied.

7   75/117/EEC.
8   76/207/EEC.
9   2002/73/EC.
10   2006/54/EC.
11   *Barber v GRE Assurance Group* [1990] IRLR 240, ECJ.

The Equal Treatment Directive

13.8   Until the Amsterdam Treaty amended the Treaty of Rome on 1 May 1999, the ETD had no Treaty basis. The UK as a member state was supposed to implement the ETD into national law. Wherever possible, therefore, national law had to be interpreted consistently with the ETD and EU case-law. However, where an unimplemented part of the ETD gave rights which cannot be read into the SDA 1975 (or other national law), the position was more complicated. Individuals in ETs and other national courts could use the ETD, but only against any employer which was an 'emanation of the state'.[12] Where the employer was a private one, then probably the only option was to sue the government for damages for non-implementation of the ETD.[13] Although the ETD is supported by the Treaty (ie the amended article 141), the position does not appear to have changed. Article 141(3) now reads:

> The Council ... shall adopt measures to ensure the application of the principle of equal opportunities and equal treatment of men and women in matters of employment and occupation, including the principle of equal pay for equal work or work of equal value.

EU legislation: race discrimination

Freedom of movement

13.9   Article 39 (formerly article 48) of the Treaty of Rome requires freedom of movement for workers within the EU. Article 39(2) states:

> such freedom of movement shall entail the abolition of any discrimination based on nationality between workers of the member states as regards employment, remuneration and other conditions of work and employment.

Article 39 has direct effect, which means that workers can rely on it.[14] On the whole, this is unnecessary because workers in the UK have access to the RRA 1976. However there may be occasions when article 39 gives wider rights than the RRA 1976.

The Race Directive

13.10   More significantly, in 2000 the European Council issued a Directive on Equal Treatment Between Persons Irrespective of Racial or Ethnic

---

12 See para 3.12.
13 See para 3.10.
14 *Van Duyn v Home Office* [1975] Ch 358, ECJ.

Origins.[15] This is variously known as the 'Race Directive', 'Race Discrimination Directive' or the 'Race Equal Treatment Directive'. Although most of its requirements were already in the RRA 1976, there were a few areas – particularly in relation to the definitions – where the existing wording of the RRA 1976 had to be changed. When implementing the Directive, the government could introduce more favourable rights, but it could not reduce the protection which already existed under the RRA 1976.[16]

13.11   Unfortunately, by choosing to implement the Directive by regulations rather than primary legislation, the government was unable to go beyond what the Directive requires. As a result, the changes only applied to discrimination on grounds of race or ethnic or national origins, but not to discrimination on grounds of nationality or, according the government, colour. This not only creates two-tier rights, but it makes things extremely complicated.

13.12   The Directive explicitly prohibits discrimination related to 'racial or ethnic origin' and it rejects any theories which attempt to determine the existence of separate human races. Taken together with the General Framework Directive and the objectives cited in the recitals to both Directives to formulate a coherent set of policies aimed at combating discrimination, it seems inconceivable that discrimination on grounds of colour is not covered by the Race Discrimination Directive. This issue has now been addressed by the courts.[17] The text in this chapter will indicate where different rights may exist.

Who is covered?

13.13   The RRA 1976 and SDA 1975 are wider in scope than the Employment Rights Act (ERA) 1996. They protect job applicants, apprentices, employees, former employees,[18] contract workers and those working on a contract personally to execute any work,[19] in relation to employment at an establishment in Great Britain.[20] Volunteer workers will be covered if in reality they work under a contract, as may be indicated by a mutual

---

15 2000/43/EC.
16 Race Directive article 6.
17 See para 13.23 below.
18 See para 13.38.
19 SDA 1975 s82(1); RRA 1976 s78(1).
20 Compare RRA 1976 s8 and SDA 1975 s10 for what is considered to be employment in an establishment in Great Britain. See para 13.30.

obligation to provide and undertake work personally, and receipt of pay as opposed to reimbursement of expenses.[21]

13.14　　The protection of contract workers is becoming increasingly important with the fragmentation of the labour market. Broadly speaking, contract workers are those who are employed by one organisation ('the employer') but supplied to do work for another ('the principal') under a contract between the two.[22] Precisely who can be considered as a contract worker depends on the facts but it will probably cover workers supplied by an employment agency to work for a different company,[23] workers supplied by concessionaires to work for department stores in specific concessions, and workers employed in contracted-out services.[24] The importance of the protection is that it means a worker who is discriminated against by the principal, as opposed to his/her employer, still has a legal claim.

13.15　　Employment agencies must not discriminate in their provision of services.[25] Any person providing or making arrangements for the provision of training facilities is also covered.[26] This protects trainees on work experience and work placement programmes.

13.16　　Barristers must not discriminate against pupils or tenants, nor must anyone discriminate in which barristers they instruct.[27] Trade unions must not discriminate in access to membership or against members, for example, in the way they offer access to benefits or services.[28]

Illegal contracts

13.17　In unfair dismissal law, an employee may be unable to bring a claim if s/he knew about an illegality in his/her contract and actively participated in it, eg accepting cash payments under the counter, which were not recorded on his/her payslips.[29] In a discrimination case which

---

21　*South East Sheffield Citizens Advice Bureau v Grayson* [2004] IRLR 353, EAT.

22　RRA 1976 s7; SDA 1975 s9.

23　*BP Chemicals Ltd v Gillick* [1995] IRLR 128, EAT.

24　The key case is *Harrods Ltd v Remick* [1997] IRLR 583; (1997) 76 EOR 41, CA. See also *MHC Consulting Services v Tansell* [1999] IRLR 677; (1999) 88 EOR 55, EAT under the DDA 1995 where the supply went through a third party (an agency), and *Jones v Friends Provident Life Office* [2004] IRLR 783, NICA.

25　RRA 1976 s14; SDA 1975 s15.

26　RRA 1976 s13 as amended; SDA 1975 s14 as amended.

27　SDA 1975 s35A; RRA 1976 s26A.

28　RRA 1976 s11; SDA 1975 s12.

29　See para 6.19.

is based on a statutory tort as opposed to the contract of employment, illegality of the contract is less of a problem. As long as the illegality is not so inextricably bound up with the worker's illegal conduct that allowing him/her to win his/her claim would seem to condone the conduct, the worker can still claim.[30] In one case, a woman could therefore bring a pregnancy dismissal claim even though she knew HM Customs & Revenue was being defrauded and did nothing about it. Her acquiescence in the employer's illegal performance of the contract was in no way causally linked with her sex discrimination claim, which concerned a dismissal for redundancy and incapability after the employer discovered she was pregnant.[31]

Migrant workers

13.18 Where migrant workers are permitted to work in the UK, they have the same protection against discrimination as everyone else. However, recent rules introduced to increase employers' liability for employing illegal workers are likely to have repercussions for non-British workers who are entitled to work. The Immigration, Asylum and Nationality Act 2006 makes employers liable for a civil penalty of up to £10,000 for every illegal migrant they have employed. The penalty notice is served by officials of the UK Border Agency (formerly known as the Border and Immigration Agency). Employers have a 'statutory excuse' defence if they have taken the correct steps to verify and keep copies of relevant documentation (passports, work permits, residence cards etc). A pre-employment check must be carried out before work starts and annual checks (at least) for those with restrictions on their right to live or work in the UK. There is also an offence punishable with an unlimited fine and/or prison of deliberately employing an illegal migrant. It may well be race discrimination to make assumptions about who needs to prove their right to work and who does not. Employers are therefore advised to check everyone's documents at the point of recruitment. The UK Border Agency has issued a statutory Code of Practice, which may be taken into account in any tribunal race discrimination claim: *Guidance for Employers on the Avoidance of Unlawful Discrimination in Employment Practice While Seeking to Prevent Illegal Working*. The Code (indexed as the 'Anti-discrimination Code of Practice for Employers (Feb 08))' as well as useful 'Summary Guidance for Employers on

---

30 *Hall v Woolston Hall Leisure Ltd* [2000] IRLR 578, CA. For an example of illegality, see *Vakante v Addey and Stanhope School and others* (2004) 751 IDS Brief 11, EAT.
31 *Hall v Woolston Hall Leisure Ltd* [2000] IRLR 578, CA.

Preventing Illegal Working (April 09)' are available on the UK Border Agency website.[32]

13.19   Immigration law is beyond the scope of this book, but there are other occasions where it interrelates with employment rights. For example, if an employer dismisses an employee on the incorrect understanding that s/he is no longer permitted to work in the UK, this cannot be a fair reason for dismissal.[33] Moreover, it may be unlawful race discrimination to refuse to employ a worker who needs a work permit on a mere assumption that the BIA would be unlikely to grant a work permit.[34] Equally, it may be race discrimination to avoid employing workers of certain nationalities altogether on the assumption that there will be difficulties regarding their work status. For the position on transfers of businesses under the TUPE Regulations 2006, see para 10.37.

Vicarious liability

13.20   Employers are liable for the discriminatory acts of their employees carried out in the course of employment regardless of whether they knew or approved those acts, unless they took all reasonably practicable preventative steps.[35] The scope of employers' liability is a particularly important issue in claims of sexual or racial harassment.[36] Employers are also liable for the acts of their agents.[37] There are statutory provisions on where employers' liability lies in the case of the police.[38]

Sex Discrimination Act 1975

13.21   The SDA 1975 prohibits discrimination against women, men, married persons or civil partners. It is not prohibited to discriminate against an unmarried person although this may be unlawful under the ETD article 2(1). In addition, a worker must not be discriminated against on grounds that s/he intends to undergo, is undergoing or

---

32 Via links at www.ukba.homeoffice.gov.uk/sitecontent/documents/employer-sandsponsors/preventingillegalworking/

33 *Kelly v University of Southampton* UKEAT/0295/07.

34 *Osborne Clarke Services v Purohit* UKEAT/0305/08; [2009] IRLR 341, EAT.

35 RRA 1976 s32; SDA 1975 s41.

36 See para 17.110 below for more detail.

37 RRA 1976 s32; SDA 1975 s41. See *Caniffe v East Riding of Yorkshire Council* [2000] IRLR 555; (2000) 93 EOR 50, EAT regarding the preventative steps defence regarding employees' actions.

38 RRA 1976 s76A; SDA 1975 s17.

has undergone gender reassignment.[39] Gender reassignment means any process or part of a process undertaken under medical supervision, but not necessarily surgery, for the reassignment of someone's sex by changing physiological or other characteristics.[40] For the purposes of sex discrimination law, a trans person must be regarded as having the sexual identity of the gender to which s/he has been reassigned.[41] The Gender Recognition Act (GRA) 2004 enables trans people to obtain legal recognition of their acquired gender on the issue of a full gender recognition certificate by a Gender Recognition Panel.[42] This means the person is treated entirely as of his/her acquired gender. Sections 1–3 of the GRA 2004 set out the basis on which a certificate will be issued. The GRA 2004 was passed following comments by the European Court of Human Rights that to deny this right could be a breach of article 8 of the European Convention on Human Rights (the right to respect for private life).[43] There is a useful guide on the site of the Government Equalities Office, *Gender reassignment – a guide for employers.*[44]

13.22   Discrimination against gay and lesbian workers is not covered by the SDA 1975 unless it amounts to gender discrimination. However, such discrimination is specifically outlawed by the Employment Equality (Sexual Orientation) Regulations 2003.[45]

Race Relations Act 1976

13.23   The RRA 1976 prohibits discrimination on 'racial grounds' or against members of any 'racial group'. Section 3 defines 'racial' in these contexts as 'by reference to colour, race, nationality or ethnic or national origins'. However, the Race Relations Act 1976 (Amendment) Regulations 2003[46] apply only to discrimination related to race, ethnic or national origins. Nationality and more importantly, colour, are excluded. This is quite ludicrous.[47] The EU almost certainly intended colour discrimi-

---

39 SDA 1975 s2A(1).

40 SDA 1975 s82(1).

41 *A v Chief Constable of West Yorkshire Police and another* [2004] IRLR 573, HL.

42 The Panel's guidance on applying for a certificate is available on www.grp.gov.uk

43 *Goodwin v UK* [2002] IRLR 664, ECtHR.

44 Available at www.equalities.gov.uk/PDF/Gender%20reassignment%20-%20a%20guide%20for%20employers%202005.pdf or via a link on its Gender Reassignment page.

45 SI No 1661. See paras 17.74–17.90.

46 SI No 1626.

47 See comments at paras 12.13 and 13.11–13.12 above.

nation to be included in the Race Discrimination Directive. The President of the EAT has firmly stated that 'it is very hard to conceive of a case of discrimination on the ground of colour which cannot also be properly characterised as discrimination on the ground of race and/or ethnic origin....We have no doubt that the European Court of Justice would not give even the time of day to a submission that a claim of 'colour discrimination' did not attract the operation of the Directive.'[48] The RRA 1976 should therefore be interpreted to include colour discrimination within the amended sections. Nevertheless, to avoid arguments, the EAT recommends that claimants add to any claim of colour discrimination that it is 'discrimination based on colour and/or race and/or ethnic origin'.

13.24   The real meaning of 'national origins' becomes more important as a result of the two-tier definition. Does it mean a worker's nationality at birth when that has changed? Or does it mean the nationality of the parents or grandparents of a British worker? Or is it entirely separate from the concept of nationality? The Court of Session has suggested that it includes 'nations' with a historical or geographical meaning but which cannot confer citizenship as such, eg a worker discriminated against specifically as English, although s/he is a British national.[49]

13.25   A British national from Northern Ireland who is discriminated against on the ground of being 'Irish' is covered by the RRA 1976.[50] English-speaking Welsh people are not considered a different racial group from Welsh-speaking Welsh people.[51] If a worker is discriminated against in England, for example, because s/he is from Scotland, Wales or Northern Ireland, s/he should probably claim race discrimination on grounds of national origins as opposed to nationality or ethnic origin.[52]

13.26   For the purposes of the RRA 1976, a particular racial group may comprise two or more distinct racial groups. For example, a person of Cypriot nationality could claim s/he has suffered discrimination not only as a Cypriot, but as a non-British national or as someone not of EU nationality.[53]

---

48 *Abbey National PLC and Hopkins v Chagger* UKEAT/0606/07; 0037/08 and 0041/08, see paras 32–35; [2009] IRLR 86, EAT disagreeing with the earlier EAT decision in *Okonu v G4S Security Services (UK) Ltd* [2008] ICR 598.
49 *BBC Scotland v Souster* [2001] IRLR 150, CS.
50 *Bogdenie v Sauer-Sundstrand Ltd* (1988) 383 IDS Brief 15, EAT.
51 *Gwynedd CC v Jones and Doyle* (1986) 336 IDS Brief 15, EAT.
52 *BBC Scotland v Souster* [2001] IRLR 150, CS.
53 *Orphanos v Queen Mary College* [1985] IRLR 349, HL.

Ethnic groups

13.27 There are seven essential characteristics which a group must have to fall within the meaning of 'ethnic group' under the RRA 1976.[54] In summary, these are:

1) a long shared history;
2) its own cultural tradition;
3) a common language;
4) literature;
5) religion;
6) a common geographical origin; and
7) being a minority or oppressed group within a larger community.

It does not matter if the size of a particular ethnic group has diminished due to intermarriage or lapsed observance, provided there remains a discernible minority.[55]

13.28 Jewish and Sikh people are covered by the RRA 1976, but Rastafarian[56] and Muslim[57] people are not.[58] 'Gypsies' in the narrow sense of 'a wandering race (by themselves called "Romany") of Hindu origin' are an 'ethnic group', although a prohibition against 'travellers' may refer to all those of a nomadic way of life and amount only to indirect discrimination against those of Romany origin.[59]

Discrimination on the ground of religion

13.29 The RRA 1976 does not prohibit religious discrimination as such, but where there is discrimination in connection with religion, it may be possible to claim indirect discrimination against a racial group protected by the RRA 1976.[60] An employer who attacks a religious practice which is particularly associated with a worker's racial (ethnic or national) group is likely to discriminate indirectly. For example:

- a rule against wearing turbans may indirectly discriminate against Sikhs;

---

54 *Mandla v Lee* [1983] IRLR 209; [1983] ICR 385, HL.
55 *Commission for Racial Equality (CRE) v Dutton* [1989] IRLR 8, CA.
56 *Dawkins v Department of the Environment* (1993) 49 EOR 377 and [1993] IRLR 284, CA.
57 *Nyazi v Rymans* (1988) EAT 6/88.
58 But the Employment Equality (Religion or Belief) Regulations 2003 SI No 1660 will apply. See paras 17.49–17.73.
59 *CRE v Dutton* [1989] IRLR 8, CA.
60 See para 13.52 onwards for definition of indirect racial discrimination.

- imposing a short dress as uniform would indirectly discriminate against a Muslim female worker of Pakistani national origin;
- a requirement that a manager work on Saturdays may indirectly discriminate against Jewish workers;[61]
- a rule that no holidays are taken over summer peak periods and therefore not on Eid may indirectly discriminate against workers of Asian national origin.[62]

Religious discrimination was explicitly outlawed in December 2003 by the Employment Equality (Religion or Belief) Regulations 2003.[63]

Employment outside Great Britain

13.30   The RRA 1976 and SDA 1975 cover discrimination in relation to employment in Great Britain.[64] Employment is at an establishment in Great Britain if the employee works wholly or partly in Great Britain or, where s/he works wholly outside Great Britain,[65] if s/he is ordinarily resident in Great Britain when s/he applies for or was offered the job or at any time during the employment, and the work is for the purposes of the employer's business at an establishment in Great Britain.[66]

Private households

13.31   The RRA 1976 does not apply to direct or indirect discrimination in employment in private households except in relation to race or ethnic or national origins. Victimisation is covered in all cases.[67] Workers in private households are usually domestic servants or private chauffeurs. Sometimes it is difficult to know whether the worker is employed for the purposes of a private household or not. For example, it will depend on all the facts whether a chauffeur, employed to drive a company director to and from work as well as the director and his/her spouse on leisure trips, is employed by the company rather than in the director's private household.[68]

61   *Tower Hamlets LBC v Rabin* (1989) 406 IDS Brief 12, EAT.
62   *J H Walker Ltd v Hussain* [1996] IRLR 11; (1996) 66 EOR 50, EAT.
63   SI No 1660. See paras 17.49–17.73 on religious discrimination.
64   RRA 1976 s4; SDA 1975 s6.
65   Under the RRA 1976, this is only in relation to race or ethnic or national origins.
66   RRA 1976 s8; SDA 1975 s10. See also RRA 1976 s6 re training in employment for skills to be used outside Great Britain.
67   RRA 1976 s4(3).
68   See *Heron Corporation v Commis* [1980] ICR 713, EAT.

Crown employees and armed services

13.32 The RRA 1976 and SDA 1975 generally cover employment by the Crown. Many government appointments are therefore covered as employees. Certain office-holders are also covered.[69] There are special rules applicable to serving members of the armed forces.

Police and prison officers

13.33 Members of the police force are generally covered[70] but discrimination in height requirements between male and female prison officers is allowed,[71] as are requirements for height, uniform or equipment within the police force.[72]

Ministers of religion

13.34 Depending on the nature of the arrangements, a church minister can be an employee and bring a claim under the discrimination legislation.[73] Discrimination is permitted in certain circumstances under the SDA 1975, where employment is for the purposes of an organised religion.[74]

Prohibited actions

13.35 Unlike the law on unfair dismissal, the law on discrimination covers all aspects of employment, including recruitment, promotion and dismissal. Section 4 of RRA 1976 and section 6 of SDA 1975 prohibit discrimination in the arrangements made for determining who should be offered employment, in the terms on which employment is offered, in refusing to offer employment, and in access to opportunities for promotion, transfer, training or any other benefits, facilities or services. Whereas the RRA 1976 prohibits race discrimination in pay and contract terms, the SDA 1975 does not,[75] this being covered by the EqPA 1970.

---

69 RRA 1976 ss75–76ZA; SDA 1975 ss85–85B; Race Relations (Prescribed Public Bodies) (No 2) Regulations 1994 SI No 1986.

70 RRA 1976 ss76A–76B; SDA 1975 s17.

71 SDA 1975 s18.

72 SDA 1975 s17.

73 *Percy v Church of Scotland Board of National Mission* [2006] IRLR 195, HL.

74 See SDA 1975 s19 for details.

75 Except against transsexuals.

13.36   Finally, RRA 1976 s4(2)(c) and SDA 1975 s6(2)(b) prohibit discrimination 'by dismissing him/her, or subjecting him/her to any other detriment'. Under the SDA 1975, a 'dismissal' includes expiry and non-renewal of a fixed-term contract and also constructive dismissal.[76] The same applies under the RRA 1976 for discrimination on grounds of race or ethnic or national origins.[77] For discrimination on grounds of nationality (or colour), there is no equivalent definition of 'dismissal' and case-law is divided on whether constructive dismissal is covered. The latest view is that constructive dismissal is covered,[78] but if this is wrong, the discriminatory acts complained of should be those leading to the worker's resignation. This has implications for time limits.[79]

13.37   The law is not clear on what amounts to 'subjecting' the worker to 'any other detriment'. Basically it means putting the worker at a disadvantage,[80] but a worker is unlikely to win a discrimination case on a trivial matter. The worker must show that 'by reason of the act or acts complained of a reasonable worker would or might take the view that s/he had thereby been disadvantaged in the circumstances in which s/he had thereafter to work'. It could include a disciplinary warning, demotion, or offensive remarks, though the latter may be covered by the specific offence of harassment.[81] An unjustified sense of grievance cannot amount to a detriment, but there need not be any physical or economic consequences. The test is whether the worker's opinion that the treatment was to his/her detriment is a reasonable one to hold.[82]

13.38   Acts of discrimination against a former employee taking place after his/her job has ended are covered provided the discrimination arises out of and is closely connected with the employment relationship.[83] Examples could be giving a discriminatory reference, refusal to return the worker's property, or conducting a post-dismissal appeal in a discriminatory way.

---

76   SDA 1975 s82(1A).

77   RRA 1976 s4(4A).

78   *Derby Specialist Fabrication Ltd v Burton* [2001] IRLR 69; LA 5/01, EAT.

79   See para 21.15.

80   *Jeremiah v Ministry of Defence* [1979] 3 All ER 833; [1979] IRLR 436, CA. Here, men were required to work in a dustier part of the factory than women.

81   See para 17.91 onwards.

82   *Shamoon v Chief Constable of the RUC* [2003] IRLR 285, HL. For more detail, see paras 17.97–17.99.

83   SDA 1975 s20A; RRA 1976 s27A; *Relaxation Group plc v Rhys-Harper; D'Souza v Lambeth LBC; Jones v 3M Healthcare Ltd and others; and related cases* [2003] IRLR 484; (2003) 121 EOR 21, HL; *Metropolitan Police Service v Shoebridge* (2004) 743 IRLB 15; November 2004 *Legal Action* 17, EAT.

The meaning of 'discrimination'

13.39　There are three kinds of unlawful discrimination: direct discrimination, indirect discrimination and victimisation. Each of these has a precise legal meaning, which is set out below. There is also a specific offence of harassment. Note that 'institutional racism' is not a legal concept and it is not helpful to refer to it.[84] In summary, the meaning of each form of discrimination is as follows:

a) *Direct discrimination* is where one worker is treated differently from another because of race or his/her sex or because s/he is married or a civil partner. It is usually helpful to ask the question:[85] 'Had this worker been of a different race/sex, would the employer have treated him/her the same way?'

　　If different requirements are imposed on workers according to their race or sex, this is direct discrimination. For example: If an employer required all male workers to be more than six feet tall and all female workers to be more than five feet tall, a male job applicant of five feet five inches, who was therefore refused a job, would suffer direct discrimination.

　　There is no defence, although there are some exceptions for genuine occupational qualifications or requirements and for positive action (see chapter 14).

b) *Indirect discrimination* is where an apparently neutral provision, criterion or practice, is applied, which puts or would put workers of a certain race or sex at a disadvantage compared with others. For example: An employer requires all workers to be more than six feet tall. Women would be disproportionately less able to meet this requirement. A female job applicant below six feet would suffer indirect discrimination.

　　Provisions, criteria or practices which can be objectively justified are not unlawful indirect discrimination.

c) *Victimisation* is when a worker is treated differently because s/he has previously complained of discrimination, given evidence for another worker in a discrimination case or done any other 'protected act'. For example: an employer sacks a worker because s/he complained of race discrimination.

　　The only defence for the employer is if the worker made a false allegation and did not act in good faith.

84　*Commissioners of Inland Revenue v Morgan* [2002] IRLR 776, EAT; *Hendricks v Commissioner of Police for the Metropolis* [2003] IRLR 96, CA.

85　Unless it is discrimination on grounds of someone else's race.

d) *Harassment* used to be a form of direct discrimination. A specific offence of harassment has now been introduced in some of the legislation. For details, see para 17.91 onwards.

Direct discrimination

13.40　This is the most obvious form of discrimination. It entails differential treatment on grounds of race, sex, marital or civil partnership status. The formal definition is in RRA 1976 s1(1)(a) and SDA 1975 ss1(2)(a), 2 and 3(1)(a). RRA 1976 s1(1)(a) states:

> A person discriminates against another if on racial grounds he treats that other less favourably than he treats or would treat other persons.

SDA 1975 s1(2)(a) is similar except that it prohibits discrimination against a woman 'on the ground of her sex'. Discrimination against men is also prohibited[86] and SDA 1975 s3 prohibits less favourable treatment of a person on the ground that s/he is married or a civil partner. It is not unlawful under the SDA 1975 to discriminate against someone on the ground of his/her unmarried status, though the Equal Treatment Directive[87] article 2 says there must be no discrimination 'by reference in particular to marital or family status'. Arguably this could include unmarried status. Segregating a person on racial grounds is regarded as less favourable treatment under RRA 1976 s1(2).

13.41　Direct discrimination is best thought of in terms of comparative treatment. Comparisons between workers of different racial groups or of a different sex, marital or civil partnership status must be made where the relevant circumstances are the same or not materially different[88] so that the comparison is significant. A worker will usually have a stronger case if s/he can point to an actual person of different race or sex who was treated more favourably in similar circumstances. However, it is not essential to find an actual comparator if it can be shown that the employer 'would have treated' someone of different race or sex more favourably. This is called a hypothetical comparator.

13.42　A possible example of direct discrimination is where an employer does not appoint a woman with appropriate qualifications and experience for a job. If the woman was not appointed because she was a woman, then direct discrimination has occurred. This is so regardless of whether an actual man with similar or lesser qualifications and

---

86　SDA 1975 s2.
87　76/207/EEC.
88　SDA 1975 s5(3); RRA 1976 s3(4).

experience has applied and been appointed, although the woman would find it harder to prove her case if there was no actual comparable man.[89]

13.43   In certain cases it is impossible to make a literal comparison with someone of the opposite sex, eg unfavourable treatment of pregnant women[90] or cases concerning dress and appearance. Where women are not allowed to wear trousers or men are required to cut their hair, there is no discrimination if workers of the opposite sex have been required to meet comparable or equivalent standards of smartness.[91] So far, the Human Rights Act (HRA) 1998 does not appear to have helped on this issue.[92] In cases involving transsexuals, there should be some flexibility.[93]

13.44   Where there is more than one ground for an employer's action, it is sufficient if race or sex was 'an important factor'.[94]

Direct discrimination on grounds of gender reassignment

13.45   It is unlawful to treat a worker less favourably on grounds that s/he intends to undergo, is undergoing or has undergone gender re-assignment.[95] The comparison is with the way the employer treats or would treat a worker who is not a transsexual. It would be discriminatory to treat a worker's time off for gender reassignment less favourably than a routine sickness absence.[96] It may also be discriminatory to treat such absence less favourably than an absence for some other cause would be treated, eg paid or unpaid leave, but this depends on whether it is reasonable to do so.[97]

89   See chapter 16 for relevant evidence to prove direct discrimination.
90   See para 11.3 onwards. No comparison with a man is required.
91   See *Schmidt v Austicks Bookshops* [1977] IRLR 360; [1978] ICR 85, EAT; *Smith v Safeway plc* [1996] IRLR 456, CA; *Department for Work and Pensions v Thompson* [2004] IRLR 348, May 2004 *Legal Action* 30, EAT. Note the different approach taken by the Northern Ireland High Court in *McConomy v Croft Inns Ltd* [1992] IRLR 561.
92   See para 3.21.
93   See comments in the Government Equalities Office Guide, para 13.19 above.
94   *Owen & Briggs v James* [1982] ICR 618; [1982] IRLR 502, CA; *Nagarajan v Agnew* [1994] IRLR 61, EAT.
95   SDA 1975 s2A(1).
96   SDA 1975 s2A(3)(a).
97   SDA 1975 s2A(3)(b).

Direct discrimination on grounds of someone else's race

13.46 Unlike the SDA 1975, the wording of the RRA 1976 does not require the discrimination to be on grounds of the worker's own race. It is therefore direct discrimination to discriminate against a worker due to the race of another. For example, where a worker is dismissed because s/he refuses to carry out a discriminatory instruction to exclude black customers,[98] or a white worker is harassed because s/he has a black boyfriend/girlfriend or because s/he is friendly with a black member of staff. In some of these situations, the law on victimisation would more obviously apply (see para 13.85 below). Note that the principle does not extend to all situations where an employer is significantly influenced by racial considerations. For example, it would not in itself be direct race discrimination for an employer to dismiss a worker for racially abusing a colleague or customer on grounds of their race.[99]

The employer's state of mind

13.47 Employers often tell the ET that they are not personally prejudiced and insist that they acted with the best of intentions in everything they did. This is irrelevant.[100] What counts is what the employer does, not what s/he thinks. If an employer in fact treats a black worker worse than s/he would treat a white worker, this is direct race discrimination in any of the following situations:

- the employer intended to treat the black worker worse out of personal racial prejudice or malice;
- the employer was acting on stereotyped assumptions about members of the relevant racial group. Even if true of the group generally, it may not be true of a significant number of individuals within that group;[101]
- the employer intended to treat the black worker worse, but out of a non-malicious or even benevolent motive;

---

98 *Showboat Entertainment Centre Ltd v Owens* [1984] IRLR 7, EAT; *Zarczynska v Levy* [1978] IRLR 532, EAT; *Weathersfield Ltd t/a Van & Truck Rentals v Sargent* [1999] IRLR 94, CA.

99 *Redfearn v Serco Ltd t/a West Yorkshire Transport Service* [2006] IRLR 623, CA.

100 The key cases on this are *R v Birmingham CC ex p EOC* [1989] IRLR 173, HL; *James v Eastleigh BC* [1990] IRLR 288, HL; *Swiggs v Nagarajan* [1999] IRLR 572; (1999) EOR 51, HL.

101 *R (on the application of the European Roma Rights Centre and others) v Immigration Officer at Prague Airport and another* [2005] IRLR 115; (2005) 139 EOR 26, HL.

- the employer in fact treated the black worker worse but without realising it, ie unconscious discrimination.

Examples of direct race discrimination where the employer was not personally prejudiced are: where a head teacher refused to appoint a teacher because the pupils wished to be taught English by someone of English national origin, or where a Pakistani worker was not re-employed because the employer feared industrial unrest among fellow Pakistani workers resulting from an earlier incident between him and a white foreman.[102] The same principles apply to direct sex discrimination.

13.48   There is a long-established 'but for' test, which usually helps to identify direct discrimination.[103] The question is whether the worker, but for his/her race or sex, would have been treated differently by the employer. The advantage of this test is that it focuses on actions not motives and the ET need not try to assess the employer's state of mind.

13.49   Unfortunately, the beautifully clear 'but for' test has been undermined by some recent cases, which prefer to look at 'the reason why' the employer has acted as s/he has.[104] This alternative test rather begs the question, and does not provide much help in practice for analysing evidence. Even worse, it is likely to mislead advisers and tribunals into wrongly looking for conscious racial motivation. Arguably, the attack on the 'but for' test arises from a distortion or extension of its formulation. The original test is expressed in the active tense, ie 'but for the worker's race or sex, would the employer have treated him/her the same way?' This formulation should answer any objections that it goes too far. But in several of the cases where it has been criticised, it has effectively been looked at passively, ie 'but for the worker's race or sex, would the same thing have happened to him/her?' This latter formulation is incorrect in that, for example, it would embrace indirect discrimination. It is also interesting that most of the cases which have attacked 'but for' have concerned either victimisation (which is a different legal definition to direct discrimination), or the treatment of women in relation to sexual relationships at work, (which may be better suited to the definition of harassment).[105] A full discussion of the pros and cons of the 'but for' test and the extent to which it still applies

---

102 *Din v Carrington Viyella* [1982] IRLR 281; [1982] ICR 256, EAT.

103 *R v Birmingham CC ex p EOC* [1989] IRLR 173, HL; *James v Eastleigh BC* [1990] IRLR 288, HL.

104 This view was rejected by the majority in *James*, n100.

105 Although when the definition of direct discrimination applies as opposed to harassment is completely untested. See paras 17.99 and 17.104.

is beyond the scope of this book. However, in the vast majority of cases, the 'but for' test (correctly formulated), is still a safe way of identifying direct discrimination.

13.50   Unconscious discrimination is hard to prove but it is a concept which the law recognises. The Court of Appeal has talked about the possibility of 'a conscious or unconscious racial attitude which involves stereotyped assumptions about members of that [racial] group'.[106] The most explicit and enlightened guidance on this point was given by the House of Lords in *Swiggs v Nagarajan*.[107] Although the case concerned victimisation, the guidance was intended also to apply to direct discrimination:

> All human beings have preconceptions, beliefs, attitudes and prejudices on many subjects. It is part of our make-up. Moreover, we do not always recognise our own prejudices. Many people are unable, or unwilling, to admit even to themselves that actions of theirs may be racially motivated. An employer may genuinely believe that the reason why he rejected an applicant had nothing to do with the applicant's race. After careful and thorough investigation of the claim, members of an employment tribunal may decide that the proper inference to be drawn from the evidence is that whether the employer realised it at the time or not, race was the reason why he acted as he did ... Members of racial groups need protection from conduct driven by unconscious prejudice as much as from conscious and deliberate discrimination.

Unfortunately, many ETs fail to understand that much discrimination occurs due to unconscious stereotyping, for example, unconsciously undervaluing the performance or capability of a black worker. ETs repeatedly find that racial discrimination has not occurred because they believe in the 'honesty' of the employers' witnesses. Yet a manager who honestly believes a black worker is not fitted for promotion may nevertheless have reached a different 'honest' view of a white worker, when confronted with the same objective evidence.[108] In some cases, it may be worth explicitly drawing the above passage to the ET's attention at the outset of a hearing.

Defences to direct discrimination

13.51   An employer cannot claim that for some reason s/he was justified in directly discriminating. Only indirect discrimination can be justified. Direct discrimination is absolutely unjustifiable, although in certain

106 *West Midlands Passenger Transport Executive v Singh* [1988] IRLR 186, CA.
107 [1999] IRLR 572; (1999) EOR 51, HL.
108 See also para 16.17.

specified circumstances it is permitted, eg where authenticity is required for an acting role or to preserve privacy and decency between the sexes. These limited exceptions (which are basically common sense) together with positive action provisions are set out in chapter 14.[109]

Indirect discrimination

13.52 This is a more difficult concept for practitioners and tribunals alike. The definition of prohibited discrimination was extended in the RRA 1976 to include indirect discrimination, as it was recognised that the law against direct discrimination did not go far enough to eliminate institutionalised disadvantage in the workplace. The great difficulty of indirect discrimination is that it is not always easy to detect and advisers need to be particularly alert.

13.53 Indirect discrimination occurs where there is apparently equal treatment of all groups, but the effect of certain requirements, conditions or practices imposed by employers has an adverse impact disproportionately on one group or other. For example, a requirement that all job applicants speak fluent English, while applied equally to everyone, would disproportionately bar persons born in non-English-speaking countries from employment.

13.54 It is important to stress to ETs that the prohibition on indirect discrimination does not reduce standards or entail any kind of reverse discrimination. This is a common misconception. If a discriminatory requirement or condition can be justified, then it is not unlawful. The law simply prohibits unjustifiable requirements or conditions which have a discriminatory effect.

The definition

13.55 Unfortunately, for the reasons set out at para 13.11 above, there are two different definitions of indirect discrimination in the RRA 1976. The concept is the same, but the slight differences in wording make very real differences in what needs to be proved. It also needs to be borne in mind that the vast majority of established case-law is based on the original and more restrictive definition, which is still contained in RRA 1976 s1(1)(b).

---

109 There is also a specific defence available under the SDA 1975 where transsexuals are discriminated against in terms of time off. This may breach EU law.

13.56   Section 1(1)(b) of RRA 1976 sets out the definition for indirect discrimination which applies to nationality (or colour).[110] It states:

> A person discriminates against another if he applies to that other a require-
> ment or condition which he applies or would apply equally to persons not
> of the same racial group as that other but –
> (i)   which is such that the proportion of persons of the same racial group
>   as that other who can comply with it is considerably smaller than the
>   proportion of persons not of that racial group who can comply with it;
>   and
> (ii) which he cannot show to be justifiable irrespective of the colour, race,
>   nationality or ethnic or national origins of the person to whom it is
>   applied; and
> (iii) which is to the detriment of that other because he cannot comply with
>   it.

13.57   Section 1(1A) of RRA 1976, which applies to race or ethnic or national
origins, states:

> A person also discriminates against another if he applies to that other a pro-
> vision, criterion or practice which he applies or would apply equally to
> persons not of the same race or ethnic or national origins as that other,
> but –
> (a) which puts or would put persons of the same race or ethnic or national
>   origins as that other at a particular disadvantage when compared with
>   other persons,
> (b) which puts or would put[111] that other at that disadvantage, and
> (c) which he cannot show to be a proportionate means of achieving a
>   legitimate aim.

13.58   There is a similar definition under SDA 1975 s1(2)(b), which states:

> A person discriminates against a woman if he applies to her a provision,
> criterion or practice which he applies or would apply equally to a man,
> but –
> (i)   which puts or would put women at a particular disadvantage when
>   compared with men,
> (ii) which puts her at that disadvantage, and
> (iii) which he cannot show to be a proportionate means of achieving a
>   legitimate aim.

There is an equivalent definition for indirect discrimination against
married people or civil partners under SDA 1975 s3(1)(b).

13.59   Put more simply, what needs to be proved (subject to specific points
on the wording) is:

110 See comments at para 13.21 above.
111 'or would put' inserted by the Race Relations Act 1976 (Amendment)
    Regulations 2008 SI No 3008.

- the existence of a provision, criterion or practice, or (under RRA s1(1)(b)) requirement or condition;
- which puts the worker at a disadvantage or (under RRA s1(1)(b)) with which s/he cannot comply, eg s/he does not have a required qualification;
- others of the worker's race, sex, marital or civil partnership status would also be particularly disadvantaged by such a provision, criterion or practice, requirement or condition. This can be proved with statistics, reports or expert evidence;
- if this much is proved, the employer must then justify imposing the provision, criterion or practice, requirement or condition by showing that it is a proportionate means of achieving a legitimate aim.

Identifying the provision, criterion or practice, requirement or condition

13.60   Almost any situation causing concern will be covered by the words 'provision, criterion or practice'. They encompass the old wording of 'requirement or condition',[112] which is still partly relevant under the RRA 1976 in relation to nationality (or colour). Although far more restrictive, the words 'requirement or condition' are wider than might be expected. A 'requirement or condition' bears its natural meaning and should not be narrowly construed.[113] It is not always easy to identify which is the relevant requirement or condition imposed by the employer. Formulating the requirement wrongly can make the difference between winning and losing a case.[114] Common requirements or conditions which may be discriminatory under the RRA 1976 are those requiring certain dress,[115] languages, qualifications, experience, duration or area of residence. Those under the SDA 1975 could relate to height, mobility, shift-working or full-time work. Length of service may be discriminatory against women and black workers.[116]

13.61   A 'provision, criterion or practice' can encompass situations where the worker is disadvantaged because s/he does not have a 'preferred' qualification for the job or because s/he scores badly on one of several

---

112 SDA 1975 s82.
113 *Clarke v Eley (IMI) Kynoch* [1982] IRLR 482; [1983] ICR 165, EAT; *Home Office v Holmes* [1984] IRLR 299; [1984] ICR 678, EAT.
114 *Francis v British Airways Engineering Overhaul* [1982] IRLR 10, EAT.
115 *Kingston and Richmond Health Authority v Kaur* [1981] IRLR 337; [1981] ICR 631, EAT.
116 See appendix B for checklists on common discriminatory requirements and circumstances where they may be applied.

redundancy selection criteria, none of which are compulsory for him/her to meet in themselves. If the qualification or criterion in question is one which s/he and others of his/her sex or racial group are less likely to have, this can be indirect discrimination. However, where the worker is restricted to proving a discriminatory 'requirement or condition' because s/he falls within RRA 1976 s1(1)(b), s/he will fail. A requirement or condition must be an absolute bar, not a preference.[117]

13.62   If the worker can prove the employer was in fact operating the preference as a bar, s/he could get round the problem. This would be suggested if no one who fails to meet the preference for the job is short-listed. Alternatively, the employer may operate the preference differentially along racial lines so that, eg white applicants are short-listed even though they cannot meet the preference whereas black candidates are not. This would be direct discrimination.

Causing a disadvantage

13.63   The relevant time to measure whether the provision, criterion or practice, requirement or condition causes a disadvantage is the date on which the worker suffers a detriment because of its application.[118] For example, a woman of Asian origin who qualified as a teacher in Kenya could not comply with a requirement for a clerical post of having English O level. It was irrelevant that she had the ability to gain an O level and could in the past or in the future have obtained one. At the time that the requirement was applied, she could not meet it.[119]

13.64   In another case,[120] part-timers were selected first for redundancy. At the time of the redundancy dismissals, Mrs Clarke was a part-time worker. It was irrelevant that she could have changed to full-time working several years ago once her children had grown up, since she had not in fact done so and at the time of the selection, she was still a part-timer.

13.65   The test is whether someone is in practice disadvantaged, not whether in theory there is a difficulty.[121] For example, a Sikh could in theory comply with a requirement that he wear no turban. He need only

---

117 *Perera v Civil Service Commission* [1983] IRLR 166; [1983] ICR 428, CA; *Meer v Tower Hamlets LBC* [1988] IRLR 399, CA.

118 *Clark v Eley* (IMI) Kynoch [1982] IRLR 482, EAT.

119 *Raval v DHSS and the Civil Service Commission* [1985] IRLR 370; [1985] ICR 685, EAT.

120 *Clarke v Eley (IMI) Kynoch* [1982] IRLR 482, EAT.

121 *Mandla v Lee* [1983] IRLR 209; [1983] ICR 385, HL; *Price v The Civil Service Commission* [1977] IRLR 291; [1978] ICR 27, EAT.

take it off. However, in practice, he could not comply and would be disadvantaged. The test is whether someone can comply 'consistently with the customs and cultural conditions of the racial group'.[122]

13.66   The worker need not prove that s/he was actually put at a disadvantage. It is sufficient if s/he would have been put at a disadvantage. For example, a worker can bring a claim if s/he is deterred from applying for a job because the advertisement requires a qualification or experience which is indirectly discriminatory.[123]

Measuring the disadvantage of others of the worker's race or sex

(1) The pool in which comparison is made

13.67   According to which definition applies, a worker must show that within a 'pool' chosen for comparison:

- those of the worker's race or ethnic or national origins or sex would be put at a particular disadvantage by the provision, criterion or practice; or
- a considerably smaller proportion of those of the worker's nationality (or colour) than others could comply with the requirement or condition.

13.68   The question is within what section of the community does the proportionate comparison fall to be made or disadvantage need to be shown?[124] For example, is the detriment, disadvantage or ability to comply measured among the total female and male population or only those in a particular town or a specific workplace or with appropriate qualifications?[125] The appropriate 'pool' will depend on the facts of each case and which section of the public is likely to be affected by the requirement.[126] In choosing the pool, people must be compared in the same, or not materially different, relevant circumstances.[127] In many cases, for example, the appropriate pool will be those who, apart

---

122 *Mandla v Lee* [1983] IRLR 209; [1983] ICR 385, HL.

123 RRA s1(1A) as amended, following the case of *Centrum voor gelijkheid van kansen en voor racismebestrijding v Firma Feryn NV* C-54/07 [2008] IRLR 732, ECJ. The SDA 1975 has not been amended, but the position under EU law should be the same.

124 Question 6 in *Raval v DHSS and the Civil Service Commission* [1985] IRLR 370; [1985] ICR 685, EAT.

125 *Pearse v City of Bradford MC* [1988] IRLR 379, EAT; *Price v The Civil Service Commission* [1977] IRLR 291; [1978] ICR 27, EAT.

126 *London Underground Ltd v Edwards* [1998] IRLR 364, CA.

127 RRA 1976 s3(4), SDA 1975 s5(3).

from the discriminatory requirement, have the required qualifications for the post.[128]

13.69   Clearly the outcome will vary according to the pool chosen. The ET's selection of the appropriate pool is a matter for its discretion[129] However, the pool must not be such that it incorporates the act of discrimination. For example, in one case[130] only those who had been resident in the EU were eligible for lower college fees. It would have been misleading to choose as a pool, people who had actually applied to the college, because many would have been deterred from applying.

(2) Proving particular disadvantage

13.70   Indirect discrimination is concerned with whether a provision, criterion or practice, requirement or condition adversely affects one particular sex or racial group more than others. The original definition of indirect discrimination, which still survives in RRA 1976 s1(1)(b), required comparing proportions who are affected. This suggests a statistical exercise and much case-law has developed around it. The far looser wording under RRA 1976 s1(1A) and the SDA 1975, allows other kinds of evidence to prove particular disadvantage. Nevertheless, statistics are likely to retain a central role.

13.71   Comparing proportions (fractions or percentages) of those affected rather than absolute numbers makes a difference.[131] For example, a Spanish national may claim indirect discrimination because s/he cannot speak fluent English as his/her potential employer requires. The appropriate comparison is not the total number of Spaniards who can speak fluent English as against the total number of non-Spaniards who can speak fluent English. The proper comparison is the proportion of all Spanish people who can speak fluent English as against the proportion of all non-Spanish people who can do so. The calculation could be done as follows:

A = The total number of Spaniards within the chosen pool (eg 100)
B = The number of Spaniards within the pool who can speak fluent English (eg 5)
C = The total number of non-Spaniards in the pool (eg 100,000)
D = The number of non-Spaniards in the pool who can speak fluent English (eg 20,000).

128 *Jones v University of Manchester* [1993] IRLR 218; (1993) 20 EOR 48, CA.
129 *Kidd v DRG (UK)* [1985] IRLR 190; [1985] ICR 405, EAT.
130 *Orphanos v Queen Mary College* [1985] IRLR 349, HL.
131 Although the High Court in *Schaffter* (see note 133) said that it was relevant to the ETD if, in absolute numbers, substantially fewer women than men could comply with a requirement.

It would be meaningless to look at absolute numbers and compare five Spanish people who can speak fluent English with 20,000 non-Spanish people who can do so, since there are far fewer Spanish people in the world anyway. Therefore proportions are calculated, ie B is divided by A and D is divided by C to get the fractions to be compared. Percentages can be calculated by multiplying each fraction by 100. In this example, 5 per cent of Spanish people as against 20 per cent of non-Spanish people can speak fluent English. (See appendix A at p713 for an illustrative table.)

13.72   Since many workers born in countries other than Spain also could not meet a fluent English requirement, looking at the statistics in this way may be misleading. It may be more accurate to describe the Spanish worker as 'non-English'[132] and compare the extent to which non-English workers, as opposed to English workers, could meet such a requirement. Note that the comparison cannot simply be made between Spanish workers and English workers: a comparison must be made between those of a particular racial group against everyone else.

13.73   What amounts to a 'considerably smaller' proportion? The percentages should be looked at in terms of each other; it does not matter if the practice under attack has no relevance to the vast bulk of humanity.[133] Thus a difference of one or two per cent with very small percentages would be no less significant than a difference between 30 and 60 per cent.

13.74   Looking at it statistically, a useful measure of what amounts to a significant difference used to be the '4/5th' or '80 per cent' rule, which was commonly used in the USA. If the smaller percentage is less than 80 per cent of the larger percentage, the difference is significant. There is alternatively a well-established statistical formula which determines whether a difference is statistically significant in accordance with the laws of probability as opposed to merely random.[134]

13.75   However, UK courts have rejected the idea of following any rigid rule or formula, suggesting that ETs simply apply a common-sense approach in assessing what is a considerably smaller proportion.[135] In making this assessment, the meaning of the word 'considerably' should not be

132 RRA 1976 s3(2). A racial group can comprise two or more distinct racial groups.

133 *R v Secretary of State for Education ex p Schaffter* [1987] IRLR 53, QBD.

134 For an explanation in the context of a Northern Ireland case under the Fair Employment (Northern Ireland) Act 1989, see (1993) 49 EOR 28.

135 *R v Secretary of State for Employment ex p Seymour-Smith and Perez* [1995] IRLR 464, CA; *McCausland v Dungannon DC* [1993] IRLR 583; (1994) 53 EOR 50, NICA. Most helpful is *London Underground Ltd v Edwards* (No 2) [1998] IRLR 364, CA.

exaggerated.[136] The ECJ has said that the significance of statistical comparisons should be assessed by reference to factors such as the number
of individuals counted and whether they illustrate purely fortuitous
or short-term phenomena.[137] A lesser disparity which persisted over a
long period could be sufficient.[138] An ET can take into account the
make-up and overall numbers of the workforce under consideration;
the fact that no man is disadvantaged and the inherent likely effect of
the requirement or condition under challenge.[139]

13.76   Under RRA 1976 s1(1A) and the SDA 1975, the worker need only
show that others of his/her race, ethnic or national origin or sex are at
a particular disadvantage. This suggests a much looser test, even if
statistics are still used. Also, the definition deliberately allows for non-
statistical evidence, eg expert reports on the impact of the provision, criterion or practice. One of the earliest reported cases to consider closely
what needs to be proved to show group disadvantage was one concerning religious discrimination.[140] In that case, the EAT said that
while not everyone in the relevant group need be disadvantaged, it
must be more than one or two. There must be enough people of the
particular group who are disadvantaged for an employer to reasonably appreciate there might be disparate adverse impact on that group.

13.77   It can make a big difference whether the impact of a provision, criterion or practice is assessed by comparing those of each race or sex
who are advantaged by it (eg who can comply) as opposed to comparing those who are disadvantaged by it (eg who cannot comply or who
suffer a detriment). Although the original definition and case-law
measured those who are advantaged, the current wording in the definitions (which was changed to reflect the EU Directives) clearly indicates the measure should be those who are disadvantaged.

13.78   Note that the Part-time Workers (Prevention of Less Favourable
Treatment) Regulations 2000 prohibit discrimination against part-
timers, regardless of their sex or marital status.[141]

---

136 *R v Secretary of State for Employment ex p Seymour-Smith and Perez* [1995] IRLR
   464, CA.
137 *Enderby v Frenchay Health Authority and Secretary of State for Health* [1993] IRLR
   591, ECJ.
138 *R v Secretary of State for Employment ex p Seymour-Smith and Perez* [1999] IRLR
   253, ECJ.
139 *Avon & Somerset Constabulary v Chew* (2002) 680 IRLB 12; 701 *IDS Brief* 5; May
   2002 *Legal Action* 10, EAT.
140 *Eweida v British Airways PLC* UKEAT/0123/08; [2009] IRLR 78, EAT and see
   para 17.58 below.
141 See paras 11.92–11.99.

Justifiable or a proportionate means of achieving a legitimate aim

13.79 The final question is whether the provision, criterion or practice, requirement or condition is justifiable or, using the wording of the more recent definition, a proportionate means of achieving a legitimate aim. The concept of justifiability is central to the law on indirect discrimination. In practice there are numerous, often hidden, provisions, criteria and practices with discriminatory effect in every workplace. The possibility of bringing a successful case often turns on whether the provision, criterion or practice is justifiable.

13.80 Justifiability is very much a question of fact. It is difficult to gain guidance from past cases since tribunals have applied different tests for what is justifiable. At one time an employer needed to produce only what right-thinking people would consider were 'sound and tolerable reasons' for applying a requirement.[142] Now it is not so easy. What an ET would consider justifiable requires 'an objective balance between the discriminatory effect of the condition and the reasonable needs of the party who applies the condition'.[143] An employer must show that:

- the requirement was objectively justifiable regardless of race or sex;
- the requirement served a real business need of the employer;[144] and
- the need was reasonable and objectively justifiable on economic or other grounds, eg administrative efficiency; it is not sufficient that the particular employer personally considers it justifiable.[145]

The greater the discriminatory effect of the requirement, the greater the objective need an employer must show s/he has.[146] It is not enough that the employer has very good reasons for his/her actions. The ET must take into account the discriminatory effect on the worker. This is the central concept of 'proportionality', for which there is a three-stage test:

---

142 *Ojutiku and Oburoni v MSC* [1982] IRLR 418; [1982] ICR 661, CA.

143 *Hampson v Department of Education and Science* [1989] IRLR 69, CA.

144 *Bilka-Kaufhaus GmbH v Weber von Hartz* [1986] IRLR 317; [1987] ICR 110, ECJ; *Rainey v Greater Glasgow Health Board* [1987] IRLR 26; [1987] ICR 129, HL.

145 *Bilka-Kaufhaus GmbH v Weber von Hartz* [1986] IRLR 317; [1987] ICR 110, ECJ; *Rainey v Greater Glasgow Health Board* [1987] IRLR 26; [1987] ICR 129, HL. (Note that these were equal pay cases.) *Hampson v Department of Education and Science* [1990] IRLR 302, HL.

146 *Hampson v Department of Education and Science* [1990] IRLR 302, HL; *Barry v Midland Bank PLC* [1999] IRLR 581, HL.

1) Is the objective sufficiently important to justify limiting a fundamental right (ie not to be discriminated against)?
2) Is the measure rationally connected to the objective?
3) Are the means chosen no more than is necessary to accomplish the objective?[147]

It is for the tribunal to make its own judgment, upon a fair and detailed analysis of the working practices and business considerations involved, as to whether the provision, criterion or practice is justified. Unlike the test for unfair dismissal, it is not enough for the employer's decision to be within a band of reasonable responses.[148]

13.81   The Race Discrimination Directive states at article 2(b) and the Equal Treatment Amendment Directive (ETAD) at article 2(2):

> ... unless the provision, criterion or practice is objectively justified by a legitimate aim and the means of achieving that aim are appropriate and necessary.

EU case-law, as well as the Directives, requires the employer to show the provision, criterion or practice was reasonably 'necessary'. Unfortunately, when the government introduced the definition in the RRA 1976 s1(1A) and SDA 1975, it simply stated that the employer must show the provision, criterion or practice is 'a proportionate means of achieving a legitimate aim'. The European Commission has issued a 'reasoned opinion' stating that the UK has not properly implemented the Race Discrimination Directive by this wording.

13.82   Examples of factors which may justify a discriminatory requirement are hygiene, safety, consistency of care, consistency of management and important economic and administrative considerations. Each case will depend on its precise facts and the principle of balance. A government cannot rely on budgetary considerations to justify a discriminatory social policy. Non-government employers can put cost into the balance with other factors, but cannot rely purely on cost considerations.[149] Note that the Employment Act 1989 exempted turban-wearing Sikhs from any statutory requirements to wear safety helmets on constructions sites and declared that any requirement imposed by an employer to that effect would not be justifiable indirect discrimination.[150]

---

147 *R (on the application of Elias) v Secretary of State for Defence* [2006] IRLR 934, CA.
148 *Hardys & Hansons plc v Lax* [2005] IRLR 726, CA.
149 *Cross and others v British Airways plc* [2005] IRLR 423, EAT.
150 Employment Act 1989 ss11 and 12. The employers' liability for injury is, as a consequence, restricted.

13.83   Often employers lose sight of their aims when imposing discriminatory requirements. Where an employer seeks to justify a requirement, it is worth establishing first what business need the employer purports to have, and then examining whether the imposition of the requirement serves (or is necessary to serve) that need at all. A public authority's failure to follow its duties under RRA 1976 s71 or SDA 1975 s76A (see paras 13.97–13.104) may be relevant to whether it can justify indirect discrimination.[151]

13.84   Once it is shown that there is a prima facie discriminatory requirement, the employer must prove it is justifiable.[152] This is sometimes forgotten by ETs who may expect workers to show why the requirement is not justifiable and to suggest alternative ways for employers to achieve needs. Obviously it is helpful if workers can show how employers could meet their needs by taking action with less discriminatory effect, but workers should not be required to provide such evidence. There have been a number of cases over the last few years concerning the justification of indirect discrimination in the relatively newer areas of age and religious discrimination. These are reported in more detail in chapter 17, but what is interesting is the number of times a case is overturned on appeal because, although the tribunals have found the employers' aims to be legitimate, they have failed to focus their minds on whether the means used were proportionate.

Victimisation

13.85   It is unlawful to victimise a worker because s/he has made a complaint of discrimination or done any other 'protected act' under the RRA 1976 or SDA 1975. The primary purpose of the victimisation provisions is to ensure that workers are not penalised or prejudiced because they have taken steps to exercise their statutory rights or are intending to do so, and that they are not deterred from their fundamental right to challenge discrimination in the tribunals.[153] This protection is particularly important for workers who risk dismissal by bringing up controversial issues, but do not have the requisite length of service to qualify for a claim of unfair dismissal. The law protects

---

151 *R (on the application of Elias) v Secretary of State for Defence and Commission for Racial Equality* [2005] IRLR 788, HC.

152 See para 16.42 on the burden of proof.

153 *Chief Constable of West Yorkshire Police v Khan* [2001] IRLR 830, HL; *Coote v Granada Hospitality Ltd* [1998] IRLR 656, ECJ; *St Helens Borough Council v Derbyshire and others* [2007] UKHL 16.

workers complaining about discrimination against themselves as well as workers speaking out on behalf of others. For example, a white worker must not be victimised for supporting a black worker who has brought a grievance of race discrimination. Similarly a trade union representative could claim victimisation if s/he is put under particular pressure by the employer when s/he takes up race or sex discrimination cases.[154] Victimisation protects those raising the issue formally or informally, not purely in ET proceedings.

13.86   It is unlawful under RRA 1976 s2 to treat people less favourably because they have done any 'protected act', ie if they have brought proceedings under the RRA 1976 or have given evidence or information in proceedings (brought by themselves or anyone else) under the RRA 1976, or intend to do any of those things. More generally, it is unlawful to treat people less favourably because they have done, or intend to do, anything under or by reference to the RRA 1976 or because they have alleged, or intend to allege, that anyone has committed an act which would in fact amount to a contravention of the RRA 1976. It is also unlawful for an employer to victimise a worker because s/he suspects the worker has done or intends to do a protected act. Section 4 of SDA 1975 grants similar protection in relation to the SDA 1975, the EqPA 1970 and the Pensions Act 1995 (sex discrimination in occupational pensions). Note that victimisation of a worker who complains of sexual harassment may fall under the definition of further harassment under SDA s4A(1)(c), as opposed to the main victimisation provisions. It may be unclear on the facts which definition should apply. If in doubt, the worker should claim in the alternative under both sections.

13.87   The precise scope of doing anything 'under or by reference to' the statutes is uncertain. A Leeds ET thought that the activities of three local authority race trainers in pursuance of the authority's obligations under RRA 1976 s71 were protected acts under RRA 1976 s2(1)(c) and their dismissal when the authority changed hands was unlawful victimisation. Other examples of 'protected acts' could be encouraging a colleague to take up a discrimination case; issuing a press statement referring to breaches of the RRA 1976 or SDA 1975; or approaching the Equality and Human Rights Commission (EHRC) or a Race Equality Council. A worker cannot bring a claim for victimisation regarding what employers say in documents written for the tribunal proceedings, eg refusal to disclose documents or applications for costs,

---

154 S/he may also be able to claim discrimination for taking up trade union activities. See para 2.1 onwards.

because these matters are protected by an immunity. But this does not mean the worker has no remedy if the employer behaves badly during proceedings – s/he can apply for the response to be struck out or for costs, or s/he can seek extra compensation for injury to feelings and aggravated damages.[155]

13.88   Victimisation by an employer does not always take the obvious form of dismissing or disciplining a worker. It may take many less obvious and more subtle forms, for example:

- pressurising a worker to drop an allegation of discrimination;
- writing direct to the worker (even though s/he is represented) and to his/her work colleagues, warning of the risk that if the worker's ET claim succeeds, staff may lose their jobs and service-users suffer. (This is as distinct from a reasonable although firm attempt to persuade a claimant to settle his/her claim.);[156]
- withdrawing or reducing trade union facilities to a shop steward who is gathering evidence for a discrimination or equal pay claim;
- refusing holiday leave requests on the desired dates;
- writing a poor reference or refusing to provide one at all.

13.89   Since a worker first has to prove that s/he has done a 'protected act', which led to the victimisation, it is advisable that any complaint of discrimination or statement of intention to bring proceedings or give evidence should be put in writing at the time. If appropriate, such written statement should be accompanied by a reminder to the employer of the right not to be victimised under the relevant sections.

13.90   As a matter of evidence, it is difficult to prove that the reason the employer has treated the worker unfavourably is because the worker has done a protected act. For example, an employer dismissing a worker because s/he has made an allegation of racial harassment may purport to do so because his/her work is poor.

13.91   Employers often say they are not punishing the worker for doing the protected act, but for some other aspect of his/her behaviour. For example, in one case,[157] Mr Aziz was a taxi driver and member of TST, a company promoting the interests of taxi drivers in Coventry. He made secret tape recordings of other TST members, as he felt he was being discriminated against. He later decided to make a race discrimination claim against TST. When the recordings were disclosed

---

155 *South London & Maudsley NHS Trust v Dathi* [2008] IRLR 350, EAT.
156 *St Helens Metropolitan Borough Council v Derbyshire and others* [2007] IRLR 540, HL.
157 *Aziz v Trinity Street Taxis* [1988] IRLR 204, CA.

during the case, he was expelled from TST. Mr Aziz claimed that he was victimised by being expelled. He claimed that the protected act was making the tape recordings with a view possibly to bringing a race discrimination case. He lost his case because the ET found that the reason for his expulsion was the fact that the recordings were underhand and a breach of trust. The ET accepted that TST would still have expelled Mr Aziz even if the purpose of the recordings was nothing to do with the race relations legislation.

13.92   Unfortunately, it can be hard to prove that victimisation has taken place. A worker must show four things:

1) s/he has done a 'protected act', ie an act within RRA 1976 s2(1)(a)–(d) or SDA 1975 s4(1)(a)–(d);
2) s/he has been treated less favourably as a result. The comparison is with the way another worker who had not done the protected act would have been treated;[158]
3) the less favourable treatment was 'by reason that' the worker has done the protected act, ie motivated by it (even if unconsciously);[159]
4) the worker has suffered a detriment, eg dismissal, non-promotion or refusal of a reference. Where the victimisation is less concrete, eg a verbal threat or undue pressure, this can still be a detriment if a reasonable employee would consider it so.[160]

The second stage above resembles the 'but for' test for direct discrimination.[161] But the third stage is more difficult. In the *Khan* case,[162] Sgt Khan brought a race discrimination case in the ET regarding his failed promotion. Before the ET hearing, he applied for another post. When asked for a reference, his Chief Constable replied, 'Sgt Khan has an outstanding tribunal application against the Chief Constable for failing to support his application for promotion. In light of that, the Chief Constable is unable to comment any further for fear of prejudicing his own case before the tribunal.' Sergeant Khan claimed victimisation. The House of Lords said there was no doubt that had Sgt Khan not brought his original ET case, he would have been supplied with a reference. But the reason for the Chief Constable's refusal of a

---

158 *Chief Constable of West Yorkshire Police and others v Khan* [2001] IRLR 830, HL.
159 *Chief Constable of West Yorkshire Police v Khan* [2001] IRLR 830; (2002) 101 EOR 30, HL; *Swiggs v Nagarajan* [1999] IRLR 572, HL; *St Helens Metropolitan Borough Council v Derbyshire and others* [2007] IRLR 540, HL.
160 *St Helens Metropolitan Borough Council v Derbyshire and others* [2007] IRLR 540, HL; see para 13.36 above on 'detriment'.
161 See para 13.48.
162 [2001] IRLR 830; (2002) 101 EOR 30, HL.

reference was simply to preserve his position in the pending litigation. It was not motivated by the fact in itself that Sgt Khan had brought an RRA 1976 case. The House of Lords said the test that would usually work was to ask whether the employer would still have refused the reference request if the litigation had finished, whatever the outcome. If the answer was no, then it would usually follow that the reason for the refusal was the current existence of the proceedings – not the fact that the worker had brought them in the first place.

13.93   This decision does not mean that employers have a free hand to victimise workers as long as an ET case is running.[163] The point here was that the content of any reference was precisely the matter awaiting adjudication in the existing ET case. The Chief Constable, having taken legal advice, refused the reference because he feared prejudicing his own case before the ET.

13.94   An employer has a defence to a victimisation claim in relation to a worker's allegation under the RRA 1976, SDA 1975, EqPA 1970 or Pension Act 1995, where such allegation was false and not made in good faith.[164] Therefore as long as the worker genuinely believes the discrimination of which s/he complains has occurred, even if the ET disagrees, s/he should be protected.

13.95   However, if the worker complains of discrimination which would not be covered by the relevant Acts even if s/he proved it happened, s/he will not be protected.[165] For example, a black worker who is dismissed for complaining of a racial assault taking place outside the course of employment (and therefore not covered by the RRA 1976) cannot complain of victimisation.[166]

13.96   As is apparent from all of the above, the difficulties in proving motive or causation severely limit the effectiveness of the victimisation provisions in practice. Even so, it is often easier to prove victimisation than direct discrimination in the ET. Victimisation is a major practical problem in the workplace, but tends to be overlooked as an industrial relations issue. It is remarkable how often equal opportunities policies and training deal with direct and indirect discrimination but fail to address victimisation.

---

163 See *St Helens Metropolitan Borough Council v Derbyshire and others* [2007] UKHL 16, where the House of Lords is anxious to ensure *Khan* is not misinterpreted.

164 RRA 1976 s2; SDA 1975 s4.

165 *Waters v Commissioner of Police of the Metropolis* [1997] IRLR 589; (1997) 76 EOR 40, CA.

166 Although s/he could claim direct discrimination if a white worker bringing an equally serious complaint would not have been dismissed.

Duty of public authorities

Race Relations Act 1976 s71 and the Race Relations (Amendment) Act 2000

13.97   The Race Relations (Amendment) Act (RR(A)A) 2000 extended the scope of the RRA 1976 to forbid discrimination by the police and other public authorities in carrying out any of their functions. This is set out in an expanded section 19 of the RRA 1976 and is relevant to the non-employment parts of the RRA 1976, which are beyond the scope of this book.

13.98   The RR(A)A 2000 also introduced a new section 71 into the RRA 1976, which places a positive duty on a public authority 'in carrying out its functions to have due regard to the need (a) to eliminate unlawful race discrimination; and (b) to promote equality of opportunity and good relations between persons of different racial groups'. This would include the authority's employment functions. Schedule 1A lists which authorities are subject to the section 71 duty: it includes central and local government, the NHS, water, fire and police authorities, and educational bodies.

13.99   Specific duties for public authorities have been set out in regulations.[167] Authorities were required to publish a Race Equality Scheme by 31 May 2002 and must review their list of functions, policies and proposed policies for relevance to the general statutory duty every three years. This is to ensure their Race Equality Scheme is kept up to date and effectively implemented. Also, with a few listed exceptions, the authorities in their capacity as employers had to put monitoring in place by May 2002. Authorities must monitor existing staff, job applicants, staff applications for training and promotion. Authorities with 150 or more full-time staff must also monitor disciplinaries, grievances, performance appraisals, training and leavers. Results must be published annually.[168]

13.100   The EHRC (and previously the CRE) has enforcement powers if these duties are not carried out. The CRE produced a statutory Code of Practice on the Duty to Promote Race Equality and four non-statutory guides which give practical guidance to help authorities meet their duty. There is a separate Code and guidance for authorities in Scotland.[169] In 2004, the CRE issued compliance proceedings against 52

167 Race Relations Act 1976 (General Statutory Duty) Order 2001 SI No 3457; Race Relations Act 1976 (Statutory Duties) Order 2001 SI No 3458.

168 SI 2001 No 3458, art 5.

169 The Code and guides are on the EHRC website, www.equalityhumanrights.com, search 'codes'.

public authorities for failing to comply with their duty. The CRE also noted that while most organisations have published Race Equality Schemes, many have failed to implement them effectively.[170] In terms of individual discrimination cases, an employer's failure to follow its section 71 duties, including any failure to carry out risk assessments before introducing new policies, may be particularly relevant to whether it can justify indirect race discrimination.[171] There have been a number of very interesting judicial review cases, where the courts have quashed decisions made by public authorities because they were not preceded by equality impact assessments.[172] Unfortunately, none of these were in the employment context.

13.101   The statutory Code is a useful negotiating tool, expanding on the basic obligations to monitor and publish results annually. It also provides a basis for asking questions in a RRA 1976 questionnaire[173] and for cross-examination. The Code's recommendations include:

- When a public authority publishes results, it should explain how it is dealing with trends or problems highlighted by its monitoring. (Clause 5.7)
- It may be useful to combine and analyse monitoring data with other data, eg on sex and disability. (Clause 5.7)
- If monitoring shows that current employment policies and practice are leading to unlawful discrimination, the authority should take steps to end the discrimination. As a first step, the authority should examine each of its procedures closely to find out how discrimination might be happening. (Clauses 4.29–4.30; 5.10–5.11.)
- Consulting people through various methods, especially those likely to be affected by a policy, and taking account of their views. (Clauses 4.20–4.22)

SDA 1975 – The gender duty

13.102 The SDA 1975, s76A[174] imposes a gender equality duty on public authorities, which is further set out for England and Wales in the Sex

---

170 For a survey on implementation, see 'Race equality: an ongoing obligation' (2006) 154 EOR 13.

171 See para 13.79 above.

172 See *R (C) v Secretary of State for Justice* [2008] EWCA Civ 882; *R (Kaur and Shah) v L B Ealing* [2008] EWHC 2062 (Admin); *R (Watkins-Singh) v Governing Body of Aberdare Girls High School* [2008] EWCA 1865 (Admin).

173 See para 21.2 above.

174 Section 76A was introduced by the Equality Act 2006.

Discrimination Act 1975 (Public Authorities) (Statutory Duties) Order 2006 and the Sex Discrimination (Public Authorities) (Statutory Duties) (Scotland) Order 2007.[175] The gender duty is similar to the public duties under the RRA 1976 and DDA 1995. The duty came into force on 6 April 2007. With limited exceptions,[176] it applies to all public authorities. When carrying out their functions, including the employment function, authorities must have due regard to the need to (a) eliminate unlawful discrimination and harassment, and (b) promote equality of opportunity between men and women.

13.103   This means they should consider their policies and working practices in relation to all aspects of the employment relationship. Many public authorities[177] including local authorities, NHS Trusts and government departments are also subject to specific duties which differ slightly in England, Wales and Scotland (except for non-devolved bodies). In England, the specific duties include publishing a Gender Equality Scheme by 30 April 2007 and revising the Scheme every three years. In Scotland, the Scheme was to be published by 29 June 2007 and an equal pay policy statement by 28 September 2007, with progress reviews every three years. The Welsh specific duties were initially delayed, but public authorities in Wales were meanwhile advised to develop a Gender Equality Scheme. Authorities must consult their employees and any trade unions in preparing the Scheme. The Scheme must contain overall objectives to meet the gender duty including the need to address any sex-related pay differences.[178] The Scheme should involve arrangements for assessing the impact of the authority's activities on gender equality, an action plan, and the gathering and use of information. The EOC's Codes of Practice (see below) at sections 3.12–3.23 (England and Wales) and 3.16–3.26 (Scotland) give useful guidance on how information should be gathered and reviewed. The authority should publish a report annually which summarises the actions it has taken towards meeting the listed objectives.[179]

13.104   The former Equal Opportunities Commission published two statutory Codes of Practice on the Gender Equality Duty, one for England and Wales and one for Scotland.[180] The Codes give practical guidance to

175 SI No 2930 and SSI No 32 respectively.
176 Set out in SDA 1975 s76A(3) and (4).
177 A full list can be found in appendix D of the EOC's Codes of Practice – see below.
178 SI No 2930 reg 2(4) and (5).
179 SI No 2930 reg 6; SSI No 32 reg 5(1).
180 The Codes and guidance are available on the EHRC website, www.equalityhumanrights.com, search 'codes'.

public authorities on the general and specific duties. For example, the England and Wales Code encourages monitoring at paras 2.63, 2.73, 3.12, 3.16, 3.23, 3.55 and 4.5. As with other statutory Codes, they do not create legal obligations in themselves, but must be taken into account by any court or tribunal where relevant. If you are running an individual case of sex discrimination against a public authority, it is worth checking to what extent the employer has complied with any relevant recommendations in the Codes.

CHAPTER 14

Permitted race and sex discrimination

Chapter 14: Key points

- Under the Sex Discrimination Act 1975 and the Race Relations Act 1976 except in relation to race or national or ethnic origins, discrimination in recruitment, transfer, promotion or training is permitted if it falls within the list of genuine occupational qualification (GOQ) exceptions in the statutes.
- The GOQ exceptions do not apply where the employer already has workers of the necessary race or sex who could carry out the relevant duties without undue difficulty.
- Supplementary GOQs apply in respect of transsexual workers, but not where the worker has successfully applied to the Gender Recognition Panel for legal recognition of his/her acquired gender.
- Under the Race Relations Act 1976, in relation to race or ethnic or national origins, the GOQ exceptions do not apply. Instead there is a genuine and determining occupational requirement (GOR) exception. This works as a general exception.
- The GOR exception applies to dismissal as well as to recruitment and promotion, etc.
- Both GOQ and GOR exceptions should rarely apply, as they allow discrimination.
- The most commonly used GOQ exception is a form of positive action, ie to recruit someone of a particular race or sex to provide personal (face-to-face) services to others of that group.
- Limited additional positive action is permitted by way of targeted training and encouraging applications for recruitment.

Genuine occupational qualifications

14.1   Under Race Relations Act (RRA) 1976 s5 and Sex Discrimination Act (SDA) 1975 s7, discrimination is permitted in certain circumstances[1] where being of a particular racial group or gender is a genuine occupational qualification (GOQ) of the job. The GOQ defence may apply to discrimination in refusing to offer someone employment or in the arrangements made for determining who should be offered employment or in access to opportunities for promotion or transfer or to training for employment.

14.2   Under the RRA 1976, the GOQ exception does not apply to discrimination on grounds of race or ethnic or national origins. In such

---

1   RRA 1976 s5(1); SDA 1975 s7(1).

cases, a genuine and determining occupational *requirement* (GOR) exception applies instead.[2]

14.3   The GOQ defence is *not* available in the following circumstances:

- under the SDA 1975, where discrimination is against a worker because s/he is married or a civil partner;
- where discrimination occurs in the terms of employment offered or afforded to workers, or in access to benefits, facilities or services (other than promotion, transfer or training), or in dismissing someone or subjecting them to any other detriment;
- to the filling of a vacancy at a time when the employer already has workers of the particular race/sex who are capable of carrying out the duties in question, whom it would be reasonable to employ on those duties and who could carry out those duties without undue inconvenience to the employer.[3] For example, in *Etam plc v Rowan*,[4] a shop selling women's clothes refused to employ a male shop assistant because the job was likely to involve contact with women in a state of undress.[5] The GOQ defence failed because the part of a sales assistant's job which involved contact with women in changing rooms could have been carried out by other (female) shop assistants without causing undue inconvenience to the employer.

For a full list of GOQs, it is important to read the wording of the sections. In summary, they are as follows.

14.4   Under the RRA 1976:

- for reasons of authenticity as an actor, entertainer, artist's or photographer's model;
- for reasons of authenticity, working in a place where food or drink is served to the public in a particular setting; or
- to provide personal services promoting the welfare of persons of the same racial group.[6]

14.5   Under the SDA 1975:

- for reasons of authenticity as an actor or entertainer or for reasons of physiology (excluding physical strength or stamina);
- to preserve decency or privacy because of likely physical contact or

---

2   See para 14.8.
3   RRA 1976 s5(4), SDA 1975 s7(4).
4   [1989] IRLR 150, EAT.
5   SDA 1975 s7(2)(b)(i) and (ii).
6   See para 14.10 below.

contact with persons in a state of undress or using sanitary facilities or, where work is in a private home, because of close physical or social contact with someone living in the home;

- because it is necessary to live on work premises and there are no separate sleeping and sanitary facilities and it is not reasonable to expect the employer to supply these;
- where the work is in a single-sex establishment or part of an establishment for persons requiring special care, supervision or attention, eg a hospital or prison;
- where the job is one of two to be held by a married couple or by a couple who are civil partners; or
- to provide personal services promoting the welfare or education or similar services to persons of the same sex.[7]

An employer can invoke the GOQ defence even where only some of the duties of the job are covered by the section,[8] although of course it is then more likely that the duties can be covered by other workers.

Transsexuals

14.6   GOQs also apply to permit discrimination in certain circumstances against workers because they intend to undergo, are undergoing or have undergone gender reassignment.[9] Again, it is advisable to read the precise wording but broadly speaking the position is as follows. Discrimination is permitted if being a man or being a woman is a GOQ for the job (as in the single-sex GOQs[10] set out above) provided the employer can also show the treatment is reasonable.[11] Unlike the usual position, the GOQ defence is additionally available where the employer dismisses a worker.[12] There are four supplementary GOQs[13] which also apply to dismissal as well as recruitment, promotion, transfer and training. In brief these are:

- where the job-holder may have to carry out intimate physical searches pursuant to statutory powers;[14]

---

7   See para 14.10 below.
8   RRA 1976 s5(3); SDA 1975 s7(3).
9   See SDA 1975 ss7A and 7B.
10   SDA 1975 s7 and listed above.
11   SDA 1975 s7A(1).
12   SDA 1975 s7A(2).
13   SDA 1975 s7B.
14   SDA 1975 s7B(2)(a).

- where work is in a private home, because of physical or social contact with someone living in the home;[15]
- because it is necessary to live on work premises and it is not reasonable to expect the employer to make alternative arrangements or equip the premises to preserve decency and privacy.[16] Unlike the above two supplemental GOQs, this GOQ only applies while the worker is undergoing or intending to undergo gender re-assignment;
- where the work provides vulnerable individuals with personal welfare or other services and in the reasonable view of the employer, these could not be effectively provided whilst the worker is undergoing gender reassignment. Again this GOQ does not apply to a worker who has already undergone gender reassignment.[17]

The exception to the single-sex GOQs, where there are other employees who could reasonably carry out the relevant duties,[18] applies only to the first of these supplementary GOQs, ie there is no GOQ defence where the employer has other employees who could carry out the intimate searches without undue inconvenience.[19]

14.7 A post-operative transsexual should usually be regarded as having his/her reassigned gender.[20] For this reason, it is probably inappropriate to try to invoke the GOQ exceptions to allow discrimination on the basis that the worker is a transsexual or of the sex of his/her birth.[21] Moreover, if the worker has successfully applied to the Gender Recognition Panel for legal recognition of his/her acquired gender, these supplementary GOQs will not apply.[22]

Genuine and determining occupational requirements

14.8 As a result of amendments required by the EU Race Directive, the GOQ exception does not apply to discrimination on grounds of race or ethnic or national origins. Instead there is now a genuine and

---

15 SDA 1975 s7B(2)(b).
16 SDA 1975 s7B(2)(c).
17 SDA 1975 s7B(2)(d).
18 SDA 1975 s7(4) and above.
19 SDA 1975 s7B(4).
20 See para 13.21.
21 *A v Chief Constable of the West Yorkshire Police* [2003] IRLR 32, CA.
22 SDA 1975 s7B(3) and see para 13.21.

determining occupational requirement (GOR) exception.[23] This applies to discrimination in recruitment, promotion, transfer, training and dismissal,[24] where being of a particular race or of particular ethnic or national origins is a 'genuine and determining occupational requirement' and it is 'proportionate' to apply that requirement in the particular case. This is intended to be a very limited exception which should only apply where it is appropriate and necessary for the worker to be of a particular race or ethnic or national origins. There is no GOR exception under the SDA 1975.

Positive action

14.9   The codes of practice encourage positive action.

Personal services

14.10   Section 5(2)(d) of RRA 1976 says that being of a particular racial group is a GOQ where:

> ... the holder of the job provides persons of that racial group with personal services promoting their welfare, and those services can most effectively be provided by a person of that racial group.

Section 7(2)(e) of SDA 1975 is similar in relation to gender except that it refers to personal services promoting 'welfare or education or similar personal services'. To gain the protection of the subsections the following must be satisfied.

- The job must involve wholly or partly the provision of 'personal services'. The post-holder must be directly involved in the provision of the services,[25] ie in face-to-face contact with the recipient. Purely administrative and managerial positions such as assistant head of a local authority housing benefit department[26] are not covered.

---

23   RRA 1976 ss4A and 5.
24   Though since the GOQ exception did not apply to dismissal, it is questionable whether the new exception conforms with the non-regression principle in regard to dismissal. See para 12.2.
25   *Tottenham Green Under Fives' Centre v Marshall* [1989] IRLR 147; [1989] ICR 214, EAT.
26   *Lambeth LBC v CRE* [1990] IRLR 231, CA.

- Those services must be such that they are most effectively provided by a person of the same sex or racial group.[27] It is not necessary to show that the services can be provided only by a person of the same sex or racial group. It is recognised that 'where language or a knowledge and understanding of cultural and religious background are important, then those services may be most effectively provided by a person of a particular racial group'.[28]
- The EAT has said that the provider of services must be of a particular racial group which is the same group as that of the recipients and not simply black.[29] However, Balcombe LJ in the Court of Appeal suggested obiter that in some circumstances, eg a health visitor, personal services may be most effectively provided to persons of 'a racial group defined by colour', eg black people, by a person of the same colour, regardless of which ethnic group each person came from.[30]
- There must be no other workers already employed who could, without undue inconvenience, provide those services.[31]

Encouraging applications/offering training

14.11   Under RRA 1976 s38 and SDA 1975 s48, an employer can:

- encourage people of only a particular sex or racial group to apply for jobs; and
- offer training only to people of a particular sex or racial group;

provided that in the previous 12 months the number of women or people of that racial group doing the work in question was comparatively small, either generally or in the employing organisation in particular.

14.12   Note that, although it is permissible to encourage job applicants who are women or of a particular racial group, it is not permissible to

---

27 *Tottenham Green Under Fives' Centre v Marshall* [1989] IRLR 147; [1989] ICR 214, EAT.

28 *Lambeth LBC v CRE* [1990] IRLR 231, CA.

29 *Tottenham Green Under Fives' Centre v Marshall* [1989] IRLR 147; [1989] ICR 214, EAT; *Lambeth LBC v CRE* [1990] IRLR 231, CA.

30 *Lambeth LBC v CRE* [1990] IRLR 231, CA. See also *Hartup v Sandwell MBC*, EAT 20 July 1993 (479/92), summarised at (1993) 504 IDS Brief 16, where the EAT accepted that 'a particular racial group' can compromise two or more distinct racial groups.

31 RRA 1976 s5(4); SDA 1975 s7(4).

discriminate at the point of taking someone on. Employers can there-fore place advertisements expressly encouraging applications from women and particular racial groups or ask job centres to tell such people that applications from them are particularly welcome, but it should be made clear that selection will be on merit, regardless of race or sex.

Special needs

14.13   It is not unlawful under RRA 1976 s35 to afford someone of a partic-ular racial group access to facilities or services to meet his/her special needs in regard to education, training or welfare.

Discriminatory advertisements

14.14   Under RRA 1976 s29 and SDA 1975 s38 it is unlawful to publish or have published an advertisement which indicates or might reason-ably be understood as indicating an intention to discriminate, unless a GOQ or other exceptions apply. Proceedings in respect of unlawful advertisements can only be brought by the Equality and Human Rights Commission[32] and not by individuals. However, a discriminatory adver-tisement may be evidence supporting an individual's claim of unlaw-ful discrimination if a person goes on to apply for the job and is unsuccessful. Following an amendment to the definition of indirect dis-crimination under the RRA 1976 in order to comply with the Race Discrimination Directive, an individual can also bring a claim if s/he was deterred from applying for a job by an indirectly discriminatory requirement contained in an advertisement.[33] As the Equal Treatment Directive is worded in a similar way, individuals ought to be allowed to bring similar claims for indirect sex discrimination in advertisements, but this is untested.

Statutory authority

14.15   There are certain exceptions regarding acts of discrimination done in pursuance of statute or a statutory instrument.[34]

---

32   Equality Act 2006 s25, replacing the previous equality commissions.
33   See para 13.66.
34   RRA 1976 s41 as amended by SI 2003 No 1626; SDA 1975 s51.

National security

14.16   Discriminatory acts done to safeguard national security are excluded from the RRA 1976 and SDA 1975.[35]

Pregnancy or childbirth

14.17   Section 2(2) of SDA 1975 permits (but does not require) special treatment afforded to women in connection with pregnancy or childbirth.

---

35   RRA 1976 s42; SDA 1975 s52.

Discrimination on grounds of disability

Chapter 15: Key points

- The Disability Discrimination Act 1995 does not only apply to employees.
- There is a complex definition of disability under the Disability Discrimination Act 1995. It can often cover workers who would not be perceived by themselves or their employers as disabled, eg those with back injuries, depression and other temporary health problems.
- It is usually necessary in a case to prove a worker has a disability even where that seems obvious.
- HIV, multiple sclerosis and cancer are deemed a disability on diagnosis. Those registered as blind or partially sighted are also automatically covered.
- Failure to make reasonable adjustment is at the heart of the Disability Discrimination Act 1995. Employers are expected to make risk assessments and take proactive steps to assist a worker where reasonable adjustment is needed.
- An employer is not obliged to make reasonable adjustment if s/he does not know the worker has a disability and it is not obvious.
- Direct discrimination means different treatment on grounds of disability. There is no justification defence.
- The previously important definition of 'disability-related' discrimination' has effectively been rendered useless by the case of *Lewisham LBC v Malcolm*.
- Victimisation is where a worker is punished for complaining about discrimination.
- Public authorities have a disability equality duty.
- Guidance for running a discrimination case is at chapter 21. Evidence to prove disability discrimination is at para 16.47 onwards. Checklists are in appendix A.

The legal framework

15.1   As with the Race Relations Act (RRA) 1976 and Sex Discrimination Act (SDA) 1975, the Disability Discrimination Act (DDA) 1995 covers discrimination in relation to premises, education, goods, facilities and services and other areas as well as employment. In Europe, disability discrimination is covered by the General Framework Directive (2000/78/EC). The original body with overall responsibility for keeping the workings of the DDA 1995 under review and promoting the equal opportunities for disabled people was the Disability Rights Commission (DRC). The Equality and Human Rights Commission (EHRC) took over the DRC's remit from October 2007.[1] On 8 June 2009, the UK ratified the UN Convention on the Rights of Persons with Disabilities together with the optional protocol. It is far too early to say whether this will create any additional rights in terms of the employment sphere.

15.2 The employment part of the DDA 1995 came into force on 2 December 1996. Various regulations have been made giving more specific detail of legal requirements in certain areas.[2] A revised Code of Practice on Employment and Occupation was issued under DDA 1995 s53 and replaced the original Code in 2004.[3] As with the Codes under the RRA 1976 and SDA 1975, this Code must be taken into account by an employment tribunal (ET) on any relevant point, but it is not legally actionable in itself.[4]

15.3 The Code of Practice covers a range of matters, but is particularly useful regarding the scope of the employer's duty to make reasonable adjustments. The other key document is the revised *Guidance on matters to be taken into account in determining questions relating to the definition of disability*.[5] The Employment Appeal Tribunal (EAT) has encouraged ETs to refer explicitly to any relevant provision of the Code or the Guidance.[6]

15.4 The DDA 1995 covers far more people than may be realised. According to a report by the Department for Work and Pensions in February 2003, every three months 2.6 per cent of workers (over 600,000 people) become sick or disabled using the definition of disability under the DDA 1995. This compares with only 0.3 per cent (73,000) who would qualify for statutory sick pay or incapacity benefit. Approximately 5,000 cases are now lodged each year in the ETs under the DDA 1995.

---

1 See para 12.25.
2 For example, the Disability Discrimination (Meaning of Disability) Regulations 1996 SI No 1455 and the Disability Discrimination (Employment) Regulations 1996 SI No 1456.
3 The hard copy, 222 pages, can be ordered online from The Stationery Office: www.tso.co.uk (tel: 0870 600 5522).
4 DDA 1995 s53(4)–(6).
5 Issued under DDA 1995 s3, revised in May 2006. This can be ordered from The Stationery Office, see n3 above. It is also available on the EHRC website, www.equalityhumanrights.com
6 *Goodwin v The Patent Office* [1999] IRLR 4, EAT.

15.5   Although the definition of discrimination under the DDA 1995 differs significantly from the definition in the RRA 1976 and SDA 1975, many other aspects of the scope of the legislation and ET procedure are identical. It may be useful in these other areas to cross-refer to the guidance on law and practice in running cases under the RRA 1976 and SDA 1975. For an overall checklist on the DDA, see p715 below.

Which workers are covered?

15.6   There is no longer a small employers' exemption. As with the other discrimination legislation, the DDA 1995 protects job applicants, apprentices, people on work placements,[7] contract workers[8] and those working personally on a contract to execute any work as well as employees.[9] The DDA 1995 also covers partners in firms, barristers and pupils.[10] Police officers and police cadets are covered,[11] but armed services personnel are not.[12] With limited exceptions, employers are liable for the discriminatory acts of their employees or agents, regardless of whether they knew of or approved those acts.[13]

15.7   Trade organisations (eg organisations of workers) must not discriminate in access to membership or in terms of membership.[14]

Statutory authority

15.8   A discriminatory act will not be unlawful if it is done in pursuance of a statute or statutory instrument or to safeguard national security.[15]

---

7   DDA 1995 s14C; Code paras 9.42–9.50.
8   DDA 1995 s12(1). *MHC Consulting Services Ltd v Tansell* [1999] IRLR 677, EAT. Also see para 13.14, although the wording is slightly different to that under RRA 1976 s7 and SDA 1975 s9.
9   DDA 1995 s68.
10 DDA 1995 ss6A–C, 7A–D; Code paras 9.25–9.41.
11 DDA 1995 s64A; Code paras 9.23–9.24.
12 DDA 1995 s64(7).
13 DDA 1995 s58. See para 13.20 for the law on equivalent provisions under the RRA 1976 and SDA 1975.
14 DDA 1995 ss13, 14, 14A–D.
15 DDA 1995 s59.

Charities and supported employment

15.9 Charities are permitted to discriminate in pursuance of their charitable purposes if those are connected with disability.[16] Providers of supported employment under the Disabled Persons (Employment) Act 1944 may treat a particular group of disabled workers more favourably than others.[17]

Prohibited actions

15.10 Section 4 of DDA 1995 prohibits discrimination against a disabled person in the arrangements made for deciding who should be offered employment, in the terms on which employment is offered, in refusing to offer employment, in access to opportunities for promotion, transfer, training or other benefit, in contract terms or by dismissing the worker (including constructive dismissal)[18] or subjecting him/her to any other detriment or harassment. Discrimination in occupational pension schemes and in group insurance services, whether by the employer, pension scheme trustees or group insurers, is also covered.[19] Acts of discrimination against a former employee taking place after his/her job has ended are covered provided the discrimination arises out of and is closely connected to the previous employment relationship.[20] Examples could be giving a discriminatory reference, refusal to return the worker's property, or conducting a post-dismissal appeal in a discriminatory way.[21]

15.11 Employment must be at an establishment in Great Britain.[22] Employment is at an establishment in Great Britain if the employee works wholly or partly in Great Britain or, where s/he works wholly outside Great Britain, if s/he is ordinarily resident in Great Britain when s/he applies for or was offered the job or at any time during the employment, and the work is for the purposes of the employer's business at an establishment in Great Britain.[23]

---

16 DDA 1995 s10(1).

17 DDA 1995 s10.

18 DDA 1995 s4(5)(b).

19 DDA 1995 ss17–18; Code Chapter 10.

20 DDA 1995 s16A; Code para 8.28.

21 For case examples before DDA 1995 s16A was passed, see *Relaxation Group plc v Rhys-Harper; D'Souza v Lambeth LBC; Jones v 3M Healthcare Ltd and others; and related cases* [2003] IRLR 484; (2003) 121 EOR 21, HL.

22 DDA 1995 s4(6).

23 DDA 1995 s68(2) and (2A).

The meaning of 'disability'

15.12   Except in obvious cases, one of the most important and difficult issues is whether a worker is covered by the DDA 1995. The DDA 1995 effectively covers many workers with long-term ill-health, which would not conventionally be seen as a 'disability'. The most frequently claimed disabilities in the first few years of the DDA 1995 were back or neck impairments, and depression. It is dangerous to generalise about when the DDA 1995 applies and each case will depend on a close examination of its facts. A worker with a back impairment, for example, may or may not be covered by the DDA 1995, depending on the duration and severity of the problem. It is necessary to go through the stages of the statutory definition set out below, taking into account the clarification in the Guidance.[24] Whether the worker is recognised as disabled in other contexts, eg for the purposes of social security benefits, requires a different legal test.[25]

15.13   The DDA 1995 prohibits unlawful discrimination against a 'disabled person' in employment.[26] Section 1 defines a disabled person as a person who has a disability. Section 1(1) reads:

> Subject to the provisions of Schedule 1, a person has a disability for the purposes of this Act if he has a physical or mental impairment which has a substantial and long-term adverse effect on his ability to carry out normal day-to-day activities.

Each element of this definition should be separately considered.[27] Schedule 1 provides some guidelines, and further clarification can be found in the Disability Discrimination (Meaning of Disability) Regulations 1996[28] and in the *Guidance on matters to be taken into account in determining questions relating to the definition of 'disability'*. The following text should be read together with paras 16.47–16.67 on evidence to prove disability.

15.14   Although far more conditions are covered by the DDA 1995 than advisers or workers may at first realise, there is no doubt that many workers with obvious disabilities have struggled to prove they are within the Act. Employers almost automatically deny a worker has a relevant disability once a case starts. The effect of this and the detailed

---

24   See para 15.3 above.
25   *Hill v Clacton Family Trust Ltd* [2005] EWCA Civ 1456; (2006) 798 IDS Brief 11, CA.
26   DDA 1995 s4.
27   See checklist on p714.
28   SI No 1455.

stages of the definition, has led to some seemingly obvious cases being excluded. The EAT stressed in *Goodwin* that although the Guidance should be looked at in deciding whether someone has a disability, it should not be used as an obstacle if it is obvious that they do.[29] For further assistance regarding who may be covered by the DDA 1995, see *Proving disability and reasonable adjustments: a worker's guide to evidence under the DDA* by Tamara Lewis, which contains a digest of 26 common and less common impairments.[30]

15.15   Workers with multiple sclerosis, HIV or cancer,[31] or those registered with a local authority or certified by a consultant ophthalmologist as blind or partially sighted, are deemed disabled without the need to prove the stages of the definition.[32]

Physical impairment

15.16   'Physical impairment' includes sensory impairment and severe disfigurement, although not tattoos or ornamental body piercing.[33] Provided all aspects of the definition are met, conditions such as ME (chronic fatigue syndrome),[34] asthma and back disorders can be covered. Seasonal allergic rhinitis, for example hay fever, is expressly excluded.[35] Addictions to alcohol, nicotine or other substances are also not covered unless the addiction was originally the result of administration of medical treatment or medically prescribed drugs.[36] It is not necessary to consider how a physical or mental impairment was caused. So for example, depression[37] or liver disease resulting from alcohol dependency would count as an impairment.[38]

---

29 *Goodwin v The Patent Office* [1999] IRLR 4, EAT.

30 Available at www.equalityhumanrights.com/uploaded_files/dda_workers_guide_reasonable_adjustments.doc

31 DDA 1995 Sch 1 para 6A(1) with effect from 5 December 2005.

32 Disability Discrimination (Blind and Partially Sighted Persons) Regulations 2003 SI No 712.

33 Disability Discrimination (Meaning of Disability) Regulations 1996 SI No 1455 reg 5.

34 *O'Neill v Symm & Co Ltd* [1998] IRLR 232, EAT.

35 Disability Discrimination (Meaning of Disability) Regulations 1996 SI No 1455 reg 4(2).

36 Disability Discrimination (Meaning of Disability) Regulations 1996 SI No 1455 reg 3.

37 *Power v Panasonic UK Ltd* [2003] IRLR 151, EAT.

38 Guidance Part I para 11.

15.17   The concept of 'impairment' is not defined by the DDA 1995. It does not equate with a clinical condition – it is a functional concept rather than a medical one, ie focussing more on adverse effects.[39] Indeed, sometimes it can be hard to distinguish an impairment from its effects. An impairment can be something which results from an illness or which is the illness itself, ie it can be cause or effect.[40] One situation where this analysis helps in finding a physical impairment is where a worker genuinely suffers physical symptoms, but these result from psychological distress rather than any organic physical cause.[41] Of course the psychological condition may amount to a mental impairment. It also seems that a person can be regarded as having had a disability if s/he suffered from a combination of impairments with different effects, to different extents, over periods of time which overlapped, even though none of the individual impairments had sufficient adverse effect on its own.[42]

Mental impairment

15.18   'Mental impairment' includes learning disabilities.[43] The requirement that a mental illness be clinically well-recognised was removed in December 2005. It is no longer necessary to name a precise condition which is recognised by a respected body of medical opinion, eg by being listed in the World Health Organisation's international classification of diseases. However, it will still be necessary to provide evidence of a particular impairment and its effects (though note comments in the previous paragraph). Workers suffering from schizophrenia, manic depression or severe psychoses will usually be covered. It should now be much easier to bring ordinary depression under the DDA 1995, although it should be distinguished from a worker simply feeling fed-up or a bit stressed. Ordinary depression may fail to meet other aspects of the definition of disability, eg it may not have a substantial adverse effect for as long as 12 months. However, it should still be covered if it is likely to recur. Certain personality disorders are

---

39   *Ministry of Defence v Hay* [2008] IRLR 928, EAT.
40   *McNicol v Balfour Beatty Rail Maintenance Ltd* [2002] IRLR 711; November 2002 *Legal Action* 19, CA.
41   *McNicol v Balfour Beatty Rail Maintenance Ltd* [2002] IRLR 711; November 2002 *Legal Action* 19, CA; *College of Ripon & York St John v Hobbs* [2002] IRLR 185, EAT; May 2002 *Legal Action* 12. See also *Millar v Inland Revenue Commissioners* [2006] IRLR 112, CS.
42   *Ministry of Defence v Hay* [2008] IRLR 928, EAT.
43   Guidance Part I para 13.

specifically excluded, for example, a tendency to set fires or steal, to physical or sexual abuse, voyeurism or exhibitionism.[44] Where a worker displays an excluded disorder as a result of a non-excluded impairment, the question is why s/he has been discriminated against. For example, a worker who is dismissed for committing indecent exposure as a result of depression is protected only if the dismissal is wholly or partly for the depression as opposed to wholly for the exhibitionism.[45]

Affecting normal day-to-day activities

15.19   The impairment must affect normal day-to-day activities in respect of one of the following capacities: mobility (including ability to stand), manual dexterity, physical co-ordination, continence, ability to lift, carry or move everyday objects, speech, hearing or eyesight, memory or ability to concentrate, learn or understand, or perception of the risk of physical danger.[46] Ability to understand includes understanding of normal social interaction and the subtleties of human non-factual communication.[47] Part D of the Guidance provides extremely useful guidelines and illustrations on what are 'normal day-to-day activities'. The activity must be one which is carried out by many people on a daily or frequent or fairly regular basis, although not necessarily by a majority of people. Travel by tube or aeroplane is a normal activity[48], as is taking exams.[49] An activity is still normal if it is only normal for one sex.[50]

15.20   Impairments which only affect ability to carry out particular hobbies (eg piano playing) or sports are not covered.[51] The Guidance says that inability to carry out a particular form of work is not covered, because no particular form of work is 'normal' for most people. For example, in one old case, a garden centre worker was unsuccessful because although he could not lift heavy bags of soil, he could still lift everyday

---

44   Disability Discrimination (Meaning of Disability) Regulations 1996 SI No 1455 reg 4(1).

45   *Edmund Nuttall Ltd v Butterfield* [2005] IRLR 751, EAT.

46   DDA 1995 Sch 1 para 4(1).

47   *Hewett v Motorola Ltd* [2004] IRLR 545, EAT, a case concerning Asperger's syndrome.

48   *Abadeh v British Telecommunications plc* [2001] IRLR 23, EAT; May 2001 *Legal Action* 14.

49   *Paterson v The Commissioner of Police of the Metropolis* UKEAT/0635/06; [2007] IRLR 763, EAT; *Legal Action* May 08.

50   *Epke v Commissioner of Police of the Metropolis* [2001] IRLR 605, EAT.

51   See also *Coca-Cola Enterprises Ltd v Shergill* (2003) 727 IDS Brief 13, EAT; May 2003 *Legal Action* 21.

objects.[52] On the other hand, the key decision of the ECJ in *Chacon Navas v Eurest Colectividades SA*[53] suggests that 'day-to-day activities' in the DDA 1995 must encompass activities which are relevant to participation in professional life. Therefore, while inability to do a specialised work activity such as delicate work with specialised tools may not be considered a disability, inability to do a work activity which is common to many jobs, would be covered, eg using a word processor, answering the telephone, interacting with customers. Adverse effects on normal activities such as mobility, which occur only when working at nights, would also be covered because many people do work nights.[54]

15.21   A worker may tell an adviser or the tribunal that his/her day-to-day life is unaffected by his/her disability. This can be misleading. A worker may play down the effect of his/her disability.[55] Or it may be that a worker has rearranged his/her life to avoid carrying out a certain activity and feels that s/he is coping. The focus should be on what the worker cannot do; or cannot do without difficulty, as opposed to what s/he can do.[56] For example, an ET must take account of a worker's overriding tiredness when undertaking certain activities.[57] It should also recognise that someone is disabled even if s/he can get around a problem, eg by using a shoulder bag when s/he is unable to carry a bag in his/her hand.[58] An ET should not place too much emphasis on the way a worker appears to cope at the hearing because this can be misleading.[59]

Substantial effect

15.22   The Guidance at Section B expands on the meaning of 'substantial' adverse effect. It is unnecessary that a worker is completely unable to

---

52   *Quinlan v B&Q plc* (1998) 614 IDS Brief 14, EAT.
53   [2006] IRLR 706, ECJ, applied by the EAT in *Paterson v The Commissioner of Police of the Metropolis* UKEAT/0635/06; [2007] IRLR 763, EAT. See also para 15.30 below.
54   *Chief Constable of Dumfries & Galloway Constabulary v Adams* UKEATS/0046/08.
55   *Goodwin v The Patent Office* [1999] IRLR 4, EAT.
56   *Goodwin v The Patent Office* [1999] IRLR 4, EAT; *Vicary v British Telecommunications plc* [1999] IRLR 680 EAT; May 2000 *Legal Action* 12; *Leonard v Southern Derbyshire Chamber of Commerce* [2001] IRLR 19, EAT; May 2001 *Legal Action* 14.
57   *Leonard v Southern Derbyshire Chamber of Commerce* [2001] IRLR 19, EAT; May 2001 *Legal Action* 14.
58   *Vicary v British Telecommunications plc* [1999] IRLR 680 EAT; May 2000 *Legal Action* 12.
59   *Leonard v Southern Derbyshire Chamber of Commerce* [2001] IRLR 19, EAT; May 2001 *Legal Action* 14.

carry out the activity, but the effect must be clearly more than trivial.[60] A substantial effect could include where a worker can carry out the activity, but only for short periods of time or more slowly than usual or only in a particular way or under certain environmental conditions. It may be that a worker can carry out the activity, but it is tiring or painful to do so. Alternatively, the worker may have been medically advised to refrain from the activity altogether. To assess whether an effect is substantial comparison is made, not with the population at large, but with how the worker would carry out the activity if s/he did not have the impairment.[61] Section D of the Guidance gives examples linked to each of the listed capacities for day-to-day activities (at para 15.19 above) where it is unclear whether an impairment has substantial effect. For example, it would be reasonable to regard as having substantial adverse effect:

- difficulty going up or down stairs;
- difficulty using one or more forms of public transport;
- difficulty co-ordinating the use of a knife and fork at the same time;
- difficulty carrying a moderately loaded tray steadily;
- difficulty asking specific questions to clarify instructions.

It would not be reasonable to regard as having substantial adverse effect:

- experiencing some discomfort as a result of travelling in a car for more than two hours without discomfort;
- inability to thread a small needle;
- inability to carry heavy luggage;
- inability to converse in a foreign language;
- a minor lisp or other speech impediment.

The Guidance should be looked at in full and advisers should always consider each case on its particular facts, rather than generalise from the examples. The Guidance stresses these are simply indicators, not a rigid test. Remember also that a physical impairment may have mental effects and a mental impairment may have physical manifestations.[62]

15.23   Severe disfigurement is deemed to have 'substantial' adverse effect.

---

60   *Goodwin v The Patent Office* [1999] IRLR 4, EAT.
61   *Paterson v The Commissioner of Police of the Metropolis* UKEAT/0635/06; [2007] IRLR 763, EAT.
62   Guidance, Section D.

15.24   The fact that medical treatment or medication controls or corrects the impairment is irrelevant (except for someone whose sight impairment is corrected by glasses or lenses).[63] The effect without the correcting measures should be assessed. So, for example, a worker is still protected, even if his/her diabetes is controlled by insulin or his/her depression is controlled by counselling sessions with a clinical psychologist.[64] Plates and pins inserted into an ankle some time previously should also be taken into account if they continue to give support.[65] The test is whether the impairment is 'likely' to have substantial adverse effect if the medication or controlling measures were not taken.[66] The EAT has suggested that an ET should consider both the effect of a worker's impairment while on medication and the 'deduced effects' but for the medication.[67] This is obviously difficult and medical evidence may be needed.[68]

15.25   A worker with a progressive condition, eg motor-neurone disease or muscular dystrophy, is deemed disabled as soon as the condition has any effect on the worker's ability to carry out day-to-day activities, even if the effect is not yet substantial. The worker must prove it is likely that at some stage in the future, the progressive condition will lead to an impairment with a substantial adverse effect.[69] The Guidance says 'likely' means 'more probable than not' but the House of Lords has said it only means 'could well happen', which is a lower threshold.[70] If the condition has not yet had any effect at all, the worker is not protected.[71] This causes real problems for workers who are discriminated against by their employers simply because they have been diagnosed with a condition, but who are not covered by the DDA 1995 until the condition starts to affect any of their day-to-day activities.

15.26   It does not matter whether the activity which is initially affected, but not substantially, is different from the activity which will in future be substantially affected, if both arise from the same impairment.[72]

---

63   DDA 1995 Sch 1 para 6.
64   *Kapadia v Lambeth LBC* (1999) 625 IRLB 2, EAT.
65   *Carden v Pickerings Europe Ltd* [2005] IRLR 720, EAT.
66   For the meaning of 'likely' when used in the DDA 1995, see observations in the next paragraph.
67   *Goodwin v The Patent Office* [1999] IRLR 4, EAT.
68   See para 16.56.
69   DDA 1995 Sch 1 para 8; See also para 16.57 on evidence.
70   Guidance para C2; *SCA Packaging Ltd v Boyle* [2009] UKHL 37.
71   DDA 1995 Sch 1 para 8.
72   *Kirton v Tetrosyl Ltd* [2003] IRLR 353, CA.

Long-term effect

15.27   The DDA 1995 does not protect those with short-term or temporary disability. To be considered long-term, the effect of the impairment must have lasted or be likely to last at least 12 months or for the rest of the worker's life. If an impairment ceases to have substantial adverse effect but is likely to recur, it is treated as continuing. This covers workers with impairments with fluctuating or recurring effects, eg rheumatoid arthritis or a recurrent depressive disorder.[73] Conditions which recur only sporadically or for short periods (eg epilepsy or, presumably, migraine) can still be covered, depending on the facts.[74] The likelihood must be assessed as it existed at the date of the discrimination and not in the light of what has actually happened by the time of the tribunal hearing.[75] The tribunal can consider medical evidence obtained after the event, as long as it relates to the circumstances at the time. For the meaning of 'recurring and long-term effect' see the Guidance, Section C.

Past disability

15.28   A worker who has recovered from a past disability is protected if s/he is discriminated against in connection with that disability.[76] The DDA 1995 does not protect workers who are discriminated against because they are incorrectly perceived to have a disability.

The EU definition and policy developments

15.29   Following a consultation, the Disability Rights Commission recommended in 2006 that the definition of disability be amended so that a person who is discriminated against due to any impairment is covered. By removing the requirement to prove substantial adverse effect over 12 months or more, many people unjustly excluded on technicalities would be brought within the protection. The emphasis would move to whether the employer's behaviour was reasonable and justifiable. At the time of writing, the Equality Bill[77] has not followed this

---

73   *Crossingham v European Wellcare Lifestyles Ltd* [2006] All ER (D) 279 (Oct), EAT.
74   Guidance paras C4–C5.
75   *Richmond Adult Community College v McDougall* [2008] IRLR 227, CA; *Legal Action* May 08.
76   DDA 1995 Sch 2.
77   See para 12.24 above.

recommendation, but proposes only to remove the requirement that the adversely affected day-to-day activities fall within the strict list of capacities.

15.30   There are few guidelines from the ECJ regarding the meaning of 'disability' under the Directive. It has suggested that disability be understood as 'a limitation which results, in particular, from physical, mental or psychological impairments and which hinders the participation of the person concerned in professional life'.[78] There is nothing in the Directive to prohibit discrimination on grounds of sickness as such (unless within the meaning of 'disability'). United Kingdom law cannot provide lesser rights than in the Directive, but it can of course choose to provide greater rights and a wider coverage. Although the ECJ's wording seems narrower than the definition in the DDA 1995, it may be wider in one respect. It indicates that the measure of whether a worker is disabled may be the effect on participation in professional life, whereas case-law under the DDA 1995 says that a particular type of work is not a 'normal' activity (see para 15.20 above).

The meaning of 'discrimination'

15.31   The definition of discrimination is different in some respects from the definition in the RRA 1976 and SDA 1975 and it is essential not to become confused. There are five kinds of unlawful discrimination under the DDA 1995:

1) failure to make reasonable adjustments;[79]
2) direct discrimination;[80]
3) disability-related discrimination;[81]
4) harassment. This is similar under all discrimination legislation;[82]
5) victimisation.[83]

15.32   An employer has no duty to make reasonable adjustments if s/he does not know, and cannot reasonably be expected to know the worker is disabled and needs the adjustment.[84] Therefore, although workers may be

---

78 *Chacón Navas v Eurest Colectividades SA* [2006] IRLR 706, ECJ.
79 DDA 1995 ss3A(2), 4A and 18B(2) replacing the former ss5(2) and 6.
80 DDA 1995 s3A(5).
81 DDA 1995 s3A(1) replacing the former s5(1).
82 DDA 1995 s3B; Code paras 4.38–4.39. See paras 17.91–17.125 below.
83 DDA 1995 s55; Code paras 4.33–4.36.
84 See para 15.41.

reluctant to reveal they have a disability, it may be important to tell the employer, and in writing, to gain the protection of the DDA 1995.

15.33   The DDA 1995 does not prohibit positive discrimination in favour of disabled workers, as it is not unlawful to discriminate against a worker on grounds that s/he is not disabled. However, local government employers may be restricted due to the provisions of the Local Government and Housing Act 1989.[85]

Failure to make reasonable adjustments

15.34 The duty on employers to make reasonable adjustments is at the heart of the DDA 1995. Section 4A of DDA 1995 states:

> (1) Where–
>   (a) a provision, criterion or practice applied by or on behalf of an employer, or
>   (b) any physical feature of the premises occupied by the employer, places the disabled person concerned at a substantial disadvantage in comparison with persons who are not disabled, it is the duty of the employer to take such steps as it is reasonable, in all the circumstances of the case, for him to have to take in order to prevent the provision, criterion or practice, or feature, having that effect.

The steps which the DDA 1995 suggests the employer may have to take include adjusting premises, acquiring or modifying equipment, providing a reader or interpreter, modifying instructions and assessment procedures, adjusting hours of work or training, allowing time off for care, arranging training, providing supervision or other support, reallocating duties, assigning him/her to a different workplace, transferring him/her to fill an existing vacancy.[86] The Code makes further suggestions, eg permitting flexible working, allowing a period of disability leave, modifying disciplinary or grievance procedures, adjusting redundancy selection criteria and modifying performance-related pay arrangements.[87] Sometimes it may be necessary for an employer to take a combination of steps.[88]

15.35   There is no open-ended duty to make adjustments; the duty is owed in relation to a particular employee or job applicant whom the employer knows to have a disability and is likely to be disadvantaged.[89]

---

85 See commentary in (1996) 65 EOR 38.
86 DDA 1995 s18B(2); Code para 5.18.
87 Code para 5.20.
88 Code para 5.19.
89 DDA 1995 s4A(2).

A worker who fails to get a job or who is not promoted or trained or who suffers any other detriment as a result of the employer's failure to make reasonable adjustments may bring a discrimination case. Adjustments are not confined to those needed to enable a worker to function in his/her job; they include countering a disadvantage in terms and conditions.[90] Failure to make a reasonable adjustment can never be justified.[91] It is for the tribunal to decide, using an objective test, whether it thinks that an adjustment would have been reasonable. It is not simply a matter of what the employer reasonably thinks.[92] The duty exists only where it is the disabled person who is put at a disadvantage by workplace practices or features. There is no duty to make reasonable adjustments to enable a non-disabled worker to look after a disabled relative.[93]

15.36   The duty to make reasonable adjustments is unique to the DDA 1995 and central to its effectiveness. In the key case of *Archibald v Fife Council,*[94] the House of Lords said that the DDA 1995 is different from the SDA 1975 and the RRA 1976 in that employers are required to take steps to help disabled people, which they are not required to take for others: 'The duty to make adjustments may require the employer to treat a disabled person more favourably to remove the disadvantage which is attributable to the disability. This necessarily entails a measure of positive discrimination.' Factors which are particularly relevant in deciding whether it was reasonable for the employer to have made the necessary adjustment are the extent to which the adjustment would prevent the disadvantage, the practicability of the employer making the adjustment, the employer's financial and other resources, the availability of financial or other assistance to make the adjustment, and the cost and disruption entailed.[95] The effect of making the adjustment on other employees may also be relevant.[96] It is not necessary that a particular step is guaranteed to work. It is enough if there is a substantial possibility that it will work.[97]

90 *The Chief Constable of Lincolnshire Police v Weaver* UKEAT/0622/07.
91 When reading older cases, bear in mind that the law changed on this point on 1 October 2004.
92 *Smith v Churchills Stairlifts plc* [2006] IRLR 41, CA.
93 Though there must not be direct discrimination against such a worker on the ground that s/he has a disabled relative. See para 15.44. The SDA may also help regarding caring requirements, see para 11.80 onwards.
94 [2004] IRLR 652; 132 EOR 24; November 2004 *Legal Action* 19, HL.
95 DDA 1995 s18B(1); see Code paras 5.24–5.42.
96 Code, para 5.42; *The Chief Constable of Lincolnshire Police v Weaver* UKEAT/0622/07.
97 *H M Prison Service v Beart* [2003] IRLR 238, CA confirming the EAT's decision at (2002) 713 IDS Brief 5.

15.37   The Code of Practice clarifies further when the duty to make adjustments may arise. The following are a few examples of possible adjustments from the Code. Note that whether it is reasonable to expect the employer to make such adjustments will depend on all the facts of the case. Possibilities are:

- allowing the worker to work flexi-time to enable additional breaks to overcome fatigue or changing the worker's hours to fit with the availability of a carer or to avoid travel on public transport during rush hours;
- where no reasonable adjustment can keep the worker in his/her original post, transferring him/her to an available suitable alternative post with retraining and modified equipment;
- training other employees on conducting meetings in a way which enables a deaf worker to participate effectively;
- discounting periods of disability-related absence when selecting for redundancy;
- allowing a phased return to work with a gradual build up of hours.

An employer may be under a duty to make physical arrangements for the worker to go to the toilet or to accommodate an external carer to help the worker do so. However, this does not go as far as a duty actually to provide the carers to attend to a worker's personal needs.[98]

15.38   Failure to assess what is required to eliminate a disabled person's disadvantage is probably not in itself a breach of the duty to make reasonable adjustments.[99] But if an employer fails to consult, s/he seriously risks failing to take appropriate steps through ignorance. Depending on the facts, the duty may require moving the employee without competitive interview to a post at a slightly higher grade.[100] It will rarely be a reasonable adjustment to pay full sick pay which has otherwise run out in respect of disability-related absences, especially if the original sick pay was generous.[101] However, it may be a reasonable adjustment to pay a worker fully if s/he is off sick due to the employer's failure to make a reasonable adjustment which would enable him/her to return to

98 *Kenny v Hampshire Constabulary* [1999] IRLR 76, EAT.
99 *Mid Staffordshire General Hospitals NHS Trust v Cambridge* [2003] IRLR 566, EAT; *Southampton City College v Randall* [2006] IRLR 18, EAT; Code para 5.20, apparently superseded by *Tarbuck v Sainsbury's Supermarkets Ltd* [2006] IRLR 664; November 2006 *Legal Action* 15, EAT and *Spence v Intype Libra Ltd* UKEAT/0617/06.
100 *Archibald v Fife Council* [2004] IRLR 652; (2004) 132 EOR 24; November 2004 *Legal Action* 19, HL.
101 *O'Hanlon v Commissioners for H M Revenue and Customs* [2007] IRLR 404, CA.

work.[102] There is no absolute rule that disability-related absences must be disregarded for the purpose of totting-up and triggering a review process or dismissal under a sickness absence procedure.[103] To what extent disregarding disability-related absences for this and other purposes may be a reasonable adjustment depends on the facts of the particular case. If an employee needs redeployment as a result of his/her disability, s/he must be given equal priority (at least) with other categories of redeployee, eg redundant employees.[104] It would also be a reasonable adjustment before dismissing a worker to consult him/her regarding his/her continued prospects for employment.[105] It does not necessarily excuse an employer from making a reasonable adjustment that disciplinary action which may lead to dismissal is pending.[106] It depends on the difficulty of effecting the adjustment, the likelihood of dismissal and the fairness of the disciplinary process. Provision of awareness training for other employees in relation to the worker's disability could also be a reasonable adjustment.[107]

15.39   Research suggests that adjustments are not necessarily expensive. There may also be financial assistance available, eg grants under the Access to Work Scheme as well as advice and information from specialist bodies, eg the Royal National Institute for the Blind (RNIB) and the Disability Employment Advisers at the local Job-centre Plus offices. When considering the reasonableness of an adjustment, the cost of not making the adjustment may also be a relevant factor, eg it may be more expensive to medically retire a worker than make the needed adjustments to keep him/her in work. Special rules exist where an employer may need to alter premises which s/he occupies under a lease.[108] For examples of reasonable adjustments for over 24 different impairments and references to specialist sources of information, see *Proving disability and reasonable adjustments: a worker's guide to evidence under the DDA* by Tamara Lewis.[109]

102 *Nottinghamshire County Council v Meikle* [2004] IRLR 703; (2004) 132 EOR 27, CA.

103 *Royal Liverpool Children's NHS Trust v Dunsby* [2006] IRLR 351, EAT, although this case concerned whether disability-related discrimination was justified which, unlike the test for reasonable adjustment, requires a subjective test.

104 *Kent CC v Mingo* [2000] IRLR 90; (2000) 89 EOR 55; May 2000 *Legal Action* 12, EAT.

105 *Rothwell v Pelikan Hardcopy Scotland Ltd* [2006] IRLR 24, EAT.

106 *H M Prison Service v Beart* [2003] IRLR 238, CA.

107 *Simpson v West Lothian Council* (2005) 137 EOR 26, EAT; EATS/0049/04.

108 See Code Chapter 12.

109 Available at www.equalityhumanrigts.com/uploaded_files/dda_workers_guide_reasonable_adjustments.doc. And see paras 16.65–16.60.

15.40   In considering whether an employer has met any duty of reasonable adjustment, the ET must apply an objective test. Although it should scrutinise the employer's explanation, it must reach its own decision on what steps were reasonable and what was objectively justified. When running a case, a worker needs to make some suggestions as to what adjustments should have been made.[110]

15.41   The employer is under no duty to make reasonable adjustments if s/he does not know and cannot reasonably be expected to know that the worker or job applicant is disabled and does not know and cannot reasonably be expected to know that the worker is likely to be substantially disadvantaged as a result.[111] A worker does not have to tell an employer that s/he is disabled, but if s/he needs adjustments to be made, s/he would be wise to tell the employer clearly in writing that s/he is disabled and any adjustment s/he knows would help. Although an employer has a duty to make reasonable enquiries based on information given to him/her, there is no absolute onus on the employer to make every enquiry possible.[112] Early cases suggested, rather alarmingly, that employers do not always need to take a very proactive approach in finding out. However, there may now be higher expectations of employers. The Code says employers must do all they can reasonably be expected to do to find out if someone has a disability and is likely to need reasonable adjustments.[113] If information is given confidentially to the employer's occupational health department, the employer cannot be taken to have that knowledge.[114] Failure to make reasonable adjustments can, if sufficiently serious, amount to a fundamental breach of the implied term of trust and confidence, entitling an employee to resign and claim constructive dismissal.[115]

---

110 See para 16.65.

111 DDA 1995 s4A(2); see Code paras 5.12 and 5.16. *Eastern & Coastal Kent Primary Care Trust v Grey* UKEAT/0454/08; [2009] IRLR 429, EAT.

112 *Ridout v T C Group* [1998] IRLR 628; (1998) 82 EOR 46, EAT; *O'Neill v Symm & Co Ltd* [1998] IRLR 232; *Hanlon v University of Huddersfield* (1998) 619 IDS Brief 6, EAT.

113 Code para 5.12.

114 *Hartman v South Essex Mental Health & Community Care NHS Trust* [2005] IRLR 293, CA: although not a DDA 1995 case, establishes this principle, contrary to Code paras 5.15–5.16 and *L B Hammersmith & Fulham v Farnsworth* [2000] IRLR 691, EAT.

115 *Greenhof v Barnsley Metropolitan Borough Council* [2006] IRLR 98, EAT.

Direct discrimination

15.42   Section 3A(5) of DDA 1995 states:

> A person directly discriminates against a disabled person if, on the ground of the disabled person's disability, he treats the disabled person less favourably than he treats or would treat a person not having that particular disability ...

This concept is similar to that of direct discrimination under the RRA 1976. It is important to focus on the idea of a comparator, who the employer has treated or would treat differently in similar circumstances. Ideally (although this is not essential), the worker can find an actual comparator, eg a colleague without a disability or with a different disability. For example, a disabled worker is sacked because his/her total sickness absence amounts to three months, whereas a non-disabled worker who is off sick for three months is not sacked. This suggests the employer has treated the disabled worker less favourably purely because s/he is disabled, unless the employer can prove a credible reason for the different treatment, which is unrelated to disability. It is still possible, though harder, to prove direct discrimination where there is no comparator, eg no one else has been off sick for three months,[116] Stereotypical assumptions made about a worker because of his/her disability may also be direct discrimination, eg an assumption that a disabled person will have a poor sick record.[117]

15.43   The importance of direct discrimination is that there is no justification defence available to the employer. The scope of direct disability discrimination has not widely been tested because the definition of disability-related discrimination, as previously understood, was more helpful. Now this other definition has been rendered ineffective, as explained below, the scope of direct discrimination will become more important. The examples given in the Code for direct discrimination[118] assume a wide definition of direct discrimination which may not be confirmed by the tribunals.

15.44   Unlike some of the other discrimination strands,[119] the definition of direct disability discrimination refers only to discrimination on grounds

---

116 See paras 16.11–16.34 for types of evidence relevant to proving direct discrimination.

117 *Tudor v (1) Spen Corner Veterinary Centre Ltd (2) Tschimmel* (2006) 809 IDS Brief 19; (2006) 787 IRLB 4, ET is an interesting ET level example of a directly discriminatory assumption.

118 Code, paras 4.5–4.23.

119 Eg under the RRA 1976, but not under the SDA 1975. For 'strands' see Glossary at p744.

of the worker's own disability and not that of anyone else. This is contrary to the General Framework Directive.[119] It now remains to be seen whether the DDA 1995 can be interpreted to give effect to the Directive.[121]

Disability-related discrimination

15.45   Section 3A(1) of DDA 1995 states:

> A person discriminates against a disabled person if –
> (a) for a reason which relates to the disabled person's disability, he treats him less favourably than he treats or would treat others to whom that reason does not or would not apply; and
> (b) he cannot show that the treatment in question is justified.

This concept was intended to be different to that of direct discrimination. The key case of *Clark v Novacold*[122] established that the comparison was with how the employer would treat a worker to whom the disability-related reason did not apply, eg, someone who was able to climb stairs or see a computer screen.[123] It is useful to consider again the example where an employer dismisses a disabled worker because s/he has been off sick for 3 months. If the employer would have dismissed the worker for 3 months' absence, whether or not s/he was disabled, the employer has not directly discriminated against the disabled worker. However, if the reason for the disabled worker's absences was related to his/her disability, under the *Clark* interpretation, it would be 'disability-related discrimination'. Unlike with direct discrimination, employers had a defence of justification available to direct-disability discrimination.

15.46   Unfortunately, this understanding of the meaning of disability-related discrimination has been swept away by the House of Lords in *Mayor and Burgess of the London Borough of Lewisham v Malcolm*.[124] The practical effect of the *Malcolm* decision is that the meaning of disability-related discrimination is reduced to the far more limited scope of direct discrimination.

---

120 Directive 2000/78/EC. *Coleman v Attridge Law* C-303/06 ECJ; [2008] IRLR 722; *Legal Action* Nov 2008.

121 The ET in Coleman said that it can, but leave to appeal has been granted. *Coleman v (1) EBR Attridge Law LLP (formerly Attridge Law) (2) Law* 2303745/2005/ET.

122 [1999] IRLR 318, CA.

123 See Code paras 4.27–4.32.

124 [2008] UKHL 43; [2008] IRLR 700; November 2008 *Legal Action* 14. Applied to employment by *Child Support Agency (Dudley) v Truman* UKEAT/0293/08; [2009] IRLR 277, EAT.

15.47   The Equality Bill (see para 12.24) attempts to reinstate the old definition of disability-related discrimination as well as adding the concept
of indirect discrimination to the DDA 1995. It remains to be seen
whether these amendments will come into force. Until the law is
amended to correct difficulties arising from the *Malcolm* case, most
claims can be re-expressed as failure to make reasonable adjustment.
For example, if a worker is demoted because s/he cannot do his/her job,
which in turn is because a reasonable adjustment has not been made,
his/her claim could be for the failure to make the reasonable adjustment as opposed to for the demotion, and compensation would include
financial loss arising from the demotion. Similarly a disability-related
dismissal due to the worker's absence on sick leave could amount to a
failure to make reasonable adjustments if adjustments such as allowing a staged return to work or offering alternative employment would
have avoided the dismissal.[125] Note that simply 'not dismissing' is not
an adjustment in itself.[126] The great danger is that this reformulation
may lead to time-limit problems.[127] It may also be possible to refor-
mulate some disability-related discrimination claims as harassment. For
example, disciplinary action because a worker is unable to arrive on
time or perform to a certain level due to his/her disability could, if
conducted in an oppressive way, amount to unwanted conduct for a
reason relating to the worker's disability, which had the effect of creating
a humiliating environment. How far this can be argued is uncertain.
The scope of the specific definition of 'harassment' under the discrimination legislation has hardly been explored.[128] Another option is
to consider is whether direct discrimination can be proved.

Victimisation

15.48   Victimisation under DDA 1995 s55 is when a worker is punished or
treated differently as a result of complaining about discrimination or
raising the issue or doing any other 'protected act'. It is the equivalent to unlawful victimisation under the other discrimination legislation and the same case-law should apply to all the legislation.[129]

---

125 *Fareham College Corporation v Walters* UKEAT/0396/08; UKEAT/0076/09.
126 *Clark v Novacold* [1999] IRLR 318, CA; *Stockton on Tees Borough Council v Aylott*
     UKEAT/0401/08.
127 See para 21.24 regarding time-limits and appendix A, p722 for an illustration.
128 See comments at para 17.104.
129 See paras 13.85–13.96.

Public authorities' disability duty

15.49 Section 49A(1) of DDA 1995, imposes a disability equality duty on public authorities, which is further set out in the Disability Discrimination (Public Authorities) (Statutory Duties) Regulations 2005 and the Disability Discrimination (Public Authorities) (Statutory Duties) (Scotland) Regulations 2005.[130] The duty is similar to those under the RRA 1976 and SDA 1975. The general duty came into force on 5 December 2006. With limited exceptions, it applies to all public authorities including local authorities, NHS Trusts, schools and universities, government departments and the police. When carrying out their functions, including the employment function, authorities must have due regard to the need to eliminate discrimination and harassment of disabled people, and to promote equality of opportunity; the need to take steps to take account of disabled people's disabilities, even where that involves treating disabled people more favourably than other people; the need to promote positive attitudes towards disabled people; and to encourage participation by disabled people in public life.

15.50 This means authorities should consider their policies and working practices in relation to all aspects of the employment relationship. Many public authorities[131] including those listed above are also subject to specific duties which include publishing a Disability Equality Scheme by 4 December 2006 (except for some schools) and revising the Scheme every three years. In April 2007, the DRC published a list of 60 authorities which had failed to produce a Disability Equality Scheme by the initial deadline.[132] Disabled people must be involved in all aspects of the development of the scheme.[133] The Scheme should involve arrangements for assessing the impact of the authority's activities on disability equality, an action plan, and gathering and use of information. This entails monitoring and analysing recruitment, development and retention of disabled employees.[134] The Codes of Practice (see below) at sections 3.56–3.107 give useful guidance on how information should be gathered and reviewed. Publication of the Disability Equality Scheme should be the start of the process of meeting the general equality duty, not the end point.

130 SI No 2966 and SSI No 565 respectively.
131 For full list see SI No 2966 and SSI No 565, listed also in the Codes of Practice.
132 Public Bodies' Response to the Disability Equality Duty: An Audit of Compliance with the Requirement to Publish a Disability Equality Scheme at www.officefordisability.gov.uk/docs/ded_report_2007combined.pdf
133 SI No 2966 and SSI No 565, regs 2(2) and 2(3)(a), and expanded in the Codes.
134 SI No 2996 and SSI No 565, regs 2(3)(d)-(e).

15.51   The former Disability Rights Commission published two statutory Codes of Practice on the duty to promote disability equality, one for England and Wales and one for Scotland.[135] The Codes give practical guidance to public authorities on the general and specific duties. As with other statutory Codes, they do not create legal obligations in themselves, but must be taken into account by any court or tribunal where relevant. If you are running an individual case of disability discrimination against a public authority, it is worth checking to what extent the employer has complied with any relevant recommendations in the Codes.

135 These can be bought from The Stationery Office at www.tso.co.uk (tel: 0870 600 5522), and are on the EHRC website at www.equalityhumanrights.com/uploaded_files/PSD/ded_code_englandandwales.doc and www.equalityhumanrights.com/uploaded_files/PSD/ded_code_scotland.doc

Evidence in discrimination cases

Chapter 16: Key points

- Once the claimant proves a prima facie case, the burden of proof moves to the employer to prove s/he did not discriminate.
- Where appropriate, the employment tribunal must take account of the employer's failure to answer a discrimination question-naire or follow a relevant part of the discrimination Codes in deciding whether the employer has a case to answer.
- Employers rarely admit discrimination and often deny it, even to themselves.
- The employment tribunal can infer direct discrimination from a variety of factors, eg a pattern of incidents, racist remarks, inad-equate explanations, statistics, wholly unexplained unreasonable behaviour, and most importantly, actual or evidential compara-tors.
- The best evidence is an actual comparator, ie another worker of a different race, sex, religion, age, sexual orientation or without a dis-ability, who has been treated differently (ie better) in compara-ble circumstances.
- A hypothetical comparison can be made where there are no actual comparators or only evidential, ie loosely comparable, compara-tors.
- In indirect discrimination cases, it is important to produce sta-tistics and evidence showing the adverse impact of the provision, criterion or practice, in all relevant pools.
- In disability discrimination cases, medical evidence is often nec-essary to prove the worker has a disability under the Disability Discrimination Act 1995.
- Specialist websites are useful sources of information regarding the effect of a disability and possible reasonable adjustments.
- Medical evidence is usually necessary to claim compensation for injury to health (personal injury) in discrimination cases. See also paras 19.27–19.35 for necessary evidence on this.

The burden of proof in discrimination cases

16.1   The standard of proof in discrimination cases is the normal civil stan-dard, namely whether, on the balance of probabilities (ie 'more likely than not'), discrimination occurred. The employment tribunal (ET) should be reminded of this at the hearing.

16.2   As a result of various EU Directives, the burden of proof has partially transferred from the worker to the employer. This applies to cases under the Sex Discrimination Act (SDA) 1975; Disability Discrimination Act (DDA) 1995; the regulations relating to age, religious and sexual orientation discrimination; and the Race Relations Act (RRA) 1976 in respect of race, ethnic or national origins.[1] To paraphrase:

> ... where the claimant proves facts from which the ET could conclude in the absence of an adequate explanation that the employer committed an unlawful act, the ET must uphold the complaint unless the employer proves s/he did not commit that act.[2]

16.3 The Court of Appeal in *Igen Ltd and others v Wong; Chamberlin Solicitors and another v Emokpae; Brunel University v Webster*[3] set out guidance on the stages which an ET should follow. Although the guidelines were expressed in terms of a sex discrimination case, the same would apply to the other types of discrimination. The Court of Appeal said the ET must go through a two-stage process: At stage 1, the claimant must prove facts from which the ET *could* conclude, in the absence of an adequate explanation from the respondent (employer), that the respondent had discriminated against the claimant. In deciding whether the claimant has proved these facts, the ET can take account of the respondent's evidence. At stage 2, the respondent must prove s/he did not commit that discrimination. Although there are two stages, ETs will generally wish to hear all the evidence in one go, including the respondent's explanation, before deciding whether the requirements of each stage are satisfied.

16.4 The full guidelines are as follows:

1) Pursuant to SDA 1975 s63A, it is for the claimant who complains of sex discrimination to prove, on the balance of probabilities, facts from which the tribunal could conclude, in the absence of an adequate explanation, that the respondent has committed an act of discrimination against the claimant which is unlawful by virtue of Part II or which by virtue of section 41 or section 42 of the SDA 1975 is to be treated as having been committed against the claimant. These are referred to below as 'such facts'.

2) If the claimant does not prove such facts s/he will fail.

3) It is important to bear in mind in deciding whether the claimant has

---

1 Which should include colour – see para 13.23.

2 RRA 1976 s54A; SDA 1975 s63A; DDA 1995 s17A(1C); Employment Equality (Religion or Belief) Regulations 2003 SI No 1660 reg 29; Employment Equality (Sexual Orientation) Regulations 2003 SI No 1661 reg 29; Employment Equality (Age) Regulations 2006 SI No 1031 reg 37.

3 [2005] IRLR 258; (2005) 757 IRLB 4; 140 EOR 20; May 2005 *Legal Action*, CA.

proved such facts that it is unusual to find direct evidence of sex discrimination. Few employers would be prepared to admit such discrimination, even to themselves. In some cases the discrimination will not be an intention but merely based on the assumption that 's/he would not have fitted in'.

4) In deciding whether the claimant has proved such facts, it is important to remember that the outcome at this stage of the analysis by the tribunal will therefore usually depend on what inferences it is proper to draw from the primary facts found by the tribunal.

5) It is important to note the word 'could' in SDA 1975 s63A(2). At this stage the tribunal does not have to reach a definitive determination that such facts would lead it to the conclusion that there was an act of unlawful discrimination. At this stage a tribunal is looking at the primary facts before it to see what inferences of secondary fact could be drawn from them.

6) In considering what inferences or conclusions can be drawn from the primary facts, the tribunal must assume that there is no adequate explanation for those facts.

7) These inferences can include, in appropriate cases, any inferences that it is just and equitable to draw in accordance with section 74(2)(b) of the SDA 1975 from an evasive or equivocal reply to a questionnaire or any other questions that fall within section 74(2) of the SDA 1975.

8) Likewise, the tribunal must decide whether any provision of any relevant code of practice is relevant and, if so, take it into account in determining, such facts pursuant to section 56A(10) of the SDA 1975. This means that inferences may also be drawn from any failure to comply with any relevant code of practice.

9) Where the claimant has proved facts from which conclusions could be drawn that the respondent has treated the claimant less favourably on the ground of sex, then the burden of proof moves to the respondent.

10) It is then for the respondent to prove that s/he did not commit, or as the case may be, is not to be treated as having committed, that act.

11) To discharge that burden it is necessary for the respondent to prove, on the balance of probabilities, that the treatment was in no sense whatsoever on the grounds of sex, since 'no discrimination whatsoever' is compatible with the Burden of Proof Directive.[4]

12) That requires a tribunal to assess not merely whether the respon-

4 97/80/EC.

dent has proved an explanation for the facts from which such inferences can be drawn, but further that it is adequate to discharge the burden of proof on the balance of probabilities that sex was not a ground for the treatment in question.

13) Since the facts necessary to prove an explanation would normally be in the possession of the respondent, a tribunal would normally expect cogent evidence to discharge that burden of proof. In particular, the tribunal will need to examine carefully explanations for failure to deal with the questionnaire procedure and/or code of practice.

16.5   The residual situation under the RRA 1976 for discrimination not related to race, ethnic or national origins is that the burden of proof remains on the worker throughout. Guidance is in the older case of *King v Great Britain-China Centre*.[5] Essentially, the first four stages set out above can be followed. The divergence comes once the claimant has proved facts from which race discrimination could be inferred. The employer's explanation will still be important, but if the explanation is inadequate, it does not automatically follow that race discrimination is proved. Having said that, if the worker establishes such a prima facie case and there is no credible explanation from the employer, it is almost a matter of common sense that race discrimination is inferred and an ET should not be reluctant to grasp the nettle.[6]

16.6   The question under either burden of proof is, what facts are sufficient to prove a case in the absence of an adequate explanation from the employer (stage 1)? This is often referred to as proving a 'prima facie' case. Ideally, the worker can identify an actual comparator of a different race, sex, etc who has been treated differently or better in similar circumstances.[7] However, by way of an example, it may not be enough to shift the burden of proof for a black worker simply to show a white comparator was promoted to a post for which s/he had applied. It seems s/he would also have to show that s/he met the stated requirements of the post and was at least as well qualified as the white comparator.[8] Other examples where it may be legitimate for an ET to find a prima facie case so that the burden of proof shifts are:

- where a black woman is not selected for one of five posts following

5 [1991] IRLR 513, CA. Approved by the House of Lords in *Zafar v Glasgow CC* [1998] IRLR 36, HL.
6 *King v Great Britain-China Centre* [1991] IRLR 513; *Grewal v Walsall MBC* (1995) 514 IRLB 19, EAT.
7 See paras 13.41 and 16.19 onwards on comparators.
8 *Dresdner Kleinwort Wasserstein Ltd v Adebayo* [2005] IRLR 514, EAT.

a reorganisation in circumstances where all the successful candidates are white men with whom she is equally qualified. It may be different if a number of equally qualified white candidates have also been rejected;[9]

- where a woman is allocated only three projects out of over 200 following her gender reassignment, compared with a large allocation previously;[10]

- where an employer dismisses a black employee for an offence which has equally been committed by his/her white colleagues; has failed to investigate his/her allegation of race discrimination and has been evasive in replying to his/her questionnaire.[11]

Where there is no actual comparator, the worker needs to prove a prima facie case from other evidence,[12] eg a woman who is well-qualified for a job and meets the person specification, is not even interviewed. Further examples of the type of evidence which could lead to an inference of discrimination are set out in the rest of this chapter.

16.7   In deciding whether the claimant has proved a prima facie case, although the ET must disregard the employer's explanation, it can take into account other evidence from the employer which discredits or puts the claimant's facts into context, for example, evidence that the alleged discriminator treats all employees equally badly.[13]

16.8   An ET can conflate the two stages and go straight to the issue of whether the employer can explain the treatment complained of.[14] This is particularly appropriate where the facts are not in dispute and it is hard to separate the two stages because there is only a hypothetical comparator.

16.9   Some employers argue at the ET hearing that it is not necessary for them to provide any explanation because the worker has not even made out a prima facie case. However, discrimination cases are best looked at as a whole. The ET will usually want to hear the employer's evidence and explanation and the worker should have the opportu-

---

9 *Network Rail Infrastructure Ltd v Griffiths-Henry* [2006] IRLR 865; May 2007 *Legal Action*, EAT.

10 *EB v BA* [2006] IRLR 471; May 2007 *Legal Action*, CA.

11 *Dresdner Kleinwort Wasserstein Ltd v Adebayo* [2005] IRLR 514, EAT.

12 *Shamoon v Chief Constable of the RUC* [2003] IRLR 285, HL.

13 *Laing v Manchester City Council* [2006] IRLR 748; May 2007 *Legal Action* 14, EAT; *Madarassy v Nomura International plc* [2007] IRLR 246; May 2007 *Legal Action* 14, CA.

14 *Madarassy v Nomura International plc* [2007] IRLR 246; May 2007 *Legal Action* 14, CA; *Brown v London Borough of Croydon* [2007] IRLR 259, CA.

nity of questioning the employer's witnesses.[15] Very often a claimant may not be sure what lies behind something that concerns him/her and it can only be decided after evidence has been given.[16]

16.10   In indirect discrimination cases, the burden of proof is on the worker to show that there is a provision, criterion, practice, requirement or condition with discriminatory impact which disadvantages him/her and others of his/her sex, sexual orientation, marital or civil partnership status, race, religion or age. Once this is proved, if the employer seeks to claim that a discriminatory practice is justifiable, it is for the employer to prove it. If indirect race discrimination is proved in relation to nationality (or possibly colour), the burden is on the employer to show it was not intentional, so that damages may not be awarded.[17] Possibly due to a drafting error, it seems that the burden of proof is not reversed in victimisation cases under the Race Relations Act 1976.[18]

Helpful kinds of evidence in race and sex discrimination cases

Direct discrimination

16.11   In *King*,[19] the Court of Appeal said that as direct evidence of discrimination is rarely available, the necessary evidence will 'usually depend on what inferences it is proper to draw from the primary facts'. In other words, the ET must look for clues and draw conclusions. The concept of the ET drawing 'inferences' is central to running a discrimination case. Since such an indirect approach is necessary, a wide range of evidence may seem relevant. Choosing which evidence to use in a case is important. A good case can become discredited by taking weak points. Excessive and inconclusive evidence clouds the real issues and lengthens the hearing, increasing the risk of a costs award if the claim fails.

---

15 *JSV Oxford v DHSS* [1977] IRLR 225, EAT; *Laher v Hammersmith and Fulham LBC* (1995) 514 IRLB 4, EAT.

16 *The Court of Appeal approving the EAT in Balamoody v UKCC for Nursing, Midwifery and Health Visiting* [2002] IRLR 288, CA.

17 See para 13.23 regarding 'colour' and para 19.37 regarding compensation.

18 *Oyarce v Cheshire County Council and Equality and Human Rights Commission* [2008] EWCA Civ 434; [2008] IRLR 653; November 2008 *Legal Action* 13, CA.

19 *King v Great Britain-China Centre* [1991] IRLR 513, CA.

Other acts of discrimination

16.12   Every act of discrimination within the three months[20] prior to lodging an ET1[21] may form the basis of a claim. However, acts or indicators of discrimination falling outside the time limit may be mentioned in the claim purely as evidence in support of the discriminatory acts founding the claim.[22] For clarity, it should be stated which acts form the basis of the claim. Earlier alleged acts of discrimination will usually be helpful only if they took place relatively recently and relate to the same managers. Acts of discrimination or evidence of discriminatory attitudes occurring after the acts founding the claim are also admissible as supporting evidence of a tendency to discriminate.[23] Indicators from a time before or after a particular decision, eg not to promote, may indicate that an ostensibly fair decision was made on racial grounds.[24]

16.13   Where the worker mentions a number of out-of-time incidents as evidence supporting the claim, the ET should not look at each incident in isolation to decide if it was itself discriminatory. In such a case, it is important to draw the ET's attention to the Employment Appeal Tribunal's (EAT) guidance in *Qureshi v (1) Victoria University of Manchester (2) Brazier*, a case under the RRA 1976.[25] The ET should find the primary facts about all the incidents and then look at the totality of those facts, including the employer's explanations, in order to decide whether to infer the acts complained of in the ET1 were on racial grounds. To adopt a fragmented approach 'would inevitably have the effect of diminishing any eloquence that the cumulative effect of the primary facts might have on the issue of racial grounds'.

The employer's explanation

16.14   The employer's likely explanation for what has happened must be anticipated, as it will have to be discredited. If, for example, a worker has clearly committed a dismissable offence or is obviously the least qualified and experienced for an appointment or promotion, then it

---

20 Subject to any extension of time limits under the statutory dispute resolution procedures if they still apply.

21 Claim to employment tribunal.

22 *Eke v Commissioners of Customs and Excise* [1981] IRLR 334, EAT; *Qureshi v (1) Victoria University of Manchester (2) Brazier* EAT/484/95, approved and quoted at length in *Anya v University of Oxford* [2001] IRLR 377, CA.

23 *Chattopadhyay v Headmaster of Holloway School* [1981] IRLR 487, EAT.

24 *Anya v University of Oxford* [2001] IRLR 377, CA.

25 EAT/484/95. The guidance is set out in detail and approved by the Court of Appeal in *Anya v University of Oxford* [2001] IRLR 377.

will be extremely difficult to prove unlawful discrimination, even if it could be shown that the employer was generally prejudiced against workers of the same sex, sexual orientation, age, race or religion. The issue is less favourable treatment and if, for example, a man would similarly have been dismissed for the same offence, it is irrelevant that the employer was pleased to have the opportunity to dismiss a woman.

16.15 Where the alleged act of discrimination is dismissal, ETs often suspect that the case is an attempt to claim unfair dismissal for a worker without the necessary qualifying service. It must therefore be remembered that the ET is not interested in whether or not the dismissal was fair, but whether it was on the discriminatory ground.[26] Direct discrimination is not about unfair treatment, it is about different treatment. However, unreasonable conduct by an employer is not completely irrelevant. An inference of unlawful discrimination can be drawn from the employer's inability to explain unreasonable treatment of the worker.[27] Also, in some cases it can be argued that the dismissal was so patently unfair as to be irrational unless explained by hidden grounds. An ET should not assume without evidence that the employer behaves equally badly to employees of all races.[28] Even so, it is advisable for the claimant to prove that the employer is not normally unreasonable with other workers or to show some further evidence indicating unlawful discrimination.

16.16 Discrimination cases are more than usually dependent on the quality of the employer's evidence at the hearing, which makes their outcome hard to predict. Much will depend on how well the employer's explanation stands up to cross-examination. Any contradiction between different witnesses for the employer, or between the explanation given at the hearing and that in any contemporaneous document or in the defence or questionnaire reply, may well lead the ET to infer race, sex, religion, age or sexual orientation discrimination. However, it will not usually be enough simply to discredit the employer's version of events; some other indication of unlawful discrimination may be required.

16.17 When listening to the employer's explanation, the ET should not simply consider whether the witnesses sound credible or honest.

---

26 *Zafar v Glasgow CC* [1998] IRLR 36, HL.
27 *Bahl v The Law Society* [2004] IRLR 799, CA; *Igen Ltd and others v Wong; Chamberlin Solicitors and another v Emokpae; Brunel University v Webster* [2005] IRLR 258; (2005) 757 IRLB 4, CA; *Chief Constable of West Yorkshire v Vento* [2001] IRLR 124, EAT.
28 *Anya v University of Oxford* [2001] IRLR 377, CA.

A witness can be credible, honest – and mistaken.[29] The fact that the employer had a genuine belief that the claimant was guilty of misconduct does not mean s/he has discharged the burden of proving s/he did not discriminate. That would fail to appreciate the insidious nature of discrimination.[30] Witnesses do not generally advertise their prejudices.[31] Indeed, very little discrimination today is overt or even deliberate.[32] Witnesses can be unconsciously prejudiced.[33]

16.18   An ET should recognise that an employer may discriminate against one minority ethnic group even though s/he may not discriminate against another. The fact that a person is married to a black woman, for example, is not indicative of whether he would racially abuse an Irish worker.[34] There is no legal reason why a manager could not discriminate against a worker of the same racial group as him/herself, but it is a factor to be taken into account.[35] The ET will no doubt be wondering why such discrimination would have happened. However, it is quite possible to envisage that a black business-person may hire a white salesperson in order to appeal to white customers; or that a junior black manager may feel isolated and under pressure to be accepted within a white dominant organisation.

Comparative treatment

16.19   The central concept in direct discrimination is that of actual or hypothetical comparative treatment. The worker must prove s/he was less favourably treated than an actual or hypothetical comparator. Such comparison must be made where the relevant circumstances of the worker and the comparator are the same or not materially different.[36] For example, if a female police constable fails her probation on grounds of dishonesty, the comparator is an actual or hypothetical male police constable who has his probation confirmed, despite having committed

---

29 *Anya v University of Oxford* [2001] IRLR 377, CA. Applied to DDA 1995 cases by *Williams v YKK (UK) Ltd* (2003) 714 IRLB 12, EAT.

30 *Dresdner Kleinwort Wasserstein Ltd v Adebayo* [2005] IRLR 514, EAT.

31 *Glasgow CC v Zafar* [1998] IRLR 36, HL.

32 *Anya v University of Oxford* [2001] IRLR 377, CA.

33 *Swiggs v Nagarajan* [1999] IRLR 572 HL and para 13.50 above.

34 *Robson v Commissioners of the Inland Revenue* [1998] IRLR 186; (1998) 77 EOR 46, EAT.

35 *Graham v Barnet LBC* (2000) 647 IRLB 8, EAT.

36 RRA 1976 s3(4); SDA 1975 s5(3); Employment Equality (Religion and Belief) Regulations 2003 SI No 1660 reg 3(3); Employment Equality (Sexual Orientation) Regulations 2003 SI No 1661 reg 3(2); Employment Equality (Age) Regulations 2006 SI No 1031 reg 3(2).

the same kind of dishonesty. Obviously if an actual worker of a different sex, sexual orientation, race, religion or age can be identified who, in similar circumstances, was treated more favourably, then the case will be much stronger. It then becomes a question of whether the employer can provide a credible innocent explanation for the different treatment.

16.20   In most cases it is impossible to find a real life comparator where all the relevant circumstances are the same, so the ET must consider how a hypothetical comparator would have been treated.[37] Indeed, even where the worker has real comparators, it is safest also to claim that, in the alternative, s/he was less favourably treated than a hypothetical comparator would have been. A hypothetical comparator is simply someone who is the same as the worker in all relevant ways except that s/he is of a different race, sex, age, etc. To decide how a hypothetical comparator would have been treated, it is necessary to look at all the evidence pointing to race, sex, age, etc discrimination, eg dubious remarks, inadequate explanations and general statistics. In particular, the ET can look at how the employer has treated others in loosely similar but not identical circumstances.[38] As long as the ET understands that these comparisons are not being put forward as actual comparators, it is perfectly legitimate to use them as 'building blocks' in constructing how the hypothetical identical comparator would have been treated.[39] Often the term used for these less precise comparators is 'evidential comparators'.[40] Using the example above, it would be useful to look at a male police constable who had passed his probation when there was evidence that he was useless at the job. Although incapability is not the same as dishonesty, it would be one indicator of whether the employer is generally lenient towards men as opposed to women.

16.21   Where an actual comparator or even a loosely similar comparator is found, try to anticipate the employer's explanation for treating him/her better than the worker. For example, the explanation could be differences in:

- relevant experience;

37 *Balamoody v UKCC for Nursing, Midwifery and Health Visiting* [2002] IRLR 288, CA; *Chief Constable of West Yorkshire v Vento* [2001] IRLR 124, EAT; *Shamoon v Chief Constable of the RUC* [2003] IRLR 285, HL.
38 *Chief Constable of West Yorkshire v Vento* [2001] IRLR 124, EAT; *Shamoon v Chief Constable of the RUC* [2003] IRLR 285, HL.
39 *Chief Constable of West Yorkshire v Vento* [2001] IRLR 124, EAT.
40 *Shamoon v Chief Constable of the RUC* [2003] IRLR 285, HL.

- relevant qualifications;
- prior disciplinary record;
- status;
- whether an internal or external candidate for a post.

16.22   In a recruitment case, if a job centre or recruitment agency was involved, it should be asked what job description the employer supplied. Where someone fails to gain a post after interview, despite having equal or better qualifications and experience than the person appointed, it is common for the employer to say that the successful candidate interviewed better. This is extremely difficult to contradict. All notes made by the interview panel in relation to each candidate during or after the interviews should be obtained. Also, while the interview is still fresh in his/her mind, the worker should note down the questions and answers as near verbatim as possible.

16.23   It may be relevant to know how the employer generally treats male and female workers or workers from different racial groups, in circumstances other than those of the alleged discriminatory act. It may be that an employer generally speaks more politely to white workers than to black workers, or that black workers are penalised for arriving late to work whereas white workers are not. In *West Midlands Passenger Transport Executive v Singh*,[41] the Court of Appeal said that evidence of discriminatory treatment against a group may be more indicative of unlawful discrimination than previous treatment of the particular worker, which may be due to personal factors other than discrimination. Sometimes it is appropriate, as in *Singh*, to request statistics showing comparative treatment of groups of workers.

16.24   It may also be helpful to show the worker has been treated differently from an expected norm, eg the employers have not followed their own written disciplinary or grievance procedure on this occasion.

Statistics

16.25   The *Singh* case established the potential importance of statistical evidence in cases of direct discrimination. The Court of Appeal said:

> Direct discrimination involves that an individual is not treated on his merits but receives unfavourable treatment because he is a member of a group. Statistical evidence may establish a discernible pattern in the treatment of a particular group.[42]

41 [1988] IRLR 186, CA.
42 *West Midlands Passenger Transport Executive v Singh* [1988] IRLR 186, CA at 188.

Mr Singh claimed racial discrimination in his failure to gain promotion to the post of senior inspector. The court said that if statistics revealed a regular failure of members of a certain group to gain promotion to certain jobs and an under-representation in such jobs, it may give rise to an inference of discrimination against members of the group.

16.26   Statistics can be obtained in various ways, eg through a questionnaire (see para 21.2) or by way of additional information or disclosure (see paras 21.42–21.48). If statistical evidence is not available because, for example, an employer has not monitored the workforce and applications for employment and promotion, the ET could be invited to draw an adverse inference from this fact. Unfortunately, although monitoring is recommended by the Race Relations Code of Practice and encouraged by the higher courts,[43] most ETs will not draw an inference from failure to monitor. This may change in respect of public authorities who are now obliged to monitor under the public sector race duty and should also be doing so as good practice under the gender duty.[44]

Failure to follow the Codes of Practice

16.27   The race, sex and disability Codes of Practice are admissible in evidence and an ET must take into account relevant provisions of the Codes in determining any question in the proceedings.[45] The Codes make recommendations on good practice in recruitment and promotion procedures. In cases concerning discrimination in these areas, the employer's practices and procedures should be examined to see whether the guidelines of the Codes have been followed. Questions in the questionnaire (see para 21.2) and requests for additional information and disclosure (see paras 21.42–21.48) should be aimed at establishing what procedures were adopted and these will be a matter for cross-examination at the hearing.

16.28   The Commission for Racial Equality's Code of Practice encourages record-keeping by employers, and para 4.70 of the Code recommends that in any disciplinary matter, the employer should consider the possible effect on a worker's behaviour of racial abuse or other racial provocation. Furthermore, any complaint of racial discrimination by a

43 Monitoring was approved by the Court of Appeal in *Singh* [1988] IRLR 186, CA and by the EAT in *Carrington v Helix Lighting* [1990] IRLR 6, EAT.

44 See paras 13.97–13.104.

45 RRA 1976 s47(10), SDA 1975 s56A(10) and DDA 1995 s53(8); *Igen Ltd and others v Wong; Chamberlin Solicitors and another v Emokpae; Brunel University v Webster* [2005] IRLR 258; (2005) 757 IRLB 4; (2005) 140 EOR 20; May 2005 *Legal Action* 25, CA; *Noone v North West Thames Regional Health Authority* [1988] IRLR 195, CA.

worker should not be treated lightly. The ET's attention should be drawn to those provisions, where the worker has complained of discrimination at some stage during his/her employment, including the final disciplinary hearing, and has been ignored.

16.29   An ET should not infer that discrimination has occurred purely from an employer's failure to follow his/her own equal opportunities policy,[46] but poor practice in recruitment procedures is likely to be a significant factor. Where relevant, it is also worth referring to the EC Code on Sexual Harassment for its definition, recommendations on preventative action and action in response to a complaint.[47]

Racist remarks/overt indications of prejudice

16.30   Although prejudice need not be present to prove discrimination,[48] it strengthens the case if it is demonstrably present. Difficulties often arise because it is only the worker's word and s/he can be accused of making up such remarks while giving evidence. It is therefore important that any crucial remarks are mentioned in the ET1 form from the start.

16.31   Another difficulty is that certain words, 'jokes' or actions may not be taken as indicative of a racist, sexist or ageist, etc attitude by the ET. Even if they are, a tribunal will not automatically conclude that prejudiced attitudes lead to discriminatory treatment. In an appointment or promotion case, an employer's comment that someone 'who would fit in' was wanted should be regarded as a danger signal.[49] In certain cases, racist or similar comments may themselves constitute one of the acts of discrimination basing the claim.[50]

16.32   Things said by an employer in a 'without prejudice' negotiation can sometimes be very revealing. Normally without prejudice discussions are kept off the record from the ET,[51] but the rule will not apply if 'unambiguous impropriety' took place, eg racist remarks were made during the conversation.[52]

46 *Qureshi v Newham LBC* [1991] IRLR 264, EAT.

47 *Grimaldi v Fonds des Maladies Professionelles* [1990] IRLR 400, ECJ; *Wadman v Carpenter Farrer Partnership* [1993] IRLR 374, EAT.

48 See para 13.47.

49 *Baker v Cornwall CC* [1990] IRLR 194, CA at 198; *King v The Great Britain-China Centre* [1991] IRLR 513, CA.

50 Provided they amount to a detriment or harassment. See paras 13.35 and 17.89 onwards.

51 See paras 9.19–9.20.

52 On both points, see *BNP Paribas v Mezzotero* [2004] IRLR 508; November 2004 *Legal Action* 16, EAT.

Previous complaints of discrimination

16.33 Recorded previous complaints of unlawful discrimination against relevant managers should constitute useful evidence, particularly if the employer has failed to investigate such allegations (see para 16.28). There are many and obvious reasons why a worker may not complain of discrimination while still employed. The EC Code specifically addresses this issue with regard to sexual harassment. Nevertheless, a worker who alleges that discrimination has been occurring for some time is likely to be heavily cross-examined on why s/he did not complain at the time, the implication being that s/he has made it up after the event. The worker should be prepared to answer this question at the hearing. For the same reason, even if discrimination has not previously been mentioned, it is advisable for a worker to raise it at any dismissal hearing.

16.34 Where a worker during employment seeks advice in respect of discrimination, legal proceedings will usually be regarded as a last resort. However, s/he should be advised of the risks of not recording the allegation in writing, should some issue of discrimination ultimately end up in the ET. If appropriate, the employer's attention could be expressly drawn to the prohibition on victimisation in the legislation. If the statutory dispute resolution procedures still apply, the worker will have to bring a grievance first in any event, though this only applies to discrimination other than dismissal. The worker also risks having compensation reduced if s/he wins a later discrimination case if s/he unreasonably did not bring a grievance first.[53]

Pregnancy

16.35 Useful evidence to prove pregnancy discrimination includes remarks indicating the employer or relevant manager is unhappy about the pregnancy; a generally unhelpful attitude to time off for antenatal care or discussions about maternity leave and return; less favourable treatment of the woman compared with other staff; different treatment of the woman compared with how she was treated on similar issues before she became pregnant; a generally unfavourable environment in the workplace or in the woman's own department towards pregnant women or mothers of young children. The Equal Opportunities Commission's (EOC) formal investigation into pregnancy discrimination is useful evidence of a wider pattern.[54]

53 See chapter 22.
54 See para 11.1 above.

Indirect discrimination

Proving others of the worker's group are disadvantaged

16.36   Traditionally, statistical evidence is necessary in an indirect discrimination case to prove the provision, criterion or practice, requirement or condition particularly disadvantages those of a specific sex, sexual orientation, race, religion or age. Changes in the wording of the definition of indirect discrimination in recent years mean that other types of evidence to prove disadvantage may sometimes be acceptable, eg expert evidence and research reports. Nevertheless, where possible, it is advisable still to present statistical evidence, as alternative methods may be less convincing and are little tested in the courts.[55] The ET can take account of its own knowledge and experience in determining whether a provision, criterion, practice, requirement or condition has disparate impact[56] and may do so, particularly as to whether women need to work part-time due to childcare. On the other hand, an ET may unexpectedly insist on evidential proof of apparently obvious facts. It is well-established that determining the correct pool for comparison of the impact on people of different groups is a question of fact for the ET.

16.37   The ET may choose a pool not anticipated by the worker and catch him/her unprepared. It may be possible to avoid this difficulty by agreeing a pool with the employer prior to the hearing, by holding a pre-hearing review on the point or even adjourning the main hearing once the pool is decided if the necessary statistics are not available. However, it is wise to prepare statistics on all the potential pools. Clearly some pools will be more helpful than others, and less helpful pools which the ET might choose should therefore be anticipated with, if possible, explanations as to why they are misleading or irrelevant, for example, because they incorporate discrimination.

Where to find statistics or other evidence on impact

16.38   As stated above, statistics need to be gathered to show adverse impact within every likely pool for comparison. The statistics must relate to those within and those outside the relevant racial, religious, age, gender or sexual orientation group and within the possible pools. One of the difficulties with indirect discrimination cases is that statistics are rarely available to meet the exact purpose. Where directly relevant statistics

---

55 See paras 13.70–13.77.
56 *Briggs v North Eastern Education and Library Board* [1990] IRLR 181, NICA.

are not available, other statistics or evidence, from which the relevant facts may be inferred, should be used.

16.39   Statistics on any workplace pool can be obtained through the questionnaire procedure, eg by asking how many of the existing workforce, by reference to sex and marital status, work part-time or full-time and how many women left after having children.

16.40   Statistics and evidence can be obtained from various sources, eg the Low Pay Commission, the Child Poverty Action Group, Stonewall, the Muslim Council, the Board of Deputies, the Trades Union Congress (TUC), trade unions and university research departments, libraries, the Joint Council for the Welfare of Immigrants and community groups. The Equality and Human Rights Commission (EHRC) will advise on available reports and statistical sources and has publications on its website.[57] The EOC used to publish a useful annual booklet on its website, *Facts about Women and Men in Great Britain.*[58] A series of spreadsheets giving detailed historical employment statistics by reference to sex is linked to the *Labour Market Statistics First Release Historical Supplement.*[59] The website for the Office for National Statistics is also useful, though bewildering.[60] The former Department of Employment's *Gazette* used to summarise workforce surveys and is available in most libraries, as are the Labour Force Surveys and General Household Surveys which contain detailed statistics on patterns of full-time and part-time work by single and married men and women.[61] The Learning and Skills Council certainly used to produce Key Statistics booklets on the workforce and unemployment, using information from a wide range of data sources.[62] For evidence of the difficulty of getting childcare on either side of the working day, see two research reports for the Joseph Rowntree Foundation: *Around the clock: childcare services at atypical times* and *Combining self-employment and family life.*[63] Research reports or articles in specialist publications such as the *Nursing Times* on the position of black workers in the NHS, are useful for direct and indirect discrimination cases. The Equal Opportunities Review (EOR) and IDS Diversity at Work[64] are excellent reference sources with their own research features and detailed listings of recently published reports. Local authority social services should have statistics on childcare

57 www.equalityhumanrights.com
58 The 2006 edition is available at www.equalbutdifferent.org.uk/pdfs/men%20 and%20women.pdf
59 Available at www.statistics.gov.uk/OnlineProducts/LMS_FR_HS.asp#summary
60 At www.statistics.gov.uk. See also its annual 'Social Trends' 2005 edn: www.statistics.gov.uk/downloads/theme_social/social_trends35/social_trends_35.pdf
61 The regional trends survey may show large regional variations in patterns of working women.
62 Website: www.lsc.gov.uk
63 Summary available free at www.jrf.org.uk/node/530

facilities and take-up. In view of the extended right to request flexible working (para 11.101), Carers UK has information and statistics regarding carers on its website, including research into the general profile of caring, and employment and caring.[65] It estimates 58 per cent of carers are women. It also has *Facts about working carers: evidence from the 2001 census for England and Wales.*[66] Statistics from the 2001 census indicate the age group in which the largest proportion of people provide care is the 50s and that 24.6 per cent of women compared with 17.9 per cent of men in that age group are carers.[67] There have been numerous research reports in relation to age discrimination (direct and indirect discrimination issues). Many of these are listed in the bibliography to Help the Aged's guide: *How to recognise cases of age discrimination: An Adviser's Toolkit.*[68] or are available on the website of the Age and Employment Network.[69]

16.41   Where there is no statistical or research evidence precisely on the point required, verbal evidence from 'experts' or respected members of the community may be useful.

Justifiability

16.42 The greater the discriminatory effect, the better the justification the employer needs. Although the onus is on the employer to justify the provision, criterion or practice, it is still useful for the worker to produce evidence of the extent of its discriminatory effect. It will also be useful if the worker is able to put forward any reasonable alternative ways with less discriminatory effects by which the employer could have achieved his/her objectives.

16.43   The Codes of Practice may provide guidance on what should be considered unjustifiable. For example, under para 4.20 of the CRE Code, employers should consider whether it is reasonably practicable to adapt recruitment arrangements to enable workers to meet their cultural and religious needs.

---

64 Published by Michael Rubenstein Publishing, tel: 0844 800 1863 and Incomes Data Services Ltd, tel: 020 7449 1107 respectively.

65 Home page: www.carersuk.org; research at www.carersuk.org/Policyandpractice/Research

66 At www.carersuk.org/Newsandcampaigns/makeWORKwork/Factsaboutworkingcarers

67 At www.statistics.gov.uk search 'carers' or at
www.statistics.gov.uk/CCI/nugget.asp?ID=347&Pos=&ColRank=1&Rank=358

68 See bibliography, appendix F, for details of availability.

69 At www.taen.org.uk

Victimisation

16.44 The worker first needs to prove that the 'protected act' took place. This may be difficult if his/her complaint of discrimination was made verbally. In order to show the worker was victimised as a result, it is useful to prove that the employer's behaviour towards the worker was different before and after doing the protected act. It is worth doing a chronology of the key facts. The timing of events is particularly revealing in victimisation cases. It is also helpful to prove the employer has treated the worker less favourably than s/he has treated other workers (who have not made allegations of discrimination) in similar circumstances. This is the same concept of comparators as for direct discrimination cases.[70]

Failure to respond to the questionnaire

16.45 Under RRA 1976 s65(2)(b), SDA 1975 s74(2)(b), Employment Equality (Sexual Orientation) Regulations 2003[71] reg 33(2)(b); Employment Equality (Religion or Belief) Regulations 2003[72] reg 33(2)(b) and Employment Equality (Age) Regulations 2006[73] reg 41(2)(b), if the employer 'deliberately and without reasonable excuse' fails to answer the questionnaire within eight weeks or answers in a way that is 'evasive or equivocal', the ET may draw an inference that the employer committed an unlawful act of discrimination.[74] The higher courts have encouraged both the use of the questionnaire procedure[75] and ETs to draw inferences from vague or unsatisfactory replies.[76] It should be borne in mind when drafting the questionnaire that it should not be so onerous that an employer has a 'reasonable excuse' for not answering.[77] Failure to answer a questionnaire does not automatically lead to an inference that discrimination has occurred without any other evidence. Rather controversially, the EAT has recently suggested that

---

70 See para 16.19 onwards.

71 SI No 1661.

72 SI No 1660.

73 SI No 1031.

74 *King v Great Britain-China Centre* [1991] IRLR 513; [1992] ICR 516, CA.

75 *Carrington v Helix Lighting* [1990] IRLR 6.

76 *Igen Ltd and others v Wong; Chamberlin Solicitors and another v Emokpae; Brunel University v Webster* [2005] IRLR 258; (2005) 757 IRLB 4; (2005) 140 EOR 20; May 2005 *Legal Action* 25, CA; *Berry v The Bethlem & Maudsley NHS Trust; Hinks v Riva Systems and Lumsden* (1997) 31 EOR DCLD 1, EAT.

failure to answer the questionnaire is only relevant to the extent that it potentially sheds light on the mental processes of the alleged discriminator.[78] This seems to go too far and may not be consistent with the view of the Court of Appeal in *Igen Ltd v Wong*.[79] An inference can also be drawn under the same sections from an evasive or equivocal reply to any direct questions put in writing in any other place, eg an ordinary letter, by the worker to his/her employer, or by the employer's complete failure to reply, or any contradiction between the employer's written case in the tribunal response and in additional information and the witnesses' oral evidence.[80]

Witnesses

16.46   The principles are the same as in other ET cases. However, there is little doubt that independent witnesses in discrimination cases (particularly if they are of a different sex, sexual orientation, age, race or religion to the worker) can vastly increase the chances of success. If witnesses are called on any point of detail, the adviser should check what they will say if asked whether they believe unlawful discrimination has taken place. Witnesses may not understand what amounts to discrimination under the law. Although it is only a matter of their opinion, it will harm the worker's case if his/her witnesses consider that discrimination has not occurred.

Helpful kinds of evidence in disability discrimination cases

16.47   The Code of Practice under the DDA 1995 is admissible in evidence and under DDA 1995 s53(6) an ET must take into account any relevant provision.[81] The Guidance relating to the definition of disability must also be taken into account.[82] Chapter 15 refers in detail to the provisions of the Code and Guidance.

---

77 See para 21.2 onwards for more details on the questionnaire procedure.

78 *D'Silva v NATFHE and others* UKEAT/0384/07; [2008] IRLR 412, EAT.

79 See n75. See observations in Central London Law Centre's questionnaire guides, listed in bibliography, appendix F.

80 *Dattani v Chief Constable of West Mercia Police* [2005] IRLR 327, EAT.

81 *Goodwin v The Patent Office* [1999] IRLR 4, EAT; *Clark v TDG Ltd (trading as Novacold)* [1999] IRLR 318; (1999) 85 EOR 46, CA.

82 DDA 1995 s3(3); *Goodwin v The Patent Office* [1999] IRLR 4, EAT.

The DDA 1995 questionnaire procedure

16.48 The questionnaire procedure under the DDA 1995 is basically the same as under the SDA 1975 and RRA 1976. Under DDA 1995 s56(3)(b) if the employer 'deliberately and without reasonable excuse' fails to answer the questionnaire within a reasonable time or answers in a way that is 'evasive or equivocal', the ET may draw an inference that the employer committed an unlawful act of discrimination.

Victimisation

16.49 Evidence relating to victimisation will be similar to that necessary under the SDA 1975 and RRA 1976 (see para 16.44 above).

Proving the disability

16.50 In most cases, the worker will need to prove that s/he has a disability as defined by the DDA 1995. The employer's first response in defending a case is almost always to deny the worker has a disability within the meaning of the Act and to require him/her to prove it. Even if the employer concedes the worker has a disability, some level of evidence will be necessary to satisfy the ET. For the law on each stage of the definition, see paras 15.12–15.27. See also the checklist on the definition of disability in appendix A. The following is a guide to gathering evidence by reference to the stages of the definition, bearing in mind the developing case-law.

Mental impairment

16.51 Since December 2005 onwards, it has no longer been necessary to prove that a mental illness is clinically well-recognised. Nevertheless, it is still important to get medical evidence of the impairment and its effects, and it is usually helpful (though no longer essential) if a well-recognised illness can be identified. Workers and their GPs tend to use words like 'anxiety', 'stress' and 'nervous debility'. These are the names of symptoms, but not necessarily of impairments in themselves. Simply producing copies of medical certificates using such vague terms at the ET will not be enough. Note also that the ET must not try to judge for itself whether the worker has a mental illness from the way s/he gives evidence on the day.[83] Evidence of mental impair-

---

83 *Morgan v Staffordshire University* [2002] IRLR 190, EAT.

ment apart from illness, eg learning difficulties, can be provided by an educational psychologist or other suitable expert, not only by doctors.[84]

Substantial adverse effect on ability to carry out day-to-day activities

16.52   The worker must prove the impairment has a substantial adverse effect on his/her ability to carry out normal day-to-day activities. Remember this means 'normal' activities and not hobbies. Specialist work activities may or may not be covered, so it is best to get as many examples as possible on activities in and outside work. A good starting point is to go through paras D20–D27 of the Guidance with the worker, discussing the examples listed under each heading. Do not stop with those examples. They should give the worker and the adviser ideas for other examples. Although it is an undesirably negative approach, the more examples of things the worker cannot do, the easier it is to prove disability. Explain to the worker that unfortunately this is how the law works.

16.53   It is not simply a question of what the worker cannot do at all. There is also an adverse effect if s/he can only do certain activities with difficulty, eg in pain, extremely slowly, with great tiredness, or in an unusual way. For example, a worker may be able to walk up ten steps, but only if s/he pauses for breath at each step. Or a worker may be able to carry a bag, but only if it is on his/her shoulder rather than in his/her hand.

16.54   There is a risk that a tribunal will reach the wrong conclusions regarding the effects of a worker's disability from observing the way s/he looks or behaves at the hearing. An ET should certainly be very cautious about substituting its observations for what is stated in the report of a jointly-instructed expert.[85] It is important to anticipate and ask the worker to explain any potentially misleading impressions, eg the fact that the worker sits for a long period while giving evidence, does not mean that s/he is not in pain, or s/he may have taken pain-killers.

16.55   Do not make assumptions that because the worker has a well-known disability, the ET will accept s/he is disabled or assume that s/he cannot do certain activities. Most disabilities have a huge range of effects on the individual, from extremely mild to very severe. Each worker must be consulted as an individual. However, it does help if the

---

84 *Dunham v Ashford Windows* [2005] IRLR 608, EAT.
85 *Mahon v Accuread Ltd* UKEAT/0081/08.

adviser has some knowledge, to ask the right questions. Introductory knowledge can often be gained from the many excellent websites of specialist organisations. Such organisations can be found by doing an internet search, eg using an internet search engine, typing in the name of the disability 'AND organisation'. See also Central London Law Centre's *Proving disability and reasonable adjustments: A worker's guide to evidence under the DDA.*[86]

16.56   Remember that a worker is covered whose symptoms are controlled by medication or other medical treatment if, apart from that treatment, his/her impairment would have substantial adverse effects.[87] It is particularly important to get clear medical evidence to prove such 'deduced' effects. It is not enough for the worker to make his/her own speculation in the ET as to what would happen if the treatment stopped.[88]

Progressive conditions

16.57   A worker with a progressive condition is covered as soon as there are any symptoms, provided s/he can prove it is more likely than not that s/he will go on to develop a substantial adverse effect.[89] It is not enough for the worker simply to prove s/he has a progressive condition such as rheumatoid arthritis. Such a condition will not necessarily become serious for every individual. The best way to prove it is likely to become serious is to get a medical report on the worker's own condition. This can be difficult, especially if using the doctors treating him/her, as they may not want to be negative. In some cases, it will be enough to provide statistical evidence showing how the condition in question usually develops. But it is risky to rely on this alone without reference to the worker's own particular circumstances.

Medical evidence

16.58   It has become unusual now to run a DDA 1995 case without the use of medical evidence. This does make the procedure more expensive and time-consuming. See para 20.111 below for the position on getting the cost of a report covered by the ET. Usually it is sufficient to produce a report, without bringing the doctor to the ET hearing. However, if

---

86 Available on the EHRC website. Details in Bibliography, appendix F.

87 See para 15.24.

88 *Woodrup v Southwark LBC* [2003] IRLR 111, CA.

89 See para 15.25.

there is a difference of opinion between doctors separately instructed by the worker and the employer, it may be a disadvantage not to have oral evidence. Where a jointly-instructed expert's report has confirmed the worker's symptoms, the worker should not be cross-examined at the hearing on the basis that s/he is exaggerating his/her symptoms without forewarning, so s/he has a chance to ask the expert to attend.[90]

16.59   The EAT has set out guidelines for getting medical evidence in *De Keyser Ltd v Wilson*.[91] The key points are:

- it is preferable for an expert to be jointly instructed by the employer and worker;
- if one side cannot afford to share the cost of a joint expert, so that the other side goes ahead and instructs their own expert, it is still a good idea if both sides agree the terms of instruction;
- the letter instructing an expert should set out in detail the questions which s/he should answer and avoid partisanship;
- the ET may set a timetable for instructing experts and getting their reports (unfortunately this is often unrealistic as doctors are busy people and cannot be forced to keep to deadlines);
- if each side instructs their own expert, the experts should be encouraged to meet on an off-the-record basis and agree as many issues as possible. (It is rather unrealistic to expect this to happen, both in terms of the experts' time and willingness, and the costs to the parties.)

16.60   Although the EAT sets an ideal of a jointly instructed expert, it is still very common for each side to call their own expert. This is especially so where the worker wants to get a medical report from the GP or specialist who has been treating him/her. It is a matter of judgement on each case which is the most appropriate course.

16.61   When asking a doctor to provide a report, remember that the letter of instructions to the doctor may have to be disclosed to the employer and the ET. Make sure the letter does not appear biased. Bearing in mind what the law requires to be proved, ask the doctor a series of precise questions as to his/her medical assessment.

A doctor can only advise on medical aspects of a case, not on an interpretation of the law.[92] Ask the doctor to state on what basis s/he knows the worker and is aware of his/her condition. Enclose a written authority from the worker to write the report. It will normally also be necessary to agree to pay the doctor's reasonable costs, but check what

90 *Mahon v Accuread Lt*d UKEAT/0081/08.
91 [2001] IRLR 324.
92 *Vicary v British Telecommunications plc* [1999] IRLR 680, EAT.

these are first. A sample letter to a doctor is in appendix A at p716.

16.62 The worker needs to decide whether to get a report from his/her GP or specialist consultant or from an independent specialist who s/he has not met before. In the latter case, the independent specialist could be jointly instructed (see para 16.60 above). The worker's choice depends partly on the nature of the evidence and the seriousness of the case. It is usually tempting for workers to use their own doctors or specialists, but this is not always a good idea. A GP can confirm the history of his/her treatment of the worker and what s/he was told at the time, but may not have specialist knowledge of the particular condition, and may not be seen as independent. Sometimes workers' own doctors are reluctant to give bad news, and they create a falsely optimistic (or self-protective) report, which does not help workers prove their true situation. They may also rely on sketchy and out-of-date notes. On the other hand, a worker's own doctor or specialist obviously has credibility from having seen the worker over a period of time and it may be unnecessary for the worker to attend a special examination.

16.63 If the worker produces a report, it is quite likely the employer will in turn want to get his/her own report. This will mean the worker has to attend an examination with a possibly hostile doctor. If there is a case management discussion and no expert has yet been instructed, the ET may well follow the *De Keyser* guidelines and suggest the employer and worker jointly instruct an independent doctor and share the expense. If this happens, make sure the selection of the doctor is not made solely by the employer, that the doctor has not had other dealings with the employer, and that the doctor's instructions are in neutral terms and come equally from each party.

16.64 Finding an independent medical expert can be difficult. A consultant with the relevant speciality can usually be found by asking the GP or one of the teaching hospitals, but this may not be the best route. The expert must also be willing and able (ideally with experience) to write a suitable report, reliable in terms of timescale, and not too expensive. There are some directories of experts, eg 'The Expert Witness Directory', which has a website listing experts by field of expertise.[93]

Reasonable adjustments

16.65 It is best to take a methodical approach when trying to persuade a tribunal that the employer has failed to make reasonable adjustments.

93 At www.legalhub.co.uk

This is because the ET needs to identify (1) the provision, criterion or practice or physical feature of the premises which is causing the worker difficulty, (2) the nature and extent of the disadvantage suffered by the worker as a result of these factors, (3) any non-disabled comparators who are not placed at a disadvantage (where appropriate), (4) proposed adjustments and consider to what extent they might alleviate the disadvantage.[94] When running a tribunal case (though not necessarily at the time the problem at work arose), the worker must give at least a broad idea of what kind of adjustments would have been useful, so that the employer knows what allegation s/he has to meet.[95] Once a potentially reasonable adjustment has been identified, the burden of proof is reversed for the employer to prove s/he did not fail in his/her duty to make reasonable adjustments. The amount of detail which the worker needs to give to reverse the burden of proof depends on the nature of the disability – a subtle disability requiring specialised adjustments would require more than basic detail.[96]

16.66   Although the worker needs only give a broad idea of potential adjustments, his/her case will be stronger if s/he can put forward several specific and sensible suggestions. Specialist organisations will have ideas and their websites can be useful. Medical experts and the Disability Employment Advisers or Access to Work Advisers based at Jobcentres may also help. The Access to Work Advisers can also give information regarding what grants the employers could have obtained to pay for adjustments.[97] Ideas for adjustments for over 26 different impairments are listed in Central London Law Centre's publication *Proving disability and reasonable adjustments: A worker's guide to evidence under the DDA*[98] and web-based guides such as *Guidance on employers for working with cancer*.[99]

Remedies and compensation

16.67   Medical evidence could be needed on several aspects of assessing compensation. In terms of loss of earnings, the question is when a worker

---

94 *The Environment Agency v Rowan* [2008] IRLR 20, EAT; May 2008 *Legal Action* 15.
95 *Project Management Institute v Latif* [2007] IRLR 579 EAT.
96 *E A Gibson Shipbrokers Ltd v Staples* UKEAT/0178/08 and UKEAT/0179/08.
97 For details of Disability Employment Advisers and Access to Work Advisers, see the Jobcentre Plus website at www.jobcentreplus.gov.uk
98 Available on EHRC website. See bibliography, appendix F, for details.
99 At www.cipd.co.uk/guides

would have returned to work, and for how long, had s/he not been discriminated against. With progressive diseases, a doctor may need to assess for how long the worker could continue in employment, even assuming all reasonable adjustments were made.

16.68   Where the worker has lost his/her job and cannot find a new job, statistical or expert evidence may be necessary to prove difficulties on the job market for people with the relevant disability. For this, it is worth checking the websites of specialist organisations. The worker also needs to prove what efforts s/he has in fact made to get a new job. Where the worker is so distressed by the manner of his/her dismissal or other unlawful treatment by the employer that it interferes with his/her ability to get a new job, medical evidence should be obtained as confirmation.

16.69   The worker will also need to provide evidence of his/her injury to feelings, as in all discrimination cases. If the worker has seen his/her GP with resulting depression, a GP report should be obtained. If the worker has suffered psychiatric damage to his/her health, an expert medical report is essential.[100]

Injury to feelings, mitigation and other evidence

16.70   Medical reports are not essential for ordinary injury to feelings claims, but the worker is likely to be awarded a higher sum if s/he did visit his/her GP with distress resulting from the discrimination and a GP's report can be obtained. To claim compensation for more serious injury to health, eg psychiatric damage, a formal medical report will be essential.[101] The Judicial Studies Board (JSB) give guidelines regarding psychiatric damage in personal injury cases, which may be useful for discrimination cases too.[102] Many of the principles relevant to obtaining medical evidence in a disability discrimination case will also be relevant to proving injury to feelings or health in all the discrimination strands (see paras 16.58–16.64 above).

16.71   Sexual harassment cases usually cause severe injury to feelings, sometimes amounting to post-traumatic stress syndrome. General research reports and statistical evidence of the level of sexual harassment of women at work and its effects may also be useful. Some ETs

---

100 See paras 19.27–19.35.
101 *Sheriff v Klyne Tugs* [1999] IRLR 481, CA; and paras 19.27–19.35.
102 See para 19.29–19.32 for areas requiring evidence.

take pregnancy dismissal cases less seriously than other forms of discrimination. Again, a report from the worker's own GP plus any expert evidence that this can be a time when women feel particularly vulnerable, would be helpful.[103]

16.72   Women who are pregnant or with young babies, as well as black and other minority ethnic or disabled workers, will find it harder to obtain new employment. This can be relevant to the level of compensation in dismissal cases including unfair dismissal. As well as detailed evidence of the particular worker's attempts to find fresh employment, reference to the general problems of the subject group may be of assistance.[104]

16.73   The EAT has said that compensation in discrimination cases where no upper limit applies cannot be dealt with briefly and informally. Careful preparation will be necessary for a remedies hearing. In cases under the DDA 1995, a medical expert may well be required as to the worker's likely future health, since this would be relevant to an assessment of future loss of earnings.[105]

---

103 See EOC's formal investigation into pregnancy discrimination, para 11.1 above.
104 Jobcentres are sometimes willing to write a letter on the general job prospects facing the worker.
105 *Buxton v Equinox Design Ltd* [1999] IRLR 158, EAT.

Other areas of discrimination and stress

continued

Chapter 17: Key points

Age, retirement and pensions

- Age discrimination in employment has been unlawful since 1 October 2006. It protects workers of all ages until retirement.
- Unlike in the other discrimination strands, there is a potential justification defence to direct age discrimination.
- Provided employers follow the correct procedures, it is not age discrimination or unfair dismissal to force an employee to retire at or over the age of 65.
- It is age discrimination to force office-holders or other workers to retire on age grounds, even over the age of 65, unless justified.
- Employers can choose to agree with employees or other workers to continue working beyond 65.
- It is unlawful sex discrimination to apply different retirement ages to men and women.
- Certain but not all age discrimination in pensions is permitted. Men and women are entitled to equality in their occupational pension schemes.[1]

Religion and belief, sexual orientation discrimination

- Discrimination on grounds of religion or belief and sexual orientation has been unlawful since December 2003.
- The structure of the Employment Equality (Religion or Belief) Regulations and the Employment Equality (Sexual Orientation) Regulations mirrors the structure of the Race Relations Act 1976.
- 'Belief' includes non-religious belief, eg pacifism; whether it covers fundamental political beliefs is untested.
- The statutory dispute resolution procedures will usually apply (until abolished) if an employee wishes to claim discrimination.
- The questionnaire procedure should be used as with all discrimination cases.

Harassment

- There is a specific offence of harassment in the discrimination legislation, although under the Race Relations Act 1976 it is confined to race or ethnic or national origins.

1 This area of law is complex and developing.

- In other cases under the RRA 1976, the worker must prove that the harassment amounts to direct discrimination or victimisation in the usual way.
- The harassment must be carried out in the course of employment.
- It may be possible to hold the employer liable for harassment by clients and customers. There is also a specific offence of third party harassment under the SDA 1975.
- The employer's failure to deal, or his/her mode of dealing, with an allegation of harassment may itself be a discriminatory act.
- The harassment, or the employer's failure to deal with a complaint about it, may also constitute fundamental breach of contract entitling the worker to resign and claim constructive dismissal.
- Other civil and criminal causes of action outside discrimination law may exist, although none are easy.
- Bullying or harassment which is not attributable to the worker's race, sex, disability, religion, sexual orientation or age may also give rise to a criminal or civil claim. In some circumstances a worker may resign and claim constructive dismissal.

General guide to useful evidence

- Evidence proving that the harassment occurred, eg visits to a GP, people the worker told at the time, first-hand witnesses, diary, groundless disciplinary action brought by the harasser against the worker.
- Evidence of any efforts to inform management and the response.
- Evidence of any substantial preventative measures taken by the employer, eg equal opportunities training of staff.
- Compare what actually happened with the recommendations in the EC Code on Sexual Harassment.

HIV, health and safety, stress and smoking

- Workers with AIDS or HIV infection are covered by the Disability Discrimination Act 1995.
- Workers must not be discriminated against because they have AIDS or HIV. Employers must make reasonable adjustments.
- Employers should make a risk assessment of risks to the health and safety of their employees.
- In extreme cases, an employee subjected to severe stress at work may be able to resign and claim constructive unfair dismissal.

- A worker can bring a personal injury claim in the civil courts for physical or psychiatric injury caused by stress at work, but it is hard to win such cases.
- A worker cannot bring a personal injury claim for psychiatric injury caused by dismissal or the manner of dismissal, as opposed to the employer's actions during the employment.
- In the employment tribunal, an employee can claim compensation for psychiatric injury caused by discriminatory treatment (including dismissal) under the Race Relations Act 1976, Sex Discrimination Act 1975, Disability Discrimination Act 1995, Employment Equality (Sexual Orientation) Regulations 2003, Employment Equality (Religion or Belief) Regulations 2003, Employment Equality (Age) Regulations 2006.
- It is prohibited to smoke in workplaces in England, Wales and Scotland.

Age discrimination, retirement and pensions

The legal framework

17.1   Age discrimination in employment and vocational training became unlawful in October 2006. The Employment Equality (Age) Regulations 2006[2] were passed to implement the age provisions in the EC's General Framework Directive[3] There is no statutory Code, but ACAS has issued guidance, *Age and the Workplace: Putting the Employment Equality (Age) Regulations 2006 into practice.*[4] This is worth looking at although it is mainly addressed to employers. In the year 2007/8, 2949 age discrimination claims were started in the employment tribunals.

17.2   In many ways, the Regulations have a similar content and structure to the Race Relations Act (RRA) 1976 and Sex Discrimination Act (SDA) 1975. It is therefore helpful to read chapters 13, 16 and 19 for equivalent case-law and the approach to evidence. However, there are some important differences, some of which are highlighted below.

17.3   As with all discrimination law, the Regulations protect employees in the widest sense, including those employed personally on a contract to do any work, job applicants, apprentices and contract

2 SI No 1031.

3 2000/78/EC.

4 Available on its website at www.acas.org.uk/media/pdf/s/3/ Age_and_the_Workplace.pdf

workers.[5] Office-holders, barristers, partners in firms and the police are also covered.[6] The Regulations cover discrimination in recruitment, during employment, by dismissal, including constructive dismissal, and after the employment relationship has ended provided that any post-termination discrimination arises out of and is closely connected with the former employment relationship.[7] The law does not simply protect older workers. It is unlawful to discriminate against workers of any age. However, workers aged 65 and above have very limited protection (see para 17.24 onwards).

17.4   The burden of proof is as under the RRA 1976 and SDA 1975.[8] Employment tribunal (ET) time limits and available remedies are as for the RRA 1976.[9] The questionnaire procedure is also available[10] and an inference can be drawn from failure to reply properly within eight weeks. For more detail on the kind of evidence necessary to prove age discrimination together with references for research reports, see Help the Aged's guide: *How to recognise cases of age discrimination: An adviser's toolkit* by Tamara Lewis.[11]

The meaning of 'discrimination'

17.5   The usual concepts of discrimination apply, ie direct discrimination, indirect discrimination, victimisation and harassment.[12] Resisting instructions to discriminate is also covered (see below). Direct discrimination occurs where a worker is treated less favourably on grounds of his/her age.[13] For example, an employer selects the oldest workers for redundancy. Unlike race discrimination, the definition does not cover less favourable treatment on grounds of someone else's age. This may be contrary to the Directive as is an equivalent provision under the Disability Discrimination Act 1995.[14] It is also unlawful to treat someone less favourably on grounds of his/her

5 Employment Equality (Age) Regulations 2006 (EE(A) Regs) regs 2(2) and 9; see para 13.14 for meaning of 'contract worker' under RRA 1976 and SDA 1975.

6 EE(A) Regs 2006 regs 12–17.

7 EE(A) Regs 2006 regs 7 and 24.

8 EE(A) Regs 2006 reg 37; paras 16.1–16.10.

9 EE(A) Regs 2006 regs 38 and 42; chapter 19.

10 EE(A) Regs 2006 reg 41; paras 21.2–21.12; plus a specialist Age Questionnaire guide from Central London Law Centre, appendix F, at pp784–785.

11 Available at www.taen.org.uk/publications/ad_guide_for_advisers.pdf

12 EE(A) Regs 2006 regs 3–6.

13 EE(A) Regs 2006 reg 3(1)(a).

14 See para 15.44.

apparent age,[15] eg an employer refuses to recruit a worker because s/he guesses the worker is of a certain age or because s/he mistakenly thinks the worker is older than the worker in fact is.

17.6   Unlike all the other discrimination strands, there is a potential justification defence to direct age discrimination. Employers can justify direct discrimination if they can prove the less favourable treatment is a proportionate means of achieving a legitimate aim. Exactly the same defence is available for indirect discrimination cases. See paras 17.11–17.14 below for further comments on the defence.

17.7   Indirect discrimination is where the worker is put at a disadvantage because of the application of a provision, criterion or practice which puts or would put those of the same age group at a particular disadvantage compared with others.[16] For example, an employer requires job applicants to have lengthy prior experience. This would put younger candidates at a disadvantage as they have had less time to acquire such experience. Alternatively, an employer wants recent graduates for a job. This would exclude the majority of older candidates. For a list of possible indirectly discriminatory requirements on age grounds, see appendix B. If an employer introduces a requirement that, in order to get a pay rise, its employees must obtain a particular qualification, an older employee cannot argue that this is indirect discrimination purely because it will take a few years to get the qualification and s/he will have less time left in employment before retirement to enjoy the benefits of the rise. This is just a consequence of being older, but it is not a consequence of age discrimination.[17]

17.8   The definition is similar to that in other discrimination strands, except that the concept of 'age group' is unique. It seems the worker can choose to describe his/her own age group as appears appropriate. For example, a worker aged 55 could describe his/her age group as '55', 'over 50', '50–60', etc. The Regulations do not state explicitly that the comparison must be with everyone of an age not within the worker's age group. Arguably, therefore, the worker can choose the age group of those s/he is comparing him/herself with, eg 'under 50' or '20–30'. Obviously the choice of age groups will be determined by the evidence available to show disparate impact on those of the worker's age. Until there is any caselaw on this point, advisers cannot be sure what tribunals will expect.

---

15 EE(A) Regs 2006 reg 3(3)(b).

16 EE(A) Regs 2006 reg 3(1)(b).

17 *Chief Constable of West Yorkshire Police and West Yorkshire Police Authority and others v Homer* UKEAT/0191/08; [2009] IRLR 262, EAT; June 2009 *Legal Action* 37.

17.9   The employer has a justification defence to indirect age discrimination. The wording is the same as for the defence to direct age discrimination and also reflects the defence for indirect discrimination in
the other discrimination strands. See paras 17.11–17.14 below for further comments on the defence.

17.10   Victimisation protects a worker against less favourable treatment
because s/he has complained about age discrimination.[18] It is also
unlawful to treat a worker less favourably because s/he has not carried
out an instruction to discriminate or because s/he has complained
about such an instruction.[19]

The defence to direct and indirect age discrimination

17.11   As mentioned above, an employer can defend a case of direct or indirect age discrimination by showing the treatment, provision, criterion
or practice is a proportionate means of meeting a legitimate aim.[20]
This derives from article 6 of the Directive, which states that a difference of treatment on age grounds is not unlawful if it is objectively
and reasonably justified by a legitimate aim, and if the means of achieving that aim are appropriate and necessary. The Directive (unlike the
Age Regulations) goes on to give examples of potentially justifiable
differences of treatment. If any of these examples are quoted against
the worker, remember that they are only examples, they do not appear
in the Age Regulations, and must still be justified on the facts of the particular case.

17.12   Because it is unique to have a defence available to direct discrimination, there has been uncertainty whether direct age discrimination
cases ought to be harder to justify than indirect discrimination cases,
despite the wording of the defence being the same. Indeed, it is strongly
arguable that the defence should rarely succeed in direct discrimination cases, because it inevitably involves making generalisations based
on age as opposed to assessing the capabilities of individuals. In its final
consultation on the Regulations, the government said, 'treating people
differently on grounds of age will be possible but only exceptionally and
only for good reasons'.[21] In early cases, the EAT has rejected the idea that

18 EE(A) Regs 2006 reg 4; and see paras 13.85–13.96 for victimisation under the
RRA 1976 and SDA 1975.

19 EE(A) Regs 2006 reg 5. There is no exact equivalent under the other discrimination strands, where the definitions of direct discrimination and victimisation
could be used instead.

20 EE(A) Regs 2006 reg 3(1).

21 *Equality and Diversity: Coming of Age.* DTI consultation, July 2005.

direct age discrimination can only be justified in exceptional circumstances. However, it has expressed a tentative view that it may be harder to justify direct discrimination because the overall effect of a measure will be greater than for indirect discrimination, and this will be relevant to the assessment of proportionality.[22] On a judicial review brought by the National Council on Ageing (operating through its membership organisation, Heyday), the High Court asked the ECJ to comment on the defence to direct age discrimination. The ECJ stated that the defence need not be restricted to a precise list of potential grounds for justification such as is contained in article 6 of the Directive.[23] Unfortunately the other comments of the ECJ were less clear. Paragraph 46 of its judgment can be read to suggest that – allowing a certain degree of flexibility – employers can only justify direct discrimination if it is in pursuit of legitimate aims of a 'public interest nature'. It is hard to be sure what such aims would be and it seems a strange idea that private sector employers would have to be considering the public interest. The case will now revert to the High Court and doubtless it will spawn further case-law regarding the nature of the direct discrimination defence.[24]

17.13   Subject to how the law develops regarding permitted defences to direct discrimination, the following observations may apply to direct or indirect age discrimination. Test cases on indirect sex discrimination under the SDA 1975 suggest that an employer may use costs savings as one of several reasons justifying discrimination, but not as the sole reason.[25] Where costs are put forward as one of several reasons, the actual amount of the savings should be examined and also put in the context of other employment considerations. An even more controversial area is whether customer preference or corporate image will be an acceptable defence. Where this is based on stereotypes and used to justify direct discrimination, it should be challenged. Defences such as health and safety or proximity to retirement age, although more superficially attractive, may well be based on assumptions and generalisations about the health and abilities of workers of a certain age, and how

22 *Seldon v Clarkson Wright & Jakes (EHRC intervening)* UKEAT/0063/08; [2009] IRLR 267, EAT; *Legal Action* May 2009. This case was decided before the ECJ judgment in the *Heyday* case.

23 *R (on the application of the Incorporated Trustees of the National Council on Ageing (Age Concern England)) v Secretary of State for Business, Enterprise and Regulatory Reform.* C-388/07 [2009] IRLR 373, ECJ.

24 The *Heyday* case is concerned with the specific issue of whether the government can justify the default retirement age – see para 17.24.

25 See para 13.82.

long workers of any age are likely to remain in a particular job. If a certain level of health or fitness is genuinely needed for a job, it is better that an employer applies a medical or fitness test to all job candidates, than make assumptions that workers over a particular age will not be suitable. A general health test may still be indirectly discriminatory, in that it may screen out more older workers than young ones, but it will be fairer than a directly discriminatory rule, in that it assesses the actual individual. Last In First Out may be justifiable as one of several redundancy selection criteria but probably not as the sole criterion.[26]

17.14   The onus is on the employer to prove the defence, but the worker should be ready to challenge the employer's justification and demand proof of any assumptions made about the link between age and performance. Early cases have revealed that a great deal of stereotyping around age still exists. In one case, for example, the EAT overturned a stereotyped assumption made by an employment tribunal that partners in a solicitors' firm would, by the age of 65, be more likely to be underperforming than younger partners.[27] For more detail on various defences and sources for challenging the myths and stereotypes on which many of the defences apply, see Help the Aged's guide: *How to recognise cases of age discrimination: An adviser's toolkit* by Tamara Lewis.[28]

Harassment

17.15   Harassment is also forbidden. This is where, on grounds of age, the harasser engages in unwanted conduct which has the purpose or effect of violating the worker's dignity or creating an intimidating, hostile, degrading, humiliating or offensive environment for him/her. As to whether the conduct has such an effect, the test is whether, having regard to all the circumstances, including in particular the worker's perception, it should reasonably be regarded as having that effect.[29]

17.16   Examples of harassment, deliberate or unintentional, could be teasing, offensive jokes, hostile or patronising remarks, exclusion from team meetings or social occasions, remarks about physical appearance linked to age, being made to do menial tasks and run errands, bullying, and making someone feel they ought to leave. Of course, the

---

26 *Rolls Royce PLC v UNITE the Union* [2009] EWCA Civ 387; [2009] IRLR 576, CA upholding the High Court's decision at [2009] IRLR 49, HC. See also 17.22.

27 *Seldon v Clarkson Wright & Jakes (EHRC intervening)* UKEAT/0063/08; [2009] IRLR 267, EAT; May 2009 *Legal Action* 18.

28 Available at www.taen.org.uk/publications/ad_guide_for_advisers.pdf

29 EE(A) Regs 2006 reg 6.

worker may be happy with a certain level of joking and banter, especially on occasions such as birthdays. But if it is unwanted and if it is reasonable to consider that it creates a humiliating or offensive environment, etc then it is unlawful. For further detail on the law of harassment, see para 17.91 onwards.

Where discrimination is allowed

17.17   There are a number of exceptions where age discrimination is allowed. In some cases, these are thought to go beyond what is permitted by the General Framework Directive and may be subject to challenge.[30]

17.18   An employer may discriminate against a worker because s/he does not possess a certain characteristic related to age or because the employer is satisfied on reasonable grounds that s/he does not possess such a characteristic.[31] Possessing the characteristic must be a genuine and determining occupational requirement (GOR) and it must be proportionate to apply the requirement in a particular case. For example, a TV production company may require a young actor to play the role of a young person in a film. A similar GOR exception is common across all the discrimination strands, but seems superfluous under the Age Regulations, where there is already a defence to direct discrimination.

17.19   Positive action in training or encouraging job applications is permitted where a particular age group has been disadvantaged in the past.[32] Other exceptions relate to statutory authority and national security,[33] statutory and enhanced redundancy pay,[34] and the national minimum wage.[35] Moreover, an employer may pay a worker a lower hourly rate on age grounds if the worker is in a lower national minimum wage band than his/her comparator and the worker is paid less than the normal adult minimum wage.[36] For example, in the year starting October 2008, waiter A (aged 19) falls within the 18-21 band (minimum rate £4.77 per hour). Waiter B (aged 25) is within the adult band (minimum rate £5.73 per hour). An employer is entitled to pay B £7 per hour and pay A, on grounds of his age, £5 per hour. However, if the

30 See chapter 3 regarding use of EU law.
31 EE(A) Regs 2006 reg 8.
32 EE(A) Regs 2006 reg 29.
33 EE(A) Regs 2006 regs 27 and 28.
34 EE(A) Regs 2006 reg 33. See para 18.22.
35 See para 4.29.
36 EE(A) Regs 2006 reg 31.

employer pays A £6 per hour, the exception does not apply, because A is now paid more than the adult minimum rate. Waiter A can claim direct discrimination and the employer will have to justify the pay difference in the usual way.

17.20 Regulation 32 exempts certain benefits based on length of service. It is common for employers to give pay increments or other enhanced benefits for each year of employment. This indirectly discriminates against younger workers. The Age Regulations permit these enhancements for the first five years of a worker's service. After that, an employer must justify applying length of service criteria to pay or benefits, but the usual objective test for justification does not apply. The employer need only show that it reasonably appears to him/her that the service criterion fulfils a business need, eg by encouraging loyalty or motivation or rewarding experience.[37]

17.21 Service requirements can also discriminate against other workers who are less likely to build up long service, eg women, because of career breaks, or black workers, because of previous discrimination. Indirect discrimination cases can therefore be brought under other discrimination legislation. The *Cadman* test case under the Equal Pay Act (EqPA) 1970 concerned what level of justification is necessary for pay increments which indirectly discriminate against women.[38] The decision in that case indicated that justification is usually self-evident but can be challenged in special circumstances. It is interesting to consider whether that means the general service-related benefits exemption under the Age Regulations, which does not allow for consideration of special circumstances in individual cases, could be challenged as contrary to the Directive.

17.22 The reg 32 exemption explicitly does not include any benefit awarded to a worker because s/he has stopped working for the employer,[39] eg redundancy pay. But redundancy selection criteria could be considered a 'benefit' and would be covered, presumably because the worker has not yet been selected for dismissal. This means that criteria such as LIFO, which disadvantage younger workers, require a lower standard of justification under the Age Regulations.[40] However, if LIFO also discriminated against women or black workers, it would need proper justification under the usual test in the SDA 1975 or RRA 1976, since there is no equivalent exemption for service-related benefits in those statutes.

---

37 EE(A) Regs 2006 reg 32.
38 See para 5.45.
39 EE(A) Regs 2006 reg 32(7).
40 *Rolls Royce PLC v UNITE the Union* [2009] EWCA Civ 387; [2009] IRLR 576, CA.

17.23   Certain discrimination in pensions is permitted, but this is a very complex area and beyond the scope of this book.[41] It is also lawful to cease life assurance cover after early retirement on ill-health grounds once workers reach 65 or the organisation's normal retirement age.[42] The rules regarding retirement and recruitment at or within six months of retirement age are set out below.

Retirement

Overview

17.24   In the years leading up to the implementation of the Age Regulations, there was extensive debate regarding the desirability of retaining a national retirement age. Disappointingly, the final decision was to set a default retirement age of 65 for employees, although this is to be reviewed in 2010. Allowing a retirement age undermines the legislation in many respects. The National Council on Ageing in the *Heyday* case has challenged the lawfulness of the default retirement age.[43] In this case, the ECJ said that the issue of retirement age falls within the scope of the Directive, but it is for the national courts to decide whether the government's approach is justifiable.[44] This will require a high standard of proof. The matter now awaits a decision by the High Court.

17.25   The default retirement age of 65 for male and female employees is not a compulsory retirement age and is not to be confused with the state pension age. An employer can choose to keep on an employee past the age of 65 if both parties so wish. However, an employee who is forced to retire at or over the age of 65 (or any earlier non-discriminatory normal retirement age), will be unable to claim age discrimination or unfair dismissal provided the employer has followed the correct procedures (set out below). Pending the High Court's decision in the *Heyday* case (above), it may be wise to lodge any such claim with the tribunal and ask for it to be stayed (put on hold). The President of the

---

41 The Employment Equality (Age) (Amendment No 2) Regulations 2006 SI No 2931. Local government pensions are also affected by the Local Government (Early Termination of Employment) (Discretionary Compensation) Regulations 2006 SI No 2914, see also para 17.42 onwards.

42 EE(A) Regs 2006 reg 34.

43 Along with a challenge regarding the direct discrimination defence. See para 17.12.

44 *R (on the application of the Incorporated Trustees of the National Council on Ageing (Age Concern England)) v Secretary of State for Business, Enterprise and Regulatory Reform* C-388/07 [2009] IRLR 373, ECJ; *Palacios de la Villa v Costefiel Servicios SA* C-411/05 [2007] IRLR 989, ECJ.

Employment Tribunals in England & Wales has issued a second Practice Direction ordering that all claims raising the same issue regarding reg 30 of the Regulations be stayed pending the High Court decision.[45] An employee will still be able to claim discrimination under the other strands if applicable, eg under the SDA 1975 if the employer tended to force women to retire at 65 but allow men to work longer, or under the DDA 1995 if the employee was made to retire simply because of his/her disability.

17.26   An employer will be unable to set a lower normal retirement age (NRA) unless this is objectively justifiable. In this respect, the law represents a small improvement on the previous position. It will now be very hard for an employer to justify setting a NRA below 65.

17.27   The retirement rules apply to employees, parliamentary staff and those in Crown employment.[46] They do not apply to non-employees, eg office-holders, partners in solicitors' firms or other workers. Non-employees cannot claim unfair dismissal in any event. But if they are forced to retire on grounds of their age, it will be direct age discrimination unless justified in the usual way.

The employer's duty to notify the intended retirement date

17.28   An employer who intends to retire an employee must give the employee written notice of the date on which s/he intends the employee to retire and the employee's right to request not to retire on that date.[47] The notification must be made 6–12 months before the proposed retirement date, even if the employee has already been told the date or it is in his/her contract. If the employer fails to give this notification within the timescale, the employee can claim up to eight weeks' compensation, according to what the tribunal thinks is just and equitable.[48] A week's pay is gross pay subject to the current maximum applicable to statutory redundancy pay[49] The tribunal claim must be made before the end of three months starting from the last day the employer was permitted to make the notification. If the employee did not then know the date of intended retirement, the time limit is counted from the date when s/he did know or should have known.[50]

---

45 At www.employmenttribunals.gov.uk/RulesLegislation/directionsEW.htm
   See also *Johns v Solent SD Limited* UKEAT/0449/07.
46 EE(A) Regs 2006 reg 30 and Sch 6 para 1(1).
47 EE(A) Regs 2006 Sch 6 para 2.
48 EE(A) Regs 2006 Sch 6 para 11(3).
49 See para 18.17.
50 EE(A) Regs 2006 Sch 6 para 11(2).

17.29   An employer who has not made the notification by six months before the proposed retirement date has a continuing duty to do so up to 14 days before retirement.[51] If the employer fails to notify the employee after this time, the employee can claim automatic unfair dismissal.[52] Nevertheless, it is uncertain how much an employee would actually be awarded by way of loss of earnings for such a claim.

The right to request not to retire

17.30   An employee can ask his/her employer at any time to continue working past retirement age. But if the employee makes a request under the statutory procedure, the employer is forced to hold a meeting and discuss the matter. Unfortunately, that is as far as it goes. The employer can choose whether to agree to continued working and need not give reasons for refusing. If the employer fails to follow the procedure, the dismissal will be automatically unfair.[53]

17.31   Under the procedure, the employee must make a written request which states that it is made under EE(A) Regs 2006 Sch 6 para 5 and which proposes to continue working after retirement for a stated period or indefinitely. If the employer has not provided a written notification of the intended retirement date, the employee must identify the date on which s/he believes the employer intends to retire him/her. The request must be made more than three months but not more than six months before the intended retirement date or, if the employer has not given the correct notification under EE(A) Regs 2006 Sch 6 para 2, any time during the six months before the intended retirement date.

17.32   The employer must hold a meeting to discuss the request within a reasonable time of receiving it and both parties must take reasonable steps to attend. If it is not practical to hold a meeting within a reasonable time, the employer can consider the matter without one. The meeting is unnecessary if the parties agree continued working and the employer gives the employee a written notice to that effect.

17.33   The employer must give written notification of his/her decision as soon as reasonably practicable after the meeting. If the request is accepted, the decision must state the employee can continue working indefinitely or until a specified date. If it is refused, the decision must state this and confirm the retirement date. The employer need not give reasons for refusal although the ACAS guidance (see para 17.1

51 EE(A) Regs 2006 Sch 6 para 4.
52 Employment Rights Act (ERA) 1996 s98ZG.
53 ERA 1996, s98ZG.

above) says it would be good practice to do so. The employee can appeal in writing as soon as reasonably practicable after the decision. S/he must set out the grounds of appeal (even though s/he may not have been given reasons for refusal). The employer must hold an appeal meeting. The same rules apply as for the initial meeting. Again, the employer need not give reasons for refusal.

17.34　　If the employee's termination date falls before the employer has given his/her initial decision under this procedure, the employee's contract of employment continues in force until the date after the written decision is given. But the original termination date remains unchanged for the purposes of ascertaining the intended retirement date under the unfair dismissal rules.[54]

17.35　　The employee has the right to be accompanied to the meeting by a work colleague of his/her choice.[55] If the employer refuses to allow this, the employee can bring a tribunal claim for up to two weeks' gross pay subject to the ceiling applicable for statutory redundancy pay (see para 18.17).[56] It is automatically unfair to dismiss the employee or his/her companion and unlawful to subject either of them to a detriment for exercising this right.[57]

17.36　　A request under the procedure can only be made once in respect of a single retirement date though there is nothing to prevent further informal discussions. If the employer does agree that the employee can continue working beyond retirement, the employer needs to go through the notification and duty to consider procedures all over again in respect of future retirement dates unless the future date is no later than six months from the original date.

Unfair dismissal and retirement

17.37　The rules regarding unfair dismissal and retirement are set out at ERA 1996 ss98ZA–98ZH. The following is a summary. The references to 'retirement age' below in paras 17.37–17.39 mean:

- the default retirement age of 65; or
- any higher NRA set by the employer for employees generally; or
- any lower NRA set by the employer which is non-discriminatory and objectively justifiable.

---

54 EE(A) Regs 2006 Sch 6 para 10.
55 EE(A) Regs 2006 Sch 6 para 9.
56 EE(A) Regs 2006 Sch 6 para 12.
57 EE(A) Regs 2006 Sch 6 para 13.

It is automatically unfair dismissal to force an employee to retire before retirement age. Unless objectively justified, it will also be age discrimination.

17.38   It is not age discrimination to dismiss an employee, person in Crown employment or member of parliamentary staff genuinely for retirement at or over the age of 65.[58] This will also be a fair dismissal if the correct procedures are followed. It is therefore important to consider whether the dismissal was genuinely for retirement. There are rules about this. The law will consider the dismissal was genuinely for retirement, and the employee cannot argue otherwise, if:

- the employer gave the statutory notification under EE(A) Regs 2006 Sch 6 para 2 (see para 17.28 above);
- the job ended on the intended retirement date, ie in this instance, the date notified by the employer under EE(A) Regs 2006 Sch 6 para 2;
- the job ended at or above the employee's retirement age (see previous paragraph).[59]

If the job ended before the retirement age[60] or intended retirement date,[61] the law assumes the reason was not retirement, and the employer cannot argue otherwise. In other situations, eg the employer made no EE(A) Regs 2006 Sch 6 para 2 notification but the job ended at retirement age and on the intended date, the tribunal will look at all the circumstances and decide whether the reason was genuine.[62] In particular, it will take account of:[63]

- whether the employer at least made a Sch 6 para 4 notification, ie more than 14 days in advance;
- if so, how far in advance of the retirement date the notification was given;
- whether the employer followed the procedure to consider the employee's request to continue working.

If the employer asserts that the dismissal was for retirement, but the tribunal decides that it was not, the dismissal is very likely to be unfair.

17.39   If the tribunal decides the dismissal was genuinely for retirement and at retirement age, it will be a fair dismissal if the employer gave the

58 EE(A) Regs 2006 reg 30.
59 ERA 1996 ss98ZB(2), 98ZD(2) 98ZE(4) and s98ZH.
60 ERA 1996 ss98ZA, 98ZC.
61 ERA 1996 ss98ZB(3), 98ZD(3), 98ZE(5).
62 ERA 1996 ss98ZB(5), 98ZD(5), 98ZE(7).
63 ERA 1996 s98ZF.

correct notification under EE(A) Regs 2006 Sch 6 paras 2 or 4 of the retirement date and the right to request continued working, and if the employer followed the correct procedure if the employee did request continued working (see paras 17.30–17.36 above).

17.40   The statutory dispute resolution procedures[64] do not apply to retirement dismissals. However, if a tribunal finds that a dismissal was not genuinely for retirement, then the procedures do apply (until abolished) and the employer can be penalised for failing to follow the statutory dismissal and disciplinary procedure (DDP).

Recruitment at retirement age

17.41   It is not unlawful to discriminate in recruitment against a job applicant on age grounds who is older than 65 or any higher NRA operated by the employer or who would reach that age within six months of his/her application for the job.[65] As with retirement age, this exception only applies to employees, parliamentary staff or those in Crown employment.[66]

Pensions and sex discrimination

17.42   The subject of pensions is very complicated and beyond the scope of this book. However, the following is an introduction to the issues arising in connection with pensions and sex discrimination. For a brief guide to claiming compensation for pension loss in an unfair dismissal claim, see paras 18.40–18.48.

17.43   Originally the legislation did not prohibit all forms of discrimination in connection with retirement and pensions, so in many cases the only protection was under EU law. Partly as a result of different state pension ages, occupational pension schemes have tended to discriminate. Article 141[67] covers discrimination in private pensions, including contracted-out schemes, and whether or not they are contributory, as an equal pay issue.[68] Statutory schemes are not covered and this may in some circumstances exclude a local authority scheme.[69]

---

64 See chapter 22 and 22.67 regarding abolition date..

65 EE(A) Regs 2006 reg 7(4) and (8).

66 EE(A) Regs 2006 reg 7(5).

67 See paras 5.9–5.10 above.

68 *Barber v Guardian Royal Exchange Assurance Group* C-262/88 [1990] IRLR 240, ECJ; *Worringham & Humphreys v Lloyds Bank Ltd* [1981] IRLR 178, ECJ.

69 *Griffin v London Pensions Fund Authority* [1993] IRLR 248, EAT.

17.44 There have been a series of decisions by the ECJ on what amounts to discrimination in a pension scheme. It seems that article 141 only prohibits discrimination in contributions and benefits under the scheme.[70] Restrictions on a part-time employee joining a pension scheme may be indirect sex discrimination under article 141 unless the employer can objectively justify the restriction.[71] Equally it may breach the Part-time Workers (Prevention of Less Favourable Treatment) Regulations 2000.[72]

17.45 Highly complex case-law has dealt with how far back in time discriminatory schemes can be rectified.[73] It is not simply a matter of the usual EqPA 1970 time limits.[74]

17.46 The large number of ECJ cases finding discrimination in pensions unlawful led to the Pensions Act 1995 and the Occupational Pension Schemes (Equal Treatment) Regulations 1995.[75] As well as providing for equal treatment between men and women in access to and terms of membership of occupational pension schemes (subject to certain exclusions), the Pensions Act 1995 provides for equal state pension age to be phased in from 2010 to 2020.

17.47 The legislation is modelled on the EqPA 1970 in that it imports an 'equal treatment rule' into a woman's pension where she is or was employed on like work, work rated as equivalent under a job evaluation scheme or work of equal value, unless the trustees of the scheme can prove a genuine material factor defence other than sex.[76] It would be unlawful to discriminate directly, eg by refusing entry to women, or indirectly, eg by unjustifiably excluding part-time workers.

17.48 The law on equality of pensions (access, benefits and contributions), time limits and retrospective claims is complex and undergoing change. Full guidance is beyond the scope of this book. The Employment Tribunals Service (ETS) website[77] has a comprehensive section on part-time pension cases, with case-law and practical guidance. Note

---

70 *Newstead v Department Transport* C-192/85 [1988] IRLR 166, ECJ.

71 *Bilka-Kaufhaus GmbH v Weber Von Hartz* C-170/84 [1986] IRLR 317, ECJ.

72 SI No 1551. See paras 11.92–11.99.

73 See *Bestuur van het Barber Algemeen Burgerlijk Pensioenfonds v Bearne* C-7/93 [1994] PLR 211, ECJ; *Coloroll Pension Trustees Ltd v Russell* C-200/91 [1994] IRLR 586, ECJ; *Preston v Wolverhampton Healthcare NHS Trust* [2000] IRLR 506; November 2000 *Legal Action* 26, ECJ; [2001] IRLR 237, May 2001 *Legal Action* 14, HL.

74 See para 5.71.

75 SI No 3183.

76 Pensions Act 1995 s62.

77 At www.employmenttribunals.gov.uk Click 'Part-time workers' on title bar.

also that occupational pensions may be adversely affected on the transfer of an employer's business, even if the Transfer of Undertakings (Protection of Employment) Regulations 2006 apply.[78] It would be wise for workers to clarify at the time of any sale of the business the effect on their pension. The Pensions Act 2004 provides a minimum level of protection on a transfer. It also created a new Pensions Regulator and Pensions Protection Fund.

Religious discrimination

The legal framework

17.49 As part of the European Council's General Framework Directive,[79] discrimination on grounds of religion was made unlawful in December 2003 by the Employment Equality (Religion or Belief) Regulations (EE(RB) Regs) 2003.[80] ACAS has issued guidance on the Regulations: *Religion or belief and the workplace: putting the Employment Equality (Religion or Belief) Regulations 2003 into practice.*[81] The guidance deals with issues such as dress, prayer needs and requirements for time off. It contains an appendix with information about the ten most commonly practised religions and beliefs in Britain. In the year 2007/8, 709 employment tribunal cases were started concerning religion or belief. There are two research papers available on the ACAS website: *Sexual orientation and religion or belief discrimination in the workplace [Ref: 01/07]* and *The experiences of sexual orientation and religion or belief discrimination employment tribunal claimants [Ref: 02/07].*[82]

17.50 The Regulations mirror those relating to sexual orientation and are structured in a very similar way to the RRA 1976 and SDA 1975. It is therefore worth reading chapters 13, 16 and 19 for equivalent case-law and the approach to evidence. As with those statutes, employees in the widest sense are covered, ie including those employed personally on a contract to do any work, as well as apprentices and contract workers.[83]

---

78 SI No 246. See chapter 10.

79 2000/78/EC.

80 SI No 1660.

81 Available on the ACAS website at
www.acas.org.uk/media/pdf/f/l/religion_1.pdf

82 Summary available at
www.acas.org.uk/media/pdf/d/j/SORB_summaries_1.pdf

83 EE(RB) Regs 2003 regs 2(3) and 8. See para 13.14 for meaning of 'contract workers' under the RRA 1976 and SDA 1975.

The police are also covered.[84] The employing organisation is vicariously liable for discrimination carried out in the course of employment by its managers or junior staff against the worker.[85]

17.51 As with all discrimination law, the Regulations cover discrimination in recruitment, during employment, by dismissal including constructive dismissal,[86] and after the employment relationship has ended, provided that any post-termination discrimination arises out of and is closely connected with the former employment relationship.[87]

17.52 The burden of proof is as under the RRA 1976 and SDA 1975.[88] ET time limits and available remedies are as for the RRA 1976.[89] The questionnaire procedure is also available[90] and an inference can be drawn from failure to reply properly within eight weeks.

Religion or belief

17.53 It is unlawful to discriminate on grounds of religion or belief. This means any religion, religious or philosophical belief.[91] This seems to cover fringe religions and membership of religious cults. The ACAS guide lists the following as some of the most commonly practised religions and beliefs in Britain: Baha'i, Buddhism, Christianity, Hinduism, Islam, Jainism, Judaism, Rastafarianism, Sikhism, Zoroastrianism and other ancient religions, eg Druidry, Paganism and Wicca. The tribunals may consider a number of factors when deciding what is a religion or belief, eg collective worship, a clear belief system, profound belief affecting way of life or view of the world. The government has suggested 'any philosophical belief must attain a certain level of cogency, seriousness, cohesion and importance, must be worthy of respect in a democratic society and must not be incompatible with human dignity' – humanism might meet this description, but support for a political party or a belief in the supreme nature of the Jedi Knights would not.[92]

---

84 EE(RB) Regs 2003 reg 11.

85 EE(RB) Regs 2003 reg 22; see para 13.20 for the equivalent under the RRA 1976 and SDA 1975.

86 EE(RB) Regs 2003 reg 6(5).

87 EE(RB) Regs 2003 reg 21.

88 EE(RB) Regs 2003 reg 29; paras 16.1–16.10.

89 EE(RB) Regs 2003 regs 20–34; chapter 19.

90 EE(RB) Regs 2003 reg 33, Sch 2; paras 21.2–21.12; plus specialist guides from Central London Law Centre, appendix F, at pp784–785.

91 EE(RB) Regs 2003 reg 2(1) as amended by the Equality Act 2006.

92 Baroness Scotland, House of Lords. *Hansard* HL Debates col 1110, 13 July 2005.

The original definition, prior to its amendment on 30 April 2007, referred to 'religious or similar philosophical belief'. Although the government insists that the word 'similar' was superfluous and its removal has no significance, the tribunals may consider that 'philosophical belief' now has a wider meaning and could indeed cover fundamental political beliefs. Membership or non-membership of the Masons may be protected as a religion or belief.[93] Some commentators have suggested beliefs such as pacifism, environmentalism[94] or even vegetarianism may be covered, but the latter is uncertain.

17.54   It is also unlawful to discriminate on grounds of lack of a religion or belief.[95] A religious belief can be intensely personal and subjective. As long as a belief is asserted in good faith, it need not be shared by others for it to be a religious belief, nor need it be a mandatory requirement of an established religion. For example, a Christian worker may believe she ought to wear a cross visibly over her clothing, even though she knows it is not required by scripture or as an article of faith.[96]

The meaning of 'discrimination'

17.55   The usual concepts of discrimination apply, ie direct discrimination, indirect discrimination, victimisation and harassment.[97] Direct discrimination is where the worker is treated less favourably on grounds of religion or belief.[98] This includes discrimination against a worker because of someone else's religion or belief, eg because s/he has Muslim friends or because s/he refuses to carry out an employer's instruction to discriminate against Muslims. Originally discrimination on grounds of perceived belief was covered, but amendments made in April 2007 appear to have inadvertently removed this protection.[99] Dismissing a worker for promoting his/her religion is not direct religious discrimination.[100]

---

93 *Gibson v Police Authority for Northern Ireland and others* FET 15.9.06, case no:00406/00, although as an ET level case in Northern Ireland, it is only illustrative.

94 *Nicholson v Grainger PLC*, successful in the employment tribunal but under appeal.

95 EE(RB) Regs 2003 reg 2(1) as amended.

96 *Eweida v British Airways PLC* UKEAT/0123/08; [2009] IRLR 78, EAT; May 2009 *Legal Action* 16.

97 EE(RB) Regs 2003 regs 3–5.

98 EE(RB) Regs 2003 reg 3(1)(a); see also paras 13.38–13.48 under the RRA 1976 and SDA 1975.

99 EE(RB) Regs 2003 reg 3 reworded by the Equality Act 2006.

100 *Chondol v Liverpool City Council* UKEAT/0298/08; June 2009 *Legal Action* 37.

17.56   It is not unlawful to discriminate on grounds of the discriminator's own belief or lack of belief.[101] Usually this exemption is not a
problem and it is just a matter of how the claim is put. For example, a
Catholic employer who refuses to employ a worker because s/he is
not Catholic, ie because the worker is not of the employer's own
religion, is also discriminating because of the worker's own lack of
belief (or different religion). Such discrimination would be covered
on the latter basis. However, if a Catholic employer refuses to employ
a worker because s/he is gay and it is against the employer's own
religious beliefs that people should be gay, the worker could not claim
religious discrimination.[102]

17.57   Victimisation protects a worker against less favourable treatment
because s/he has complained about discrimination.[103] Indirect discrimination is where the worker is put at a particular disadvantage
because of the application of a provision, criterion or practice which
the employer cannot show to be a proportionate means of achieving a
legitimate aim.[104] Any unjustifiable restriction on religious practices,
eg dress requirements or Sabbath working, may be indirect religious discrimination.[105] This concept is already familiar from indirect race
discrimination law.[106] At a stretch, it is arguable that such restriction
would also be direct religious discrimination on grounds of religious
belief. This depends on whether direct discrimination covers the man-
ifestation of a belief, so that refusal to allow a religious practice becomes
direct discrimination in itself. The advantage of direct discrimination is
that there is no defence of justification. This question arose in the heavily publicised *Azmi* case,[107] but was left undecided by the Employment
Appeal Tribunal (EAT). Instead, the EAT resolved the issue by looking
at the correct comparator for direct discrimination. It said that where a
Muslim woman is not permitted to wear the veil, the comparator is a
woman, whether Muslim or not, who for reasons other than religious
belief wants to wear a face covering and is not permitted to do so. This
approach makes it difficult to use direct discrimination where an
employer refuses to permit religious practices.

101 EE(RB) Regs 2003 reg 3(1) as amended.
102 Although on this example, it might be sexual orientation discrimination.
103 EE(RB) Regs 2003 reg 4; and see paras 13.85–13.96 under the RRA 1976 and
    SDA 1975.
104 EE(RB) Regs 2003 reg 3(1)(b); see also paras 13.52–13.84 under the RRA 1976
    and SDA 1975.
105 See appendix B and paras 17.64–17.72 for examples.
106 See para 13.29.
107 *Azmi v Kirklees Metropolitan Council* [2007] IRLR 485, EAT.

17.58   To prove indirect discrimination, a worker needs to show the employer's rules disadvantage not only him/her but also others of the same religion or belief. This may be a problem where the worker holds a very subjective and personal belief which is not strictly-speaking part of the requirements of his/her religion. For example, in one case a Christian worker believed she should wear a cross visibly over her clothes, but was unable to prove that other Christians would hold the same views. It would not be enough if she could find one or two other like-minded souls who shared this belief. There must be some evidence of group disadvantage, ie it must be possible to make some general statements which would be true about a group (eg Christians) such that an employer ought reasonably to appreciate that any particular provision, criterion or practice may have adverse impact on that group.[108]

17.59   There can be difficulties where a worker does not want to perform certain duties because of his/her religion and this clashes with the rights of other protected groups, eg women or gay workers. Where a public employer wants to promote equal opportunities in its services, it may be justifiable for it to refuse to allow a worker to avoid providing certain services, such as civil partnership ceremonies, for religious reasons.[109]

Harassment

17.60   Harassment is also forbidden, where the harasser on grounds of religion or belief engages in unwanted conduct which has the purpose or effect of violating the worker's dignity or creating an intimidating, hostile, degrading, humiliating or offensive environment for the worker.[110] The test is whether, having regard to all the circumstances and particularly the worker's perception, the conduct should reasonably be considered as having such an effect.[111] The ACAS guide says harassment may consist of intentional and obvious bullying, or unintentional or subtle behaviour. It may involve nicknames, teasing, name

---

108 *Eweida v British Airways PLC* UKEAT/0123/08; [2009] IRLR 78, EAT; May 2009 *Legal Action* 16.

109 *L B Islington v Ladele (Liberty – Intervenor)* UKEAT/0453/08; May 2009 *Legal Action* 17. Similarly in *McClintock v Department for Constitutional Affairs* [2008] IRLR 29, EAT.

110 EE(RB) Regs 2003 reg 5(1). See paras 17.100–17.101 for exact wording.

111 EE(RB) Regs 2003 reg 5(2); see also para 17.91 onwards on harassment generally.

calling or other behaviour which is not intended to be malicious, but nevertheless is upsetting. It may not be targeted at the individual but may consist of a general culture, eg which tolerates the telling of religious jokes. The harassment need not be on grounds of the worker's own religion or belief; it can be on grounds of that of a friend, relative or work colleague.[112]

17.61   Examples of harassment, deliberate or unintentional, could be:

- anti-Muslim remarks or so-called 'jokes' and 'banter' referring to terrorist attacks, or demonstrating general prejudice towards Muslims as a group (Islamophobia);
- allowing excessive expression of overt football allegiances where these are a proxy for sectarian rivalry, eg as may happen in Glasgow as between Celtic and Rangers fans;
- harassing Jewish workers because of their (perceived) support for Israel; allowing hostility towards the State of Israel to develop into an atmosphere of anti-Semitism;
- a devout Christian haranguing colleagues for being insufficiently religious.

Where discrimination is allowed

17.62   There are a few exceptions, eg for limited positive action[113] and for national security.[114] There are special rules allowing Sikhs wearing turbans not to wear safety helmets on construction sites.[115]

17.63   An employer may discriminate where, having regard to the nature of the employment or the context in which it is carried out, being of a particular religion or belief is a genuine and determining occupational requirement (GOR) and it is proportionate to apply such a requirement in the particular case, or it amounts to such a GOR because the employer has an ethos based on religion or belief.[116] The need for the requirement to be 'proportionate' suggests that whereas, eg a Roman Catholic school may be able to insist on its teachers being Roman Catholic, it may not be able to so insist with cleaners or gardeners.

---

112 *Saini v All Saints Haque Centre and others* UKEAT/0227/08; [2009] IRLR 74, EAT; June 2009 *Legal Action* 37.
113 EE(RB) Regs 2003 reg 25.
114 EE(RB) Regs 2003 reg 24.
115 EE(RB) Regs 2003 reg 26.
116 See exact wording of EE(RB) Regs 2003 reg 7; for an early case on 'ethos', see *Glasgow City Council v McNab* [2007] IRLR 476, EAT.

Special situations

Dress codes and appearance

17.64   Many religions have obligations in terms of dress and appearance. How people dress will depend on their level of observance. Examples of religious dress are as follows:

- As part of the five Ks of their faith, strictly practising male Sikhs do not shave or cut their hair, which is covered with a turban. They wear a 'Kara' (metal bracelet) and a 'Kirpan' (short ceremonial sword under clothing).
- Many Sikh women cover their hair with a scarf ('dupattah' or 'chooni').
- Rastafarians wear uncut hair, plaited into dreadlocks. They often wear a hat (usually, red, gold and green).
- Muslim men usually wear western shirts and trousers (not shorts), though a few may wear traditional dress. Some men will keep their heads covered at all times. Many Muslim men also grow a beard, which is considered obligatory within some schools of thought.
- Muslim women may dress modestly, covering arms and legs. Some may wear a 'hijab' (headscarf). More unusually, in some communities, women may wear a 'burqa' or 'chador', which covers them from head to ankle and conceals the shape of their body. Muslims may wear jewellery signifying marriage or religious devotion.
- Many Hindu women wear modest dress, covering their legs, eg a sari or top over loose trousers. They often wear a 'bindi' (a red dot on the forehead). Many married women wear a necklace ('mangal sutra') or other wedding jewellery, eg bangles or nose rings, as well as a wedding ring.
- Some Hindu men wear a small tuft of hair ('shikha') similar to a ponytail, although this is often hidden under the remaining hair.
- Orthodox Jewish men keep their head covered at all times, usually wearing a skullcap ('kappel', 'kippah' or 'yarmulke'). Orthodox women will dress modestly, avoiding trousers or short sleeves and skirts. They may cover their heads with a scarf.

17.65   Employers imposing rigid dress codes forbidding jewellery, headwear, beards or long hair for men, or who impose uniforms with short sleeves or skirts, may indirectly discriminate against members of certain religious groups. Whether or not it is unlawful, will usually depend on the employer's reason for imposing the rule. Reasons such as safety or hygiene are the most likely justification, but there are ways around most difficulties. In one well-publicised case,[117] the EAT upheld an ET decision that it was justifiable to require a bi-lingual support worker to remove her veil when teaching school pupils, so that children could receive optimal communication from visual clues. This is not to say that an employer could justify refusing to allow the veil in other jobs. Differential rules may also amount to direct discrimination, eg if the employer allows Sikh men to wear turbans but does not allow Muslim women to wear hijabs. For the position regarding the wearing of the veil in the tribunal, see para 21.71.

Prayer breaks

17.66   Observant Muslims need to pray five times per day at fixed times. The times are: dawn, just after midday, mid-afternoon, immediately after sunset and at night, just before going to bed. The number of occasions which fall at work therefore depends on the worker's shifts and the season. The prayer breaks take about ten minutes on each occasion, the same time it may take any worker to make coffee, have a chat or go to the toilet. Devout Hindus may also pray three times per day: at sunrise, noon and sunset. Unjustified refusal to allow time off to pray will be indirect discrimination. It is difficult to see how such a refusal could be justified, although if the employer refuses to allow any workers to take breaks of any kind, the worker may have to offer to make up the time. It is helpful that a worker is entitled to at least one 20-minute break away from the work station every six hours under the Working Time Regulations 1998 (see para 4.75). If the employer allows other workers to take breaks for different reasons, eg cigarette breaks, refusal of a prayer break could also be direct discrimination. Employers are probably not required to provide a prayer room, but if there is an available quiet space, it would almost certainly be discriminatory not to allow the worker to use it.

Sabbath working

17.67   Workers may need certain days off for religious holidays (para 17.68 below) or because of the Sabbath. The Muslim holy day is Friday and many Muslim men try to attend midday prayer at a mosque every Friday. For Jewish people, the Sabbath ('Shabbat') is Saturday, but it starts at sundown on Friday. Observant Jews must arrive at home before Sabbath begins, which means leaving work in the early afternoon during winter. A requirement to work Friday, Saturday or Sunday may

117 *Azmi v Kirklees Metropolitan Council* [2007] IRLR 485, EAT.

therefore indirectly discriminate against certain workers. Whether or not such a requirement is justifiable depends on the nature of the job and whether other arrangements can be made.

17.68   In *Copsey v WBB Devon Clays Ltd*,[118] a case brought before the EE(RB) Regs 2003 came into force, an evangelical Christian was dismissed for refusing to work Sundays on religious grounds. He claimed unfair dismissal, arguing that the relevant legislation should be interpreted in the light of article 9 (freedom of religion) of the European Convention on Human Rights. Unfortunately, several decisions by the European Commission for Human Rights say that article 9 is not even engaged on an issue of working hours, as the worker can simply find alternative employment. The three Court of Appeal judges in *Copsey* differed as to whether the Commission's decisions must be followed. However, they all agreed the practical issue under unfair dismissal law was to balance the employer's interests with those of the worker, giving particular emphasis to the need for an employer to do his/her best to accommodate the worker's needs, especially when changing previously suitable contractual hours. The Court of Appeal's judgment is very interesting to read and its principles would presumably also apply when considering whether indirect religious discrimination under the EE(RB) Regs 2003 is justified.

17.69   There are also long-standing rules under the ERA 1996, allowing shop and betting workers to refuse to work on Sundays (see para 6.88).

Religious holidays and time off

17.70   Every religion has a range of holidays of varying importance. Each individual will have his/her own feelings as to which holidays s/he feels obliged to observe. Very often the holidays are part of a cultural as well as a religious tradition and there are social and family pressures to observe the day, even if the individual is not particularly religious. The dates of the holidays can be hard to ascertain in advance, as many follow the lunar year. Jewish holidays start at sundown the previous evening. Advance dates of Jewish holidays can be found on the following websites: www.jewishgen.org/jos/josfest.htm or www.bod.org.uk (click 'Jewish Calendar').

17.71   The two most important festivals for Muslims are Eid-al-Fitr, which marks the end of Ramadan; and Eid-al-Adha. The exact date depends on a sighting of the new moon and is not known far in advance. 'Eid' means festival. Muslim workers would need at least one day off on

118 [2005] IRLR 811, CA.

each occasion to celebrate appropriately. Major Hindu festivals include Divali (or Deepavali) in October/November; which marks the end of the Hindu year; Holi (in February/March); Raksha bandhan (in August); and Navratri (in September/October). The main Sikh festivals include the Birthday of Guru Nanak (in October/November); Vaisakhi, the New Year festival, normally on 13 April; and Bandhi Chhord (October/November), at the same time as Divali – many Sikhs celebrate both. There are 13 key days which a minority of observant Jews would follow. The most important and universally observed dates requiring time off work are Yom Kippur (the Day of Atonement) and Rosh Hashannah (the New Year). These fall in September/October. Pesach (or Passover), near Easter, and Chanukah, near Christmas, are also commonly celebrated. Other holidays include Sukkot, Shavuot and Tish'ah B'av. Greek Orthodox Easter is a different date from that usually observed for Easter by other Christian religions.

17.72   Not all religious holidays require time off work, but most do. Difficulties arise when employers object to granting time off, saying that the worker has benefited from time off over Christmas and Easter. This is rather unfair when such holidays are traditional bank holidays for all workers regardless of their religion. In most circumstances, refusal to allow the worker time off for a religious holiday would be discriminatory. It should not be underestimated how important many of these religious holidays are to the individual and his/her family. The question is whether the time should be paid or unpaid, or whether it should come out of the worker's annual holiday entitlement. Legally, this is difficult to answer. Requiring the time to come out of existing holiday entitlement is arguably indirect discrimination, because the worker is disadvantaged by using up one of his/her holiday days to meet religious obligations, which may not even be of a recreational or festive nature (eg a fast day). The best solution would appear to be paid leave. Arguably this discriminates against those who are not of a religion requiring additional holidays, but it is doubtful this is a comparable situation. It is thoughtless, unfair and possibly discriminatory to fix social events, important meetings or one-off training on important religious holidays. Dates should routinely be checked in advance.

Sources of further information

17.73   The Muslim Council of Britain has produced a Good Practice Guide for Employers and Employees: *Muslims in the Workplace*.[119] The Board of

---

119 Available at www.mcb.org.uk/faith/approved.pdf

Deputies has published *Employment. A Practical Guide for Employers and Jewish Employees.*[120]

Discrimination against gay men and lesbians

The legal framework

17.74   In a Trades Union Congress (TUC) survey at the end of 1998 of 440 gay, lesbian and bisexual workers, 44 per cent said they had suffered discrimination at work because of their sexuality.[121] In a UNISON survey in 2003, 52 per cent of its members said they had experienced harassment because they were lesbian or gay. Yet despite evidence of the desperate need, no government was prepared to legislate against such discrimination until the intervention of Europe. As part of the European Council's General Framework Directive,[122] discrimination on grounds of sexual orientation was made unlawful from December 2003 by the Employment Equality (Sexual Orientation) Regulations (EE(SO) Regs) 2003.[123] ACAS has issued guidance on the regulations: *Sexual Orientation and the Workplace: Putting the Employment Equality (Sexual Orientation) Regulations 2003 into Practice.*[124]

17.75   The government estimates that between 1.3 and 1.9 million workers are covered by the law and that up to 390,000 employees have experienced discrimination at work due to their sexual orientation. In the year 2007/8, 582 employment tribunal cases were started concerning sexual orientation discrimination. There are two research papers available on the ACAS website: *Sexual orientation and religion or belief discrimination in the workplace [Ref: 01/07]* and *The experiences of sexual orientation and religion or belief discrimination employment tribunal claimants [Ref: 02/07].*[125]

17.76   The regulations mirror the religion and belief regulations and are structured in a very similar way to the RRA 1976 and SDA 1975. It is therefore worth reading chapters 13, 16 and 19 for equivalent case-

---

120 This can be downloaded from
     www.boardofdeputies.org.uk/file/Employment.pdf
121 (1999) 86 EOR 13.
122 2000/78/EC.
123 SI No 1661.
124 Available at www.acas.org.uk/media/pdf/e/n/sexual_1.pdf
125 Summary available at www.acas.org.uk/media/pdf/d/j/
     SORB_summaries_1.pdf

law and the approach to evidence. As with those statutes, employees in the widest sense are covered, ie including those employed personally on a contract to do any work, as well as apprentices and contract workers.[126] The police are also covered.[127] The employing organisation is vicariously liable for discrimination carried out in the course of employment by its managers or junior staff against the worker.[128]

17.77   It is unlawful to discriminate on grounds of sexual orientation. 'Sexual orientation' means orientation towards others of the same sex or opposite sex or both.[129] According to the explanatory notes to the regulations, it does not extend to sexual practices or preferences, eg sado-masochism or paedophilia.

17.78   As with all discrimination law, the Regulations cover discrimination in recruitment, during employment, by dismissal including constructive dismissal,[130] and after the employment relationship has ended, provided that any post-termination discrimination arises out of and is closely connected with the former employment relationship.[131]

17.79   The burden of proof is as under the RRA 1976 and SDA 1975.[132] ET time limits and available remedies are as for the RRA 1976.[133] The questionnaire procedure is also available[134] and an inference can be drawn from failure to reply properly within eight weeks.

The meaning of 'discrimination'

17.80   The usual concepts of discrimination apply, ie direct discrimination, indirect discrimination, victimisation and harassment.[135] Direct discrimination is where the worker is treated less favourably on grounds of sexual orientation.[136] This includes discrimination based on a

---

126 EE(SO) Regs 2003 regs 2 and 8. See para 13.14 for meaning of 'contract workers' under the RRA 1976 and SDA 1975.

127 EE(SO) Regs 2003 reg 11.

128 EE(SO) Regs 2003 reg 22; see also para 13.20 for the equivalent under the RRA 1976 and SDA 1975.

129 EE(SO) Regs 2003 reg 2.

130 EE(SO) Regs 2003 reg 6(5).

131 EE(SO) Regs 2003 reg 21.

132 EE(SO) Regs 2003 reg 29; paras 16.1–16.10.

133 EE(SO) Regs 2003 regs 20–34; chapter 19.

134 EE(SO) Regs 2003 reg 33, Sch 2; paras 21.2–21.12 and specialist guides from Central London Law Centre, see appendix F at pp784–785.

135 EE(SO) Regs 2003 regs 3–5.

136 EE(SO) Regs 2003 reg 3(1)(a); see also paras 13.40–13.51 under the RRA 1976 and SDA 1975.

perception of the worker's sexual orientation, whether correct or false. A worker who is discriminated against because of a false perception that s/he is gay would therefore be protected. It also means that a worker may not need to disclose his/her sexual orientation when bringing an ET claim. Discrimination against a worker because of someone else's sexual orientation is also covered, eg because s/he has gay friends or because s/he refuses to carry out an employer's instruction to discriminate against gay men or lesbians. In this respect, the wording copies that of the RRA 1976 regarding discrimination 'on grounds of race', ie the worker's own or someone else's race.

17.81   Indirect discrimination is where the worker is put at a particular disadvantage because of the application of a provision, criterion or practice which the employer cannot show to be a proportionate means of achieving a legitimate aim.[137] Victimisation protects a worker against less favourable treatment because s/he has complained about discrimination.[138]

Harassment

17.82   Harassment is also forbidden, where the harasser, on grounds of sexual orientation, engages in unwanted conduct which has the purpose or effect of violating the worker's dignity or creating an intimidating, hostile, degrading, humiliating or offensive environment for the worker.[139] The test is whether, having regard to all the circumstances and particularly the worker's perception, the conduct should reasonably be considered as having such an effect.[140] The TUC says the most common form of discrimination faced by lesbian and gay workers is harassment, and the majority of successful tribunal claims have concerned this. The ACAS guide states that harassment may comprise intentional and obvious bullying, or unintentional or subtle behaviour. It may involve nicknames, teasing, name-calling or other behaviour which is not intended to be malicious, but nevertheless is upsetting. It may not be targeted at the individual but may consist of a general culture, eg which tolerates the telling of homophobic jokes. Harassment can be based on the sexual orientation of the worker or of

---

137 EE(SO) Regs 2003 reg 3(1)(b); see also paras 13.52–13.84 under the RRA 1976 and SDA 1975.

138 EE(SO) Regs 2003 reg 4; see also paras 13.85–13.96 under the RRA 1976 and SDA 1975.

139 EE(SO) Regs 2003 reg 5(1). See paras 17.100–17.101 for exact wording.

140 EE(SO) Regs 2003 reg 5(2); see also paras 17.91 onwards on harassment generally.

someone else, eg a friend or relative. It is also unlawful to harass some-one on the misconception that they are gay or even using homophobic abuse when knowing perfectly well that they are not gay.[141]

17.83   Examples of harassment, deliberate or unintentional, could be:

- 'outing' (ie revealing the sexuality of) a lesbian, gay or bisexual worker for malicious reasons or against his/her wishes;
- spreading rumours that a gay man has HIV just because he takes sick leave or loses weight;
- where lesbian, gay or bisexual workers complain of harassment, accusing them of being over-sensitive, having no sense of humour or bringing it on themselves by hiding (or revealing) their sexual ori-entation.

17.84   Much has been made of the possible conflict with the law against reli-gious discrimination, ie can a worker be prevented from making homo-phobic observations if these are an expression of his/her religious views? It is hoped that this will rarely occur in practice. The ACAS guide notes that although some religions have strong views about sexual orientation, most do not advocate persecution of people because of their sexual orientation. Everyone has the right to be treated with dig-nity and respect in the workplace, whatever his/her race, sex, age, dis-ability, religion or sexual orientation. Workers need not be friends, but they should treat each other professionally. In one case, it was found not to be unlawful indirect religious discrimination for a Coun-cil to require all its marriage registrars to perform civil partnership ceremonies when needed. It was justifiable for the Council to want to provide its services in a non-discriminatory manner and to include the gay community. It would have undermined the Council's com-mitment to equal opportunities if it had allowed a Christian Registrar to be excused those duties.[142]

Where discrimination is allowed

17.85   There are a few exceptions, eg for limited positive action[143] and for national security.[144] The Regulations also allow the granting of

---

141 *English v Thomas Sanderson Ltd* [2008] EWCA Civ 1421; [2009] IRLR 206, CA; May 2009 *Legal Action* 16.
142 *L B Islington v Ladele (Liberty – Intervenor)* UKEAT/0453/08; [2009] IRLR 154, EAT; May 2009 *Legal Action* 17 .
143 EE(SO) Regs 2003 reg 26.
144 EE(SO) Regs 2003 reg 24.

benefits to married people or civil partners to the exclusion of others.[145]

17.86 An employer may discriminate where being of a particular sexual orientation is a genuine and determining occupational requirement (GOR) and it is proportionate to apply such a requirement.[146] Controversially, however, there is a specific exception under EE(SO) Regs 2003 reg 7(3) where employment is for the purpose of an organised religion. In such a case, the employer may apply a requirement relating to sexual orientation (i) so as to comply with the doctrines of the religion, or (ii) because of the nature of the employment and the context in which it is carried out, so as to avoid conflicting with the strongly held religious convictions of a significant number of the religion's followers.

17.87 In a test case,[147] various trade unions argued that the regulation 7(3) GOR was too wide and outside the Directive. The High Court disagreed, but it did say that regulation 7(3) must be construed strictly and purposively, to ensure compatibility with the Directive. The term 'for the purposes of an organised religion' does not mean 'for the purposes of a religious organisation'. In particular, employment in a faith school is not likely to be for the purposes of an organised religion. This decision confirms the intentions of the government.[148] It seems that regulation 7(3) covers jobs such as minister of religion but not cleaners or even teachers in a religious school.

Special considerations

17.88 A survey in 2003 showed that nearly 40 per cent of UNISON's lesbian and gay members were not 'out' to all their managers, and over 80 per cent were not out to their client group. Men were twice as likely to be out at work as women. This has implications for the nature of workplace policies, the purpose of monitoring, and the willingness of individuals to complain about discrimination or harassment. The

---

145 EE(SO) Regs 2003 reg 25. The previous exclusion, referring only to marital status and before the Civil Partnership Act 2004 came into force, was unsuccessfully challenged as contrary to the Directive in the *Amicus* case, see below n147.

146 EE(SO) Regs 2003 reg 7.

147 *R (on the application of Amicus – MSF section and others) v Secretary of State for Trade and Industry and Christian Action Research Education and others* [2004] IRLR 430, HC.

148 See Lord Sainsbury in the House of Lords debate on 17 June 2003, extracts at 119 EOR 26–27.

Regulations do not require employers to monitor sexual orientation. Whether or not they should monitor this and what its purpose would be, are difficult questions given that, unlike with race and gender, workers may choose to hide their sexual orientation at work. The TUC has produced a useful guide, which also covers transsexual workers: *Monitoring LGBT workers*.[149]

17.89　The statutory entitlements to dependant, parental, adoption and 'paternity' leave are all available where there are same-sex partners. Any additional policies offered by the employer should state that they are equally available to same-sex partners, eg compassionate and bereavement leave; parental and adoption leave; carers' leave; perks such as private healthcare insurance, free travel and discounts on company goods. Granting benefits only to those with heterosexual partners would probably be direct discrimination.

Criminal convictions

17.90　Historically, gay men have been vulnerable to criminal convictions in respect of offences which are no longer unlawful or have no heterosexual equivalent. Employers who refuse to recruit anyone with any kind of criminal conviction or arrest record may therefore indirectly discriminate against gay men, unless the particular job justifies their policy. The ACAS Code suggests that employers take into account the fact that laws relating to gay men have changed significantly over time and many convictions are unlikely to have any bearing on the individual's skills and suitability for the job. The Human Rights Act 1998 may also be helpful in unfair dismissal cases where homosexual workers are dismissed in connection with sexual activity.[150] Article 8 of the European Convention on Human Rights, which is concerned with the right to a *private* life, may not help where the employer dismisses for an offence which is committed in public, eg in a public lavatory,[151] but in order to be a fair dismissal, the conviction would still need to be detrimental to the worker's ability to carry out his job.

149 Available at www.tuc.org.uk/equality/tuc-9303-f0.cfm
150 See para 3.20 above.
151 *X v Y* [2003] IRLR 561, EAT.

Harassment

Meaning of harassment under discrimination legislation[152]

17.91   Until various changes to discrimination law made during 2003 as a result of the EU Race Discrimination and General Framework Directives,[153] there was no explicit definition of harassment within the RRA 1976, SDA 1975 or DDA 1995. Nevertheless, harassment was unlawful under those statutes and a large body of case-law developed. Some of this old case-law will be applicable to the new concept, but much of it will be too restrictive as the new definition has wider scope.

17.92   In 1991 the European Commission adopted a Recommendation on the Protection of the Dignity of Women and Men at Work. Annexed to the Recommendation is a Code of Practice on measures to combat sexual harassment. The exact legal effect of the code is unclear, but the ET should take it into account where relevant in sexual harassment cases.[154] The Code covers the definition of harassment, preventative steps and handling grievances.

17.93   It is useful first to consider the old way in which the discrimination statutes covered harassment, as this may still apply to forms of less favourable treatment falling outside the new definition. Moreover, this old method still applies under RRA 1976 where harassment is not on grounds of race or ethnic or national origins.

The old method

17.94   Under the old method, harassment fell within the definition of direct race or sex discrimination (and sometimes victimisation), taking the form of a prohibited act under RRA 1976 s4 or SDA 1975 s6. For example, on grounds of race or sex, the worker was not promoted, was denied benefits or, most commonly, was subjected to 'any other detriment' such as disciplinary action, verbal abuse or physical assault.

17.95   The test is the normal one for direct discrimination, ie has the worker been less favourably treated on grounds of his/her sex than

---

152 This section should be read together with chapter 13 on race and sex discrimination law and paras 17.49–17.90 on religion and belief and sexual orientation discrimination.

153 See chapter 12.

154 *Grimaldi v Fonds des Maladies Professionelles* [1990] IRLR 400, ECJ; *Wadman v Carpenter Farrer Partnership* [1993] IRLR 374, EAT.

someone of the opposite sex has or would have been treated? Where the treatment is gender-specific or based on stereotypical assumptions about gender characteristics, then as a matter of fact, it will probably, but not automatically, be less favourable treatment between the sexes.[155] Where the treatment appears 'neutral', eg the employer shouts at the worker or tears up his/her letters, it will be harder to prove that a worker of a different sex would have been treated differently.

17.96 If the harasser continues or intensifies the harassment or otherwise punishes the worker after s/he complains to the harasser or to management of the harassment, this may be unlawful victimisation as well as further direct discrimination.

Detriment

17.97 A 'detriment' simply means 'putting at a disadvantage'.[156] There does not need to be any physical or economic consequences. The EC Code (see para 17.92) suggests it is purely a subjective test whether sexual harassment has occurred, as does some of the case-law. But the leading cases on the meaning of 'detriment' import an objective measure. They say it is necessary to show that by reason of the acts complained of, a reasonable worker would or might take the view that s/he had been disadvantaged in the circumstances in which s/he had thereafter to work.[157] An unjustified sense of grievance cannot amount to a detriment. On the other hand, the test should be applied from the worker's viewpoint, ie is his/her opinion that the treatment was to his/her detriment a reasonable one to hold?[158]

17.98 Several cases have dealt with how serious the detriment must be to amount to an unlawful act. A single incident of harassment can amount to a detriment 'provided it is sufficiently serious'. A one-off racist or sexist 'joke' or remark will not always be enough in itself, but the surrounding circumstances may make it so. For example, an offensive or demeaning sexual comment made by a junior employee to a supervisor in front of others could be unlawful.[159] Where there is a series of incidents, it is important not to look at each one separately, since there

---

155 *MacDonald v Advocate-General for Scotland; Pearce v Governing Body of Mayfield School* [2003] UKHL 34; [2003] IRLR 512.
156 *Jeremiah v Ministry of Defence* [1979] 3 All ER 833; [1979] IRLR 436, CA. See also para 13.37.
157 *Shamoon v Chief Constable of the RUC* [2003] IRLR 285, HL.
158 *Shamoon v Chief Constable of the RUC* [2003] IRLR 285, HL.
159 *Insitu Cleaning Co Ltd v Heads* [1995] IRLR 4, EAT.

can be a cumulative effect which exceeds the sum of each incident.[160] Incidents trivial in themselves can acquire a measure of seriousness if they appear to be recurrent.[161] Once unwelcome sexual interest has been shown by a man in a female employee, other incidents which would normally appear quite unobjectionable, eg asking to look at personal photographs, can take on a different significance.[162]

17.99   Note that where the new definition applies and treatment amounts to 'harassment', it can no longer be claimed as a 'detriment'.[163] This prevents both legal schemes being used at once. Arguably, if the facts do not fit the new definition, the old method can still be used. If in doubt, a claim should be made in the alternative, eg 'I have been subjected to harassment contrary to RRA 1976 s3A and/or direct discrimination in the events described above, contrary to RRA 1976 ss1(1)(a) and 4(2)(d)'.

The specific definition of harassment

17.100 The specific definition of harassment is almost identical under RRA 1976 s3A (where it is on grounds of race or ethnic or national origins), DDA 1995 s3B, EE(RB) Regs 2003[164] reg 5; EE(SO) Regs[165] reg 5; and EE(A) Regs 2006[166] reg 6. Section 4A of SDA 1975 contains this common definition together with two additional definitions, as explained below. See chapters 13, 15 and the rest of this chapter for the overall ambit of each piece of discrimination law and examples of harassment on each of the grounds.

17.101 Under the specific definition, the harasser harasses a worker if:

- on grounds of race or ethnic or national origins, sexual orientation, religion or belief, age, or for reasons related to the worker's sex or that of another person or the worker's disability,
- s/he engages in unwanted conduct,
- which has the purpose or effect of –
  (a) violating the worker's dignity, or
  (b) creating an intimidating, hostile, degrading, humiliating or offensive environment for the worker,

---

160 *Reed and Bull Information Systems Ltd v Stedman* [1999] IRLR 299, EAT.
161 *Scott v Commissioners of Inland Revenue* [2004] IRLR 713, CA, obiter.
162 *Reed and Bull Information Systems Ltd v Stedman* [1999] IRLR 299, EAT.
163 RRA 1976 s78; EE(SO) Regs 2003 reg 2(3); EE(RB) Regs 2003 reg 2(3).
164 SI No 1660.
165 SI No 1661.
166 SI No 1031.

- and it should reasonably be regarded as having that effect, having regard to all the circumstances including, in particular, the perception of the harassed worker.

Generally, this includes harassment based on the race, sexual orientation, religion etc of someone else, eg a friend or relative of the worker. But the definition under the DDA 1995 requires harassment to be related to the worker's own disability. Harassment of the worker because of the disability of a friend or relative is unlawful under the General Framework Directive (2000/78/EC).[167] The question now arises whether the DDA 1995 can be interpreted consistently with the Directive so as to cover such 'associative' harassment.[168]

17.102 The other difficulty with the definition of harassment is that, apart from in relation to disability and sex, it prohibits harassment 'on grounds of' race, religion, age, etc whereas the various EU Directives speak of harassment 'related to' race, etc. Unlike with the definition of direct discrimination, which was previously used for harassment situations, it should not be necessary to make comparisons with how someone of a different race or sex, etc would have been treated.[169] However, the phrase 'on grounds of' still has a more restricted meaning than the Directives' wording, 'related to'. It suggests that the harassment must be caused by race or religion, etc as opposed to simply connected with it. In practice, this can make a big difference.[170] Indeed, the definition of harassment in the SDA was redrafted to replace 'on grounds of' with 'related to' from 6 April 2008 following a judicial review brought by the former EOC.[171] The parallel definitions under the other discrimination legislation could be challenged on the same basis. The wider wording in the Directives may also be able to challenge situations where an employer permits a member of the public to harass a worker, even though the employer's conduct is not in itself on grounds of race, etc. A new definition of third party harass-

---

167 *Coleman v Attridge Law* [2008] IRLR 722. See also para 15.44 regarding the same point on direct disability discrimination.

168 An ET has said that it can, but the decision is under appeal. *Coleman v (1) EBR Attridge Law LLP (formerly Attridge Law) (2)* Law 2303745/2005/ET.

169 *Wandsworth NHS Primary Care Trust v Obonyo (No 1)* UKEAT/0237/05; 155 EOR 28, EAT.

170 For examples where it may make a difference, see *Equal Opportunities Commission v Secretary of State for Trade and Industry* [2007] IRLR 327, HC, concerning the former definition of harassment under the SDA.

171 *Equal Opportunities Commission v Secretary of State for Trade and Industry* [2007] IRLR 327, HC.

ment has been introduced into the SDA 1975, again as a result of the EOC judicial review. For more details of harassment by the public, see para 17.125 below.

17.103   There is an additional category of sexual harassment if the harasser engages in any form of unwanted verbal, non-verbal or physical conduct of a sexual nature with the same purpose or effect.[172] There is a final category of harassment under the SDA 1975, where a worker is treated less favourably on grounds that s/he has rejected or submitted to the unlawful harassment.[173] It is also unlawful to subject a worker to harassment on the ground that s/he intends to undergo, has undergone or is undergoing gender reassignment or to treat him/her less favourably because s/he has rejected or submitted to such unwanted conduct.[174]

17.104   Although 'harassment' is traditionally understood as meaning behaviour such as verbal or physical abuse, the legal definition is much wider. 'Unwanted conduct ... creating a hostile etc environment' could presumably include actions such as oppressive disciplinary action, which would normally be covered by the definition of direct discrimination. It may be especially tempting to claim under the heading of 'harassment' in those tricky cases where the wider definition is needed. The scope of the definition and its relationship with the definition of direct discrimination is untested, but as both cannot apply at once, it will sometimes be safest to make the tribunal claim in the alternative.[175]

The harassment is unwanted

17.105   It is crucial under the specific definition as well as under traditional harassment law to prove the behaviour was unwanted. Harassers often try to suggest that black workers don't mind racist banter or women are happily flirting back.

17.106   The harasser sometimes argues that the worker did not complain for a long time and as soon as s/he did complain, the harasser stopped. The EAT has said that some conduct is obviously unwelcome unless invited. On the other hand, with less obvious behaviour, the question would be whether the woman, by words or behaviour, made it clear that she found the conduct unwelcome. She need not make a public fuss

172 SDA 1975 s4A(1)(b).
173 SDA 1975 s4A(1)(c).
174 SDA 1975 s4A(3) and (4).
175 As explained in para 17.99. See also para 13.37.

to indicate her disapproval; walking out of the room might be sufficient, provided that any reasonable person would understand her to be rejecting the conduct.[176]

17.107 Unfortunately a woman's sexual attitudes may be considered relevant. In some old cases which were taken under the direct discrimination definition, the EAT said that evidence of a worker's mode of dress at work[177] and evidence showing that a woman talked freely about sexual matters to fellow workers[178] can be relevant both to whether she suffered a detriment and to compensation for injury to feelings. Somewhat inconsistently, the EAT also acknowledged that 'a person may be quite happy to accept the remarks of A or B in a sexual context, and wholly upset by similar remarks made by C'.[179] These cases should be challenged as out of date, following the principles set out in the 1991 EC Code.

The reasonableness test

17.108 The other big issue on the specific definition is the requirement that the unwanted conduct must be 'reasonably regarded' as violating dignity or creating an offensive environment. Although the worker's perception is heavily taken into account, this does mean there is an element of objectivity in the test. This reasonableness test is contrary to previous case-law, the EC Code, and does not appear in the Equal Treatment Amendment Directive (ETAD). Although the test only applies where the harasser's conduct has an unintended effect, motive is generally irrelevant in discrimination law.

17.109 The EC code defines sexual harassment as:

> ... unwanted conduct of a sexual nature or other conduct based on sex affecting the dignity of women and men at work ... a range of behaviour may be considered to constitute sexual harassment. It is unacceptable if such conduct is unwanted, unreasonable and offensive to the recipient. The essential characteristic of sexual harassment is that it is unwanted by the recipient, that it is for each individual to determine what behaviour is acceptable to them and what they regard as offensive.

Employers' liability

17.110 Under discrimination law, the employing organisation is legally responsible for any discriminatory action by one employee against another,

176 *Reed and Bull Information Systems Ltd v Stedman* [1999] IRLR 299, EAT.
177 *Wileman v Minilec Engineering* [1988] IRLR 144; [1988] ICR 318, EAT.
178 *Snowball v Gardner Merchant* [1987] IRLR 397; [1987] ICR 719, EAT.
179 *Wileman v Minilec Engineering* [1988] IRLR 144; [1988] ICR 318, EAT.

provided that the action is carried out in the course of employment. This is often called 'vicarious liability'. The organisation is vicariously liable even if it did not instruct, authorise, approve or even know of the discrimination.

17.111   When is a discriminatory act carried out outside the course of employment? The most important case on this issue is *Jones v Tower Boot Co Ltd*,[180] where Mr Jones was subjected to a number of horrific incidents of verbal and physical racial abuse. These took place in work time and on work premises. The employers argued that they could not be liable for such clearly unauthorised acts carried out by fellow employees. The Court of Appeal disagreed, saying that the words 'in the course of employment' should be given their natural meaning. The whole point was to widen the net of responsibility beyond the guilty employees themselves, by making employers additionally responsible.

17.112   Discrimination carried out in work time and on the premises by fellow employees therefore seems to be covered, even if it is extremely serious and wholly unrelated to the employment, eg physical assault. But harassment often takes place out of work time or during rest breaks. It will then be for each ET to decide on the facts whether it took place during 'the course of employment'.[181] An incident which occurs during a chance meeting between work colleagues at a supermarket, for example, would almost certainly not be covered.[182] Similarly, an incident when one employee visits another where s/he is living outside work hours and on a purely social basis will probably not be covered.[183] On the other hand, harassment during business trips, office Christmas parties, organised leaving parties or a social gathering of work colleagues in the pub immediately after work, may well be 'in the course of employment'.[184]

The employer's defence

17.113   The employer is responsible regardless of whether s/he knew or approved of the unlawful act, unless s/he 'took such steps as were reasonably practicable' to prevent unlawful acts of discrimination.[185] It is for the employer to prove this defence.[186]

180 [1997] IRLR 168; (1997) 71 EOR 40, CA.
181 *Jones v Tower Boot Co Ltd* [1997] IRLR 168; (1997) 71 EOR 40, CA.
182 *Chief Constable of the Lincolnshire Police v Stubbs* [1999] IRLR 81, EAT.
183 *Waters v Commissioner of Police of the Metropolis* [1997] IRLR 589, CA.
184 *Chief Constable of the Lincolnshire Police v Stubbs* [1999] IRLR 81, EAT.
185 RRA 1976 s32(3); SDA 1975 s41(3); DDA 1995 s58(5); EE(SO) Regs 2003 reg 22(3); EE(RB) Regs reg 22(3).
186 *Waters v Commissioner of Police of the Metropolis* [1997] IRLR 589, CA.

17.114   It is important to remember that the employer's responsibility is to take preventative action; it is not a defence that the employer acted promptly once s/he discovered the discrimination, eg by sacking the harasser (although this may prevent liability for further discrimination).

17.115   There are no rigid guidelines on the necessary level of preventative action, but this defence does not often succeed. A written equal opportunities policy is unlikely to suffice unless it is very actively implemented. As one ET put it when allowing the defence: 'Harassment [in the workplace] is a live issue, not a dead letter.'[187] A useful measure of adequate preventative action is contained in the recommendations of the EC Code on Sexual Harassment.

Employer's reaction to a complaint of harassment

17.116   In some cases, particularly in small organisations, the perpetrator is in reality the employer and there is no one more senior for the worker to turn to. In many cases, however, the perpetrator is a colleague or intermediate manager and the worker may complain about his/her treatment to more senior management. As protection against victimisation, it would be wise to make the complaint in writing.

17.117   The employing organisation will not only be vicariously liable for the harassment itself, but it may also be guilty of direct discrimination and/or victimisation in the way it reacts to the complaint. The discrimination could occur both in the way the complaint is investigated (or not investigated) and also in the subsequent reaction, eg transfer or dismissal of the worker.

17.118   To show that this is direct race discrimination, for example, it is necessary to prove that a worker of a different race bringing an equivalent complaint would not have received the same reaction; for example, the complaint would have been treated more seriously and investigated more thoroughly and the worker would have been kept better informed. Further, s/he would not have been transferred or dismissed as a consequence.[188]

17.119   It is not necessary to have evidence of any such comparable incident in the past. As with any direct race discrimination case, the ET can infer from the evidence generally that a complaint from a white person would have been dealt with in a more favourable manner.

---

187 *Graham v Royal Mail and Nicholson* (1994) 20 EOR DCLD 5, ET. Though see the research report on women in the Royal Mail during the 1990s referred to in (1999) 83 EOR 3.

188 Similar comparisons would be made for direct discrimination on other grounds, though under the SDA 1975, it may be a further form of harassment under section 4A(1)(c).

17.120   The ETs have been undecided about what is a sensible actual or hypothetical comparison. Is the question how the employer would have treated a white worker complaining of: (a) racial harassment by a colleague or manager, (b) non-racial harassment or violence from a colleague or manager, or (c) any serious grievance? The first option does not seem to be a helpful comparison because it is far less common for such a situation to occur in most workplaces. The second or third scenarios provide a more logical comparison, but even then, it is not really comparable as there is not the same stigma attached.

17.121   Whether or not the employer can be accused of direct discrimination in the handling of and response to the complaint, his/her treatment of the worker may amount to victimisation, ie penalising him/her for raising the issue. Victimisation only applies where the worker's complaint related to treatment which would, if proved, be unlawful discrimination. For example, a black worker who is sacked for complaining about a racial assault which took place outside the course of employment probably cannot claim victimisation under the RRA 1976, although s/he may be able to claim direct discrimination if the employer would not have sacked a white worker who complained about an assault outside work by a colleague.

17.122   A worker may also be able to claim unlawful detriment or dismissal under the health and safety or whistleblowing legislation[189] if s/he is penalised by his/her employer for complaining about harassment. This is useful where the victimisation provisions of the discrimination legislation do not apply, eg because the harassment occurred outside the course of employment, or was not based on race, sex or any of the unlawful grounds.

Constructive dismissal

17.123 As well as any discrimination claim, if an employer commits a repudiatory or fundamental breach of contract, an employee may resign and claim constructive unfair dismissal[190] provided s/he meets the unfair dismissal eligibility requirements. What amounts to a repudiatory breach is a question of fact, but in the key case of *Western Excavating (ECC) v Sharp*,[191] Lawton LJ said that:

> Persistent and unwanted amorous advances by an employer to a female member of his staff would clearly be such conduct.

189 See para 6.77 onwards and 6.91 onwards.
190 See paras 6.35–6.44.
191 [1978] IRLR 27; [1978] ICR 221, CA.

In *Bracebridge Engineering v Darby*,[192] the employer's failure to treat seriously and fully investigate the worker's allegations of assault clearly amounted to a repudiatory breach of the implied term of trust and confidence and the obligation not to undermine the confidence of female staff.

Harassment by the public

17.124 The employer is not vicariously liable under discrimination law for harassment by members of the public. However, an employer may be guilty of discrimination in his/her reaction to harassment by the public or a complaint about it. For example, it would be direct discrimination to ignore racial harassment from the public against a black member of staff but to take action when a white worker makes an equivalent complaint. In addition, failure to take appropriate action may entitle an employee to resign and claim constructive unfair dismissal.

17.125 In the well-publicised case of *Burton & Rhule v De Vere Hotels*[193] some black waitresses employed by a hotel claimed race discrimination against the hotel after they were subjected to racially offensive remarks by a speaker (Bernard Manning), who had been booked by guests hiring the hotel. The hotel itself had not treated the waitresses any differently from how it would have treated white waiters or waitresses. Nevertheless, the EAT said that an employer could be liable for the harassment itself if s/he could have anticipated it would happen and taken action to prevent the worker being subjected to it. Unfortunately this approach, though morally desirable, was legally wrong and was disapproved by the House of Lords.[194] *Burton* was decided as a direct discrimination case. It is arguable that the specific definition of harassment can make employers legally responsible for harassment by the public, eg if an employer's policy of not challenging racist clients creates an offensive environment for the worker.[195] However, there may still be problems in showing that the harassment was 'on grounds of' race. This difficulty is avoided under the DDA 1995 and SDA 1975, where the definitions use the wider phrase 'related to' rather than 'on grounds of'. This replicates the wording of the EU Directives. Indeed, the

192 [1990] IRLR 3, EAT.
193 [1996] IRLR 596, EAT; (1996) 70 EOR 48.
194 *MacDonald v Advocate-General for Scotland; Pearce v Governing Body of Mayfield School* [2003] UKHL 34; [2003] IRLR 512.
195 *Gravell v London Borough of Bexley* UKEAT/0587/06.

definition in the SDA 1975 was amended following a judicial review by the EOC (see para 17.101 above). There is also a new offence of third party harassment in the SDA 1975 alone. Under s6(2A)–(2D), an employer subjects a woman to harassment where a third party subjects the woman to harassment in the course of her employment, and the employer has failed to take such steps as would have been reasonably practicable to prevent the third party from doing so. This does not apply unless the employer knows that the woman has been subject to harassment in the course of her employment on at least two other occasions by a third party, not necessarily the same one. A 'third party' means anyone other than the employer or someone employed by the employer. The employer's responsibility for third party harassment also extends to where the harassment is on grounds of gender reassignment. It is a mystery why it is necessary for the harassment to have already occurred at least twice, before an employer can be liable. Arguably this restriction is unlawful under the Equal Treatment Directive (2002/73/EC). Where the employer cannot be made liable for third party harassment under the discrimination legislation, it is a question of exploring claims in the civil or criminal courts (see below).

Civil or criminal claims outside the discrimination legislation

17.126 Sometimes due to the limitations of the discrimination legislation, other legal claims in the civil courts may be appropriate. These can also apply where the harassment, eg assault or general bullying, is not based on race, sex, disability or other protected grounds. Usually an ET claim under the RRA 1976, SDA 1975, DDA 1995, age, religious or sexual orientation regulations is preferable.[196] It offers a simpler and quicker procedure, with the benefit of the statutory questionnaire procedure. Where the worker is not eligible for public funding (legal aid) or backed by a trade union or the Equality and Human Rights Commission (EHRC), the costs risk of losing in the county court or High Court makes it an unrealistic option. However, advisers may want to explore whether the worker has legal protection insurance or, if not, the option of a conditional fee arrangement ('no win no fee') with after-the-event insurance against costs risks. Furthermore, as an industrial court, the ET may be more willing than a county court or High Court to understand and believe the claim (although

---

196 Consider also the implications of *Sheriff v Klyne Tugs (Lowestoft) Ltd* [1999] IRLR 481, CA at para 19.28 below.

this may be too optimistic a view). The following suggestions are not a full list of civil and criminal possibilities.

Common law claims

17.127 Where the harassment involves physical contact, particularly if there is a severe assault, the worker may have a claim for damages at common law in civil assault against the perpetrator. Even where there is no physical contact, a claim in tort may be possible where the perpetrator intentionally inflicts injury (physical or psychiatric) by his/her words or actions.[197] An employee can also claim against his/her employer for negligence if the employer fails to protect him/her against victimisation or harassment which causes physical or psychiatric injury.[198] The employer will not be liable unless s/he knows or ought to know that harassment is taking place and fails to take reasonable steps to prevent it.[199] Common law claims are an under-used remedy and the possibility should not be overlooked. The advantage of such claims is that they are heard in the civil courts where public funding (legal aid) may sometimes be available and it is unnecessary to prove the assault was on grounds of race, sex, disability, etc. Longer time limits also apply. It may also help if the assault was by a member of the public or otherwise outside the course of employment. The disadvantages are set out in the previous paragraph.

Protection from Harassment Act 1997

17.128 Although the Protection from Harassment Act (PHA) 1997 was not designed for employment situations, it can apply. The following is a summary of the provisions in relation to England and Wales. For the slightly different provisions in Scotland, see sections 8–16 of the Act. Under PHA 1997 s1 a person must not pursue a course of conduct which s/he knows or a reasonable person would know amounts to harassment of another person.[200] A 'course of conduct' means conduct on at least two occasions.[201] This needs to be carried out by the same person or if more than one, there must be some link, eg they are

---

197 *Burris v Adzani* [1995] 1 WLR 1373, CA.
198 *Waters v Commissioner of Police of the Metropolis* [2000] IRLR 720, HL. See also para 17.149 onwards on stress claims.
199 *Waters v Commissioner of Police of the Metropolis* [2000] IRLR 720, HL.
200 PHA 1997 s1(1) and (2).
201 PHA 1997 s7(3). *Banks v Ablex Ltd* [2005] IRLR 357, CA.

acting in concert or one is acting under instructions from the other.[202] Harassment is not defined except to say that it includes alarming the person or causing the person distress and the conduct can include speech.[203] The conduct is not unlawful if it was reasonable in the particular circumstances.[204] Presumably therefore reasonable disciplinary action, although causing distress, would be excluded. On the other hand, a series of unjustified warnings may on the facts amount to harassment.

17.129   Under PHA 1997 s4 it is also an offence to cause another person on at least two occasions to fear that violence would be used against him/her. There is an exception for reasonable self-defence.[205]

17.130   The worker can claim against the individual harasser or, in some circumstances, against the employer. The concept of vicarious liability under PHA 1997 is different from that under the discrimination legislation. Nevertheless, an employer can be vicariously liable under the PHA 1997 for harassment carried out by his/her employees, provided there is sufficiently close connection between the work the harasser is employed to do and the harassment.[206] Depending on the facts, it is likely that the employer would be vicariously liable for a manager harassing a subordinate, and possibly, for harassment by a colleague at the same level working in the same team. If harassment is by a third party, eg an independent contractor, the worker may similarly be able to sue the third party's employer.

17.131   Breach of PHA 1997 s1 or s4 is a criminal offence liable to imprisonment or a fine.[207] A civil claim can also be made for damages for financial loss and anxiety.[208] The High Court or county court can also issue an injunction restraining the perpetrator from continuing to harass.[209]

17.132   The PHA 1997 may be very helpful where the harassment is not covered by the discrimination legislation, eg because it cannot be proved that it is on grounds of race, sex or disability, etc or because it took place off work premises and possibly outside the course of employ-

202 *Dowson and others v The Chief Constable of Northumbria Police* [2009] EWHC 907 (QB).

203 PHA 1997 s7.

204 PHA 1997 s1(3)(c). There are also other exceptions.

205 PHA 1997 ss2(2), 4(3) and (4). Together with other exceptions.

206 *Majrowski v Guy's and St Thomas's NHS Trust* [2006] IRLR 695; November 2006 *Legal Action* 13, HL.

207 PHA 1997 s3(2).

208 PHA 1997 s3(3).

209 Advisers should check the exact position on this.

ment, or was perpetrated by a member of the public. The other great advantage is the potential to obtain a restraining injunction, which is not available under the discrimination statutes in the ET. Although the time limits are longer, it will usually be important to act quickly, especially if an injunction is sought. The disadvantage of the PHA 1997, as with all non-ET claims, is the more formal procedure and the costs risks. The scope of the PHA 1997 for use in employment cases is still being tested.

Criminal prosecution

17.133 Criminal prosecution is outside the scope of this book. Workers do sometimes invite the police to prosecute for criminal assault where physical harassment has taken place, but there are difficulties in following this route. The facts are harder to prove due to the stricter rules of evidence and the criminal standard of proof. Moreover, the worker is simply a witness in a police action and loses control of the process. An unsuccessful criminal case is likely to jeopardise any parallel civil claim.

Bullying

17.134 Bullying or harassment, even if it is not attributable to the worker's race, sex, disability, religion, belief, sexual orientation or age is now recognised as a workplace problem in itself. If the bullying is carried out by the employer or if the employer fails to deal adequately with a complaint, an employee may be able to resign and claim constructive unfair dismissal.[210] If the worker is penalised for complaining about such bullying, s/he may be able to make a whistleblowing claim.[211] If the bullying is serious, the worker may also be able to bring a civil or criminal claim as set out above.[212]

Workers with HIV or AIDS

17.135 It is estimated that by 2009 there will be over 80,000 people living with HIV in the UK, one quarter undiagnosed.[213] Many of these people are

210 Subject to the usual rules.
211 See para 6.91 onwards.
212 For example, see *Green v D B Group Services (UK) Ltd* [2006] EWHC 1898 (QB); 812 IDS Brief 3, HC.
213 Statistics on Terrence Higgins website at www.tht.org.uk

afraid to reveal their condition to their employer. Medical advances mean that far more of these have long-term prospects and are able to work. It is important that employers understand this. The TUC has produced a basic leaflet, *Tackling HIV Discrimination at Work*,[214] and the National AIDS Trust has a range of useful publications on its website including *HIV and Recruitment for employers*.[215] There is also useful ACAS guidance within its advisory booklet *Health and Employment* (May 2006).[216] Helpful organisations with sources of specialist information include AVERT, the Terrence Higgins Trust and the National AIDS Trust.[217] The Health and Safety Executive has produced a leaflet: *Blood-borne viruses in the workplace: Guidance for employers and employees*.[218] As applicable, cases can be brought using discrimination and unfair dismissal law. For a variety of reasons, only a handful of cases concerning AIDS or HIV have reached the ETs, so there is little indication of what approach an ET will take.

Unfair dismissal

17.136   The Data Protection Code (at part 4) provides guidance to employers for the appropriate collection and use of information regarding a worker's health. The Code and Supplementary Guidance is available on the Information Commissioner's website.[219] HIV infection is not itself usually sufficient reason to justify dismissal.[220] Where a worker who is an employee becomes ill, the usual rules on unfair dismissal for ill-health apply, including adequate consultation with doctors and the employee.[221] Because of the variable state of health of AIDS/HIV sufferers, proper consultation is particularly important.

17.137   In the rare event that an employee with AIDS/HIV constitutes a demonstrated health risk to others, dismissal for 'some other substantial reason' may be fair, although an employer should discuss with the employee the possibility of transfer to alternative employment.

---

214 Available at www.tuc.org.uk/equality/tuc-12059-f0.pdf
215 Available at www.nat.org.uk/Media%20library/Files/PDF%20documents/
    Recruit-Employers.pdf
216 At www.acas.org.uk/CHttpHandler.ashx?id=257&p=0
217 At www.avert.org and www.tht.org.uk and www.nat.org.uk
218 Available at www.hse.gov.uk/pubns/indg342.pdf
219 See para 1.56 above.
220 See ACAS guidance, n215.
221 See paras 7.9–7.25.

Where no health risk exists, but another employee harasses or refuses to work with someone with AIDS/HIV, the employer should make reasonable attempts at conciliation and to supply information on the transmission of AIDS/HIV in order to allay fears. If these steps fail and neither employee can be transferred, it may well be fair to discipline or even dismiss the employee who is refusing to work. An employer's failure to offer reasonable support to an employee being harassed could lead to a constructive dismissal claim.

17.138   If there are a large number of workers objecting, the employer may argue that it is impracticable to transfer or dismiss all of them and it is therefore reasonable to dismiss the employee with AIDS/HIV. However, since an ET is not entitled to take account of a threat of industrial action in determining fairness,[222] it is arguable that it should not take account of pressure falling short of such a threat.[223]

17.139   If there is customer pressure, the employer should again try to consult to allay fears. If that fails, and there is nowhere else to employ the employee, dismissal will probably be fair.

Disability discrimination

17.140 Under the DDA 1995, HIV infection is deemed a disability on diagnosis.[224] The DDA 1995, which covers a wide range of workers and not purely employees, gives more powerful protection than unfair dismissal law.[225] Not only must the worker not be dismissed purely because s/he has AIDS or HIV infection, s/he must also not be unjustifiably treated less favourably for a related reason. Also, the employer must make any necessary reasonable adjustments required by his/her condition,[226] eg allowing time off for medical appointments where necessary; ensuring drinking water is available; flexibility over eating times; providing a safe and confidential place to keep medication; being flexible about hours if necessary.[227]

---

222 ERA 1996 s107.
223 See R A Watt, 'HIV, Discrimination, Unfair Dismissal and Pressure to Dismiss', ILJ Vol 21 No 4 Dec 1992.
224 DDA 1995 Sch 1 para 6A.
225 For an example, see *High Quality Lifestyles Ltd v Watts* [2006] IRLR 850, EAT.
226 See paras 15.34–15.41.
227 For more details, see *Proving disability and reasonable adjustments: A worker's guide to evidence under the DDA* by Tamara Lewis, (appendix F, pp784–785).

Other discrimination

17.141   Because of the popular misconception that only gay men are likely to have AIDS/HIV, male workers may be discriminated against solely because they are gay.[228] Therefore if a gay man is treated adversely because of an assumption that he is likely to have AIDS/HIV, this is probably direct discrimination contrary to the EE(SO) Regs 2003. Similarly, if an employer refuses to recruit job applicants from central African countries or requires only such applicants to undergo HIV tests (because AIDS is widespread in some of those countries), this is unlawful direct discrimination under the RRA 1976.

HIV testing

17.142   It is probably a fundamental breach of contract (and therefore constructive dismissal) to require an employee to undergo an HIV test, even if there is a contractual right to do so, unless there is reasonable ground for suspecting that the employee is infected and that there may be a real risk to the health and safety of others.[229] However, in the latter case, it is probably fair to dismiss an employee who refuses to have the test, provided that the employer has explained why the test is necessary and warned that a refusal will lead to dismissal. Article 8 of the European Convention on Human Rights (the right to respect for private life) may be relevant to cases.

17.143   It is a breach of the implied duty of trust and confidence for an employer to disclose that an employee has AIDS/HIV without the employee's consent. In rare cases, disclosure may be permitted where it is only to persons who have a real need to know and it is in the public interest, for example, where health risks are concerned. The Data Protection Code does not deal specifically with whether the employer has a legal right to conduct medical testing, but it does deal with how the results of any test are processed and stored.

Health and safety

17.144   Health and safety at work is generally beyond the scope of this book. The following is a brief introduction to some areas which overlap with employment law.

228 See para 17.83.
229 See *Bliss v South East Thames Regional Health Authority* [1985] IRLR 308; [1987] ICR 700, CA, on requiring a surgeon to undergo a medical examination.

17.145   All employers have a duty to take reasonable care for the health and safety of their employees. This is a general common law duty as well as a specific statutory duty under the Health and Safety at Work Act 1974.[230] Breach of this duty may enable employees to resign and claim constructive unfair dismissal (see para 17.155 below). Alternatively, where a worker has suffered physical or psychiatric damage, s/he may be able to claim compensation in the civil courts in contract or tort. Such claims are known as personal injuries claims. These claims are hard to bring because public funding (legal aid) is not usually available. Most private solicitors will not take on stress cases in particular, unless the worker has trade union funding, legal expenses insurance, agrees a conditional fee arrangement ('no win no fee') or pays privately.

Risk assessments

17.146   Under the Management of Health and Safety at Work Regulations 1999,[231] an employer must 'make a suitable and sufficient assessment of the risks to the health and safety of his employees, to which they are exposed while they are at work'.[232] An employer with five or more employees must record any significant findings in the assessment and note any groups of employees identified as especially at risk.[233] An employer must also assess the heath and safety risks of persons not in his/her employment arising out of or in connection with the conduct of the business.[234]

17.147   Risk assessments should include the risk of employees developing stress-related illness as a result of their work.[235]

17.148   Employees also have a responsibility to tell their employer of any situation which would represent a serious and immediate danger to health and safety or about any short-comings in the employer's health and safety arrangements.[236] In support of this responsibility is the protection against detriment or dismissal for raising such issues in the appropriate way.[237]

230 Section 2.
231 SI No 3242.
232 Management of Health and Safety at Work Regulations (MHSW Regs)1999 reg 3(1)(a); for risk assessments and pregnancy, see para 11.71.
233 MHSW Regs 1999 reg 3(6).
234 MHSW Regs 1999 reg 3(1)(b).
235 See the Health and Safety Executive Management Standards, Step 1 at www.hse.gov.uk/stress/standards/step1/index.htm
236 MHSW Regs 1999 reg 14(2).
237 ERA 1996 ss44, 100 and 43A. See paras 6.77–6.82 above.

Stress cases

17.149 The Health and Safety Executive (HSE) defines stress as the adverse reaction people have to excessive pressure or other types of demand placed on them. The HSE says stress is a serious problem. It has commissioned research which indicates that up to 5 million people in the UK feel 'very stressed' by their work, with about half a million experiencing work-related stress at a level they believe is making them ill. The case-law shows a variety of causes of stress, eg excessive workload, dissatisfied customers, bullying and traumatic nature of work. The HSE has published Management Standards, which are a useful measure for assessment and support. Details of the HSE research, Management Standards and other guidelines are available on its website.[238]

17.150   A worker who has suffered psychiatric damage caused by stress at work may be able to claim compensation in contract or tort. These claims are heard in the county court or High Court. Essentially, the employee needs to prove:[239]

- the employer was negligent or in breach of a contractual duty;
- the psychiatric damage was caused by stress at work and not domestic or other factors;
- the damage to the particular employee was reasonably foreseeable by the employer, taking account of the workload and the employee's characteristics. The fact that an employee is working considerably more than a 48-hour week, taken together with other factors, may increase the likelihood that the injury was foreseeable.[240]

17.151 There have been several test cases in recent years. Few have won. Those cases that have succeeded, have often concerned the treatment of an obviously vulnerable employee returning to work after a nervous breakdown brought on by stress at work.[241] The most well-known of such cases was *Walker v Northumberland CC*.[242] More recently the key

---

238 At www.hse.gov.uk/stress/index.htm

239 *Hartman v South Essex Mental Health and Community Care NHS Trust and the five linked cases* [2005] IRLR 293, CA.

240 *Hone v Six Continents Retail Ltd* [2006] IRLR 49, CA, but see *Pakenham-Walsh v Connell Residential (Private Residential Company) and another* [2006] EWCA Civ 90, and *Sayers v Cambridgeshire County Council* [2007] IRLR 29, HC. For the 48-hour week, see para 4.68 above.

241 *Young v Post Office* [2002] IRLR 660, CA; *Walker v Northumberland CC* [1995] IRLR 35, HC.

242 [1995] IRLR 35, HC.

case has been *Barber v Somerset County Council*.[243] Liability for psychiatric injury caused by stress is generally no different in principle from liability for physical injury.[244]

17.152 The best test is to measure the employer's conduct against that of a reasonable and prudent employer taking positive thought for the safety of his/her workers in the light of what s/he knows or ought to know.[245] The Court of Appeal in *Sutherland v Hatton*[246] provides useful practical guidance, but every case still depends on its own facts.[247] Provision of a counselling service does not discharge an employer's duty of care where only management can improve the worker's situation.[248] However, an employer cannot be taken to have knowledge of information supplied on a confidential medical questionnaire to the employer's occupational health service.[249]

17.153 For civil claims in the context of harassment at work, see para 17.126 onwards.

Stress-related illness caused by dismissal

17.154 Bizarrely, where an employee's psychiatric injury is caused by dismissal or the manner of dismissal, s/he cannot bring a common law claim in the county court or High Court for breach of contract (eg the implied term of trust and confidence)[250] or get compensation for the injury as part of unfair dismissal compensation.[251] As already mentioned, s/he can bring a common law claim for financial loss or psychiatric injury caused by breach of the implied term of trust and confidence in the employer's actions preceding and independent of any subsequent dismissal.[252] The dividing line may not always be clear. In contrast, a worker who wins a discrimination case in the ET may claim compensation for injury to feelings, which includes injury to

---

243 [2004] IRLR 475, HL.

244 *Hartman v South Essex Mental Health and Community Care NHS Trust* [2005] IRLR 293, CA; *Harding v The Pub Estate Company Ltd* [2005] EWCA Civ 553.

245 *Barber v Somerset County Council* [2004] IRLR 475, HL.

246 [2002] IRLR 263, CA.

247 *Barber v Somerset County Council* [2004] IRLR 475, HL.

248 *Intel Corporation (UK) Ltd v Daw* [2007] IRLR 355, CA.

249 *Hartman v South Essex Mental Health and Community Care NHS Trust* [2005] IRLR 293, CA.

250 *Johnson v Unisys Ltd* [2001] IRLR 279, HL. See also para 1.33 above.

251 *Dunnachie v Kingston upon Hull City Council* [2004] IRLR 727, HL; May 2004 *Legal Action* 35; and para 18.27 below.

252 *Eastwood and another v Magnox Electric plc; McCabe v Cornwall County Council and others* [2004] IRLR 733, HL.

health caused by the unlawful acts of discrimination whether these comprise dismissal or prior acts.[253]

Stress and constructive dismissal

17.155 In theory, an employee who is subjected to severe stress at work can resign and claim constructive unfair dismissal. S/he could claim breach of the implied terms of trust and confidence, and the employer's duty to provide a safe working environment. However, such a claim may be as hard as proving stress in the civil courts after the decision of the EAT in *Marshall Specialist Vehicles Ltd v Osborne*.[254] Ms Osborne resigned because of overwork which she claimed led to a nervous breakdown. The ET implied a contract term that the employer would take reasonable steps to avoid imposing a workload which would foreseeably cause mental or physical injury. The EAT overturned the ET decision and said there was no such term. There was only the general implied term to take reasonable care for the safety of employees. The EAT said an employee must:

- prove the risk of injury was foreseeable (as in *Sutherland v Hatton* above);
- establish the employer was in breach of his/her duty (as in *Sutherland*);
- prove the breach was a fundamental breach of the contract of employment.

The NHS Injury Benefits Scheme

17.156 Any NHS employees who lose pay because of illness or injury caused by work, including stress, can claim up to 85 per cent of their pay under this Scheme. See para 7.24 for more details.

Disability discrimination

17.157 A worker who has a stress-related illness, whether or not it is caused by his/her work, may fall within the definition of a disabled person under the DDA 1995. If so, his/her employer must make any reasonable adjustments required, eg reducing workload or hours or allowing a staged return to work.[255]

---

253 See para 19.27.
254 [2003] IRLR 672, EAT.
255 See chapter 15 for more details.

Smoking at work

17.158   In order to protect workers from passive-smoking, smoking in enclosed public spaces, workplaces and work vehicles was made unlawful in England (from 1 July 2007) and Wales (from 2 April 2007). 'No smoking' signs must be displayed. There are some exemptions, for example for people living in other people's workplaces, such as prison inmates or residents of care homes, but for the residents, not for the prison officers or carers. The ban is set out in the Health Act 2006 and five sets of supporting regulations.[256] Council officers (usually Environmental Health) can enter premises, even on an anonymous basis, to monitor compliance. Employers can be fined for not enforcing the ban.

17.159   ACAS recommends that employers draw up a non-smoking policy. Special smoking rooms on the premises are not allowed, but employers can decide whether to allow smoking outside the building. There is no implied contractual right to smoke at work and the introduction of a smoking ban will be regarded simply as a new works rule rather than a variation of contract.[257] Provided the employer gives adequate notice, it is very unlikely that an employee would win a case for constructive dismissal or unfair dismissal if an employer refused to allow cigarette breaks or smoking outside doorways. Nor can a worker claim disability discrimination as a smoker, since addiction to nicotine is explicitly excluded from coverage by the DDA 1995.[258]

17.160   Conversely, an employee may be able to claim constructive dismissal or unfair dismissal if an employer fails to take care of his/her health and safety by not properly implementing the ban or allowing smoking outside in areas where smoke filters through to the employee.[259]

17.161   The position is similar in Scotland, where smoking has been banned since March 2006 under the Smoking, Health and Social Care (Scotland) Act 2005 and the Prohibition of Smoking in Certain Premises (Scotland) Regulations 2006.[260] There is an informative website produced by the Scottish Executive which contains individual guidance.[261]

---

256 The Smoke-free (Premises and Enforcement) Regulations 2006 SI No 3368; The Smoke-free (Vehicle Operators and Penalty Notices) Regulations 2007 SI No 760; The Smoke-free (Penalties and Discounted Amounts) Regulations 2007 SI No 764; The Smoke-free (Exemptions and Vehicles) Regulations 2007 SI No 765; The Smoke-free (Signs) Regulations 2007 SI No 923.

257 *Dryden v Greater Glasgow Health Board* [1992] IRLR 469, EAT.

258 See para 15.16 above.

259 *Waltons and Morse v Dorrington* [1997] IRLR 488, EAT.

260 SSI No 90.

261 At www.clearingtheairscotland.com/

Procedures

Unfair dismissal remedies

Chapter 18: Key points

- An employment tribunal can order re-employment (reinstatement or re-engagement) but cannot force the employer to take the employee back. It can only award more compensation, ie an 'additional award', if the employer refuses (unless it was impracticable to re-employ).
- In practice, few re-employment orders are sought or made.
- Unfair dismissal compensation normally comprises a basic award and a compensatory award.
- The basic award is based on age, years of service and gross pay (subject to a £350 weekly maximum for dismissals from 1 February 2009, and £380 maximum for dismissals from 1 October 2009).
- The compensatory award is subject to an overall ceiling (£66,200 for dismissals in year starting 1 February 2009). It mainly comprises loss of earnings and pension. The latter can be valuable but complex to calculate.
- The compensatory award may be reduced for contributory fault, failure to mitigate or procedural-only unfairness. There is a strict order in which any such deductions must be calculated.
- The compensatory award may be increased or reduced by up to 25 per cent for the employer's or employee's failure to follow guidance in ACAS's Code of Practice on Disciplinary and Grievance Procedures. Where the statutory dispute resolution procedures still apply, the award can be increased or decreased by 10–50 per cent.
- There is recoupment of certain benefits claimed by the employee. The employer deducts these from the compensatory award and reimburses the Department for Work and Pensions.
- Compensation for injury to feelings is not awarded for unfair dismissal.
- There is a minimum basic award and/or no ceiling on the compensatory award in a few special areas.
- Where the employer is insolvent, the state pays limited debts to the employee.
- For discrimination remedies, see chapter 19. See para 20.165 regarding tax on termination.

Overview

18.1   An employment tribunal (ET) which finds unfair dismissal cannot force an employer to take the employee back, although it can make an order for reinstatement or re-engagement and award extra compensation (an 'additional award') if the employer refuses to comply. Re-employment orders are unusual. Most employees who win unfair dismissal cases get financial compensation. This consists of a basic award and a compensatory award.

18.2   An employee is entitled to have an ET decide whether s/he has been unfairly dismissed, even if his/her employer offered a financial settlement equal to the maximum possible award.[1] However, there may be a costs risk if the employee rejects a very large offer, particularly if the employer is prepared to admit s/he has unfairly dismissed the employee.

Reinstatement and re-engagement

18.3   If the employee wins his/her case, the ET must explain its powers to order reinstatement or re-engagement and ask the employee if s/he wants re-employment.[2] This duty exists even if the employee did not indicate a desire for re-employment on his/her tribunal claim form. An ET's decision on compensation will not necessarily be invalid if it failed to ask about re-employment, but it may be invalid if the failure led to injustice.[3]

18.4   If the employee does now want to get his/her job back, the ET will decide whether to order reinstatement or re-engagement or neither. If neither of the re-employment orders is practicable or desired by the employee, the ET will make an award of compensation.[4] It was envisaged when ETs were first introduced that re-employment orders would be the primary remedy. Realistically, however, the parties tend not to want to work with each other again after the conclusion of an ET hearing, making re-employment orders rare. Only eight orders were made in the year 2007/08.[5]

1 *Telephone Information Services Ltd v Wilkinson* [1991] IRLR 148, EAT and Employment Rights Act (ERA) 1996 s94. It is uncertain whether the change in costs rules since this case was decided would alter the position – see para 20.142 onwards on costs.

2 ERA 1996 s112(2).

3 *Cowley v Manson Timber Ltd* [1995] IRLR 153, CA.

4 ERA 1996 s112(4). See para 18.14 below.

5 Employment Tribunal and EAT statistics (GB) 1 April 2007 – 31 March 2008

What are reinstatement and re-engagement orders?

18.5   Under an order for reinstatement, the employer must treat the employee in all respects as if s/he had not been dismissed.[6] The ET will decide the date when the employee will return to work and the amount of the missing wages and benefit that the employer must pay for the period between dismissal and reinstatement, including restoring any rights that the employee would have acquired during the period of absence. Notice pay or other ex gratia payments and any earnings from a new employer will be deducted.[7]

18.6   An order for re-engagement is more flexible. The ET can decide the employee must be engaged by the employer, its successor or an associated employer in employment comparable to previously or in other suitable employment.[8] On making an order, the ET needs to specify the terms on which re-engagement will take place, including the employer's identity, the nature of the employment and its pay, the date when the employee will start work and the amount payable by the employer in respect of any benefit including pay which the employee might reasonably have expected to have had but for the dismissal, giving credit for notice pay, ex gratia payments and new earnings.[9] The employee is entitled to put forward his/her views on the terms of the order.[10]

18.7   Except where the ET takes into account any contributory fault by the employee (see para 18.50 below), an order for re-engagement should be on terms which are, so far as is reasonably practicable, no less favourable than an order for reinstatement would have been.[11] This means that (apart from this exception) with both types of order, an employee should get all his/her back-pay between the date of termination and the date of re-employment.

18.8   Where re-employment has been ordered, the ET cannot reduce the back-pay for the employee's failure to mitigate, eg failure to look for another job.[12] This contrasts with the position on the compensatory award, where an employee does not want re-employment.[13] Again, unlike the ordinary position with a compensatory award, there is no

6 ERA 1996 s114.
7 ERA 1996 s114(4).
8 ERA 1996 s115(1).
9 ERA 1996 s115(2) and (3).
10 ERA 1996 s116(3)(a).
11 ERA 1996 s116(4).
12 *City and Hackney Health Authority v Crisp* [1990] IRLR 47, EAT.
13 See para 18.32.

upper limit on the back-pay which can be ordered. If the dismissal was automatically unfair under ERA 1996 s98A because the employer failed to follow the statutory dismissal and disciplinary procedure (DDP), the tribunal will also make an award of four weeks' pay, unless this would result in injustice to the employer.[14] This means gross pay subject to the usual statutory weekly maximum.[15] This also applies to unfair retirement dismissals under ERA 1996 s98ZG.[16]

18.9   ETs sometimes like to avoid making orders by pressing the parties to agree certain steps. This can cause difficulties when one or other side does not stick to the agreement. In the case of re-engagement, an ET must make an order and not simply order the employer 'to offer to re-engage' on specified terms.[17]

Will the ET order re-employment?

18.10   In exercising its discretion whether to order re-employment, an ET must first consider reinstatement and if it decides not to order that, then it must consider re-engagement.[18] In both cases, the ET must take into account:[19]

- whether the employee wants an order and what type of order;
- whether it is practicable for the employer to comply with an order;
- whether it would be just to make an order if the employee has caused or contributed to some extent to the dismissal.

At this stage, the ET only needs to make a provisional assessment of whether it is practicable to re-employ the employee, and this should encourage the ET to be positive.[20] The ET can reconsider after it has made an order, if the employer refuses to re-employ on grounds of practicability.

18.11   It is unlikely to be practicable to re-employ if the working relationship has completely broken down[21] or if the job no longer exists. The

---

14 ERA 1996 s112(5)–(6). Note that the statutory dispute resolution procedures will now only apply to a few residual cases.

15 ERA 1996 s227(1)(ba). See para 18.17 for the current rate.

16 ERA 1996 s112(5)–(6) and s227(1)(ba).

17 *Lilley Construction Ltd v Dunn* [1984] IRLR 483, EAT.

18 ERA 1996 s116(1) and (2).

19 ERA 1996 s116(1) and (3).

20 *Timex Corporation v Thomson* [1981] IRLR 522, EAT; *Port of London Authority v Payne and others* [1994] IRLR 9, CA.

21 *ILEA v Gravett* [1988] IRLR 497, EAT; *Central & North West London NHS Foundation Trust v Abimbola* UKEAT/0542/08.

employer does not have to dismiss others to make way for the employee.[22] However, it is irrelevant that an employer has engaged a permanent replacement unless it was not practicable to get the dismissed employee's work done otherwise, or the replacement was engaged after a reasonable period during which the employee had not indicated s/he wanted re-employment, and it was no longer reasonable to cover the work other than with a permanent replacement.[23] This is a good reason for noting it on the tribunal claim if the employee wants re-employment or, even better, writing a letter immediately after dismissal, putting the employer on notice.

The employer refuses to comply with the order

18.12　The ET's order for reinstatement or re-engagement will have set a start date. If the employer refuses to comply with the order, there will be another compensation hearing. At this hearing, the onus will be on the employer to prove that it was not practicable to re-employ after all.[24] Obviously it will be hard for the employer to convince the ET, when s/he was unable to prevent the ET making the order in the first place.

18.13　　If the ET is satisfied that it was not practicable to re-employ, it will order compensation for unfair dismissal in the usual way (see para 18.14 below).[25] But if the ET still believes re-employment was practicable, it will also award an 'additional award' of no less than 26 weeks' and no more than 52 weeks' pay.[26] A week's pay[27] is paid gross[28] and is subject to the same weekly maximum as the basic award.[29] In this latter situation, the usual ceiling on the compensatory award can be exceeded to the extent necessary to ensure that, added to the additional award, the total is not less than the back-pay which would have been payable had the employer re-employed.[30] This is to ensure an

22 *Freemans plc v Flynn* [1984] IRLR 486, EAT.
23 ERA 1996 s116(5) and (6).
24 ERA 1996 s117(4).
25 ERA 1996 s117(3)(a).
26 ERA 1996 s117(3)(b).
27 Calculated in accordance with the rules at ERA 1996 ss220–227.
28 The author can find no authority for this, except for the general wording of the ERA 1996 provisions regarding compensation and by analogy to the basic award. See *Secretary of State for Employment v John Woodrow & Sons (Builders) Ltd* [1983] IRLR 11, EAT.
29 ERA 1996 s227(1)(b). See para 18.17.
30 ERA 1996 s124(4). *Parry v National Westminster Bank plc* [2005] IRLR 193, CA.

employer has no financial incentive for avoiding re-employment. Any award of four weeks' pay made for an automatic unfair dismissal under ERA 1996 s98A (if still in force), or retirement dismissals under s98ZG[31] will be deducted from the compensatory award.[32] This is presumably because the employee can claim the minimum basic award instead.[33]

Compensation

18.14 Compensation consists of two elements: the basic award and the compensatory award. Although it is relatively easy to make an approximate assessment of the value of an employee's claim for settlement purposes (apart from any lost pension element), it is surprisingly difficult to work out and prove the exact sums with the precision necessary for an ET hearing. See appendix A for a compensation checklist, sample calculation and model schedule of loss.

The basic award and redundancy payment

Basic award

18.15 The basic award was introduced to compensate employees for the loss of job security following dismissal. The basic award is calculated broadly in the same way as a redundancy payment.[34]

18.16 The basic award is calculated by reference to the period ending with the effective date of termination[35] during which the employee has been continuously employed. It allows for one-and-a-half weeks' pay for each year of employment in which the employee was not below the age of 41, one week's pay for each year of employment when the employee was below 41 but not below 22, and half a week's pay for each year of employment below the age of 22. A maximum of 20 years' employment will be counted. The table at appendix E can be used to calculate a basic award or redundancy pay.

18.17 A week's pay is gross pay subject to a maximum figure[36] which is index linked to the retail price index. It is increased each February. For dismissals from 1 February 2009, the upper limit was £350. This

31 See para 18.8.
32 ERA 1996 s123(8); s117(2A).
33 See para 18.20.
34 ERA 1996 s119 (basic award) and s162 (redundancy pay).
35 See para 20.29; ERA 1996 s97.
36 ERA 1996 s227(1)(a).

was increased to £380 for dismissals from 1 October 2009 and there will be no increase in February 2010.[37] If the employee was paid below the national minimum wage, the basic award must be calculated on the basis of that minimum.[38] If there are fixed working hours, a week's pay is the amount payable by the employer under the contract of employment. If the employee's pay varies with the amount of work done ('piece rate') the amount of a week's pay is calculated by reference to the average hourly rate of pay over the last 12 weeks of employment,[39] and where there are no normal hours, a week's pay will be the average weekly pay over the last 12 weeks of employment. Roughly speaking, the 12 weeks are counted back from the termination date.[40]

18.18   The basic award may be reduced if the employee:

- behaved before the dismissal or before the notice was given in such a way that it would be just and equitable to do so;[41]
- received a redundancy payment, whether paid under statute or otherwise;[42]
- received an ex gratia payment, unless it would have been paid in the future, even if the dismissal had been fair;[43] or
- unreasonably refused an offer of reinstatement, in which case the ET will reduce the basic award by such amount as it considers just and equitable.[44]

18.19   A minimum basic award[45] applies in certain cases, eg dismissal due to trade union membership or activities;[46] for being a health and safety representative or carrying out such duties; for being a trustee of an occupational pension scheme, or an employee representative for the purposes of collective redundancy or Transfer of Undertakings (Protection of Employment) Regulations (TUPE) consultation or a workforce representative under the Working Time Regulations.[47] The

---

37 The Work and Families (Increase of Maximum Amount) Order 2009 SI No 1903. This effectively brings forward the February 2010 rise and is awaiting parliamentary approval at the time of writing.

38 *Paggetti v Cobb* [2002] IRLR 861, EAT.

39 ERA 1996 s222(3).

40 For precise timing, see ERA 1996 ss222(4), 226(3) and 97.

41 ERA 1996 s122(2).

42 ERA 1996 s122(4).

43 *DCM Optical Clinic plc v Stark* UKEAT/0124/04.

44 ERA 1996 s122(1).

45 Before any reduction under ERA 1996 s122.

46 Trade Union and Labour Relations (Consolidation) Act (TULR(C)A) 1992 s156.

47 ERA 1996 s120.

minimum award is reviewed every February, and for dismissals in the year starting 1 February 2009 it is £4,700.

18.20 If the employee was automatically unfairly dismissed under ERA 1996 s98A because the employer failed to comply with the statutory DDP (if still applicable)[48] or unfairly dismissed for retirement under s98ZG, the basic award (before any deductions in respect of redundancy or under a designated dismissal procedures agreement) must be no less than four weeks' gross pay (unless this would result in an injustice to the employer).[49]

Statutory redundancy pay

18.21 Employees often think that redundancy payments will be higher than they are. As noted above, statutory redundancy pay is calculated in the same way as the basic award. The payment is calculated by a combination of age, years of service and weekly gross pay, subject to the weekly maximum, roughly speaking at the termination date.[50] The relevant date is similar to the effective date of termination.[51] It is easiest to use a table such as that reproduced at appendix E below to work out the figure by which weekly pay must be multiplied. There is also an interactive ready reckoner available on the Department for Business Innovation & Skills (BIS) website.[52]

18.22 The statutory calculation discriminates both directly and indirectly on age grounds, but the government decided this was justifiable because older workers find it much harder to obtain new employment. The Employment Equality (Age) Regulations 2006[53] (EE(A) Regs) allow employers to pay an enhanced contractual redundancy payment, provided this applies to the whole scheme, by lifting the ceiling on a week's pay or multiplying the weekly amount by more than one year for each year's service or multiplying the total by a certain number.[54] If an employer wishes to give an enhanced redundancy payment calculated on any other basis, s/he needs to justify the age discrimination in

---

48 See chapter 22.

49 ERA 1996 s120(1A)–(1B).

50 In fact a combination of the 'relevant date' under ERA 1996 s145 and the 'calculation date' under ERA 1996 s226.

51 See para 20.29 and ERA 1996 s145.

52 At www.berr.gov.uk/employment/employment-legislation/employment-guidance/page33157.html and see appendix E.

53 SI No 1031.

54 EE(A) Regs 2006 reg 33.

the usual way.[55] It may well be justifiable for an employer to adopt a redundancy pay scheme which discriminates directly or indirectly on age grounds if the purpose is to reward loyalty, help older workers who are vulnerable in the job market or to encourage turnover so as to facilitate career progression of younger staff.[56] Similarly, it may be justifiable for an employer to take account of immediate entitlement to a pension.[57] But in all cases, an employer does need to prove with evidence that the means chosen to achieve the legitimate aim were proportionate. There are great dangers that stereotyped assumptions can be made, eg as to at what age employees' job performance deteriorates.

18.23   On making a redundancy payment, the employer must give the employee a written statement indicating how the amount was calculated.[58] If the employer is insolvent and will not pay, the employee can apply to the Redundancy Payments Office for payment out of the National Insurance Fund.[59] S/he can also do this if the employer simply fails or refuses to pay and s/he has taken all reasonable steps (other than legal proceedings) to get payment from the employer.

18.24   Any sum received as contractual redundancy pay will be set off against the statutory amount.

The compensatory award

18.25   The idea of the compensatory award is to compensate the employee for the financial loss suffered as a result of being dismissed, including expenses incurred and loss of fringe benefits.[60] The point is to compensate the employee, but not to award him/her a bonus, and not to penalise the employer. The ET must award what it considers to be 'just and equitable' having regard to the loss and it has wide discretionary powers. The award is subject to an overall ceiling which is revised every February. For dismissals in the year starting 1 February 2009 it is £66,200. The ceiling does not apply to dismissals for health and safety or whistleblowing reasons[61] or to compensation for

---

55 See chapter 17 regarding age discrimination.
56 *MacCulloch v Imperial Chemical Industries plc* UKEAT/0119/08; [2008] IRLR 846, EAT.
57 *Loxley v BAE Systems Land Systems (Munitions and Ordnance) Ltd* UKEAT/0156/08; [2008] IRLR 853, EAT.
58 ERA 1996 s165(1).
59 ERA 1996 s166 and para 18.69.
60 ERA 1996 s123(1) and (2).
61 Under ERA 1996 ss100 and 103A, see also s124(1A).

unlawful discrimination.[62] When employees hear about this ceiling, they tend to expect it is the sum they will get. In reality, apart from highly paid employees, the awards never reach the ceiling. Statistics are available on average awards made by tribunals, but this is also a poor guide. It is important that employees understand that the compensatory award is worked out by reference to a number of set factors, the most important of which is probably their loss of earnings and pension.

18.26   The compensatory award often includes compensation under these headings:

- loss of earnings;
- loss of fringe benefits;
- loss of pension;
- expenses for job-hunting or, rarely, the cost of setting him/herself up in business[63] or moving to find employment;[64]
- loss of statutory rights.

When an ET makes an award, it must set out the heads of compensation, so that everyone can understand how it arrived at the total figure.[65]

Compensation for injury to feelings

18.27   Compensation for injury to feelings and other non-economic loss cannot be awarded for unfair dismissal cases.[66] Injury to feelings and aggravated damages can be awarded to an employee who wins his/her case for detriment short of dismissal on grounds related to trade union membership or activities.[67] They can also be awarded for other cases concerning detriment short of dismissal,[68] eg due to whistleblowing[69] or for taking up a right under the Working Time Regulations. The *Vento* guidelines[70] apply to the size of any injury to feelings award.[71]

---

62 See chapter 20.

63 *Hill v Roland Berger Technics Ltd* [1982] IRLR 498, EAT.

64 *Co-operative Wholesale Society Ltd v Squirrell* (1974) 9 ITR 191, NIRC; *Nohar v Granitstone (Galloway) Ltd* [1974] ICR 273, NIRC.

65 *Norton Tool Co Ltd v Tewson* [1972] IRLR 86, EAT.

66 *Dunnachie v Kingston upon Hull City Council* [2004] IRLR 727; May 2004 *Legal Action* 35, HL.

67 *Cleveland Ambulance NHS Trust v Blane* [1997] IRLR 332, EAT.

68 See para 6.64 onwards for full list of detriments.

69 *Virgo Fidelis Senior School v Boyle* [2004] IRLR 268, EAT.

70 See para 19.16 below.

71 *LB Hackney v Adams* [2003] IRLR 402, EAT; *Virgo Fidelis Senior School v Boyle* [2004] IRLR 268, EAT.

Loss of earnings

(1) Past and future loss

18.28   Usually the largest part of an employee's compensatory award is the amount for loss of earnings. In theory, the ET will award loss of earnings from the effective date of termination until the hearing date ('past loss') and thereafter until the ET decides that the loss would have stopped or it becomes too speculative to award any further loss ('future loss'). If the employee has obtained a new job at a lower rate of pay, the ET will estimate how long s/he is likely to be earning less, and award the difference. Once a new job is secured which is as well or better paid, the compensation calculation will usually stop at that point, rather than the higher pay eating into the earlier losses, but ultimately it is up to the tribunal.[72]

18.29   Where the employee was dismissed without notice or pay in lieu, s/he will be awarded loss of earnings through the notice period. Any earnings from a new job need not be deducted.[73] Similarly, even if s/he did get paid in lieu of notice, s/he need not set off any higher earnings in the notice period against his/her claim for loss of earnings after the notice period.[74] This should not be confused with a wrongful dismissal claim for unpaid notice, where earnings during the notice period would be set off.[75] Further, an employee will not be awarded loss of earnings for unfair dismissal through the notice period if s/he would have been off sick and only receiving statutory sick pay (SSP) at that time.[76] However, if the employee only has a statutory notice entitlement, a way round this might be a wrongful dismissal claim for full pay for the notice period, since special rules apply (see para 1.39).

18.30   If the employee has not found a new job, the ET, in assessing how long s/he is likely to remain unemployed, will take into consideration the employee's age[77] and personal characteristics,[78] and the availability of work in the locality. Owing to the speculative nature of this part of the award, it is important to present compelling and persuasive

---

72 *Whelan v Richardson* [1998] IRLR 114, EAT; *Dench v Flynn & Partners* [1998] IRLR 653, CA.

73 *Norton Tool Co Ltd v Tewson* [1972] IRLR 86, NIRC; *Voith Turbo Ltd v Stowe* [2005] IRLR 228, EAT; *Stuart Peters v Bell* UKEAT/0272/08 (constructive dismissal), though *Morgans v Alpha Plus Security Ltd* [2005] IRLR 234, EAT disagrees.

74 *Voith Turbo Ltd* [2005] IRLR 228, EAT. But see *Morgans.* [2005] IRLR 234, EAT.

75 See para 1.31.

76 *Burlo v Langley and another* [2007] IRLR 145, CA.

77 *Isle of Wight Tourist Board v Coombes* [1976] IRLR 413, EAT.

78 *Fougère v Phoenix Motor Co* [1976] IRLR 259, EAT.

evidence; this should include the opinion of the local job centre or other job agencies and the efforts made to secure employment. Where many years' future loss is sought, it may be advisable to secure a formal expert report on the prospects of finding new employment. In unusual cases, where loss of earnings is likely to be career-long, a discount may be made to represent the value of a large cash award up front.[79] Conversely, an ET can award a premium of approximately 2.5 per cent for delayed payments. This is particularly appropriate in a case where some items have been discounted for accelerated payments. It is not the same as an award for interest (at a much higher rate), which is available only in discrimination cases.[80]

18.31   Future loss of earnings will not be awarded after a date on which an ET decides the employee would not continue to have been employed anyway, eg if three months after his/her dismissal, the employer closed down, or if the employee was suffering from progressive ill-health which at one point would permanently stop him/her working.

18.32   Employees cannot assume that the ET will award all of their past loss of earnings, ie up to the date of the ET hearing. Employees have a duty to 'mitigate' their loss,[81] ie to try to find a new job and not simply to sit back and await compensation from the tribunal. This is a real problem in practice. It is crucial that an adviser informs employees at the outset that this is how compensation works and that they should look for fresh employment and keep records of all their attempts, including copies of letters written, diary notes of appointments and hard copies of e-mails (as these tend to be deleted). It would be wise for employees to register with a local or specialist job agency, read specialist press and apply for vacancies. The ET will be unsympathetic to employees who did not even try to get another job, eg due to fear of a bad reference. It is better that employees apply for a job and if they get rejected on grounds of poor references, they could write to their ex-employer about this, reminding the employer that they are trying to mitigate their loss and possibly, ask for an open reference.[82]

18.33   The ET will expect a degree of flexibility from employees as time goes on if they are getting nowhere. Employees need not necessarily accept the first job which is offered, if it is on low pay, since they may

79 *Kingston upon Hull CC v Dunnachie; HSBC Bank plc v Drage* [2003] IRLR 384, EAT; *Bentwood Bros (Manchester) Ltd v Shepherd* [2003] IRLR 364, CA, but generally this occurs most in discrimination awards, see para 19.10.

80 *Melia v Magna Kansei Ltd* [2005] IRLR 449, EAT.

81 ERA 1996 s123(4).

82 See also paras 1.50–1.55 on references.

be acting reasonably in mitigating their loss by looking for a job with equivalent pay to previously.[83] For a period of time, it is unreasonable to expect an employee to lower his/her sights, but after a while, it may be reasonable for him/her to accept a job of lesser pay and status.[84] There is always a risk that if an employee is offered a job and turns it down because of low pay or other unsuitability, the ET may decide to stop awarding compensation from the date of the offer. When employers lose cases, they tend to fight very hard on the issue of compensation, and go to the ET armed with evidence of suitable available vacancies. If there is a potential problem, it may be useful to take the case of *Wilding v British Telecommunications plc*[85] to the ET, as a corrective to the ET being too tough on the employee. The Court of Appeal set out these guidelines in *Wilding*:

- It is the duty of an employee to act as a reasonable person who was not expecting compensation from the former employer.
- The onus is on the employer as the wrongdoer to show that the employee failed to mitigate.[86]
- If the employee turned down a job offer, eg from the former employer, the test is whether the employee acted unreasonably, taking into account all the circumstances.
- The court or tribunal must not be too stringent in its expectations of the employee, who is, after all, the injured party.

18.34   The ET must take the employee's age, health and other personal circumstances into account in deciding whether s/he has failed to mitigate.[87] The ET should not refuse to award compensation for loss of earnings because the claimant is unfit to work, if the claimant's ill-health was caused by the dismissal.[88] Depending on the situation, it may be reasonable for an employee to mitigate his/her loss by setting up in business[89] rather than immediately looking for a job with a new employer. It may also be reasonable to undergo retraining or study in order to change careers and improve long-term earning capacity, but there must be good reasons to make this choice in the particular case.[90]

---

83 *A G Bracey Ltd v Iles* [1973] IRLR 210, EAT.
84 *Orthet Ltd v Vince-Cain* [2004] IRLR 857, EAT.
85 [2002] IRLR 524, CA.
86 See also *Bessenden Properties Ltd v Corness* [1974] IRLR 338, CA.
87 *Fougère v Phoenix Motor Co Ltd* [1976] IRLR 259, EAT.
88 *Dignity Funerals Ltd v Bruce* [2005] IRLR 189, CS.
89 *Gardiner-Hill v Roland Berger Technics Ltd* [1982] IRLR 498, EAT.
90 *Orthet Ltd v Vince-Cain* [2004] IRLR 857, EAT.

18.35   If the employee gets a new job but has been dismissed or resigned by the time of the ET hearing, it will depend on the facts whether the ET will order the original employer to pay compensation for lost earnings beyond the date when the new job started.[91] If the new job did not last long and was always unsuitable, it could be argued that the employee finding him/herself out of a job again is all part of the loss arising from the original dismissal. A reasonable but unsuccessful attempt to mitigate does not break the link between the original dismissal and the resulting loss.[92] However, a longer period of new employment, where the employee loses the job through his/her own fault, probably would break the link.

(2) Calculating the weekly loss

18.36   The calculation is based on how much the employee would have earned had s/he remained in the old job including regular overtime and bonuses. The employee needs to produce evidence of this. The ET must take account of likely pay rises (even if not contractual), including anticipated overtime payments.[93] The award will be greater where the increase is certain rather than probable. If the employer can show that overtime would have diminished or ceased, the award will be reduced accordingly. If the employee would have been unable to work for the original employer anyway because of sickness and would only have been entitled to SSP, then s/he will not be awarded loss of earnings for that period.

18.37   Unlike the basic award, the award for loss of earnings is calculated net of tax and National Insurance contributions. If the employee was paid below the statutory minimum wage, the calculation of lost earnings must be based on the minimum wage.[94]

Loss of fringe benefits

18.38   The compensatory award includes an element for the loss of fringe benefits in respect of both the immediate and the future loss period. The value of these can be hard to quantify, though it is usually the cost to the employee of replacing them. The following fringe benefits have been taken into consideration by ETs:

---

91 *Dench v Flynn & Partners* [1998] IRLR 653, CA; *Cowen v Rentokil Initial Facility Services (UK) Ltd (t/a Initial Transport Services)* UKEAT/0473/07.
92 *Witham Weld v Hedley* EAT 176/95.
93 *York Trailer Co v Sparks* [1973] IRLR 348, NICA.
94 *Paggetti v Cobb* [2002] IRLR 861, EAT.

- entitlement to holiday pay;
- tips or other gratuitous payments which would have been earned during the compensatory period;[95]
- the loss of a company car, which is usually assessed by reference to the AA annual guidelines;[96]
- cheap loans (ie the value in comparison with bank loans);[97]
- accommodation, if it is free or subsidised;
- medical insurance, which is assessed by reference to the cost to the employee of acquiring the same medical protection.

Loss of statutory rights

18.39 Loss of long notice entitlement, maternity rights and the right to claim unfair dismissal should be reflected in the compensatory award. The loss of unfair dismissal protection[98] is now usually compensated at around £300.[99] This tends to be known as an award for 'loss of statutory rights'. The ET is unlikely to make this award if the employee has already been employed in a new job for one year by the time of the hearing. In addition, if the employee has built up a long statutory minimum notice period, s/he can also claim for the fact that s/he will have to start again in any new job. This award is usually valued at half of the entitlement to the statutory notice which had been acquired, calculated as a net sum.[100] This means no more than a six-week multiplier, ie half the maximum statutory notice period.[101] The reason for the reduction is to reflect the double contingency that the employee will get a new job and then that s/he will be dismissed before acquiring a similar level of notice entitlement. It can be difficult to claim this latter award, and advisers should take copies of the case-law with them to the ET.[102] Employers – and even tribunals – sometimes argue that the employee has already been paid his/her notice pay and should not get a double award. This is misconceived. The point is to compensate an employee for being vulnerable in his/her new job – just as an employee

95 *Palmanor v Cedron Ltd* [1978] IRLR 303, EAT.

96 *AA Schedule of estimated standing and running costs of vehicles.*

97 *UBAF Bank v Davis* [1978] IRLR 442, EAT.

98 *Head v S H Muffet* [1986] IRLR 488, EAT.

99 See *Dugdale plc v Cartlidge* UKEAT/0508/06 and 0522/06.

100 *Daley v Dorsett (Almar Dolls)* [1981] IRLR 385, EAT.

101 *Arthur Guinness Son & Co v Green* [1989] IRLR 288, EAT.

102 *Daley v Dorsett (Almar Dolls)* [1981] IRLR 385, EAT and *Arthur Guinness Son & Co v Green* [1989] IRLR 288, EAT in particular, as the latter post-dates the unhelpful comments in *Head v S H Muffet* [1986] IRLR 488, EAT.

has already had his/her unfair dismissal claim in respect of the old job, but still routinely gets awarded the £300.

Loss of pension rights

18.40 If the employee had an occupational pension with his/her employer, the pension loss caused by the dismissal needs to be added into the compensatory award. The employee may also suffer some loss of the Second State Pension (formerly SERPS). Unfortunately this loss is the hardest to quantify, yet may be the most valuable part of the employee's claim. The burden of proof is on the employee to prove the loss, so s/he must obtain the necessary pension documents from the employer when preparing the case, and work out how to quantify the loss.

18.41 The ETs have published a set of guidelines to help ETs and the parties alike in making the calculation: *Compensation for loss of pension rights*[103] was written by a committee of ET Chairmen (David Sneath and Colin Sara), the Government Actuary and a member of his department. These guidelines are still the most commonly used reference point by tribunals and advocates, though they need not be followed because they have no statutory force and are based on broad assumptions which may not apply to the particular case.[104] An ET must first consider any credible evidence and arguments put forward by the parties.[105] It is beyond the scope of this book to give practical guidance to calculating pension loss. The following is simply an introduction to the main concepts.

18.42 If pension loss is likely to be substantial, it may be worth getting expert advice from an actuary on the value of lost rights. An alternative approach would be to obtain quotations for the cost of replacing the lost pension. Calculations need to be made as to what pension the employee is now likely to receive and what pension s/he would have received had it not been for the dismissal. Insurance companies can quote for topping up the pension to the latter level. A tribunal can award compensation for pension loss beyond the date of its award for loss of earnings and it can also give greater value to the loss of final salary pension scheme than a money purchase scheme.[106]

---

103 Third edition published in 2003 by The Stationery Office. They can be ordered online from www.tso.co.uk/bookshop or downloaded from www.employment-tribunals.gov.uk/pdfs/comp_loss_pension_rights.pdf

104 *Bingham v Hobourn Engineering Ltd* [1992] IRLR 298, EAT.

105 *Port of Tilbury (London) Ltd v Birch and others* [2005] IRLR 92, EAT.

106 *Roberts v Aegon UK Corporate Services Ltd* UKEAT/0277-8/08.

18.43   The ET guidelines are too complex to summarise in this text and it is recommended that readers buy a copy (they are not too expensive). The following simply provides an overview of the key principles and cannot be relied on in itself.

18.44   The way to calculate financial loss differs according to whether the employee was employed on a final salary ('defined benefit') scheme; or a money purchase ('defined contribution') scheme. In a final salary scheme, the amount of pension is based on a proportion of the employee's earnings at the leaving date for each year of service. The proportion is most often $\frac{1}{60}$ per year worked in the private sector; and $\frac{1}{80}$ in the public sector. In a money purchase scheme, the amount of pension is based on the investment of sums contributed by the employee and possibly the employer over a number of years. Stakeholder pensions are money purchase schemes. Employers must provide access to stakeholder schemes, but need not contribute.

18.45   Where an employee leaves a money purchase scheme early, eg due to dismissal, s/he retains the value of the sums invested to the termination date, but loses the prospective value of further contributions from the employer. There may also be a financial penalty for leaving early. The financial loss is therefore fairly easy to calculate. The position is more complicated with a final salary scheme. The early leaver will usually be entitled to a deferred pension, but one which will be of lesser value than had s/he not been dismissed. The difference can be hard to quantify and will depend on whether the tribunal uses the simplified or the substantial loss approach. The ET need not follow either approach, but it must explain its reasons for rejecting both or for choosing one of them.[107]

18.46   The simplified approach will be appropriate most often. The substantial loss approach applies where there is likely to be career loss because: (a) the employee had worked for the employer for a long time and was in a stable relationship, whereby s/he was unlikely to have left voluntarily or been made redundant; and (b) the employee is unlikely to find new employment before pension age, or s/he has found new employment but it is without a pension and the new salary is not any higher to compensate for that. Where the simplified approach applies, compensation for loss of pension falls into three categories:

1) loss of pension from dismissal until the tribunal hearing;
2) loss of future pension from after the tribunal hearing;
3) loss of enhanced rights of the pension which has so far accrued.

107 *Greenhoff v Barnsley Metropolitan Borough Council* (2006) 813 IDS Brief 5; EAT/0093/06, lays down guidelines.

Categories 1 and 2 apply to loss with both final salary and money purchase schemes. Broadly speaking, the guidelines calculate the loss as the amount of pension contributions the employer would have made in the relevant period. This calculation works for future loss which is unlikely to exceed two years. There may be a deduction for accelerated receipt. Category 3 applies to final salary schemes. The idea is to calculate the difference between the deferred pension the employee will actually receive and the one s/he would have received had s/he not been dismissed, allowing for contingencies. The guidelines reproduce the government actuarial tables to make this calculation. The guidelines recommend no compensation under this category if the employee is within five years of retirement or if his/her employment would have terminated within one year anyway.

18.47　　The calculation for the substantial loss approach encompasses all three categories of the simplified approach. In essence, it calculates the difference between the deferred pension now and what it would have been had the employee left at retirement age, less any expected final salary pension in a new job. There is then a deduction for the 'withdrawal factor', ie the contingency that the employee would have left the old job or will leave the new job before retirement age.

18.48　　The effect of dismissal on the state pension also needs to be considered in many cases. Most obviously, if the employee was not in an occupational pension scheme at all, or alternatively was in an occupational scheme which was not contracted out, s/he is liable to lose the Second State Pension (formerly SERPS) element for the period s/he is out of work. The guidelines set out a method for calculating this loss.

Adjustments to the compensatory award

18.49　　Payments under any private or occupational pension scheme which the employee decides to take early as a result of the dismissal are not set off against the compensatory award.[108]

18.50　　If the ET finds the dismissal was to any extent caused or contributed to by any action of the employee, it can reduce the compensatory award proportionally as it thinks fit. This is known as 'contributory fault' and the ET usually makes a percentage reduction, eg 25 per cent or 50 per cent, but in very rare cases, it can deduct 100 per cent. The employee's conduct must have been culpable or blameworthy. This does not necessarily include merely unreasonable conduct – it depends on the extent of the unreasonableness.[109] Potentially, actions arising from an

---

108 *Knapton and others v ECC Card Clothing Ltd* [2006] IRLR 756, EAT.
109 *Nelson v BBC* (No 2) [1979] IRLR 346, CA.

employee's alcoholism could amount to contributory fault.[110] Contributory fault for incompetence would be rare, unless the employee was deliberately lazy or negligent.[111]

18.51   The decision to reduce the award and the degree of contribution is discretionary and can only be challenged before the Employment Appeal Tribunal (EAT) if it is legally perverse (ie no ET properly directing itself could have reached the same decision). Such a challenge is very difficult to succeed in, though the employee must have been given the opportunity to give evidence on the matter in the ET. The ET must also identify the conduct which has been taken into account.[112]

18.52   The compensatory award can only be reduced if the conduct actually causes or contributes towards the dismissal.[113] Unfortunately, the ET can in addition reduce the basic award for conduct not necessarily relating to the dismissal.[114] Compensation cannot be reduced for post-dismissal misconduct.[115]

18.53   If the statutory DDP or grievance procedure still apply to a particular case, failure to follow the procedure can affect compensation.[116] If the procedure is not completed due to a failure by either the employer or employee to comply with a requirement of the procedure, the compensatory award must be increased or reduced by 10–50 per cent respectively.[117] This increase or reduction does not apply if there are any exceptional circumstances which would make it unjust or inequitable. From 6th April 2009 (and subject to transitional provisions where the statutory dispute resolution procedures still apply), a new ACAS regime came into force.[118] If the employer or employee unreasonably fails to follow the ACAS Code of Practice on Disciplinary and Grievance Procedures, the compensatory award may be increased or decreased by up to 25 per cent respectively. Case-law developed on the factors relevant to the level of appropriate percentage adjustments under the statutory dispute resolution procedures is likely to be useful on the appropriate level under the ACAS regime.[119]

---

110 *Sinclair v Wandsworth Council* UKEAT/0145/07.
111 *Slaughter v C Brewer & Sons* [1990] IRLR 426, EAT.
112 *Lindsay v General Contracting Ltd t/a Pik a Pak Home Electrical* (2002) 686 IRLB 8, EAT.
113 Ibid.
114 See para 18.18, and ERA 1996 s122(2), although the wording is wider.
115 *Mullinger v Department for Work and Pensions* UKEAT/0515/05.
116 See chapter 22.
117 Employment Act (EA) 2002 s31; ERA 1996 s124A(a).
118 TULR(C)A 1992, s207A; details in chapter 22.
119 See paras 22.53–22.55 for more detail.

18.54   So-called '*Polkey* reductions' are more common than those for contributory fault. A dismissal may be unfair for procedural reasons only,
even though the actual reason for dismissal is fair.[120] In such cases,
the compensatory award may be reduced by a percentage to reflect
the likelihood that the employee would still have been dismissed, even
if fair procedures had been followed. A percentage reduction can be as
high as 100 per cent, although the ET might still award loss of earnings
for the time it would have taken to go through proper procedures.
Most often a reduction will be in the area of 25–50 per cent.

18.55   It is often difficult to decide whether unfairness is 'procedural' or
a matter of substance. Either way, the tribunal must consider this
question of whether and when the employee would have been dismissed if the employer had acted fairly. Sometimes this is obvious,
eg the employee would have left anyway in 6 months time, eg because
of retirement or closure of the workplace. It is also fairly obvious where
the only unfairness in a redundancy dismissal is the failure to consider alternative employment, but there were no suitable available
vacancies anyway. But sometimes it is less clear what would have happened, eg if the dismissal was only unfair due to unfair redundancy
selection criteria, would the employee still have been selected for
redundancy if fair criteria had been used? A tribunal must not refuse
to make a percentage cut down just because there is an element of
speculation – a degree of uncertainty is an inevitable feature of the
exercise. On the other hand, if the evidence is such that the whole
exercise of trying to reconstruct what might have been is riddled with
uncertainty, no deduction should be made.[121]

18.56   If the employer ought to have started consultation much earlier,
when s/he first knew redundancy was likely, and as a result, the
employee loses time when s/he could have started looking for a new
job, compensation can extend to pay for that lost time.[122]

Order of deductions

18.57   The order of the various deductions, and the imposition of the overall
ceiling,[123] makes a big difference to the final award. There have been

---

120 See para 6.58.
121 See *King v Eaton (No.2)* [1998] IRLR 681, CS; *Software 2000 Ltd v Andrews and others* [2007] IRLR 568, EAT; *Virgin Media Ltd v Seddington and Eland* UKEAT/0539/08.
122 *Coney Island Ltd v Elkouil* [2002] IRLR 174, EAT.
123 See para 18.24.

several cases on what order should be followed. The ET should approach the calculation as follows:[124]

1) calculate the loss which the employee has sustained in consequence of the dismissal in so far as the loss is attributable to action taken by the employer. For example, loss of earnings and pension, and job-hunting expenses;
2) deduct all sums paid by the employer as compensation for the dismissal, eg pay in lieu of notice[125] or an ex gratia payment, but exclude at this stage any redundancy pay to the extent it exceeds the basic award. Also deduct earnings in a new job;[126]
3) any *Polkey* reduction should then be made;
4) increase or reduce the sum by 10–50 per cent for failure to comply with a statutory dispute resolution procedure (if still applicable) or by up to 25 per cent for failure to comply with a relevant part of the ACAS Code on Disciplinary and Grievance Procedures;[127]
5) add 2–4 weeks' pay if, when proceedings were begun, the employer was in breach of his/her duty to give the employee a written statement of employment particulars or change under ERA 1996 s1 or s4;[128]
6) make any reduction for contributory fault;
7) deduct any redundancy payment to the extent it exceeds the basic award;
8) if the sum calculated in accordance with the above is in excess of the statutory ceiling, the final stage is to reduce it to bring it down to the statutory maximum.[129]

Recoupment

18.58   Any income support or Jobseeker's Allowance received by the employee should not be set off against the sum awarded by the ET. However the effect is the same from the employee's point of view, because the employer must repay the sum to the Department for Work and Pensions (DWP) before passing on the balance of the award to the

---

124 *Digital Equipment Co Ltd v Clements (No 2)* [1998] IRLR 134, CA read together with the EAT's decision at [1997] IRLR 140 and updated to incorporate ERA 1996 s124A.
125 *Heggie v Uniroyal Englebert Tyres Ltd* [1999] IRLR 802, CA.
126 Though see para 18.28 above.
127 ERA 1996 s124A; TULR(C)A 1992, s207A(5); para 18.53.
128 EA 2002 ss31(5) and 38 and see para 1.26 above.
129 *Leonard and others v Strathclyde Buses* [1998] IRLR 693, CS.

employee.[130] This is known as recoupment. The ET will ask the employee whether s/he has received these benefits and, if so, its judgment will set out two figures: the monetary award (ie the total compensation awarded) and the prescribed element.

18.59   The prescribed element is the amount awarded for loss of earnings between the dismissal date and the final ET hearing, subject to any reductions made, eg for contributory fault. It will also be reduced proportionately if the statutory cap had to be applied to the overall award.[131] The judgment will specify the amount of the prescribed element and the period to which it relates. The ET must send a copy of the judgment with these details to the DWP as soon as reasonably practicable after sending it to the parties.

18.60   On receiving the judgment, the employer can immediately pay the balance of the monetary award to the employee. S/he must not pay the prescribed element until s/he has received a recoupment notice from the local DWP or notification that no recoupment applies. The notice should be served on the employer within 21 days of any reserved judgment or the conclusion of the hearing or nine days of an oral judgment, whichever is later.[132] The employer then pays the recouped amount back to the DWP and the balance of the prescribed element to the employee. The employee gets a copy of the notice and should notify the local office in writing if s/he disagrees with the amount of benefit stated as paid. It almost always takes the DWP much longer to serve the recoupment notice and it may be necessary to write to the relevant office, reminding it of the timescale in the Regulations. If the delay continues, the employee could use the DWP's complaints' procedure.

18.61   If the employee was receiving a large amount of income support or income-based Jobseeker's Allowance (JSA), his/her claim could therefore be worth very little. In particular, where the employee has claimed mortgage interest as part of his/her income support or income-based JSA, recoupment may swallow most of the award. If the case is settled before the hearing, the recoupment provisions do not apply. It is in the interests of both parties to settle and to reach an agreement on compensation, bearing in mind that there will no recoupment on the settlement sum. The parties often agree to split the difference on the amount which would have been recouped. It is safer if the settlement is for a single figure and does not itemise the specific claims that are

130 Employment Protection (Recoupment of Jobseeker's Allowance and Income Support) Regulations 1996 SI No 2349.
131 *Mason v Wimpey Waste Management Ltd* [1982] IRLR 454, EAT.
132 SI No 2349 reg 8.

being settled, such as notice pay, holiday pay, wages, etc just in case the recoupment provisions could be applied as a result, although this is unlikely. Incapacity benefit is not subject to recoupment, but must be deducted from the compensatory award.[133] Housing benefit paid following the dismissal is not deducted.[134]

Interest

18.62   Interest is payable on ET awards which remain unpaid 42 days after the decision on compensation is promulgated, ie recorded as sent to the parties.[135] Where there is an appeal whose outcome does not affect the level of compensation, the interest still accrues from that date. Where the appeal alters the award of compensation, interest runs on the altered award but still from 42 days after the original decision was promulgated. Unfortunately, if an ET has only made a decision on liability, which is appealed by the employer, no interest can run until a decision on compensation is made, usually not until the appeal has been disposed of.

18.63   Interest runs on a daily basis on unpaid parts of the award and the rate is that applicable from time to time under the Judgments Act 1838 s17. The ET decision will stipulate the applicable interest rate (8 per cent at the time of writing).

Interim relief

18.64   The law gives special protection in respect of certain dismissals, especially where these relate to acting as a workplace representative of various kinds. As well as a minimum basic award and no ceiling on the compensatory award (in some cases)[136] there are also provisions for interim relief.

18.65   Where an employee is dismissed (though not selected for redundancy) for one of the following reasons, s/he can claim interim relief:[137]

---

133 *Morgans v Alpha Plus Security Ltd* [2005] IRLR 234, EAT. Note that Employment and Support Allowance is replacing Incapacity Benefit for new claimants from 27 October 2008.
134 *Savage v Saxena* [1998] IRLR 182, EAT.
135 Employment Tribunals (Interest) Order 1990 SI No 479.
136 See paras 18.19 and 18.25.
137 ERA 1996 s128.

- taking on the role and activities of a health and safety representative;
- being a trustee of an occupational pension scheme;
- being an employee representative for collective consultation on redundancies or TUPE;
- being a workforce representative under the Working Time Regulations;
- for whistleblowing;
- for various reasons related to a trade union.[138]

18.66 Interim relief cases happen very fast. The employee must apply for interim relief together with his/her tribunal claim for unfair dismissal by the end of seven days following the effective date of termination.[139] If the statutory DDP applies, the appeal stage is treated as having been complied with where an application for interim relief has been made.[140] If the dismissal is for trade union membership or activities, s/he must also produce a certificate from an authorised union official.[141] The ET must then decide the issue as soon as possible, giving the employer at least seven days' notice of the hearing.

18.67 If the ET decides it is likely that the employee will succeed in his/her unfair dismissal case at the eventual hearing, it can order interim relief, ie reinstatement or re-engagement (if the employer agrees) or otherwise a continuation of contract order (CCO).[142] A CCO orders the employer to pay the employee's wages and other benefits from dismissal until the eventual ET decision or settlement. The payments are not repayable, even if the employee ultimately loses.

Enforcement

18.68 If an employer does not pay an ET award or compensation under a settlement or compromise agreement, it is possible to enforce payment in the county courts or High Court. Since 1st April 2009, sums payable under an ET judgment have been recoverable directly by way of an order in the county court or High Court (England and Wales)

---

138 ERA 1996 s128 and TULR(C)A 1992 s161.
139 ERA 1996 s128(2); TULR(C)A 1992 s161(2).
140 Employment Act 2002 (Dispute Resolution) Regulations 2004 SI No 752 reg 5(1).
141 TULR(C)A 1992 s161(3).
142 ERA 1996 ss129–130; TULR(C)A 1992 ss163–164.

or decree of the sheriff court (Scotland).[143] This removes the need to register the judgment and pay a fee first. Settlements and compromise agreements are enforced by bringing a claim in the county court or High Court, as appropriate, usually for damages for breach of contract. This has also been simplified in respect of non-payment of ACAS Settlements (with some exceptions).[144] Following research showing a high level of unpaid tribunal awards, the government has announced its intention that High Court Enforcement Officers will take on recovery of tribunal awards and settlements.[145]

Employer insolvency and debts covered by the state

18.69   If the employer becomes insolvent, certain debts can be claimed from the National Insurance Fund (NIF). These include unpaid wages up to eight weeks; up to six weeks' holiday pay in the previous 12 months; and statutory notice pay. All these are subject to a weekly limit, which was £350 from 1 February 2009 and £380 from 1 October 2009.[146] Statutory redundancy pay and any ET basic award (though not the compensatory award) can also be recovered from the NIF. The correct application form needs to be completed and sent to the Redundancy Payments Office or, in some cases, the employer's representative. Generally speaking, the NIF will only pay if the employer is insolvent and not just because s/he has stopped trading. However, redundancy pay is also reimbursed where the employer simply refuses to pay and the employee has taken all reasonable steps to recover the payment from the employer.[147] For more details, see *Redundancy and Insolvency: A Guide*

143 Tribunals, Courts and Enforcement Act 2007 s27.

144 For details, see Tribunals, Courts and Enforcement Act 2007, s142. For more information regarding enforcement generally, though before these changes, see *Enforcing ET Awards and Settlements* by Philip Tsamados, 2nd edn, Central London Law Centre.

145 Press release at www.justice.gov.uk/news/newsrelease190509a.htm Ministry of Justice research report available at www.justice.gov.uk/publications/docs/employment-tribunal-awards.pdf and 'Justice Denied', a Citizens Advice Report available via www.citizensadvice.org.uk/index/campaigns/policy_campaign_publications/evidence_reports/er_employment/justice_denied

146 These increases apply when February and then October 2009 constitute the 'appropriate date' as defined by ERA 1996 s185.

147 ERA 1996 s166.

For Employees by the Insolvency Service.[148] There is also useful guidance and links on the Directgov site.[149] See para 10.34 for the position regarding the transfer of an insolvent business.

148 Available at www.insolvency.gov.uk/pdfs/guidanceleafletspdf/guidefor
    employees.pdf
149 Att www.direct.gov.uk/en/Employment/RedundancyAndLeavingYourJob/
    DG_10026695

CHAPTER 19

Discrimination remedies

Chapter 19: Key points

- When a worker wins a discrimination case, the employment tribunal can make recommendations and award compensation.
- The recommendations are for action to be taken by the employer to reduce the effect of the discrimination.
- Compensation consists of financial loss, injury to feelings and interest.
- Injury to feelings can comprise separate awards for hurt feelings, aggravated damages and injury to health.
- Injury to health compensation is compensation for personal injury and the principles for its calculation are similar to those for personal injury claims (for physical or psychiatric injury) in the civil courts.
- There is no compensation awarded for unintentional indirect race discrimination except in relation to race or national or ethnic origins.
- There are special considerations related to the duty to mitigate when awarding loss of earnings in pregnancy dismissal cases.

General guide to useful evidence

- Payslips, contract documents, information regarding any new employment, and other evidence regarding financial loss.
- Report from GP and/or consultant psychiatrist regarding injury to feelings and/or health, visits and treatment, prognosis, recommendations for and cost of future treatment.
- Evidence from the worker, doctor or other relevant witness regarding each of the factors in the Judicial Studies Board guidelines for personal injury.
- Evidence of any conduct by the employer leading to aggravated damages. This evidence was probably given during the hearing on liability, but must now be highlighted.
- See also paras 16.67–16.73.

19.1 When an employment tribunal (ET) has made a finding of unlawful discrimination, it may make such of the following as it considers just and equitable:[1]

- a declaration of the rights of the parties in respect of the matter to which the complaint related;
- a recommendation;
- an order for compensation, although not for unintentional indirect discrimination under the RRA 1976 except where it relates to race or national or ethnic origins.

Recommendations

19.2 The ET may recommend that, within a specified period of time, the employer take action to obviate or reduce the adverse effect of the act of discrimination proved.[2] If 'without reasonable justification' the employer fails to comply with the recommendation, the ET can award compensation or additional compensation, save for certain forms of unintentional indirect discrimination.[3] The ET cannot insist on a recommendation being carried out.

19.3 Examples of recommendations are that the employer makes a full written apology to the worker, that s/he removes discriminatory documents, warnings, adverse reports, etc from the worker's personnel file, or that s/he notes on it that the worker has been discriminated against previously. An interesting example of a recommendation approved by the Employment Appeal Tribunal (EAT) was that an employer interview separately a number of individuals implicated by the ET's decision and discuss with them those parts of the decision that affected them as individuals.[4]

19.4 The ET is hampered in what it can recommend. In *Noone v North West Thames Regional Health Authority (No 2)*,[5] the ET recommended

1 Race Relations Act (RRA) 1976 s54; Sex Discrimination Act (SDA) 1975 s65; Disability Discrimination Act (DDA) 1995 s8; Employment Equality (Religion or Belief) Regulations (EE(RB) Regs) 2003 SI No 1660 reg 30; Employment Equality (Sexual Orientation) Regulations (EE(SO) Regs) 2003 SI No 1661 reg 30; Employment Equality (Age) Regulations (EE(A) Regs) 2006 SI No 1031 reg 38.

2 RRA 1976 s56(1)(c); SDA 1975 s65(1)(c); DDA 1995 s8(2)(c); EE(RB) Regs 2003 reg 30(1)(c); EE(SO) Regs 2003 reg 30(1)(c); EE(A) Regs 2006 reg 38(1(c).

3 See para 19.37 below.

4 *Chief Constable of West Yorkshire Police v Vento (No 2)* [2001] IRLR 124, EAT. This point does not seem to have been appealed to the Court of Appeal.

5 [1988] IRLR 530; (1989) 23 EOR 46, CA.

that if another post of consultant microbiologist became available, the health authority should seek the secretary of state's permission to dispense with the normal NHS advertising requirements and offer the post to Dr Noone. The Court of Appeal rescinded the recommendation because it undermined fair recruitment procedures to the detriment of the NHS, the professions concerned with it, the public and would-be applicants for the post.

19.5   Two other recommendations proposed by the health authority were substituted. These were that the health authority draw to the attention of any future appointments committee considering an application by Dr Noone the provisions of the RRA 1976 and remind them that Dr Noone's previous application had failed on the ground of race. This case probably means that, whatever the industry, an ET cannot recommend that the worker be given the next available vacancy.

19.6   The ET cannot make general recommendations on good practice in the workplace, for example, that an equal opportunities policy is introduced or that there is monitoring or training of staff. Neither can it recommend a pay rise as this should be covered by an award of compensation.

19.7   Sometimes settlement can be negotiated on action which an employer is willing to undertake. Not only will this not be subject to the above limitations, but it will also be enforceable.

The award of compensation

19.8   Unlike for unfair dismissal, there is no longer an upper limit on the compensatory award. Although the ET may select which of the three remedies it orders, according to what is 'just and equitable', if it does make a financial award, this must not be limited by such considerations.[6] An award of compensation should comprise all loss[7] directly caused by the act of discrimination including past and future loss of earnings, loss of opportunity and injury to feelings.[8] The overriding principle laid down by the European Court of Justice (ECJ) is that

6 *Hurley v Mustoe (No 2)* [1983] ICR 422, EAT.

7 RRA 1976 s56(1)(b). As the RRA 1976 creates a statutory tort, the Court of Appeal in *Essa v Laing* [2004] IRLR 313 (an RRA 1976 case) rejects the view that loss needs to be reasonably foreseeable. Other discrimination legislation has similar wording.

8 RRA 1976 ss56(1)(b) and 57(4); SDA 1975 ss65(1)(b) and 66(4); DDA 1995 s17A(4); EE(SO) Regs 2003 regs 30(1)(b) and 31(3); EE(RB) Regs 2003 regs 30(1)(b) and 31(3); EE(A) Regs 2006 regs 38(1)(b) and 39(3).

compensation must enable the loss and damage actually sustained as a result of the discrimination to be made good in full in accordance with the applicable national laws.[9]

19.9 Loss of earnings may be claimed where appropriate, eg the discriminatory action is dismissal or refusal to promote to a higher paid post. Where a candidate is not short-listed for interview, an ET may award compensation representing loss of opportunity, so that the potential loss of earnings will be reduced by a percentage representing the likelihood of the candidate actually obtaining the job had s/he not been discriminated against. Where the discriminatory action is just a small aspect of a wider situation or occurs in a procedural step, there is a risk that the tribunal will decide the worker would still have been disadvantaged even if s/he had not been discriminated against. For example, an employer discriminates by assessing a worker badly against redundancy selection criteria, but even without such discrimination, the worker would still have scored less than others. In such a case, compensation may be reduced to reflect the percentage chance that the worker would have been dismissed anyway.[10] However, this type of reduction in compensation would be unusual in other types of discrimination case, because it is not normally possible to say what would have happened to a worker had s/he not been discriminated against.[11]

19.10 Discrimination cases sometimes attract awards for lengthy future loss of earnings, either because the discrimination has caused psychological damage or because workers covered by the legislation tend to be those who, for various reasons, will find it harder to find a new job. Unfortunately, complexities have crept into the calculation of lengthy future loss from personal injury cases. Employers argue there should be a discount for the value of receiving a large capital sum up front ('accelerated receipt').[12] Also, in rare cases, calculations may be made by reference to the Ogden tables to represent the risk of mortality.[13] General guidance can be found in Facts and figures 2008/9.[14] The Ogden

9 *Marshall v Southampton Area Health Authority (No 2)* [1993] IRLR 445, ECJ.

10 *Abbey National PLC & Hopkins v Chagger* UKEAT/0606/07; 0037/08; 0041/08; [2009] IRLR 86, EAT.

11 *Chagger* UKEAT/0606/07; 0037/08; 0041/08; [2009] IRLR 86, EAT.

12 See para 18.30. If using the Ogden tables and arguing for career-long loss, it is important to read the comments in *Abbey National PLC & Hopkins v Chagger* UKEAT/0606/07; 0037/08; 0041/08; [2009] IRLR 86, EAT.

13 6th edition (May 2007) available via a link on www.gad.gov.uk/Services/Other_Services/Compensation_for_injury_and_death.asp

14 Edited by Robin de Wilde. Sweet & Maxwell. Contains a copy of the 6th edition of the Ogden tables.

Tables should not be used unless a career-long loss of earnings has been established.[15] But if the Tables are used, the party wanting to use them should submit a schedule well in advance, say 14 days after the employer's tribunal response (ET3), and the other party should submit a counter schedule within 14 days afterwards.[16]

19.11   Where there are findings of discrimination against individually named respondents as well as against an employing organisation, the ET can make orders of compensation specifically against the individuals. It is becoming increasingly common for ETs to make the major award against the employer, but to order a smaller additional sum, eg £500, to be paid by the named individuals.[17] The ET can make the award on a 'joint and several' basis, ie so that the full award can be claimed from either the employer or the individual if one of them is or becomes insolvent.[18] The award should still be apportioned, and the apportionment should be based on the culpability of each respondent, not their relative financial strength. A manager can be personally liable, not only for his/her own discriminatory actions, but for those of other staff if s/he has consciously encouraged a discriminatory atmosphere.[19]

19.12   Large ET awards following dismissal may be taxable where they exceed £30,000.[20] If the award comprises past and future loss of earnings, which have been calculated net of tax by the ET, the worker is in effect taxed twice on the same sum. To compensate the worker properly, the ET should award a grossed up figure, but this does not apply to injury to feelings awards, which should not be taxable.[21] Tax can be complicated on high discrimination awards and is not within the scope of this book.

15 *Kingston-upon-Hull CC v Dunnachie (No 3); Drage v HSBC Bank plc* (2003) 742 IDS *Brief* 9, EAT.

16 *Kingston-upon-Hull CC v Dunnachie; Drage v HSBC Bank plc* [2003] IRLR 384, EAT – though the EAT's suggestion of 14 days is a little early. See also *Birmingham City Council v Jaddoo* UKEAT/0448/04.

17 This is one reason to name individuals in the ET1. See para 21.40.

18 *Way and another v Crouch* [2005] IRLR 603, EAT.

19 *Gilbank v Miles* [2006] IRLR 538, CA.

20 Income Tax (Earnings and Pensions) Act 2003 ss401 and 403. See also para 20.165.

21 *Orthet Ltd v Vince-Cain* [2004] IRLR 857, EAT. Income Tax (Earnings and Pensions) Act 2003 s406. Some commentators consider the case is wrong on this.

Injury to feelings and aggravated damages

19.13   Unlike in ordinary unfair dismissal cases, an ET may make an award for injury to feelings where it finds unlawful discrimination. Injury to feelings are awarded to reflect the degree of hurt felt by the particular claimant as a result of the discrimination. This can include upset, frustration, worry, anxiety, mental distress, fear, grief, anguish, humiliation, unhappiness, stress, depression, affront, bitterness, shock and so on.[22] It can also cover loss of a chosen career which gave job satisfaction.[23] It is not enough in itself to harbour a legitimate and principled sense of grievance. Injury to feelings need to be proved, although usually this is not difficult.

19.14   There is often extra compensation for 'aggravated damages', ie where a worker's sense of injury is 'justifiably heightened by the manner in which or motive for which' the employer did the wrongful act.[24] In England and Wales, aggravated damages should not be aggregated with and treated as part of the damages for injury to feelings.[25] They should be listed separately in the claimant's schedule of loss.[26] In Scotland, aggravated damages cannot be awarded as a separate head of damages, but the injury to feelings award can include an element in recognition of this aspect.[27]

19.15   It is uncertain whether, in very limited circumstances, an ET can award 'exemplary damages', ie an award which is purely to punish the employer.[28] In any event, particularly bad behaviour by the employer is likely to upset the worker more and lead to aggravated damages. Indeed, in *Alexander*,[29] the Court of Appeal said:

> ... compensatory damages may and in some cases should include an element of aggravated damages where, for example, the defendant may have behaved in a high-handed, malicious, insulting or oppressive manner in committing the act of discrimination.

22 Referred to at various times by *Vento v Chief Constable of West Yorkshire Police (No 2)* [2003] IRLR 102, CA; *Ministry of Defence v Cannock* [1994] IRLR 509, EAT.
23 *Ministry of Defence v Cannock* [1994] IRLR 509, EAT.
24 *Alexander v The Home Office* [1988] IRLR 190, CA. For examples, see para 19.22 below.
25 *Scott v Commissioners of Inland Revenue* [2004] IRLR 713, CA; *Virgo Fidelis Senior School v Boyle* [2004] IRLR 268, EAT.
26 See pp739–742 for a sample.
27 *D Watt (Shetland (Ltd)) v Reid* EAT/424/01.
28 See para 19.36 below.
29 [1988] IRLR 190, CA.

In practice, ETs have awarded compensation for aggravated damages in a range of circumstances (see below).

The size of the injury to feelings award

19.16   The size of the award is largely in the ET's discretion. After many years of uncertainty, the Court of Appeal laid down guidelines in the important case of *Chief Constable of West Yorkshire Police v Vento (No 2)*.[30] The Court of Appeal identified three broad bands for injury to feelings, as distinct from compensation for injury to health:[31]

- A top band, normally between £15,000 and £25,000, for the most serious cases, eg a lengthy campaign of harassment. Only in the most exceptional case should an award for injury to feelings exceed £25,000.
- A middle band between £5,000 and £15,000 for serious cases which do not merit the top band.
- A lower band of £500–£5,000 for less serious cases, eg where the act of discrimination is an isolated or one-off occurrence. Awards less than £500 should generally be avoided altogether.

19.17   As previously stated, these bands relate only to injury to feelings, and any award for aggravated damages and injury to health would be separate and additional. The guidelines were set in 2003 and some tribunals (though not others) have been willing to increase the figures to take account of inflation. Using the Retail Prices Index from the end of 2003 to the end of 2008, there is a good argument that compensation should be increased by 18.5 per cent.[32]

19.18   ETs still have an enormous amount of discretion in how much they award and the EAT will rarely interfere. It is, therefore, very hard for advisers to predict the size of an award as, for example, one ET may legitimately award £7,000 on a middle band case, where another would award double that on the same set of facts.

19.19   One of the first cases to go to the EAT was *(1) Armitage (2) Marsden (3) HM Prison Service v Johnson*.[33] The case merely illustrates when an ET is entitled (if it chooses) to make a high award. Mr Johnson, a black prison auxiliary, was awarded £20,000 for injury to feelings for a

---

30 [2003] IRLR 102; (2003) 114 EOR 27; May 2003 *Legal Action* 21, CA.

31 See para 19.27 below.

32 Estimate given in 189 Equal Opportunities Review at p11. Naomi Cunningham and Michael Reed have also tracked down the Bank of England's on-line inflation calculator at www.bankofengland.co.uk/education/calculator/index1.htm

33 [1997] IRLR 162; (1997) 71 EOR 43, EAT.

campaign of racial harassment lasting 18 months, plus £7,500 aggravated damages for the employer's rejection of his grievance and putting it down to a character defect. The employer's investigation, instead of providing a remedy for the wrongs suffered by the worker, added to his injury. Further, £500 was also awarded against two prison officers personally. The EAT decided the ET was entitled to award £28,500 (even if it was a little on the high side) for such a serious (although not the worst possible) case of discrimination. The EAT said that, in general, injury to feelings awards should bear some broad similarity to the range of awards in personal injury cases. It should also relate to the value of the sum, in terms of purchasing power or earnings, in real life.

19.20   The EAT in *Tchoula*,[34] a case decided before *Vento*, also provides an interesting overview. The EAT reviewed a large number of the ET awards to date and divided them into higher and lower categories. The interesting thing about Tchoula is that although the EAT reduced the worker's award for injury to feelings and aggravated damages from £27,000 to £10,000, it awarded as much as £10,000 for what it considered to be a lower category case. Although Mr Tchoula did suffer considerable injury to feelings, the discrimination had not contributed to his marriage breakdown nor caused depression. The discrimination lasted only over a period of ten days, and although he had lost his job and the opportunity to continue in the security industry, he wanted to better himself anyway.

19.21   The EAT refused to overturn another large ET award of £20,000 for injury to feelings and £5,000 aggravated damages in *Chan v Hackney LBC*.[35] Mr Chan was forced into medical retirement after months of sustained pressure. The EAT said it was legitimate to take into account the treatment of Mr Chan outside the time limit as context for the impact on his feelings of the acts of race discrimination within the time limit.

19.22   So far, the highest awards have been in race discrimination and sexual harassment cases. Factors which lead to high awards tend to be a long period or numerous incidents of discrimination; false accusations made in public; loss of a valued job or career; a particular vulnerability of the worker, eg due to age or work environment; and most importantly, evidence of severe injury to health and feelings or family difficulties. Harassment of a pregnant woman could lead to a high award where it causes additional stress because it threatens the

---

34 *ICTS (UK) Ltd v Tchoula* [2000] IRLR 643; November 2000 *Legal Action* 26, EAT.
35 EAT/120/97; November 1997 *Legal Action* 15, EAT; May 1997 *Legal Action* 10, ET.

well-being of the unborn child.[36] One-off acts of discrimination or only short periods of harassment will not necessarily fall into the lowest Vento band as the overall seriousness should be taken into account.[37] Aggravating factors may be conscious victimisation,[38] ignoring or mishandling a grievance or a character attack on the worker. It could also, depending on the facts, lead to aggravated damages to promote the discriminator while the worker's harassment grievance has not yet been fully investigated.[39] The employer's behaviour in the ET proceedings will also be relevant,[40] including repeated unmerited threats of costs in the correspondence. If an employer unreasonably disputes that a disabled worker is disabled under the DDA 1995, thus requiring him/her to go through unnecessary medical examinations, this could lead to an award of aggravated damages.

19.23   *Vento*[41] sets the lower band of awards at £500–£5,000 and suggests this is only applicable for minor cases and one-off occurrences.[42] The first case regarding the absolute minimum suitable award was decided prior to the lifting of the ceiling and should really be considered as out of date. This case was *Alexander v The Home Office*,[43] where a black prisoner was deprived of work in the prison kitchen on the ground of his race. The Court of Appeal increased the county court judge's award from £50 to £500, saying that:

> For the injury to feelings, however, for the humiliation, for the insult, it is impossible to say what is restitution and the answer must depend on the experience and good sense of the judge and his assessors. Awards should not be minimal, because this would tend to trivialise or diminish respect for the public policy to which the Act gives effect. On the other hand ... to award sums which are generally felt to be excessive does almost as much harm.[44]

---

36 *Gilbank v Miles* [2006] IRLR 538, CA.

37 For example, see *Wallington v Sand B Car Hire Kent Ltd* EAT 0240/03; *Carney v Rouf and another* EAT 0353/04; (2005) 777 IDS Brief 11; (2005) 139 EOR 26, EAT.

38 *ICTS (UK) Ltd v Tchoula* [2000] IRLR 643; November 2000 *Legal Action* 26, EAT.

39 *British Telecommunications plc v Reid* [2004] IRLR 327; (2004) 126 EOR 28; May 2004 *Legal Action* 32, CA.

40 *Zaiwalla & Co v Walia* [2002] IRLR 697; (2002) 111 EOR 24; November 2002 *Legal Action* 18, EAT.

41 *Chief Constable of West Yorkshire Police v Vento (No 2)* [2003] IRLR 102; (2003) 114 EOR 27; May 2003 *Legal Action* 21, CA.

42 See para 19.16 above.

43 [1988] IRLR 190, CA.

44 [1988] IRLR 190 at 193 per May LJ.

Since the Court of Appeal relied on the judge's finding that Mr Alexander 'had not suffered any substantial injury to his feelings', £500 should be regarded as the absolute minimum appropriate award for injury to feelings. This view has been confirmed by the EAT in *Sharifi v Strathclyde Regional Council*.[45] See also the views of the EAT in *Murray v Powertech*,[46] where the ET's award was increased to £1,250, and *Doshoki v Draeger Ltd*[47] where the award was increased from £750 to £4,000. In another case, £1,500 awarded for injury to feelings for sexual harassment for a 'short period' was increased by the EAT to £8,500.[48] The EAT said harassment over a three month period is not 'short'. The tribunal should also have taken into account that the harassment was not perpetrated by a junior employee but by one of the owners of the business.

19.24   It is surprising, in the light of these cases, that awards as low as £1,000–£2,000 or less are still made. It is advisable not to take it for granted that the ET will appreciate the likely impact of the discrimination on the worker's feelings, but to give explicit evidence on this from the worker and other witnesses including medical evidence where appropriate. It is also wise to be ready to make arguments on the case-law and to point out that in *Alexander*, £500 was considered a minimum award, ie where there is in reality little or no injury to feelings (a very unusual situation) and at a time before the removal of the ceiling on the compensatory award. Many years have passed and the value of money has increased even since the *Murray*[49] case.

19.25   Unfortunately ET practice in the size of injury to feelings awards is extremely variable and difficult to predict. Some ETs clearly believe they are awarding a large sum when they award, say, £5,000 for serious injury. It is therefore important to draw the ET's attention to the higher awards, especially in comparable cases, and the bands in *Vento*. Awards made by other ETs, unless appealed, have no precedent value when considered in isolation. But it is not at all helpful to look at reports of average awards as these tend to keep the figures low and ignore the factors in the particular case.[50] Media reports are highly misleading as they often report settlements rather than ET awards and in any event

45 [1992] IRLR 259; (1992) 44 EOR 36, EAT.
46 (1992) 44 EOR 35, EAT.
47 [2002] IRLR 340; (2002) 104 EOR 22; November 2002 *Legal Action* 18, EAT.
48 *Carney v Rouf and Islam* EAT 0353/04; (2005) 777 *IDS Brief* 11; (2005) 139 EOR 26; May 2005 *Legal Action*, EAT.
49 *Murray v Powertech* (1992) 44 EOR 35, EAT.
50 EOR publishes a very useful annual compensation round-up with individual case examples, eg see 189 – 190 EORs (June - July 2009) for 2008.

tend to include figures for the entire compensatory award, which may consist primarily of loss of earnings.

19.26   Although it is hard to appeal against an award for injury to feelings on the grounds that it is too low, where there is strong evidence of injury and an extremely low award, this should be considered. Where there have been a number of acts of discrimination, particularly if there is victimisation as well as direct discrimination or if there is discrimination based on different characteristics (eg race and disability), the tribunal should separately consider the injury to feelings arising from each action rather than taking a loose overview.[51] Having considered these elements separately, a tribunal must still stand back and look at the global figure, ensuring there is no double counting and that the overall award is not disproportionate.

Injury to health (personal injury)

19.27   Injury to feelings, when it becomes sufficiently severe, can be considered as an injury to health. It is now common in serious cases to argue for injury to health as a separate category. It does not matter exactly where the line is drawn, and 'stress and depression' can be included in injury to feelings, but the ET will not allow 'double recovery', ie the worker to be compensated twice for the same injury.[52] In setting its bands of compensation for injury to feelings, *Vento*[53] did indicate that injury to health was a separate matter.

19.28   Unfortunately, seeking compensation for injury to health in an ET is not a simple matter, because traditionally, claims for damage to health are brought as negligence or contract claims in the civil courts.[54] An ET can award compensation for any personal injury caused by the tort of racial discrimination.[55] The same would apply in sex, sexual orientation, religion, age or disability discrimination cases. This means that if the discrimination has seriously damaged the worker's health, physically or psychiatrically (and not solely his/her feelings), a claim for damages for personal injury (ie injury to health) must be added to any discrimination case which is brought. Examples could include nervous

---

51 *Al Jumard v Clywd Leisure Ltd* UKEAT/0334/07; [2008] IRLR 345, EAT; *Legal Action* Nov 2008.

52 *HM Prison Service v Salmon* [2001] IRLR 425, EAT.

53 *Chief Constable of West Yorkshire Police v Vento (No 2)* [2003] IRLR 102; (2003) 114 EOR 27; May 2003 *Legal Action* 21, CA.

54 See also paras 17.149–17.155 on stress.

55 *Sheriff v Klyne Tugs (Lowestoft) Ltd* [1999] IRLR 481; (1999) 88 EOR 51, CA.

breakdown, severe depression or post-traumatic stress syndrome. If a worker omits to add such a claim, but his/her discrimination case is decided by the ET or settled, s/he will very probably be unable to make any future personal injury claim arising from the discriminatory actions by the employer.[56] This is because the issue could and should have been argued in front of the ET – an employer is entitled to know that all claims have been dealt with in one place, so there is some finality to the issues.

19.29   Employment lawyers have had to become familiar with the basic principles of quantifying damages in personal injury cases, especially those related to psychiatric illness. A formal medical report is usually essential for making such a claim. In personal injury cases, there is a vast body of reported awards for pain and suffering caused by different injuries. These are collated and set out in such sources as *Kemp & Kemp: Quantum of Damages*[57] and formulated into guidelines by the Judicial Studies Board (JSB): *Guidelines for the assessment of general damages in personal injury cases.*[58]

19.30   The JSB guidelines are often referred to in the ET when assessing injury to health in discrimination cases. Chapter 3 of the current guidelines deals with psychiatric damage and lists the following factors to be taken into account:

i)   the claimant's ability to cope with life and work;

ii)   the effect on the claimant's relationships with family, friends and those with whom s/he comes into contact;

iii) the extent to which treatment would be successful;

iv)   future vulnerability;

v)   prognosis;

vi)   whether medical help has been sought;

vii) whether the injury results from sexual and/or physical abuse and/or breach of trust, and if so, the nature of the relationship between the claimant and the discriminator, the nature of the abuse, its duration and the symptoms caused by it.

19.31 The guidelines put awards into four categories, with estimates of the current value of awards in each category, ie severe (£35,000–£74,000),

---

56 *Sheriff v Klyne Tugs (Lowestoft) Ltd* [1999] IRLR 481; (1999) 88 EOR 51, CA. Advisers should read *Sheriff* for its implications.

57 Published by Sweet & Maxwell (looseleaf), www.sweetandmaxwell.co.uk

58 These can be purchased as a book (9th edn (2008) published by Oxford University Press at http://ukcatalogue.oup.com/product/9780199548583.do) or accessed through a Lawtel subscription (www.lawtel.com).

moderately severe (£12,250–£35,000), moderate (£3,750–£12,250) and minor (£1000–£3,750). Cases of work-related stress resulting in a permanent or long-standing disability preventing a return to comparable employment are likely to be moderately severe. Where there is marked improvement by the hearing and a good prognosis, the case is likely to be moderate. There are also specific categories for post-traumatic stress disorder. When arguing for a certain sum in the ET, it may be useful to find some cases in *Kemp & Kemp* within the relevant range, which are similar to the claimant's case.

19.32   There are well-established principles in personal injury law regarding what should happen in cases where the claimant has a vulnerable personality or a pre-existing condition caused by other factors.[59] This is rather complex, but can be broadly summarised as follows:

- *The eggshell skull or personality principle*: If the injury to the claimant is greater than normal because s/he has a vulnerable personality, the employer is nevertheless responsible for all the injury caused, even though it was unforeseeable.
- *The aggravation or exacerbation principle*: If the claimant already had some symptoms arising from a pre-existing illness, the employer is only liable for the additional injury s/he has caused.
- *Pre-existing risk of injury*: If the claimant had a pre-existing condition which made it likely s/he would have gone on to suffer a similar psychiatric illness even if the unlawful act had not occurred, his/her compensation will be reduced by a percentage to reflect that possibility.
- *The acceleration principle*: If the claimant had a pre-existing condition, but the symptoms occurred sooner due to the unlawful act, the employer is only liable for losses during the 'acceleration period'.

19.33   In all these situations, it is important to provide evidence as to what the claimant's condition and prognosis would have been, had s/he not been discriminated against. As yet, there are few employment law authorities on the application of the principles to discrimination cases. In *Sadler v Portsmouth Publishing and Printing Ltd*,[60] the claimant had a significant history of depressive episodes prior to her illness caused by sexual harassment. Based on medical evidence, the ET found the claimant had a 33 per cent chance of becoming ill anyway due to her pre-existing condition. Further, her current illness was caused 80 per cent by her underlying condition and made worse by the sexual

59 For a detailed source on this, see Butterworths Personal Injury Litigation Service, www.lexisnexis.co.uk
60 UKEAT/0280/04.

harassment by 20 per cent. The ET applied both discounts to the award for personal injury (injury to health) and to the award for loss of earnings. The EAT said this was incorrect: only the 80 per cent could be deducted from the personal injury award and only the 33 per cent could be deducted from the financial losses.

19.34   Note that the ET can only deal with the personal injury claim where it is attached to a discrimination claim. If the worker brings no discrimination claim, s/he would take his/her claim for personal injury in the county court or High Court in the usual way.[61]

19.35   Despite the practical difficulties, there are some advantages in bringing such cases in the ET. Community Legal Service funding (legal aid) is not usually available for most types of personal injury case and it can be difficult to find solicitors willing to do cases on conditional fee arrangements ('no win, no fee') unless the claim is substantial or the worker has legal expenses insurance. In the ET, at least the worker has access to a relatively less expensive and less formal procedure. Also, under discrimination law it is only necessary to prove the psychiatric injury was directly caused by the act of discrimination.[62] It is not necessary to show the type of injury was reasonably foreseeable. This is helpful where a worker is more badly hurt by, say, a single act of discrimination, than anyone might have expected.

Exemplary damages

19.36   Exemplary damages are awarded to punish a wrongdoer. It is untested by the appeal courts whether they can be awarded in cases of discrimination in employment.[63] In 2008, exemplary damages were awarded by an employment tribunal in a case against the MoD concerning sex and sexual orientation discrimination. This has been appealed and the outcome should be interesting.[64] The key case of *Rookes v Barnard*[65] established that exemplary damages can be awarded in any of three situations:

- where there has been oppressive, arbitrary or unconstitutional action by servants of the government; or

61 Though see paras 17.149–17.155 regarding civil claims for non-economic loss.
62 *Essa v Laing Ltd* [2004] IRLR 313, CA. The case relates to the RRA 1976, but presumably also applies under the other discrimination statutes and regulations.
63 *Kuddus v Chief Constable of Leicester Constabulary* [2001] UKHL 29, establishes the possibility; and see the EAT's comments in *Virgo Fidelis Senior School v Boyle* [2004] IRLR 268 at 278.
64 *Fletcher v Ministry of Defence* (2009) 189 EOR 11.
65 [1964] AC 1129, HL.

- where the defendant's conduct has been calculated to make profit which will exceed the compensation payable; or
- where statute says they can be awarded.

Indirect race discrimination

19.37   No award of compensation may be made in respect of indirect race discrimination (except in relation to race or ethnic or national origins) if the employer proves that the requirement or condition was not applied with the intention of treating the worker unfavourably on grounds of race.[66] The equivalent provision under the SDA 1975 was removed in 1996, probably due to its incompatibility with EU law. No award of compensation may be made for unintentional indirect discrimination on the ground of age, sexual orientation, religion or belief, unless the ET thinks it just and equitable to award compensation as well as making any declaration or recommendation.[67] This does not seem to add anything to the general requirement that the tribunal's order for remedies is just and equitable (see para 19.1 above).

19.38   There is case-law regarding the meaning of 'unintentional' indirect discrimination under both the RRA 1976 and the SDA 1975. In one case,[68] a single-parent train operator resigned when London Underground imposed a new flexible rostering scheme in order to save costs. This was found to be intentional indirect discrimination because although the employer did not introduce the scheme with the intention of discriminating against women, it did insist on the worker complying with it, while knowing of the unfavourable consequences for her.

19.39   In another case,[69] to increase efficiency a company decided no holidays could be taken during the May to July peak period. When Eid fell in June 1992, the company refused to make an exception to its policy, even though its Muslim employees offered to work extra hours to compensate. The discrimination was found to be intentional, even though the motive was purely to increase efficiency, because the employer wanted to bring about the state of affairs constituting the adverse treatment and knew that one racial group (ie Asians) would be disproportionately affected.

---

66 RRA 1976 s57(3).
67 EE(A) Regs 2006 reg 38(2); EE(SO) Regs 2003 reg 30(2) and EE(RB) Regs 2003 reg 30(2).
68 *London Underground Ltd v Edwards* [1995] IRLR 355; (1995) 62 EOR 39, EAT.
69 *J H Walker Ltd v Hussain* [1996] IRLR 11; (1996) 66 EOR 50, EAT.

Compensation for pregnancy discrimination

19.40 In the 1990s, many cases were brought against the Ministry of Defence (MOD) by servicewomen formerly discharged on grounds of pregnancy. Compensatory awards tended to be very high, mainly because they referred back to many years of lost earnings and concerned unique difficulties for wives of service personnel in finding fresh employment. A few cases laid down some guidelines applicable to assessing compensation, including the MOD cases specifically and pregnancy discrimination cases generally.[70]

19.41 Points made by the cases include the following:

- In awarding compensation for loss of earnings after birth, an ET should consider the chance that a woman would not have returned to work anyway, taking account of work and family demands.[71] It would not be exceptional or even unusual to assess the chance of a woman's return as 100 per cent.[72] Evidence as to what the woman did in fact do, having been dismissed, does not necessarily mean she would have done the same had she not been dismissed.[73]
- The order of deductions where a woman mitigates her loss by obtaining new employment at lesser pay is first to deduct her new earnings from the sum she would have received had she remained in her original employment and then to make any deduction assessed to reflect the chance she would not have returned to her original employment.[74]
- Concerning the duty to mitigate,[75] a woman must actively seek employment six months after the birth of her child if she wishes to obtain compensation for loss of earnings after that date.[76] However, expectations of what a worker should do to find work should not be unreasonable, as she is the wronged party.[77] Furthermore, an ET is entitled to take into account its own knowledge and experience

---

70 See *Ministry of Defence v Cannock* [1994] IRLR 509; (1994) 57 EOR 51, EAT, as improved and modified by a different EAT in *MOD v Hunt* [1996] IRLR 139, EAT. Also see *MOD v Wheeler, Donald, Nixon and Joslyn* [1998] IRLR 23, CA.

71 *Ministry of Defence v Cannock* [1994] IRLR 509; (1994) 57 EOR 51, EAT.

72 *MOD v Hunt* [1996] IRLR 139, EAT.

73 *MOD v Hunt* [1996] IRLR 139, EAT.

74 *MOD v Wheeler, Donald, Nixon and Joslyn* [1998] IRLR 23, CA.

75 See para 18.32.

76 *Ministry of Defence v Cannock* [1994] IRLR 509; (1994) 57 EOR 51, EAT.

77 *MOD v Hunt* [1996] IRLR 139, EAT at para 11.

of difficulties in the labour market facing women with young children.[78]

- The burden of proving failure to mitigate is on the person alleging it, ie the employer. If no evidence is given on the failure to mitigate, eg what steps should have been taken and when, the ET cannot fill the gap by making assumptions about when the worker could have found fresh employment.[79]
- An ET should not allow a woman to be questioned on whether the pregnancy was planned or unplanned.

Interest

19.42 An ET has a discretion whether to award interest, although arguably the decision in *Marshall v Southampton Area Health Authority (No 2)*[80] suggests it must always be awarded. The rules are complicated and should be referred to for the precise calculation method.[81] However, broadly speaking, interest on an injury to feelings award runs from the date of the discrimination and, for any financial loss, runs from a date midway between the act of discrimination and the date of calculation by the ET. The rate is that of the Court Special Investment Account under rule 27(1) of the Court Fund Rules 1987 or in Scotland, the rate fixed, for the time being, by the Act of Sederunt (Interest in Sheriff Court Decrees or Extracts) 1975.[82] The special interest rate for England and Wales was reduced to 6 per cent on 1 February 2002 and to 3 per cent on 1 February 2009, but check the latest rate. It is difficult to find a source for the interest rates but the website of the Court Funds Office seems the best bet, at least for England and Wales.[83] To calculate interest on injury to feelings, multiply the daily rate by the number of days between the discrimination and the hearing. To find out the daily rate, divide the amount of the injury to feelings award by 365 and multiply by the interest rate, eg 3 per cent. To calculate interest on financial loss,

---

78 *MOD v Hunt* [1996] IRLR 139, EAT at para 85.

79 *MOD v Hunt* [1996] IRLR 139, EAT, at para 2. Though it is still wise to bring evidence of efforts to mitigate.

80 [1993] IRLR 445, ECJ.

81 Employment Tribunals (Interest on Awards in Discrimination Cases) Regulations 1996 SI No 2803.

82 SI No 821. Employment Tribunals (Interest on Awards in Discrimination Cases) Regulations 1996 SI No 2803 reg 3(2).

83 At www.courtfunds.gov.uk/cfo/investments_interest.htm It also contains details of past rates. We believe the special rate referred to there is the one under r27(1), but it is not completely clear.

multiply the daily rate by half the number of days between the discrimination and the hearing. To find out the daily rate, divide the sum awarded for financial loss by 365 and multiply by the interest rate. If the rate of interest has varied during the period for which it must be calculated, the ET may apply a median or average rate for the sake of simplicity.[84]

19.43 An ET must consider whether to award interest, even if it is not invited to do so,[85] and in its written reasons must set out how interest was calculated or, if none has been awarded, explain why not. It is a good idea to include interest in the Schedule of Loss.[86]

19.44 Interest on unpaid awards runs from the date of the award unless full payment of the award is made within 14 days of the relevant decision day.[87]

Costs against the employer

19.45 Costs may be awarded against either party on the same basis as in unfair dismissal actions.[88] However, costs are far more frequently awarded against unsuccessful workers in discrimination cases than against unsuccessful employers, even though it must almost always be unreasonable for employers to defend proceedings where they have knowingly discriminated and certainly in cases of sexual harassment.[89]

Enforcement

19.46 For information regarding what to do if the employer refuses to pay the award or settlement, see para 18.69.

---

84 Employment Tribunal (Interest on Awards in Discrimination Cases) Regulations 1996 SI No 2803 reg 3(3).
85 Employment Tribunal (Interest on Awards in Discrimination Cases) Regulations 1996 SI No 2803 reg 2(1)(b); *Fasuyi v Greenwich LBC* EAT/1078/99.
86 See example at pp739–742.
87 Employment Tribunal (Interest on Awards in Discrimination Cases) Regulations 1996 SI No 2803 reg 8.
88 See para 20.142 onwards.
89 See para 21.86.

Running an unfair dismissal case

continued

continued

Chapter 20: Key points

- Winning an unfair dismissal case is mostly about the quality of the evidence, which is gathered during case preparation.
- It is essential that a detailed statement is taken from the employee as soon as possible while memory is fresh.
- A case is started when the employee's written claim on the standard ET1 form arrives at the tribunal. The form must be sent to the correct tribunal office. Time limits are very strict.
- As soon as the employer's response (on the ET3 form) is received, the employee should ask the employer for documents and additional information. If these are not supplied voluntarily, the tribunal must be asked for an order.
- Contemporaneous documents are usually more influential evidence than witnesses.
- Contact possible witnesses at an early stage, while they are still enthusiastic, and take a signed statement. A witness order can be obtained if a witness will not come to the tribunal without one. It is generally unwise to force a hostile witness to come.
- If the employee is ordered to supply any documents or additional information to the employer, s/he must comply with the order in time. Otherwise costs may be ordered against him/her, or the claim may be struck out.
- The employment tribunal must give 14 days' notice of any hearing (though not of a case management discussion). Once a hearing date is fixed, it is extremely difficult to get it changed.
- If a representative is noted on the ET1, all correspondence will go to the representative. Make sure the employee is kept informed and told the hearing date. If no representative is noted, make sure the employee gets in touch whenever s/he receives a letter and in any event, every few weeks.
- Every case is allocated an officer from the Advisory, Conciliation and Arbitration Service (ACAS), who will get in touch regarding possible settlement. Conversations through ACAS should not be disclosed to the employment tribunal.
- There are many advantages in settling a case, provided it is for a reasonable sum. It avoids recoupment (see para 18.58) and can include wording for an agreed reference.
- An employee must try to get a new job (even if less well paid) and keep records of all attempts. If the employee does not try very hard, s/he may not be awarded much compensation.

- The employee and any witnesses give oral evidence at the tribunal. Witness statements are usually exchanged 7–14 days before the hearing.

Preliminary steps

20.1   At the outset it should be established what the employee wants to achieve. If the employee only wants his/her job back or a good reference or payment of outstanding wages, holiday or notice pay, it is not advisable to commence a claim for unfair dismissal. Nothing is more likely to annoy the employer. However, commencing a claim might induce a settlement which incorporates the monies owing and includes an agreed reference. Unfortunately, if the case does not settle, an ET cannot order a good reference to be given.

20.2   If the priority is to get the employee's job back, negotiations with the employer should start immediately, possibly with the intervention of an Advisory, Conciliation and Arbitration Service (ACAS) conciliation officer or some other party, eg another employee. ACAS launched a new free pre-claim conciliation service in April 2009, where parties want to negotiate before a tribunal claim has even been lodged. The employee, or indeed the employer, can ask for ACAS to get involved by telephoning the nearest ACAS office. ACAS officers will usually deal with the matter over the phone. It is unclear whether they will take the same hands-off role as they do once a claim has started,[1] ie merely acting as an intermediary for any negotiation, but this is likely. The greater the delay in starting negotiations, the less the likelihood of success. If an employee simply wants a good written reference or payment of monies owed, a telephone call or polite letter should be the first step. Only if the employer refuses, should the employee threaten employment tribunal (ET) proceedings. Where a stronger approach is necessary, it is sometimes effective to send a draft tribunal claim under cover of a 'without prejudice'[2] letter proposing settlement.

20.3   Before the employee decides to start a case, s/he should be advised on his/her chances of success, what is involved and the likely compensation. The employee should be warned that it is particularly important s/he makes efforts to find a new job, as otherwise his/her compensation will be reduced for failure to mitigate.[3] S/he must keep

1 See para 20.156 below.
2 See para 9.19 and glossary at p782.
3 See para 18.32.

records of all efforts to find work. Stress that any e-mails must be printed out as soon as they are sent. It is common for these to get lost later and some e-mail providers delete sent e-mails after a certain number of days.

20.4   As soon as an employee comes for advice, the adviser should work out and diarise the last day for lodging a tribunal claim (usually known as an 'ET1'). The employee should also make a note. Once ET proceedings are started, they move very quickly. It can take as little as three months from the date the ET1 is lodged to the hearing. If information and documents need to be gathered, this must be started immediately. All time limits and dates for chasing up requests made to the employer should be diarised.

Collecting information before lodging the ET1

20.5   Before starting the claim, the adviser should get all relevant documents in the employee's possession, eg a statement of the main terms and conditions of employment and/or contract of employment, staff handbook, works rules, letter of appointment, letter of dismissal, P45 (which should state the last date worked), payslips, warning letters and appraisal reports. There may well be other relevant documents.

20.6   It is very important to obtain all documents which may form the employment contract (see para 1.2 above). If the employee signed any statement, document or letter during employment, it is essential to see this prior to lodging the ET1 if at all possible. It may contain information relevant to the strength of the case.

20.7   The terms of the contract will be particularly vital in relation to a constructive dismissal claim, where the employee must show a fundamental breach of contract. If, eg the employee relies on a change of workplace as such a breach, but the contract contains a mobility clause, there will be no breach of contract and the claim will fail.

20.8   Once all the employee's documents are gathered, it is good practice for the adviser to take a full statement of all the material facts, concentrating on the reason for dismissal and the events immediately preceding it. The old-fashioned word for this is a 'proof'. The final disciplinary hearing leading to dismissal is usually very important and the adviser should obtain a near verbatim account while the employee's memory is relatively fresh. Probe the employee on the facts, particularly on the weaknesses. The names and addresses of possible witnesses to significant incidents and in relation to any warnings should be collected. It is usually easier to establish names and addresses at an early stage than months later when a witness order is needed.

20.9 The employee should sign and date the statement and keep a copy. It should be explained that the statement is only for private use as the adviser's working document. The statement is useful when negotiating, since an understanding of the facts and thereby the issues, allows negotiation from a position of strength. If the adviser does not have time to take a neat statement at this stage, s/he should at least take full and systematic notes covering all the issues. However, since witness statements[4] eventually need to be written in most cases, it may save time in the long run to take notes in the shape of a statement and type these up from the outset.

Statutory dispute resolution procedures

20.10 Certain steps must be taken while the statutory dispute resolution procedures still apply. Although they were abolished on 6th April 2009, the transitional provisions mean they may still need to be followed in some limited circumstances.[5]

The first letter and written reasons for the dismissal: ERA 1996 s92

20.11 Before starting the claim, the employee should write to the employer requesting written reasons for the dismissal. The first letter to the employer is important.[6] As well as requesting information which will be instrumental in the conduct of the case and its final outcome, it creates an initial impression on the employer which may encourage settlement later on. The employee should ask for any key documents which s/he needs at this stage, although this is not the time to ask for absolutely everything relevant to running a case, and the employer cannot be compelled to provide documents before a case starts.[7] The employee may have no contractual documents and be uncertain whether any exist. The employer should therefore at least be asked for copies of the relevant procedures and the employee's statement of particulars of employment.[8] The employee can gain additional compensation of 2–4 weeks' pay if s/he wins his/her unfair dismissal case, if at the time s/he started it, the employer was in breach of his/her duty

---

4 See paras 20.101–20.110.
5 See chapter 22 for detail of the procedures and abolition dates.
6 See p751 for an example.
7 See paras 20.62–20.66 on disclosure.
8 See para 1.24.

under Employment Rights Act (ERA) 1996 s1 (to supply written particulars within two months of starting employment) or s4 (to provide a written statement within one month of any change of particulars).[9] Presumably the employer cannot avoid the penalty by providing written particulars after dismissal. The point is untested, but if wrong, the employee may not want to ask for the particulars until s/he has started the case.

20.12   If the employee qualifies to claim unfair dismissal, s/he is entitled to receive an adequate and truthful statement of the reasons for dismissal on request.[10] The entitlement is often referred to as requesting 'section 92 written reasons' or 'written reasons for dismissal'. The employer must supply the reasons within 14 days of the employee's request. In order to prove that a request was made, it is best to make it in writing and send it by recorded delivery, fax or e-mail.

20.13   If the employer unreasonably refuses to supply written reasons within 14 days or supplies reasons which are inadequate or untrue, the employee is entitled to compensation of two weeks' gross pay.[11] There is no limit on a week's pay.[12] An employer who fails to supply reasons within 14 days due to a genuine oversight, but supplies them when s/he realises the oversight, will not be held to have unreasonably refused.[13] It is not enough for an employer to acknowledge the request within the 14 days and supply reasons later unless, eg the person taking the decision to dismiss was on holiday. No compensation can be claimed for not providing written reasons unless the employer has been requested to provide them (except where a woman was dismissed while pregnant or on maternity leave).

20.14   The written reasons must be adequate so that it is clear to the employee and to anyone else why the employee was dismissed and upon which of the potentially fair reasons for dismissal[14] the employer relies.[15] The purpose of the right is to make the employer state truthfully the reason for dismissal. Any statement given by the employer is admissible in unfair dismissal proceedings and will be important in determining the fairness of the dismissal.[16] In deciding whether to award compensation for inadequate or untrue reasons, the ET is not

9 See para 1.26.
10 ERA 1996 s92.
11 ERA 1996 s93(2).
12 By omission from ERA 1996 s227.
13 *Ladbroke Entertainments v Clark* [1987] ICR 585, EAT.
14 Under ERA 1996 s98(2); see para 6.49.
15 *Horsley Smith & Sherry v Dutton* [1977] IRLR 172, EAT.
16 ERA 1996 s9(5).

concerned with whether the reasons given were intrinsically good or bad.[17] If the reason was bad, the dismissal will be unfair, but there will be no award for the written reasons claim.

20.15 The time limit for a claim for failure to supply adequate and true reasons is the same as for unfair dismissal. Even if reasons are supplied within 14 days, an ERA 1996 s92 claim should usually be added to the unfair dismissal claim (see p000 for an example). One can never be sure what will emerge during the unfair dismissal hearing about the truth of the reasons given.

20.16 Women dismissed while pregnant or on maternity leave are entitled to written reasons, whether or not they request them, and regardless of their length of service.[18] This is logical because they can claim unfair dismissal for reasons related to pregnancy or maternity, even if they do not have the necessary length of service for ordinary unfair dismissal claims. If the reasons are not supplied, a claim should be made as in usual cases. Even though it is not necessary, it is probably worth asking the employer for reasons where they are not volunteered.

The ET Rules of Procedure

20.17 Although this chapter is concerned with running unfair dismissal cases (and therefore refers to 'employees' throughout), the procedural rules are basically the same with all ET cases. However, different cases and types of claim do vary in length and complexity. Additional points relevant to discrimination cases are in chapter 21 and to equal pay claims in chapter 5.[19]

20.18 The procedural rules regarding the preparation and hearing of cases in England, Wales and Scotland are contained in the Employment Tribunal (Constitution and Rules of Procedure) Regulations (ET Regs) 2004.[20] Previously there were separate rules for Scotland, which has developed certain different practices in its tribunals. Although there is great similarity, there are some practical differences which may not be covered by this book. There are also three practice directions concerning procedures applicable to Scottish tribunals.[21] The ET Regs

17 *Harvard Securities v Younghusband* [1990] IRLR 17, EAT.
18 ERA 1996 s92(4).
19 See also paras 18.64–18.67 regarding interim relief.
20 SI No 1861, as amended by SI No 2351.
21 Access via www.employmenttribunals.gov.uk/RulesLegislation/rulesThat Govern.htm Practice Directions issued for England & Wales are also linked to this.

2004 contain a large number of changes from the 2001 Regulations, which they replaced. The changes were designed to make the steps of case preparation more open, efficient, consistent and understandable. The tribunal has great powers and flexibility to make decisions, but fair process, notification and consultation of parties is built in at every stage. Much of the jargon has been replaced with plain English, largely following the wording in the Civil Procedure Rules (CPR) 1998.[22] Unfortunately the plain English is often very confusing, as words such as 'response' and 'additional information' are given a technical meaning as well as their general usage.

20.19   The 'overriding objective' of the procedural rules is to enable tribunals to deal with cases justly. This means, so far as is practicable:

- ensuring the parties are on an equal footing;
- dealing with the case in ways which are proportionate to the complexity or importance of the issues;
- ensuring the case is dealt with expeditiously and fairly; and
- saving expense.[23]

20.20   An ET must give effect to the overriding objective when exercising its procedural powers. This is constantly referred to by the tribunal when making decisions as to what orders should be made for documents and information, and deciding the length and conduct of the hearing.

20.21   The overriding objective was introduced in July 2001. There are understandable resource pressures on the tribunal system, partly due to constantly expanding areas of employment law. Nevertheless, it is a pity that processing cases swiftly and cutting time and costs is made a measure of justice.

20.22   There is a risk in some cases that the ETs' eagerness to save time and cut costs may lead to inadequate justice, because the parties are not given enough time or information to prepare and run cases properly. As employers are generally already in possession of the information needed to run a case, employees are usually the more disadvantaged by such pressures. In truth, the tribunal system is vastly under-resourced and with more claims being lodged every year, attempts to push through cases with minimal preparation and inadequate time allocation for hearings are inevitable. The Employment Appeal Tribunal (EAT) has recognised, albeit in the context of a discrimination case, that there can be a tension between what expedition requires and what fairness requires. If so, in the end, justice should be preferred to expe-

---

22 SI No 3132. See Glossary at p773.
23 ET Regs 2004 reg 3.

dition.[24] Article 6 (the right to a fair hearing) of the European Convention on Human Rights has also become an important counter-balance.[25]

The tribunal claim (ET1)

Starting a case

20.23   A case is started when the employee (known as the 'claimant')[26] presents the Secretary of the Tribunals with a written claim containing the necessary information.[27] This is known as the 'claim',[28] but it is also often referred to by the number of the standard form, ie 'ET1'.[29]

20.24   The Tribunals Service has a very useful website[30] with details of how to apply. There is an ET1 form which can be downloaded and installed on your computer or alternatively claimants can apply interactively on-line. The claim can be posted, hand-delivered, e-mailed or faxed.[31] If faxed, do not send a duplicate copy by post as both claims are likely to be separately registered with different case numbers and there is a possibility of confusion. If posted, the claim should be addressed to the Secretary to the Employment Tribunal.

20.25   In England and Wales, the claim must go to the correct ET office, which can be ascertained through the website from a list showing jurisdiction according to the postcode where the claimant worked.[32] Alternatively, claimants can telephone the ET enquiry line on 0845 795 9775. In Scotland, all applications go to the Central Office in Glasgow.[33] If more convenient, the claim form can be taken into the Aberdeen, Dundee or Edinburgh office, and they will forward it to Glasgow. Claims submitted on-line automatically go to the correct tribunal office.

---

24 *Senyonjo v Trident Safeguards Ltd* UKEAT/0316/04. See also EAT's comments in
   Sodexho v Gibbons [2005] IRLR 836, EAT.
25 See paras 3.18–3.19 above.
26 Until 1 October 2004, known as the 'applicant'.
27 ET Regs 2004 Sch 1 r1. See para 20.34 below.
28 Until 1 October 2004, known as the 'originating application'.
29 Formerly known as 'IT1'.
30 At www.employmenttribunals.gov.uk
31 Details on the ET website www.employmenttribunals.gov.uk..
32 At www.employmenttribunals.gov.uk/HearingCentres/hearingCentres.htm
33 Address on the ET website.

20.26   The employee needs to think carefully before starting a case. Although technically s/he can withdraw at any time, the longer the case goes on, the greater risk that costs will be awarded against him/her for unreasonable conduct.[34]

Time limits

20.27   The time limit for lodging an unfair dismissal claim is within three months from dismissal,[35] which is far shorter than that for other civil claims. The time limit is strictly enforced with an extension only in exceptional circumstances.

20.28   The period of three calendar months runs from the effective date of termination (EDT). If the EDT is 20 May, the claim must be presented on or before midnight on 19 August.[36] The claim should be sent to the relevant ET in good time, and if it has not been acknowledged within the time limit, a check should be made before the expiry of the time limit with the relevant ET office to confirm that it has arrived. It is legitimate to expect first class post to arrive on the second day after posting, provided that it is not a Sunday or bank holiday.[37] If it is unexpectedly delayed, this may be a ground for allowing a late claim, but it is extremely risky to rely on this. An ET1 sent by e-mail would ordinarily be expected to arrive 30–60 minutes after transmission.[38] If using the on-line form on the Tribunals Service website and it does not go through, the claim will not be presented unless it can be proved it arrived at least at the server hosting the website.[39] If you do e-mail the form through the Tribunals Service website, you should get a receipt. Perhaps the easiest and safest routine is to fax the claim form during office hours and telephone the ET office about 20 minutes later for confirmation of safe receipt of all the pages (taking the name of the clerk spoken to). It is also worth keeping a copy of the fax confirmation slip, but this may not be sufficient evidence in itself if the claim gets lost.

---

34 See paras 20.142–20.155 on costs.

35 Subject to the statutory dispute resolution procedures (if they still apply), see below.

36 *Post Office v Moore* [1981] ICR 623, EAT.

37 *Consignia plc v Sealy* [2002] IRLR 624, CA; *Coldridge v H M Prison Service* UKEAT/0728/04 and 0729/04.

38 *Initial Electronic Security Systems Ltd v Avdic* [2005] IRLR 671, EAT.

39 The case-law seems to conflict on this. *Tyne and Wear Autistic Society v Smith* [2005] IRLR 336, EAT; *Mossman v Bray Management Ltd* UKEAT/0477/04/TM.

20.29   For time limit purposes, the EDT means:

- when the contract is terminated by notice, the date that the notice expires;[40]
- when the contract is terminated without notice, the date on which termination takes effect.[41] With a summary dismissal for gross misconduct, this will be the last day worked.

However, where there is no gross misconduct and notice is required, if the employer pays money in lieu of notice, the EDT can be ambiguous. Either the employer has terminated the contract of employment with immediate effect and made a payment in lieu of notice, or the employer has terminated the contract from the end of the notice period, but does not require the employee to attend work in the interim.[42] The dismissal letter or P45 may indicate which is the case. Usually when the employer pays in lieu of notice, the EDT is the last day actually worked[43] and it is safest when calculating time limits to work from this date. A useful rule of thumb is to present the claim within three months of the last day actually worked (unless the employee is off sick or on holiday during his/her last week). By doing this, the claim will always be in time. If the employee is absent due to sickness or holiday at the end of his/her employment, the EDT takes place when the contract of employment actually terminates. Be careful that there is no ambiguity as to when the job actually ends.

Late claim

20.30   Exceptionally, the ET will admit a late claim provided it was not reasonably practicable to present the claim in time, and it was presented within such further period as the ET considers reasonable.[44] It is for the employee to show that it was not reasonably practicable to present the claim in time.[45] It is very difficult to make unfair dismissal claims out of time.

20.31   It may be that the employee was mentally incapable[46] or physically unable to keep within the time limit, or maybe was unable to do so

40 ERA 1996 s97(1)(a).

41 ERA 1996 s97(1)(b).

42 *Adams v GKN Sankey* [1980] IRLR 416, EAT.

43 *Dixon v Stenor* [1973] ICR 157; [1973] IRLR 28, NIRC.

44 ERA 1996 s111.

45 *Porter v Bandridge* [1978] ICR 943; [1978] IRLR 271, CA.

46 *Schulz v Esso Petroleum Co Ltd* [1999] IRLR 488, CA; *Imperial Tobacco Ltd v Wright* UKEAT/0919/04/DM.

because s/he was unaware of the right to claim unfair dismissal or how to do so or what the time limits were. What is relevant is the employee's state of mind and the extent to which s/he understood his/her position.[47] Ignorance of the law or of facts will be an acceptable excuse only if, tested objectively, 'a reasonable employee' would not be expected to know of the law[48] or be put on enquiry because of the facts.[49] Ignorance of a fact which is crucial to a claim can make it not reasonably practicable,[50] eg because a redundant employee finds out only after the expiry of the time-limit that s/he was immediately replaced by someone else. The employee cannot rely on the fact that it was his/her solicitor who wrongly put in a late claim on his/her behalf[51] – his/her remedy is to sue the solicitor for negligence. However, if a solicitor simply gave wrong advice and the employee retained responsibility for lodging the claim form, the employee may be able to argue that it was not reasonably practicable for him/her to get the claim in on time.[52] If the employee was misled by the advice of a Citizens Advice Bureau, the position is less clear-cut. It will depend on who gave the advice within the Bureau and in what circumstances.[53] Where the DDP applied under the statutory dispute resolution procedures, it may be grounds for an extension of time that the outcome of the internal appeal was notified only shortly before the normal time-limit. In such a case, reasonable practicability is assessed by reference to the period after the conclusion of the appeal rather than the whole three month period.[54]

20.32   Even if the employee shows that it was not reasonably practicable to present the claim in time, s/he must do so within a further

---

47 *London International College Ltd v Sen* [1993] IRLR 333, CA; *Palmer and another v Southend-on-Sea Borough Council* [1984] IRLR 119, CA; *Marks & Spencer plc v Williams-Ryan* [2005] IRLR 563, CA.

48 *Porter v Bandridge* [1978] ICR 943; [1978] IRLR 271, CA. Though see *Biggs v Somerset CC* [1996] IRLR 203, CA.

49 *Churchill v A Yeates & Sons* [1983] ICR 380; [1983] IRLR 187, EAT.

50 *Cambridge and Peterborough NHS Foundation Trust v Crouchman* UKEAT/0108/09.

51 *Dedman v British Building and Engineering Appliances Ltd* [1973] IRLR 379, CA.

52 *Royal Bank of Scotland v Theobald* UKEAT/0444/06; (2007) IDS Employment Law Brief 9, EAT.

53 *Marks & Spencer plc v Williams-Ryan* [2005] IRLR 563, CA. Regarding advice from employment consultants generally, see *Ashcroft v Haberdashers Aske's Boys School* UKEAT/0151/07; [2008] IRLR 375, EAT.

54 *Ashcroft v Haberdashers Aske's Boys School* UKEAT/0151/07; [2008] IRLR 375, EAT; *Royal Bank of Scotland v Bevan* UKEAT/0440/07.

reasonable period. The employee must act promptly once s/he discovers that the claim is out of time.[55]

Statutory dispute resolution procedures

20.33 Where the statutory dispute resolution procedures still apply, the time limits for starting tribunal claims may in some circumstances be extended by three months from the expiry of the normal time limit. It is vital to be sure the statutory procedures apply, before relying on any possible extension of the time limits. This can be a complex question. If in any doubt at all, always play safe and keep to the normal time limit. For detail of the procedures, when they apply, the effect on time limits and transitional provisions following their abolition, see chapter 22.

Drafting the tribunal claim

20.34 Under the ET Regs 2004, the following information must be set out in a tribunal claim:[56]

- The worker's name and address. The worker is called the 'claimant'.
- The employer's name and address. The employer is called the 'respondent'.
- Details of the claim. This simply means identifying which employment right has been breached,[57] although fuller details may subsequently be required by the ET and should normally be given from the outset.[58]

20.35 In residual cases where the statutory dispute resolution procedures still apply to the claim, the form must also set out:

- Whether or not the claimant is or was an employee of the respondent. This is important to certain employment rights and also to the application of the statutory dispute resolution procedures, but it is not always clear-cut.[59] If the claimant is or was an employee of the respondent, s/he must also state:
- whether the tribunal claim includes a complaint that s/he has been

---

55 *Golub v University of Sussex* (1981) 13 April, unreported, CA; *James W Cook & Co (in liquidation) v Tipper and others* [1990] IRLR 386, CA.

56 ET Regs 2004 Sch 1 r1.

57 *Grimmer v KLM Cityhopper UK* [2005] IRLR 596, EAT.

58 See para 20.38 below.

59 See paras 6.4–6.12 above.

dismissed, eg unfair dismissal or dismissal under the discrimination legislation. This is asked because, if the claimant was dismissed, the statutory DDP probably applies;

- in a case where s/he is bringing any claims other than or additional to dismissal, whether s/he has raised the subject matter of the claim with the respondent in writing at least 28 days prior to presenting the tribunal claim. If not, s/he must explain why not. This is designed to see whether the claimant is barred from bringing certain claims because of non compliance with the statutory grievance procedure.

20.36   Claimants must use the standard tribunal form (ET1). This should ensure that all the essential information is included, although if anything is omitted, it will not necessarily debar the claim.[60] There are two available forms, one which is to be used where the statutory dispute resolution procedures still apply, and the new form, where they do not.

20.37   The forms can be downloaded from the Tribunals Service website or completed on-line. It is possible to send the form by e-mail through the system; alternatively, print it out and send, fax or deliver it to the tribunal. Whichever way you choose, the most important thing is make sure you get a receipt immediately (see para 20.28).

20.38   At Box 5.2 of the new form, claimants must set out the background and details of their claim. The employee can make several claims on a single ET1 form, for example a claim for unfair dismissal, notice pay and written reasons for dismissal; or for race discrimination and unfair dismissal.[61] It is important to remember that the tribunal claim will be the first document read by the ET panel before the hearing starts and will give them a strong early impression of the merits of the case which can be difficult to shake afterwards. It is therefore foolish to give only very brief details of the claim.[62] A well-written ET1 can also assist the case preparation to run more smoothly, eg by making a pre-hearing review less likely, eliciting a more detailed response from the employer, making it easier to obtain interim orders from the tribunal and improving the chances of settlement. The ET1 should state fully all the material facts and dates (without going into laborious detail). If there are obvious weaknesses in the case, they cannot be hidden and it may be best to refer to them in the ET1 and offer as convincing an explanation as possible. At box 6 of the new form, it is optional whether

---

60 *Richardson v U Mole Ltd* [2005] IRLR 668, EAT.
61 See p754 for a sample form.
62 See also para 20.42 regarding problems in amending a claim later.

the claimant states what compensation or remedy s/he is seeking. Probably it is safer not to complete this at such an early stage. In an unfair dismissal case, if the claimant knows she wants reinstatement, it is a good idea to indicate this at the outset in box 4.9.

20.39   It helps when completing the form to bear in mind the relevant law and therefore what issues are relevant or irrelevant. For example, if the employer is a large company, this should be stated in the ET1, since the tribunal must consider fairness in the light of the employer's size and administrative resources. If the employer is small, it does not help the employee to draw attention to this in the ET1.

20.40   In an unfair dismissal case, it is best to complete the ET1 bearing in mind what the employer must do for a dismissal to be fair. The employee can then draw attention to what the employer ought to have done but did not. For example, in a conduct case, it is of little assistance to focus on the employee's innocence of the misconduct or to refer to matters occurring after dismissal, eg the police's decision to drop charges. What is relevant is the employer's genuine and reasonable belief at the time of dismissal, the extent of the investigations into the employee's guilt and the opportunity afforded to the employee to offer an explanation. The ET1 should focus on these points, eg highlighting inadequacies in the investigation. For the above reasons, it is almost always better for an adviser who understands the law to write the ET1 rather than ask the employee to write his/her own, even if the adviser intends to amend it. Sample tribunal claims are in appendix A, but these should not be copied slavishly. Every case is unique.

20.41   If the adviser puts him/herself down as representative, s/he will receive all correspondence from the ET or employer and must keep the employee informed. The ET will expect the adviser or someone else from the adviser's organisation to represent the employee at hearings unless notified otherwise. If no representative is noted on the form, correspondence goes to the employee, who must be forewarned to keep in close touch, even if nothing happens for four or five weeks. An adviser can later take over the running of a case, simply by writing to the ET and to the employer to notify them of this.

Amending the tribunal claim

20.42   A tribunal claim can be amended at any time, but the employee needs the tribunal's permission.[63] In deciding whether to allow an amend-

---

63 ET Regs 2004 Sch 1 rr10(2)(q) and 11(1).

ment, the ET must take account of all the circumstances and balance the hardship and injustice of refusing the amendment against that of allowing it.[64] Where the amendment is to add new facts and grounds, the ET must decide if the new claim is in time and, if not, whether the amendment should now be allowed. If the claim arises out of the same facts as the original claim but simply adds factual details or attaches a new legal label, the ET should very readily allow the amendment even outside the time limit.[65] For example, an employee may describe a sequence of events leading to a dismissal which s/he labels as unfair under the Disability Discrimination Act 1995. The same facts could also support a claim of unfair dismissal, provided s/he was eligible. On the other hand, if the amendment is to introduce an entirely new cause of action dependent on quite different facts, it is more difficult. The greater the difference between the factual and legal issues raised by the new claim and the old, the less likely it is that an amendment will be allowed, but it is always a matter for the tribunal's discretion.[66] It is important to remember that whether the new claim would be out of time if it were a free-standing claim (including whether the test for extending time for the relevant claim would be satisfied) is only one factor.[67] Other factors would be why the new claim was not originally included; how late in the day the amendment is now sought; whether the respondent would be surprised by the new allegation or prejudiced by its late addition and, as already mentioned, the balance of hardship to each party. As well as legal difficulties, claimants can sometimes be discredited in terms of evidence if they appear to have changed their mind from what they originally wrote in the tribunal claim. Overall, it can be difficult for several reasons to amend a claim out of time. It is therefore important to spend enough time with the employee at the outset to identify and evaluate all possible claims.

20.43   An ET can order an additional party to be joined at any time,[68] eg in a TUPE case where it becomes clear that the other party to the transfer should be joined or in a discrimination case, when it is necessary to join an individual discriminator.

---

64 *Selkent Bus Co Ltd v Moore* [1996] IRLR 661, EAT. *Transport and General Workers Union v Safeway Stores Ltd* UKEAT/0092/07.

65 *Selkent Bus Co Ltd v Moore* [1996] IRLR 661, EAT; *Transport and General Workers Union v Safeway Stores Ltd* UKEAT/0092/07.

66 *Transport and General Workers Union v Safeway Stores Ltd* UKEAT/0092/07.

67 *Transport and General Workers Union v Safeway Stores Ltd* UKEAT/0092/07 reviews the authorities on this.

68 ET Regs 2004 Sch 1 r10(2)(k).

Procedure for accepting the claim

20.44   On receiving the claim, the tribunal decides whether to accept it. If everything is in order, the claimant will be sent a standard acknowledgement form (ET5). A copy of the claim will be sent to the respondent, who has 28 days to respond. The case will be allocated a case number, which must be quoted on all correspondence or telephone contact with the tribunal.

20.45   All or part of the claim will be rejected if the form does not include all the required information or if it appears that the claimant failed to send his/her employer a written grievance where the statutory grievance procedures apply.[69] The claimant will be informed of this with written reasons for the decision and information on how the decision can be reviewed or appealed. Where a claim is rejected in this way, it is treated as never having been presented.[70] It is probably only worth seeking a review or appealing if the tribunal has made a legal mistake and time limits have now expired in respect of taking the simpler route of resubmitting the claim.

20.46   If it is just a matter of completing the form properly, then the claimant can simply add in the missing information and resubmit the claim immediately, provided the tribunal time limit has not by then passed. On the other hand, if the statutory grievance procedure under the statutory dispute resolution procedures still applies and the claimant has not yet sent his/her employer a written grievance regarding the subject matter of the tribunal claim, s/he must now do so and wait 28 days before resubmitting the tribunal claim. The time limit for resubmitting the tribunal claim will be extended by three months from the normal time limit in respect of the matters of grievance. Problems will arise if, by the time the tribunal sends the claim back, the time limit for sending a grievance letter has passed, ie one month from expiry of the normal time limit. This is discussed in more detail at paras 22.62–22.64. The tribunal is supposed to inform the claimant as soon as reasonably practicable if the claim is rejected,[71] but this is not a complete safeguard. There are rules as to whether the ET can hear the claim where it mistakenly accepts an ET1 as presented and no step 1 grievance letter has been sent.[72]

---

69 ET Regs 2004 Sch 1 r3.
70 ET Regs 2004 Sch 1 r3(7).
71 ET Regs 2004 Sch 1 r3(5).
72 See para 22.58.

The employer's response (ET3)

20.47   The employer must send the tribunal his/her response[73] to the claim on a standard ET3 form. The employer must indicate whether s/he intends to resist the claim and, if so, must indicate on what grounds.[74] If the employer does not give sufficient details, so that the claimant does not fully understand what the employer's defence is, a letter should be written to the ET pointing this out and requesting additional information. In an unfair dismissal case, the employer must prove that dismissal was for one of the potentially fair reasons.[75]

20.48   Employers must present their response to the ET within 28 days of the date they were sent a copy of the claim. If they want an extension of time, they must write to the ET within the 28 days, explaining their reasons, and (if legally represented) sending a copy to the claimant, notifying the claimant that s/he can write to the ET to object to the extension within seven days and that s/he must copy any such objection to the other parties. If the employers are not legally represented, the tribunal will notify the claimant of the application.[76] The ET will only extend time if it is just and equitable to do so and will notify the parties if the request to extend time is refused. ETs must issue a default judgment once the time limit for presenting a response (and any permitted extension) has passed or if the respondents have presented a response but indicated that they do not intend to resist the claim.[77] The only exceptions are where the tribunal does not have jurisdiction to hear the claim, or where it appears the respondent did not receive the claim form or if a settlement has been reached. The Employment Judge can make an order for additional information if needed to issue the default judgment. The default judgment can relate solely to liability or, if the value of the claim is clear, eg notice pay, it can also relate to compensation. The ET can issue a default judgment on its own initiative, but the claimant can write to the ET after the 28 days are up to request that a judgment is entered. Either way, the most likely result is that the employer will very promptly provide an ET3 or seek a review and will be allowed to proceed. In considering the review, the

---

73 Previously called 'Notice of Appearance' or IT3.

74 ET Regs 2004 Sch 1 r4(3).

75 ERA 1996 s98; para 6.49 above.

76 ET Regs 2004 Sch 1 r4(4) – 4(4E).

77 ET Regs 2004 Sch 1 r8. The tribunal's obligation to issue default judgments was tightened by SI 2008/3240 in respect of proceedings issued on or after 6th April 2009.

ET should take account of all the circumstances, including the reason for the delay in providing the response, the prejudice to each side of allowing or refusing the late response, and the merits of the response.[78] Nevertheless, it is still worth applying for a default judgment, if only to put pressure on the employer to respond quickly.

20.49 An employer cannot take any part in the case until s/he has presented a response and it has been accepted (except to apply for a review of a default judgment or request written reasons for it).[79] Once the response is submitted and accepted, the ET sends a copy on to the claimant. It is then that the further preparatory stages can take place. All the information in the ET3 should be checked with the claimant, listing what points are not accepted. Rather than make separate notes, it saves time later to type the employee's comments into his/her original proof/statement (see para 20.8). Check all the small details on the ET3 form as well as the grounds on which the employer intends to resist the claim. If the employer's reasons for justifying the dismissal are vague or unclear, it may be wise to ask for additional information (see para 20.58 below).

Case management

Overview, stages and timescale

20.50 Case management is concerned with preparing the case for the hearing, eg collecting information and documents from the other side and fixing hearing dates.[80] These steps are sometimes known as interim or interlocutory matters. In non-discrimination cases, this preparation is usually dealt with in correspondence direct between each side and the ET is asked for an order only if agreement cannot be reached. In discrimination cases or other cases which are particularly large or complex, the ET usually holds one or more case management discussions,[81] where these matters are dealt with orally in front of an Employment Judge.[82] Some regions are now using telephone conferencing. Correspondence with the ET can take place by e-mail, although some documents will still be sent out hard copy because they need to be signed

---

78 *Moroak t/a Blake Envelopes v Cromie* [2005] IRLR 535, EAT.
79 ET Regs 2004 Sch 1 r9.
80 See p690 for the stages of running a basic ET case.
81 Previously known as 'directions hearings'.
82 In Scotland, case management discussions are relatively rare.

by a Judge. Claimants are advised to check their emails every day if they want to communicate this way.

20.51   Once the ET1 and ET3 are submitted, generally no further special forms or formats are used.[83] Any correspondence with the other side or the ET simply takes the form of an ordinary letter. Although no legalistic formats are required, there are certain conventions which tend to be followed. The ET does not want to get into lengthy correspondence to and fro with the claimant. It is important to remember that the case is not argued on paper. The claimant definitely does not, for example, provide a written response to the ET3 or to any additional information provided by the employer. The opportunity to do that is shortly before the hearing, when s/he can write a witness statement (see para 20.101 below). In the meantime s/he is simply gathering information from the employer by means of additional information, written answers and documents, and s/he is providing information if requested by the employer. Any correspondence between a party and the ET will be copied to the other party (apart from requests for a witness order).

20.52   The ET has general case management powers. In England and Wales, ETs are more proactive than in Scotland. An ET can make orders at a case management discussion or a hearing or, in the absence of the parties, when considering the paperwork. In the latter case, the parties will be given an opportunity to object (see para 20.71 below). It is common for the ET to make orders regarding the provision of additional information, written answers, witness statements and documents.[84] Usually the following stages are followed (more details will be set out below):

- The claimant writes to the employer asking for certain additional information, answers to questions or documents within a certain timescale, normally 14 days.[85] The letter may be copied to the ET. Ideally the claimant writes this letter as soon as s/he receives the ET3.
- If the employer does not supply the requested information and documents, the claimant writes to the ET, explaining this and asking for an order, giving reasons why the information is needed. This letter is copied to the employer together with a letter setting out specific information required by the rules.

83 Though there may be a form for responding to an employer's counter-claim to a breach of contract claim.
84 Though such orders are less common in Scotland.
85 See example, p766.

- The ET sends the employer an order to supply the additional information or documents by a certain date, usually in 14 days' time. A copy of the order is sent to the claimant. Alternatively the ET may refuse to make an order or cut down the information requested.
- If the order is not complied with, the ET can be asked to make an order for costs or to strike out all or part of the employer's ET3 or to debar the employer from defending altogether. Striking out is unusual on this ground.[86]
- Some orders for additional information or documents warn the employer that 'unless' the order is complied with on time, the ET3 will be struck out. If the original order did not contain this warning, an ET cannot strike out without first writing to the employer, inviting him/her to give reasons why s/he should not be struck out.[87] The employer then tends to supply the ordered information.
- If the employer wants to vary or set aside the order, s/he must apply before the time for compliance.[88] The application must be copied to the claimant, who must be notified of his/her right to object within seven days.

Each of these steps can happen in reverse if the employer asks the claimant for information. Timescales in any orders should be taken extremely seriously, as ETs have been known to order costs against claimants who have failed to comply. It is no defence that the representative is inexperienced or, for example, a very busy trade union official.

20.53   Many ETs send out standard case management letters, setting out steps which must be taken, eg concerning when documents should be shown to the other side, whether witness statements should be prepared and when trial bundles should be agreed. Regardless of whether there has been a standard letter, on receiving the ET3, the adviser should write to the employer asking for any additional information and documents which s/he requires.

20.54   Do not delay in writing the first letter to the employer requesting additional information and documents. It is important to allow enough time to prepare the case. Many steps need to be taken after getting documents and information from the employer, including discussing these with the claimant, writing witness statements and agreeing a trial bundle. Some ETs fix hearing dates very quickly and the claimant

---

86 ET Regs 2004 Sch 1 r13; see paras 20.55–20.57 above.
87 ET Regs 2004 Sch 1 r19(1).
88 ET Regs 2004 Sch 1 r12(3).

may not have left enough time to gather the information needed. Although the employer should always be asked for the information voluntarily first, there is a risk in delaying going for an order if the information is not supplied within the 14 days. If there is a real indication that the information is coming shortly, then it is worth waiting, because there is always the fear that the ET will refuse to order some of the requested information. But there is a risk of getting strung along for a long period, at the end of which no information is volunteered and time has run out to get an order.

Striking out

20.55   At any time, on its own initiative or, more usually, on the application of either party, an ET can make any orders it considers appropriate.[89] It can also strike out all or part of a tribunal claim or response on grounds that it is scandalous or vexatious or has no reasonable prospects of success, or that the way the worker or employer is conducting the proceedings is scandalous, unreasonable or vexatious.[90] It can also strike out for non compliance with an order. Before striking out, the ET must give the relevant party the opportunity to give reasons why the order should not be made.[91] Striking out is a very serious step and should not be taken lightly.[92] It should be rare in whistleblowing or discrimination cases to strike out on the ground of no reasonable prospects for success, as these issues are particularly fact-sensitive and dependent on evidence being heard.[93] Where striking out is considered for procedural abuses, the crucial issue is whether a fair trial is still possible and whether a lesser sanction may be appropriate.[94] A striking out order is unlikely to be made if it is still possible to have a fair hearing, eg because by the time the ET threatens to strike out, the employer finally produces the ordered information and documents.[95] A rare exception was one case where the employer ignored various interim orders and eventually produced a lengthy witness statement on the first day of the hearing, having previously served no witness statements. The EAT

89 ET Regs 2004 Sch 1 r10(1).
90 ET Regs 2004 Sch 1 r18(7).
91 ET Regs 2004 Sch 1 r19(1).
92 *De Keyser Ltd v Wilson* [2001] IRLR 324, EAT; *Blockbuster Entertainment v James* [2006] EWCA Civ 684.
93 *Ezsias v North Glamorgan NHS Trust* [2007] EWCA Civ 330; (2007) 830 IDS Brief 829, CA.
94 *Bolch v Chipman* [2004] IRLR 140, EAT.
95 *National Grid Company plc v Virdee* [1992] IRLR 555, EAT.

agreed that the ET was entitled to strike out the employer's defence, because the employer had gained an unfair advantage by having already seen the claimant's witness statements, and also because there was no guarantee that the claimant's pro bono representative would still be available if the hearing was adjourned for the claimant to deal with the unexpected witness statement.[96]

20.56   An 'unless order' under r13(2) is more draconian – it is an order which states that unless it is complied with, the claim or response (as relevant) will be struck out on the date of non-compliance without the need for a hearing or to give notice to the relevant party.

20.57   The ET can be asked to review its decision to strike out a claim, whether a striking out order was made under r18(7) or the striking out occurred automatically following an 'unless order'.[97] When deciding whether to overturn the striking-out, the tribunal should have regard to the nine factors set out in part 3.9(1) of the Civil Procedure Rules (CPR – see Glossary at p773).[98]

Requesting additional information

20.58   The ET can order the employee or employer to supply additional information.[99] This replaced the concept prior to the 2004 Regulations of requesting 'further and better particulars', but some Employment Judges and representatives still refer to 'particularising' the claim. The ET can make an order on its own initiative or at the request of either party.

20.59   The concept of 'further and better particulars' was rather restricted and it is unclear whether 'additional information' is meant to be the same concept in plain English, or whether it is a looser concept representing the natural meaning of those words. Where the same phrase appears in the CPR, it has a wider meaning – additional information can be ordered in relation to any matter in dispute, whether or not it is referred to in the statement of case (the civil equivalent of claim and response).[100] Under the old concept of further and better particulars, all that could be asked for was more details of the employer's defence as

---

96 *Premium Care Homes Ltd v Osborne* UKEAT/0077/06.

97 See para 20.135 below; *Uyanwa-Odu and another v Schools Offices Services Ltd and another* UKEAT/0295/05; *Neary v (1) The Governing Body of St Albans Girls' School (2) Hertfordshire County Council* UKEAT/0281/08.

98 Neary UKEAT/0281/08.

99 ET Regs 2004 Sch 1 r10(2)(b).

100 CPR 18.1.

set out in the ET3.[101] The questions were to clarify the text of the ET3 and the employer's case, so that the claimant was not caught by surprise and know broadly what defence his/her employer will put forward. For example, if the employer says in the ET3, 'We warned the claimant on numerous occasions as to her conduct at work', a relevant request would be, 'Please state in respect of each warning the date when the claimant was warned, by whom, and the nature of the warning given'. Clarification on essential points should always be requested, in order to be fully prepared. The concept of 'additional information' does seem to allow wider questioning and need not strictly relate to matters set out by the employer in the response. Even so, this procedure cannot be used to ask for detailed evidence and employers are quick to refuse to give information on this ground. The idea is to ask for information to identify the issues and clarify what the employer is saying so that the claimant knows what case s/he has to meet. Where the employee needs information which cannot be obtained on any restrictive definition of 'additional information', s/he can simply ask for written answers (below). In practice, the letter to the employer may request additional information and written answers under a combined heading.

20.60   The ET tends to be reluctant to order too much additional information and frequently amends the request. So the temptation to ask for too much should be avoided unless it is necessary because of the vagueness of the ET3.

Written answers

20.61   The procedural rules say that the ET can order a party to provide written answers to questions put by the ET.[102] This is just given as an example of the type of order which an ET can make, and there is no reason why the questions cannot also be put by the other party. Certainly before the updating of the rules, it was common for this to be done.[103] Under this procedure, the employee can ask the employer[104] a series of questions which will clarify any issue likely to arise for determination or for the information which is likely to assist the ET in dealing with the claim. It would be permissible to ask of the employer in a dismissal case involving fighting at work, 'What action was taken against

101 See as an example, p764, question 1.
102 ET Regs 2004 Sch 1 r10(2)(f).
103 Under rule 4(3) of the 2001 Rules of Procedure, also known as 'interrogatories'.
104 Or vice versa.

the other person involved in the fight?' and 'In the last five years have there been other incidents of fighting at work? If so, when, who was involved and were they dismissed; if not, what action was taken against them?'[105] However, the ET is unlikely to allow lengthy and detailed questioning. The aim is not to conduct the whole case on paper, cross-examination is usually reserved for the full ET hearing. Nevertheless, the procedure is very useful because it does not have the strict and technical rules sometimes applied to 'additional information'. If the employer refuses to answer on the ground that 'You are not entitled to this because you have asked for evidence about matters not contained in the ET3', the answer is that this objection is not valid in respect of a request for written answers.

Disclosure

20.62   Disclosure is the method by which the employee can find out about and obtain documents which are in the employer's possession. Strictly speaking, an order for disclosure only obliges the employer to produce a list of the requested documents. This is combined with an order for inspection, which allows the documents to be seen and copies taken at the employee's expense. In practice, the ET often simply asks the employer to send copies to the employee and to give formal inspection if requested. This is useful because the employer tends not to ask for copying costs in this situation and s/he can always be asked to bring the originals to the hearing. If there is any suspicion at all about whether documents are genuine or have been manipulated, the originals should be inspected at this stage. This will involve a visit to the offices of the employer or employer's representative.

20.63   All courts prefer documents to witnesses and the ET is no exception. This is particularly true of contemporaneous documents. Cases are often won or lost on the strength of the documents before the ET and it is essential that all relevant documents are available at the hearing. The practice regarding disclosure has become more formal than it used to be. An ET can order such disclosure and inspection as might be granted by a county court,[106] ie as set out by Part 31 of the Civil Procedure Rules.[107] Reflecting these Rules, the ET's standard letter commonly states something like this:

105 For a further example, see p764, question 2.
106 ET Regs 2004 Sch 1 r10(2)(d).
107 Available at www.justice.gov.uk/civil/procrules_fin/index.htm

Each party must within 14 days let the other know what documents it will rely on at the hearing and what other documents it has which could adversely affect its own or the other side's case or could support the other side's case. A formal order for disclosure and inspection of documents will be made upon application by either party.[108]

It may be worth waiting 14 days to see what the employer volunteers, but whatever any standard letter says, an adviser must also specifically ask the employer for what s/he wants and thinks that the employer has.

20.64   The ET is more ready to order disclosure than additional information although it will not allow wide-ranging and speculative requests. The documents must be relevant for the fair disposal of the case. A document is relevant if it advances the employee's case or damages the employer's case.[109] The case-law on what documents are relevant is particularly developed in relation to discrimination cases.[110]

20.65   In unfair dismissal cases it is usually relevant to seek disclosure of all contractual documents or statements of terms and conditions and any personnel file and written warnings relied on. If the employee has a long history of grievances, disputes and disciplinary action, it may be unwise to ask for the whole personnel file and it is better just to specify documents which are relevant to the current claim. It is always a good idea to request, 'any other documents in the employer's possession, power or control which are relevant to the case'. The ET will usually order this category of documents and it prevents the employer holding back useful documents or surprising the employee with unseen documents on the day of the hearing. Letters between the parties or to ACAS concerning possible settlement of the claim must not be produced on disclosure or put before the ET unless each party expressly agrees.[111] See para 21.44 below regarding confidential documents.

20.66   Under the standard case management tribunal letter, the employee also must disclose relevant documents. Usually s/he does not have anything which the employer does not also have, but most ETs now expect the employee to disclose correspondence relating to his/her efforts to find a new job. This can be updated just before the hearing by inclusion in the trial bundle. Especially in discrimination cases,

---

108 In Scotland the position is looser. Practice Direction 1 for Scotland (available on the ETS website), requires legally represented parties to send a list of documents to be relied on at the hearing to the other side no later than 14 days before the hearing.

109 *Compagnie Financiére du Pacifique v Peruvian Guano Co* (1882) 11 QB 55, CA.

110 See para 21.44 below.

111 Or otherwise waives privilege. See paras 9.19–9.20.

employees often have diaries which they wrote at the time. A diary probably has to be disclosed, but check whether it contains privileged information, eg notes of legal advice, and whether it was written at the time or only after the case started as an aide-mémoire. Where there are tape recordings or electronic documents which need to be seen in their original form, consider how these will be produced in the tribunal, whether transcripts are necessary and who will prepare and pay for them. Electronic documents include e-mails, word-processed documents and databases, which may be stored on servers and back-up systems and even 'deleted'. The employee needs to agree with the employer in what form such documents should be disclosed (printed out, via e-mail, etc).[112] If tampering is suspected of documents which have been created on computer, ask for these to be e-mailed to the claimant's/representative's office. The dates that documents were generated can often be checked electronically.

Applying for an order

20.67   If the employer will not voluntarily supply the requested documents and information or takes too long in doing so, it is necessary to apply for an order. Do not delay in applying. If the application is made too close to the hearing, an order is unlikely to be made, either because of slow ET administration, or because it is decided to leave matters to the hearing date. The procedure is set out in Schedule 1 rule 11. To apply for an order, the claimant must write to the ET, setting out what s/he wants by way of additional information, documents, etc and explaining how the order 'would assist the tribunal or chairman in dealing with the proceedings efficiently and fairly'. A general explanation will probably not be enough, so it is best to set out briefly (rather than giving too much away to the respondent) why each item is relevant to the issues.

20.68   The order will usually be considered by the ET on the paperwork. However, if a case management discussion or other hearing is already scheduled where the order will be considered, the claimant must write at least ten days in advance, unless it is not reasonably practicable to do so or the Employment Judge decides it is in the interests of justice to allow shorter notice.[113] The same applies if the respondent wants an order against the claimant. The idea is that no one is caught by surprise.

20.69   At the same time as writing to the ET, the claimant must write to the respondent, informing him/her of the details of the application for

112 CPR PD 31 para 2A deals with electronic disclosure.
113 ET Regs 2004 Sch 1 r11(2).

an order and why it is sought. The letter must also state that any objection to the application must be sent to the ET within seven days of receiving a copy of the application (or before any earlier hearing date), and that the objection must be copied to the ET and all other parties, including the claimant.[114] The claimant must confirm in writing to the ET that this requirement has been complied with. The simplest way to do this is for the claimant to note on the letter to the ET that s/he has simultaneously written to the respondent in accordance with rule 11(4).[115] Then the letter to the ET can be copied to the respondent together with a covering letter containing all the information about how the respondent can object. It makes sense for a representative who runs many ET cases to have a standard covering letter.[116] If the claimant is unrepresented, s/he need only send the respondent a copy of his/her letter to the ET. The ET will write direct to the respondent regarding the other matters.

20.70   The request for an order will be considered by an Employment Judge. It is not unusual for a request to be refused or reduced. This is a real concern because it is hard to challenge. The ET can always be asked to reconsider its decision to refuse an order[117] and it is best to do this as soon as possible and put forward some additional arguments. The ET cannot change an earlier decision which has affected the parties' preparation of their cases unless there has been a material change in circumstances.[118]

20.71   If an order is made without having given the respondent a chance to make representations, the respondent may apply to set it aside or vary it.[119] Equally, the claimant may want the ET to set aside or vary an order which has been made against him/her if s/he has had no chance to comment in advance. If so, the claimant must write to the ET before the deadline for compliance with the order, explaining why s/he wants the order changed. The claimant must copy his/her letter to the employer and make the normal notifications in accordance with rule 11 (para 20.70 above). For an overview of this procedure and what happens if a party does not comply with an order, see paras 20.50–20.54.

---

114 ET Regs 2004 Sch 1 r11(4).
115 See p770 for precedent.
116 See p766 for precedent.
117 ET Regs 2004 Sch 1 rr10 and 11; *Hart v English Heritage (Historic Buildings & Monuments Commission for England)* [2006] IRLR 915, EAT.
118 *Goldman Sachs Services Ltd v Montali* [2002] ICR 1251, EAT.
119 ET Regs 2004 Sch 1 r12(2).

20.72   The ET cannot be asked formally to review[120] a case management order or refusal to make an order.[121] It is possible to appeal to the EAT, but only if there is an error of law or perversity and the employee's case is clearly prejudiced. An EAT appeal is rather a drastic step to reverse a decision to grant or refuse an order, but if that is the intention, remember to ask the ET immediately the order is made for written reasons for its decision or order. If the order is made at a hearing, you must ask for the reasons then.[122]

20.73   Case management orders, as with other ET correspondence, are contained in letters signed by administrative officers. The Employment Judge who made the decision may not be identified. Although some regions are willing to identify who made the decision, some are not. The EAT has stated very firmly that all judicial orders made by Employment Judges, whether interlocutory or otherwise, should identify the Judge and be signed by him/her.[123]

Orders against third parties

20.74   The ET also has power to order a third party to disclose documents or provide additional information.[124] For example, an employment agency could be ordered to provide documents relating to the wording of a job advertisement if that wasn't in the employer's possession.

Witness orders

20.75   An employee can apply for a witness order requiring the attendance of any person as a witness[125] if that person can give relevant evidence which is necessary (because it is disputed) and s/he will not attend voluntarily.[126] A witness can also be ordered to produce documents. This is useful where documents are held by someone other than the employer, who will not provide copies voluntarily. A request for an order should be sent to the ET in good time for the hearing, setting out

---

120 See para 20.134.

121 ET Regs 2004 Sch 1 r34.

122 See ET Regs 2004 Sch 1 r30; and para 20.137 onwards regarding the EAT Rules.

123 *Ilangartne v The British Medical Association* EAT/508/98; see November 1999 *Legal Action* 17.

124 ET Regs 2004 Sch 1 r10(2)(d) states that an order can be made against 'any person'.

125 ET Regs 2004 Sch 1 r10(2)(c).

126 *Dada v Metal Box Co* [1974] IRLR 251; [1974] ICR 559, NIRC.

the name and home or work address of the witness. It should very briefly summarise why the evidence is relevant and necessary and state that the witness is not prepared to attend the hearing voluntarily.[127] The ET will then serve the witness order direct on the witness and send a copy to the employee and/or his/her representative. There is a financial penalty (currently £1,000) if the witness fails to attend, unless the witness successfully applies to the ET before the hearing for the order to be set aside.

20.76   An order should be obtained only if the witness is co-operative, but does not want to attend without an order (usually to protect the witness, so that the employee can tell his/her employer that s/he is not attending the hearing voluntarily). A witness who does not want to attend at all or is forced to do so is invariably a bad witness. It will also be hard to get a statement from an unwilling witness in advance of the hearing, so there is no certainty as to what s/he will say. There is an extra complication in that the tribunal will probably have ordered witness statements to be exchanged in advance and may be reluctant to allow in a late statement. Unlike requests for case management orders, the letter sent to the ET asking for a witness statement is not copied to the employer.

Hearing dates and adjournments

20.77   The author believes that in Scotland the ET consults each side about availability before fixing a hearing date. But usual practice in England and Wales is for the ET to fix the date and then send each side a notice of hearing. Each party must receive at least 14 days' notice of a hearing date.[128] It is not necessary to give 14 days' notice of a case management discussion. Advisers should read the notice of hearing carefully to check what kind of hearing is referred to. Sometimes parties fail to notice that it is calling them to a pre-hearing review or a case management discussion (or both) and not the main hearing.

20.78   ETs used to consult over convenient hearing dates, but this is now very rare. However, the standard directions letter may ask how long the parties think the case will last. If the date, once fixed, is inconvenient, an adjournment (the technical term for postponement) should be requested immediately. If there is a case management discussion (see para 20.85), dates are often fixed on the spot, so it is important to come with diaries and a note of dates to avoid for all witnesses.

127 See p771 for an example.
128 ET Regs 2004 Sch 1 r14(4).

20.79　　Once a date is notified, it is essential to check immediately with the employee and other witnesses that they can attend. It is extremely hard to get an adjournment, even with both parties' consent, unless, eg a key witness is ill or not enough days have been allocated. The ET is usually unsympathetic if a representative is unavailable, stating that another representative can surely be found. This is most unreasonable with small voluntary sector organisations and also fails to recognise the realities of how trade union representation is organised. The person who suffers is usually the low-paid employee who cannot afford to pay for representation and whose case will suffer from losing the adviser who has been involved from the beginning. There have been a few successful appeals against such refusals in discrimination cases where law centres and other voluntary advice centres have been involved.[129]

20.80　　Due to the pressures on the ET system to process cases quickly, there have been a number of cases where postponements have been unreasonably refused. In certain circumstances, inadequate and late disclosure of documents by the employer may be a ground for adjournment if it prevents the claimant from dealing with his/her claim properly.[130] However, a postponement is unlikely unless it causes real problems. It is quite common for a few extra documents to be produced by the employer at the last minute. In a key case under the Human Rights Act 1998,[131] the Court of Appeal said that although an adjournment is a discretionary matter for the tribunal, some adjournments must be granted if not to do so amounts to a denial of justice. To comply with the right to a fair trial under article 6 of the European Convention on Human Rights,[132] if a party is unable to be present through no fault of his/her own, s/he must usually be granted an adjournment, however inconvenient to the ET and other side. However, the onus is on the party wanting an adjournment to prove a genuine need for it.

20.81　　To improve the chances of persuading an ET to grant a postponement, or a successful appeal otherwise, it is important generally to conduct the case promptly and efficiently, to request any necessary postponement as soon as the problematic date is notified, to explain fully in a letter to the ET why the postponement is needed and why it will harm the employee's case if the representative is unavailable. It is

---

129 *Christou v Morpheus and Symes* EAT/498/99; November 1999 *Legal Action* 17; *Yearwood v Royal Mail* EAT/843/97, May 1998 *Legal Action* 15; *De Souza v British Telecom and Lyon* (1997) 588 *IDS Brief* 15, EAT.

130 *Eastwood v Winckworth Sherwood* EAT 0174/05 sets out guidelines.

131 *Teinaz v Wandsworth LBC* [2002] IRLR 721, CA.

132 See paras 3.18–3.19 above.

also helpful to indicate available future dates as flexibly and imminently as possible.[133] The employer needs to be notified of the application to postpone in the usual way.[134] In any event, it is worth telephoning the respondent first to try to get an agreement for the postponement.

20.82   Where a postponement is requested because the claimant is medically unfit to attend, it is crucial to get a strong letter from the claimant's doctor, specifying exactly what is wrong, stating that the claimant cannot attend the hearing and explaining how his/her ill-health prevents him/her from doing so. It is not enough for the doctor to say the claimant is unfit to attend work, since that is a different matter. The letter or report should not use vague words like 'stress' and 'anxiety', but should be clear about symptoms, their causes and severity.[135] Doctors often do not realise the importance of addressing specific issues in their letter. It is essential to explain to them exactly what is needed and why. If the ET has doubts, it can ask for further medical evidence. However, it is absurd to criticise a party for not attending the hearing to give evidence of his/her condition when a doctor has advised him/her on medical grounds not to attend.[136]

20.83   Where possible, it is advisable to make any postponement request well in advance of the hearing. Once the hearing date is imminent, the ET clerks should be chased to ensure the application gets put in front of an Employment Judge as soon as possible. Do not assume that marking a fax 'urgent' will suffice. If the request is left too late, it is more likely that the ET will defer the decision to the tribunal on the day. This is problematic because everyone must come ready to go ahead and costs can be wasted if the adjournment is agreed. It also makes it less likely that the request will be granted. The ET has a discretion to order that the claimant pay the costs of the respondent if caused by the adjournment.[137]

20.84   If the adviser knows in advance of any notice of hearing that there will be problems with certain dates, s/he should write and inform the ET before the dates are set. Finally, if the ET refuses without giving reasons, the adviser should ask for written reasons if s/he intends to appeal.

---

133 *Tillingbourne Bus Co Ltd v Norsworthy* [2000] IRLR 10, EAT indicates relevant considerations for the ET.

134 See para 20.69.

135 *Andreou v Lord Chancellor's Department* [2002] IRLR 728, CA.

136 *Teinaz v Wandsworth LBC* [2002] IRLR 721, CA.

137 See para 20.142 onwards on costs.

Case management discussion

20.85 This is an informal hearing before an Employment Judge sitting alone, attended by each party or his/her representatives, at which the preparation of the case is moved on. It used to be called a 'hearing for directions' or an 'interlocutory hearing'. A case management discussion is not often held in straightforward unfair dismissal cases, but can be requested at any time by either party or initiated by the ET itself, to identify the issues[138] and deal with all or any outstanding procedural issues that are not being resolved in correspondence, eg disclosure of documents, fixing hearing dates, or ordering that cases be heard together. A number of ET regions will automatically have a case management discussion in discrimination cases.

20.86 Once the ET has sent notification of a case management discussion, it is worth trying to agree as much as possible with the employer's representative regarding which documents will be disclosed, when to exchange witness statements, etc. This reduces the chances of getting unsatisfactory orders from the tribunal at the discussion and may even obviate the need for the discussion altogether. If agreement cannot be reached, the claimant should come to the discussion with a typed draft of the issues involved and the orders s/he is seeking. Ideally these should be sent to the employer in advance. This helps the claimant (especially if unrepresented) keep to his/her own agenda. It is common for the Employment Judge to encourage the parties to agree arrangements voluntarily. It is a good idea to be co-operative where possible, but if one of the Judge's suggestions would seriously harm the claimant's case, and the claimant wants to preserve the right to appeal, then s/he should not agree and the Judge should be required to make an order.

20.87 Case management discussions are sometimes conducted by telephone conferencing, usually where both parties are represented. The conference is set up by the ET.

Combined cases

20.88 Where similar issues of fact or law are concerned, the ET may order that cases against the same employer be considered together.[139] This is sometimes loosely referred to as 'consolidation'. The ET can do this of its own accord or on application by either party. Separate claims by

138 See para 21.49 in a discrimination context.
139 ET Regs 2004 Sch 1 r10(2)(j).

the claimant made in separate ET1 forms at different times can also be combined. For example, in a discrimination case, there may be an initial ET1 regarding the original discrimination and a further ET1 when an employee is dismissed, concerning victimisation and unfair dismissal. Each party will have the opportunity to argue for or against consolidation and careful consideration should be given to whether tactically it would help the individual cases or save costs. The commonest instances of consolidation are for multiple redundancy or equal pay claims.

Pre-hearing review – jurisdiction

20.89   A pre-hearing review can be requested by either side or ordered by the ET on its own initiative.[140] A pre-hearing review is an interim hearing, where the ET can decide any interim or preliminary matter, normally on an issue of jurisdiction. This type of pre-hearing review was formerly named a 'preliminary hearing'.

20.90   The pre-hearing review usually takes the form of a full hearing with witnesses, except that it tends to be much shorter. The pre-hearing review will be heard by an Employment Judge alone, unless a party requests a full tribunal panel at least ten days before and the ET considers it desirable to have a panel because issues of fact are to be decided.[141] Preparation is as for a full hearing, except that the evidence is collected relating to the preliminary issue alone. If the claimant and any other witnesses are to give evidence, it is normally a good idea to prepare witness statements even if the ET has not made any order to do so. The outcome of the pre-hearing review is usually very important to the claimant as it tends to concern whether the ET has jurisdiction to hear his/her case. For example, pre-hearing reviews are often held where there is a dispute over whether the employee has been employed for one continuous year, was an employee, worked under an illegal contract, commenced proceedings within the time limit, etc. Many of these hearings can be quite lengthy and complex, particularly if they concern TUPE issues. Hearings concerning late claims and time limits tend to be shorter and more informal, relying mainly on the arguments put by the parties' representatives rather than being dependent on a dispute over what happened. If the claimant is successful in the pre-hearing review and can therefore continue with all or part of his/her case, the Employment Judge will usually go on to deal with

140 ET Regs 2004 Sch 1 r10(2)(o).
141 ET Regs 2004 Sch 1 r18(3).

case management arrangements. The claimant should be prepared for this.

20.91   The ET often consults the parties about whether to order a pre-hearing review. If there is no prior consultation, write in promptly when one is ordered if you have any concerns. It is not always sensible and cost-effective to hold a pre-hearing review on a preliminary issue. Sometimes the evidence needed to address the preliminary issue over-laps awkwardly with the evidence relevant to the substantive case. There is also a risk that fact findings will be made at the pre-hearing review based on inadequate evidence, because it was unclear that certain issues would arise. Such fact findings could then bind the ET at the final hearing.

Pre-hearing review – striking out and costs deposits

20.92   The general rules and procedure for pre-hearing reviews are set out above. In addition, an ET can at a pre-hearing review amend or strike out any part of the claim or response on various grounds, most notably that it is scandalous or vexatious or has no reasonable prospect of success or for non compliance with an order or practice direction.[142]

20.93   If the ET considers that the claim or response has little reasonable prospects of success, it can give a costs warning and order the claimant or employer (as applicable) to pay a deposit of £500 as a condition of being permitted to continue with the case.[143] At this stage, the ET must take account of the party's ability to pay. If the claimant goes ahead after being ordered to pay a deposit and eventually loses his/her case, there is a greater chance of having costs awarded against him/her. If no costs are awarded against the claimant at the final hearing, s/he will get the deposit back.

20.94   It is important for the claimant to demonstrate that s/he under-stands the law and that, if his/her version of the facts is proved, it could arguably amount to unfair dismissal. The ET will rarely require a deposit if evidence in dispute is clearly central to the case and there is a sub-stantial disagreement over what happened, since it needs a full hearing with witnesses to make fact findings. This should be borne in mind when attending a pre-hearing review. Whether or not a deposit has been required, any costs ultimately ordered can substantially exceed £500. Costs may be awarded against an unsuccessful party even if there has been no pre-hearing review, but there is an increased likelihood

142 ET Regs 2004 Sch 1 r18(7). See para 20.55.
143 ET Regs 2004 Sch 1 r20.

of costs for unreasonably persisting with the case where a review was held and deposit required.[144] No member of the ET which heard the pre-hearing review will be part of the ET panel at the final hearing.

20.95   Employers sometimes automatically call for a pre-hearing review related to costs as a tactic to put pressure on the claimant. The best way to prevent a pre-hearing review even being held is to write a good ET1, which demonstrates a good understanding of the law and makes the relevant points.[145] When the claimant receives a copy of an employer's letter asking for a pre-hearing review, s/he should immediately write back pointing out that the ET1 sets out a legitimate claim, and copy the letter to the ET.

Preparation for the hearing

Trial bundles

20.96   In England and Wales, ETs expect a joint bundle of documents to be agreed with the employer. In Scotland, each side brings their own bundle of 'productions'. Normally a copy should be given to the other side in advance as a matter of courtesy, though often this does not happen. The trial bundle usually contains the ET1 and ET3 (though some ETs think this is superfluous, it is useful to share the same numbering), and relevant correspondence from the case preparation, eg additional information and documents which each side think are relevant. Not every document produced on disclosure need go into the trial bundle. Witness statements should be kept separate. Four copies of the bundle must be produced for the ET's use (three ET members and the witness table). Some ETs now expect an additional copy to be brought for any member of the public sitting in the hearing. If agreement cannot be reached on the bundle, the employee's representative should prepare his/her own bundle. The bundle should have the ET1 and ET3 at the front and then the documents in chronological order, numbered on each page and indexed at the front. Sometimes the ET orders the employer to prepare the joint bundle, but it is always better to prepare the trial bundle oneself. However tempting it is to agree to an offer from the employer's representative to do the work (and bear the costs), this usually means getting the bundle at the very last minute and in a shape which is not user-friendly.

144 ET Regs 2004 Sch 1 r47(1). See para 20.142 onwards on costs generally.
145 See paras 20.38–20.40.

Evidence related to compensation

20.97   The employee should disclose to the employer before the hearing and put into the trial bundle details of all efforts made to secure new employment, eg letters, e-mails, copies of advertisements, details of employment agencies contacted, Job Centre information about jobs applied for and expenses. If the employee wins and only wants compensation, the ET will want to know that s/he has made genuine efforts to obtain another job and mitigate his/her loss.[146] The ET clerk will also want to know for recoupment purposes, details of the benefit office dealing with the employee's claim for Jobseeker's Allowance (JSA) or income support. Where it has been particularly hard to gain new employment due to the way dismissal took place, a report from a doctor or employment agency may help. If other factors caused difficulties, eg the employee's age, disability, race or having a young child, specialist evidence and reports will be useful.

Schedule of loss and mitigation or statement of remedy

20.98   It is now common for the ET to order the claimant to provide a statement of what remedy s/he is claiming and a schedule of his/her losses to date. This often has to be provided at the same time as additional information and disclosure, and updated shortly before or at the hearing. There is no standard format for such a schedule or agreement on how detailed it should be, though some tribunal regions send out a precedent. Essentially it should contain details of the claimant's estimate of what s/he would be earning had s/he not been dismissed; the date of any new job and its pay; and any other losses, eg pension rights or job-hunting expenses. It should contain the heads of compensation claimed, eg loss of statutory rights. Some ETs expect the claimant to fill in details which are matters for the ET's discretion, eg the number of weeks' future loss of earnings which is claimed. It is probably safer simply to write 'Future loss @ £00 (specify sum) for the number of weeks which the ET decides'. Where the schedule is used at the hearing, it is a nice idea to add two extra columns for the ET to complete – one to contain the employer's contentions under each heading, and the final column to contain the ET's decision. Various model schedules of loss are in appendix A. Some ETs also ask for mitigation to be included in the schedule. This means a list of the steps taken by the claimant to mitigate his/her loss,[147] eg letters written and interviews attended for a new job.

146 See para 18.32.
147 See para 18.32.

Other preparation

20.99   Witness statements should be prepared for each witness, signed and dated, and exchanged with the employer in advance of the hearing (see below). Each side should bring four extra copies of their own witness statements to the hearing for the ET panel and witness box. The witness statements should not be added into the trial bundle. Each witness should be told where and when to attend the ET. Maps for each ET office can be printed from the Tribunals Service website.[148] It is a good idea to explain the procedure to witnesses and to show them a copy of the trial bundle or at least the key documents, so that they understand the context of the case and see any documents on which they might be cross-examined. The adviser should prepare for his/her role as representative and in particular note down the key points on which s/he wants to cross-examine the employer's witnesses. The adviser ought to be able to anticipate what the employer will say at the hearing, especially if witness statements have been exchanged in advance. The adviser should also meet the employee and go through any unexpected points in the employers' witness statements.

20.100   If an adviser has not run a case before, it is a good idea to visit another ET hearing to see what happens. The employee may find this useful too. Arrive before 10 am when the hearings start and ask the clerk at reception which would be the most relevant case to watch or look on the list of cases on the notice board, which indicate the legal issues involved. The clerks are usually very helpful if asked for assistance.

Witness statements

20.101   ETs in England and Wales, now routinely expect the parties to provide written 'witness statements' for their witnesses. Witness statements should only be produced in Scotland if ordered by the tribunal.[149] The idea is that each witness will put his/her evidence in chief in a statement. Usually the witness will be asked to read out the statement at the hearing, but sometimes the ET will prefer to read the statement to itself (see para 20.121).

20.102   Advisers can usually ask a few supplementary questions and interrupt to draw the ET's attention to relevant pages of the trial bundle. The witness will then be cross-examined in the usual way. The purpose of

148 At www.employmenttribunals.gov.uk
149 According to the Tribunals Service website.

this approach is to speed up the proceedings and to let the parties know in advance what the evidence is going to be. ETs expect all the parties' evidence to be in the witness statements apart from any new issues arising from the other side's witness statements. The ET will get annoyed if the claimant or employer's witness statements are sketchy and too many extra questions are asked which could have been included in the first place. To avoid any extra verbal questions, some ETs order that further or supplementary witness statements are exchanged within seven days of the exchange of the original witness statements. However, this does seem rather clumsy and excessive in terms of paperwork. If it does happen, be careful to include all evidence in the statements as the ET is unlikely to allow any supplementary questions at the hearing.

20.103 Usually there has been some agreement between the parties or suggestion (or an order) by the ET that the witness statements should be exchanged seven or 14 days in advance of the hearing. It may be proposed in an ET standard letter, or otherwise the adviser could suggest this at the time of requesting additional information and documents. The agreed trial bundle should be completed before the witness statements are exchanged, so that there are no surprise documents produced by the employer after the claimant has set out his/her full story. This is also necessary if page references for key documents are to be inserted in the witness statements. It is useful both for forewarning the employee and preparing cross-examination to obtain the employer's statements in advance. However, with a weak case where the employee is hoping for a last-minute settlement, the disadvantage of exchange is that it reveals the employee's entire case and how few witnesses s/he may have.

20.104 It is important to exchange witness statements simultaneously with the employer, so there is no risk of last-minute alterations. It is usually best to suggest the employer deliver his/her statements by messenger and the claimant will hand over his/her own witness statements to the messenger by way of exchange. Alternatively it can be done by return of fax or e-mail. If attaching to an e-mail, make sure 'track changes' is not visible when the statement is printed out!

20.105 It may not be possible to get a witness statement in advance where a witness has been compelled to attend by a witness order or only traced at the last minute. Although an ET may be reluctant to exclude evidence from a witness altogether if there is no statement, it may ask one to be written up on the spot, and may order costs if time is wasted as a result. The ET has specific power to order statements but should not do so in every case particularly when the parties are not legally represented.[150] Where the adviser is not using witness statements, s/he will still need a clear written note of the employee's evidence in a sensible order, from which s/he will ask questions at the hearing.

20.106   Although technically an ET can choose to read and take account of a written witness statement where the witness does not come to the hearing, such an approach is not very effective or persuasive because it cannot be tested in cross-examination. The ET often says it will 'go to its weight', ie the ET will read the witness statement, but is unlikely to place much reliance on it. It would therefore be unusual for a party to use a witness statement without calling the witness to attend.

How should a witness statement be written?

20.107   Ideally a witness statement should be set out clearly, with typed and numbered short paragraphs and sub-headings to break up the text. It is useful to cite the page in the trial bundle where documents are referred to. Wide margins and double-spacing enables annotations to be made by the ET panel and representatives as evidence is given during the hearing. Dates and names should always be stated in full. The witness's evidence should be written in a logical order, usually explaining background details first and then telling the story chronologically. Care should be taken with accuracy and consistency of detail. Always bear in mind what are the relevant legal and factual issues, and provide the evidence which is relevant to those. For example, in an unfair dismissal case, draw attention to lack of warnings or inadequate investigation. In a discrimination case, always draw attention to different treatment.[151] If there are problem areas, as a matter of tactics it may be useful to lessen the impact of cross-examination by dealing with those areas in the statement.

20.108   Ensure the employee fully agrees with the content of the statement, that s/he understands all the words used and can easily read them. Most people stumble when reading under stress. Short words and sentences make reading easier. Try to use the words and expressions that the employee usually uses him/herself to describe the events. It is unwise to ask the employee to write his/her own statement with a view simply to tidying it up. The statement will probably be poorly structured, include irrelevant information and exclude relevant information.

150 *Eurobell Holdings plc v Barker and another* [1998] ICR 299, EAT; TLR 12 November 1997. Though witness statements have become far more common since this case.

151 See p748 for sample unfair dismissal witness statement and pp719 and 722 for discrimination examples.

20.109   Tell the employee in advance that there is nothing wrong with the adviser having written the statement in consultation with him/her. Otherwise if asked directly at the hearing whether s/he wrote the statement, the worker may become anxious and not tell the truth.

20.110   If the employee or other witness cannot read, or cannot read English, but can definitely understand English and the content of his/her statement, then the ET should be asked whether the statement can be read out by the adviser, with the employee indicating his/her understanding at regular intervals. See para 21.62 where the witness statement needs to be written in a different language.

Expenses

20.111 The parties, their witnesses and professional representatives on the staff of a Citizens Advice Bureau or acting for the Free Representation Unit or Bar Pro Bono Unit may claim expenses for attending ET hearings.[152] Forms can be obtained from the ET clerk and claims must be submitted within one month. The amounts and types of expenses covered are complicated and do change, so it is advisable to check. A guidance note entitled *Expenses and allowances payable to parties and witnesses attending an employment tribunal* can be obtained from the ET office or downloaded from the Tribunals Service website.[153] The current position appears to be roughly as follows. The first £5 of any travel expenses will not be covered unless the person was ordered to attend by a witness order. Car travel is paid at 15 pence per mile, but parking costs and congestion charges are not met. Taxi fares are only paid in exceptional circumstances, eg the person has a medical condition which prevents him/her using public transport. Prior written approval must be obtained from the Regional Secretary of the Tribunal where a long taxi journey is needed. Travel from overseas may be covered if the ET agrees it is in the interests of justice, but only with prior consent. Loss of earnings up to a maximum of £45 per day will be reimbursed if the employer certifies the loss has occurred; paid holiday or special leave is not covered. Overnight expenses are paid where essential, subject to certain limits, which may be exceeded if there are special requirements for people with a disability. There are allowances for registered

---

152 According to the tribunal's guidance note on expenses. It is unclear why law centre employees should be excluded from this. It may only be an administrative rule, but the author is unable to find the answer to this.

153 At www.employmenttribunals.gov.uk/Documents/Publications/ExpenseAllowances.pdf But check if there has been an update, search 'expenses' on the ET site.

childminders and adult carers of up to £5.35 per hour, except during a period covered by loss of earnings. The Employment Judge's permission will be need in advance of a hearing to use a friend or relative as an interpreter. This is not usually a good idea, but if it is allowed, s/he can claim the usual witness expenses, but not a fee for interpreting. If a professional interpreter is required, notify the tribunal's office, which will make arrangements. If a Judge orders the production of essential medical reports or evidence, repayment will be made in line with indicative Tribunal Service rates – check these with the tribunal before costs are incurred. Where an adviser is unable to find an expert or interpreter for the ET rates, s/he should make a note of everywhere s/he has tried and the charges quoted. In some circumstances, failure to reimburse fully may be a denial of the right to a fair trial under article 6 of the European Convention on Human Rights.

The hearing

Arrival

20.112　On the day of the hearing, arrive early and check in with the clerk at reception. The clerk will indicate whether the case has been allocated to a particular tribunal panel or whether the case is unallocated, ie 'floating' or a 'floater'. The cases are usually also listed on a notice board in the reception area. Allocated cases usually start at 10 am. An unallocated case joins a queue and will be heard by the first ET panel to come free. This may involve a long delay. Many cases float each day. If a party has not arrived by the time of the hearing, the ET should usually telephone and make further enquiries before proceeding in his/her absence.[154]

20.113　Claimants and respondents usually have separate waiting rooms and, in many tribunals, there are a number of private meeting rooms available for use. Visit the employer in the respondents' waiting room to sort out any last-minute problems and to see what witnesses are there. This is often an opportunity to discuss settlement. Give the employer's representative copies of any cases that will be discussed in the closing speech. The clerk will visit each side in their waiting rooms to collect the trial bundles and witness statements for the ET panel. If there is any doubt whether a witness will be called, hold back

---

154 *Cooke v Glenrose* UKEAT/0064/04; [2004] IRLR 866, EAT; *Euro Hotels (Thornton Heath) Ltd v Alam* UKEAT/0006/09.

the relevant witness statement in case the ET reads it first. The names and references of any cases to be referred to in closing should also be given to the clerk together with copies of the cases. The clerk will ask whether the witnesses will swear or affirm when giving evidence. If witnesses require any holy book other than the New Testament, the clerk should be told at this point, eg the Old Testament for Jewish witnesses; the Guru Granth Sahib, sometimes called the Adi Granth, for Sikhs and the Mahabharata or within that, the Bhagavadgita, for Hindus. Muslim witnesses may prefer to affirm rather than invoke the Koran in this context or where they do not have facilities to wash first. See paras 21.65–21.71 regarding accessibility of tribunals to people wearing religious dress or with a disability.

20.114 The time before the hearing starts can be used to clear up last-minute queries and to calm the employee and witnesses. Cases often settle on the morning of the hearing, so the representative should have in mind what the employee wants and terms of settlement, and should bring precedents for settlements and consent orders, and a calculator. If part of the settlement would be an agreed reference, which is common, a draft should have been prepared in advance.[155]

Composition of the ET panel

20.115 With limited exceptions, tribunal cases are heard by a three-person panel, unless the parties agree otherwise (which they are rarely asked to do). The panel is chaired by an Employment Judge, who is a solicitor, barrister, advocate or legal executive of at least five years' standing, and has two wing or 'lay' members. The lay members are drawn from each side of industry (employer and employee-orientated background), but are not there to represent an interest group and must take a neutral position in deciding cases. ET decisions can be by a majority but are usually unanimous.

20.116 Certain claims, eg for breach of contract, payslips, section 1 statements of particulars, unlawful deductions or leave entitlement under the WTR 1998,[156] can be heard by an Employment Judge sitting alone. The parties' consent is not needed, although they should be consulted.[157] The case-law is uncertain as to whether, if there is no challenge

---

155 See para 20.163 below regarding consent orders at tribunal.
156 Employment Tribunals Act 1996 s4(3) as amended by the Employment Tribunals Act 1996 (Tribunal Composition) Order 2009, SI No 789.
157 Employment Tribunals Act 1996 s4(2)–(3); *Sterling Developments (London) Ltd v Pagano* [2007] IRLR 471, EAT.

by the parties, the Judge must explicitly consider his/her discretion to order a full panel, eg because there is a dispute on the facts.[158]

The ET's approach

20.117   The original intention was for the hearing of unfair dismissal claims to be expedient, simple and informal. Unfortunately ETs vary enormously in their practice, from far too informal to the strict formalities of civil courts. As an ET has a wide discretion to conduct hearings as it likes, there is not much that can be done except be prepared for anything! Always call the Employment Judge 'Sir' or 'Madam' and remain seated. The other representative can be addressed by name (Mr/Ms/Mrs ...), although barristers tend to call each other 'my friend' or 'my learned friend'. The room is set out informally and no one wears a wig and gown. However, the witnesses and representatives should dress smartly and behave appropriately. Remember it is a court of law and everyone in the room is very visible to the tribunal panel. A hearing can be conducted by electronic communications,[159] eg telephone or video link with a witness who has moved abroad.

20.118   If the employee's claim is prejudiced by the ET's conduct, eg continuous interruptions from the panel or refusal to allow certain evidence to be called, this can be a ground of appeal. The representative must object at the time and ask the ET to note the objection. If there is an appeal, the Employment Judge's notes if relevant will be ordered. An appeal can also be made if it is felt that the ET is biased or any member has a conflict of interest, eg has some connection with the employer. If it is intended to appeal on any of these points, an objection must usually first be raised in the ET. Only object if it is felt that it is really necessary, as it will alienate the ET and appeals are difficult when concerning the conduct of ETs.[160] Because of the potential consequences, the representative should ask for five minutes to consult the claimant privately before making any objection.

20.119   At the start of the hearing, the ET will deal with any preliminary matters such as arguments about the documents or matters of jurisdiction, although the latter will usually have been resolved at a separate

---

158 ETA 1996 s4(5); *Sogbetun v London Borough of Hackney* [1998] IRLR 676, EAT; *Gladwell v Secretary of State for Trade and Industry* UKEAT/0337/06; (2006) 818 IDS Brief 9, EAT; *Sterling Developments (London) Ltd v Pagano* [2007] IRLR 471, EAT.

159 ET Regs 2004 Sch 1 r15(1).

160 Though the Human Rights Act 1998 may be of assistance. See paras 3.18–3.19 above.

pre-hearing review. The parties should normally have written to each other about any outstanding matters at least ten days before the hearing, so no one is caught by surprise.[161] The ET will itemise the issues to be decided (eg in an unfair dismissal case, the main issues are – what was the reason for dismissal? Was it fair to dismiss for that reason, taking account of the band of reasonable responses?). The ET usually informs the parties at this stage how it wants the hearing conducted and says whether it wants to hear evidence about remedy (efforts to get new employment) at the same time or only if and when the claimant wins. If the ET does not say, then ask.

The order of events

20.120 If there is a dispute over whether there was a dismissal, the employee goes first. Otherwise the employer starts in an unfair dismissal case.[162] The ET will not usually want to hear an opening statement. Assuming the employer starts, s/he will call his/her witnesses first. Each witness will be asked to stand and take the oath or affirm to tell the truth. The witness will then sit. The ET will check his/her address. Then the witness will give his/her 'evidence in chief'.

20.121 If a witness statement has been prepared, most of the evidence in chief will consist of the statement. The representative should hand extra copies to the ET panel and a clean copy for the witness box, unless the clerk has already done this. By way of introducing the statement, the adviser asks the witness to confirm his/her name and address, that it is his/her statement and that its contents are believed to be accurate and true. Usually the witness reads out the statement, pausing when asked to look at documents referred to in the trial bundle. Occasionally the ET may read the statement to itself, but apparently the President has given a direction that witnesses should usually read out their own witness statements. The adviser can ask some supplementary questions, though not too many.[163] In Scotland, witness statements are used less often, and the evidence in chief may be given by the witness answering the representative's questions.

20.122 The representative must not 'lead' his/her own witness, ie must not ask a question in such a way that it suggests to the witness what the answer should be. For example, s/he must ask 'What did you do next?' as opposed to 'Did you then go to see the HR director?'. However, if the

---

161 See para 20.69.
162 See Burden of Proof at para 9.1 above.
163 See paras 20.101–20.110.

facts to be established are not in dispute by the other side, the representative can lead, eg 'I think we all agree that you went on holiday from 1 to 14 August'. Whether there are any facts that can be agreed should be checked with the other side before the hearing. If this has been done, it is wise to indicate to the ET that leading questions are being put because the facts are agreed.

20.123   After the evidence in chief is finished the employee's representative can then ask questions. This is called cross-examination and 'leading questions' are permitted. After that, the employer's representative can ask a few more questions, simply clearing up anything that arose in cross-examination. This is called re-examination. Either before or after re-examination, the ET panel usually questions the witness. During cross-examination, the Employment Judge may also have asked some questions for clarification. In Scotland, the ET panel tends to ask more questions than in England and Wales.

20.124   The same process is followed with each witness. After all the employer's witnesses have given evidence, the employee is immediately called to give evidence and then any of the employee's witnesses. In Scotland, witnesses must stay outside the room until after they have given evidence. In England and Wales, witnesses are allowed to sit in the room throughout and usually do. The Scottish system seems preferable, as it is hard for witnesses not to influence each other, especially if they are still employed. Although there is now an explicit power in the new rules to request that a particular witness be excluded from the room while others give evidence, this would require a culture change in England and Wales. It is difficult to know how to go about making such requests more routine, without antagonising the ET in a particular case. The ET is likely to consider such a request unreasonable, simply because it is unusual.[164]

20.125   It is useful to prepare in advance of the hearing a chronology, ie a list of the important dates, as well as a list of the names and job title of the main characters, particularly those who will be giving evidence. These can be handed to the ET and the employer's representative at the outset. Ideally the content would be agreed with the employer's representative in advance, but this rarely happens unless the ET has made a specific order.

164 Power to exclude witnesses is in ET Regs 2004 Sch 1 r27(4).

The closing speech

20.126 Each party has a right to address the ET, usually in a closing speech.[165] This is sometimes called 'closing submissions' or 'final submissions'. In England and Wales, the party which started usually addresses the ET last. In Scotland, it tends to be the opposite. The length of the speech depends on the complexity of the case, but the ET should not be bored. The main point of the closing speech is to relate the key points of evidence to the relevant law. If the employer's representative will have the last word, the employee's should anticipate and deal with the employer's strong points in his/her closing speech. It is best to prepare the closing speech in advance, amending it through the course of the hearing to reflect what emerges. If the hearing lasts more than one day, it is useful to produce written submissions. These usually make more impact than an improvised purely oral speech.

20.127 The ET should be reminded of the main issues and related evidence. Where there is a conflict of evidence, it can be suggested why the ET should prefer the employee's witnesses. To ensure that the ET addresses its mind to certain key issues, it should expressly be invited to make findings of fact on those matters. It may even be helpful to circulate a skeleton argument, ie a list of the main legal and factual issues which are expanded in the closing speech.

20.128 If any reported cases are referred to, remember that only the decision of the most senior court on a particular issue is important. Most unfair dismissal cases are decided on their facts and case-law need not be routinely referred to. On the whole, it is not necessary to read extracts from the case-law unless there is an unusual or difficult legal issue. The ET will be familiar with the main cases and legal principles and a key authority may just be referred to by name. Copies of the full case report (from IRLR or ICR) should be handed to each member of the ET and employer's representative unless it is a very well-known case such as *Polkey*.[166] If references are made to reported cases, advisers should make sure that they fully know and understand them.

20.129 Sometimes there is only enough time at the hearing date to finish the evidence and a new date would need to be fixed for closing speeches. Provided the parties agree, the ET may suggest each side send in written closing submissions within seven or 14 days. The ET should order

---

165 ET Regs 2004 Sch 1 r27(2).
166 *Polkey v AE Dayton Services* [1987] IRLR 503, HL. See para 6.58.

that the submissions are exchanged between the parties so that each side has the opportunity to comment on the other's submissions.[167]

The judgment

20.130 In England and Wales, the ET's judgment is often given verbally at the end of the hearing, after a short break to make up its mind. It will subsequently be confirmed in writing and sent to the parties. Sometimes the tribunal suggests the representatives wait at the tribunal while the judgment is typed up, so they can take it away with them. If a barrister represents the claimant and the instructing solicitor has not come to the tribunal, the latter must remember to get the hard copy of the judgment from the barrister. The judgment simply states the ET's decision and may include compensation, a declaration or recommendation (eg in a discrimination case), and any costs order.[168] In a complex case or where time has run out, the judgment may be 'reserved', ie made at a later date and sent to the parties. This can mean a wait of a few months. A long and unreasonable delay in providing the judgment, even by as much as a year, will not in itself constitute a ground for appeal. Only in exceptional cases will unreasonable delay amount to a real risk that someone has been deprived of their right to a fair hearing under article 6 of the European Convention on Human Rights.[169] In Scotland, the ET rarely announces its judgment at the end of the hearing.

20.131 When the ET reserves its judgment, it must send it to the parties subsequently together with written reasons.[170] When the judgment is given orally at the end of the hearing, the reasons may be given orally at the same time. If the claimant wants the reasons put in writing, s/he must ask for this at the hearing or make a written request within 14 days of the date the judgment is sent to the parties.[171] This time limit can be extended if the ET thinks it just and equitable. It is essential to ask for written reasons if planning to appeal.[172] The written reasons must include the issues relevant to the claim, relevant fact findings, a concise statement of the law, how the fact findings and law have been applied to determine the issues, the reason why any issues

167 *Mayor and Burgesses of Haringey LBC v Akpan* (2002) 693 IRLB 11, EAT.
168 ET Regs 2004 Sch 1 r28 and r29.
169 *Bangs v Connex South Eastern Ltd* [2005] IRLR 389, CA.
170 ET Regs 2004 Sch 1 r30(2).
171 ET Regs 2004 Sch 1 r30(2), (5).
172 See para 20.138.

were not determined and if compensation has been awarded, details as to how it has been calculated.[173] The ET's decision is usually unanimous, although it may be by a majority. It is important not to get confused between the written judgment and the written reasons (if any), which are usually contained in separate documents – both will be needed if the claimant wants to appeal.

20.132   The tribunal may have taken evidence regarding compensation (remedies) at the same time as it heard evidence relevant to liability. If not, if the ET decides the dismissal is unfair at the end of the hearing, it may then go on to deal with the evidence about compensation, or it may adjourn and suggest that the parties reach agreement on compensation. The parties may be able to reach agreement immediately by talking in the waiting rooms. If so, any agreement should be written, signed and shown to the ET. The clerk will make copies. Alternatively, the ET may send the parties away, on the basis that settlement discussions will take place outside the ET on another day. As long as the ET has reached a final decision on liability, ie that the employee was successful, then it should only be the compensation which is settled. In some circumstances, this may prevent the original judgment regarding liability being appealed. Time should not be allowed to drift. If no agreement can be achieved, then the claimant can simply write to the ET asking the case to be relisted for a hearing on compensation. Delays in fixing the compensation hearing can cause financial distress to the employee and may also deprive him/her of the benefit of interest on an unpaid award. Sometimes there will be concerns about the employer's continuing ability to pay any award. For this reason, even where the ET does not reach a decision at the end of the hearing and reserves its judgment, it may well set a provisional date for a remedies hearing (without prejudging its decision), in case the employee wins.

Appeals and reviews

20.133   An employee who is unhappy with the ET's judgment, including any costs order, may be able to ask the ET to review its decision or, alternatively, appeal to the EAT, or both. Whereas there is a 42-day time limit for lodging an appeal, there is only 14 days to seek a review. It is possible to appeal to the EAT against an interim order refusing additional information or disclosure or a request to postpone. It is also

173 ET Regs 2004 Sch 1 r30(6).

possible to ask the ET to reconsider if the employee has not had a chance to make representations,[174] but it is not possible to use the review process for these matters.

Review by the ET

20.134 The ET has power on its own initiative or, more likely, at a party's request, to review an ET judgment on one of the following grounds:

- the decision was wrongly made as a result of an administrative error, eg by ET staff or one of the parties;[175]
- a party did not receive notice of the proceedings leading to the decision;
- the decision was made in the absence of a party;
- new evidence has become available since the conclusion of the hearing, provided its existence could not have been reasonably known or foreseen at the time of the hearing and is likely to have an important influence on the result of the case; or
- the interests of justice require such a review,[176] eg a crucial new case has just been reported, or the ET made a mathematical error in calculating compensation or has made a decision on compensation without asking the parties for their comments.

20.135 If the employee wants a review, s/he must apply for it orally at the hearing or in writing, stating the grounds in full, within 14 days of the date when the judgment was sent to him/her.[177] The ET can extend the 14-day time limit if it is just and equitable to do so.[178] The ET can refuse to hold the review if it has no reasonable prospects of success. Otherwise the review will normally be heard by the ET which decided the case. On hearing the review, the ET can confirm, vary or revoke its decision and order a rehearing before the same or a different tribunal. It is important to read the ET's notification of the review carefully, as the ET may move on to a rehearing of the full case on the same day, immediately following a successful review. An ET has power to review its decision to strike out all or part of a claim, whether for non-payment of a deposit, or for reasons under rule 18(7), eg vexatious conduct or

---

174 See paras 20.71–20.73.
175 *Sodexho Ltd v Gibbons* [2005] IRLR 836, EAT.
176 ET Regs 2004 Sch 1 r 34(3).
177 ET Regs 2004 Sch 1 r35(1)–(2).
178 ET Regs 2004 Sch 1 r35(1).

non-compliance with an order.[179] Default judgments and decisions not to accept a claim or response can also be reviewed, although the grounds are a little different.[180] Note that clerical errors, eg numerical mistakes in calculating compensation, can simply be corrected by the ET under the 'slip rule' without any review.[181]

Appeal to the EAT

20.136　The procedural rules for appeals are set out in the Employment Appeal Tribunal Rules (EAT Rules) 1993 as supplemented by the Practice Direction (Employment Appeal Tribunal – Procedure) 2008 (EAT PD).[182] It is advisable to read the very helpful and clear practice direction. EAT procedure is not within the scope of this book and the following is simply an introduction, assuming the employee is the 'appellant', ie the person bringing the appeal. However, the employee also needs to know what forms to complete and timescales to meet where s/he is responding to an appeal brought by the employer.

20.137　If the appeal is against a judgment, it must be lodged within 42 days from the date the written judgment was sent to the parties. However, if written reasons were requested orally at the hearing or in writing within 14 days of the judgment being sent out (but no later) or if the ET reserved its reasons and gave them subsequently in writing, the 42 days runs from the date the written reasons were sent to the parties.[183] An appeal against an order must also be lodged within 42 days of the order being sent out.[184] The date the judgment, reasons or order are sent out is normally recorded on the document in question. If the document containing the judgment or its reasons is sent on a Wednesday, the Notice of Appeal must arrive at the EAT on or before the Wednesday six weeks later.[185] However, due to slightly different wording in the rules, it is possible that the time limit for an order sent out on a Wednesday would expire on the Tuesday six weeks later. Advisers should play safe. Note that the EAT's day (unlike the ET's) ends at 4 pm for these purposes and both the Notice of Appeal and all the supporting

---

179 *Sodexho Ltd v Gibbons* [2005] IRLR 836, EAT. See also para 20.57.

180 ET Regs 2004 Sch 1 rr33–35.

181 ET Regs 2004 Sch 1 r37(1).

182 Both available on the EAT website at
　　www.employmentappeals.gov.uk/RulesLegislation/rulesLegislation.htm

183 EAT PD para 3.3.

184 EAT PD para 3.2.

185 EAT PD para 1.8.1.

documents must have arrived by that time.[186] The EAT has power to allow late appeals, but in practice will only do so in exceptional circumstances.[187] Moreover, unlike for ET claims, an appeal posted 1st class is not deemed to arrive on the 2nd day after posting.[188]

20.138   The Notice of Appeal must be substantially in accordance with the prescribed forms and attach copies of the judgment or order appealed against, the ET's written reasons (almost always in a different document), the ET1 and ET3 or a written explanation why any of these cannot be attached.[189] Otherwise the appeal will not be validly lodged. It is therefore crucial to ask the ET for its written reasons within the specified time limits.[190] An ET must supply written reasons for a judgment if requested within the correct time-limit, but it is optional whether the ET gives written reasons for an interim order where these were given orally.[191] If written reasons cannot be attached, eg because the ET has refused to issue them, the employee must apply to the EAT to exercise its discretion either to dispense with the reasons or to require the ET to provide them.[192] If the employee has also applied to the ET for a review, a copy of the application and any outcome must also be attached.[193] Copies of relevant orders including case management orders should be included. Finally, if the employee wants the EAT to look at evidence which is not contained in the written reasons, s/he must apply with the Notice of Appeal for admission of such evidence or for the relevant parts of the Judge's notes to be supplied.[194]

20.139   The Notice of Appeal must clearly identify the point of law which is the ground of appeal and the order which the EAT is asked to make. If the employee wishes to appeal on grounds of perversity, the Notice must set out full particulars of the matters relied on.[195] The employee

---

186 EAT PD para 1.8.2; *Woodward v Abbey National plc; J P Garrett Electrical Ltd v Cotton* [2005] IRLR 782, EAT.

187 EAT PD paras 3.7 – 3.9; EAT Rules r37(1); *United Arab Emirates v Abdelghafar* [1995] IRLR 243, EAT; *Jurkowska v Hlmad Ltd* [2008] IRLR 430, CA; *Muschett v L B Hounslow, Khan v London Probation Service, Ogbuneke v Minster Lodge and ors, Tallington Lakes Ltd v Reilly and another* UKEAT/0281/07, 0285/07, 0400/07, 1870/06.

188 *Bost Logistics Ltd v Gumbley and others; Sybersolve Solutions Ltd v Eleode* UKEAT/0113/08.

189 EAT PD para 2.1.

190 See para 20.131.

191 ET Regs 2004 Sch 1 r30.

192 EAT PD para 2.3.

193 EAT PD para 2.2.

194 EAT PD para 7.1.

195 EAT PD para 2.6.

cannot generally reserve the right to add or amend details later, but an early application for leave to amend may be accepted.[196] The EAT will sift the Notices of Appeal, rejecting those with no chance at all. Often a short preliminary hearing (about one hour) is held to decide whether an appeal has reasonable prospects of success. The Notice of Appeal will be sent to the employer, who may (and sometimes must) within 14 days lodge concise written submissions as to why there is no reasonable prospect of success.[197] The employer can also cross-appeal. The employer will be notified of the date for the preliminary hearing. Normally only the employee (as the appellant) has the right to speak, although increasingly both parties are allowed to do so. If the appeal gets past the preliminary hearing and is allocated to a full hearing, the employer will be sent all the employee's documents and must lodge an Answer within 14 days.[198] The employee will have 14 days to serve a Reply to any cross-appeal. Obviously all these steps may happen in reverse if the employer is the one who is appealing.

20.140   Appeals against ET interim orders will be fast-tracked. A hearing date will be fixed or, especially for fast-track cases, the case will be put into a warned list.[199] Skeleton arguments must be lodged and exchanged 14 days before the full appeal and lodged ten days before any preliminary hearing.[200] This time limit is often treated casually by barristers, but there is a risk of costs orders or even dismissal of the appeal if it is ignored. The employee, as the appellant, is primarily responsible for preparing the appeal bundles in consultation with the employer. Only relevant documents should be included and there is a special order in which they should be put. Four copies of the bundle must be lodged with the EAT within specific time limits.[201] The full appeal usually consists of legal arguments put forward by each party (or their representatives). Witnesses do not give evidence. The EAT panels tend to be very courteous – and very clever! So it is important to be well researched in the relevant law.

20.141   Employees often cannot understand that they may not automatically appeal when they lose. An appeal to the EAT is not a fresh rehearing of the entire case. It is a legal argument between the representatives for each party, largely based on the pleadings and the ET's decision on

196 EAT PD para 2.7.
197 EAT PD para 9.8.
198 EAT PD para 10.
199 EAT PD paras 9.20 and 12.
200 EAT PD para 13.
201 For full details of the documents and time limits, see EAT PD para 6.

the facts. Normally the ET's notes of oral evidence will only be glanced at by the EAT, if at all. The appeal is confined to errors of law. Where there is no legal error, the employee must show that the ET's decision on the factual evidence was legally perverse, ie that no reasonable ET could possibly have come to the same decision. It is very hard to show this and the EAT is reluctant to interfere with the ET's general discretion.

Costs

20.142   Unlike most civil courts, the ET does not usually order that the unsuccessful party pays the costs of the winner. However, in certain circumstances the ET may order costs, usually because a party is running or defending a hopeless case, or because s/he fails to comply with tribunal orders, or because s/he behaves badly in conducting the case or because his/her poor case preparation leads to unnecessary postponements or adjournments of the hearing. Costs orders (expenses orders in Scotland)[202] can be made only where the receiving party has been legally represented.[203] A qualified solicitor without a practising certificate would not constitute a legal representative.[204] Nor would his/her costs be paid simply because s/he had instructed a barrister who did constitute a legal representative (although the costs of the barrister can be paid).[205] If the receiving party was not legally represented, a preparation time order may be made instead.[206] Wasted costs orders can also be made personally against some representatives.[207] To put it in context, in 2007/8, ETs made 327 costs awards against claimants, well under 0.5 per cent of the total cases disposed of in that year. Only 94 of those awards were for more than £2000, but there were 19 awards over £8000. Fewer costs awards were made against respondents.[208]

202 ET Regs 2004 Sch 1 rr38–41 and 46–47.
203 ET Regs 2004 Sch 1 r38(2) and (5).
204 *Ramsay & others v Bowercross Construction Ltd & others* UKEAT/0534-5/07.
205 *Ramsay* UKEAT/0534-5/07.
206 ET Regs 2004 Sch 1 rr42–47.
207 ET Regs 2004 Sch 1 r48.
208 See Employment Tribunal and EAT statistics (GB) 1 April 2007 – 31 March 2008 available at www.employmenttribunals.gov.uk/Documents/Publications/EmploymentTribunal_and_EAT_Statistics_v9.pdf

Costs orders

20.143 The ET can order a party (called 'the paying party') to make a payment in respect of costs incurred by the other party ('the receiving party'). It has a discretion to award costs in the following situations:

- a party has not complied with an order or practice direction;[209]
- a full or interim hearing is postponed or adjourned at the request of the paying party. If costs are awarded, they will be those which are incurred by the receiving party as a result of the postponement or adjournment.[210] If the hearing is postponed as a result of the employer's unreasonable failure to produce evidence about job availability, when the employee had indicated in advance his/her desire for reinstatement or re-engagement, costs must be awarded;[211]
- the paying party has acted vexatiously, abusively, disruptively or otherwise unreasonably in bringing the proceedings or was misconceived in doing so. 'Misconceived' includes having no reasonable prospect of success;[212]
- the paying party or his/her representative has acted vexatiously, abusively, disruptively or otherwise unreasonably in conducting the proceedings or was misconceived in doing so.[213]

20.144 The tribunal must first decide whether any of these categories apply and secondly decide whether to use its discretion to award costs and if so, how much to award.[214] There is a greater risk now than in the past that costs will be awarded against the employee. Nevertheless, if a case is run properly, tribunal orders and hearing dates are adhered to, and the case is reasonably arguable, it is unlikely costs will be awarded. Many of the reported cases where costs have been awarded seem to involve highly unsympathetic and sometimes vindictive behaviour by the claimants (although that may just have been the tribunal's interpretation). Employees should not be intimidated out of running legitimate cases because of fear of costs or letters routinely sent by some employers' solicitors threatening costs. The Court of Appeal has firmly stated that costs awards remain exceptional and are rarely awarded in ET proceedings.[215]

209 ET Regs 2004 Sch 1 r40(4).
210 ET Regs 2004 Sch 1 r40(1).
211 See ET Regs 2004 Sch 1 r39 for precise wording.
212 ET Regs 2004 Sch 1 rr2 and 40(3).
213 ET Regs 2004 Sch 1 r40(3).
214 *Monaghan v Close Thornton Solicitors* EAT/3/01.
215 *Lodwick v London Borough of Southwark* [2004] IRLR 554, CA; *Gee v Shell UK Ltd* [2003] IRLR 82, CA.

20.145   Costs should not be lightly awarded for 'unreasonable' behaviour. Although there is no precise definition of this phrase, the ET rules place a high threshold on the award of costs, and 'unreasonable' should be interpreted in the context of the other words in that rule.[216] The fact that the employee's case is weak, does not necessarily mean it is 'misconceived', although it is obviously important to be very careful. If faced with a costs application against the employee at the end of a case which s/he has lost, it is important to explain why the case previously appeared to have reasonable prospects of success. It is worth referring to these comments from the case of *E T Marler Ltd v Robertson*:[217] 'Ordinary experience of life frequently teaches us that that which is plain for all to see once the dust of battle has subsided was far from clear to the contestants when they took up arms.' Moreover, costs should only be awarded from the point when a case becomes misconceived or behaviour becomes unreasonable.[218]

20.146   It is unwise to lodge an extremely weak case in the tribunal, in the hope that the employer will make a settlement offer and with the intention of withdrawing before the hearing if no offer is forthcoming. The employer would be able to apply for costs for a misconceived case having been started and conducted up to the date of withdrawal. On the other hand, if the employee runs a reasonable case and withdraws for good reasons, costs should not be awarded just because s/he has withdrawn. The question is not whether the withdrawal of the claim is in itself unreasonable, but whether, in all the circumstances of the case, the employee has conducted the proceedings unreasonably.[219] Withdrawal can lead to costs savings and it would be unfortunate if claimants were deterred from dropping claims because of a fear of costs ordered due to the withdrawal.[220]

20.147   The ET can order the employee to pay some or all of the employer's costs (or vice versa). Unlike costs awarded due to an adjournment, costs are not confined to those incurred by the employer as a result of the employee's conduct.[221] The nature, gravity and effect of the worker's conduct are all relevant factors.[222]

---

216 *Ganase v Kent Community Housing Trust* UKEAT/1022/01.

217 As quoted with approval in *Lodwick v London Borough of Southwark* [2004] IRLR 554, CA.

218 *Ramsay & others v Bowercross Construction Ltd & others* UKEAT/0534-5/07; *McPherson v BNP Paribas (London Branch)* [2004] IRLR 558, CA.

219 *McPherson v BNP Paribas (London Branch)* [2004] IRLR 558, CA.

220 *McPherson v BNP Paribas (London Branch)* [2004] IRLR 558, CA.

221 ET Regs 2004 Sch 1 r40 and *McPherson v BNP Paribas (London Branch)* [2004] IRLR 558, CA.

222 *McPherson v BNP Paribas (London Branch)* [2004] IRLR 558, CA.

20.148   The amount of the costs must be assessed by the county court if above £10,000, ie independently adjudicated by the county court, unless agreed.[223] The employer's estimate of his/her costs should not be agreed unless it seems very low. It is worrying that the ET can order costs as high as £10,000 without formal assessment. Even so, the employer should be required to provide in advance an itemised schedule as to how the costs were incurred. Legal costs should be broken down by the standing and hourly rate of each fee earner and the type of activity, eg telephone, meetings, letters in and out, documents read. The ET may have regard to a party's ability to pay when considering whether to make a costs order or how much to order.[224] The ET can also take account of the fact that the claimant is represented by a trade union which is likely to pay any costs awarded against its members.[225]

20.149   A party can apply for costs at any time during the proceedings. The application can be made by writing to the tribunal or orally, at the end of a hearing. An application cannot generally be made later than 28 days from the issue of the final judgment in the case.[226] The paying party must be given the chance to comment before any order is made against him/her.[227] If costs are awarded against the employee, s/he is entitled to written reasons for the order, provided s/he requests the reasons within 14 days of the costs order.[228] The reason and basis for the order should be clearly specified by the ET, particularly when a substantial sum (in the thousands) is awarded[229] and the ET must explain how it calculated the costs.[230]

20.150   Although there is an occasionally used procedure for taking a costs deposit from a party where a case has little reasonable prospect of success,[231] costs may be awarded as set out above regardless of whether a deposit was ever required or even applied for. Nevertheless, if a deposit was ordered and the party has lost, s/he is at greater risk of a costs award. If the case is lost on substantially the same grounds as founded

223 ET Regs 2004 Sch 1 r41(1).
224 ET Regs 2004 Sch 1 r41(2). *Jilley v Birmingham and Solihull Mental Health NHS Trust* UKEAT/0584/06 and 0155/07.
225 *Walker v Heathrow Refuelling Services Co Ltd and others*, UKEAT/0366/04.
226 ET Regs 2004 Sch 1 r38(7).
227 ET Regs 2004 Sch 1 r38(9).
228 ET Regs 2004 Sch 1 r38(10).
229 *Lodwick v London Borough of Southwark* [2004] IRLR 554, CA.
230 *D36 Ltd v Castro* (2005) 754 IRLB, EAT.
231 See paras 20.92–20.94.

the decision to order a deposit, the ET must consider whether it was unreasonable of the party to have persisted with the case.[232]

20.151   Usually settlement negotiations are 'without prejudice', ie off the record as far as the ET is concerned. But some employers write a letter headed 'without prejudice save as to costs' or a completely open letter offering a certain sum. They threaten to draw this to the attention of the ET on the question of costs should the employee lose, or win and get a lesser award. Such letters are adapted from civil court practice, where costs are routinely awarded, and are known as '*Calderbank* offers'. The EAT has said they have no place in the ET system. However, general intransigence or pressing for an unreasonably high award after its excessiveness has been pointed out could amount to unreasonable behaviour and lead to costs.[233] The EAT has said in the past that an employee has an absolute right to have his/her unfair dismissal claim decided and an ET therefore should not award costs simply because the employee has turned down an open offer of compensation which turns out to equal or exceed the eventual ET award.[234] The position may be different if the employer concedes unfair dismissal. There is some contradiction between this principle and the more recent cases mentioned above considering *Calderbank* offers. Overall, the safest approach is for the employee to be seen to take a reasonable approach in running the case and in his/her approach to negotiations; there may be a difference between a reasonable unwillingness to settle at all unless unfairness is admitted, and a willingness to settle, but only for ridiculous figures.

20.152   ETs should not casually warn claimants of costs risks at the hearing if they pursue particular arguments or even their whole case. Costs are not routinely ordered and this is unfair pressure unless there truly is such a risk.[235]

Preparation time orders

20.153 A tribunal can make a preparation time order that the paying party makes a payment in respect of the preparation time of another party.

232 ET Regs 2004 Sch 1 r47.
233 *Monaghan v Close Thornton Solicitors* UKEAT/0003/01; May 2002 *Legal Action* 13. See also *Power v Panasonic (UK) Ltd* UKEAT/0439/04 and *Kopel v Safeway Stores plc* UKEAT/0281/02; (2003) 742 IDS Brief 7, EAT, although the claimants' whole approach was misconceived in those cases.
234 *Telephone Information Services v Wilkinson* [1991] IRLR 148, EAT; *Billany v Knutsford Conservative Club Bailli* case no: [2003] UKEAT 0065_03_0807.
235 *Gee v Shell UK Ltd* [2003] IRLR 82, CA.

An order may be made where the receiving party was not legally represented at the hearing or in proceedings determined without a hearing.[236] A costs order and a preparation time order cannot be made in favour of the same party.[237] Preparation time means time spent up to, but not including, the hearing by the party's legal or other advisers or by the party or his/her employees in relation to the proceedings.[238] The ET will assess the number of hours spent on preparation, based on its estimate of a reasonable and proportionate time to have spent on the particular case and information on time spent provided by the party claiming costs.[239] From 6 April 2009, an hourly rate of £29 has applied, going up by £1 annually each year on 6 April. The ET cannot order more than £10,000. The grounds for making a preparation time order and principles applicable are otherwise the same as for costs awards (para 20.142 onwards, above).

20.154 Preparation time orders were introduced with the new ET procedural rules in 2004. Apparently the purpose was to acknowledge the cost of tribunals to unrepresented parties and not-for-profit representatives. However, it is a lesser entitlement, both in terms of the hourly rate, and the fact that it excludes time at the hearing itself. There also appears to be an unintended gap, where an employee is represented at the hearing by a legally qualified representative on a not-for-profit basis, eg a solicitor employed in a law centre. If understood correctly, a preparation time order could be awarded if the law centre sent an unqualified representative, but not if it sent a solicitor or barrister. The alternative, a full costs order, is usually refused by tribunals on the ground that the worker does not 'incur' any costs when represented by a law centre. Case-law is complicated on this and there are various theories on ways around the problem, which are not within the scope of this book.

Wasted costs orders against representatives

20.155 An ET can order a representative to pay all or part of the wasted costs of any party, if these have been incurred as a result of any improper, unreasonable or negligent act or omission by the representative.[240]

236 ET Regs 2004 Sch 1 r42(2).
237 ET Regs 2004 Sch 1 r46(1); *Ramsay & others v Bowercross Construction Ltd & others* UKEAT/0534-5/07.
238 ET Regs 2004 Sch 1 r42(3).
239 ET Regs 2004 Sch 1 r45 sets out the calculation rules.
240 ET Regs 2004 Sch 1 r48.

A high standard of misconduct is required, not simply running a hopeless case or acting unreasonably or negligently, but having lent assistance to proceedings which amount to an abuse of the court.[241] Orders can be made against legal and non-legal representatives, but not against a representative who is not acting for profit with regard to the proceedings, eg a law centre or trade union representative. It does cover representatives acting on a contingency fee arrangement ('no win no fee'). The ET must give the representative an opportunity to comment before making an order and may take account of his/her ability to pay.

Settlement

ACAS, compromise agreements and consent orders

20.156   An ACAS officer is attached to most ET claims, including all unfair dismissal or discrimination claims, and has a statutory duty to promote a settlement. The ACAS officer usually contacts each party by letter or telephone and the claimant can choose whether to use him/her as an intermediary or negotiate direct with the employer. Communications to an ACAS officer are not admissible in evidence before the ET, unless the party expressly agrees.[242] Most settlements do not take place until each side has a better idea of the strengths of their case following the interim processes. In reality, most settlements occur shortly before the hearing itself. The role of ACAS is usually referred to as' conciliation' and the ACAS officer is a 'conciliation officer'. In the last few years, the option of 'mediation' has been introduced, either through ACAS or independent mediators or, in pilot schemes, through the tribunal. As this is most suited to discrimination claims, it is discussed in more detail at para 21.52.

20.157   The ACAS officer has no duty to see that the terms of a settlement are fair and must not advise on the merits of the claim.[243] There is therefore no need to enter into a discussion about the evidence and it is best to focus on issues of compensation. There is a risk that what is said to ACAS about the employee's case may be passed on to the employer's representative. Remember that the ACAS officer's job is to

---

241 *Mitchells Solicitors v Funkwerk Information Technologies York Ltd* UKEAT/0541/07.
242 Employment Tribunals Act 1996 s18(7).
243 *Clarke and ors v Redcar and Cleveland Borough Council; Wilson and ors v Stockton-on-Tees Borough Council* [2006] IRLR 324, EAT.

encourage settlement – it is not to worry about whether the employee has secured a good deal. There are many advantages in settling a claim, as it avoids the risk of losing, the unpleasantness of the hearing, the operation of the recoupment provisions and may be the only way to negotiate a good reference.

20.158   A settlement agreement reached through ACAS is recorded on a COT3 form and signed, but it is binding and effective as soon as it is verbally agreed, even if the form is never later signed.[244] It is essential to have clear instructions from the employee on whether to settle and on what terms and to be absolutely clear to ACAS when any discussion is subject to final confirmation. The COT3 form is used to record the settlement terms and is signed by the employee and employer or their representatives. ACAS will not normally rubber stamp a settlement if reached in direct negotiation with the employer's representative, but will accept some direct communications are necessary to clarify or hurry things along. Once there is a COT3 settlement, the ACAS officer notifies the ET. If the hearing date is very close, check that ACAS has done this and it may even be wise to write to the ET to confirm that an ACAS settlement has been reached.

20.159   Once the tribunal has been notified of a settlement, it sends out a letter stating that it has updated its records and closed its file; the file is kept in archive for one year and then destroyed. The tribunal does not issue an order or judgment in these circumstances. Many employers' representatives are uncomfortable with this and therefore insist on it being part of the settlement terms that the claimant writes to the tribunal asking for his/her case to be withdrawn.[245] If s/he wishes, the employer can then subsequently write to the tribunal asking for the claim to be dismissed. Alternatively, if the written settlement recorded by ACAS contains an agreement that the proceedings will, following withdrawal of the claim by the claimant be dismissed, the ET will automatically dismiss the proceedings on withdrawal.[246]

20.160   The important point is that the claimant does not agree to withdraw the claim until after the employer has paid the settlement sum. For example, 'the claimant undertakes to write to the tribunal withdrawing the claim within 7 days of payment of the settlement sum and meanwhile, the case is adjourned generally'. This preserves the claimant's right to reopen the case if the employer does not pay, or to sue for the agreed sum, whichever s/he thinks will most effectively

244 *Gilbert v Kembridge Fibres* [1984] IRLR 52, EAT.
245 Under ET Regs 2004 Sch 1 r25.
246 ET Regs 2004 Sch 1 r25A.

secure him/her the money. Some employers offer to pay only because they cannot face the idea of a tribunal hearing, but have no intention of actually paying up. The possibility of reopening the case can be important to make such employers honour the settlement.

20.161   Usually a settlement is not binding in respect of ET claims unless it is agreed through ACAS. However, ACAS need not be involved where a 'compromise agreement' is reached directly between the parties. A compromise agreement is a written agreement which relates to the employee's complaint before the ET and states that the employee has received independent advice from a qualified lawyer (a solicitor holding a practising certificate or a barrister who is covered by professional indemnity insurance), a legal executive, officers, officials or employees of an independent trade union who have been certified by the trade union as competent to give advice or an advice centre employee or volunteer who has been certified as competent to give advice. In these circumstances it will be a binding settlement.[247]

20.162   If a settlement is reached at the tribunal, eg on the morning of the hearing, it is important to get it validly written out and signed on the spot. If there are the appropriate representatives, a compromise agreement could be drafted. If not, an ordinary signed agreement could be made, although the employer is unlikely to find this satisfactory. The best option is to ask the tribunal to make a consent judgment, as this is the easiest to enforce in a county court if the employer does not pay.[248] The parties should write out the agreed terms, sign them and ask the tribunal to make an order. There are two ways to do this – either the terms are set out fully in the tribunal's order or they are set out in a schedule which is attached to the order. The latter option is preferable as it can contain matters outside the tribunal's jurisdiction, eg agreement to provide a reference, and it should avoid any risk of recoupment. The tribunal should then be asked to make a decision that the claim is stayed (or adjourned) pending payment. As explained above, this means the claimant can ask for the hearing to be relisted if the employer fails to pay and it maintains the incentive on the employer to comply with the settlement terms. Otherwise the claimant's only option will be to sue in the county court, which will take a long time and meanwhile the employer may even become insolvent. Typical wording for the order could be: 'Terms of settlement having been agreed between the parties, the claim is stayed against the respondent. Liberty

---

247 ERA 1996 s203.
248 See para 18.00 regarding enforcement..

for the claimant to restore on or before (date)[249] and if no application is received by that date, the claim is dismissed against the respondent upon withdrawal by the claimant'. Some tribunals will not agree to stay the claim and insist on withdrawal immediately, although it is not clear why they should not be able to adjourn the hearing as they might on any other ground. Wording then could be: 'Terms of settlement having been agreed between the parties (as annexed), the claim in case number (insert) is dismissed on withdrawal by the claimant'. Of course the actual terms of settlement also need to be written out and the clerk can be asked to make copies for the tribunal and each party.

The settlement terms

20.163 Care should be taken that the employee fully understands the implications and meaning of any settlement before an agreement is concluded. If possible, only the particular ET claim should be settled. In practice, many employers insist on a wider settlement, ie that in return for payment of the specified sum, the employee waives any other claim arising out of the contract of employment or its termination. Compromise agreements (although not necessarily COT3s) must precisely itemise the claims to be settled,[250] and may not be effective to exclude potential complaints which have not yet arisen.[251] As well as explaining to the employee precisely what a 'full and final' settlement means, it is safest to ask explicitly whether money is owing, eg in respect of wages, bonuses and commission, notice pay or holiday pay. Ask about the employee's health and whether s/he has had any accidents at work. Whatever his/her reply, there should be an express exclusion for any personal injury (PI) or industrial injury claims.[252] If there seems to be a potential PI claim, the employee should get advice on this before concluding a settlement. This is because the exclusion may not be sufficient to safeguard his/her right to bring such a claim or the employer may refuse to agree such an exclusion or to exclude any potential PI claims of which the employee is aware at the time of settlement. It may also be possible to do a global settlement including the value of the PI claim. In addition, there should be an explicit excep-

---

249 Usually one week after the payment date.
250 *Hinton v University of East London* [2005] IRLR 552, CA.
251 *Lunt v Merseyside TEC Ltd* [1999] IRLR 459, EAT, though doubted, probably wrongly, by *Hilton UK Hotels v McNaughton* 0059/04; 794 IDS Brief 3, EAT.
250 But see para 19.28 where settling discrimination claims.

tion for pension rights. ACAS officers often suggest the personal injury and pension exclusions in their standard wording.

20.164   It is advisable to specify in the COT3 or settlement agreement a date for payment. The actual wording of an agreed reference should be incorporated as well as the basis on which it will be supplied.[253] The following considerations should be taken into account:

- Does the employee wish to ask for an open ('to whom it may concern') reference as well as asking the employer to write a reference in the agreed terms on request?
- Does the employee wish to suggest that if the employer is asked for a verbal reference, s/he will only provide a written reference, or that s/he will respond verbally with the same content and spirit and without addition?
- Does the employee wish to suggest that if the employer is asked for a reference which asks specific questions, s/he may not answer at all, or s/he may answer if asked, or only with the employee's prior written consent, or that s/he will answer with the same spirit and content as the agreed terms and without addition? What should the employer say if asked for more information?
- It should be specified that the reference will be supplied on headed notepaper and duly signed and dated. The employee may wish to specify who should or who should not deal with reference requests.

It should be remembered that an employer cannot be asked to lie in a reference and can only be controlled so far. Often it is important to preserve some remnants of goodwill to improve the chances of fair behaviour in response to reference requests. Alternatively, it may focus the employer's mind, if s/he has asked for confidentiality, for example, to state that if the spirit or content of the reference agreement is not adhered to, then the employee will no longer be bound by confidentiality.

20.165   Employers often propose lengthy and complex settlement agreements with onerous and unsuitable terms. It is essential to understand what these mean and ensure the employee understands and consents.[254] An employee also needs to be advised of any tax implications and the effect of receiving a lump sum on any benefits currently claimed. The tax position on settlements may not be straightforward and is beyond the scope of this book. Very generally speaking, payments made wholly in respect of an unfair dismissal or discrimination

---

253 See appendix C, p771, for an example.
254 See appendix A, p738 for a checklist on settlement terms.

claim will be tax free as long as they do not exceed £30,000.[255] However, some parts of the settlement may comprise contractual earnings due, eg outstanding wages or holiday pay, which would be taxable in any event. Employers sometimes seek indemnities in respect of any tax which unexpectedly later becomes due. If the employee is in a strong position, s/he should insist the employer bears the risk of unforeseen tax. If the employee does agree to provide an indemnity, this certainly should not include an agreement to cover any tax penalties, interest or fines, resulting from the employer's default or slowness in dealing with the matter, or the employer's costs in dealing with HM Revenue & Customs, and the employee should reserve his/her right to make representations or challenge any liability or assessment with HMRC before the employer pays it.[256]

---

255 Income Tax (Earnings and Pensions) Act 2003 ss401 and 403. See also para 19.12 above regarding tax of the injury to feelings element in discrimination awards.

256 A useful article, Tax tips and traps on termination by Timothy Brennan is in the *Employment Lawyers Association Briefing*, Vol 14, No 6, July 2007, p91.

Running a discrimination case

continued

Chapter 21: Key points

- The procedure for running a discrimination case is basically the same as that for running an unfair dismissal case, but with greater emphasis on obtaining evidence.
- It is essential in a discrimination case to send the employer a questionnaire containing a set of questions to elicit evidence, especially information about comparators.
- There are time limits for service of the questionnaire. Ideally a questionnaire should be served well before any tribunal case is started.
- An employer cannot be forced to answer a questionnaire, but an employment tribunal should usually draw an adverse conclusion if the employer fails to answer fully or at all within eight weeks.
- The statutory dispute resolution procedures (applicable to employees) have been abolished but they may still apply to discrimination cases in transitional situations.
- There are strict time limits for starting a discrimination claim in the employment tribunal. Where there are several acts of discrimination or different legal claims, it is essential to think separately about the time limit and possible extension for each individual claim, as these may vary.
- Claims can be brought against individual discriminators as well as against the employer.
- Case management discussions are usually held in discrimination cases, which deal with matters such as what additional information and disclosure is needed. The discussions can be tricky to handle and it is important to be well-prepared.
- Restricted reporting orders can be obtained in cases involving sexual misconduct or offences, disability cases where evidence of a personal nature is given, and possibly other cases of particular sensitivity.
- The employment tribunal should be informed of and accommodate accessibility issues affecting any disabled party, witness or representative.
- The claimant usually gives evidence first in a discrimination case. S/he should be prepared for aggressive cross-examination by the respondent's representative.

21.1   In running discrimination cases, the basic principles are similar to those for unfair dismissal, dealt with in chapter 20 above. This chapter, which should be read in conjunction with chapter 20, highlights the procedural and technical differences that arise in cases under the Race Relations Act (RRA) 1976, Sex Discrimination Act (SDA) 1975, Disability Discrimination Act (DDA) 1995, Employment Equality (Sexual Orientation) Regulations (EE(SO) Regs) 2003[1] Employment Equality (Religion and Belief) Regulations (EE(RB) Regs) 2003[2] and Employment Equality (Age) Regulations (EE(A) Regs) 2006.[3] In addition, where the worker intends to claim compensation for injury to health or needs to prove s/he is disabled under the DDA 1995, s/he may need to obtain medical evidence at an early stage (see chapter 16). Claims relying on rights under directly effective EU law are made through the relevant domestic legislation and usual employment tribunal (ET) procedures apply.[4]

The questionnaire

21.2   Effective use of the special questionnaire procedure under discrimination law[5] offers an important opportunity to obtain information from which inferences may later be drawn.[6] It is very hard to win a discrimination case where no questionnaire has been submitted. Questionnaires are particularly necessary as a way to gather evidence which is not contained in documents and therefore cannot be obtained on disclosure. There are also several advantages of the procedure over the more limited potential of a request for additional information in respect of the ET3:

- any questions can be asked, not those limited to clarification of what is already in the ET3;
- questions may be detailed and concern matters of evidence;
- a questionnaire submitted at a very early stage can help decide whether a case should be pursued at all and, if so, how it should be formulated.

1 SI No 1661.

2 SI No 1660.

3 SI No 1031.

4 See paras 3.1–3.12.

5 RRA 1976 s65; SDA 1975 s74; DDA 1995 s56, Equal Pay Act (EqPA) 1970 s7B; EE(SO) Regs 2003 reg 33; EE(RB) Regs 2003 reg 33; and EE(A) Regs 2006 reg 41.

6 For detailed guidance on the questionnaire procedure and precedents, see specialist questionnaire guides listed in the bibliography at pp784–785 below.

Time limits

21.3 A questionnaire must be served on the employer within three months of the act of discrimination (or any extended time limit under the statutory dispute resolution procedures)[7], unless an ET1 has already been presented, in which case the questionnaire must be served within 21 days of the date of presentation (28 days under the DDA 1995).[8] The ET has a discretion to grant leave for service of a questionnaire out of time,[9] but it may refuse to do so or take the opportunity to reduce the permissible questions. The Employment Appeal Tribunal (EAT) has said that it is a 'sensible and necessary part of the procedure that a worker can ask leave to serve a follow-up questionnaire after the initial one, provided that notice is given to the employer of the request for leave so that s/he can argue that any question is 'unnecessary or too wide or oppressive'.[10] It may also be possible to elicit follow-up information via a request for additional information or disclosure, or if the employer is a public authority, by a freedom of information request (see para 1.179).

Procedure

21.4 Questionnaires are best submitted on the standard forms,[11] although in emergencies it is sufficient to accompany the questions with a statement of the alleged unlawful treatment on a letter headed, as appropriate, 'Race Relations (Questions and Replies) Order 1977 SI No 842', 'Sex Discrimination (Questions and Replies) Order 1975 SI No 2048' or 'Disability Discrimination (Questions and Replies) Order 1996 SI No

---

7 If they still apply.

8 Race Relations (Questions and Replies) Order 1977 SI No 842; Sex Discrimination (Questions and Replies) Order 1975 SI No 2048; Disability Discrimination (Questions and Replies) Order 2004 SI No 1168; EE(SO) Regs 2003 reg 33(4); EE(RB) Regs 2003 reg 33(4); EE(A) Regs 2006 reg 41(4); EqPA 1970 s7B.

9 SI No 842 article 5(b); SI No 2048 article 5(b); SI No 2793 article 3(b); EE(SO) Regs 2003 reg 33(4)(b)(ii); and EE(RB) Regs 2003 reg 33(4)(b)(ii).

10 *Carrington v Helix Lighting* [1990] IRLR 6, EAT. See also *National Grid Company v Virdee* [1992] IRLR 555 paras 44 and 46, EAT.

11 RRA 1976 s65; SDA 1975 s74; DDA 1995 s56; EqPA 1970 s7B. The RR65 form is available at www.equalityhumanrights.com/Documents/CRE/PDF/rr65.pdf The SD74 form is available at www.equalities.gov.uk/docs/Sex%20 Discrimination%20Questionnaire%20(SD74).doc The DL56 form is available at www.equalityhumanrights.com/Documents/Disability/Employment/DL56.pdf The sexual orientation, religion and age questionnaire forms are available on the BIS (formerly BERR) site under publications at www.berr.gov.uk/files/file25460.pdf, www.berr.gov.uk/files/file25462.pdf and www.berr.gov.uk/files/file32724.pdf respectively.

2793', etc. It is advisable to send the questionnaire by recorded delivery to the employer, marked for the attention of a particular person, eg the managing director or head of human resources.

21.5   The questions and answers are admissible as evidence at the hearing. Unlike with additional information and disclosure, the ET cannot make an order compelling the respondent to answer the questionnaire. Many employers do not realise this and it is worth fostering the illusion by requesting an answer within 14 days of service. The only sanction is the ET's ability to draw an inference from the failure to reply within eight weeks.[12] Originally no timescale was suggested in the legislation, but an eight-week period was introduced for questionnaires relating to sexual orientation, sex, age, religion, equal pay and race, ethnic or national origins. This is a pity. Eight weeks is far longer than necessary or useful and does put a premium on serving questionnaires at a very early stage.

21.6   An inference can also be drawn from an evasive or equivocal reply. If the employer does not reply after a chasing letter or if s/he replies selectively, another letter should be written, stating that the failure to reply adequately will be drawn to the attention of the ET which will be invited to draw an adverse inference.[13] Failure to answer the questionnaire properly should be taken very seriously by the ET.[14]

Drafting the questionnaire

21.7   The questionnaire form contains two standard printed questions, but the main point is to think of additional questions, which can be set out at (or attached to) the standard paragraph 4 (equal pay, age, religion and sexual orientation questionnaires) or paragraph 6 (race, sex or disability questionnaires). Broadly speaking, questions fall into three categories:

a) those concerning the facts and circumstances of the particular treatment of the worker bringing the claim;

b) questions to discover how other workers have been treated in similar circumstances and, in particular to find out comparable details of any comparator and how s/he has been treated; and

c) general (normally statistical and procedural) questions about the workplace revealing how the employer treats other workers.[15]

12 See paras 16.45 and 16.48.

13 See p711 for an example.

14 See para 16.45; *Igen Ltd and others v Wong; Chamberlin Solicitors and another v Emokpae; Brunel University v Webster* [2005] IRLR 258, CA.

15 See appendix A pp700–710 for examples and tips on drafting questionnaires.

As a general rule, it is useful to ask in respect of any major decision affecting a worker (eg dismissal), who made the decision, when and for what reasons.

21.8 Since an ET may draw an inference only if the employer had no reasonable excuse for failing to answer a questionnaire adequately and if it is just and equitable to do so,[16] it is important not to hand the employer an easy excuse by drafting an unclear or unreasonable questionnaire. Employers often say they cannot answer the questions because they do not understand in what way they are alleged to have discriminated. This objection is illogical and runs counter to one of the main purposes of the procedure: to assist in the formulation of the claim. Unfortunately it is an objection which frequently wins sympathy in the ET and therefore the statement at paragraph 1 (equal pay, age, religion or sexual orientation questionnaires) or paragraph 2 (race, sex or disability questionnaires) of the questionnaire form should clarify the allegations as far as possible.

21.9 The facts set out eventually in the ET1 should normally be identical to paragraph 1 or paragraph 2 of the questionnaire. Certainly no key facts should be omitted from either statement, as the worker is likely to be cross-examined on any difference between the statements and any difference between either statement and his/her oral evidence. If the information requested in the questionnaire is too wide-ranging and/or difficult to collate, it will irritate the ET and provide an easy excuse for the employer not to answer. Either the extent of the requested statistics should be confined from the outset to the minimum necessary, or at a later stage the employer can be offered the opportunity of providing more limited information if s/he raises this objection. In particular, it should be carefully considered over what period, at what intervals and within what geographical or departmental area to request statistics. Where the employer objects that statistics are not kept, s/he can be asked whether information is kept on computer or, with smaller employers, suggest a head-count.

21.10 Either at the outset, or after an employer objects that certain information is confidential, it may be possible to agree that names of other workers be deleted.[17] However, sometimes it is not possible to disguise the identity of other workers, especially where particular comparators are the subject of enquiry. A particular problem may arise if

---

16 RRA 1976 s65(2)(b); SDA 1975 s74(2)(b); DDA 1995 s56(3)(b); EE(SO) Regs 2003 reg 33(2)(b); EE(RB) Regs 2003 reg 33(2)(b); EE(A) Regs 2006 reg 41(2)(b).
17 See para 21.44 below for confidentiality in relation to disclosure.

the employer objects to providing information regarding named comparators due to the Data Protection Act (DPA) 1998.[18] The prime response to this is that disclosure is allowed for the purpose of actual or prospective legal proceedings under DPA 1998 s35(2) as well as for establishing legal rights. Further, though this is superfluous, disclosure is allowed where the persons referred to give explicit consent. An allegedly worried employer should therefore be invited to seek such consent. The employer may also dispense with such consent where reasonable.[19]

21.11   Race and colour are vague concepts which usually require clarification. To avoid misunderstanding or deliberate evasion in response to questionnaires under the RRA 1976, it should be specified under which 'racial categories' information is to be provided. For example, where there is any doubt whether the employer discriminates solely against African/Caribbeans or against all non-whites or only against workers born abroad, the questions should cover all the options. This is especially important given the two-tier rights under the RRA 1976, where the worker may wish to claim discrimination on grounds of race as well as colour, or national origins as well as nationality. This suggests that statistics should be asked in all the relevant categories, even though the employer may not have monitored each separately.

21.12   A worker can choose whether to send the questionnaire to the employer before or after s/he has started an ET case. It is usually best to send the questionnaire long before lodging the ET1. This forces employers to answer before they can counter-attack by asking the worker to give more information regarding his/her claim. In general, sending the questionnaire as early as possible enables the worker to keep the initiative on the case and ensures there is time before the hearing to follow up the information provided. Also, if an ET is to draw an adverse inference from an employer's failure to answer a lengthy questionnaire adequately, it should be served sufficiently in advance of the hearing for the employer to be expected to collate the information. The other advantage of an early questionnaire is that the reply should be received before the deadline for starting a tribunal case. This enables the worker to make a more informed decision on the chances of success, whether to go ahead and on what grounds.

---

18 See paras 1.56–1.74 and particularly paras 1.63–1.68.

19 DPA 1998 s7(4)–(5). See sample letter at p712 and more detailed comments in the Questionnaire Guides referred to at n6 above.

The tribunal claim (ET1)

The time limit

21.13 The ET1 must be presented within three months of the act of discrimination (or any extended time limit under the statutory dispute resolution procedures, if they still apply in the particular case). Earlier incidents can be referred to as supporting evidence.[20] If further discrimination takes place against a worker who is still employed after s/he has started an ET case, in theory it should be possible to amend the original ET1 to add the later claims.[21] However, it is probably safer to lodge a new ET1 within the time limit and ask for the two cases to be considered together.

21.14 The act of discrimination is not always easy to identify, so advisers must be alert about the time limit. Time usually runs from when a decision not to promote or appoint is made (not when it is communicated),[22] or from when a warning is given, and not from the end of any appeal or grievance procedure. However, if the failure of the grievance procedure or appeal was itself on grounds of race, religion, sex, sexual orientation, age or related to disability, then that is a further act of discrimination from which another three-month period runs. It is unwise to rely on this to extend time, as usually it is the original action which constituted the discrimination, not the decision on appeal or grievance, which tends to be a rubber-stamping exercise. Therefore if there is a lengthy appeal or grievance process, it is important not to allow the original incident to fall out of time.

21.15 Apart from under the RRA 1976 in respect of nationality (and possibly colour), a worker who resigns can claim that the constructive dismissal was itself an act of discrimination.[23] In respect of nationality (and colour), case-law is divided as to whether constructive dismissal is covered in itself, or whether the worker can only claim in respect of the discriminatory actions which prompted the resignation. In the latter instance, time limits would have to be counted from the employer's actions not from the date the worker resigned.[24]

---

20 *Eke v Commissioners of Customs and Excise* [1981] IRLR 334, EAT.

21 *Okugade v Shaw Trust* UKEAT/0172/05; *Prakash v Wolverhampton City Council* UKEAT/0140/06.

22 *Virdi v Commissioner of Police of the Metropolis and another* [2007] IRLR 24, EAT; May 2007 *Legal Action* 15.

23 RRA 1976 s4(4A)(b); SDA 1975 s82(1A)(b); DDA 1995 s4(5)(b); EE(SO) Regs 2003 reg 6(5)(b); EE(RB) Regs 2003 reg 6(5)(b); EE(A) Regs 2006 reg 7(7)(b).

24 *Commissioner of Police of the Metropolis v Harley* [2001] IRLR 263; November 2001 *Legal Action* 18, EAT.

21.16   In some situations, discrimination continues over a period of time, sometimes up to the date of leaving employment. The time for lodging an ET1 then runs from the end of that period.[25] The common, although technically inaccurate, name for this is 'continuing discrimination'. Advisers should be careful if relying on showing continuing discrimination for time limit purposes as it is sometimes hard to distinguish it from a single act of discrimination with continuing effects. For example, a failed promotion attempt resulting in continued employment at a lower grade and wage is not in itself continuing discrimination.[26] If a worker is out of time, s/he should make another attempt at promotion on which it may be appropriate to base a claim provided this latest failure also appears discriminatory on the facts. On the other hand, if an employer maintained a rule that only workers of a particular race or sex would be promoted to certain posts, that would be continuing discrimination.

21.17   In *Calder v James Finlay Corporation Ltd*,[27] a woman was twice refused a mortgage subsidy from her employer which was available to men. The EAT said that although the unsuccessful requests took place more than three months prior to her claim, the rules of the scheme barring women constituted a discriminatory act extending throughout Mrs Calder's employment until she left. Similarly, in *Barclays Bank v Kapur*,[28] the employer kept in force 'a discriminatory regime' throughout the workers' employment in that their past service in banks in Africa was not credited towards their pensionable service. The ET had jurisdiction to hear the claim even though the workers entered the discriminatory scheme several years earlier, which was when the decision not to include their service was taken.

21.18   The *Calder* and *Kapur* cases concerned formal rules which were discriminatory. This principle was taken further in *Owusu v London Fire and Civil Defence Authority*.[29] Mr Owusu, a clerical worker, complained of the failure to regrade him at any stage since his transfer several years earlier and the failure to let him act-up when such opportunities arose (all of which had arisen more than three months before he lodged his tribunal claim). The EAT accepted there could be a continuing act of discrimination if Mr Owusu proved a discriminatory

---

25 RRA 1976 s68(7); SDA 1975 s76(6); DDA 1995 Sch 3 para 3; EE(RB) Regs 2003 reg 34(4)(b); EE(SO) Regs 2003 reg 34(4)(b); EE(A) Regs 2006 reg 42(4)(b).
26 *Amies v ILEA* (1976) 121 SJ 11; [1977] ICR 308, EAT.
27 [1989] IRLR 55, EAT.
28 [1989] IRLR 387, CA; [1991] IRLR 136; (1991) 36 EOR 33, HL.
29 [1995] IRLR 574, EAT.

policy, rule or practice (however informal) which, when followed or applied, excluded him from regrading or acting-up opportunities. However, it would be necessary to prove a linking practice as opposed to a series of one-off decisions, even if they were each discriminatory.

21.19   The *Owusu* case was approved of by the Court of Appeal in *Cast v Croydon College*,[30] which confirmed that there could be a continuing policy or regime, even if it was not formal or written, and even if it was only confined to one post or role. Mrs Cast asked her line manager before she went on maternity leave whether she could return to work afterwards on a part-time or job-share basis. He refused, even though the college had a written policy generally receptive to job-sharing at all levels. Mrs Cast unsuccessfully repeated her request to her manager twice after her return. A few months later she resigned. Subsequently she lodged her ET claim. The ET said that the time limit was three months from the first refusal, before Mrs Cast even went on maternity leave. Mrs Cast's claim was therefore well out of time. The Court of Appeal disagreed. It said that the several refusals of Mrs Cast's request indicated the existence of a discriminatory policy in relation to her post (manager of the college's information centre). This policy continued until Mrs Cast left and her claim was therefore in time, regardless of the date of any particular request and refusal.

21.20   The Court of Appeal also considered the position if there had not been a continuing policy or practice, but simply a succession of independent refusals. Any refusal within the last three months would be in time provided it was the result of a fresh consideration by the employer (even if it was a decision made by the same manager and on the same facts). On the other hand, if the manager simply referred back to his previous decision or expanded on his reasons, this would not be a fresh consideration, and time would run from the earlier decision. Mrs Cast therefore had an alternative argument that the time limit should be counted from the last (and not the first) of her line manager's refusals.[31]

21.21   The most useful case of all is *Hendricks v Commissioner of Police of the Metropolis*,[32] where the Court of Appeal further extended the *Owusu* principle. It said a worker need not be restricted to proving a

---

30 [1998] IRLR 318; (1998) 80 EOR 49, CA.

31 See also *Akhtar v Family Services Unit* (1996) 70 EOR 56, CA, and the slightly different approach in a non-employment case, *Rovenska v General Medical Council* [1997] IRLR 367, CA.

32 [2003] IRLR 96; May 2003 *Legal Action* 20, CA, confirmed by *Lyfar v Brighton and Sussex University Hospitals Trust* [2006] EWCA Civ 1548; May 2007 *Legal Action* 15, CA.

discriminatory policy, rule, regime or practice, if s/he could show that a sequence of individual incidents were evidence of a 'continuing discriminatory state of affairs'. In other words, Ms Hendricks must prove a general link between the incidents so that they amounted to 'an act of discrimination extending over a period', as opposed to a succession of unconnected and isolated specific acts. Her case was in fact unusual and extreme. She was complaining of nearly 100 incidents of bullying and harassment by a large number of colleagues over an 11-year period and ongoing discrimination by management in failing to give support and unjust appraisals. If there is continuing discrimination, the continuing act is not broken by absences, eg on holiday or maternity leave during which nothing happens.[33]

21.22   A close sequence of discriminatory actions, eg a series of threats, warnings and abuse, as is common in harassment cases, may well constitute continuing discrimination in the legal sense, although to be safe the ET claim should be lodged within three months of each incident. In practice, it is usually enough if the most serious incidents (and those easiest to prove) are in time. The other actions can still be referred to as supporting evidence. In this kind of case, the ET is also likely to be sympathetic to exercising its discretion to allow in late claims; even more so if there is medical evidence of the worker's distressed state of mind.

21.23   In harassment cases, time limits are often missed because, for example, the worker goes off sick and then resigns. No further acts of discrimination are likely to have occurred during the worker's absence, but an adviser may mistakenly calculate the three months from the resignation rather than from the last incident at work.[34] Another trap into which advisers can fall occurs where the harassment stops once the worker complains, but the employer takes some time to investigate and the longer-term outcome is unsatisfactory. By the time the worker realises s/he is unhappy with the solution, three months may have passed from the harassment itself.[35]

21.24   A discriminatory act may consist of an omission to do something, eg failure to promote a worker on racial grounds or failure to make a

---

33 *Spencer v H M Prison Service* UKEAT/0812/02/MH; (2004) 132 EOR 27; November 2004 *Legal Action* 18, EAT.

34 Although *Spencer v H M Prison Service* (above) may help.

35 Continuing failure to implement promised remedial measures may amount to continuing discrimination, thus extending the time limit: *Littlewoods Organisation plc v Traynor* [1993] IRLR 154; (1993) 49 EOR 35, EAT. The ambit of this decision is unclear and advisers should still be careful, especially given the principles in the following paragraph.

reasonable adjustment. A deliberate omission takes place on the date the discriminator decides on it. In the absence of any specific evidence, this means the date when the discriminator takes any step inconsistent with doing the omitted act or otherwise, the date by which s/he might reasonably have been expected to do the omitted act.[36] This is most likely to come up under the DDA 1995 where the worker claims for failure to make reasonable adjustments. To be safe on time limits, it would be wise to submit any ET claim within three months of the date when the employer first refuses to make the required adjustment or, if earlier, when it might reasonably be expected that the adjustment would have been made. If in doubt, count the three months from when the employer should first have become aware of the need for the adjustment.

21.25 The case-law on time limits and on out-of-time claims (below) shows a reluctance by the higher courts to be rigid about time limits in discrimination cases. But it can still be a source of major difficulty in the ETs. Employers tend to argue fiercely that as many incidents as possible are out of time. Although several of the above cases may come to the rescue where a worker seems to be out of time, it is still far easier to run and prove a case where the relevant incidents occurred within the last three months. For example, the concept of continuing discrimination may seem to rescue a situation, but in fact it is much harder to prove that there is a linking practice, than that discrimination occurred on separate occasions.

Claims outside the time limit

21.26 An ET may allow a claim outside the time limit if it is just and equitable to do so.[37] This is a wider and therefore more commonly granted discretion than for unfair dismissal claims. The ET must weigh up the reasons for and against extending time and explain its thinking.[38] An ET ought to consider the checklist under Limitation Act 1980 s33, suitably modified for ET cases, although the ET will not make a mistake as

---

36 RRA s68(7); SDA s76(6); DDA 1995 Sch 3 para 3(3) and (4); EE(SO) Regs 2003 reg 34(4); EE(RB) Regulations 2003 reg 34(4); EE(A) Regs 2006 reg 42(4); *Matuszowicz v Kingston upon Hull City Council* [2009] EWCA Civ 22; [2009] IRLR 288, CA.

37 RRA 1976 s68(6); SDA 1975 s76(5); DDA 1995 Sch 3 para 3(2); EE(SO) Regs 2003 reg 34(3); EE(RB) Regs 2003 reg 34(3); EE(A) Regs 2006 reg 42(3).

38 *Osaje v Camden LBC* (1997) EAT/317/96; November 1997 *Legal Action* 16; *Arube v Devon Probation Service* [2001] IRLB 14, EAT, May 2001 *Legal Action* 14.

long as it does not omit a significant factor.[39] The factors to take into account under the Limitation Act 1980 (as modified) are these:

- the length of, and reasons for, the worker's delay;
- the extent to which the strength of the evidence of either party might be affected by the delay;
- the employer's conduct after the cause of action arose, including his/her response to requests by the worker for information or documents to ascertain the relevant facts;
- the extent to which the worker acted promptly and reasonably once s/he knew whether or not s/he had a legal case;
- the steps taken by the worker to get expert advice and the nature of the advice s/he received. A mistake by the worker's legal adviser should not be held against the worker[40] and appears to be a valid excuse.

The ET should consider whether the employer is 'prejudiced' by the lateness,[41] ie whether the employer was already aware of the allegation and so not caught by surprise, and whether any harm is done to the employer or to the chances of a fair hearing by the element of lateness. Where the delay is because the worker first tried to resolve the matter through use of an internal grievance procedure, this is just one factor for the ET to take into account.[42] If the delay was because the worker tried to pursue the matter in correspondence before rushing to an ET, this should also be considered.[43] Where the claimant has a mental disability, a tribunal may choose to take account of the fact that s/he was reluctant to admit to him/herself that s/he had a disability or that severe depression made it difficult for him/her to make decisions about taking legal action.[44] An ET will probably also take into account the apparent strength of the case.

21.27   Where a claim is outside the time limit because a material fact emerges much later, eg the job for which a black worker applied is filled several months later by a white person with lesser qualifications or experience, an ET should consider whether it was reasonable of

---

39 *Chohan v Derby Law Centre* [2004] IRLR 685, EAT.

40 *Chohan v Derby Law Centre* [2004] IRLR 685, EAT; *Virdi v Commissioner of Police of the Metropolis and another* [2007] IRLR 24; May 2007 *Legal Action* 15, EAT.

41 *Osaje v Camden LBC* (1997) EAT/317/96; November 1997 *Legal Action* 16; *Arube v Devon Probation Service* [2001] RLB 14, EAT, May 2001 *Legal Action* 14.

42 *Apelogun-Gabriels v Lambeth LBC and another* [2002] IRLR 116, CA.

43 *Osaje v Camden LBC* (1997) EAT/317/96; November 1997 *Legal Action* 16.

44 *Department of Constitutional Affairs v Jones* [2008] IRLR 128, CA; *Legal Action* May 2008 and *Carter v (1) London Underground Ltd (2) Transport for London* UKEAT/0292/08 respectively.

the worker not to realise s/he had a prima facie case until this happened.[45] Alternatively, it could be argued that the claim is not out of time at all because the act of discrimination has not 'crystallised', ie finally taken place, until the eventual appointment.[46] This is rather an unusual argument and should not be relied on.

21.28   It is often worth trying to get in an out-of-time claim, if the above factors are persuasive, as some ETs are prepared to exercise their discretion favourably. In particular, where there are several discriminatory acts, with only the most recent in time, the ET may well grant leave to allow in the earlier acts. This is especially so where the earlier acts will be raised in the case anyway as matters of evidence supporting the latest claim.[47] In this type of case, the ET1 should be clearly drafted so that it is plain that the earlier discriminatory acts are meant to be claims in their own right and not just supporting evidence.

21.29   It is also wise expressly to ask permission in the ET1 for the earlier claims to be allowed in under the ET's discretion. However, whether or not this request is made in the ET1 itself, it should be sought by the worker's representative at the very latest at the start of the hearing. The onus is on the worker's representative to seek permission. The ET is not obliged to offer to use its discretion and if nothing is said, the earlier acts may be treated purely as evidence.[48] Frequently, however, the question will already have been dealt with during the preparation of the case.

21.30   At a case management discussion, the ET may order the worker to set out which of the claimed incidents of discrimination are in time.[49] The ET may also order a pre-hearing review to make decisions on whether part or all of the claim is in time. However, if the main incident is in time and the earlier incidents will be heard as evidence anyway, a pre-hearing review is unnecessary as it will make no difference to the ground covered by the final hearing.[50] The ET can decide after it has heard all the evidence at the final hearing whether to allow in the earlier incidents as grounds of the claim. Also, if the worker alleges continuing discrimination on the *Hendricks* principle (see para 21.21 above), the ET cannot decide at a pre-hearing review whether the evidence proves the discriminatory incidents were in fact linked.

45 *Clarke v Hampshire Electro-Plating Co Ltd* [1991] IRLR 490, EAT.
46 *Clarke v Hampshire Electro-Plating Co Ltd* [1991] IRLR 490, EAT.
47 Chapter 16 on relevant evidence, para 16.12 on other acts of discrimination.
48 *Dimtsu v Westminster CC* [1991] IRLR 450, EAT.
49 See p722 for sample written submission on time limits.
50 The EAT in *Sutcliffe v Big C's Marine* [1998] IRLR 428 and the Court of Appeal in *Smith v Gardner Merchant Ltd* [1998] IRLR 510 at 512 have both commented against the general desirability of having pre-hearing reviews in this context.

Statutory dispute resolution procedures

21.31 The statutory dispute resolution procedures described in chapter 22 used to apply to discrimination cases in some situations, although not where the claimant was not an employee of the respondent.[51] The procedures have now been abolished, but because of complicated transitional provisions, they may still apply to a particular case. The procedures allow an extension of tribunal time limits in certain circumstances, which can lead to complicated calculations in claims concerning several discriminatory actions. Add to this the rules on the transitional provisions and there are real dangers of making a mistake. For more details and examples, see chapter 22. Meanwhile bear in mind these dangers:

- a claim concerning a discriminatory warning and dismissal will have different time limit rules for each action, since the warning is covered by the statutory grievance procedure and the dismissal by the DDP.
- where a claim regarding discrimination during work is made both against an individual respondent and against the employing organisation, the grievance procedure and thus extension of time applies to the latter claim but not to the former.[52]
- similarly, where a claim regarding discrimination during work is brought by a contract worker[53] against both his/her employer and the principal for which s/he works, the statutory grievance procedure applies in respect of the claim against the employer and the time limit is extended by three months, but it does not apply to the simultaneous claim against the principal.

Time limits on EU claims

21.32 Complex questions arise with regard to time limits where a worker can claim directly under EU law. A discussion of the legal position on this is beyond the scope of this book.[54]

---

51 See also para 22.46 regarding discrimination by fellow employees.

52 *Bisset v Martins and Castlehill Housing Association Ltd; Martins v Bisset and Castlehill Housing Association Ltd* UKEAT/0022/06 and UKEAT/0023/06.

53 See para 13.14.

54 *Harvey* (see p787 below) deals with this issue. Useful cases include *Emmott v Minister for Social Welfare* [1991] IRLR 387; [1993] ICR 8, ECJ; *Biggs v Somerset CC* [1996] IRLR 203, CA; *Preston v Wolverhampton Healthcare NHS Trust (No 2)* [2001] IRLR 237, HL.

Drafting the ET1

21.33 See paras 20.36–20.37 above for details regarding the standard forms (ET1) for tribunal claims. At box 5.2 of the new form and 6.2 of the old form, the claimant is asked to describe the incidents (with dates) which s/he believes amounted to discrimination.

21.34 It is very important to be sure about the extent of the worker's claim and set it out correctly from the outset. The ET may not allow any amendments of the ET1 later, especially to add entirely new grounds.[55]

21.35 If the worker is claiming indirect discrimination or victimisation as well as direct discrimination, s/he must specify this.[56] Equally, if s/he is complaining of discriminatory treatment during employment and on dismissal, it needs to be clear whether s/he is saying the dismissal is some form of discrimination or victimisation, or whether it is purely an unfair dismissal. As long as the worker has clearly described all the relevant facts in a way which makes it clear what s/he is claiming, s/he should be allowed to amend later to add the correct legal label. For example, if the worker wrote on the ET1 that s/he alleged sex discrimination in promotion and that is what led to the subsequent dismissal, s/he should be able to add the label 'victimisation' later. Conversely, there may be difficulty amending if all the employee has done is describe the discriminatory promotion, his/her complaints and the subsequent dismissal, without making any link.

21.36 The safest route is to think through the case and get it right from the outset. Even if the ET does allow later amendments, the original version of the ET1 will still be visible and any significant changes will damage the worker's credibility.

21.37 If victimisation is claimed, the protected act should be cited. In indirect discrimination claims, because of the uncertainty about which provision, criterion or practice, requirement or condition and which pool the ET will approve, it is probably best to express the claim in broad or alternative terms. All key matters on which the worker will rely should be mentioned concisely in the tribunal claim with dates. It is important to include any racist or sexually offensive remarks. However, if workers do omit to mention historic incidents in their ET1 which provide further supporting evidence of discrimination, they should not be debarred from including such evidence for the first time in their witness statement for the hearing.[57] Nevertheless, this is a dangerous

---

55 See paras 20.42–20.43 for general principles regarding amendments.

56 *Office for National Statistics v Ali* [2005] IRLR 201; (2005) 137 EOR 25; May 2005 *Legal Action* 25, CA.

57 *Senyonjo v Trident Safeguards Ltd* UKEAT/0316/04.

strategy and may lead to an award of costs against them for unreasonable conduct of the proceedings. If unfair dismissal is being claimed in addition to discrimination, this should be added in a separate paragraph specifying in which way the dismissal was unfair, to clarify that it is recognised as a different issue.[58]

21.38   As there are two-tier rights under the RRA 1976,[59] it is usually advantageous for the worker to claim on grounds of race or ethnic or national origins, as opposed to purely on grounds of colour or nationality (assuming this is possible on the facts). Depending on the facts, the worker can (for example) simply refer to 'race' discrimination in the ET1.[60] If s/he is later required to be more specific, s/he can state the discrimination was on grounds of race and/or colour and/or ethnic origin.

21.39   If the worker has mentioned an actual comparator in the ET1, s/he should still preserve the right to argue that s/he has been less favourably treated than a hypothetical comparator would have been.[61]

Naming individual respondents

21.40   In the questionnaire and in the ET1, individuals may be named as respondents, as well as the employing organisation. The latter should always be named, but whether the former are added depends on several considerations.

- Naming individuals ensures that the claim succeeds against somebody if the employing organisation might escape liability because the employer took all reasonably practicable steps to prevent the discrimination happening.[62] If the claim succeeds against the employer and named individuals, the award can be made enforceable in its entirety against any of the respondents.[63] This is the most obvious reason for naming individuals. Therefore if during the course of the case, the employing organisation accepts vicarious liability for any discriminatory actions of the discriminator, the ET often puts pressure on the worker to withdraw the claim against individuals. However, as set out below, there are other powerful reasons why the individuals should remain as respondents. An ET should not be allowed simply to strike out the case against

58 See para 20.38 onwards for drafting an ET1 in unfair dismissal claims.
59 See para 13.23.
60 See p711 for a sample pleading.
61 See para 16.19 on comparators and p711 for a sample pleading.
62 See para 13.20.
63 See para 19.11.

individual respondents at a case management discussion without the worker's consent: this is a judicial decision which should be handled appropriately and would require grounds.[64]

- It usually ensures that the named individuals will give evidence at the hearing, so the desirability of their attendance must be considered.

- In harassment cases, it is possible that the employer will require the individual to obtain separate representation in case there is a conflict of interest. The worker may gain useful additional or conflicting information from separated sources.

- In harassment cases, it ensures the individual perpetrator is personally accountable and unable to hide behind the employer. An element of compensation (or part of any settlement) may also be awarded (or agreed) against the perpetrator.

- Where there has been deliberate and malicious discrimination, costs may be awarded against an individual respondent for unreasonably defending the proceedings.[65] This is valuable because, where, as is common, the employer supports and funds the individual's case, it can be implied that s/he has underwritten the individual's costs,[66] including those ordered against the individual. However, where the individual is not joined as respondent, unless it can be argued that the principle of vicarious liability extends to vicarious liability for the conduct of proceedings, the employer could avoid a costs order by claiming that s/he was entitled to rely on statements from the individual that s/he (the individual) had not discriminated.

- If the employing organisation is likely to go into liquidation with no funds for unsecured creditors, it ensures that the claim can proceed[67] and that there is a likelihood of recovering money, assuming the named individual has any assets. If the employing organisation goes into liquidation or ceases trading completely unexpectedly and no individual respondent has been named, the claimant can try to join an individual respondent at a later stage.[68]

---

64 See para 21.53 on the ET's powers to strike out parts of the claim.

65 See para 20.142 onwards on costs.

66 *Bourne v Colodense* [1985] ICR 291; [1985] IRLR 339, CA.

67 Leave from the High Court may be necessary to proceed against a company in liquidation or administration, depending on the type of insolvency or liquidation proceedings.

68 Employment Tribunal (Constitution and Rules of Procedure) Regulations (ET Regs) 2004 SI No 1861 Sch 1 r10(2)(k).

- Individuals should be named as respondents only if there is a strong case against them, as the ET will be reluctant to make a specific finding against them. Caution should be used in naming more than one individual since ETs react badly to any suggestion of a conspiracy. There may also be a risk of costs if naming certain individuals appears frivolous, vexatious, unreasonable or misconceived.

Written reasons for dismissal

21.41 Where the alleged act of discrimination is dismissal, a worker should usually request written reasons under Employment Rights Act (ERA) 1996 s92 provided s/he was an employee and had sufficient service.[69] In discrimination cases this may be a particularly significant piece of evidence. Even if the reply is received within the 14 days, one should always add an ERA 1996 s92 claim to the ET1 since, if the discrimination is proved, the worker is very likely to receive an award for untrue reasons.

Case management

Additional information and written answers

21.42 The considerations and procedure are the same as for unfair dismissal.[70] However, in discrimination cases it is especially important to secure as much information as possible of the employer's defence and this opportunity should not be lost. Although questions cannot be as free-ranging as on the questionnaire (see para 21.2 above), the advantage is that the ET can be asked to order the employer to reply.

21.43 The employer often asks the worker to provide very detailed additional information regarding his/her claim. For comments on this, see para 21.50 below.

Disclosure

21.44 Disclosure of documents is a crucial part of the information gathering process in most discrimination cases.[71] The ET will not permit wide, trawling exercises for helpful evidence. What will be relevant and useful needs to be thought out (see a sample at pp712–713 below).

69 See para 20.11.
70 See paras 20.58–20.61.
71 See also paras 20.62–20.66 for general principles.

If documents are necessary for disposing fairly of a case or for saving costs, the ET should order their disclosure, even if they are confidential.[72] Where there is a problem about confidentiality, the ET can look privately at the documents to see if they are necessary and to decide whether the same information can be obtained in any other way.

21.45 If an ET refuses to order disclosure of something important, one should write asking the same Employment Judge to reconsider the decision, explaining why the disclosure is needed and citing any relevant case-law.[73] It may be best to request an oral hearing and to give notice to the employer of the request. The EAT has said that given the evidential difficulties in discrimination cases, tribunals should be generous in orders for disclosure against the employers. Such cases are not the same as normal litigation, where a party must make out a credible case before the process of disclosure begins.[74] If the ET continues to refuse disclosure, unless there are powerful grounds for appeal, it is often best to request the document again during the final hearing, when it becomes clear whether it is relevant. This is feasible in discrimination cases because they tend to last several days.

21.46 The ET can order disclosure of relevant statistics provided that they do not relate solely to the question of the employer's credit, but go to an issue in the case, eg whether the employer, intentionally or otherwise, operated a discriminatory policy which manifested itself on other occasions and may have manifested itself in respect of the present complaint.[75]

21.47 The disclosure process usually refers to documents. However, for the sake of convenience, the ET can order that the employer supply a digest of information contained in bulky documents. In this way, information generally only available from a questionnaire can be made the subject of an order for disclosure. Where the statistical information is known to the employer but is not contained in existing documents, the ET cannot order the employer to draw up such a schedule under the disclosure procedure.[76] It may be possible to obtain an order for such information by way of a written answer or as additional information.

72 *Nassé v Science Research Council; Vyas v Leyland Cars* [1979] IRLR 465; [1979] ICR 921, HL.

73 For example *Enfield LBC and others v Sivanandan* May 2000 *Legal Action* 11; (2000) 637 IRLB 13; *Nassé v Science Research Council; Vyas v Leyland Cars* [1979] IRLR 465; [1979] ICR 921, HL if the problem is confidentiality.

74 *Enfield LBC and others v Sivanandan* May 2000 *Legal Action* 11; (2000) 637 IRLB 13, EAT.

75 *West Midlands Passenger Transport Executive v Singh* [1988] IRLR 186; [1988] ICR 614, CA.

76 *Carrington v Helix Lighting* [1990] IRLR 6, EAT.

21.48   Original documents should always be inspected, as tampering is not uncommon in discrimination cases, and a request should also be made that the originals be brought to the hearing. If documents have been electronically generated, it may be worth asking for them to be sent by e-mail, as it may be possible to check the date of creation.

Case management discussions

21.49   ETs usually hold case management discussions in discrimination cases.[77] Their purpose is normally to clarify the issues, sort out what disclosure, additional information and written answers should be ordered, decide on exchange of witness statements, estimate the length of hearing and fix dates. The request for disclosure and additional information should be sent to the employer at least ten days before the case management discussion, so that an order can be requested if necessary.[78] Depending on tactics, it may also be useful to mention any unanswered items in the questionnaire, since, although the ET cannot make an order, the Employment Judge may well encourage the employer to reply. This is risky though, because the Judge may express the view that the questions are irrelevant.

21.50   Many employers take the opportunity to seek clarification of the case against them and the adviser should go prepared for some tricky questions. The ET may insist on the worker setting out every incident of discrimination on which s/he relies. The latter can be very awkward as, although the major incidents will have been pleaded in the ET1, quite often the worker will mention additional, more minor, examples of less favourable treatment during the main hearing. If taken by surprise at the case management discussion, do not attempt to answer on the spot. Ask for 14 days to supply voluntary additional information. This is particularly important if a representative but not the worker attends the case management discussion, as is common. The worker or adviser may find that statements or explanations made casually at a case management discussion find their way into the ET's subsequent order or account of the meeting and cause problems later, eg by artificially narrowing the case. Case management discussions in discrimination cases should be prepared for very carefully as they can have a major impact on shaping the case. The Employment Judge can exert considerable pressure to formulate the issues on the spot, and if

---

77 Previously called directions hearings. See paras 20.85-20.87 for general tactics for case management discussions generally.
78 ET Regs 2004 Sch 1 r11(2).

the worker or his/her representative is unprepared or unassertive, the nature of the case can change.

21.51   Unfortunately many ETs take an excessively formalistic approach, requiring very detailed and legalistic particularisation of discrimination claims. This approach defeats the objective of accessibility and informality in the ET system. The Employment Judge at a case management discussion almost invariably states that s/he is simply identifying the legal questions in issue so that they are clear for everyone and the employer knows what case has to be defended. This can be useful if the tribunal claim was badly written, but it is frustrating and often confusing to be asked to rephrase issues when they are already clearly itemised in the claim form. The EAT has said there is a difficult balance to be drawn between requiring particularity on the one hand, and going too far, so as to render the proceedings technical, legal and pure matters of form, on the other. ET procedures are designed to give relative ease of access to unrepresented parties to make their complaints. When too much is put in writing, ultimately the trial of an action will dissolve into an examination of a whole series of documents rather than concentrating on the main issues in the case. Everything should be made clear by the time of the full hearing by means of an exchange of witness statements, following full and proper disclosure.[79]

Mediation

21.52   In some tribunal regions, the tribunal may ask the parties at the case management discussion whether they are interested in judicial mediation. If so, and the case is deemed suitable for mediation, a date will subsequently be fixed and all case management orders will be put on hold. The mediation, which is free, will be carried out by a trained Employment Judge and can last up to 2 days. The idea is to enable the parties to reach a settlement of the case and agree a way forward if the employee is still employed. The Judge is supposed to remain neutral and avoid expressing any opinion on the merits of the case. His/her role is simply to help the parties identify the issues and find a resolution. If the mediation is unsuccessful, the tribunal proceedings will go ahead with a different Employment Judge and the contents of the mediation will be kept confidential. The judicial mediation scheme started as a pilot in three Regions (Birmingham, London Central and Newcastle) in 2006 for cases involving race, sex or disability discrimination. It was rolled out to all tribunals in England and Wales in

---

79 *Enfield LBC and others v Sivanandan*, May 2000 *Legal Action* 11, (2000) 637 IRLB 13, EAT.

January 2009 for certain cases. Work is currently underway to develop a similar scheme in Scotland.[80] As well as judicial mediation, ACAS and private organisations may offer mediation at any stage before or during the proceedings, although this will need to be paid for. Whether or not mediation is a good idea is hard to say. A lot depends on whether the employer is in good faith, what the worker wants and whether s/he can cope with a tribunal hearing. Settlement can be achieved without a mediation meeting – there is always the normal option of negotiating via the representatives, usually over the telephone, through ACAS. The advantage of a meeting is that both parties come to it with an intention to settle, which makes an agreement more likely. The disadvantage is that some employers (or their lawyers) may use the opportunity to weaken the worker's resolve and effectively circumvent the worker's representative. Also, a worker may give too much away. Strictly-speaking, if the mediation fails, the employer cannot quote what the worker said at the mediation to the employment tribunal. But in reality, it will be useful for the employer to hear what the worker says and see how s/he reacts under pressure. The Employment Lawyers Association published a report in July 2008 regarding its members' reactions to the pilot scheme.[81] Although this reported a generally positive response, it needs to be treated with some caution, as it is likely to be a response predominantly from lawyers used to acting for employers. It is well worth reading the individual comments in the appendix as an indication of the pros and cons of going down this road.

Striking out

21.53 Sometimes an ET at an interim stage tries to strike out some of the worker's supporting allegations on grounds that they are irrelevant. This would mean the worker cannot deal with those matters at the full hearing and will be unable to obtain related disclosure at the preparatory stages. The EAT has said that an ET should be careful not to overstep the line between legitimate case management and over-simplifying the case by striking out proper claims to save time.[82] Although it may be desirable that cases should be kept within proper bounds, the worker must not be prevented from putting his/her full case. An ET certainly should not refuse to allow in relevant evidence of past acts of

---

80 Employment Tribunals Act 1996 s7B.

81 Judicial Mediation in the Employment Tribunals at www.elaweb.org.uk/medialibrary.axd?id=806919716

82 *Hambly v Rathbone Community Industry Ltd* (1999) 617 IRLB 10, EAT.

discrimination simply to save time.[83] If the ET does have a good reason to disallow some of the allegations, it must follow the correct procedure.[84] An ET has power to strike out or amend all or part of a claim on grounds that it is scandalous, vexatious or has no reasonable prospects of success.[85] The worker must have been given the chance to argue against the striking out.[86] Where a discrimination case looks extremely weak on the ET1, an ET may be tempted to strike out the whole claim, but this should not occur except in the most obvious case. Discrimination cases are generally fact-sensitive and their proper determination is vital in a pluralistic society.[87] For general principles on striking out, see para 20.55.

Restricted reporting orders

21.54   In a case involving allegations of 'sexual misconduct' (eg a sexual harassment case) the ET has power at any time to make a restricted reporting order (RRO), which specifies that certain parties must not be publicly identified.[88] It can also revoke the order at any time. A party can apply orally or in writing for an RRO or the ET may make an order on its own initiative. The ET can make a temporary RRO without notifying the other parties. Within 14 days, a party can apply to have the temporary order revoked or converted into a full order. If no application is made, the temporary RRO will lapse. If an application is made, it will remain in force until the application is determined. Whether or not a temporary RRO is made, an ET must give all parties a chance to make representations at a pre-hearing review or the full hearing, before making a full order. Any other interested person, eg the press, can also apply to make representations to the ET before a full RRO is made.

21.55   The RRO can cover the person making the allegation or anyone affected by it.[89] This may include direct witnesses of the misconduct, but should not usually include those less directly involved, eg managers conducting an investigation, or the employing organisation

---

83 *Senyonjo v Trident Safeguards Ltd* UKEAT/0316/04 would be helpful on this.

84 *Hambly v Rathbone Community Industry Ltd* (1999) 617 IRLB, 10, EAT.

85 ET Regs 2004 Sch 1 r18(7)(b).

86 ET Regs 2004 Sch 1 r18(6).

87 *Anyanwu v South Bank Students' Union and South Bank University* [2001] IRLR 305, HL.

88 ET Regs 2004 Sch 1 r50.

89 ETA 1996 s11(1)(a).

itself.[90] The order also should not be too wide-ranging in terms of which incidents are covered.[91]

21.56   Where there are allegations of a 'sexual offence', the ET must delete from the public record any information likely to lead members of the public to identify any person affected by or making such allegation.[92] This may be called a register deletion order (RDO). The precise meanings of 'misconduct' and 'offence' are uncertain, but the latter probably refers to a criminal offence. Similar rules apply in the EAT.

21.57   ET hearings are open to the public and reporters are in regular attendance in some tribunals, often arranging for photographers to ambush unwitting claimants as they leave the building. As there is no power for an ET to exclude the public or the press and as the RRO is effective only until the judgment on liability and remedy is sent to the parties,[93] the protection is of limited value. However, the inability to identify the parties while the hearing is taking place will certainly deter a proportion of the daily reporters.

21.58   Ironically, although the reporting restrictions were brought in with a view to protecting complainants of sexual harassment,[94] it is very often the perpetrators who seek and obtain an order against the claimant's will. Many claimants have experienced heavy-handed attempts from their employers to silence them from the moment they raised the allegations, as well as intimidation from the harasser not to speak out. By the time they reach an ET, they wish the matter to be out in the open. The higher courts have yet to consider fully how tribunals should approach a clash between a party who wants full and open reporting (usually the claimant) and another party, who wants the protection of an RRO (usually the alleged perpetrator). This could raise interesting issues about the balance between article 8 (the right to private life), article 10 (the right to freedom of expression) and article 6 (entitlement to a fair and public hearing) of the European Convention on Human Rights.[95]

90 *R v London (North) Industrial Tribunal ex p Associated Newspapers Ltd* [1998] IRLR 569, HC; *Leicester University v A* [1999] IRLR 352, EAT.

91 *R v London (North) Industrial Tribunal ex p Associated Newspapers Ltd* [1998] IRLR 569, HC; *Leicester University v A* [1999] IRLR 352, EAT.

92 ET Regs 2004 Sch 1 r49.

93 ET Regs 2004 Sch 1 r50(8)(b) and (11).

94 See parliamentary debate in *Hansard*, 16 June 1993, p951.

95 See para 3.20. *Tradition Securities & Futures SA and others v Times Newspapers Ltd and others* UKEATPA/1415/08 and UKEATPA/1417/08; [2009] IRLR 354, EAT.

21.59 An RRO may also be made under the DDA 1995 where evidence of a personal nature is likely to be heard.[96] Unlike in cases of sexual misconduct, only the claimant or the ET (but not the respondent) can request an RRO.

21.60 In sensitive cases other than under the DDA 1995 and where there is no sexual misconduct or offence, the ET and EAT can still order an RRO or RDO by using their general power to regulate their own procedure.[97] The worker would need to show that fear of publicity would otherwise deter him/her from bringing a case. The tribunals' power derives from the EU directives which require member states to provide an effective remedy and make judicial processes 'available' to those claiming discrimination covered by the directives.[98] It applies to both public and private sector workers. A worker claiming discrimination on grounds of gender reassignment[99] or sexual orientation, for example, may well be deterred from claiming by fear of publicity.

Preparation for the hearing

Witness statements

21.61 In England and Wales, it is now fairly standard for the evidence of witnesses to be put into written 'witness statements', which are usually exchanged 7–14 days before the hearing. Witness statements are less commonly used in Scotland. Well-written witness statements can be very effective in helping to win discrimination cases. As opening speeches are rare, the claimant's witness statement will be particularly important in creating a strong first impression and providing an overall picture of what the case is about. Paragraphs 20.101–20.110 set out the basic procedure and considerations.

21.62 The following additional tips are useful in writing statements in discrimination cases:

- If the worker is likely to be the first witness, explain important background at the start of the statement, eg how the workplace is structured, the hierarchy, and the worker's job.

96 ET Regs 2004 Sch 1 r50(1)(b).
97 Under ET Regs 2004 Sch 1 r10(1) and ETA 1996 s30(3) respectively. *X v Stevens* [2003] IRLR 411, EAT; *Chief Constable of West Yorkshire Police v A* [2000] IRLR 465, EAT.
98 Equal Treatment Directive 76/207/EEC article 6; General Framework Directive 2000/78/EC article 9; Race Discrimination Directive 2000/43/EC article 7.
99 *Chief Constable of West Yorkshire Police v A* [2000] IRLR 465, EAT.

- The worker's evidence should be set out clearly and usually in chronological order, though sometimes it is clearer to group 'themes', eg keeping a history of failed promotion attempts separate from the chronology of a dismissal for alleged misconduct.
- If possible without destroying the sense and logical order, indicate some of the discriminatory elements early in the statement. For example, in a race discrimination case, draw attention to a white dominant work hierarchy or to any racist remarks early on.
- Ensure the worker understands and agrees with the content of his/her statement. Try to use his/her normal way of speaking and avoid jargon. If the worker fully understands English but cannot read it, it will be necessary to explain this to the ET at the hearing and ask to read the statement for him/her. If the worker's English is very limited, a statement in English will probably be unsuitable. An interpreter will then be necessary in the ET and s/he can translate the statement into English for the tribunal. It would be sensible also to prepare a written translation in advance. The interpreter will have to take an oath or affirmation that s/he will well and faithfully interpret to the best of his/her skill and understanding.
- Draw attention to legally relevant facts. For example, in a case of direct race discrimination, always point out where the employer's behaviour is different from the norm.[100] In direct discrimination cases, different treatment is more relevant than unfair treatment.
- In a DDA 1995 case, a worker may face difficult questioning related to the definition of 'disability'. The worker may not answer properly under the stress of a hearing. It is also well-known that some people play down the effect of their disability. A well-written witness statement addressing each aspect of the definition, having discussed the matter carefully with the worker when s/he is not under the pressure of cross-examination in a public forum, may be crucial.
- Include facts relevant to proving the worker's injury to feelings and, if applicable, health.[101] If the employer has particularly upset the worker by aggressive behaviour, highlight this, as it will be relevant to aggravated damages.

Preparing the worker

21.63   It should be clearly explained to the worker what has to be proved and that the issue is discrimination, not fairness. In particular, it should be

---

100 See sample extracts from RRA 1976 witness statement at pp719–722 below.
101 See chapter 19 regarding what needs to be proved.

stressed that it is necessary to prove that the reason for what happened was the worker's race, religion, sex, sexual orientation, age, or related to disability. Advise the worker to keep to the relevant incidents, not to quote weak examples or accuse irrelevant people of racism or sexism. Certain cross-examination techniques are very common and the worker should be warned. In particular, s/he is likely to be asked in respect of all key persons for the employer whether they are (for example) racist or have discriminated. Explain the legal significance of saying that someone may have discriminated and that it is not the same as saying that someone is prejudiced. If the legal issues are not explained, the worker may find that as a result of being pinned down at the outset, s/he unwittingly makes concessions or gives evidence which (wrongly) appears to contradict how the case has been set out. On the other hand, be careful not to confuse the worker.

21.64   Most discrimination hearings are traumatic experiences, whatever the results, so the worker should bring along a friend or relative, especially where s/he may otherwise be the only woman or black person in the room. Sexual harassment cases will be particularly unpleasant and the worker should be warned about possible lines of cross-examination (see paras 17.105–17.107).

Accessibility of tribunals and legal advice

Disabled workers

21.65   ETs are a service provider covered by the DDA 1995.[102] Their relevant services include receiving and dealing with claims and appeals; setting up hearings in an appropriate venue and heard by suitably qualified and trained tribunals; notifying the decision; providing information about rights of appeal and complaint. A service provider must take reasonable steps to:

- change any practice, policy or procedure which makes it impossible or unreasonably difficult for disabled people to make use of its services;
- provide an auxiliary aid or service if it would make it easier for disabled people to make use of its services;
- provide a reasonable alternative method of making its services available to disabled people where a physical feature makes things impossible or unreasonably difficult. The service provider must

102 DDA 1995 ss19–21.

also take reasonable steps to remove or alter such a feature or provide reasonable means of avoiding it.

21.66   The former Disability Rights Commission in conjunction with the Council on Tribunals produced guidance to assist tribunals to facilitate the full participation of disabled people (parties, witnesses, representatives and public) in the tribunal process. *Making tribunals accessible to disabled people: guidance on applying the Disability Discrimination Act* can be downloaded from the Council on Tribunals' website. There is also the recently updated disability section (chapter 5) of the Equal Treatment Benchbook, which is written for Judges, but useful for everyone to be aware of.[103] These are extremely useful documents, both for use when seeking any adjustment by the ET and to alert advisers to issues they may not have thought of. The adviser should take copies to any interim or final hearing where a claimant or witness is disabled. The right to a fair hearing under article 6, together with article 14 (non-discrimination) of the European Convention on Human Rights would also be important if problems arise. Many of the recommendations in the Council's guidance and the Equal Treatment Benchbook would also be relevant to solicitors and barristers in providing advice to disabled clients.

21.67   The guidance recognises that the practical and procedural requirements of the tribunal process are likely to present additional barriers for disabled people, eg physical barriers to access, not just for wheelchair users (eg accessible waiting and hearing rooms, parking facilities, toilets); communication with ET staff and written information in inaccessible formats; difficulties sitting still for long periods of time or without breaks; and for users with learning difficulties or mental health issues, possible difficulty understanding the process or progress of their case and generally additional stress.

21.68   The guidance states that ETs must treat each individual as an individual and not assume global solutions will work. Tribunals and tribunal staff must give proper consideration to requests for reasonable adjustments and if any particular adjustment is refused, explain why. These are some issues the ET should bear in mind:

• Time limits for making a claim or various interim steps may not provide enough time for claimants with mental illnesses, learning difficulties or literacy problems to seek advice or for visually impaired parties to get documents in an accessible format.

103 Available at www.council-on-tribunals.gov.uk/publications.130.htm and www.jsboard.co.uk/etac/etbb/index.htm respectively

- Forms, letters and guides should be provided in alternative formats and hearing venues should be accessible to users with a range of impairments.
- Hearings should be guaranteed to start at a certain time and not float, where a party has difficulty sitting or is in pain generally or liable to get more than usually stressed, eg due to learning difficulties.

21.69   The Disability Rights Commission's Legal Bulletin, Issue 3 of December 2002, provides some interesting case studies of where adjustments have been made. For a claimant and expert witness with hearing impairments, the ET funded a lipspeaker and a palentypist (a stenographer who types the evidence simultaneously so the witnesses can read it off a laptop). There were five-minute breaks every 45 minutes for the lipspeaker and palentypist, and the desks in the hearing room were rearranged to accommodate them. For claimants or witnesses with learning difficulties, letters should be written in plain English, simply structured, and a copy sent on tape. Copies should also be sent to any support workers. The witness should be able to visit the hearing room one week in advance and practise taking the oath. The hearing itself should be conducted slowly and informally with breaks. Cross-examination should be kept to short and simple questions. A friend or helper could be allowed to sit next to the witness while giving evidence.

21.70   Advisers should inform the ET ahead of the hearing about any special requirements which an individual may have. It is worth letting the employer's representative know in advance too. A good time to discuss arrangements would be at any case management discussion. There is a box on the standard claim form inviting the claimant to state any assistance s/he requires if s/he has a disability.

Religious dress

21.71   The Judicial Studies Board provides guidance for judges in courts and tribunals generally regarding religious dress in its Equal Treatment Bench Book.[104] The general principle is that a Muslim woman should be permitted to wear the veil unless really necessary, eg for the purposes of identifying a person or assessing her facial expression when answering crucial questions relating to issues of credit. Even then, the matter should be handled with sensitivity and careful thought given to whether the veil presents a true (rather than imagined) obstacle to the judicial task.

104 April 2007 revision available at www.jsboard.co.uk/etac/etbb/index.htm

Expenses

21.72   Interpreters may be needed for witnesses who do not speak English as a first language as well as for deaf or blind workers. It is usually unhelpful to use an unofficial interpreter, especially one known to the worker, although the risk with professional interpreters is that they may not speak the correct dialect. These days the tribunal provides a language interpreter if requested in advance. The claimant would need to get permission from the tribunal before the hearing if s/he wants to use a friend or relative instead and no interpreter's fee will be paid by the tribunal (only travel and normal expenses). Para 20.111 sets out more details of expenses which can be claimed from the tribunal. These include the cost of a helper accompanying a witness because of a medical condition, as well as reasonable charges for the attendance of medical professionals or the production of medical reports where that is essential to the case and if ordered by the ET in advance. The tribunal has indicative pay rates for medical evidence – ask the clerk to see these before incurring costs. As the rules on which expenses are covered and in what circumstances often change, it is essential to check the latest position with the ET itself before relying on getting costs fully covered.

The hearing

Start of hearing: preliminary issues

21.73   Sometimes the ET will decide certain issues relating to jurisdiction immediately before starting the full hearing. This is the time to ask leave to allow out-of-time claims if such leave has not previously been requested.[105] It is advisable to warn the employer's representative in advance if this is intended. Otherwise, if there is a need to adjourn because the employer is taken by surprise, the costs of the adjournment may be awarded against the claimant. Any last-minute application for an order, eg for specific documents, should usually have been notified ten days in advance, but the tribunal can waive this requirement.

Opening

21.74   As the burden of proof is on the worker, usually the worker and then his/her witnesses go first. Although traditionally, the party who starts

---

105 *Dimtsu v Westminster CC* [1991] IRLR 450, EAT. See paras 21.28–21.29 above.

gives an opening speech, these days the ET normally wants to go straight to the witnesses. If the worker's representative does get a chance to say a few words, keep it short, but use the opportunity to make some contextual points.

21.75 In most direct discrimination cases, it is worth reminding the ET at the outset that in order to succeed, prejudice need not be demonstrated, nor need unlawful discrimination be a conscious or intentional act. It could also usefully be reminded that the standard of proof is only the balance of probabilities. Even though it is serious to allege discrimination against an employer, it is equally serious to fail to find discrimination where it has occurred.

21.76 Where a discrimination claim is combined with one of unfair dismissal, it is unclear who should start and the ET has the right to govern its own procedure. For the reasons set out above, it is usually worth arguing for the right to go first. In England and Wales, this also means the worker will give the final closing speech. Sometimes, however, it may be best to let the employer start, for example, where the worker will make a bad witness but the employer has clearly breached procedures. If the worker starts in such a case, the ET may form an adverse view early on which distracts it from the employer's conduct.

Strategy

21.77 Although the issues will probably have been clarified at a case management discussion (see above), employers' representatives sometimes object at the beginning of a hearing that they do not fully understand what case they have to meet and in what way they are alleged to have discriminated. ETs sometimes go along with this approach and require workers' representatives to commit themselves to precise allegations, even when the case is clearly pleaded and no request for clarification has been made at interim stages. The adviser should therefore be prepared to answer the following sort of question put at the start of the hearing.

- Is it alleged that the worker was discriminated against because s/he is of African national origin or because s/he is black?
- Precisely who are you alleging discriminated against the worker? In promotion cases, which members of the selection panel are you alleging discriminated?
- In what way did the employer discriminate? What is every matter relied on?

The difficulty with the last question is that the worker will be confined to every matter that s/he can remember to list at the outset. In respect of the first two questions, the issues should be kept open by putting matters in the alternative. Some ETs recognise that in a promotion case, for example, the worker cannot know how a decision was made, who influenced whom, who may have been prejudiced, who may have unconsciously discriminated, etc and permit the worker simply to say it was some or all of the panel. If an ET insists on the worker saying which of a selection panel discriminated, unless one panel member clearly had a decisive influence, it may be best to name all panel members, reserving the right to drop the allegations against some. The worker's representative may also wish to register a formal protest against being forced to take a position, to safeguard the possibility of a later appeal.

21.78   As a general rule, it is best to run cases in a low-key way. Fierce cross-examination and use of emotive words such as 'racist' or 'liar' will usually alienate the ET. In any opening speech, the ET's expectations should not be needlessly raised. It may be planned to reveal overt prejudice, but legally this need not be shown, so do not promise more than may be possible to deliver. The ET may find it easier to accept that senior managers have acted with benevolent motives or through a desire to have someone who 'fits in' rather than through racial or sexual hostility.

21.79   In most cases, it is not certain whether the act of direct discrimination was conscious or unconscious, intended or not. The ET must not be relied on to understand what unconscious discrimination is or that it can happen. Many ETs still look for indications of deliberate discrimination (whether the motives were good or bad) and focus on the honesty and sincerity of the employer's witnesses. This issue must be taken on explicitly. It should be explained that an employer may not be aware that s/he has discriminated and that the proper approach for the ET to take in determining direct discrimination or victimisation cases, ie whether inferences can be drawn from the primary facts, does not require it to make a finding as to whether the unlawful discrimination was conscious or not.[106]

21.80   The main opportunity to make comments will be in the closing speech, although this may be too late if the ET has listened to the evidence with the wrong perspective. Sometimes an ET can be reminded indirectly of the correct approach by the way the employer's witnesses are cross-examined, eg a witness can be asked (if relevant) whether s/he accepts discrimination can sometimes be unconscious.

106 See para 16.17.

21.81   On the whole, the fewer people that have to be proved discriminatory or prejudiced, the easier it is to convince an ET, except where the main point is that a whole workplace was hostile towards workers of a particular race or sex. Unless there is extremely strong evidence, probably in the form of a direct witness, any suggestion of a conspiracy or policy in the employing organisation to discriminate should be avoided. As a final note of caution, in running the case, be careful not to lose sight of the main issues in a mass of detail.

Dismissals

21.82   Where an unfair dismissal claim is also before the ET, it usually entails quite different considerations, unless the claim is purely that the dismissal was unfair by reason of being discriminatory. The issues should be kept separate in the opening and closing speeches.

21.83   Where the worker does not have sufficient service to qualify for claiming unfair dismissal, ETs tend to be very suspicious, seeing the discrimination claim as an attempt to circumvent the qualifying period under the ERA 1996. Great care must be taken when running such a case not to deal with issues which relate solely to fairness.[107] Constantly draw attention to differences from the norm. Even so, in some circumstances it may be appropriate to argue that matters such as the employer's failure to follow disciplinary procedures, inadequate grounds for dismissal, failure to consult, etc are also matters from which an inference of less favourable treatment may be drawn.

No case to answer

21.84   At the end of the evidence of the worker and his/her witnesses, the employer may ask the ET to reject the case at that stage on the basis that the worker has not made out a prima facie case for the employer to answer. The ET should be reminded of the decision in *Laher v Hammersmith and Fulham LBC*,[108] that only in the most exceptional cases should the employer not be called to give an explanation. If the ET dismisses the case at that stage, there is a likely basis for appeal.[109]

---

107 Particularly after *Zafar v Glasgow CC* [1998] IRLR 36, HL. See para 16.15 above.
108 (1995) 514 IRLB 4, EAT. See also *JSV Oxford v DHSS* [1977] IRLR 225, EAT and see para 16.2 onwards above on the burden of proof.
109 See also the view expressed by the House of Lords in *Anyanwu v South Bank Student's Union and South Bank University* [2001] IRLR 305, HL in the context of striking out at an interim stage. See para 21.53.

21.85   Some ETs deal with the matter instead by warning the worker about the costs of proceeding further. Regardless of whether the ET actually gives a costs warning, workers' representatives should be aware of the danger of an ultimate award of costs if the ET seems sympathetic to the suggestion that there is no case to answer.

Costs

21.86   Costs are awarded on the same basis as in unfair dismissal cases,[110] although they seem to be awarded more readily against unsuccessful workers in discrimination cases. Because of the greater length of the latter, costs tend to be larger. There is little that can be done about this except to keep the issues within reasonable bounds and to be aware that if a case is clearly going badly, points should not be laboured. If a costs award has to be argued, point out the matters which called for an explanation from the employer and could only be obtained in the forum of an ET hearing. If the employer failed to answer the questionnaire, point out that this could have provided an early explanation to the worker. As a matter of public policy, discrimination cases should be heard.[111]

21.87   Costs can be awarded regardless of whether there was a previous costs deposit. In fact, costs deposits are infrequent in discrimination cases. Many ETs recognise that discrimination is overwhelmingly a matter of evidence, which can be tested only at hearing.

Appeals

21.88   For more detail on appeals to the EAT and ET reviews, see paras 20.133–20.141. As with unfair dismissal cases, an appeal to the EAT must usually be lodged within 42 days from the date the written reasons for the judgment were sent out.[112] Reviews must be requested of the ET within 14 days of the judgment being sent out.

21.89   An appeal can only be lodged if the judgment was wrong in law or perverse on the facts. It is hard to challenge discrimination

---

110 See para 20.142.

111 *Anyanwu v South Bank Students Union and South Bank University* [2001] IRLR 305, HL and para 21.53 above. See also para 20.145 for the quote cited by the CA in *Lodwick v L B Southwark* [2004] IRLR 554, CA.

112 See para 20.137 for the precise rule.

decisions for perversity, but they can sometimes be appealed for taking the wrong approach. For example:

- The ET must give adequate and intelligible reasons for its decision so each party knows why s/he has won or lost.[113]
- The ET must make findings of the primary facts and follow them through to a reasoned conclusion. It is not enough simply to set out the relevant evidential issues without deciding what happened, though there need not be a fact finding on every minor issue.[114]
- The ET should not give credence to a witness purely because s/he appears to be honest or truthful, without considering the whole of the evidence in the case. A witness may be credible and honest but mistaken. ETs must recognise that witnesses can unconsciously discriminate.[115]
- The ET must not evaluate a series of allegedly discriminatory incidents in isolation and consider whether each on its own is proved to be discrimination. The ET must also consider the 'eloquence of the whole'.[116]

113 *Anya v University of Oxford* [2001] IRLR 377, CA; European Convention on Human Rights article 6 (right to a fair trial).
114 *Anya v University of Oxford* [2001] IRLR 377, CA.
115 See paras 16.17 and 13.50.
116 *Qureshi v (1) Victoria University of Manchester (2) Brazier* EAT 484/95, quoted extensively in *Anya v University of Oxford* [2001] IRLR 377, CA. And see para 16.13.

Disciplinary, dismissal and grievance procedures

continued   637

Chapter 22: Key points

- From October 2004 to 6 April 2009, there were statutory minimum dispute resolution procedures setting out minimum steps for disciplinary and grievance procedures. The procedures only applied to employees. In many circumstances, an employee was unable to take an employment tribunal case for discrimination or other in-work matters, if s/he had not brought a statutory grievance first.
- An employee with one year's service could claim automatic unfair dismissal if the employer failed to follow the statutory dismissal and disciplinary procedures (DDP).
- There was an increase or reduction in compensation for unfair dismissal, discrimination and other specified employment tribunal claims where a party failed to comply with the statutory dispute resolution procedures.
- Although the procedures were abolished with effect from 6 April 2009, under transitional provisions, they may still apply in some cases.
- The ACAS Code of Practice on Disciplinary and Grievance Procedures sets out basic principles of fair practice and natural justice which should form part of the procedures. It is not against the law in itself to fail to follow the Code, but an ET must take account of the Code in deciding any unfair dismissal case.
- In cases where the statutory dispute resolution procedures no longer apply, a tribunal may adjust compensation by up to 25 per cent if one party unreasonably fails to follow the ACAS Code. This applies where employees bring specified cases including unfair dismissal and discrimination.
- It is also important to be familiar with the worker's own disciplinary and grievance procedure.
- An employment tribunal case can be brought for unfair dismissal, but not for 'unfair warnings'. Unfair warnings which do not lead to actual or constructive dismissal cannot usually be legally challenged unless they are discriminatory or an unlawful detriment.
- Except for gross misconduct, there should not normally be dismissal for a first offence.
- Even on allegations of gross misconduct, fair investigative and disciplinary procedures should be followed.
- Workers have a legal right to be accompanied to disciplinary and grievance hearings.

- Discrimination may be relevant to disciplinary action or the subject of grievances.
- Be very careful not to miss legal time limits while taking out grievances or appeals. The statutory dispute resolution procedures, if still applicable, extend time limits in some circumstances.
- This chapter should be read in conjunction with the chapters on unfair dismissal and discrimination as appropriate.

Disciplinary action including dismissal

Introduction

22.1   Basic principles of good practice in conducting disciplinary action are set out in the Advisory, Conciliation and Arbitration Service (ACAS) Code of Practice on Disciplinary and Grievance Procedures. When deciding unfair dismissal cases, the employment tribunal (ET) must take account of any failure by an employer to follow the Code. In October 2004, the government introduced statutory dispute resolution procedures, which were designed to improve internal procedures and encourage workplace resolution of problems. The statutory procedures included a disciplinary and dismissal procedure (DDP), which set out minimum procedural steps prior to dismissal (see para 22.37 onwards). The dispute resolution procedures were abolished with effect from 6 April 2009, but with some transitional effect (see para 22.67). Where they no longer apply, there is a new regime under which the ACAS Code is given additional importance. In specified cases, including unfair dismissal and discriminatory disciplinary action or dismissal, a successful claimant's compensation may be reduced or increased by up to 25 per cent if s/he or the employer respectively unreasonably refused to follow the Code. More detail of the Code as well as the statutory dispute resolution procedures is set out below.

22.2   There may be additional good practice steps set out in the employee's own disciplinary procedure. Where the employee has been or is likely to be dismissed, this chapter should be read in conjunction with the chapters on unfair dismissal. Where discrimination is involved, the discrimination chapters should be read. If disciplinary warnings are unfair, but not discriminatory or unlawful on any other ground (eg detriment for taking up rights under the Working Time Regulations 1998) there is generally little an employee can do except register his/her disagreement in writing or in an appeal, so that this is at least noted on the file if matters get worse in the future and s/he is ultimately dismissed. In extreme cases s/he can resign and claim constructive dismissal, but this is not usually advised.

The ACAS Code

22.3   The ACAS Code of Guidance on Disciplinary and Grievance Procedures sets out good practice guidelines for the handling of disciplinary and grievance issues in employment. The latest version of the Code (4th edn, with effect from 6 April 2009) can be downloaded from the ACAS website.[1] Although it is not against the law in itself for employers to fail to follow the Code, employment tribunals (ETs) must take this into account when deciding unfair dismissal cases.[2] The Code states explicitly that it does not apply to redundancy dismissals or to non-renewal of fixed-term contracts.

22.4   The Code has always been important for unfair dismissal cases, but it has gained new significance since 6 April 2009, since it can now affect the level of compensation in cases where the statutory dispute resolution procedures no longer apply. This is because an ET may increase or reduce an employee's compensation by up to 25 per cent in any successful case for unfair dismissal, discrimination or other specified cases, for the employer's or employee's unreasonable failure to follow the Code.[3] With one obscure exception, the types of case covered by these compensatory adjustments are the same as those covered by the statutory dispute resolution procedures (see para 22.78). Unfortunately, there seems to be a contradiction between the statutory position on compensation and the self-proclaimed scope of the Code. While the Code says it does not cover redundancy, the statutory provisions for adjustment to compensation apply to redundancy payments and to discrimination cases. So what happens with a case involving discriminatory selection for redundancy?

22.5   It is too soon to know what tribunals will consider to be an unreasonable failure to follow the Code and when they will award compensation. However, when deciding by what percentage to adjust compensation, they are likely to apply the same principles as they did under the statutory dispute resolution procedures. Under the statutory dispute resolution procedures, tribunals were obliged to adjust

---

1 At www.acas.gov.uk/CHttpHandler.ashx?id=1047&p=0
2 Trade Union and Labour Relations (Consolidation) Act (TULR(C)A) 1992 s207.
3 TULR(C)A 1992 s207A; in the case of unfair dismissal, the uplift is on the compensatory award, see para 18.53.

by 10 per cent except in exceptional circumstances and could adjust by up to 50 per cent if it was 'just and equitable in all the circumstances' to do so. Under the ACAS regime, the tribunal 'may' adjust if it considers it 'just and equitable in all the circumstances'. The case-law on adjustments under the statutory dispute resolution procedures is at para 22.53 below.

22.6   Examples of recommendations in the Code are:

   – employees and, where appropriate, their representatives, should be involved in the development of rules and procedures;
   – employers (and employees) should act consistently;
   – it is important to carry out investigations of potential disciplinary matters without unreasonable delay;
   – where practicable, different people should carry out the investigation and disciplinary hearing;
   – if there is to be a disciplinary hearing, an employee should be given sufficient information about the alleged misconduct or poor performance to prepare to answer the case;
   – the notification of the disciplinary should advise the employee of his/her right to be accompanied. The companion may be a work colleague or a trade union representative;
   – employees should be given the right to appeal against any formal decision made.

22.7   It is hard to know what kind of failures to follow the Code a tribunal will consider relevant in any particular case. The actual wording of the legislation says compensation may be adjusted where

   – 'the claim to which the proceedings relate concerns a matter to which a relevant Code applies'
   – and the employer or employee has unreasonably failed to comply with the Code 'in relation to that matter'.

So how direct does the connection need to be between the content of the Code and the claim? Clearly a concrete matter such as refusal of the right to appeal would lead to extra compensation if an unfair dismissal claim succeeded for that reason. But what if the breach of the Code was the failure to involve employees or their representatives in the development of the disciplinary rules?

22.8   Unlike the 2004 version which it replaces, the new ACAS Code is extremely short – under 10 pages. By reducing its guidance to obvious and basic steps, it has lost much of its value in setting standards. Most of the more subtle guidance has been removed to a 70 page guide:

Discipline and Grievances at Work: The ACAS Guide.[4] The Guide sets out extracts from the Code and expands it with more advice. Tribunals do not need to pay any attention to the Guide, and it is difficult to predict whether it will have any influence in cases. Nevertheless, ACAS does have recognised status in the field of industrial relations, and the Guide expands on what is usually regarded as good practice. It may be useful to quote sections from the Guide, for example, during disciplinary hearings.

The employer's disciplinary rules

22.9   Employers should have their own written disciplinary procedure, which will normally cover the disciplinary rules, and standards of expected conduct, as well as the procedures to be followed when disciplining a worker. The rules usually set out unacceptable behaviour in a number of areas, although obviously not every scenario can be covered. The written rule effectively serves as advance warning to the employee. Employers sometimes have rules that employees will be automatically dismissed for certain offences, eg fighting at work, regardless of the circumstances. Nevertheless, in an unfair dismissal case, the ET will still expect the employer to have considered the individual circumstances including, whether the employee was aware of the rule and its seriousness; the employee's general work and disciplinary record; the reason the employee broke the rule on this occasion, and any mitigating factors.

22.10   The disciplinary rules normally list examples of behaviour which is considered to be gross misconduct (see para 22.15 below).

The procedural steps

22.11   Employers should follow their own procedure when disciplining the employee, provided it complies with the general standards of fairness set by the ACAS Code and the statutory minimum dispute resolution procedures if they still apply (see para 22.33 below). The following stages are generally regarded as good practice:

- The ACAS Code says it is important to carry out necessary investigations of potential disciplinary matters without unreasonable delay, so as to establish the facts. An employee may be asked about an event so long after it occurred that s/he cannot give a proper

4 Available at www.acas.org.uk/index.aspx?articleid=2179

explanation. This can make a dismissal unfair. The investigation stage may involve holding a preliminary meeting with the employee or may simply entail gathering evidence. The Code advises that where practical, different people should carry out the investigation and the disciplinary hearing in misconduct cases.

- Minor cases of misconduct and most cases of poor performance should be dealt with through informal advice and counselling. The manager's objective should be to encourage and help the employee to improve. It is important that the employee understands what the problem is, what needs to be done to improve and over what period, and how his/her performance will be reviewed.

- Where formal disciplinary action is likely, the formal procedure should be followed. There should be a disciplinary hearing at which the employee is given the opportunity to answer the allegations and state his/her case. The ACAS Code says the employee must be informed in writing of the disciplinary hearing and told of his/her right to be accompanied. The notification should give sufficient information regarding the alleged misconduct or poor performance and its possible consequences, to enable the employee to prepare for the hearing. ACAS says it would normally be appropriate to provide copies of any written evidence including any witness statements with the notification.

- The ACAS Code says the disciplinary hearing itself should be held without unreasonable delay while allowing the employee reasonable time to prepare his/her case. At the hearing itself, the employer should explain the complaint and go through the evidence against the employee. The employee should be given a reasonable opportunity to answer questions and present his/her case.

- If disciplinary action is taken, the employee should be given an explanation why and informed of his/her right of appeal. The ACAS Code says that appeals should be heard without unreasonable delay and, where possible, dealt with by a manager who has not previously been involved in the case.

- Where serious misconduct is alleged it may be fair to suspend the employee during the investigatory or disciplinary process, although this should be for as short a time as possible and kept under review. Unless the contract says otherwise, suspension should be on full pay.

- Overall, the process should be handled without undue delay and confidentiality should be maintained. The employee should be given records of the hearings.

Forms of disciplinary action

22.12 It is long-established good practice that no employee is dismissed for a first offence unless it amounts to gross misconduct. Therefore the employee should normally have received some warnings before dismissal. It is often thought that the law requires precisely one oral and two written warnings before an employee can be fairly dismissed. This is a myth. If the employee's offence is sufficiently serious, the employer can skip the earlier warnings. The usual stages followed would be:

- *Informal action.* This is suitable for cases of minor misconduct or unsatisfactory performance. A quiet word should be enough to deal with the problem. It may be particularly helpful in small employers where problems can be dealt with quickly and confidentially.
- *First formal action.* The employer can start at this stage for more serious difficulties and it will usually take the form of a first written warning. ACAS says the warning should set out the details of the complaint, the required improvement with timescale, and the right of appeal. The warning should also state that the employee is at risk of a final written warning if there is no improvement. ACAS says the employee should be told how long the warning will remain current. It is common for a copy of the warning to be kept on file but disregarded for disciplinary purposes after a specified period, eg six months. Note that ACAS's suggestion that 6 months is an appropriate period has been moved from its Code to its informal Guide (see above).
- *Final written warning.* The employee can be given a final warning, because there is no improvement within the timescale set on the first warning, or – even if there have been no prior warnings – if the behaviour is serious enough. The warning should give similar details to those required on a first warning, but additionally in this case it should indicate the risk of dismissal if there is no improvement. The final warning should normally be disregarded for disciplinary purposes after a specified period, eg 12 months. Again, ACAS's suggestion that 12 months is an appropriate period is in its Guide but no longer in its Code.
- *Dismissal.* If the employee repeats offences or fails to improve after a final warning or if s/he commits gross misconduct, s/he can be dismissed. Alternatively, the employee's contract may allow other sanctions such as a disciplinary transfer or demotion.

22.13 Whatever disciplinary procedure applies to the employee, it is likely to set out stages similar to the above. When deciding whether to dismiss an employee, the employer may sometimes be able to rely on the fact that the employee has several live warnings, even though these concern unrelated offences. However, employers should not normally rely on warnings which have lapsed after a specified time under the procedure.[5]

What level of penalty is appropriate?

22.14 In imposing warnings or dismissing the employee, the employer must act reasonably, taking account of all the circumstances. The following factors will be relevant: the employee's length of service and work record; the nature of the job and his/her status; the seriousness of the employee's behaviour; any personal mitigating factors; the way similar offences by other employees have been dealt with previously. Additional factors will be relevant depending on the nature of the offence.[6] It is particularly important not to discriminate on grounds of race, religion, sex, pregnancy, sexual orientation, age, disability or other unlawful ground during the process. The ACAS Code recommends that, depending on the circumstances, if disciplinary action is contemplated against an employee who is a trade union representative, the case should be discussed at an early stage with an official employed by the union, after getting the employee's agreement.

Gross misconduct

22.15 Particularly serious offences are known as 'gross misconduct'. Gross misconduct (if proved) usually means the employee can be fairly dismissed for a first offence. Fair procedures in the investigation and disciplinary should be followed in the normal way, although compensation for unfair dismissal is likely to be reduced if the employee wins only because of poor procedures. Gross misconduct also means the employer can dismiss without giving notice or pay in lieu. This is called 'summary dismissal'.

22.16 Employers tend to use the phrase 'gross misconduct' very readily and this should not be automatically accepted as correct. Nevertheless, certain types of misconduct would obviously fall under this category, eg theft, sexual harassment or physical violence. Other examples

5 See paras 7.36–7.37 on this.
6 See examples in chapter 7.

are likely to be falsification of records, serious bullying or harassment, deliberate damage to property, serious insubordination, bringing the employer into serious disrepute, serious infringement of health and safety rules and serious negligence which causes or may cause loss or damage. The disciplinary procedure applicable to the employee will probably list examples of what the employer considers gross misconduct, although this is unlikely to be an exhaustive list.

Capability issues

22.17 Depending on the employer's procedures, an employee's failure to perform to the required standard may be dealt with through the normal disciplinary procedure or (often with public sector employers) through a separate capability procedure. Many employers are reluctant to rush to disciplinary action due to poor performance and often prefer several informal counselling meetings. Continuing poor performance by the employee may be due to some underlying domestic or work problems, eg ill-health or being subjected to harassment. The Disability Discrimination Act 1995 may apply in some circumstances.

22.18 The employee should not normally be dismissed for a failure to meet work standards unless s/he has been given warnings and an opportunity to improve, with reasonable timescales and targets. However, employers may be able to dismiss for a single error due to negligence with very serious consequences. Case-law suggests this is most likely where there is a danger to the health and safety of others.[7]

Appeals

22.19 The opportunity to appeal against a disciplinary decision is essential to natural justice. The ACAS Code says employees should be informed of their right of appeal and appeals should be heard without unreasonable delay. The employer's disciplinary procedure usually sets out time limits for lodging and dealing with the appeal.[8] The right to appeal is also set out in the statutory minimum dispute resolution procedures.

22.20 The appeal should be heard by someone appropriate, ideally a senior manager, who has not been previously involved in the disciplinary procedure. In small organisations it may not be possible to find such an individual, in which case the person dealing with the appeal

7 See paras 7.1–7.30 re unfair dismissal on grounds of capability, particularly 7.5.
8 Though these restrictions do not apply for the purposes of compliance with the statutory dispute resolution procedures, see para 22.71.

should act as impartially as possible. Independent arbitration may be a suitable alternative if agreed by everyone concerned. The employee is entitled to be represented at the appeal hearing. If new evidence arises during the appeal, the employee or his/her representative should be given the opportunity to comment and it may be necessary to adjourn the appeal to investigate.

22.21   The employee may appeal on a number of grounds, eg procedural irregularities, the penalty was too severe, new evidence has come to light, or it is unfair to believe that the worker had committed the offence or that his/her work was substandard. The employer's appeal procedure may set out a format for the appeal.

22.22   The employee may not want to appeal, feeling it is pointless. However, that is normally unwise. Both the ACAS Code and the statutory dispute resolution procedures seem to expect employees to appeal if they are unhappy about the decision. They therefore risk a reduction in their compensation if they win their tribunal case having failed to appeal. But if the employee does not want his/her job back after dismissal, there are dangers in appealing (see para 22.40).

22.23   The employee must be extremely careful not to miss any ET time limits if s/he intends to bring a claim. The ET claim must be lodged within the time limit (whether the normal time limit or one extended under the statutory dispute resolution procedures if they still apply), even if the appeal procedure has not been completed.

Discriminatory disciplinary action

22.24   The employee may be subjected to disciplinary action for a number of discriminatory reasons, eg:

- the employee's manager is angry with him/her because s/he has rebuffed his/her sexual approaches;
- the manager has chosen to bring formal disciplinary proceedings against a black employee for being late. However, when a white employee was equally late, the manager merely had an informal word;
- the employee is accused of inaccurate completion of timesheets. The employee is dyslexic and finds it difficult to complete forms accurately.

22.25   If the employee believes s/he is being subjected to disciplinary action for discriminatory reasons, s/he needs to decide at an early stage whether to say so at the disciplinary. If the employee later brings an ET case for discrimination, s/he may lose credibility if s/he did not raise the issue at the disciplinary. On the other hand, discrimination is a serious issue to raise which is likely to upset the employer. The employee risks being victimised as a result of raising the issue and work relations may deteriorate badly. Although victimisation is unlawful, it can be hard to prove. The employee needs to consider whether s/he has sufficient objective evidence to prove the discrimination and whether s/he wants to take on this issue.

22.26   If the employee does decide to raise the issue, s/he should do so in writing prior to the disciplinary hearing. Employers often say later that the issue of discrimination was never raised at the disciplinary. Remember that, where the statutory dispute resolution procedures still apply, if the employee intends to bring an ET claim that the disciplinary action is discriminatory, s/he must bring an internal grievance to that effect, except where the disciplinary action takes the form of dismissal. It is not compulsory under the new ACAS regime to bring a grievance about discriminatory action short of dismissal, but there is possibly a risk of reduction in compensation if the employee unreasonably fails to raise the issue of discrimination with his/her employer before going to tribunal.

22.27   See para 22.32 below regarding discriminatory handling of disciplinary action.

Grievances

22.28   The purpose of a grievance procedure is to give employees a way to raise issues with the management about their working environment or work relationships. An individual employee bringing a formal grievance, especially if it is on a controversial subject such as discrimination, does risk upsetting his/her manager. The employee needs to be clear about what s/he is trying to achieve. If the employee intends to bring a claim on a matter which is still covered by the statutory dispute resolution procedures, s/he will have to start a grievance first by sending a step 1 letter (see para 22.41 below). Under the new ACAS regime (see para 22.3 above), it is not a bar to bringing a claim if a grievance is not brought. However, the ACAS Code seems to expect formal grievances to be brought if it is impossible to resolve matters informally. There is therefore a risk of compensation being reduced if the employee wins any case when s/he had not first brought an internal grievance. There are various ambiguities in the Code, however. It is unclear whether it would be considered a breach of the Code not to attempt an informal grievance before raising a formal one, although the wording does not seem specific enough to make that a compulsory requirement. It is also unclear whether employees have to bring a grievance once they have left the employment.

22.29   An employee has an implied contractual right to have a grievance dealt with promptly.[9] The ACAS Code sets out very basic guidance to employers on handling grievances. It says employees should raise grievances formally and without unreasonable delay if they have not been able to resolve the matter informally. The formal grievance should be raised with a manager who is not the subject of the complaint. Employers should deal with grievances consistently and promptly. Employees should appeal where they feel their grievance has not been satisfactorily resolved. Where an employee raises a grievance during a disciplinary process, ACAS recommends the disciplinary process be temporarily suspended in order to deal with the grievance. If the grievance and disciplinary are related, it may be appropriate to deal with both together. Where the statutory dispute resolution procedures still apply, there are minimum steps for the handling of a grievance (see para 22.71 below).

22.30   Employers' grievance procedures often have more than one appeal stage. The stages may entail either one-to-one meetings, where the employee can be accompanied by a colleague or representative, or full hearings with witnesses, rather like a disciplinary hearing. The latter model is more common in the public sector where trade union representation is available. Some employers have different grievance procedures for different issues, eg the normal procedure plus different procedures for bullying, discrimination, sexual harassment or collective grievances. They may also have a special procedure for whistleblowing under the Public Interest Disclosure Act 1998.[10]

22.31   If the employee intends to bring an ET claim regarding the subject matter of the grievance, s/he must do so within the ET time limit (whether the normal time limit or any extension where the statutory dispute resolution procedures still apply) even if the grievance procedure has not been completed.

Discriminatory handling of disciplinary or grievance procedures

22.32   Employers may be guilty of further discrimination or victimisation in the way they deal with an employee's grievance related to discrimina-

9 See para 1.17.
10 See paras 6.91–6.98, particularly 6.94.

tion, for example by failing to investigate properly or taking an exceptionally long time to deal with the matter. In addition, it is sometimes necessary with a disabled employee to make reasonable adjustments to the disciplinary process, eg by allowing an interpreter or signer or, for someone with learning disabilities, adopting a particularly informal and unthreatening manner and process.

Statutory dispute resolution

Introduction

22.33 In October 2004, the government introduced statutory minimum disciplinary and grievance procedures (known as statutory dispute resolution procedures), which employers and employees needed to follow in most situations. The procedures and related rules were set out in the Employment Act (EA) 2002 and the Employment Act 2002 (Dispute Resolution) Regulations 2004 (EA(DR) Regs 2004).[11] The procedures applied to the large majority of employment cases including unfair dismissal and discrimination.[12] The procedures were abolished with effect from 6 April 2009, but with some transitional effect (see para 22.67). It will still be necessary to understand the procedures for a while, partly in case they apply under the transitional rules, and partly because older cases are still going through the legal system.

22.34 In summary, employers must follow a minimum dismissal and disciplinary procedure (DDP) when dismissing an employee or taking relevant disciplinary action (see below). Similarly, an employee must lodge a grievance before bringing a tribunal case for discrimination or a number of other matters. The statutory procedures were meant to be simple, but they are extremely difficult to understand and apply in practice, with many legal uncertainties. The procedures have proved unpopular with everyone: employers, employees and tribunals.

What are the procedures?

22.35 There is a statutory DDP and a statutory grievance procedure (GP). Both have a standard procedure, which must normally be followed, and a shorter modified procedure, which can be followed in limited circumstances. The steps of each procedure are set out in the checklist at

11 SI No 752.
12 See para 22.78 for full list.

para 22.71. These procedures only set out the minimum steps which are required. There may be more detailed disciplinary and grievance procedures under the employee's own contract of employment, which should still be followed.

22.36   The procedures only apply to employees. This is confusing because many workplace rights, eg protection under the Working Time Regulations, apply to workers generally and not only to employees. Discrimination law also applies to non-employees, eg to job applicants and to contract workers.

When does the statutory minimum DDP apply?

22.37   The standard DDP applies when the employer contemplates dismissing or taking relevant disciplinary action against an employee.[13] Relevant disciplinary action excludes warnings or paid suspension, and therefore includes action such as disciplinary demotion or unpaid suspension. The modified DDP applies when the employer has already dismissed the employee for gross misconduct and it was reasonable for the employer to have dismissed the employee before speaking to him/her.[14]

22.38   The DDP applies to actual dismissal, including failure to renew a fixed-term contract. It does not apply where the employee resigns and claims constructive dismissal, although it would apply to relevant disciplinary action, if that triggered the resignation. The DDP applies to dismissals for any reason, eg misconduct, redundancy (though not collective redundancies), capability, ill-health or on discriminatory grounds.

22.39   If the employer fails to follow the DDP and dismisses the employee, the employee can claim automatic unfair dismissal, provided s/he has one year's service. The employee will also get additional compensation. For more detail of the consequences of not following the DDP, see para 22.52. There are a number of exceptions where the DDP does not apply. These are set out in the checklist at para 22.72. There are a number of other situations, where the employer and employee are deemed to have completed the DDP, even though they have only followed some of the steps or have not even started the procedure (see para 22.73). These are different from the exceptions, because there may be consequences for time limits or, in some cases, compensation.

---

13 EA(DR) Regs 2004 reg 3(1).
14 EA(DR) Regs 2004 reg 3(2).

22.40   If an employee is reinstated on appeal, his/her dismissal will probably 'disappear' and s/he will be unable to claim automatic unfair dismissal as a result of any earlier breach of the DDP by the employer.[15] Nor will s/he be able to claim unfair dismissal on normal principles. However, an employer who dismisses an employee without following the DDP cannot avoid a finding of automatic unfair dismissal simply by writing to the employee rescinding the dismissal, unless the employee chooses to accept the withdrawal of the dismissal or reopens the matter by appealing.[16]

When does the statutory minimum GP apply?[17]

22.41   A grievance is an internal complaint by an employee to his/her employer about action which the employer has taken or intends to take in relation to him/her.[18] An employee must first send a grievance letter in accordance with the statutory GP if s/he wants to bring an ET claim for any of the matters listed in Schedule 4 to the EA 2002, eg equal pay, discrimination or unauthorised deductions from pay.[19] In addition, the employee will have his/her compensation reduced if s/he wins a case relating to any of the matters listed in Schedule 3, but did not comply with the grievance procedure. The only difference between the schedules is that breach of contract claims arising or outstanding on termination are not included in Schedule 4.[20] Therefore, an employee would not be debarred from claiming breach of contract if s/he had not sent a grievance letter, but may have his/her compensation reduced if s/he wins.

22.42   The GP does not apply if the employee only wants to bring a case about dismissal, since that is when the DDP applies. This includes a claim for unfair or discriminatory dismissal, including a claim that the way the dismissal was carried out was discriminatory, eg due to the discriminatory handling of a disciplinary hearing or failure to make reasonable adjustments in the process.[21] However, if the employee resigns

---

15 *Brock v Minerva Dental Ltd* UKEAT/0356/06. The case-law on 'disappearing dismissals' is rather complex and not entirely clear.

16 *Brock v Minerva Dental Ltd* UKEAT/0356/06. Though, this tactic may affect the amount of compensation awarded.

17 EA(DR) Regs 2004 reg 6.

18 See para 22.48 for the statutory definition.

19 See para 22.78 for the full list.

20 Note that notice pay claims are covered by the DDP anyway – see para 22.57.

21 *Lawrence v HM Prison Service* [2007] IRLR 468, EAT; *Department for Constitutional Affairs (formerly North Wales Magistrates Courts Committee) v Jones* UKEAT/0333/06; *Otaiku v Rotheram Primary Care NHS Trust* UKEAT/0253/07.

and claims constructive dismissal, the GP applies and s/he must bring a grievance. Where the grievance has been sent prior to resignation regarding the matters which subsequently caused the employee to resign, it is unlikely that a further written grievance alleging constructive dismissal is necessary after the resignation takes effect.[22] But it is important that the original grievance set out the employer's actions which led to the constructive dismissal. The employee can rely on the outcome of the grievance and appeal in his/her constructive dismissal claim, without having to raise another grievance about that.[23] Otherwise there would be endless grievances about rejected grievances. Arguably further grievances should also not be necessary in discrimination cases where the employee wants to complain about the rejection of a grievance or appeal being discriminatory as well as the matter which s/he was originally complaining or appealing about.

22.43   The GP does not apply to 'relevant disciplinary action', unless such action was discriminatory or on other hidden grounds. If so, both the DDP and the GP apply and there are special rules.[24]

22.44   The modified GP applies if the employee has left, where the standard grievance procedure was not previously completed, and where the parties now agree in writing that the modified procedure should apply.[25] If the employee prefers to avoid meeting the employer in this situation, s/he can suggest in the step 1 letter that the modified procedure apply, although of course the employer may not agree. The employee must be careful to include the basis of his/her grievance in the initial letter, if the modified procedure might apply.[26]

22.45   There are a number of exceptions when the GP does not apply. These are set out in the checklist at para 22.74. There are a number of other situations, where the employer and employee are deemed to have completed the GP, even though they have only followed some of the steps or not even started it (see para 22.75). These are different from the exceptions, because there may be consequences for time-limits or, in some cases, compensation. Unless one of the exceptions can be made to apply, it is not an excuse to fail to send a grievance letter just because the employee suspects or knows it is pointless, even

---

22 See comments of the EAT in *Galaxy Showers Ltd v Wilson* [2006] IRLR 83, EAT and in *Step In Time Ltd v Fox and Hunter* UKEATS/0031/08.

23 *Parsons v Burworth Estates* UKEAT/0547/08.

24 EA(DR) Regs 2004 reg 7 and para 22.75 below, final bullet point.

25 EA(DR) Regs 2004 reg 6(3).

26 See para 22.50.

if the employer has indicated s/he will not listen to the grievance. The employee is best advised to write the grievance and attend any meetings held by the employer, even if these seem to be a charade.

22.46   There is an extra complication in discrimination cases, since discrimination or harassment can be carried out by a fellow employee and not necessarily the employer. Under discrimination law, the employer is vicariously liable for such discrimination (subject to certain exceptions) and a tribunal claim can be brought against the individual discriminator as well as against the employer. It seems that it is unnecessary to have brought a statutory grievance in order to be permitted to make a tribunal claim against individual respondents.[27] As a result, the extension of time limits when a statutory grievance is submitted applies only to claims against the employer but not to claims against the individual discriminator.[28]

22.47   It can be confusing to identify whether the DDP or GP applies, or possibly both, especially where the employee has several claims. The checklist at para 22.70 gives some common examples. It is a good idea at the outset to list the employee's claims, including any separate incidents of discrimination, and consider in respect of each claim whether the GP or DDP applies and the effect on time limits.

What goes into the statutory grievance letter?

22.48   There is no guidance in the Regulations as to how much information needs to be put into a grievance letter, but many cases have considered this aspect. The grievance letter need not for these purposes comply with different or more complicated contractual procedures,[29] although failure to follow contractual procedures may be relevant in other contexts. The statutory GP says only that the employee must 'set out the grievance in writing'. The Regulations define a grievance as a complaint by an employee about action which his/her employer has taken or is contemplating taking in relation to him/her. A grievance under the procedure simply amounts to a written complaint that the employer has or has not done something in relation to the employee, and it is not necessary explicitly to ask the employer to investigate the

---

27 *Odoemelam v The Whittington Hospital NHS Trust* UKEAT/0016/06; *Bisset v Martins and another* UKEATS 0022/06 and 0023/06 although *Bisset* doubted obiter by *London Borough of Lambeth and ors v Corlett* UKEAT/0396/06.

28 See para 22.59 onwards on time limits.

29 *Shergold v Fieldway Medical Centre* [2006] IRLR 76, EAT; *Thorpe v Poat and Lake* [2006] All ER (D) 30 (Jan), EAT; UKEAT/0503/2005.

matter or hold a meeting.[30] Although the initial written grievance is commonly referred to as a 'step 1 letter', in fact it can be any kind of written statement. There is no particular form which the grievance must take, and it need not be written in any unduly legalistic or technical manner.[31] There is no formal requirement that the complaint is labelled a 'grievance',[32] but it will be safer if it is. It does not even matter if the grievance letter states that it is 'informal' and reserves the right to raise a formal grievance.[33] Indeed, the employee need not even be intending to raise a grievance in the letter.[34] The grievance letter can deal with other matters, eg a request for flexible working, and can be contained in a resignation letter, a solicitor's letter or a letter before action.[35] It can even be in a solicitor's 'without prejudice' letter,[36] although this seems risky. In one case, it was sufficient that the employee presented a complaint of bullying verbally to his manager at a meeting, which the manager noted contemporaneously, and the employee agreed the note as a written record of the grievance.[37] However, it is extremely unwise to rely on this being accepted in other cases. The statement or questions in a discrimination questionnaire do not in themselves constitute a statement of grievance,[38] nor is it enough to raise the complaint in the context of other litigation, eg a county court pleading.[39]

22.49   The only requirement is that the initial grievance letter, read in context, makes essentially the same complaint that is later the subject of the tribunal case, but in no way does it need to be identical to the later pleaded tribunal claim.[40] In an equal pay claim, it is enough for the original grievance statement to identify that it is talking about equal pay

---

30 *Galaxy Showers Ltd v Wilson* [2006] IRLR 83, EAT.

31 *Canary Wharf Management Ltd v Edebi* [2006] IRLR 416, EAT; *Galaxy Showers Ltd v Wilson* [2006] IRLR 83, EAT.

32 *Shergold v Fieldway Medical Centre* [2006] IRLR 76, EAT.

33 *Procek v Oakford Farms Ltd* UKEAT/0049/08; November 2008 *Legal Action* 12.

34 *Thorpe v Poat and Lake* [2006] All ER (D) 30 (Jan), EAT; UKEAT/0503/2005.

35 EA(DR) Regs 2004 reg 2(2); *Shergold v Fieldway Medical Centre* [2006] IRLR 76, EAT; *Mark Warner Ltd v Aspland* [2006] IRLR 87, EAT; *Commotion v Rutty* [2006] IRLR 171, EAT.

36 *Arnold Clark Automobiles Ltd v Richard Stewart and Barnetts Moro Group Ltd* UKEATS/0052/05; May 2006 *Legal Action.*

37 *Kennedy Scott Ltd v Francis* UKEAT/0204/07; November 2007 *Legal Action* 16.

38 EA(DR) Regs 2004 reg 14; *Holc-Gale v Makers UK Ltd* [2006] IRLR 178, EAT.

39 *Burns v Killgerm Group Ltd* UKEAT/0548/08.

40 *Canary Wharf Management Ltd v Edebi* [2006] IRLR 416, EAT; *Cannop and others v Highland Council sub nom Highland Council v TGWU and others* [2008] IRLR 634; *Legal Action* Dec 2008, CS; *Shergold v Fieldway Medical Centre* [2006] IRLR 76, EAT.

as opposed to, for example, a complaint about the minimum wage[41] In a discrimination claim, it is probably necessary to state the facts or different treatment are based on a particular type of discrimination, eg race or disability, and to itemise the acts of discrimination complained of, eg failed promotion. The grievance document need not be read in isolation. There may have been earlier or – less likely, later – communications which illuminate the scope of the grievance.[42] What is already in the employer's knowledge is also relevant.[43]

22.50   Before the grievance meeting, the employee must inform the employer of the 'basis' for the grievance, ie provide more detail. It is therefore usually easiest and safest if the initial letter includes both the complaint and its basis. This is particularly crucial where the modified grievance procedure is used, as the initial letter must then include the basis for the grievance. It is easy to confuse the two procedures. When reading the case-law regarding what must go into a written grievance, keep in mind whether the courts are talking about the standard or modified grievance procedure. As the modified procedure is confined to written exchanges, it is important that the written grievance sets out essential details such as who, what, where, when and why.[44] The amount of information which can be set out in a grievance obviously depends on how much is within the employer's knowledge as opposed to the employee's. As a rough guide, the initial statement of grievance should set out the key facts; contain enough detail for the employer to understand and investigate the complaint; itemise every matter of concern to the employee; and make it clear if discrimination is alleged and what kind. If it is intended to claim continuing discrimination, all the incidents should be listed, but it is not necessary to keep submitting further grievances regarding the same continuing act.[45] It is important to include any discriminatory remarks. With an equal pay claim, the basis for the grievance should include the male comparators who will be used in the tribunal case, the type of work they are doing and the nature of the pay differential, but it is not necessary to itemise

41 *Suffolk Mental Health Partnership NHS Trust v Hurst and others; Sandwell Metropolitan Borough Council v Arnold and others* [2009] EWCA Civ 309; [2009] IRLR 452, CA.

42 *Cannop and others v Highland Council sub nom Highland Council v TGWU and others* [2008] IRLR 634, CS; December 2008 *Legal Action* 12.

43 *Cumbria Protection Board v Collingwood* UKEAT/0079/08.

44 *Clyde Valley Housing Association v McAulay* UKEATS/0045/07; [2008] IRLR 616; December 2008 *Legal Action* 13, EAT.

45 *Weare v HBOS plc* UKEAT/0300/08.

each part of the pay package.[46] In a harassment case, it should set out all the important matters which the employer needs to investigate, without necessarily mentioning every little detail. If the grievance is simply based on a suspicion, it should set out the reasons for holding the suspicion.[47]

22.51   It is uncertain whether it is enough to describe the factual basis of the complaint or whether it is necessary to identify the applicable legal entitlement. The former is probably sufficient if the facts clearly describe a legal claim, but again, it is safest to label the legal entitlement where possible, eg 'unlawful deduction' or 'sexual harassment'. Where applicable, it is certainly necessary to clarify that discrimination is being complained about and what kind (race, sex etc) as opposed to simply unfairness. In summary, it is safest if a letter clearly states that it is a grievance, asks the employer to investigate, sets out the complaint fully and identifies the relevant legal entitlement, rather like the details of the intended tribunal claim. However, the case-law indicates that most of this is not necessary and there may well be tactical reasons for taking a lower key approach – but be very careful.

What are the consequences if the procedures are not followed?

22.52   The statutory dispute resolution procedures do not form part of the employee's contract of employment.[48] Failure by the employee or employer to follow the procedures is therefore only significant if the employee brings a tribunal case for unfair dismissal, constructive unfair dismissal, discrimination or the various matters covered by the statutory procedures (see para 22.78 below). If so, there are three key consequences:

- Adjustment of compensation (DDP or GP)
- Automatic unfair dismissal (DDP)
- Barred ET claims (GP)

Adjustment of compensation (DDP or GP)

22.53   If either the employer or employee fails to comply with a requirement of the DDP or GP, non-completion of the procedure will be attributed

---

46 *European Credit Management Ltd v Hosso (debarred)* UKEAT/0240/08, on the last point.
47 *City of Bradford Metropolitan District Council v Pratt* [2007] IRLR 192, EAT.
48 EA 2002 s30 has not been brought into force.

to him/her and the procedure need not go on to be completed. If the employee goes on to win any related tribunal case, the employee's compensation will be increased or reduced by 10–50 per cent (except in exceptional circumstances) according to who was at fault for the non-completion of the procedure.[49] A percentage increase is often referred to as an 'uplift' in the compensation. If it is automatic unfair dismissal, there is also a minimum four-week basic award.[50] Note that the requirements of the procedure are essentially those set out in the checklist at para 22.71 below. Although there is some ambiguity in the body of the procedures as to whether the employee must appeal an unsuccessful disciplinary or grievance, it seems clear from EA 2002 s31(2) that compensation can be reduced for failing to do so. Arguably, if the employer fails to notify the employee of the right to appeal, the employer has 'failed to complete' the procedure, and the employee need not then appeal if s/he does not want to. For dangers where the employee does not want his/her job back, see para 22.40.

22.54   The employee does not need to await the completion of the grievance procedure before starting his/her ET claim – indeed it is possible that the procedure will not yet be finished by the time limit. The employee only needs to have sent the step 1 letter and waited 28 days (see below). Nor should the employee be penalised in compensation because the procedure has not been completed by the time s/he starts his/her ET claim, so long as s/he continues to comply properly with the procedure.[51]

22.55   If the claimant wants a large uplift on his/her compensation, s/he should ensure that the necessary evidence is before the tribunal. The main factor affecting the size of the compensatory uplift for an employer's failure to follow the statutory procedure will be the degree to which the employer was 'culpable'. Ignorance of the law or a mistaken belief that one of the exceptions applied is likely to lead to a low-end uplift. Flagrant and deliberate disregard of the procedures will lead to an uplift near the top end. But complete failure to follow the procedures does not necessarily mean it will be a high uplift. It all depends on the reason for the failure. A merely technical breach which did not make much difference to the claimant's substantive rights will probably be low end. But a more substantial breach, eg failing to give the claimant sufficient information to argue against why s/he should be dismissed, is more likely to be high end. Rather controversially, the

49 EA 2002 s31.
50 Employment Rights Act (ERA) 1996 s120(1A).
51 Though some commentators worry there might be a penalty.

Scottish EAT has said that matters which do not relate to the actual conduct of the procedures should not be taken into account. It has also said that it is not relevant to take into account what has happened after the conclusion of the procedures, so it is irrelevant, eg, that either party has acted unreasonably or improperly in the conduct of the tribunal case.[52] Only in exceptional cases would it be relevant to take into account the size of the award to which the uplift will be applied.[53]

Automatic unfair dismissal (DDP)

22.56   If the employer is at fault for non-completion of a DDP in relation to dismissal, the employee can claim automatic unfair dismissal under ERA 1996 s98A (provided s/he has at least one year's service).[54] The employee cannot claim automatic unfair dismissal if the employer failed to follow the DDP solely in respect of relevant disciplinary action other than dismissal.[55] There is no automatic unfair dismissal if the procedure was in fact completed (ie finished), even if the employer failed to follow some of the general requirements such as avoiding unreasonable delays.[56] The only significance of failure to follow such requirements is that, if the procedure is not finished, it indicates who is responsible for the non-completion.

22.57   If the employee has less than one year's service, the employer can get away with not following the DDP, unless there is some other claim the employee can make based on the dismissal, which does not require one year's service, eg dismissal for asserting a statutory right or discrimination. In such a case, the employee can at least claim a percentage uplift in compensation if the employer did not follow the DDP. So, for example, if an employee brings a case under the Race Relations Act (RRA) 1976 and proves his/her dismissal was unlawful race discrimination, s/he will get extra compensation if the DDP was not followed. It seems that notice pay, as a wrongful dismissal claim,

52 The key cases regarding the uplift are *Aptuit (Edinburgh) Ltd v Kennedy* UKEATS/0057/06; November 2007 *Legal Action* 17; *McKindless Group v McLaughlin* UKEATS/0010/08; [2008] IRLR 678; November 2008 *Legal Action* 12, EAT; *CEX Ltd v Lewis* UKEAT/0013/07; *Home Office v Khan & King* UKEAT/0257/07; *Davies v Farnborough College of Technology* UKEAT/0137/07; [2008] IRLR 14, EAT; *Virgin Media Ltd v Seddington and Eland* UKEAT/0539/08.

53 *Abbey National PLC v Chagger* [2009] IRLR 86, EAT.

54 ERA 1996 s108.

55 *A to B Travel Ltd v Kennedy* UKEAT/0341/06.

56 *Selvarajan v Wilmot & others* [2008] IRLR 824; *Legal Action* Nov 2008, CA.

is covered by the DDP[57] and presumably therefore not by the statutory grievance procedure.[58]

Barred ET claims (GP)

22.58 An employee who has not sent his/her employer a step 1 grievance letter, where the GP applies, will be debarred from bringing an ET case altogether (with the exception of breach of contract claims – see para 22.41). A tribunal cannot hear the complaint, even if the ET1 was mistakenly accepted, if it was apparent in the ET1 that a step 1 letter was required but had not been submitted, or if the employer raised the failure in accordance with the ET rules of procedure.[59] This seems to mean that the employers must raise the failure in their tribunal response, although they can amend the response later if necessary (and if permitted by the ET), eg following a case management discussion.[60]

Extension of time limits where the statutory dispute resolution procedures apply

22.59 Each employment right has its own time limit. Normal time limits for starting an unfair dismissal case are set out at para 20.27 onwards and for starting a discrimination case are set out at para 21.13. Where either the DDP or statutory grievance procedure applies, the normal ET time limit in some circumstances can be extended by three months beginning with the day after the day on which it would otherwise have expired.[61] For example, if the normal time limit expires on 19 September 2008, the further three months is counted from 20 September 2008 and ends on 19 December 2008.[62] This is confusing because the normal unfair dismissal and discrimination time limits are calculated as three months less one day from the relevant date, yet the extended time is a further three months, but not less one day,

57 *London Borough of Lambeth & others v Corlett* UKEAT/0396/06.

58 Applying EA(DR) Regs 2004 reg 6(5).

59 EA 2002 s32(6). See para 20.17 for ET rules of procedure.

60 *DMC Business Machines plc v Plummer* UKEAT 0381/06; *Holc-Gale v Makers UK Ltd* [2006] IRLR 178, EAT.

61 EA(DR) Regs 2004 reg 15(1).

62 *Singh t/a Rainbow International v Taylor* UKEAT/0183/06. Although the EAT calculated three months from 19 September 2005 (the day after the original time limit) as expiring on 20 December 2005, commentators agree this was a miscalculation; *Joshi v Manchester City Council* UKEAT/0235/07.

making a total of six months less one day. This difference is due to the different wording in the legislation regarding time limits.

22.60   The unfair dismissal time limit is extended only where, at the time the time limit expires, the employee has reasonable grounds for believing that a dismissal or disciplinary procedure, (whether the DDP or other, eg contractual disciplinary procedure), is still on-going in respect of the substance of the ET complaint.[63] For example, an appeal has been lodged but not yet resolved. If the employee appealed fairly promptly after s/he had been dismissed and either the employer has responded, indicating the matter is in progress, or not much time has passed, then there should be no problems. It may be harder to show there are reasonable grounds for believing the procedure is being followed where the employee submitted an appeal a long time after dismissal and the employer has failed to respond. If the disciplinary procedure is still uncompleted after the three-month extension, there is no further extension. The employee may therefore have to start a tribunal case even though his/her appeal has not yet been heard. If the internal appeal is concluded only hours before expiry of the normal three month time-limit, there can be no extension of time under the statutory dispute resolution procedures. However, it may be a basis for extending time under the normal unfair dismissal rules on the ground that it was not reasonably practicable to get the claim in on time.[64]

22.61   In contrast, the time limit for any claim where the statutory grievance procedure must be followed is always extended by three months, once a step 1 grievance letter has been sent to the employer regarding that matter within the normal ET time limit.[65] It is irrelevant whether the grievance procedure has finished or even if the employer has stated s/he will not deal with it. If the procedure is still not finished after the three-month extension, there is no further extension and the employee must start his/her ET case.

22.62   If the employee presents his/her ET claim without having sent a step 1 grievance letter to his/her employer, the ET will send it back.[66] The ET cannot just put the claim on hold while the claimant lodges a grievance and waits 28 days.[67] As long as the claimant submitted the ET claim within the normal time limit, s/he will now get a three-month

63 EA(DR) Regs 2004 reg 15(1) and (2). Formal negotiations for a compromise agreement may amount to a 'dismissal procedure', *Eagles v Rugged Systems Ltd* UKEAT/0018/09, but don't rely on this.

64 *Royal Bank of Scotland v Bevan* UKEAT/0440/07; see para 20.31.

65 EA(DR) Regs 2004 reg 15(1) and 15(3)(b).

66 See paras 20.45–20.46.

67 *London Borough of Hounslow v Miller* UKEAT/0645/06.

extension for relodging the claim.[68] Meanwhile the claimant must send his/her employer the step 1 letter no more than one month after the end of the 'original' time limit for making the claim.[69] The 'original' time limit as opposed to the 'normal' time limit, means the primary three-month time limit plus any extension allowed by the employment tribunal under its discretion.[70]

22.63   The three-month extension gets added to the normal time limit, so that the effect in discrimination cases is to apply a six-month tribunal time limit from the date when time starts running.[71] For example, if the employee wants to claim about a discriminatory warning issued on 3 March 2009, the normal time limit would be 2 June 2009. The extended time limit for lodging the ET claim would be 2 September 2009, provided either (i) the employee sends his/her employer a step 1 letter by 2 June 2009, or (ii) lodges his/her ET claim by 2 June 2009, has it returned, then sends his/her employer a step 1 letter no more than one month after the original time-limit.

22.64   There is an additional rule where the statutory grievance procedure applies. The employee must wait until 28 days have passed since sending the step 1 letter before s/he can lodge his/her ET claim.[72] If the grievance letter is sent on a Monday, for example, the employee cannot lodge the ET claim before the Tuesday four weeks later.[73]

22.65   These extensions only operate where the DDP or GP applies. For this reason, it is crucial to know the difference between situations where the procedures apply but are deemed completed, and where they do not apply at all.[74] Unless it is certain that the statutory procedures do not apply, it will usually be safest to keep to the following steps to cover every eventuality:

- Send the employer a step 1 grievance letter within the normal unextended time limit.
- Lodge the claim within the normal unextended time limit. Where there are claims which may fall under the statutory grievance procedure, this means sending the step 1 letter sufficiently in advance of the time limit for the 28 days to pass.

---

68 EA(DR) Regs 2004 reg 15(1) and (3)(a).

69 EA 2002 s32(4)(b).

70 *BUPA Care Homes (BNH) Ltd v Cann, Spillett v Tesco Stores Ltd* [2006] IRLR 248; May 2006 *Legal Action* 22, EAT.

71 EA(DR) Regs 2004 reg 15(1).

72 EA 2002 s32(3).

73 *Basingstoke Press Ltd (in administration) v Clarke* [2007] IRLR 588, EAT.

74 See paras 22.72–22.76.

- If it is not possible to send the step 1 grievance letter more than 28 days before the time limit, lodge the ET1 within the normal time limit anyway and send a step 1 letter to the employer at the same time. Then if the ET1 is returned because the statutory dispute resolution procedures apply, it can be relodged within the extended time limit, the step 1 letter having already been safely sent.

22.66   Time limits can be very complicated where the worker has several claims including unfair dismissal. Not only do different time limits apply to each claim, counted from different starting points, but the three-month extension may apply to claims under the statutory grievance procedure, but not to the unfair dismissal.[75] In this situation, ideally the entire claim would be submitted within the time limit for the earliest claim. If this is impossible, separate claims will have to be submitted and the ET should be notified at the outset that further claims are coming and should be considered together. Unfortunately this can lead to great confusion within the ET's administration. Time-limits may also vary according to whether the statutory dispute resolution procedures still apply under the transitional provisions. This is particularly difficult in situations of continuing discrimination where it may be ambiguous whether the statutory grievance procedure still applies. For a series of examples regarding time limits and extensions, see para 22.77.

Abolition of the statutory dispute resolution procedures: transitional provisions

22.67   The statutory dispute resolution procedures will continue to apply to cases where the relevant trigger event occurred before 6 April 2009.[76] In such cases, the whole pre-6 April 2009 regime will apply, ie the statutory procedures, the rules about time limits, the rules regarding automatic unfair dismissals, the partial reversal of *Polkey* and the old tribunal Claim form. The new ACAS regime will apply where the trigger event took place on or after 6 April 2009.

22.68   The statutory DDP still applies where, on or before 5 April 2009, the employer has (a) sent the employee a Step 1 statement or held a Step 2 meeting, or (b) taken relevant disciplinary action against the employee, or (c) dismissed the employee. The position under the

---

75 See also para 21.31 regarding discrimination claims.
76 Details set out in the Employment Act 2008 (Commencement No 1, Transitional Provisions and Savings) Order 2008, SI No 3232.

statutory grievance procedure is potentially more complicated. The old regime still applies if the action about which the employee complains in his/her grievance occurred wholly before 6 April 2009. The difficulty arises where the action forming the basis of the grievance began on or before 5 April 2009 and continued afterwards. In that situation, the old regime still applies if the employee submitted a written grievance or tribunal Claim on or before 4 July 2009 (in relation to a jurisdiction with a three-month time limit, eg discrimination or constructive dismissal) or on or before 4 October 2009 (in relation to claims with a 6 month time limit, ie equal pay, redundancy or dismissal in connection with industrial action under TULR(C)A 1992 s238). Examples of how these transitional provisions apply are at para 22.77. Where they have a choice, employees can decide which regime they would prefer to apply, but they must be careful to keep within time limits.

22.69   It is not entirely clear in what circumstances the relevant 'action' would begin on or before 5 April and continue afterwards. Presumably this envisages matters such as a sequence of unlawful deductions; a series of incidents culminating in a resignation for constructive dismissal, or a continuing discriminatory state of affairs. The problem in the latter case is that it is not always certain whether a tribunal will regard a series of incidents as separate or as one continuing act. Moreover, in a case where a tribunal decides that the discriminatory actions were separate incidents over a long period of time, partly before 6 April and partly afterwards, an odd situation would arise, whereby the old regime would apply to the earlier incidents and the new regime to the later incidents.

Checklists

Which of DDP or GP applies

22.70   The following checklist covers the most common situations.

Claim	Procedure
unfair dismissal	DDP
discriminatory dismissal	DDP
constructive dismissal	GP

continued

Claim	Procedure
action short of dismissal which is discriminatory	GP. If the action is also relevant disciplinary action (unpaid suspension; demotion, etc): also DDP
discrimination case: dismissal + pre-dismissal detriments	DDP for the dismissal + GP for the other detriments
unfair dismissal + holiday pay	DDP for the dismissal + GP for the holiday pay
minimum wage	GP
unauthorised deduction from pay	GP
statutory redundancy pay and unfair dismissal on grounds of redundancy	GP for the redundancy pay[77] + DDP for the dismissal
notice pay	DDP[78]
relevant disciplinary action or dismissal for conduct, capability, redundancy, etc	Standard DDP
employee already dismissed without any hearing for gross misconduct and reasonable to dispense with a hearing.	Modified DDP
constructive dismissal; discrimination and other claims (not dismissal)	Standard GP
employee has left employer and both agree in writing to use modified procedure	Modified GP
relevant disciplinary action (not dismissal which is discriminatory	DDP and GP

---

77 Unless this amounts to a complaint about dismissal, but probably not.
78 See para 22.57.

The procedural steps

22.71 The EA 2002 sets out the statutory dispute resolution procedures at Schedule 2. The following checklist sets out the legal minimum stages for the standard and modified procedures (see paras 22.37–22.47 for when each of these apply). Remember that under the employee's own contractual procedures, s/he may have additional rights and requirements, which are relevant to an ordinary unfair dismissal claim.

Standard DDP[79]

- Step 1 letter: The employer sends the employee a letter setting out the employee's alleged conduct or characteristics or other circumstances which lead him/her to contemplate dismissing or taking disciplinary action, and inviting the employee to a meeting.[80] At this stage, the letter only needs to state the issue in broad terms. The employee must be able to understand from the letter that s/he is at risk of dismissal, where this is the case.[81] So for example, in a misconduct case, it only needs to identify the nature of the misconduct (fighting, dishonesty, etc) and to tell the employee that s/he is at risk of dismissal.[82] Some employers operate a more complex contractual procedure, with an investigatory meeting prior to the disciplinary meeting. In such circumstances, the statutory procedure may still be satisfied if the employer sends the step 1 letter with the required detail prior to the investigatory meeting and sends no further letter before the disciplinary meeting.[83]
- Before the meeting, the employer must inform the employee, verbally or in writing, of the 'basis' for the grounds in the step 1 letter.[84] The employer may choose to state both the grounds and the 'basis' for them in the original step 1 letter.[85] The 'basis' for the contemplated action does not mean all the detailed evidence which the employer is relying on, but it must include a sufficiently detailed statement of the case against the employee for him/her to properly put his/her

---

79 Set out at EA 2002 Sch 2 paras 1–3. The general requirements are at Sch 2 paras 11–13.

80 EA 2002 Sch 2 para 1.

81 *Zimmer Ltd v Brezan* UKEAT/0294/08.

82 *Alexander and another v Brigden Enterprises Ltd* [2006] IRLR 422, EAT.

83 *YMCA Training v Stewart* UKEAT/0332/06.

84 EA 2002 Sch 2 para 2(2)(a).

85 *YMCA Training v Stewart* UKEAT/0332/06.

side of the story.[86] In a misconduct case, this may mean supplying the main evidence against the employee including any statements taken, and in a redundancy case,[87] the reason why there is a redundancy situation, the selection criteria, the assessment of the employee and enough information to enable the employee to understand why s/he has been chosen rather than others. Therefore it may or may not be necessary under the statutory DDP to provide the assessment of other employees, but failure to do so may in some circumstances make the dismissal unfair on ordinary principles.[88]

- The employee must have a reasonable opportunity (ie sufficient time) to consider his/her response before the meeting.[89]
- The employee must take all reasonable steps to attend the meeting.[90]
- Step 2: The meeting is held. The timing and location of the meeting must be reasonable.[91]
- The meeting must be conducted in a manner which enables both employer and employee to explain their case.[92]
- Except where the disciplinary action consists of suspension, the meeting must take place before any action is taken against the employee.[93] As long as no action has yet taken place, it seems an employer can get away with failing to follow step 1 initially, by writing further letters and holding further meetings.[94]
- After the meeting, the employer must notify the employee of his/her decision and inform him/her of the right to appeal.[95] There is no requirement that the decision is put in writing.
- The employer is under no obligation under the DDP to supply to the employee any further evidence obtained during an investigation following the disciplinary hearing, although failure to do so may make the dismissal unfair on ordinary principles.[96]

86 *Alexander and another v Brigden Enterprises Ltd* [2006] IRLR 422, EAT; *YMCA Training v Stewart* UKEAT/0332/06.

87 *Alexander and another v Brigden Enterprises Ltd* [2006] IRLR 422, EAT; *Davies v Farnborough College of Technology* UKEAT/0137/07.

88 But see para 8.27.

89 EA 2002 Sch 2 para 2(2)(b).

90 EA 2002 Sch 2 para 2(3).

91 EA 2002 Sch 2 para 13(1).

92 EA 2002 Sch 2 para 13(2).

93 EA 2002 Sch 2 para 2(1). For the consequences of not following correct procedures in relation to unpaid suspension, see *Masterfoods (a division of Mars UK Ltd) v Wilson* UKEAT/0202/06.

94 *Smith Knight Fay Ltd v McKoy* UKEAT/0245/08.

95 EA 2002 Sch 2 para 2(4).

96 *YMCA Training v Stewart* UKEAT/0332/06.

- Step 3: If the employee wishes to appeal, s/he must inform the employer.[97] There is no requirement as to the form the appeal must take. It need not be in writing and it need not specify grounds, even if that is what the employer's contractual procedure requires.[98] Although many employers' procedures impose tight time limits on submitting appeals, there is no time limit under the DDP, except that all steps must be taken without unreasonable delay (see below).
- The employer must then invite the employee to an appeal meeting. The timing and location of the meeting must be reasonable.[99]
- The employee must take all reasonable steps to attend the appeal meeting.
- As far as is reasonably practicable, the employer should be represented by a more senior manager than attended the original meeting.[100]
- The meeting must be conducted in a manner which enables both employer and employee to explain their case.[101]
- After the appeal meeting, the employer must notify the employee of the final decision.
- Each step and action under the procedure must be taken without unreasonable delay.[102]
- If either party or the employee's companion is unable to attend the disciplinary or appeal meeting for reasons which were not foreseeable at the time the meeting was arranged, the employer must fix a new date. If the employer fixes a new date and again someone cannot attend for unforeseeable reasons, each party is deemed to have complied with the procedure and nothing further need be done.[103]
- Note that under Employment Relations Act (ERelA) 1999 s10, a worker has a right to be accompanied to a disciplinary hearing by a work colleague or trade union official. However, this is an entitlement under a different piece of legislation with different remedies if the employer fails to allow the companion.[104]

---

97 EA 2002 Sch 2 para 3(1).
98 *Masterfoods (a division of Mars UK Ltd) v Wilson* UKEAT/0202/06.
99 EA 2002 Sch 2 para 13(1).
100 EA 2002 Sch 2 para 13(3).
101 EA 2002 Sch 2 para 13(2).
102 EA 2002 Sch 2 para 12.
103 EA(DR) Regs 2004 reg 13.
104 See paras 22.80–22.83.

Modified DDP[105]

- Step 1: The employer must send the employee a letter setting out the employee's alleged gross misconduct which has led to the dismissal and the basis for considering the employee guilty of gross misconduct.
- Step 2: If the employee wishes to appeal, s/he must inform the employer.
- The employer must then invite him/her to an appeal meeting. The timing and location of the meeting must be reasonable.
- The employee must take all reasonable steps to attend the appeal meeting.
- The meeting must be conducted in a manner which enables both employer and employee to explain their case.[106]
- After the appeal meeting, the employer must notify the employee of the final decision.
- Each step and action under the procedure must be taken without unreasonable delay.[107]
- If either party or the employee's companion is unable to attend the appeal meeting for reasons which were not foreseeable at the time the meeting was arranged, the employer must fix a new date. If the employer fixes a new date and again someone cannot attend for unforeseeable reasons, each party is deemed to have complied with the procedure and nothing further need be done.[108]
- Note that under ERelA 1999 s10, a worker has a right to be accompanied to an appeal against disciplinary action by a work colleague or trade union official. However, this is an entitlement under a different piece of legislation with different remedies if the employer fails to allow the companion.[109]

Standard GP[110]

- Step 1 letter: The employee sends the employer a written grievance.[111]

105 Set out at EA 2002 Sch 2 paras 4–5. The general requirements are at paras 11–13. See para 22.37 above for when it applies.
106 EA 2002 Sch 2 para 13(2).
107 EA 2002 Sch 2 para 12.
108 EA(DR) Regs 2004 reg 13.
109 See paras 22.80–22.83.
110 Set out at EA 2002 Sch 2 paras 6–8.
111 EA 2002 Sch 2 para 6. See para 22.48 above regarding the content of a grievance letter.

- The employer must invite the employee to a meeting to discuss the grievance.[112] It is not sufficient for the employer to invite the employee to a meeting to discuss other matters unless it is made clear that part of the meeting is to discuss the grievance.[113] The timing and location of the meeting must be reasonable.[114]
- Before the meeting, the employee must inform the employer of the 'basis' for the grievance.[115] (It is simplest to include these details in the original letter.)
- The employer must have a reasonable opportunity (ie sufficient time) to consider his/her response before the meeting.[116]
- The employee must take all reasonable steps to attend the meeting.[117]
- Step 2: The meeting is held. The meeting must be conducted in a manner which enables both employer and employee to explain their case.[118]
- After the meeting, the employer must notify the employee of his/her decision and inform him/her of the right to appeal.[119] There is no requirement that this is in writing.
- Step 3: If the employee wishes to appeal, s/he must inform the employer.[120] There is no requirement that this is in writing or that grounds are given or that the appeal is lodged within a specified time, although all steps must be taken without unreasonable delay (see below).[121]
- The employer must then invite the employee to an appeal meeting. The timing and location of the meeting must be reasonable.[122]
- The employee must take all reasonable steps to attend the appeal meeting.
- So far as is reasonably practicable, the employer should be represented by a more senior manager at the appeal than at the original meeting.[123]

---

112 EA 2002 Sch 2 para 7(1).
113 *Galaxy Showers Ltd v Wilson* [2006] IRLR 83, EAT.
114 EA 2002 Sch 2 para 13(1).
115 EA 2002 Sch 2 para 7(2)(a). See para 22.50 re meaning of 'basis'.
116 EA 2002 Sch 2 para 7(2)(b).
117 EA 2002 Sch 2 para 7(3).
118 EA 2002 Sch 2 para 13(2).
119 EA 2002 Sch 2 para 7(4).
120 EA 2002 Sch 2 para 8(1).
121 See case-law on this aspect under list of procedural steps for DDP, above.
122 EA 2002 Sch 2 para 13(1).
123 EA 2002 Sch 2 para 13(3).

- The meeting must be conducted in a manner which enables both employer and employee to explain their case.[124]
- After the appeal meeting, the employer must notify the employee of the final decision.
- Each step and action under the procedure must be taken without unreasonable delay.[125]
- If either party or the employee's companion is unable to attend the grievance or appeal meeting for reasons which were not foreseeable at the time the meeting was arranged, the employer must fix a new date. If the employer fixes a new date and again, someone cannot attend for unforeseeable reasons, each party is deemed to have complied with the procedure and nothing further need be done.[126]
- Note that under ERelA 1999 s10, a worker has a right to be accompanied to a grievance hearing by a work colleague or trade union official. However, this is an entitlement under a different piece of legislation with different remedies if the employer fails to allow the companion.[127]

Modified GP[128]

- Step 1: The employee must set out in writing the grievance and its basis and send this to the employer.
- Step 2: The employer must send the employee a written response.

Exceptions to statutory dispute resolution rules

Exceptions, where the DDP does not apply

22.72   Remember that, even where the statutory dispute resolution procedures do not apply, an employer risks a finding of unfair dismissal if s/he does not follow fair procedures.

Neither the standard nor the modified DDP apply in the following situations and ET time limits will not be extended on this basis:

- The worker is not an employee.

---

124 EA 2002 Sch 2 para 13(2).
125 EA 2002 Sch 2 para 12.
126 EA(DR) Regs 2004 reg 13.
127 See paras 22.80–22.83.
128 Set out at EA 2002 Sch 2 paras 9–10. See para 22.44 above for when it applies.

- The employee does not qualify to claim unfair dismissal and the dismissal was for a reason not covered by EA 2002 Sch 3 (see paras 22.78–22.79 below).
- The employee was constructively dismissed (although a DDP would apply to any 'relevant disciplinary action' prior to the dismissal).
- All employees of the employee's description or category are dismissed and then re-engaged,[129] eg as may happen in mass dismissals to effect a change in terms and conditions.
- The employee's dismissal was one of a number of dismissals where an employer has a duty under TULR(C)A 1992 s188 to consult,[130] basically collective redundancies.[131]
- Certain types of industrial action dismissal.[132]
- The employer's business suddenly ceases to function because of an unforeseen event.[133]
- The employee cannot continue to work without contravention of a statutory duty or restriction,[134] eg health and safety legislation.
- A dismissal procedures agreement applies under ERA 1996 s110.[135]
- The modified DDP would apply, but the employee lodges a tribunal claim before the employer has sent the step 1 letter.[136]
- The employer has reasonable grounds to believe that starting the DDP would result in significant threat to any person or property.[137]
- The employer has been subjected to harassment and has reasonable grounds to believe that starting the procedure would result in him/her being subjected to further harassment.[138]
- It is not practicable for the employer to start the procedure within a reasonable period.[139] Presumably this means due to illness, closure of the business or absence, but this is untested.
- National security.[140]

---

129 EA(DR) Regs 2004 reg 4(1)(e).
130 EA(DR) Regs 2004 reg 4(1)(b).
131 See para 2.17.
132 EA(DR) Regs 2004 regs 4(1)(c), (d).
133 EA(DR) Regs 2004 reg 4(1)(e).
134 EA(DR) Regs 2004 reg 4(1)(f).
135 EA(DR) Regs 2004 reg 4(1)(g).
136 EA(DR) Regs 2004 reg 3(2).
137 EA(DR) Regs 2004 regs 11(1) and (3)(a).
138 EA(DR) Regs 2004 regs 11(1) and (3)(b). See note at para 22.76 below.
139 EA(DR) Regs 2004 reg 11(1) and (3)(c).
140 EA(DR) Regs 2004 reg 16.

Exceptions where the DDP does apply but is deemed to have been followed

22.73   As the DDP is deemed to have been followed in the following situations, it is possible that ET time limits may be extended (subject to the rules on time limits).

- The DDP has been started, but the employee or employer has reasonable grounds to believe that continuing with the DDP would result in significant threat to any person or property.[141]
- The DDP has been started, but the employee or employer has been subjected to harassment and has reasonable grounds to believe that continuing with the procedure would result in him/her being subjected to further harassment.[142]
- The DDP has been started, but it is not practicable for the employee or employer to comply with a subsequent requirement of the procedure within a reasonable period.[143]
- On two occasions, it has not been reasonably practicable for unforeseen reasons for either the employee or the employer to attend a meeting after it has been organised.[144]
- National security.[145]
- Where the employee has presented an application for interim relief,[146] having completed the disciplinary stage of the DDP, the appeal stage is deemed completed.
- Where the employee appeals under an alternative industry wide procedure.[147]

Exceptions where the GP does not apply

22.74   Although the statutory GP does not apply in the following situations, an employee should always be entitled to bring a grievance about a matter of concern. The statutory GP does not apply in these situations, and there is therefore no possibility of any extension of ET time limits on this basis:

- The worker is not an employee.

141 EA(DR) Regs 2004 reg 11(2) and (3)(a).
142 EA(DR) Regs 2004 reg 11(2) and (3)(b). See note at para 22.76 below.
143 EA(DR) Regs 2004 reg 11(2) and (3)(c).
144 EA(DR) Regs 2004 reg 13.
145 EA(DR) Regs 2004 reg 16.
146 EA(DR) Regs 2004 reg 5(1); see para 18.64.
147 See EA(DR) Regs 2004 reg 5(2)–(3) for wording.

- The complaint concerns a dismissal or failure to renew a fixed-term contract. (However, a grievance must be brought about constructive dismissal.)
- The complaint concerns 'relevant disciplinary action', ie disciplinary action, but not warnings or paid suspension. However, the GP does apply if the action was on hidden or discriminatory grounds, though it may be deemed complied with.[148]
- The complaint concerns a matter which is not covered by the dispute resolution rules at all, eg less favourable terms and conditions for a part-time worker. The full list of matters covered by the grievance procedure are set out in Schedules to the EA 2002 and are set out at para 22.78 below.
- The employee has reasonable grounds to believe that starting the GP would result in significant threat to any person or property.[149]
- The employee has been subjected to harassment and has reasonable grounds to believe that starting the procedure would result in him/her being subjected to further harassment.[150]
- It is not practicable for the employee to start the procedure within a reasonable period.[151] Presumably this means due to illness, closure of the business or absence, but this is untested. It may also include where the employee started the ET case without realising the statutory dispute resolution procedures apply and only finds out s/he should have sent a step 1 letter when it is too late to do so.
- The employee has left and since then, it has ceased to be reasonably practicable for the employee to send a step 1 grievance letter.[152]
- National security.[153]
- There are special rules concerning whistleblowing where the employee's disclosure concerns the treatment of him/herself.[154]

Exceptions where the GP does apply but is deemed to have been followed

22.75 In the following situations, as the GP applies and is deemed to have been completed, an extension of ET time limits is possible.

---

148 EA(DR) Regs 2004 regs 6(6) and 7(1).
149 EA(DR) Regs 2004 reg 11(1) and (3)(a).
150 EA(DR) Regs 2004 reg 11(1) and (3)(b). See note at para 22.76 below.
151 EA(DR) Regs 2004 reg 11(1) and (3)(c).
152 EA(DR) Regs 2004 reg 6(4); *Burt v UK Sports Centres Ltd* UKEAT/0290/08.
153 EA(DR) Regs 2004 reg 16.
154 EA 2002 Sch 2 para 15.

- The employee's grievance is part of a collective grievance, ie a trade union or employee representative sets out the grievance in writing on behalf of two or more employees.[155]
- The employee is following a grievance under a collectively agreed industry level grievance procedure between one or more employers or an employers association and one or more independent trade unions.[156]
- The GP has been started, but the employee or employer has reasonable grounds to believe that continuing with the GP would result in significant threat to any person or property.[157]
- The GP has been started, but the employee or employer has been subjected to harassment and has reasonable grounds to believe that continuing with the procedure would result in him/her being subjected to further harassment.[158]
- The GP has been started, but it is not practicable for the employee or employer to comply with a subsequent requirement of the procedure within a reasonable period. The fact that there are a large number of grievances to be dealt with by employees scattered across a large location will probably not be sufficient reason for the employer to say it is not practicable to hold the meetings within a reasonable time.[159]
- The employee has left, has sent a step 1 grievance letter before or after leaving, and it is not reasonably practicable to have a grievance or appeal meeting.[160] However, where there has been a grievance meeting, the employer must still provide a written response.[161]
- On two occasions, it has not been reasonably practicable for unforeseen reasons for either the employee or the employer to attend a meeting after it has been organised.[162]
- National security.[163]
- Where a GP applies to 'relevant disciplinary action' (because it is on hidden or discriminatory grounds), if a step 1 grievance letter is

---

155 EA(DR) Regs 2004 reg 9.
156 EA(DR) Regs 2004 reg 10.
157 EA(DR) Regs 2004 reg 11(2) and (3)(a).
158 EA(DR) Regs 2004 reg 11(2) and (3)(b). See note at para 22.76 below.
159 EA(DR) Regs 2004 reg 11(2) and 11(3)(c). *Bainbridge & ors v Redcar & Cleveland Borough Council* [2007] IRLR 494, EAT.
160 EA(DR) Regs 2004 reg 8(1).
161 EA(DR) Regs 2004 reg 8(2).
162 EA(DR) Regs 2004 reg 13.
163 EA(DR) Regs 2004 reg 16.

sent before the appeal stage of the DDP, the parties are treated as if they have complied with the entire grievance procedure.[164]

Notes on the exceptions

22.76   Several of the exceptions occur where it is not 'practicable' or not 'reasonably practicable' to have meetings and take steps. The measure of what is practicable is not defined in the legislation and is legally untested. Although it probably envisages situations such as illness, absence overseas and unavailability for other reasons, it is risky to rely on an ET accepting a particular reason.

The 'harassment' exception is more limited than it seems. This exception does not occur simply because harassment has occurred in the past. It has several precise elements:

- harassment must have occurred in the past;
- the employee (or employer) has reasonable grounds to believe that following the procedure would result in further harassment. This suggests that the employee will be penalised (harassed) because s/he has brought or followed the procedure or that the procedure will provide a specific opportunity for harassment. It does not seem to cover a situation where the employee will endure further harassment simply by virtue of the fact that s/he is still around in the workplace and has not yet resigned.

For these purposes, 'harassment' is defined as conduct which has the purpose or effect of violating the person's dignity or creating an intimidating, hostile, degrading, humiliating or offensive environment for him/her. It will only have that purpose or effect if, taking into account all the circumstances, particularly the perception of the harassed person, it should reasonably be considered as having that effect.[165]

Time limit examples under the statutory dispute resolution procedures[166]

22.77   The following are just some examples which should help to illustrate how time limits work and the pitfalls. However, the reader must always do his/her own calculations.

---

164 EA(DR) Regs 2004 reg 7.
165 EA(DR) Regs 2004 reg 11(4).
166 See para 22.59 onwards regarding extension of time limits.

(1) Unfair dismissal (relevant procedure: DDP)

Dismissal: 3 May 2009. (Step 1 letter sent 1 April 2009 so old regime applies.)

- Normal time limit: 2 August 2009.
- If a disciplinary procedure is ongoing as at 2 August 2009, time limit is extended to 2 November 2009 (even if the procedure is concluded between 3 August and 1 November 2009).
- If no disciplinary procedure is ongoing as at 2 August 2009, time limit remains 2 August 2009.

(2) Discriminatory dismissal under RRA 1976 (relevant procedure: DDP)

Dismissal: 3 May 2009. (Step 1 letter sent 1 April 2009 so old regime applies.)

- Normal time limit: 2 August 2009.
- If a disciplinary procedure is ongoing as at 2 August 2009, time limit is extended to 2 November 2009.
- If no disciplinary procedure is ongoing as at 2 August 2009, time limit remains 2 August 2009.

(3) Discriminatory warning under RRA 1976 (relevant procedure: GP)

Warning: 30 March 2009.

- Normal time limit: 29 June 2009.
- Provided step 1 grievance letter is sent to employer by 29 June 2009, ET time limit is extended to 29 September 2009. (Employee must wait 28 days after sending step 1 letter before presenting ET1.)
- If ET1 is presented to ET by 29 June 2009, but no step 1 letter has been sent to the employer, the ET will return the ET1 and the ET time limit is extended to 29 September 2009. However, the employee must now send a step 1 letter no more than one month after the original time-limit[167] and wait 28 days before relodging the claim.

---

167 See paras 22.62–22.63.

(4) Discriminatory warning and dismissal under RRA 1976 (relevant procedures: GP and DDP)

Warning: 30 March 2009; dismissal 3 May 2009. (Step 1 letter for dismissal sent 1st April 2009 so old regime applies.)

- The position on the warning is as at example (3) above. Time limit is extended to 29 September 2009 provided step 1 letter is sent no more than one month after the original time-limit.[168]
- The position on the dismissal is as at example (2) above. Time limit is extended to 2 November 2009 only if a disciplinary procedure was ongoing as at 2 August 2009. If necessary, however, separate ET1s can be lodged.

Note: If the disciplinary procedure regarding the dismissal is dealt with quickly and is completed by 2 August 2009, the time limit for the dismissal will be earlier than the time limit for the warning. To keep the whole claim together, the ET1 must therefore be submitted at the earlier time limit, ie on or before 2 August 2009

Transitional examples

(5) Unfair dismissal (relevant procedure: DDP)

Step 1 letter: 3 April 2009 (before transition date). Dismissal: 3 May 2009.

- applicable regime: old
- time limit: as (1) above.

(6) Discriminatory warning under RRA 1976 (relevant procedure: GP)

Warning: 30 March 2009 (before transition date).

- applicable regime: old
- time limit: as (3) above.

(7) Discriminatory warning under RRA 1976 (relevant procedure: GP)

Warning: 7 June 2009 (after transition date).

- applicable regime: new
- time limit: 6 September 2009.

---

168 See paras 22.62–22.63.

(8) Two unconnected discriminatory warnings (relevant procedure: GP)

First warning: 30 March 2009. Old regime. Time limit as (3), ie 29 September 2009.

Final warning: 7 June 2009. New regime. Time limit 6 September 2009.

Note: surprisingly, the time limit for the final warning is earlier than the time limit for the first warning. If the two warnings were considered part of a continuing discriminatory state of affairs, and thus an action beginning before the transition date and continuing afterwards, the time limit would be different again – see example (9). Unfortunately, it is not always clear whether a situation entails a continuing act of discrimination or separate and unconnected discriminatory acts.

(9) Continuing discriminatory action under the RRA 1976 (relevant procedure: GP)

The discriminatory action starts on 30 March 2009 (before the transition date) and continues until 7 June 2009 (after the transition date).

- Normal time limit: 6 September 2009.
- Applicable regime: depends on whether the employee submits a written grievance or tribunal claim on or before 4 July 2009.
- If the written grievance is sent to the employer on 1 July 2009: old regime; time limit 6 December 2009.
- If the tribunal claim is lodged on 1 July 2009, no previous written grievance having been sent: old regime. The tribunal will return the tribunal claim and the time limit for resubmitting it will be 6 December 2009. Meanwhile a written grievance must be sent to the employer no more than 1 month after the end of the original time limit.
- If neither a written grievance nor a tribunal claim is submitted before 5 July 2009: new regime. Time limit: 6 September 2009.

Jurisdictions covered by the statutory dispute resolution procedures and ACAS compensation regime

Jurisdictions covered by the statutory dispute resolution procedures and ACAS compensation regime

22.78 In respect of the statutory dispute resolution procedures, Schedules 3–5 to the EA 2002 are almost identical and are summarised below. It is indicated where any jurisdiction does not fall under all three schedules. Schedule 3 concerns all jurisdictions where an adjustment of compensation may be made for not following the procedures under EA 2002 s31. Schedule 4 concerns jurisdictions under EA 2002 s32 where an ET claim cannot be lodged unless there has been a previous step 1 grievance letter. Both Schedules 3 and 4 concern jurisdictions where time-limits may be extended in certain circumstances.[169] Schedule 5 concerns jurisdictions where compensation may be increased under EA 2002 s38 because at the time the case was started, the employer had not provided written particulars under ERA 1996 s1 or 4.[170] The new ACAS compensation regime applies to jurisdictions set out in TUL(R)A 1992 Schedule A2. Except for one jurisdiction indicated below, these are again identical to those in EA 2002 Schedules 3-4. Remember that in all cases, the claimant must be an employee.

The jurisdictions for all of the above are:

- discrimination law, ie claims under the EqPA 1970, SDA 1975, RRA 1976, DDA 1995, EE(RB) Regs 2003, EE(SO) Regs 2003; EE(A) Regs 2006;
- claims in respect of trade union membership and activities under TULR(C)A 1992 ss145A, 145B, 146, Sch A1 para 156;
- unlawful deductions from pay (including to recover pay below the minimum wage);
- ET claims which can be made under Working Time Regulations 1998 reg 30, regarding breaks and annual leave, etc; also for breach of the Cross-Border Railway Services (Working Time) Regulations 2008.
- claims regarding detriment for taking up rights in connection with the minimum wage under National Minimum Wage Act 1998 s24;
- redundancy pay;

169 EA(DR) Regs 2004 reg 15.
170 See para 1.24 above.

- unfair dismissal (including most automatic unfair dismissals);
- detriment related to European Works Councils or involvement in a European Cooperative Society;
- detriment (action short of dismissal) on any of the grounds listed in ERA 1996 s48, ie for whistleblowing, being an employee representative or trustee of an occupational pension scheme, for pregnancy or maternity, taking up rights in relation to maternity leave, paternity leave, adoption leave, dependant leave, parental leave, flexible working,[171] Sunday working, health and safety, study leave for young workers (special rules), under the Working Time Regulations 1998, in relation to jury service, tax credits. Chapter 6 gives more detail of the precise protection against detriment under these categories;
- detriments under European Public Limited-Liability Company Regulations 2004 reg 45; ICE Regulations 2004 reg 33; the Transnational Information and Consultation of Employees Regulations 1999 reg 32; the European Cooperative Society (Involvement of Employees) Regulations 2006 reg 34; paragraph 8 of the Schedule to the Occupational and Personal Pension Schemes (Consultation by Employers and Miscellaneous Amendment) Regulations 2006;
- breach of contract arising or outstanding on termination,[172] eg notice pay.
- the Companies (Cross-Border Mergers) Regulations 2007.[173]

Jurisdictions not covered by the statutory dispute resolution procedures and ACAS compensation regime

22.79   The statutory dispute resolution procedures do not apply to claims which are not listed in any of Schedules 3–5 to the EA 2002; the ACAS regime does not apply to claims which are not listed in Schedule A2 of TUL(R)A 1992. These include:

- refusal of dependant or parental leave (as opposed to subjecting the worker to a detriment for a reason related to these rights);
- refusal of time off for antenatal care;
- health and safety suspension for pregnancy;
- less favourable treatment as a fixed-term or part-time worker or a detriment for taking up these rights;

171 Though there was initial doubt on this.
172 This is the only category not reproduced in Schedule 4.
173 This does not fall under TUL(R)A 1992 Schedule A2.

- refusal or breach of procedure in relation to flexible working (as opposed to detriment as a result of applying for flexible working);
- refusal of the right to be accompanied to a disciplinary or grievance hearing.

The right to be accompanied to disciplinary and grievance hearings

22.80   Where a worker[174] is invited or required to attend a disciplinary or grievance hearing and reasonably requests to be accompanied at the hearing, the employer must allow the worker to choose a trade union representative or another of the employer's workers to accompany him/her.[175] This companion may address the hearing and confer with the worker during the hearing. The companion may put and sum up the worker's case and may respond on the worker's behalf to any view expressed at the hearing, but s/he may not answer questions on behalf of the worker.[176] A disciplinary hearing means a hearing which could result in a formal warning or the taking of some other action.[177] The older versions of the ACAS Code on Disciplinary and Grievances Procedures considered that hearings or meetings which could only result in informal warnings and/or counselling would not be covered. The current Code does not explicitly address this point. But some 'informal' warnings take on the characteristics of formal warnings and do attract the right to representation, eg where the informal warning is in writing, with a specified time before lapsing, and can be taken into account if further offences are committed.[178] A purely investigatory, as opposed to disciplinary, meeting is unlikely to be covered.[179] A meeting held to inform workers of their impending redundancy also would not be covered.[180]

22.81   The employer must allow a worker to take time off during working hours to accompany another of the employer's workers.[181] If the chosen

174 This entitlement is not confined to employees.
175 ERelA 1999 s10.
176 ERelA 1999 s10(2B)–(2C).
177 ERelA 1999 s13(4).
178 *London Underground Ltd v Ferenc-Batchelor; Harding v London Underground Ltd* [2003] IRLR 252, EAT.
179 *Skiggs v South West Trains* [2005] IRLR 17, EAT.
180 *Heathmill Multimedia ASP Ltd v Jones and Jones* [2003] IRLR 856, EAT.
181 ERelA 1999 s10(6).

person cannot attend the proposed time for the hearing, the employer must postpone the hearing to any reasonable time suggested by the worker within five working days of the original date.

22.82   The new ACAS Code of Guidance on Disciplinary and Grievance Procedures[182] not only refers to this right but states that employees should be advised of their right to be accompanied, when notified of a disciplinary hearing. This means there may be a compensatory uplift of up to 25 per cent where, eg, the employee wins a case of unfair dismissal or discriminatory disciplinary action, and the employer had not advised of the right or permitted the employee to be accompanied. Remember also that the worker's own disciplinary policy, especially in unionised industries, may give similar rights to representation, but without the restrictions.

22.83   A worker can complain to an ET if the statutory right is denied. The ET can award compensation of up to two weeks' pay.[183] A worker must not be subjected to any detriment because s/he has tried to exercise this right or has accompanied another worker. It would also be automatically unfair dismissal to dismiss an employee for this reason.[184]

---

182 See para 22.3.
183 ERelA 1999 s11.
184 ERelA 1999 s12.

Appendices

APPENDICES

continued

B   Indirect discrimination: possibly discriminatory requirements, provisions, criteria or practices

continued

Running ET cases: checklists and samples

STAGES OF THE BASIC PROCEDURE

This is a summary and should be read together with chapters 20–21 as applicable.

1 Interview worker, take statement, check all documents, check time limits and diarise.

2 If appropriate, request written reasons for dismissal and await reply.

3 If statutory dispute resolution procedures still apply, send step 1 grievance letter and wait 28 days before starting ET case and/or go through steps of DDP as required.

4 In a case under RRA 1976, SDA 1975, EqPA 1970, DDA 1995 or concerning discrimination on grounds of religion, sexual orientation or age, send employer a questionnaire, before starting case or within 21 days after (28 days under DDA 1995). Send follow-up letters if there is a delay in answering or answers are inadequate.

5 Start case by sending the claim (ET1) to the relevant regional office of the Employment Tribunals. Check before expiry of the time limit that ET1 has safely arrived.

6 The ET will send an acknowledgement with a case number and stating whether the claim has been accepted. Subsequent correspondence with the ET also goes to the regional office.

7 The ET will send the ET1 to the employer and will send a copy of the employer's response (ET3) to the worker's representative or to the worker direct, if unrepresented. Expect this roughly four weeks after the acknowledgement (time limits apply). Diarise likely date ET3 is due and query with ET (or consider asking for default judgment) if not then received.

8 When the ET3 is received, write to the employer asking for additional information, written answers and for documents. Set a time limit, usually 14 days. Send a copy to the ET for information.

9 If the information is not received, write to the ET and ask for an order, explaining reasons. Send a copy to the employer with the information required under rule 11. The ET will send any order it makes to the employer and a copy to the worker's representative.

10 If the employer does not supply the information as ordered, write to the ET asking that the employer be requested to show cause why the ET3 should not be struck out.

11 Optional: At stage 8, write to employer suggesting a mutual exchange of witness statements 7–14 days before the hearing.

12 Some ETs send out standard case management letters with, or soon after, the ET3 setting timescales for disclosure, exchange of witness statements, preparation of a schedule of loss etc. This does not replace the need to make any specific requests. (Stages 8–11 may still apply.)

13 In a discrimination case, expect reply to the questionnaire within 8 weeks of having sent it to the employer. If it has not arrived, write chase-up letters and further diarise.

14 At any time after the ET3 is sent out, the ET will notify each side of the hearing date. Minimum 14 days' notice must be given. Inform ET immediately if the date is unsuitable.

15 An ACAS officer will be allocated to the case at the start and will contact the worker's representative and the employer. Negotiation can be through ACAS or direct with the employer. Once an agreement is concluded, it becomes binding if each side has confirmed it verbally with ACAS. ACAS then tells the ET that the case has been settled. (Check ACAS has done this.) Alternatively, a binding settlement is reached when authorised representatives sign a compromise agreement.

16 If using ACAS, the officer will send a COT3 form for signature. This contains the agreed terms of settlement. Make sure that the worker at all stages knows the terms. If there is no settlement, the case will go to hearing. Any settlement agreed on the day of the hearing does not go to ACAS, but the ET should be asked to make an order in the agreed terms.

17 In good time for the hearing, write to the ET to request any witness orders that are wanted.

18 Prior to the hearing, prepare trial bundles, preferably in agreement with the employer. Each page of the bundle should be numbered. Make sufficient copies or ask the employer to.

19 If it has been ordered or there is agreement to do so, exchange witness statements with the other side.

20 At the end of the hearing, the ET will give its judgment or reserve judgment and write to the parties later. Request written reasons at the hearing or within the specified time limit afterwards if thinking of appealing.

21 The ET will either hear evidence relating to liability and remedies (compensation etc) all at once or, more usually, will hear just liability and then have a hearing on compensation if the worker wins. Be prepared for both.

22 Remember and diarise time limits for review (14 days) and appeal (42 days) after the judgment if unsuccessful. If successful, interest runs on compensation not paid within 42 days of the judgment. In discrimination cases, interest is paid from the date of the award if unpaid within 14 days.

23 If successful, diarise when the money from the judgment or settlement is due and chase/enforce as appropriate.

Variations:

(a) The ET may hold a pre-hearing review, usually at an early stage, at which a costs deposit may be required.

(b) The ET may hold a pre-hearing review on issues of jurisdiction at an early stage which is prepared for and conducted like a full hearing except that it is confined to the jurisdictional or preliminary issue.

(c) The ET may hold a case management discussion (especially in discrimination cases) with the representatives at any stage, just to sort out what needs to be done, eg, whether an order should be made for additional information, disclosure of documents etc.

(d) Equal value cases under the EqPA 1970 – the basic procedure applies but there are also additional special steps (see chapter 5).

INITIAL INTERVIEW WITH WORKER SEEKING ADVICE ON DISMISSAL

1 Check what worker wants.

2 Check whether correct contractual/statutory notice was given or pay in lieu (unless gross misconduct).

3 Check whether any outstanding wages or holiday pay are due.

4 Check date of dismissal and time limits for possible ET claims. Inform worker and diarise. Where there is a claim of discrimination, prepare a brief chronology, note and diarise the time limit of the last act of discrimination, if it is a continuing act of discrimination, and the earliest act of discrimination if there are several self-contained acts

5 Check whether worker qualifies for unfair dismissal (continuous service, status as employee, whether s/he was 'dismissed').

6 If applicable and if worker qualifies, consider redundancy pay claim.

7 Check possibility of unlawful discrimination (no continuous service required).

8 Where likely, eg, where there is a sex discrimination issue, check for unequal pay under EqPA 1970.

9 Check pay slips. If worker was given none, consider claim for failure to give itemised pay statements. Ask tax authorities and Department for Work and Pensions to investigate contributions record so that credited contributions can be requested if necessary. Consider risk of illegal contract.

10 Obtain all relevant documents from worker and take full statement.

11 If appropriate, write initial letter to employer requesting written reasons for dismissal, P45 and monies due.

12 Consider whether anything can be done immediately to secure a good open reference.

13 Check whether worker has appealed.

14 Ensure statutory dispute resolution procedures are correctly followed if they still apply.

15 Advise as to social security benefits or refer on for this advice.

INTERVIEW OF WORKER WITH RACE OR SEX DISCRIMINATION CLAIM

The following list suggests points that should be established by an adviser when interviewing a worker with a potential race discrimination claim. It can be adapted for sex discrimination cases. The suggestions are for guidance only and should not be followed rigidly. In each case, the facts and what needs to be proved must be carefully considered.

• Ask the worker why s/he thinks s/he was dismissed/disciplined/not promoted or appointed. This helps establish whether the worker believes it is race discrimination, although it may be necessary to ask more overtly. It also helps draw out any non-discriminatory explanation for the employer's conduct.

- Establish what is the worker's race, nationality, ethnic or national origin (as relevant under the RRA 1976); what 'racial' group it is that the employer is discriminating against.
- Ask what makes the worker think s/he has been discriminated against. Explain that this is a good question to draw out evidence indicating discrimination. Ask whether there is a direct comparison with a white worker who has been treated more favourably in comparable circumstances.
- Establish all acts of discrimination within the last three months (eg, failed promotion applications; unfair appraisals; warnings; dismissal). These can be the basis of the claim.
- Establish all acts of discrimination or evidence of prejudicial attitudes throughout the worker's employment. (Although these cannot usually form the basis of a claim if more than three months ago, they can be supporting evidence for the main claim.)
- Expressly ask the worker whether any racist remarks were made by any relevant manager, either directly to the worker or in his/her hearing. Ask whether relevant managers demonstrated prejudice in any other way, eg, by differential treatment of staff according to their 'race'.
- Ask whether the worker ever alleged race discrimination and whether that can be proved. Ask for details and the employer's reaction. (This is relevant to credibility of the worker, and of the employer if no action was taken, and to any victimisation claim.)
- Establish who made the relevant decisions and what is the decision-making hierarchy; establish whether any discriminatory patterns among the workforce can be attributed to the same decision-makers (eg, the expression of prejudice by a senior manager is relevant only if that manager has some control over this worker's fate). Avoid 'conspiracy theories', ie, accusing too many senior managers and staff of racism.
- Assess whether there are non-racial explanations for events, eg, the person promoted above the worker was better qualified or the worker was unpopular for reasons unconnected with his/her 'race'.
- Try to establish patterns. Patterns in the way the worker has been treated by certain persons in the past compared with how staff of a different racial group, eg, white, are treated, and in the way other staff of the same 'racial' group are treated and their position in the workforce.
- Establish now rather than later if there are any holes in the patterns, eg, if the managers accused have in the past made senior appointments of persons in the same 'racial' group as the worker, or if others of the same 'racial group' are generally highly placed in the employing organisation. Also look at who appointed/promoted the worker in the past and why, if it is the same manager who is now discriminating.
- If there is a history of discrimination, establish when it started and explore whether the start date makes sense, eg because a new manager took over or because it was the first time a promotion situation arose.
- Ask if the employer has an equal opportunities policy and whether it was ever brought to the worker's attention.

- Establish whether direct or indirect discrimination, or both, is possible.
- Establish whether victimisation took place, ie, whether the worker alleged discrimination in the past and/or during incidents leading to dismissal and/or in any disciplinary hearing prior to dismissal.
- Watch out for other forms of discrimination, eg, sex discrimination – in addition to or instead of race discrimination.
- Establish evidential strength – witnesses, documents, and matters from which inferences could be drawn.
- Establish what information could be usefully obtained on a questionnaire. Ask worker about distribution (and treatment – promotions/dismissals, etc) of workers of different racial groups in the workforce.
- Establish what the worker wants (particularly if still employed).

INTERVIEW OF WORKER WHO HAS BEEN MADE REDUNDANT

A worker who has been made redundant may only ask his/her adviser about the level of redundancy pay. However, s/he may have other rights, depending in part on whether s/he is an employee. The following list suggests suitable areas for exploring and should be read in conjunction with chapter 8.

1 Reasonable time off with pay during notice period to look for fresh employment.
2 Redundancy pay:
   - Check worker is eligible for statutory redundancy pay (employee; at least 2 years' service etc).
   - Check the calculation.
   - Check if s/he has a greater contractual entitlement.
   - May s/he lose the right to redundancy pay because s/he unreasonably refuses an offer of suitable alternative employment made before the expiry of his/her contract?
   - May s/he lose the right to redundancy pay if s/he has left before the expiry of his/her notice period?
   NOTE: There are rules as to the procedure to be followed if the worker wants to leave early without losing his/her pay.
3 Unfair dismissal:
   - Check worker is eligible to claim (employee; at least 1 year's service etc). Be careful to check a dismissal has taken place as opposed to an agreed termination, eg, in some early retirement/voluntary redundancy situations.
   - Would the worker win? A redundancy dismissal may be unfair if:
     – there was no genuine redundancy situation and the employer had other reasons for dismissing the worker;
     – unfair selection criteria were used or they were unfairly applied;
     – the employer did not consider alternative employment.
   NOTE: If the worker is made redundant while on maternity leave, s/he must be offered any suitable vacancy.
     – poor procedures were followed and there was no consultation with the individual or Union.
   - How much compensation is the worker likely to receive?
   NOTE: If the worker received a large contractual or voluntary redundancy

payment or if s/he obtained a new job very quickly, his/her unfair dismissal claim may be worth little or nothing.

4 Was the worker selected for redundancy for an automatically unfair reason (see paras 6.64 onwards)?

5 For example, if the worker was dismissed for a reason related to pregnancy or maternity, this may be automatic unfair dismissal, which does not require her to have had any minimum length of service.

6 Unlawful discrimination:
   - Check eligibility. (Much wider than for unfair dismissal or statutory redundancy pay.)
   - Has the worker been selected for redundancy due to his/her race, religion, sex, sexual orientation, age, disability, or because she is pregnant?
     – have objective criteria been used and objectively applied?
     – would the worker have been selected if s/he had been of a different race, religion, sex, sexual orientation, age, or not disabled?
   - Has the worker been selected on an indirectly discriminatory criterion which cannot be justified, eg, LIFO; part-timers first; 'temps' or 'casuals' first, where these groups are disproportionately black or female?
   - Have reasonable adjustments been made to the redundancy selection procedure or criteria so that a disabled worker is not put at a disadvantage, eg by discounting disability-related absences from a selection criterion based on attendance record?
   - Has the worker been selected for redundancy because of recent complaints about discrimination or harassment which have upset the employer? This would be victimisation.
   - Is access to or calculation of the redundancy payment package discriminatory?

7 Redundancies on a transfer:
   - Consider whether or not the Transfer of Undertakings Regulations apply.
   - Consider whether claim should be made against new or old employer.

8 Trade Union or employee representatives' consultation.
   - For collective redundancies.
   - Where the Transfer of Undertakings Regulations apply.

   NOTE: Any claim for breaking consultation rules is brought by the Trade Union or appropriate employee representatives on behalf of the workers.

9 Do the statutory dispute resolution procedures still apply? (They may not apply if the dismissal was one of 20 or more redundancies.) If so, have they been followed?

INITIAL INTERVIEW OF WORKER WITH POSSIBLE SEXUAL HARASSMENT CLAIM

This is a sensitive area, with difficulties of law, evidence and the worker's feelings. The checklist below suggests the information which needs to be obtained to make an informed judgement about whether the worker can bring a legal case (or even risk speaking out). It may be best not to ask all the questions in the first interview, but to fix another meeting the next day or very soon after, to speak in more detail. The last part of the checklist suggests how such an interview should be conducted. The same questions will not always be appropriate. The adviser must be thorough in his/her questioning and listen carefully to the answers. This is to ensure that the worker is consistent throughout any grievance and ET case which s/he may take. Explain to the worker some of the legal complexities so s/he understands why you are asking the questions.

1 Questions to find out background information:
   - The harasser's job title and working relationship with the worker.
   - The nature of the working day. How often the worker has contact with the harasser.
   - The general office situation, lay-out and presence of other workers.
   - The worker's start date and disciplinary record. [This is sensitive: explain the question about the worker's record is only to see how vulnerable s/he is if management raise the issue.]

2 Questions about the harassment:
   - When the harassment started.
   - Details and dates of the harassment (verbal and physical). [This requires a sensitive approach as the worker may be embarrassed, particularly with a male representative.]
   - Establish what is normal acceptable office behaviour and where the line is drawn.
   - Witnesses? Has the worker kept a diary? Has s/he seen/told her GP; any recruitment agency; family, friends or acquaintances?
   - Has the harasser done the same thing to other workers? Have others complained to management?
   - Has the worker said explicitly to the harasser or made it clear in any other way that s/he does not welcome the behaviour? [Many kinds of behaviour are obviously unwelcome and it is not essential that the worker has said as much to the harasser, but it is helpful if s/he has. Note that although this is important information to know, it is extremely sensitive as the worker may feel s/he is to blame if s/he has not said anything to the harasser. Therefore, do not ask this question until late in the interview when confidence is built. This also gives the worker time to raise it him/herself, which is preferable. If it is necessary to raise the issue first, be sure to give prior reassurance that it would be understandable if the worker had not felt able to say anything.]
   - If the worker did tell the harasser, how and when did s/he do so and what was his/her reaction?
   - Has the worker raised the matter with anyone in management or told anyone else before? [This question also needs prior reassurance.]

3 Action:
   - What does the worker want to do? [This is the most important question of all, and however bad the situation is it is not up to the adviser to impose a solution. Discuss the options including taking a grievance, going to the ET plus time limits, informal approach to the harasser, doing nothing but keeping a diary.]

4 Taking a sensitive approach:
   - Take the matter seriously and give it the necessary time.

- Be friendly and supportive but formal. Do not be authoritarian or too informal. Both could replicate the harasser's behaviour.
- Take a clear role and explain why sensitive questions are asked before asking them.
- In the first interview, allow the worker to give a broad picture before going back (in this interview or a subsequent interview) to ask for more detail.
- Do not try to get all the information in the first interview – focus on building confidence (although you must find out enough to ensure you do not miss a legal time limit). Ask more sensitive questions and deal with possible counter-allegations in later interviews after confidence in the adviser has been established.
- To maintain confidence, arrange swift follow-up interviews at the first interview. This is also essential before memories fade and witnesses lose interest.
- In case the worker is embarrassed, offer the opportunity to write down what has happened before discussing it. [NOTE: this is not a substitute for spending time talking to the worker.]
- If possible, offer the worker the chance to talk to an adviser of the same sex. [NOTE: this must not be seen as if the representative is not interested or concerned about the matter.]
- Provide reassurance that the worker is entitled to feel upset, that the harasser has behaved unacceptably and that the worker has done nothing wrong.
- Reassure the worker on confidentiality and that nothing will be done without his/her permission. It is important to take notes, but ask permission first.
- Discuss various options, taking account of what the worker wants, offering appropriate support whatever s/he decides. Take a participative and consultative approach. Address any fear of reprisals.
- Raise with the worker his/her feelings and health and direct him/her to sources of support. The adviser should not attempt to act as an amateur counsellor or suggest the worker needs counselling/psychiatric help in a way which could be understood as meaning the adviser thinks there is something wrong with the worker. Suggestions of sources of support are not an alternative to concrete remedial action.

DO NOT:
- Make assumptions.
- Suggest the worker could be to blame in inviting the harassment.
- Blame the worker for not confronting the harasser or telling the union or management earlier.
- Suggest the worker may be misinterpreting events or being over-sensitive.
- Express any view as to the effect on the harasser or the harasser's spouse/partner if the worker makes an allegation.
- Pressurise the worker into taking any form of action.
- If the adviser is a union representative, s/he should not say s/he knows the harasser and is surprised s/he has acted in that way, or express concern that the harasser is a worker of the same union.

INTERVIEW OF WORKER DISMISSED FOR POOR WORK, WITH A VIEW TO ASSESSING POTENTIAL CLAIMS FOR (A) UNFAIR DISMISSAL, (B) DISMISSAL IN FACT BECAUSE SHE IS PREGNANT, OR (C) DISMISSAL IN FACT BECAUSE S/HE IS BLACK

The following list suggests areas for questioning common to many dismissals on grounds of capability or conduct and is designed to highlight the additional questions necessary where discrimination due to pregnancy or race is suspected. Note that questions concerning discrimination are designed to find out if the worker has been treated differently, not just unfairly. The list is for guidance only.

Unfair dismissal

1 Questions to test eligibility, eg, length of continuous service, whether the worker is an employee.
2 Questions to establish the sequence of events and disciplinary process followed leading up to dismissal.
3 Obtain documents worker has: contract of employment, disciplinary procedure, dismissal letter, other letters relating to the events leading to dismissal, previous warning letters, previous appraisals.
4 Questions to establish the worker's previous work record: previous disciplinary hearings, warnings (alive or lapsed), verbal criticisms, appraisals, thankyou letters.
5 The worker's job and duties. The hierarchy and other staff in her department.
6 The nature of the allegations against the worker and his/her response – in the disciplinary hearing and, if different, to you.
7 If relevant, any training the worker has had. Has s/he recently been promoted? If so, what was his/her experience prior to promotion and is s/he being given support and guidance?
8 Dates of all relevant facts plus date of dismissal. (Relevant to show the pattern of events but also for time limits.)
9 Questions to establish whether statutory dispute resolution procedures apply and if so, whether they have been followed.
10 What does the worker want to do?

Pregnancy dismissal – extra questions to unfair dismissal list

1 Does worker think dismissal was due to her pregnancy? If so, what makes the worker think that? (This is a useful question, but explain that it is useful to know what she has in mind and that she is not being disbelieved.)
2 Questions to establish whether and when the employer and relevant manager knew the worker was pregnant, eg:
   • When is the baby due?
   • When did the worker tell the employer she was pregnant? Who did she tell? Was it verbal or in writing?
   • Has the worker had time off for pregnancy-related ill-health? If so, when and who did she tell?
   • Has the worker had time off for ante-natal care? Have there been discussions about maternity leave or benefits? With whom? When?

3 Questions to establish if the employer or relevant manager is hostile towards the worker's pregnancy, eg:
- In any of the above discussions or at any other time, has the employer expressed any irritation about time off or any other aspect of the pregnancy?
- What did the employer say when the worker first told him/her of her pregnancy?
- Has there been any problem getting time off for ante-natal care?
- Has the employer/manager's behaviour or attitude towards the worker changed in any way since s/he found out the worker was pregnant?
- What is the employer's general attitude towards pregnant workers? What about the particular manager(s) the worker is now dealing with?

4 Questions to establish either that the worker has not performed poor work at all or that other non-pregnant workers have performed equally poor work (or done worse things), yet have not been dismissed. Also ask:
- How readily does the employer usually discipline or dismiss workers?
- What sort of offences are usually considered dismissable?
- Compare the disciplinary procedure applied to the worker with any written procedure and with the normal practice adopted by the employer.

5 Where the pregnancy discrimination falls short of dismissal, eg, disciplinary action or non-promotion, ensure the worker seeks advice on maternity-related matters, eg, how to preserve her right to return after maternity leave, maternity benefits, rights to time off for ante-natal care, if relevant, rights to health and safety suspension.

6 Regarding what the worker wants to do, will she want to return to work there after her maternity leave? (This may affect how the matter is handled.)

NOTE: Adverse treatment due to pregnancy may also be sex discrimination. For this a worker need not be an employee. Also watch for dates of all adverse treatment as time limits for sex discrimination will run from each detrimental act.

Race discrimination – extra questions to unfair dismissal list

1 Note that the worker need not be an employee to claim race discrimination.

2 Does the worker believe s/he has genuinely been dismissed for poor work or for some other reason?

3 Does the worker think s/he would have been dismissed if s/he was white? If so, what makes the worker think that? (This is a useful question, but explain that it is useful to know what s/he has in mind and that s/he is not being disbelieved.)

4 Questions regarding the ethnic breakdown of the workforce and particularly of the relevant managers.

5 Questions to compare the general treatment of black and white workers, eg, as to the level of disciplinary action and dismissals; recruitment; promotion; general day-to-day behaviour by management. Has anyone else complained of race discrimination previously?

6 Questions to establish either that the worker has not performed poor work at all or that other white workers have performed equally poor work (or done worse things), yet have not been dismissed. Also ask:

- How readily does the employer usually discipline or dismiss workers?
- What sort of offences are usually considered dismissable?
- Compare the disciplinary procedure applied to the worker with any written procedure and with the normal practice adopted by the employer.

7   Questions about the previous treatment of the worker, eg, has the worker been subjected to different or racist treatment or remarks? Has the worker previously alleged race discrimination – if so, when and what happened?

8   Dates of all material incidents because the race discrimination time limit runs from each act of discrimination.

QUESTIONNAIRES – DRAFTING TIPS

The questionnaire procedure is often wasted by asking vague, unimportant and discursive questions. Some sample questionnaires are below, but the following areas of questioning should normally be adopted (particularly in a direct discrimination case). The following model is particularly suited to RRA 1976 and SDA 1975 questionnaires. A person writing a questionnaire is known as a 'complainant'.

- Analyse the strengths and weaknesses of the case, noting important facts which are unknown or where it is uncertain whether the employer will agree with or dispute a significant fact. The questionnaire can be used to find out the unknown facts and establish the employer's position.
- Regarding every important decision made by the employer, ask who made the decision, when, who was consulted, and the reasons for the decision.
- Ask questions to find out statistical patterns of discrimination in the workforce, eg, employees according to status, disciplinaries, dismissals, appointments and promotions (as relevant) by reference to race, sex, marital status, civil partnership status (as relevant).
- Identify the actions of the employer towards the worker which may be discriminatory or indicate that the worker is being treated differently from others. Ask questions to test whether the employer has treated other workers (by reference to race or sex) differently in similar circumstances. For example:
  - If the worker was disciplined for a certain level of sickness, what is the sickness level of other workers and have they been disciplined?
  - If the employer has refused to allow the worker to take three weeks holiday at one time, how much holiday at one time have other workers been allowed over the last few years? Has anyone else asked for three or more weeks at one time and been refused?
  - If the employer has not shortlisted the worker for a job because s/he lacks a certain qualification, what are the qualifications of other candidates by reference to whether they were shortlisted?
  - If the worker has never been put on any training courses, what courses have other workers doing the same job been offered?
- Anticipate possible innocent explanations by the employer for treating a worker of a different race or sex more favourably. For example:
  - Another worker with a worse sick record than the complainant may not have been so severely disciplined. An obvious reason would be a significant difference in the nature of the illness. Therefore, the question could ask not

only the number of days' sickness of other workers and whether disciplined, but the nature of sickness in each case.
- Regarding training, the explanation may be that other workers have been
employed for a longer period and have therefore received more training.
Therefore, ask in each case not only what training they have received, but
when, and their start date.
- If the worker has taken out a grievance, ask what steps were taken to investigate with dates and persons involved; who made the decision, when and on
what grounds; who was consulted, when and what were their views. Ask
the same about the grievance appeal.
- It is more effective to ask precise questions than to seek documents, but
there may be one or two crucial documents to ask for at this early stage.
- Do not ask excessive questions. The more incidents relevant to the case, the
more questions are likely to be necessary. It is dangerous to generalise, but
questionnaires involving more than 25 questions are probably too long.

For further guidance, see the series of specialist questionnaire guides produced by Central London Law Centre (tel: 020 7839 2998), including *RRA
Questionnaires: How to use the Questionnaire Procedure*, by Tamara Lewis, and
equivalent Guides under the SDA 1975, DDA 1995, Employment Equality
(Age) Regulations 2006, and a generic Guide with all strands including sexual
orientation and religion and belief (see pp784–785 below).

RRA 1976 QUESTIONNAIRE – FAILED JOB APPLICATION/ PROMOTION

*Sample questionnaire questions under paragraph 6 in case of direct or indirect race
discrimination in failed job application after interview. These questions would not be
suitable for a small informal employer.*

1 Please supply full details of the job for which the complainant applied, including duties, responsibilities and pay. Please supply a copy of the job description and contract.
2 Please state the criteria for the selection of an appointee to the post for which
the complainant applied and, in respect of each of these, please state:
  (a) when it was devised or agreed and by whom;
  (b) whether it was put in writing and, if so, when;
  (c) whether it was mandatory that applicants should comply with the said
  criterion or simply a preference.
3 Please state in detail your procedures for advertising the said post and where
and when advertisements appeared.
4 Please list all applications received for the said post, by reference to race,* academic qualifications, previous experience and whether internal or external
candidates.
5 Please denote which of those listed at 4 above were:
  (a) shortlisted,
  (b) interviewed, and
  (c) offered the job.
6 Please state who was responsible for shortlisting and the criteria applied.

7 Of each of those interviewed including the complainant, please state:
   (a)   the date of the interview;
   (b)   the name and position of each member of the interview panel;
   (c)   whether each member of the panel had at any stage received equal oppor-
         tunities training and, if so, what and when;
   (d)   the name and position of each person making the decision whether or
         not to appoint and whether there was any difference of opinion;
   (e)   precisely why the application failed or succeeded as the case may be.
8 Please give the name of any other person consulted in any way or advised of the
   decisions to appoint or not to appoint interviewees, and please state their role.
9 Why was the complainant's application unsuccessful?
10 Were there any notes or standard interview forms completed by each appointment committee member at every interview? If yes, please forward copies of all
   notes and forms relating to all interviewees including the complainant.
11 Please state by reference to race* and job title the number of employees of
   the respondents as at [appropriate date].
12 Please state by reference to race,* job title, date of appointment and place of
   work, the number of persons in the respondent company appointed from outside or promoted from within, to the position for which the complainant
   applied or above, within the five years prior to the date of this questionnaire.
13 Please denote which of the above appointments/promotions were made by
   panels including any of the members of the complainant's interview panel.
   Please identify which panel member.
14 Please state whether the respondents operate an equal opportunities policy
   and, if so, please supply a copy.
15 (If a public sector employer) Did you carry out an equality impact assessment
   before deciding upon your redundancy selection procedure and criteria? If so,
   when was it carried out? Who was involved? Of what did it comprise? What conclusions were reached?

   *   For 'race' please state under the following categories: (a) colour (b) nationality
       (c) national origins (d) ethnic origins (e) race.

RRA 1976 QUESTIONNAIRE – DISCIPLINARY DISMISSAL
*Sample questionnaire in case of direct discrimination or victimisation in dismissal.
Paragraph 2 could also stand as the grounds of an ET1.*

Paragraph 2
1 I started working for the respondents in their West End branch on 6 January
   2008. I was promoted to manager in April 2008. Throughout my employment,
   I received no warnings of any kind.
2 On 11 May 2009, I was dismissed. I believe this was discrimination. The reason
   I was given for my dismissal was that I had claimed taxi fares during the train
   strike without permission.
3 In the past I had been given travel fares in difficult travel circumstances and I
   had also given out fares to others. I understood this was in accordance with company policy. There was no secrecy involved, the petty cash slips were signed by

myself and sent to head office, and the money was given to me by the chief cashier.

4 A new area manager was appointed in March 2009. On several occasions he told me to get more white staff in the shop. My deputy manager and I were both of Asian background. About half of the remaining staff were white. I told the area manager that I was not prepared to discriminate. I said that when vacancies arose, I could only appoint the best applicants.

5 In April 2009, my deputy manager was suddenly demoted to the position of salesperson. Then on 9 May 2009 I was called to a disciplinary hearing regarding my claim for taxi fares. The disciplinary was conducted by the area manager and personnel. I told them I believed this was race discrimination. On 11 May I received a letter notifying me of my dismissal. I subsequently appealed to the regional manager. Again I told him I believed it was race discrimination. My appeal was rejected on 20 May 2009.

6 I believe I have been unlawfully discriminated against contrary to sections 1(1)(a) and 2 of the Race Relations Act 1976.

   * For 'race' please state under the following categories: (a) colour (b) nationality (c) national origins (d) ethnic origins (e) race.

Paragraph 6

1 Please state who decided to dismiss me, when and each and every reason.

2 Please state who was consulted, when and their views.

3 Please state who decided to reject my appeal and the reasons.

4 Please state who was consulted, when and their views.

5 Please state all investigations made into my allegation of race discrimination (a) during my disciplinary hearing, and (b) during my appeal. In each case, please state what investigation was made, by whom and when, and what was the finding.

6 Please confirm in relation to the allegation against me regarding claiming taxi fares:

  (a) that it is accepted I only claimed taxi fares on train strike days;

  (b) whether it is contended that I was not entitled to the fares at all or whether it is contended that I needed permission;

  (c) if the latter, whether permission would have been granted had I asked;

  (d) please clarify any other respect in which I allegedly broke company policy over claiming the fares;

  (e) please state whether the said policy is verbal or written. If written, please supply a copy. If verbal, please state how and when it was communicated to me;

  (f) please state what is the company's policy regarding when travel can be claimed and the mechanisms. Please include who has authority to give fares to each level of staff.

7 Please state all members of staff who have been given taxi fares on any occasion (i) during the transport strikes in 2009, or (ii) for any other reason, by reference to

  (a) race;*

  (b) job title and location;

(c) on whose authorisation;

(d) the reason for using the taxi;

(e) date and nature of any disciplinary action taken against them for using taxis

8 Please state all staff dismissed from London branches since 1 March 2007. In each case please state: (a) race,* (b) job title and location, (c) nature of offences leading to dismissal, and (d) date of dismissal.

9 Please state all disciplinary action, short of dismissal, taken against London staff since 1 March 2007. In each case, please state:

(a) race;*

(b) job title and location;

(c) date and level of action; and

(d) nature of offence.

10 With regard to the demotion of my deputy manager, please state

(a) who took the decision and for what reasons; and

(b) who was consulted and their views.

11 Please state all staff taken on since 1 March 2007 in London branches by reference to:

(a) race;*

(b) job title;

(c) location placed; and

(d) date taken on.

12 Please state all employees as at 11 May 2009 above the level of branch manager in the company by reference to:

(a) race;*

(b) job title;

(c) start date; and

(d) location.

13 Please state why the area manager thought there should be more white staff at my branch.

14 Does the company operate an equal opportunities policy – if so, please provide a copy.

* For 'race' please state under the following categories: (a) colour (b) nationality (c) national origins (d) ethnic origins (e) race.

RRA 1976 QUESTIONNAIRE – REDUNDANCY

Sample questionnaire questions under paragraph 6. The statement of facts is not written in a form appropriate for paragraph 2 or the grounds of an ET1.

Facts

The worker was one of 200 engineers employed across three sites in the council's maintenance department. On 10 April 2009, he was made redundant together with 21 other engineers across all the sites. He was not individually consulted and does not know how the redundancy selection criteria were applied to him or to other workers. He does not know exactly who was selected for redundancy and their racial group. However, the worker is suspicious because, on what he knows about the selection criteria, he would not have expected to be chosen. The worker also has not been redeployed.

Paragraph 6

1 Please state the redundancy selection procedure adopted for the April 2009 redundancies including the dates of all decisions and consultations and the persons involved.

2 Please state when it was first considered that redundancies might be a possibility.

3 Please state the redundancy selection criteria used, stating in the case of each criterion:
   (a) when it was decided to use that criterion and by whom;
   (b) the reason for using that criterion;
   (c) how the criterion was to be measured and by whom;
   (d) how the criterion was weighted.

4 Please state whether a decision was made in advance as to how many engineers should be made redundant. If so, when and by whom.

5 Please list all engineers employed by the council immediately before the redundancy selection procedure. For each engineer, please state:
   (a) their race;*
   (b) their job title, grade and location;
   (c) their start date;
   (d) whether or not they were made redundant;
   (e) the reasons why they were or were not selected for redundancy;
   (f) their score on each of the redundancy selection criteria;
   (g) whether they applied for redeployment;
   (h) details of any job offers made to them for redeployment;
   (i) whether or not they were in fact redeployed and if not, why not.

6 Please state specifically with regard to myself:
   (a) Who decided I would be selected for redundancy and when?
   (b) Who else was consulted, when and what were their views?
   (c) Why was I made redundant?
   (d) How did I score on each criterion?
   (e) Why was I not redeployed?

7 Please list all technical or engineering vacancies from 1 January 2009 to date by reference to job title, grade, location, date vacant, date filled.

8 Please list all staff taken on to work as engineers for the three years prior to the date of this questionnaire by reference to:
   (a) their race;*
   (b) their start date;
   (c) their job title, grade and location.

9 Please state all staff dismissed from (i) the Engineering and Maintenance Department, and (ii) the rest of the council in the three years prior to the date of this questionnaire by reference to:
   (a) their race;*

(b)   their job title, grade and location;
(c)   the dismissal date;
(d)   the reason for dismissal.
10   Please provide details of your equal opportunities policy.

* For 'race' please state under the following categories: (a) colour (b) nationality (c) national origins (d) ethnic origins (e) race.

SDA 1975 QUESTIONNAIRE – PREGNANCY

Questionnaire in case of dismissal of a pregnant woman, ostensibly on grounds of capability/conduct, but suspected to be due to pregnancy.

Paragraph 2 questionnaire

1   I have worked as Assistant Manager for Winfield Shoes in their Nottingham Branch since 12 October 2007. Throughout my employment, I received no warnings from my employers, written or verbal.
2   On 20 October 2008, I informed my manager, Tessa Hennessy, that I was pregnant. On 21 November 2008, I was off sick. I telephoned Jane Baxter of personnel and explained that I would not be in because I felt sick due to my pregnancy.
3   On 24 November 2008 I was sent a letter requiring me to attend a disciplinary hearing on 26 November 2008. This came out of the blue and was a complete shock to me.
4   At the disciplinary meeting held on 26 November 2008 I was dismissed. The reasons given to me were poor supervision of staff, poor time-keeping and taking too many personal phone calls. These allegations were untrue. My appeal to the managing director on 3 December 2008 also failed. I believe I was dismissed due to my pregnancy.

Paragraph 6 questionnaire

1   Do you accept that I told Tessa Hennessy on or about 20 October 2008 that I was pregnant? If not, when does Tessa say she first found out I was pregnant and how does she say she found out?
2   Do you accept that I told Jane Baxter on 21 November 2008, when I telephoned in sick, that I was pregnant? If not, what does Jane Baxter say I told her?
3   Please list every person within the company who knew before my dismissal that I was pregnant. In each case, please state when and how they had found out.
4   In respect of the decision to dismiss me, please state:
(a)   who took the decision and when;
(b)   who was consulted and what were their views;
(c)   every reason for my dismissal.
5   In respect of the decision to reject my appeal, please state:
(a)   who took the decision and when;
(b)   who was consulted and what were their views;
(c)   every reason for rejecting my appeal.
6   Please set out every alleged instance with dates of (a) poor staff supervision, (b) poor time-keeping, and (c) receiving personal telephone calls.

7 Please set out the company policy regarding taking personal telephone calls.

8 Do you have an equal opportunities policy – if so, please provide details.

9 Please state all dismissals and disciplinary action by the company since 1 January 2005, stating in each case

(a) job title and location of person dismissed;

(b) age of any children under five years;

(c) sex of person dismissed and whether pregnant or on maternity leave at the time;

(d) date and nature of disciplinary action; and

(e) nature of offence.

10 Please state all staff employed in the company as at 27 November 2008 by reference to (a) job title/location (b) age of children under 5 (c) sex (d) dates when pregnant or on maternity leave during employment with you (indicating which).

11 Please state all staff who have become pregnant or gone onto maternity leave since 1 January 2003 by reference to (a) job title/location (b) dates of pregnancy or maternity leave (indicating which) (c) if applicable, termination date and reason for leaving.

Notes

With reference to questions 1 to 3: In post-dismissal correspondence, the managing director denied that the company knew the complainant was pregnant prior to her dismissal. If this happens or if it is possible that the company will deny knowledge, then questions should be asked to pin down its position.

It will not always be appropriate to ask such blunt questions, but on these facts, it is possible that early questions will get a truthful answer. If there has been no prior indication from the employer that s/he will deny knowledge, it may be better not to encourage denial by such questions. Instead, if the statement at paragraph 2 sets out when the complainant did tell the employer, then the employer's response should contain any denial.

SDA 1975 QUESTIONNAIRE – SEXUAL HARASSMENT
Paragraph 2 questionnaire

The complainant worked for the respondent council in their Homeless Persons Unit. From September 2005, she was sexually harassed by her supervisor, Mr Briggs. [Cite incidents.] On 13 February 2009, the complainant informed personnel of the harassment. An investigation was carried out, during which the complainant was instructed to remain off work. On 1 March 2009, the complainant was told that the outcome of the investigation was inconclusive.

On 9 April 2009, the complainant was required by Mr Briggs to attend a disciplinary hearing for poor work performance. She was issued with a final written warning. The complainant believes Mr Briggs did this because she had told personnel about the harassment. The complainant did not take out a grievance because she feared further harassment would result from it.

Paragraph 6 questionnaire

1 Please state clearly and in detail which parts of para 2 are admitted and which are denied.

2 Please state all steps taken to investigate my allegations including all meetings and interviews with dates and persons involved.

3 In relation to every member of staff spoken to as part of the investigation, please state:
   (a) their name;
   (b) who spoke to them and on what date(s) and time(s);
   (c) whether anyone else was present;
   (d) what they were told about the allegations;
   (e) what they were asked and what they responded;
   (f) whether statements were made and their dates. (If so, please supply copies.)

4 Please state fully every finding of the council as a result of the investigation, indicating who made each finding and on what basis and on what date.

5 If any of my allegations were disbelieved, please state which and give reasons.

6 Was any action taken against Mr Briggs or any advice given to him following the investigation? If so, please specify.

7 Please state when Mr Briggs was first informed of my allegations and by whom.

8 Please state whether Mr Briggs was suspended during the investigation and if so, when.

9 With regard to Mr Briggs, please state (a) his start date, and (b) his job title and location throughout his employment with dates.

10 Please state all warnings or other disciplinary action taken against Mr Briggs at any stage in his employment including any informal counselling, giving in each case:
   (a) its date;
   (b) the level of warning;
   (c) who decided upon it;
   (d) the offence to which it related.

11 Please state all grievances, formal or informal, taken against Mr Briggs by any member of staff during his employment, in each case giving
   (a) the date;
   (b) the nature of the grievance;
   (c) whether male or female complaining; and
   (d) the outcome of the grievance.

12 Please state whether any other allegations of sexual harassment have been made by any council employee in the last six years, formally or informally. If so, please state
   (a) the date;
   (b) the name and sex of the alleged perpetrator;
   (c) whether the perpetrator was disciplined;
   (d) the job title and location of the employee making the allegation;
   (e) the sex of the employee making the allegation;
   (f) whether he/she remained with the council. If not, when did he/she leave and why. (Please also give details if she was transferred to another job within the council.)

13 Please state the number of staff in the department as at 1 March 2009 by reference to:

(a) gender; and

(b) job title and grade.

14 Please state all staff in the department in the last five years who have resigned, been disciplined or dismissed. In each case please state:

(a) whether male or female;

(b) whether resignation, dismissal or disciplinary action and date;

(c) if resignation, reason given;

(d) if dismissal or disciplinary action, nature of offence.

15 With regard to the decision to issue me with a final written warning, please state:

(a) who made the decision and when;

(b) whether anyone else was consulted. If so, when and what were their views;

(c) every reason for the warning;

(d) in relation to the criticism of my work, please specify precisely what was wrong with my work, giving dates and details.

16 Does the council operate (a) an equal opportunities policy, and (b) a harassment policy? If so, please provide a copy and details.

RRA 1976 QUESTIONNAIRE AND ET1: UNFAIR DISMISSAL, DIRECT AND INDIRECT DISCRIMINATION
ET1 grounds of claim

Note: the following grounds can also be used as para 2 of the questionnaire. If the questionnaire is sent prior to the tribunal claim, sub-paras 6-8 should be omitted.

1 The respondent operates a chain of fast-food restaurants in central London. The claimant worked as manager at various branches since his engagement in 2000. At the time of his dismissal, the claimant was working at the Piccadilly branch.

2 The claimant is of Algerian national origin.

3 On 5 November 2008, the claimant was told that his employment would be terminated by reason of redundancy on the closure of his branch on 17 November 2008.

4 The claimant was not consulted at any time prior to his dismissal as to the possibility of employment at any of the respondents' other restaurants. Other staff in the claimant's branch who were white and of British national origin were redeployed within the respondents' organisation.

5 During a conversation in September 2008, the respondent's area manager told the claimant that the respondent had started to 'professionalise' its operation and bring in managers with catering qualifications from recognised UK colleges.

6 Having regard to the size and administrative resources of the respondent, the claimant's dismissal was unfair. The claimant was unfairly selected for redundancy. Furthermore, the respondent failed to consult with the claimant concerning the possibilities of alternative employment and failed to offer such employment.

7 Furthermore, the claimant was directly discriminated against in his dismissal contrary to the Race Relations Act 1976.

8 Further or in the alternative, the claimant was subjected to indirect discrimination in his dismissal contrary to Race Relations Act 1976 in that the respondents required that he hold a UK catering qualification.

Questionnaire questions under paragraph 6

1 Please state who decided to dismiss the claimant, when and the reasons.

2 Please state who was consulted, when and their views.

3 When did the respondent take the decision to close the Piccadilly restaurant?

4 In relation to all staff employed at the Piccadilly restaurant as at 1 November 2008, please state their:
   (a) race;*
   (b) job title;
   (c) date of engagement by the respondents;
   (d) whether dismissed on closure of the branch; and
   (e) if redeployed, where.

5 Please provide a list of all the respondent's branches as at 17 November 2008.

6 Please list all vacancies within the respondent's organisation in the posts of manager, deputy manager, assistant manager or supervisor, between 1 September 2008 and 1 March 2009.

7 Please state all dismissals of staff from 17 November 2005 to date by reference to:
   (a) race;*
   (b) job title; and
   (c) reason for dismissal.

8 In relation to all appointments or promotions made to the posts of branch supervisor and above from 17 November 2005 to date, please state:
   (a) race;*
   (b) job title;
   (c) whether external appointment or internal promotion;
   (d) branch to which appointed; and
   (e) academic and catering qualifications held.

9 In relation to all existing employees as at 17 November 2008 in post as supervisor or above, please state their:
   (a) race;*
   (b) job title;
   (c) date of engagement; and
   (d) any catering qualifications held.

10 When was it decided that branch managers should have catering qualifications and by whom and for what reasons?

11 Does the respondent have an equal opportunities policy? If so, please supply a copy.

   * For 'race' please state under the following categories: (a) colour (b) nationality (c) national origins (d) ethnic origins (e) race.

ET1: RACE DISCRIMINATION

1 The claimant was employed as a project officer with the respondent council in March 2007. The claimant is black British.

2 In March 2008, one year after the claimant's appointment, a white British project officer (Sally Ward) was engaged. Ms Ward had the same grade, pay and job title as the claimant.

3 Throughout her employment, the claimant received only administrative tasks, and was not permitted to write publicity or represent the department at external meetings. In contrast, Ms Ward was given those opportunities.

4 On 30 May 2009, the claimant complained to the head of the department, Alex Stern, that her immediate supervisor was giving the best work to the white project officer, whereas she was becoming deskilled. The claimant stated she believed the differential treatment was on grounds of her race. Mr Stern did not take any action as a result of this complaint and appeared to be angry.

5 On 25 July 2009 the project officers were reduced from two to one and the claimant was made redundant.

6 The claimant suffered direct discrimination on grounds of race contrary to RRA 1976 s1(1)(a):
   (a) in nature of the work which she was allocated;
   (b) in Mr Stern's failure to deal with her complaint;
   (c) by making her redundant.

7 Further or in the alternative, the claimant was victimised contrary to RRA 1976 s2 as a result of complaining about race discrimination as set out at paragraph 4 above in that she was made redundant.

8 In these respects, the claimant compares her treatment with that of Ms Ward and/or with that of a hypothetical comparator.[1]

SAMPLE LETTER CHASING QUESTIONNAIRE REPLIES

Address the letter to the employer's representative, if known, and otherwise to the chief executive or managing director.

Dear Madam/Sir,

Thank you for your reply to the questionnaire dated 21 January 2009, nine weeks after it was sent to the Health Authority.

I am concerned that the Health Authority has not answered questions 13 to 15 inclusive. It must be possible from conducting a simple 'head count' to answer question 13. Matters raised in question 14, and certainly in question 15, must be within the memory of senior staff, at least in part.

I would remind you of the provisions of section 65 of the Race Relations Act 1976. The employment tribunal is entitled to draw an adverse inference from a late or evasive answer to a questionnaire. I will be drawing this letter to the attention of the tribunal at the hearing and I would ask the Authority to reconsider its position.

---

1 This is a reminder to the ET that if the comparison with Ms Ward does not stand up, the claimant can still claim she has been less favourably treated than a hypothetical comparator.

SAMPLE LETTER WHERE EMPLOYERS REFUSE TO ANSWER CERTAIN QUESTIONS IN QUESTIONNAIRE ON GROUNDS OF THE DATA PROTECTION ACT 1998

Note: The following letter is a model which can be adapted. There may be some further arguments which can be used. The Data Protection Act is very complicated and the scope of the exceptions set out below is untested. See paras 1.56–1.74.

Dear Madam/Sir,

Thank you for your letter dated 5 September 2008, enclosing your clients' reply to the questionnaire.

I am however concerned that some key questions have not been answered. In particular, your clients have refused to answer questions 3, 5 and 8 on grounds that disclosure is prohibited by the Data Protection Act 1998. I do not accept that the information is covered by the Act. Even if it is covered, it can be disclosed on any one of the following grounds:

1   Under section 35(2) of the Act, data are exempt from the non-disclosure provisions where the disclosure is necessary for the purpose of, or in connection with, any legal proceedings (including prospective legal proceedings). My client has served this questionnaire in order to help formulate her prospective discrimination case in the employment tribunal.

2   Alternatively, you can disclose information if the workers identified by it give their consent. Please state whether your clients have asked the relevant workers for their consent. If so,

– please state in respect of each worker, when they were asked, by whom, in what terms, and what was their response?

– please state whether the request and/or the response was in writing.

3   Your clients may disclose the information even if the relevant workers withhold their consent if it is reasonable to dispose with their consent. Please explain why your clients do not consider it reasonable to dispose with each of the relevant workers' consent.

4   Alternatively in respect of question 8, your clients could simply delete the names from the records and refer to the individuals by a number and their racial group.

I now look forward to receiving the requested information from your clients without further delay.

You will be aware that under the RRA 1976, the tribunal may draw an adverse inference from an evasive or equivocal reply to a questionnaire. No doubt you have drawn this to your clients' attention.

RRA 1976 REQUEST FOR DISCLOSURE IN PROMOTION CASE

Sample list of documents to request as disclosure in a case of alleged race discrimination in promotion or job application where the claimant failed to obtain a post after interview. For the format of requests for disclosure and orders, see appendix C.

1   Score sheets and all other notes made at any time by the members of the short-listing and interview panels relating to the candidates who applied for and were appointed to the post.

2 All documents including application forms which were before the shortlisting and interview panels for the said post.

3 Any memorandum or report written to or by any member of the interview panel relating to each of the said appointments.

4 All references written on behalf of the claimant and the successful candidate.

5 Any other notes, memoranda, letters, e-mails or documents relating to the selection process for the post, including job description and person specification.

6 The advertisements placed for the post.

7 Any rules or regulations governing procedures for the appointment of employees of the respondents.

8 Any documents relating to the respondents' equal opportunities policy.

9 All other documents in the respondent's possession or control which are relevant to the case, whether of assistance to the respondent or the claimant.

FORMULA – INDIRECT DISCRIMINATION

Note: this formula was developed in relation to the original, more restrictive definition of indirect discrimination, but it will still be useful in some circumstances for proving indirect discrimination under the new definition (see paras 13.70 – 13.72).

Indirect race discrimination: formula for comparison under RRA 1976 s1(1)(b)

members of racial group (in pool) [who can meet requirement]	those outside racial group (in pool) [who can meet requirement]
v	
all members of racial group (in pool)	all those outside racial group (in pool)

[EXAMPLES:]

Spanish people (of working age living in UK) [who speak fluent English]	non-Spanish people (of working age living in UK) [who speak fluent English]
all Spanish people (of working age living in UK)	all non-Spanish people (of working age living in UK

v

[OR]

non-English people (of working age, living in UK) [who meet requirement]	English people (of working age living in UK) [who meet requirement]
all non-English people (of working age living in UK)	all English people (of working age living in UK)

v

CHECKLIST ON THE DEFINITION OF 'DISABILITY' UNDER THE DDA 1995

NOTE: Unless the worker is obviously covered by the DDA, it will be important carefully to interview him/her with the following checklist in mind. See also para 15.12 onwards.

- Check the worker has an 'impairment' which is either physical or mental.
- Check whether it is a condition which is deemed a disability on diagnosis (HIV; Cancer; Multiple Sclerosis; certified visual impairment).
- Check none of the excluded conditions apply.[2]
- Check that the impairment has adverse effects on the worker's ability to carry out normal day-to-day activities in respect of one or more of the following capacities:[3]
  - mobility;
  - manual dexterity;
  - physical co-ordination;
  - continence;
  - ability to lift, carry or otherwise move everyday objects;
  - speech, hearing or eyesight;
  - memory or ability to concentrate, learn or understand;
  - perception of the risk of physical danger.
- Check the affected activity is a 'normal' activity as opposed to, for example, a specialised hobby or specialist work activity (though normal work activities are covered).[4]
- The focus should be on what the worker cannot do, not on what s/he can do.[5]
- Check whether the worker's ability to carry out the normal activity is 'substantially' affected, ie, the effect is clearly more than trivial.[6]
  It is unnecessary that the worker is completely unable to carry out the activity. For example:
  - the worker can only carry out the activity more slowly than usual;
  - the worker can only carry out the activity in a particular way;[7]
  - it is tiring or painful to carry out the activity;[8]
  - the worker has medical advice not to attempt the activity.[9]
- Remember that the worker may have 'played down' the true effect of his/her disability on his/her daily life, or may have adjusted his/her life to avoid the need to carry out the activity.[10]

2 *Guidance*, paras A12–A14; para 15.16 above.
3 DDA 1995 Sch 1 para 4(1).
4 *Guidance* paras D8–D9.
5 *Goodwin v The Patent Office* [1999] IRLR 4, EAT.
6 *Goodwin v The Patent Office* [1999] IRLR 4, EAT; *Guidance*, para B1.
7 *Guidance*, para B3.
8 *Guidance*, para D11.
9 *Guidance*, para D11.
10 *Goodwin v The Patent Office* [1999] IRLR 4, EAT; *Guidance*, para B8.

- Remember that if the worker has a progressive condition, s/he is protected as soon as that condition has any adverse effect, even if that effect is not yet substantial.[11]
- Consider whether the worker can only carry out an activity without substantial adverse effect due to medical treatment or an aid (except for glasses correcting eye-sight).[12]
- Note: if the worker has a severe disfigurement, it is treated as having substantial adverse effect on normal day-to-day activities, unless this is a tattoo or ornamental body-piercing.[13]
- Consider whether the effect of the impairment on the activity is long-term, ie, for 12 months or the rest of the worker's life.[14]
- Remember that impairments with recurring substantial effects may be covered, even though the effect is only for a short period at any one time.[15]
- Consider whether it is necessary to seek medical advice or obtain medical evidence on the above matters.[16]

DDA 1995 – OVERALL CHECKLIST
Note: this checklist cannot cover every aspect of the law and should be read together with chapter 15.

- Is the worker eligible to claim under the DDA 1995?
  - Check the worker has a disability under the DDA 1995.[17]
  - Check the worker's condition is not specifically excluded.[18]
- Has the employer treated the worker less favourably on grounds of disability[19]
- Has the employer discriminated by failing to comply with a duty of reasonable adjustment?[20]
  - Does the employer owe a duty of reasonable adjustment?
  - Can the worker prove the employer knew or should have known that the worker has a disability and that an adjustment may be required?
  - Has the worker been put at a disadvantage because of the failure to make reasonable adjustments?
  - Consider possible adjustments which may assist the worker.[21] (Discuss with the worker, the worker's GP and any relevant specialist organisation.)

11 DDA 1995 Sch 1 para 8; *Guidance* paras B17 – B19; para 15.25 above.
12 DDA 1995 Sch 1 para 6; *Guidance* paras B11-B15; para 15.24 above.
13 DDA 1995 Sch 1 para 6; *Guidance* paras B20-B21.
14 DDA 1995 Sch 1 para 2(1).
15 DDA 1995 Sch 1 para 2(2); *Guidance* section C; para 15.27 above.
16 See sample letter at p716 below.
17 See Checklist above.
18 See Checklist above.
19 DDA 1995 s3A(5); para 15.42 above.
20 DDA 1995 s3A(2) and 4A; para 15.34 above.
21 Checklist of suggestions at DDA 1995 s18B(2); para 15.34 above.

- Is it reasonable to expect the employer to make the adjustment?[22]
- Has the worker been harassed?[23]
- Has the worker been victimised, ie, discriminated against for complaining of discrimination under the DDA 1995?[24]
  If so, can the employer defend a claim by showing the worker's allegation was false and made in bad faith?
- Overall consider what medical and other evidence may be necessary.
- Can the cost of medical evidence be covered? Can full costs be recovered from ET?
- Is the worker willing and able to bring an ET case?
- What outcome would the worker want?
- Note time limits for starting an ET case.
- Follow statutory disputes resolution procedures if they still apply. Alternatively, ensure compliance with ACAS Code, eg by bringing a grievance.
- Consider writing a questionnaire. Note time limits.
- Does the worker have any other legal claims, eg, unfair dismissal?
- When writing the ET1, if the facts allow, state the case as under DDA 1995 s3A(1) and/or s3A(5) and/or s4A.[25]

DDA 1995 – SAMPLE LETTER TO GP

NOTE that this is not a standard letter. The letter would vary according to the facts and how obvious the worker's disability and symptoms are. In some cases, it will be appropriate to write a shorter letter focusing on very specific points of concern.

Dear Dr ...

Re: *client's full name, address and date of birth*

I am advising Claudia regarding a potential claim against her employers under the Disability Discrimination Act 1995. In order for me to assess whether Claudia is covered by the Act, I should be grateful if you would write a Report concerning her condition and covering the following points.

1   Please could you specify the nature of the impairment from which Claudia suffers.

2   Please could you comment on whether Claudia's ability to carry out day-to-day activities in any of the following respects is adversely affected to a substantial degree:

(a)   mobility;

(b)   manual dexterity;

(c)   physical co-ordination;

---

22   Consider factors in DDA 1995 s18B(1); para 15.36 above.
23   DDA 1995 s3B.
24   DDA 1995 s55.
25   See samples at pp717–719 below.

(d) continence;

(e) ability to lift or move everyday objects;

(f) speech, hearing or eyesight;

(g) memory or ability to concentrate, learn or understand;

(h) perception of the risk of physical danger.

Please could you confirm that any such effect is substantial as opposed to trivial or minor.

3   If Claudia's condition is controlled by medication or aids, please could you also state how Claudia's abilities under the above categories would be affected were she not taking any medication.

4   The Act protects workers where the effect of the impairment has lasted at least 12 months or is likely to last for 12 months or for the rest of their life, if less. Recurring effects are also covered, ie, if the effect lasts less than 12 months but is likely to recur. Please could you clarify when the substantial adverse effects started to apply to Claudia and when they ceased or, if they have not yet ceased, when they are likely to cease.

5   Claudia has told me that she has particular difficulties with mobility. Could you please especially address this point and let me know whether you would expect her:

(i)   to have difficulty using public transport;

(ii) to be able to travel a short journey in a car;

(iii) to have difficulty going up or down stairs.

Would the position be any different if she were not taking medication?

6   I attach a brief description of Claudia's job duties and areas of difficulty caused by her impairment. Do you have any suggestions as to adjustments to Claudia's working conditions which may be of assistance to her?

I enclose Claudia's written authorisation for you to disclose the above information to me. Please feel free to telephone should you wish clari?cation. Please let me know before writing your report if there will be any fee.

NOTE: *Where the adviser is aware of an area of difficulty for the claimant, s/he may wish to guide the doctor further, eg, by reference to the examples in the Guidance in section D. Paragraph 5 is an example of this.*

If the GP's letter is to be shown to the employer, the worker must think carefully about its implications. If the letter suggests that the worker cannot do the job at all, but no adjustments are feasible, this could lead to difficulties

The fee should be agreed in advance and you should check who will be responsible for its payment.

DDA 1995 – ET1

Grounds of claim where a discriminatory dismissal can be pleaded in the alternative under each of DDA 1995 s3A(5) (direct discrimination) and s3A(2) and s4A (failure to make reasonable adjustments).

1   I worked as a messenger for my employers from 17 May 2003 until my dismissal on 12 May 2009. I was dismissed because I reached 30 days sickness

absence in each of my last three years of employment under the Sickness Monitoring Procedure. However, nearly all my sickness absences were due to bronchial asthma.

2 My employers were a large company employing over 1,000 members of staff. There were ten other messengers who did the same job as I did. If any messenger was absent through sickness, the others would cover the work on overtime. There was also an agency which supplied workers at short notice in emergencies.

3 The messengers were based in a small office with poor ventilation. I told my employers several times that this aggravated my asthma.

4 Apart from my sickness, I have had no warnings throughout my employment. Indeed, I have often been complimented on my good work.

5 I believe that I was dismissed on grounds of my disability contrary to DDA 1995 s3A(5). I believe a non-disabled worker who reached 30 days' sickness for three successive years would not have been dismissed.

6 Further or alternatively, I have been discriminated against contrary to sections 3A(2) and s4A of the Disability Discrimination Act 1995 by my employers' failure to make adjustments, for example, by (i) basing me in an office with better ventilation, and/or (ii) discounting my disability-related absences when applying the Sickness Monitoring Procedure to me, and/or (iii) any other reasonable adjustment.

DDA 1995 – REFORMULATING PLEADINGS AFTER MALCOLM

Following the removal of the old concept of 'disability-related discrimination' in L B Lewisham v Malcolm (see paras 15.45–15.47), it is necessary to reframe certain discriminatory actions as failure to make reasonable adjustment. The following are some examples:

1   A worker is unable to perform her work on time because a visual impairment makes her work more slowly. As a result she is demoted. If the employer had supplied the appropriate software, the worker would have had no difficulty.

pre-Malcolm claim: the demotion is disability-related discrimination

post-Malcolm claim: failure to make reasonable adjustments by supplying the appropriate software; compensation should include compensation for the demotion because it was caused by the faiure to make reasonable adjustments.

2   A worker is dismissed because his level of sickness absences has reached the threshold of 20 days/year, at which the employer tends to dismiss employees. The worker's absences are all a result of his disability.

pre-Malcolm claim: the dismissal is disability-related discrimination.

post-Malcolm claim: failure to make reasonable adjustments by allowing a certain number of disability-related absences. Compensation should include loss of earnings arising from the dismissal which was caused by the failure to make the adjustments.

3   A worker is dismissed because of disability-related sickness absence and the difficulties of managing a phased return to work.

pre-Malcolm claim: the dismissal is disability-related discrimination

post-Malcolm claim: failure to make reasonable adjustments by allowing a phased return to work.[26]

One problem in reformulating claims in this way is time-limits. In example 1, the time-limit for complaining about the demotion would have been 3 months from the demotion. But the time-limit for complaining about failure to make reasonable adjustment is 3 months from the refusal / failure to get the software, which is much earlier.

SAMPLE WITNESS STATEMENT IN RACIAL AND RELIGIOUS HARASSMENT CASE

In reality, a claimant's witness statement may be longer than the following example. A description of the claimant's duties should also be added. The following, however, gives an idea of style and content. Note how the statement draws attention to the differences in the claimant's treatment before and after the main discriminator (Ricky Johnson) started and also compares his treatment in detail with that of a white comparator (Peter Scholar). In discrimination cases, different treatment is more significant than unfair treatment. For a witness statement in an unfair dismissal case, see appendix C, p748.

SAYED MEGALI: WITNESS STATEMENT
Background

1 I was born in Egypt and I grew up there. I came to England in 1984. I have British nationality. I am of the Muslim religion. I was employed as a room service waiter in Herberts Hotel for 16 years. I was promoted to supervisor after three years. Then after another three years I became senior supervisor. While I worked at Herberts Hotel, I never had any disciplinary action taken against me nor did I take any grievances.

2 In 2000 I left the job to return to Egypt for family reasons. When I came back to England in 2001, I started working as security guard for various agencies. On 15 October 2003, I started work as security guard for Matts Hotel.

3 I was already well-known in the hotel. I had worked as a casual waiter since 2001. I got on well with everyone. The hotel asked about me in the catering department before they took me on in security.

4 Robert Keen started one week before me as Chief of Security. Before Ricky Johnson started, I used to get on well with Robert Keen. Ricky Johnson started in July 2007 as Assistant Chief Security Officer. Ricky Johnson and Robert Keen are both white and English. I believe they are of the Christian religion.

Ricky Johnson

5 Ricky Johnson was hostile and abusive from the beginning. If there was any news story about the Middle East or Arabs or if there were Arab guests in the hotel, he used to say, 'Fucking Arabs'.

6 Gradually Robert Keen became more and more hostile to me. For example, Robert Keen kept saying, 'I am fed up with you. Why don't you go back to Egypt?' He never used to talk like that before.

7 Before Ricky Johnson came, Robert Keen was helpful when I wanted to pray.

26 See *Fareham College Corporation v Walters* UKEAT/0396/08 and 0076/09.

He even said, 'Sayed, I will be in the office for a while, you can go and pray.' He also let me take Fridays as one of my off-days so I could go to the mosque. After Ricky Johnson came, all this stopped, but Robert Keen gave Ricky Johnson every Saturday off so he could watch football.

8   One day in August or September 2007, I saw a PG Tips card with a picture of a monkey put up on the wall where we make tea. Ricky Johnson used to buy the tea. I took it down and threw it away, but a few weeks later, when a new packet of tea was bought, a new monkey card was put up. I asked Ricky Johnson if he put it there. He denied it, but I believe it was him. It never happened before he came.

9   On 30 October 2007, I wrote to the hotel manager (Frank Alexander) taking out a grievance for race and religious discrimination against Ricky Johnson. Mr Alexander acknowledged my letter on 2 November 2007 and said that his secretary would contact me to arrange an appointment to meet.

10 On 14 November 2007, I received a letter from personnel calling me to a disciplinary the next day. I had worked in security for four years and as a casual waiter for the hotel since 2001. This was the first time I had been called to a disciplinary.

11 The letter said that the disciplinary was because Ricky Johnson said I had shouted and sworn at him. I told personnel at the disciplinary that this was not true. I said that he had made the accusation because I had taken out the grievance of race and religious discrimination. At the end of the disciplinary, personnel decided to take no action.

12 I met Mr Alexander on 28 November 2007 to talk about my grievance. The meeting was for about one hour. Mr Alexander said he would investigate and come back to me, but he never did come back to me about it afterwards.

The new security guard

13 In January 2008, a new security guard, Peter Scholar, was recruited. Peter was white/English and of the Christian religion. Peter was very young, about 22 years old. He had not worked in security for as long as I had. I knew Peter Scholar. He had worked at the hotel for six months in 2007 for an independent security company employed by the hotel's building contractors. His main job was to stop the builders using the staff entrance. He had to search the builders when they went out with a bag. He also patrolled the hotel to keep an eye on the builders.

14 Right from the start, Peter Scholar was treated better than I was in many ways. He was paid more than I, even though we were supposed to be doing the same job. Then in April 2009, he was given a rise and I did not get a rise.

15 In the first week Peter Scholar started, Ricky Johnson took him to a hotel management meeting. All the senior hotel managers go to that meeting every Friday. I have never been taken to it. The previous day I had heard Ricky tell Peter he would take him to the meeting so that he could cover if Robert Keen or Ricky Johnson were not there.

16 Before Peter Scholar started, the hotel's internal telephone directory only listed Robert Keen and Ricky Johnson by name under Security. After Peter started, his name was put on the list too. I was still not named. I was just 'Back Door Security'.

17 When there is an important function in the ballroom, sometimes they need extra security. I was never given a chance to do this. It was always Robert Keen or Ricky Johnson or outside security. I was not asked. But in his first or second week, Peter Scholar was allowed to do a ballroom function.

18 I saw Ricky Johnson show Peter Scholar how to use the computer several times in his first few weeks. Ricky spent more time with Peter than he spent showing me.

19 In February 2009, the number of the safe in the security office was changed. Peter Scholar was given the new number, but I was not. I asked Robert Keen why he changed the safe number. He said it was because there were important papers there. He would not give me the number. This had never happened before. Later he told Mr Alexander he changed the safe number because of an electronic fault, but he did not say that to me and he did not give me the new safe number until Mr Alexander intervened.

20 In April 2009, Peter Scholar received a pay-rise. Most of the other hotel staff also received a rise – though some did not. Robert Keen and Ricky Johnson also received a rise, so the whole security department except me got a rise. I had received a rise every April since I started. This April I did not get a rise.

21 I have continued to be harassed by Ricky Johnson. [Give full dates and details of incidents.] Robert Keen has also started to criticise my work and threaten me with disciplinary action. [Give full dates and details of incidents.] Until Ricky Johnson started, Robert Keen had never made any serious criticisms of my work or threatened disciplinary action.

22 Until all this happened, I was never off sick from work, even for one day. All the pressure and harassment for so long have damaged my health. On 5 May 2009, my doctor told me I was not fit for work due to depression. I was off sick for four weeks.

23 I think I have been treated this way because of my Egyptian or Arab origin and also because of my Muslim religion. I also think that I have been victimised because I complained about the harassment.

24 I really did not want to go to the tribunal. I wrote so many letters. I told the hotel I would prefer to sort it out. But in the end they gave me no option. I have found it very hard to go to work over the last few years. Every day I wondered if I was going to get a letter accusing me of doing something wrong or a disciplinary. It is very stressful. In the end, I became very depressed. I have never been depressed before. I am not that kind of person. I have not taken any further grievance because I am afraid it will just lead to me getting harassed further as has happened in the past.

SIGNED ...
DATED ...

EXTRACTS FROM SAMPLE WITNESS STATEMENT OF TRADE UNION OFFICIAL IN SUPPORT OF CLAIMANT'S RACE DISCRIMINATION CASE

As well as establishing the facts and events in which the official was involved, this statement draws attention to all the ways in which the employer's behaviour differed from what normally occurs (with white staff). In discrimination cases, it is more relevant to highlight different behaviour than unfair behaviour. The statement also establishes the basis of experience from which the official is able to generalise and draw distinctions.

1   I am Branch Secretary of the [name] trade union, based at [name] Council. I have held that position for approximately four years. I have been a member of the local trade union committee since 1999. I have been involved in a multitude of investigations and disciplinaries of council staff as their trade union representative.

2   The housing department, where the claimant works, comprises 120 members of staff. Although approximately one-third of the staff are black or from minority ethnic groups, nearly all the managers are white. The trade union has taken up equal opportunities issues with management on several occasions. [*Describe incidents revealing management in a bad light on equal opportunities policies, but keep concise and relevant.*]

3   I was involved in the events concerning the claimant from the beginning. My first involvement was on [date] when the claimant was notified of disciplinary action.

4   [*Describe sequence of events with dates, official's role and how much information was given to the official and/or the claimant by management.*]

5   It is very unusual to have a disciplinary hearing without a prior investigation. Normally the investigation is carried out first and the accused person is told about the investigation and what the allegations are. The disciplinary then takes place if and when the investigation reveals there is enough to justify it. It was also extraordinary not even to know the allegations against the claimant until just before the disciplinary hearing.

6   Another unusual aspect was [*Describe all procedural irregularities which took place*].

7   [*If official has anything useful to say regarding the disciplinary allegations themselves, insert here.*]

WRITTEN SUBMISSION TO ET REGARDING DISCRIMINATION TIME LIMITS

Discrimination cases often concern a number of incidents, some or all of which apparently occurred more than three months[27] before the tribunal claim was lodged. The adviser may need to make verbal or written arguments to the tribunal at a prehearing review or at the full hearing as to why the incidents should be allowed in time as grounds of the claim. The following model may be useful, though advisers should watch out for more case-law developments on time limits. Where the statutory dispute

---

27   Possibly 6 months where the statutory dispute resolution procedures apply.

resolution procedures still apply (as in this model), time-limits are likely to be particularly complex.

ET claim (submitted 12 March 2009)

[NOTE: This does not draw attention to time-limit issues at this stage.]

1   On 11 September 2008, the claimant applied for an acting-up opportunity in his department. He was unsuccessful and the opportunity was given to a white colleague who had been with the department for a shorter period of time.

2   On 8 November 2008, acting-up opportunity arose. The claimant applied and again was unsuccessful. The opportunity was given to a white employee transferred from another department.

3   On 14 November 2008, the claimant sent his employer a grievance letter regarding his rejection from the two acting-up opportunities, which he stated he believed was due to his black African origin. On 25 November 2008, the claimant was informed that his grievance was unsuccessful. The claimant appealed the outcome of his grievance on 27 November 2008. On 15 December 2008, the claimant was informed that his appeal was unsuccessful.

4   On 2 January 2009, the claimant was made redundant. On 20 January 2009, the claimant appealed against his redundancy. The respondent has not yet set a date for hearing his appeal. The claimant believes his selection for redundancy was a further act of direct discrimination and/or victimisation.

Written submissions regarding time limits

[NOTE: These submissions should not normally be included in the ET claim, but are for any pre hearing review or the full hearing, when the issue may arise.]

The law

A   The claimant's contention will be that:

(a)   the grounds of his claim are not in fact out of time;

(b)   if the tribunal believes that any such grounds are out of time, the tribunal is asked to exercise its just and equitable discretion to allow them in as a late claim;

(c)   in any event, the claimant will refer to such matters as are out of time as supporting evidence for those grounds which are in time (*Eke v Commissioners of Customs and Excise* [1981] IRLR 334, EAT; *Anya v University of Oxford* [2001] IRLR 377, CA).

B   In deciding whether or not the claimant's claims are in time, the tribunal is asked to bear in mind that an act extending over a period should be treated as done at the end of that period (RRA 1976 s68(7)(b)). A discriminatory act extends over a period of time if it takes the form of some policy, rule or practice, in accordance with which decisions are taken from time to time (*Owusu v LFCDA* [1995] IRLR 574, EAT; approved by the Court of Appeal in *Cast v Croydon College* [1998] IRLR 318), or simply if there is a continuing discriminatory state of affairs (*Hendricks v Commissioner of Police of the Metropolis* [2003] IRLR 96, CA).

C   The tribunal is asked to exercise its discretion to allow in any out of time matters on the following grounds:

(a) As the tribunal will be aware, the legal test for whether it should allow a late claim is wider than for unfair dismissal cases. The test is not whether it was reasonably practicable for the claimant to have started his claim in time. The test is whether it is just and equitable in all the circumstances to allow a late claim.

(b) Any out of time incidents will need to be dealt with as supporting evidence in any event. The issues before the tribunal will therefore be the same and will need to be resolved in any event. There will be no additional time or cost for the respondent.

(c) The respondent has been aware from the outset of all the matters in dispute, they form a continuous sequence of events. The respondent has dealt with such matters in grievances. There is therefore no problem in having to remember facts unexpectedly raised from the past.

(d) The use of internal procedures in an attempt to resolve matters prior to resorting to the law is to be encouraged. The claimant should not be penalised for taking this course and it is one factor which the ET can take into account.

(e) For the above reasons, the respondent has not been prejudiced by the fact of any delay in starting these proceedings. By contrast, the claimant would be severely prejudiced by not having the very serious matters he raises adjudicated upon.

The grounds in this case

The claimant's claim was faxed to the Employment Tribunal on 12 March 2009.

1   *Ground*: Failure to appoint to acting-up opportunity: 11 September 2008.

This refusal is in time because it is part of a continuing discriminatory state of affairs which continued until his dismissal on 2nd January 2009, which was within three months prior to the lodging of the ET claim.

Alternatively, it is just and equitable to allow this in as a late claim. The final result of the grievance concerning this refusal took place on 15 December 2008, ie within three months prior to the lodging of the ET claim. The respondent was able to deal with the issue promptly after it occurred due to the bringing of the grievance on 4 November 2008 and will not be prejudiced by any delay in answering this complaint. Further, this matter will in any event need to be explored as part of the supporting evidence for the claims which are indisputably in time.

2   *Ground*: Failure to grant acting-up opportunity: 8 November 2008.

This claim is in time. The statutory disputes resolution procedures apply. The claimant sent the respondent a step 1 grievance letter on 14 November 2008 (within the normal time limit, ie, on or before 7 February 2009). The time limit is extended until 7 May 2009 for this claim.

3   *Ground*: Redundancy dismissal: 2 January 2009.

This claim is in time.

ET1 – UNFAIR DISMISSAL (CONDUCT) AND WRITTEN REASONS

In the following example, the ACAS regime has replaced the statutory dispute resolution procedures.

1 I started work for the respondent restaurant in May 2007 as a sous chef. I was never given a written contract.

2 Until 18 July 2009, there were no problems with my employment and I had received no disciplinary warnings of any kind. I took orders from various more senior members of kitchen staff, including the 2nd Head Chef, Basil.

3 Basil's manner in the kitchen was generally to shout and abuse more junior staff. On 18 July 2009, I was joking with some of my colleagues as I worked. Other supervisors would allow us to talk and joke as long as we got the work done. Basil entered the kitchen and poked his finger in the chest of some of my colleagues. He also waved his finger at me and he told us all to 'shut up'.

4 I was upset by his angry manner and I asked him what was wrong. He swore at me in response and I therefore swore back at him. He told us to 'f...ing shut up' and to 'f... off'. I replied to him 'f... off'. I regret doing this, but it was completely provoked by Basil's manner towards me and my colleagues. Also swearing and use of the 'f...' word is very common in the kitchen at all levels of staff.[28]

5 Basil then shouted at me to go home. When I did not want to do this, he became more angry and said that I was suspended and to go home and he called security.

6 When I came in on 19 July 2009, I found the head chef, Mo, and tried to explain what had happened. Mo's first response was that I had been there for two years and should know what Basil was like. He said 'Better look for another job'. Then he told me to return the next day at 5. Then when I went in on 20 July 2009, I was handed a letter calling me to a disciplinary hearing on 23 July 2009.

7 When I arrived on 23 July 2009, Mo and Basil were sitting there. Mo said, 'We have decided you are dismissed. We have discussed it and we have decided.' I was stunned. I had only just entered the room. I said, 'I would just like to explain something.' Mo said, 'OK, Carry on.' I said that Basil had sworn at me first. Basil said the supervisor had already told me twice to shut up. I said that had not happened. Basil did not respond. Mo then said, 'OK, thank you, sorry you have to go.' The whole meeting took about two minutes. No questions were asked of me. I did not even get the chance to sit down.

8 I then went to look for the General Manager, who I found at the bar. I told him I had been dismissed. He said he would look into the details. However, I have not heard from him since.

9 On 25 July 2009, I wrote to the General Manager and asked him the written reasons for my dismissal. I have had no response.

---

28 It is best to deal with the fact that the claimant swore in the ET1 and put it in context.

10 I believe I was unfairly dismissed contrary to ERA 1996 s98 in that:[29]

    (a) Having regard to usual language in the kitchen and in particular the generally abusive manner of Basil and the fact that he spoke to me initially on 18 July 2009 in an abusive way, there was not a fair reason to dismiss me.

    (b) I had been given no prior warnings regarding my conduct or any other matter.

    (c) there was no proper investigation and I was not given a fair hearing prior to my dismissal. In particular:

        (i) the allegations against me were not clearly put to me;

        (ii) I was given no proper chance to state my case;

        (iii) I was not listened to with an open mind.

    (d) The General Manager did not look into the matter as he promised me and I was deprived of the opportunity of an appeal.

11 Good practice guidelines in the ACAS Code of Practice on Disciplinary and Grievance Procedures were not followed as set out above.[30]

12 I further request a declaration as to the reasons for my dismissal and compensation pursuant to ERA 1996 s92.

ET1 – UNFAIR DISMISSAL (CONDUCT), NOTICE AND RIGHT TO BE ACCOMPANIED

In the following example, the ACAS regime has replaced the statutory dispute resolution procedures.

1 The claimant was employed as a part-time receptionist by the respondent Leisure Clubs from on or about the 10 April 2001 until termination on 7 July 2009. She never received any warnings throughout her employment.[31]

2 At the tennis club where the claimant was based, there were two car parks, one for members of the club and one for the staff. As a general rule, staff were asked not to park in the members' car park unless the staff car park was full.

3 In practice, however, staff frequently parked in the members' car park at different times and on occasion left their cars there overnight or for prolonged periods of time. Management were aware of this but took no action.

4 The claimant also used to park her car in the members' car park on occasion, for example, at night or when the staff car park was full, and was sometimes reminded in passing that she should use the staff car park. At no time did the

---

29 Only set out reasons in this way if confident, since there is the danger of missing something out. If uncertain, and the unfairness is apparent from the facts set out in the grounds – as in this case – it may be sufficient to state, 'for the above reasons, I believe my dismissal was unfair'. The advantage of itemising the unfairness, if you can, is that it may encourage the employer to settle.

30 The advantage of mentioning this is that it may affect compensation as well as the fairness of the dismissal. The disadvantage is that the respondents may require you to itemise in what respects the Code has not been followed.

31 Claimants 'forget' about warnings. Make sure she is correct about this statement.

claimant received a formal verbal or written warning for parking her car in the members' car park.[32]

5 On 26 June 2009 the claimant was driving into the members' car park in order to pick up a member. She was accompanied in her car by a friend. On her way in she met John Armitage, the Finance Director, who was also in his car.

6 John Armitage said something to her, but because both parties were in their cars, the claimant did not hear him properly. She believed he was saying something about the van owned by the health club, which was parked nearby, and she replied to him 'That's a delivery'. She then parked in the members' car park and went into the club to meet the member she was picking up, who was late.

7 The claimant received a letter dated 4 July 2009 which informed her that a disciplinary interview had been arranged to deal with 'continued abuse of the club car park and wilful misconduct towards a Director of the company' relating to the incident with John Armitage.

8 The disciplinary hearing took place on 7 July 2009. John Armitage conducted the interview. The claimant wanted one of her colleagues to accompany her. She was told this was unnecessary.

9 At the meeting John Armitage explained the reasons why the disciplinary meeting was taking place and said that he had told the claimant not to park her car in the members' car park, which she had then gone on to do. The claimant explained that there had been a misunderstanding about this incident, because she had not understood what he was saying at the time. If she had known what he was saying she would not have deliberately disobeyed him.

10 The claimant was summarily dismissed and did not return to work after that date. She did not appeal this decision because she was very shocked at the time and was not informed of her right to appeal.

11 The claimant was unfairly dismissed. In particular, the respondent:[33]
   (i)   failed properly to investigate the allegations against the claimant;
   (ii)   failed to reach a reasonable conclusion;
   (iii) failed to have a reasonable belief in the claimant's guilt;[34]
   (iv)   failed to follow its own contractual disciplinary procedures;
   (v)   failed to inform the claimant of her right to appeal the decision to dismiss;
   (vi)   failed to follow the ACAS Code of Practice on Disciplinary and Grievance Procedures;[36]
   (vii) allowed John Armitage to act as witness, prosecutor and judge;[35]
   (viii) it was not reasonable in all the circumstances for the respondent to dismiss and the dismissal fell outside the band of reasonable responses.

12 The claimant further claims six weeks pay in lieu of notice.

---

32 As the claimant did in fact use the members' car park, it is best to admit this from the outset and put it in context.

33 See comments at p726, n29.

34 Points (i) – (iii) relate to the steps which the employer should follow in conduct cases according to *BHS v Burchell* [1978] IRLR 379, EAT and see para 7.40.

35 See comments at n30 above.

36 Points (iv) – (vii) are appropriate on the facts of this particular case.

728   *Employment law / Appendix A*

13   The respondent failed to permit the claimant to be accompanied at the disciplinary hearing contrary to section 10 of the Employment Relations Act 1999 and contrary to the ACAS Code on Disciplinary and Grievance Procedures.[37] The claimant claims compensation.

LIST OF ISSUES FOR DISCRIMINATION CASE (WITH OTHER CLAIMS)

At case management discussions, which are usually held in discrimination cases, it is common for the Employment Judge to make a list of the 'issues' in the case. This can help clarify a muddled case which has not been thought through, but can seem an unnecessary formulation where the case is already set out precisely in the tribunal claim. It is best to go prepared with a 'draft' to hand up to the Judge and the other side, to make sure nothing gets left out. Ideally, send the draft to the other side in advance and try to get agreement to the content. The following is an example.

1   Whether the respondent subjected the claimant to direct discrimination under the Race Relations Act 1976 s1(1)(a) by giving her a written warning on 16 April 2009.

2   Whether the respondent subjected the claimant to direct discrimination under Race Relations Act 1976 s1(1)(a) by dismissing her on 23 May 2009.

3   Whether the respondent subjected the claimant to victimisation under Race Relations Act 1976 s2 by dismissed her on 23 May 2009 as a result of her allegation of race discrimination on 20 April 2009.

4   In respect of the claimant's unfair dismissal claim:
    a. Whether the respondent can prove the reason for dismissal and what is that reason.
    b. Whether it was fair to dismiss the claimant for that reason, taking account of the band of reasonable responses?

5   Whether the respondent has made an unlawful deduction from the claimant's pay contrary to Part II of the Employment Rights Act 1996 in the sum of £450 representing the claimant's wages for the period 10–23 May 2009.

VARIATION OF CONTRACT CHECKLIST

The law is complicated around what an employee can do if the employer tries to impose a change of terms and conditions in the contract of employment. In theory, no change can be made to a contract unless the employee agrees. In practice, what happens if the employer just sacks an employee who refuses to agree? Not only will the employee have no job, s/he may not be eligible to make any legal claims. Even if the employee is eligible to claim, s/he may not win.

It is commonly believed that employers only need to give 90 days' notice of a change. This is not in fact true, the employee's consent is still necessary.

The following is a guide to some important steps when thinking through the employee's legal position.

• Check the worker's employment status. If s/he is not in fact an employee, s/he will have fewer options, as s/he will not have unfair dismissal protection. Discrimination law will still apply.

37   See para 22.80.

- Check the employee's contract of employment. Is its meaning clear? Is the employer really changing the contract or is it a change which the contract allows?

WARNING: Contract terms may be written, verbal or implied. If written, they may be ambiguous. If unwritten, they may be hard to ascertain or prove.

- If the contractual position is uncertain, it may be possible to go to an ET for clarification under ERA 1996 s11 provided the disputed term is one of those which must be listed under ERA 1996 s1. (This option is irrelevant if the employer agrees the contractual position, and simply states an intention to change the contract.)

WARNING: The employee may get the wrong decision from the tribunal. This could also harm other employees, and undermine negotiating power. Also, there may also not be enough time to get a tribunal's decision.

- Is the employee eligible to claim unfair dismissal if s/he is sacked or resigns due to a contractual change? If not, his/her position is very weak.
- Even if the employee is eligible to make an unfair dismissal claim in such circumstances, is s/he likely to win it?
  - Did the employer adopt fair procedures in implementing the change? (Advance notice; consultation; flexibility)
  - Would the ET think it reasonable for the employer to impose the change? (The ET may conclude that the employer's needs are more important than the negative impact on employees. Are there better alternatives? Have other employees agreed to the change? Are there special circumstances?)
- Is the employee willing to risk losing his/her job over this?
- What is the likelihood of winning a case and what compensation is the employee likely to receive?
- What is the employee's chance of getting a new job? Will s/he get a bad reference?
- Compare the problem of working under the varied contract with any alternative/job prospects.
- Has the employee been discriminated against in the change, directly or indirectly?
  - Is s/he covered by the discrimination legislation? (Note, s/he need not be an employee or have been employed for 1 year.)
  - Is there any indirect sex discrimination, eg, introducing flexi-shifts or other changes interfering with childcare?
  - Is there any indirect race discrimination, eg, introducing duties requiring sophisticated written English skills?
  - Are the changes imposed on some staff but not on others? Is this direct discrimination? For example, an employer may make an exception for a white worker unable to work flexi-shifts for health reasons, but refuse to make an exception for a black worker with equally valid reasons.
  - Has the employer introduced duties which are hard for a disabled worker to undertake?

WARNING: Although the employee may be able to claim discrimination without resigning from his/her job, s/he may nevertheless be victimised for doing so. Victimisation and intimidation of a employee pursuing a discrimination case should be catalogued, as this too is illegal and may be the ground for a further case.

What can the employee do now?

- Agree the change (orally or in writing).
- Pin down the employer on the nature of the change and the reasons for it, either in correspondence (formal letters; informal e-mails etc) or through a grievance. The employer's reasoning helps the worker assess the strength of any tribunal claim and may give scope for a negotiated compromise.
- State disagreement with the change and attempt to negotiate.

WARNING: Once negotiation has clearly become futile, the grievance procedure is exhausted, and the employer is still insisting on the change, a employee needs to make up his/her mind swiftly whether or not s/he accepts the change. Otherwise s/he can lose the right to resign because s/he has 'affirmed' (ie, implicitly agreed by inaction).

- If relevant, a claim under ERA 1996 s11 may clarify a disputed contractual term and add negotiating pressure on the employer. If the employee is dismissed as a result, s/he may be able to claim this is automatic unfair dismissal for asserting a statutory right.
- Refuse to accept the change. If it amounts to a pay deduction, make a tribunal claim for an unlawful deduction or, less practically, a civil claim for the pay owed. If it is a change in duties, refuse to carry out the change.

WARNING: These steps risk dismissal. Dismissal for claiming an unlawful deduction is automatically unfair, but it may be hard to prove that was the reason.

- Resign and claim unfair constructive dismissal. There are many legal pitfalls for this:
  - The employee may not be eligible to claim unfair dismissal.
  - The contract may be unclear; it may be uncertain that the employer has broken it in a fundamental way.
  - The employee may not have resigned quickly enough; if s/he has taken too long to decide, the ET may consider s/he has already accepted the change.
  - The employer's behaviour may not necessarily be considered unfair by the ET.
  - The employee is out of a job and may not get much compensation even if s/he wins.
- Make a discrimination claim if applicable. This can be done whether or not s/he resigns, but it does risk victimisation or dismissal.
- The employee may also be entitled to a redundancy payment if s/he loses her job in circumstances which fit the legal definition of redundancy.[38]
- If the employer imposes the change by dismissing the employee with correct notice and then offering a new contract on different terms, the employee may be able to accept the new contract while claiming unfair dismissal in respect of the old contract.
- If the employer imposes a very radical change, the law may deem this as a dismissal and again the employee can claim unfair dismissal while remaining in the new job.

---

38 See paras 8.9–8.15.

WARNING: The employee cannot have it both ways. If s/he accepts the new terms so that s/he can remain in the job, and reserves his/her right to make a claim in respect of the variation / dismissal from the original contract, s/he cannot then renege on the new terms. Otherwise s/he can justifiably be dismissed from the new contract.

- It will be more effective if a large number of employees simultaneously bring legal action. Collective opposition and negotiation will usually be the best bet.

NATIONAL MINIMUM WAGE

The following steps need to be taken in checking whether someone has a claim:[39]

1 Is s/he a worker eligible to claim?
2 Ascertain the pay reference period. (One month or the pay interval if less.)
3 Add up the total pay in the pay reference period which can count towards the national minimum wage and make necessary deductions (see table below).
4 Calculate the number of hours in the pay reference period which must be paid at the minimum rate. (This depends on the type of work.)
5 Divide the total pay by the total hours in the pay reference period to get the actual hourly pay. Compare this with the current minimum rate.
6 If shortfall, consider options for action: taking up the issue direct or through a trade union representative, advice agency or solicitor, or approaching the enforcement agency (HMRC).

TABLE OF PAY WHICH COUNTS TOWARDS THE NATIONAL MINIMUM WAGE (OVERLEAF)

(i) Calculate the total remuneration paid. This is the total set out in Column A but does not include the items set out in Column B. (NMW Regs 1999 reg 30.)

(ii) Subtract from this total, various payments made by the worker to the employer or deductions from the worker's pay-packet, according to the rules set out in NMW Regs 1999 regs 31 – 37 (see Columns C and D). The balance should not fall below the national minimum wage.

(iii) The pay reductions in Column C should be subtracted from the total, ie the worker must receive the national minimum pay in addition to these sums.

(iv) The pay reductions in Column D should not be subtracted from the total.

---

39 Read in conjunction with paras 4.29–4.45.

Column A	Column B
Total pay received: these sums should be added together before making the deductions in column C.	**These sums do not count towards the national minimum wage. They should not be added into the total for pay received.**
• All money payments in the pay reference period, including gross pay and bonuses, performance allowances, performance-related-pay, sales commission, incentive pay. • For periods before 1 October 2009 only, tips, gratuities, service charge from customers if paid through the pay-roll, but not if through a tronc system. • The value of free accommodation up to the specified limit.	• Loan or advance of wages: reg 8(a) • Pension payment; payment on retirement; compensation for loss of office; redundancy pay: reg 8(b) and (d) • Award under a suggestions scheme: reg 8(e) • Court / tribunal award unless for a sum contractually due: reg 8(c) • Vouchers etc exchangeable for money, goods or services (reg 9(b)), eg luncheon vouchers: • Benefits in kind, except for accommodation as specified (reg 9(a)), eg car, petrol, medical insurance, meals

Column D	Column C
These sums should not be subtracted from the calculation of the total received.	**These sums do not count towards national minimum pay. They should be deducted from the calculation of the total received.**
Deductions by the employer or payments made by the worker in respect of: • Tax and national insurance. • Worker's pension contribution; union subs • To repay an advance of wages or a loan: reg 33(b); 35(b). • To recover an accidental overpayment of wages: reg 33(c); 35(c). • The worker's purchase of shares: reg 33(d); 35(d). • Goods or services from the employer, unless the worker is required to make such purchases for the job (reg 35(e)), eg the worker chooses to buy clothes from a shop where s/he works. • From 1.10.07, to a local housing authority or registered social landlord in respect of the provision of accommodation (except where the accommodation is provided in connection with the worker's employment with the authority / landlord): reg 33(e), 35(f). • The worker's conduct, or any other event, in respect of which the worker is contractually liable: reg 33(a); 35(a).	• Overtime and shift premiums, ie sums paid over the lowest rate than the worker can be paid: reg 31(1)(c) • Allowances (apart from performance) that are not consolidated into pay, eg unsocial hours allowances or London Weighting: reg 31(1)(d). • Sums paid by the employer representing amounts paid by customers in respect of service charge, gratuities, tips or cover charge: reg 31(1)(e). • Reimbursement of expenses: reg 31(1)(f); 34(1)(b). • Deductions / payments by the worker in respect of the worker's expenditure in connection with his/her employment (reg 31(1)(a); reg 34(1)(a)), eg for tools or uniform. • Deductions / payments by the worker for the employer's own use or benefit (reg 32(1)(b); reg 34(1)(c)), eg in respect of meals. • Deductions / payment by the worker for the provision of accommodation above the specified limit, but not any deductions / payments for the provision of accommodation by a local housing authority or registered social landlord, except where the accommodation is provided in connection with the worker's employment with the authority / landlord: reg 31(1)(i) and reg 2.

Case-study:

Carmen is paid £135 gross per week for a 30-hour week. In the week-ending 21 October 2009, her pay-slip showed the following deductions: £40 tax and NI; £5 union subs, £20 to recover an overpayment of wages. In addition, she earned £20 unsocial hours allowance and £7.50 performance allowance. She also receives medical insurance cover. There is a payment of £50 to her as a monthly travel ticket loan. Net pay in that week was £125.

Total pay counted towards the national minimum wage is £135 + £7.50 performance allowance. The other items do not count towards the relevant total (see table above).

£142.50 (total pay in reference period) divided by 30 (total hours in reference period) = £4.75 (actual hourly pay). Taking £5.80 as the national minimum rate (year beginning 1st October 2009), this represents a shortfall of £1.05/hour, ie, £31.50 in total in that reference period.

WHISTLEBLOWING CHECKLIST

If a worker wants to 'blow the whistle' or take up potentially controversial issues at work, it is wise to take account of the criteria in the Public Interest Disclosure Act 1998, so that s/he has protection if s/he is dismissed or penalised by the employer as a result. The following checklist does not cover all situations. See also the text on paras 6.91–6.98.

1 Check the worker reasonably believes that his/her information tends to show one of the following has taken or may take place:[40]
   - a criminal offence
   - breach of a legal obligation, including an obligation in the worker's own contract of employment
   - miscarriage of justice
   - danger to health and safety
   - damage to the environment
2 Check the worker is acting in good faith.[41]
3 Consider what outcome the worker wants.
   - is s/he willing to accept potential adverse consequences?
   - unless the complaint is about how s/he has been treated him/herself, does s/he realise s/he will only be a witness in this matter.
4 Check whether the employer has a policy which states to whom disclosure should be made and what procedure to follow. If not, see 5–7:
5 The worker should initially raise the matter with his/her employer, but exceptionally s/he can make disclosure to someone else[42] if:
   - in all the circumstances it is reasonable to make disclosure to someone else (taking account of their identity).
   - the worker reasonably believes the information/allegations are substantially true.

---

40 See paras 6.93–6.94.
41 Except where disclosure is in the course of obtaining legal advice.
42 Under ERA 1996 s43G or 43H.

- disclosure is not made for personal gain.
- the worker reasonably believes s/he will be subjected to a detriment by the employer if s/he makes a disclosure to the employer or a prescribed person;
- there is no prescribed person and the worker reasonably believes it is likely that evidence will be concealed or destroyed if s/he makes disclosure to employer; or
- it is an exceptionally serious failure.[43]

6 Alternatively the worker can raise the matter initially with a prescribed body if one exists, provided the worker reasonably believes the information/allegations are substantially true.[44]

7 If the matter is not resolved internally or by the prescribed body, the worker can raise the matter with someone else, provided the conditions at 5 above are met.

8 Remember it is unlawful if the worker is victimised or dismissed because s/he has raised these matters.

9 Consider taking advice from Public Concern at Work.

ASSESSMENT OF COMPENSATION

Unfair dismissal: compensation checklist

NOTE: This checklist refers to the most common elements comprising unfair dismissal compensation, but does not refer to all the variables. It is important to read chapter 18. The checklist is for the private use of the adviser and employee and is not for disclosure to the employer or ET. For that, see schedules of loss on pp739–740.

1   Basic award
   (a) Calculate according to age, whole years' service, gross weekly pay subject to current weekly maximum.
   (b) Check if dismissal was for a reason where a minimum basic award must be made.[44]
   (c) Make any deductions for:[46]
      (i)   unreasonable refusal of an offer of reinstatement;
      (ii) misconduct before dismissal;
      (iii) redundancy payments made.

2   Compensatory award
   Case-law on the order of adding and deducting items is extremely complex and not all variables have been tested. The following order is a rough guide, but may not be correct in every case.[47]
   (a)   Calculate how much the worker would have earned net of tax had s/he not been dismissed. Take into account any likely pay rises or overtime. Cal-

43   ERA 1996 s43H.
44   ERA 1996 s43F.
45   See paras 18.19–18.20.
46   See para 18.18.
47   See para 18.57.

culate the loss up to the hearing date and for a reasonable period into the future. Once the worker has obtained a new job at the same or greater pay, stop counting the loss.

(b)   Add any other losses, eg, pension, health insurance, company car, free meals or accommodation.

(c)   Add expenses incurred as a direct result of the dismissal, eg, the cost of job-hunting.

(d)   Add compensation for loss of statutory rights.[48]

(e)   Add compensation for loss of statutory right to a long notice period.

(f)   If the worker obtained a new job on lower pay, deduct the new net earnings.

(g)   Deduct any payments made by the former employer as a result of the dismissal, eg, notice pay or severance payments except, if a redundancy payment is made, the amount by which it exceeds the basic award.

Note: Sometimes notice pay exceeds what is actually due under the contract or statute. The extra will probably be set off against the balance of the compensatory award unless the employer explicitly made the payment in respect of the notice period.

(h)   Make any percentage deduction under the *Polkey* principle.[49]

(i)   Increase or decrease by 10–50 per cent for failure by employer or employee to comply with statutory dispute resolution procedures (if still applicable) or up to 25% for employer's or employee's failure to comply with the ACAS Code.[50]

(j)   Add 2–4 weeks' pay if, when proceedings began, employer was in breach of duty to supply section 1 or 4 statement of particulars of employment and change.[51]

(k)   Make any percentage deduction for contributory fault.

(l)   Deduct any sum by which a redundancy payment exceeds the basic award.

(m)   Apply the overall ceiling on the compensatory award (except where it does not apply).

Remember that although the employer may have to pay the total award, recoupment may well apply and leave the employee with a lesser sum.[52]

3   Additional award

If applicable, see para 18.13.

4   Other legal rights

Extra compensation may be paid for other rights claimed at the same time in the tribunal, eg, discrimination (see below) or failure to give written reasons for dismissal under ERA 1996 s92 (two weeks' pay). Also claim notice. The employee will not get paid for the notice period twice, but s/he may not win his/her unfair dismissal case.

48   See para 18.39.
49   See para 18.54.
50   See para 18.53.
51   See para 1.25 regarding this entitlement.
52   See para 18.58.

Unfair dismissal compensation: example 1 (statutory dispute resolution procedures no longer apply; ACAS Code correctly followed.)

Facts

Roger was dismissed aged 44. He was required to work his notice. Roger had worked 6½ years for his employer. His gross weekly pay was £360. His net weekly basic pay was £280 + an average of £20 net/week for voluntary and non-contractual overtime. He had no pension. Roger found a new job after eight weeks, though initially it only paid £200 net/week. It cost him £10 to look for a job (fares, telephone calls, newspapers.) 12 weeks later he was promoted, getting a rise to £330 net/week. At no stage did Roger claim social security benefits.

Roger's case is due to be heard by the tribunal on 4 September 2009, which is exactly 26 weeks from his dismissal date. Considering the facts of his dismissal, he is likely to have a 20 per cent deduction for contributory fault and his conduct prior to dismissal. There may also be a 25 per cent Polkey deduction to represent the fact that had proper procedures been followed prior to his dismissal, there is a 25 per cent chance that he would nevertheless have been dismissed on a fair basis.

Calculation of award

Basic award

£350 (maximum gross weekly pay at dismissal date) × 7½ = £2625
less
20% deduction for conduct prior to dismissal = £525
Basic award = £2100

Compensatory award

Average net earnings which Roger would have received had he not been dismissed = £300/week
8 weeks' loss of net earnings while out of work (8 × 300) = £2,400
12 weeks' loss of net earnings after new job on lesser pay (12 × (300–200)) = £120
expenses looking for a job = £10
loss of statutory rights = £300
total loss = £2830

Deductions

25% *Polkey* (75% × £2830) = £2122.50
20% contributory fault (80% × £2122.50) = £1698
Compensatory award = £1698

Total for unfair dismissal = £2100 + £1698 = £3798

Unfair dismissal compensation: example 2 (serious and flagrant breach of ACAS Code by employer)

Facts

Irina was dismissed aged 36 and required to work her notice. She had worked with her employer for two years and four months. She was paid £400 per week gross (£260 per week net). After ten weeks, she obtained a new job at the same level of pay. She had no job hunting expenses and did not claim benefits. The ET found automatic unfair dismissal because the employer failed to follow the statutory DDP.

Calculation of award

Basic award

£350 (maximum gross weekly pay) $\times$ 2 = £700

Compensatory award

Average net earnings Irina would have received had she not been dismissed = £260/week

10 weeks loss of net earnings while out of work (10 $\times$ 260) = £2600

loss of statutory rights = £300

sub-total = £2900

(unless exceptional circumstances) up to 25% increase for employer's failure to comply with ACAS Code = up to £3625.[53]

Total for unfair dismissal = between £4430 (£1240 + £3190) and £5590 (£1240 + £4350)

ASSESSMENT OF COMPENSATION FOR DISCRIMINATION

Race, sex, religion, belief, sexual orientation, age or disability discrimination: Compensation checklist

1   A single compensatory award with no upper ceiling applies.
2   Financial loss resulting from the discrimination, eg, loss of earnings on dismissal or lack of promotion, loss of pension. (Similar principles to unfair dismissal but may be longer-term future loss of earnings if severity of discrimination has damaged worker's confidence or health.)
3   Compensation for injury to feelings including aggravated damages and compensation for damage to health. Consider these as three separate headings.
4   Interest.
5   Under RRA 1976, there is no financial compensation for unintentional discrimination, except in relation to race or ethnic or national origins.
6   Note that an ET can make recommendations and award extra compensation for failure to comply with them.

53   The increase is imposed on the compensatory award ERA 1996 s124A.

SETTLEMENT TERMS CHECKLIST

Negotiating settlements has become increasingly complicated as employers produce more and more detailed and onerous written agreements. These are considerations to bear in mind:

- Generally consider the tax position, especially with large settlements.[54]
- Specify the sum to be paid and that it is free of tax. Do not agree to indemnify the employer for any attendant costs or for any tax s/he may incur as a result of making that payment. If the employer insists, narrow down the scope of the indemnity as far as possible.[55]
- Ensure there is a date for payment and supply of any reference. This should be either a specified date or 'within 14 days of receipt by the employer or if represented, the employer's representative of the COT3/settlement agreement signed by the claimant or his/her representative'. (Ideally get the claimant to sign the COT3 or agreement so there is no dispute later.)
- Specify who the settlement cheque should be made payable to and where it should be sent.
- Attach the agreed wording of the reference. Specify who should supply the reference, that it should be dated and on headed notepaper. Specify whether any other written or verbal reference may be given in any circumstances. Consider whether the worker also wants an open reference.[56]
- If the settlement is expressed to be 'full and final of all claims ...' ensure it is only 'all claims arising out of the employment or the termination thereof.'
- If the proposed wording suggests 'all claims which the worker has or may have ...', delete the words 'or may have'. Delete words like 'whatsoever'.
- Add 'with the exception of any personal or industrial injuries[57] or pension rights'
- If the employer suggests a confidentiality clause, check what is made confidential (the settlement terms? The fact of the agreement? The case itself? The whole employment?). Make any necessary exceptions (close relatives; as required by law; prospective employers; bodies such as the EHRC).
- Consider whether to ask the employer to retain confidentiality in return.
- Be careful about vague agreements not to make any 'derogatory remarks' or 'adverse comments' about the employer's business. This wording is so wide that it could, for example, prevent casual and minor critical remarks made socially about a retail employer's products. It is especially problematic if the agreement is not to say anything derogatory about unknown associated companies or individuals (employees, directors, shareholders).
- Do not agree to any penalty clause or suggestion that the worker repay the settlement sum if s/he breaks confidentiality. Apart from anything else, this could make the payment taxable. Penalty clauses may or may not be

---

54 See para 20.165 above.
55 See para 20.165 above.
56 See also para 20.164.
57 This exception may not work in respect of injuries caused by acts of discrimination.

enforceable, depending on the overall wording of the agreement, but it is unwise to take the risk.[58]

- If the employer adds clauses in restraint of trade ('restrictive covenants'), ensure the worker understands their meaning and effectiveness. These could also make the settlement partially taxable if some of the payment appears to be for agreeing to such covenants.
- If the worker owes any money to the employer or there is any suggestion the employer may wish to sue him or her, ensure the settlement is full and final of any claims either side may have.
- The worker must not agree to do anything which is outside his/her control, eg ensuring that other people keep matters confidential.
- The worker should not agree to anything where its meaning or consequences are uncertain.

SCHEDULES OF LOSS

As explained at para 20.98, these can be supplied in various forms. The following are just alternative models. The starting point is obviously the actual sums which the worker could claim (see compensation checklist at p734). The claimant would not normally put down any deductions s/he anticipates for Polkey, contributory fault or failure to mitigate. None of the following models contain the complex figures necessary to calculate pension loss.

Model 1: simple unfair dismissal schedule where claimant has new job at more pay

This is based on the Roger case-study (p736). Note that other claimants may have other losses, eg, loss of pension or loss of a long notice period

Date of birth: *add*
Effective date of termination: *add*
Actual gross weekly pay when employed by respondents = £360
Average net weekly pay when employed by respondents = £300
New job from date (ie 8 weeks) = £200 net/week, rising to £330 net/week after 12 weeks
Hearing date = 4th July (26 weeks from dismissal)

Basic award
£350 (maximum gross weekly pay) × 7 ½ = £2,625

Compensatory award
8 weeks' loss of net earnings while out of work (8 × 300) = £2,400
12 weeks' loss of net earnings after new job on lesser pay (12 × (300–200)) = £120
Expenses looking for a job = £10
Loss of statutory rights = £300

---

58 *CMC Group plc and ors v Zhang* (2006) 808 IDS Brief 8, CA; *Dunlop Pneumatic Tyre Co Ltd v New Garage and Motor Co Ltd* [1915] AC 79; *Murray v Leisureplay* [2005] IRLR 946, CA.

Model 2: simple unfair dismissal schedule where claimant does not have new job
Suppose Roger did not have a new job by the time of the hearing

Basic award
£350 (maximum weekly gross pay) × 7½ = £2,625

Compensatory award
Past loss of earnings
From dismissal date (insert date) to hearing date (insert date) = 26 weeks @
£300 net/week = £7,800

Future loss of earnings
Ongoing loss at £300/week for as long as the ET thinks appropriate.
(alternatively, Roger could speculate, eg, 18 weeks @ £300/week = £5,400)

Expenses looking for a new job = £20

Loss of statutory rights = £300

Model 3: race discrimination and unfair dismissal model for use at hearing
The following example is more complicated, as is usual in a discrimination case. The act of discrimination was the dismissal, which was also unfair. It is possible, rather than inserting figures for injury to feelings and injury to health, to note 'to be assessed by the ET'. Increasingly, however, ETs are asking how much the claimant is seeking. It may also be good tactics to suggest a high (but not unrealistic) figure in the Schedule. Suggesting unrealistic excessive figures, on the other hand, could be counterproductive. See para 19.42 regarding latest interest rates.

CLAIMANT'S SCHEDULE OF LOSS

NO.	ITEM	CALCULATION	TOTAL	COMMENT FOR ET
1	Basic award	2 whole years service @max £350/week	£700	
2	Past loss of earnings 19.9.07 – 4.11.08	58 weeks 3 days @ £305 net/week	£17,690 net of tax.	Loss from dismissal to hearing. Sums are calculated
3	Past loss of pension 19.9.07 – 4.11.08	58 weeks 3 days @ £20.11/week	£1166.38	Loss from dismissal to hearing. Calculated on basis of lost contributions.[59]
4	Interest on past losses 19.9.07 – 4.11.08 (409 days)	£18,856.38 (£17,690 + £1168.38) x 6%[60] = £1131.38, ÷ 365 x 409 = £1267.77, ÷ 2 = £633.88	£633.88	Interest from midpoint date between act of discrimination 19.9.05 and calculation date 4.11.06
5	Future loss of earnings	£305 x 52	£15,860	Medical report says Claimant will be fit to return to work in 6-12 months. It is unrealistic to suggest she will find work at once.
6	Future loss of pension	£20.11 x 52	£1045	
7	Loss of statutory rights		£300	
8	Job hunting expenses		£50	
9	Injury to feelings		£15,000	The claim falls within the mid range in *Vento* (*No 2*)
10	Aggravated damages		£5000	

59 Note that in many cases, the calculation of pension loss is more complicated.
60 The rate before February 2009.

NO.	ITEM	CALCULATION	TOTAL	COMMENT FOR ET
11	Interest on injury to feelings and aggravated damages	£18,000 x 6% = £1080 ÷ 365 x 409 = £1210	£1210	Interest from act of discrimination 19.9.05 to calculation date 4.11.06
12	Personal injury		£15,000	Moderately Severe psychiatric injury , JSB guidelines give range £10,500 - £30,000
13	Interest on personal injury	£15,000 x 6% = £900 ÷ 365 x 409 = £1008	£1008	The same period of calculation is taken as in (11) above
14	Costs of recommended cognitive therapy		£1250	
15	Adjustment for taxation		*Insert figure*	Items 1-8 are subject to tax to the extent they exceed £30,000.[61]
16	TOTAL		*Insert figure*	

61 This book does not contain the full submissions on the tax position.

Indirect discrimination: possibly discriminatory requirements, provisions, criteria or practices

RACE DISCRIMINATION

Qualifications
- formal qualifications
- qualifications only obtainable in Great Britain
- university degree
- qualifications from certain universities or organisations
- English language qualifications

Language/expression/culture/confidence
- English language fluency – written/verbal
- communication skills
- writing skills
- essay-based tests and application forms
- psychometric testing
- culturally-biased testing
- articulation/fluency in interview performance
- acquiring new technical skills knowledge, within short time periods/without special training (difficult in an unfamiliar language/with foreign technology)

Experience/service/paid employment
- previous kinds of work experience
- previous management experience
- already being at a certain grade/holding a certain high level job
- previous (fast) promotions
- previous width/variation of experience
- length of previous experience or service in certain positions/with the employer/in the industry/with past employer
- previous paid employment/paid relevant experience
- previous steady employment/no periods of unemployment
- having attended refresher/training courses (usually unavailable to night staff who tend to be black/women)
- previous acting-up experience
- being on a permanent contract rather than temporary

Dress

These could also be religious discrimination

- uniform/dress/no turbans
- clean-shaven (eg, affect Sikhs)

Attendance/shifts

- days/hours of work/shifts/flexibility (Sabbaths/religious holidays) (these could also be religious discrimination)
- not taking holiday entitlement at one time (visits to family abroad)
- limited unpaid/compassionate leave (need to visit ill family abroad)
- good attendance record (extended holidays/unpaid leave to visit family abroad)
- late travel home (danger of racial attacks)

Keeping it internal/references in and out/being part of the club

- nomination/recommendation by/reference from particular staff/management for recruitment/promotion
- word of mouth recruitment (knowing existing workers)
- favouring children from existing staff
- internal applications only
- customer satisfaction (liability to racist complaints)
- membership of certain organisations, professional bodies or trade unions/certain (culturally specific) leisure activities or interests
- using standing lists of vacancies
- using applications for one job for purpose of filling a different job

SEX DISCRIMINATION

Many of the criteria set out above would also adversely affect women or married workers. Additional criteria and practices which would specifically affect women could be:

Attendance/shifts/flexibility/mobility

Requirements and practices likely to cause difficulty for women – and sometimes for married men – usually due to child-care commitments.

Hours

- full-time work (refusal to allow job-share or part-time working)
- permitting part-time working, but requiring some hours to be worked each day
- overtime or weekend working
- shift-working, especially rotating shifts varying from day to day or week to week
- requirements to work overtime or varying shifts imposed at very short notice
- specified and inflexible start or finish times (interfering with times of taking or collecting children from school or child-minding)
- all year round working (eg, as opposed to term-time only)
- requirements entailing certain (high) attendance levels/limited absences

Mobility

- long journeys to and from work locations (necessitating earlier departures from and returns to home)
- work trips necessitating staying overnight away from home
- relocation (may be unacceptable if woman is not the primary earner in the household)

Note: Flexibility and mobility requirements often do cause women difficulties and should therefore be justified by the employer. However, it would be direct discrimination if an employer wrongly assumed a woman would be less flexible and treated her less favourably for that reason.

Miscellaneous

- age bars (women may be out of the job market during child-bearing age)
- to have acquired a certain level of experience by a certain age
- certain forms of dress or uniform (eg, may indirectly discriminate against Muslim women)
- late finishing hours (possibly dangerous travel home)
- home visits, eg, to patients or tenants unaccompanied (in some circumstances may be dangerous)

Note: Employers should provide a safe system of work for all workers, but should not directly discriminate against women unless allowed by statute (eg, in relation to pregnancy and childbirth).

RELIGIOUS DISCRIMINATION
There will be some overlap with indirect race discrimination.

Dress
- no jewellery
- no head coverings
- cut hair, be clean-shaven
- uniform which may be regarded as immodest

Alcohol and food
- canteen without suitable food options
- work meetings, business trips, outings in unsuitable venues

Attendance and breaks
- requirement to work on Sabbaths or religious holidays
- refusal prayer breaks or holidays

SEXUAL ORIENTATION DISCRIMINATION
- privileges and benefits accessible only to or in respect of married or civil partners[1]
- first choice of holidays to staff with children
- clean criminal record

AGE DISCRIMINATION
Could adversely affect older workers:
- maximum experience
- recent graduate
- qualifications only recently in existence
- formal qualifications
- high level IT skills
- having no history of unemployment
- mobility

Could adversely affect younger workers:
- minimum length of experience
- long service

For examples of indirect age discrimination, see Help the Aged's guide: *How to recognise cases of age discrimination: an adviser's toolkit* (see bibliography).

---

1   Unfortunately lawful, see para 17.83.

SITUATIONS WHERE DISCRIMINATORY REQUIREMENTS OR PRACTICES MAY OCCUR

- access to particular jobs – who is shortlisted; who is appointed
- access to promotion – who is eligible; who is shortlisted; who is promoted
- access to acting-up opportunities
- access to training schemes
- earning extra pay – determining the level of basic pay; criteria for rises; performance assessments
- opportunities to earn overtime, additional bonuses and benefits
- grading levels
- entitlement to paid time-off for trade union duties and training.[2]
- eligibility for subsidised mortgages, occupational pensions, company cars and other perks
- rules for when and for how long holidays may be taken
- sick pay entitlement
- who gets selected for redundancy
- eligibility to formal disciplinary and grievance procedures

2   See *Arbeiterwohlfahrt der Stadt Berlin eV v Bötel* [1992] IRLR 423; 38 EOR 45, ECJ.

Unfair dismissal case study[1]

This case study should be read in conjunction with chapters 6, 8 and 20. Note that the statutory dispute resolution procedures no longer apply to this study.

WITNESS STATEMENT

When writing a witness statement, bear in mind the relevant law. What makes a redundancy dismissal unfair are failure to consult, unfair selection and failure to offer alternative employment. Any facts which indicate such failings in the employee's case should be highlighted. For guidance on writing witness statements, see paras 20.101–20.110.

WITNESS STATEMENT: JENNY PENNANT

Background

1 I started work for Strass Burger House in 1989. I gained my catering qualifications from Huyton Catering College. After I completed College in 1984, I worked in a number of hotels and restaurants as a sous chef. By January 1988 I was working as the head chef of the exclusive Kyverdale restaurant.[2]

2 On 14 December 1988 I received a letter from Arthur Venger of the Strass Burger House offering me a job as head chef at the Felstead restaurant. This was the company's smallest restaurant. Over the next 12 years I worked at several of the company's other restaurants. Each move was a promotion to more prestigious premises, with an increase in pay. My last move was on 19 December 2000 when I was made the head chef of the Ashburton restaurant, the most prestigious and best restaurant in the group.

3 Strass Burger House has 150 restaurants throughout the UK. A substantial number of them are situated in London. The company also has a large head

---

1 Note that this case-study is purely fictional.

2 When writing a statement for the purpose of an unfair dismissal claim it is important to establish the previous work record (if it is good) and qualifications that the worker has acquired. If the person has worked for a long time for one employer this should be emphasised, particularly in cases of conduct/capability dismissals. Workers should set it out if they are well qualified, have had considerable experience in the industry, have worked for well-known employers, and held important positions in the past.

office at 153 Avenal Avenue, London. There is a large personnel department. Arthur Venger is Head of Human Resources.

4　I never had any time off work for sickness during the 21 years of my employment. I never had any disciplinary action taken against me or any warnings about my work. At my last annual appraisal, Mr Venger told me he wished all the workers had the same commitment to the company that I had.

My company car

5　In November 2008, at the time of the annual appraisal and pay increase, I was told that I would get a salary of £25,000 per year as well as a company car. I had been asking for a company car for some time as I often worked late and had no alternative but to catch a taxi home on those occasions. I was told that it would take about a month to get the car.

6　On 20 March 2009 I had an audit meeting. At this meeting I asked Mr Venger about my company car. He told me to 'stop going on about it' as I was becoming 'too expensive for the company'. However, I did ask him again for the car a few times because it had been promised to me.

My dismissal

7　On 28 April 2009 I was given a letter asking me to attend a meeting at 10 am on 30 April 2009, regarding my possible redundancy. At the meeting Mr Venger told me that I was being dismissed on the ground of redundancy because of the economic climate. I was devastated. I had had no idea before getting the letter that the company was thinking of making redundancies or that I might be losing my job.[3]

8　The meeting lasted about five minutes. Mr Venger seemed to be in a hurry. He had obviously made up his mind from the outset and he gave me no opportunity to argue against my redundancy. I tried to enter into a discussion about my dismissal, seeking an explanation for this decision. Mr Venger kept saying that I had been made redundant and that I should not take it personally. I asked whether there were any other jobs for me in the company but Mr Venger said that there was nothing suitable. By the end of the meeting I was very upset.

9　I went home after the meeting. That afternoon I received a letter by courier, confirming that I was being made redundant and enclosing my P45 form and my final pay-slip. I was told that I was not required to work out my notice and that I would be paid 12 weeks' pay in lieu of notice, statutory redundancy pay and £2,000 as an ex gratia payment.

10　On 1 May 2009, I wrote a letter of appeal to Ms Diana Deane, the managing director. She heard my appeal on 16 May 2009, but she confirmed the decision. She did say that she would give me a very good reference. I asked about my holiday pay. The holiday year starts 1 April and I had not yet taken any holidays this year. I am entitled to four weeks' holiday every year plus bank holidays. Ms Deane said that I would not get pay for my untaken holidays because this was at the discretion of management and I had been paid £2,000 ex gratia.

3　It is worth emphasising lack of forewarning and consultation, as these may help make the dismissal unfair.

11 I am not aware of anyone else in the company being made redundant at that time. I do not know why I was made redundant rather than any one else. I believe I had longer service than any other chef. [4]

After my dismissal

12 I was so shocked by my dismissal that I went to see my GP that same evening. It was the first time that I had seen my GP for nearly ten years. She prescribed me tablets to take for my nerves and for shock. It was the first time that I had been dismissed in all my working life.

13 About two weeks after my appeal, I saw Mr Venger's personal assistant, Patricia Reiss, in Berwick Street market. She told me that my dismissal had not been a complete surprise to her as she remembered writing to the finance company cancelling the application for my company car. She thought this was in January. [5]

Trying to find new work [6]

14 Since my dismissal I have been trying without success to secure other employment. In May 2009, I saw a full-page advert in the Hotel and Catering magazine for five different jobs at the Strass Burger House. I could have done any of these jobs but none of them were mentioned to me at the time of dismissal. I have also signed-on at a number of specialist agencies. I have been for a few interviews (give details), but I think my age is against me. [7]

Signed: *Jenny Pennant*
Dated: 10 July 2009

---

4 Unfair selection can make a redundancy dismissal unfair. Although an employer need not use length of service as a selection criterion, it is usually a factor which the ET would expect to be taken into account (unless discriminatory).

5 It is a matter of judgement whether to quote what someone else has said if unsure whether they will be a helpful witness for the claimant.

6 Especially in unfair dismissal cases, ETs expect claimants to be ready to deal with the issue of compensation if they win.

7 It is important that the worker can demonstrate that s/he has attempted to mitigate his/her losses. Prior to the hearing it will be necessary to obtain letters from specialist job agencies or the job centre, stating when the worker first signed on, what type of jobs s/he was prepared to do, what vacancies are available in the industry, and whether any jobs were offered.

LETTER OF DISMISSAL

Strass Burger House Ltd
153 AVENAL AVENUE, LONDON W1

Ms Jenny Pennant
12 Wesley Place
Hackney
London E8

30 April 2009

Dear Jenny,

Further to our meeting today, I very much regret that I have to confirm that your position as head chef is now redundant.

You have been given 12 weeks' pay in lieu of your notice entitlement and in the circumstances you are not required to attend work during this period.

I will endeavour to find you suitable alternative employment within the company. Should any position or vacancy arise we will notify you.

May I take this opportunity to thank you for the considerable service you have given to this company. If you wish to appeal, you may write to the managing director within 14 days.

Yours faithfully
Arthur Venger
Head of Human Resources

INITIAL LETTER TO THE EMPLOYER

The content and style of the initial letter depends on the circumstances. It is common to ask for written reasons for dismissal, where these have not already been clearly set out (see para 20.11). Any sums owing, eg, holiday pay or notice pay should also be requested. The following letter also asks for the employee's contract and disciplinary procedure because the employee has not retained copies of these.[8] In some circumstances, it may be better for the initial letter to come from the employee him/herself and to be written in informal terms without referring to any legislation. Such a letter would be suitable if the employee was trying to get the employer to give reasons for dismissal or answer other questions, without alerting him/her to possible legal action.

---

8   But see comments at para 20.11.

London Employment Project
12 MALVERN ROAD, LONDON E8 3LT

Arthur Venger
Head of Human Resources
The Strass Burger House Ltd
153 Avenal Avenue
London W1

1 June 2009

Dear Sir,

Re: Jenny Pennant

I act on behalf of the above named in respect of all matters pertaining to her employment at the Strass Burger House Ltd, and the termination thereof.
In order that I can advise my client further in respect of her several claims against the company, please supply the following:
1   My client's main terms and conditions of employment or her contract of employment. In particular will you supply me with the following particulars:
(a)   My client's contractual right to holiday pay, with sufficient particulars to calculate her entitlement to accrued holiday pay on the termination of her employment. Your attention is drawn to section 1(4)(d) of the Employment Rights Act 1996.
(b)   My client's disciplinary and grievance procedure.
2   Details of the company's redundancy procedure including the selection criteria.
3   The written reasons for my client's dismissal. As you are no doubt aware, if the reasons given in purported compliance of this request are inadequate or untrue, the company will have failed to discharge its legal obligation. Your attention is drawn to section 92 of the Employment Rights Act 1996.[9]
4   All monies which are owed to my client including her holiday pay.
5   My client's P45.

My client will be seeking an order for reinstatement or re-engagement as her primary remedy before the employment tribunal. To this end please supply me with all vacancies within the company, the terms and conditions attributable to each job and the salary, so that my client can consider applying for the

---

9   Even if the employer has supplied the written reasons the adviser is entitled to ask for them pursuant to ERA 1996 s92 and it will be these reasons which the tribunal will consider. If they are different to the previous statement, both can be referred to. To apply pressure on the employer, add the statement concerning the adequate and true reasons.

vacancy.[10] Meanwhile, I would invite you to reinstate my client to any suitable vacancy which you identify.

Please supply the above information within the next 14 days.

Yours faithfully
D. Rocastle
The London Employment Project

---

10 If the worker wants the job back it is important that this is made known to the employer at the earliest opportunity. It will also assist in obtaining an additional award from the tribunal (see para 18.13 above) if the employer was put on notice at an early stage.

TRIBUNAL CLAIM (ET1)

This form is compulsory and can be found on the ETS website. Use the new form as the statutory dispute resolution procedures do not apply to this case. For comments on drafting an ET claim and the standard form, see paras 20.34–20.41.

1 Your details

1.1 Title:	Mr Mrs Miss Ms ✔ Other [ ]	
1.2* First name (or names):	Jennifer	
1.3* Surname or family name:	Pennant	
1.4 Date of birth (date/month/year):	[ ] Are you: male? female? ✔	
1.5* Address: Number or Name	12	
Street	Wesley Place	
+ Town/City	Hackney, London	
County		
Postcode	E8 7ZY	

1.6 Phone number including area code (where we can contact you in the day time):

Mobile number (if different):

1.7 How would you prefer us to communicate with you? (Please tick only one box)   E-mail   Post ✔

E-mail address:

2 Respondent's details

2.1* Give the name of your employer or the organisation you are claiming against.   The Strass Burger House

2.2* Address: Number or Name	153
Street	Avenal Avenue
+ Town/City	London
County	
Postcode	W1 2GB

Phone number:

2.3● If you worked at a different address from the one you have given at 2.2, please give the full address and postcode.

Ashburton Restaurant
Grove Road
London

Postcode   WC2   4FL

Phone number:

If there are other respondents please complete **Section 11**.

3   Employment details

3.1   Please give the following information if possible.

When did your employment start?   `14-01-1989`

Is your employment continuing?   Yes   No ✔

If your employment has ceased, or you are in
a period of notice, when did it, or will it, end?   `30-04-2009`

3.2   Please say what job you do or did.   Head Chef

4   Earnings and benefits

4.1   How many hours on average do, or did, you work each week?   `65`   hours each week

4.2   How much are, or were, you paid?

Pay before tax   £ `25000` .00   Hourly
                                                            Weekly
Normal take-home pay (including   £ `      ` .00   Monthly
overtime, commission, bonuses and so on)   Yearly ✔

4.3   If your employment has ended, did you work   Yes ✔   No
(or were you paid for) a period of notice?

If 'Yes', how many weeks' or months' notice
did you work, or were you paid for?   `12` weeks   `  ` months

4.4   Were you in your employer's pension scheme?   Yes   No ✔

Please answer 4.5 to 4.9 if your claim, or part of it, is about unfair or constructive dismissal.

4.5   If you received any other benefits, e.g. company car, medical insurance, etc, from your
employer, please give details.

meals and travel

4.6   Since leaving your employment have you got another job?   Yes   No ✔
If 'No', please now go straight to section 4.9.

4.7   Please say when you started (or will start) work.

4.8   Please say how much you are now earning (or will earn). £ [   ] .00 each [   ]

4.9   Please tick the box to say what you want if your case is successful:

    a   To get your old job back and compensation (reinstatement)   ✔

    b   To get another job with the same employer and compensation (re-engagement)

    c   Compensation only

5   Your claim

5.1* Please tick one or more of the boxes below. In the space provided, describe the event, or series of events, that have caused you to make this claim:

    a   I was unfairly dismissed (including constructive dismissal)   ✔

    b   I was discriminated against on the grounds of

Sex (including equal pay)	Race
Disability	Religion or belief
Sexual orientation	Age

    c   I am claiming a redundancy payment

    d   I am owed

notice pay	
holiday pay	✔
arrears of pay	
other payments	

    e   Other complaints   ✔

5.2* Please set out the background and details of your claim in the space below. The details of your claim should include **the date when the event(s) you are complaining about happened**; for example, if your claim relates to discrimination give the dates of all the incidents you are complaining about, or at least the date of the last incident. If your complaint is about payments you are owed please give the dates of the period covered. Please use the blank sheet at the end of the form if needed.

1 The respondent is a public company operating 150 restaurants throughout the United Kingdom. A substantial number of these restaurants are situated in or around London. The respondent has a large personnel department situated at head office employing some 25 full-time employees. [FN If the employer is a large company this should be stated in the claim as the tribunal must consider, in determining the fairness of the dismissal, the size and administrative resources of the employer's undertaking.]

2 The claimant commenced employment on 14 January 1989 with the respond¬ent as a chef at its Felstead restaurant. Thereafter, the claimant was pro¬moted on several occasions and at the time of her dismissal she was employed as the head chef of the respondent's Ashburton restaurant which is the most prestigious in the group. (FN If the employee has been promoted or commended during his/her employment, state this.)

3 At no time during the claimant's employment did she receive any written or verbal warnings as to her conduct or capability. (FN Only state this if the employee is certain there have been no warnings during his/her employment.)

4 By letter dated 28 April 2009, the claimant was first informed that there was a redundancy situation and she might be dismissed. The claimant was invited to discuss this matter at a meeting on 30 April 2009 at 10 a.m. with the Head of Human Resources Arthur Venger. The claimant was told at the outset of the meeting that she was to be made redundant, before she was able to express any views.

The meeting, which lasted approximately 5 minutes, was not approached by Mr Venger with an open mind. After the meeting, the claimant went home. That afternoon, she received a letter by courier confirming her redundancy.

5 The claimant wrote a letter of appeal to the managing director, Ms Diana Deane, on 1 May 2009. Her appeal was heard on 16 May 2009 and rejected. Ms Deane also stated that the claimant was not entitled to pay for untaken holiday.

6 The claimant's dismissal was unfair under s98 of the ERA 1996 in that: (FN Depending on the facts, set out each of the considerations which the tribunal has to address in determining the fairness of the dismissal. This helps focus the ET's mind.)

(a) The dismissal of the claimant was not attributable wholly or mainly to a redundancy situation. The duties which the claimant performed pursuant to her employment contract had neither diminished nor ceased. (FN This will not be a feature of every unfair redundancy. ERA 1996 s139 and para 8.19 above)

(b) The respondent failed to consult with the claimant prior to the meeting on 30 April 2009 and gave her no warning prior to the letter of 28 April 2009 that there was a redundancy situation or that her job was at risk.

(c) The respondent unfairly selected the claimant for dismissal. (FN See paras 8.25–8.32 above.) The claimant was the longest serving chef in the company, with vast experience and a very good record.

(d) Having regard to the nature of the respondent's undertaking, and its size and administrative resources, the respondent failed adequately to discuss, seek or offer the claimant alternative employment. (FN See paras 8.29–8.32 above)

7 Further or alternatively, the claimant claims the holiday pay which is owed to her. Under the Working Time Regulations 1998, the claimant is entitled to 5.6 weeks' holiday per year including Bank Holidays. The claimant's holiday year starts on 1st April and she did not take any holidays in her final holiday year. The respondent has refused to pay the claimant in lieu of her untaken holiday. The claimant claims the sum due for untaken holidays under reg 30 of the Working Time Regulations 1998 and/or under Part II of the Employment Rights Act 1996..

8 By letter dated 1 November 2008, the claimant sought the written reasons for her dismissal. To date the respondent has failed to comply with this request. The claimant seeks a declaration as to the reasons for dismissal and compensation.

9 Further, at the time when these proceedings were started, the respondent had not provided the claimant with a statement of terms and conditions as required by section 1 of the Employment Rights Act 1996. The claimant therefore requests compensation in accordance with s38 of the Employment Act 2004.[FN See para 1.26.]

6 What compensation or remedy are you seeking?

6.1 Completion of this section is optional, but may help if you state what compensation or remedy you are seeking from your employer as a result of this complaint. If you specify an amount, please explain how you have calculated that figure.

7 Other information

7.1 Please do not send a covering letter with this form. You should add any extra information you want us to know here. Please use the blank sheet at the end of the form if needed.

8   Your representative

Please fill in this section only if you have appointed a representative. If you do fill in this section, we will in future only send correspondence to your representative and not to you.

8.1	Representative's name:	D. Rocastle
8.2	Name of the representative's organisation:	London Employment Project

8.3   Address:

	Number or Name	12
	Street	Malvern Road
+	Town/City	London
	County	
	Postcode	E8 3LT

8.4   Phone number (including area code):

Mobile number (if different):

8.5   Reference: DR/AFC/JP

8.6   How would they prefer us to communicate with them?   E-mail   Post ✔
(Please tick only one box)

E-mail address:

9   Disability

9.1   Please tick this box if you consider you have a disability   Yes
Please say what this disability is and tell us what assistance, if any, you will need as your claim progresses through the system, including for any hearings that may need to be held at Tribunal Service premises.

10   Multiple cases

10.1   To your knowledge, is your claim one of a number of claims against   Yes   No
the same employer arising from the same, or similar, circumstances?

11 Details of Additional Respondents

- Name of your employer
  or the organisation you are
  claiming against.

- Address: Number or Name

    Street

  + Town/City

    County

    Postcode

  Phone number:

- Name of your employer
  or the organisation you are
  claiming against.

- Address: Number or Name

    Street

  + Town/City

    County

    Postcode

  Phone number:

- Name of your employer
  or the organisation you are
  claiming against.

- Address: Number or Name

    Street

  + Town/City

    County

    Postcode

  Phone number:

**Please read the form and check you have entered all the relevant information.
Once you are satisfied, please tick this box.**   ✔

Data Protection Act 1998. We will send a copy of this form to the respondent(s) and Acas. We will put the
information you give us on this form onto a computer. This helps us to monitor progress and produce statistics.
Information provided on this form is passed to the Department for Business, Enterprise and Regulatory Reform
to assist research into the use and effectiveness of employment tribunals.

EMPLOYER'S RESPONSE TO THE TRIBUNAL (ET3)

Case number: 20065/09/

1   Claimant's name

1.1   Claimant's name: Jennifer Pennant

2   Respondent's details

2.1* Name of Individual,
Company or Organisation   Strass Burger House Ltd

Contact name: Arthur Venger

2.2* Address: Number or Name   153

Street   Avenal Avenue

+ Town/City   London

County

Postcode   W1

2.3   Phone number including area code
(where we can contact you in the day time):

Mobile number (if different):

2.4   How would you prefer us to
communicate with you?   E-mail   Post ✔
(Please tick only one box)

E-mail address:

2.5   What does this organisation mainly make or do?

restaurant chain

2.6   How many people does this organisation employ in Great Britain?   2000

2.7   Does this organisation have more than one site in Great Britain?   Yes ✔   No

2.8   If 'Yes', how many people are employed at the place where the claimant worked?   12

3   Employment details

3.1   Are the dates of employment given by the claimant correct?   Yes ✔   No
If 'Yes', please now go straight to section 3.3.

3.2   If 'No', please give dates and say why you disagree with the dates given by the claimant.

When their employment started

When their employment ended or will end

ET3 v03 001   ET3 v03 001

3 Employment details (continued)

Is their employment continuing?   Yes   No ✔
I disagree with the dates for the following reasons.

3.3 Is the claimant's description of their job or job title correct?   Yes ✔   No
If 'Yes', please now go straight to section 4

3.4 If 'No', please give the details you believe to be correct below.

4 Earnings and benefits

4.1 Are the claimant's hours of work correct?   Yes ✔   No

If 'No', please enter the details you believe to be correct.   [ ] hours each week

4.2 Are the earnings details given by the claimant correct?   Yes ✔   No
If 'Yes', please now go straight to section 4.3

If 'No', please give the details you believe to be correct below.

Hourly

Pay before tax   £ [   ] .00   Weekly

Normal take-home pay (including   £ [   ] .00   Monthly
overtime, commission, bonuses and so on)   Yearly

4.3 Is the information given by the claimant correct about being   Yes ✔   No
paid for, or working, a period of notice?
If 'Yes', please now go straight to section 4.4

If 'No', please give the details you believe to be correct below. If you gave them no notice
or didn't pay them instead of letting them work their notice, please explain what happened
and why.

4.4 Are the details about pension and other benefits,   Yes ✔   No
e.g. company car, medical insurance, etc, given by the claimant correct?
If 'Yes', please now go straight to section 5.

If 'No', please give the details you believe to be correct below.

5 Response

5.1* Do you resist the claim?   Yes ✔   No
   If 'No', please now go straight to section 6.

5.2● If 'Yes', please set out in full the grounds on which you resist the claim.

   1 In April 2009 the kitchen at the Ashburton restaurant was reorganised and decisions regarding menu planning, costing, standards, gross profits and budgets were, in future, to be dealt with by Ms Ethel Mann, the executive director, who was based at the Rusty restaurant.
   2 In early 2009 it was also decided that the kitchen of the Ashburton restaurant would be used as a development for senior chefs de partie and junior sous chefs at the Rusty restaurant (the largest of the respondent's restaurants) to develop their management skills. These persons were to assume responsibility for running the kitchen but would report directly to Ms Mann.
   3 As soon as the decision was made, a meeting was arranged between the claimant and Arthur Venger, the Head of Human Resources of the respondent company. This took place on 30 April 2009. The claimant was told of the reorganisation of the kitchen and how in future it would be used as a development for senior chefs in the respondent company. This meant that there was no need for a head chef at the Ashburton restaurant and in consequence thereof the position had been made redundant following the reorganisation of the kitchen. Mr Venger told the claimant that every effort would be made to find her alternative employment. These matters were explained again to the claimant by the managing director, Ms Diana Deane.
   4 There has been no suitable alternative employment available since this date.
   5 The claimant was paid £2000 ex gratia to include outstanding holiday pay. This was fully explained to her by Ms Deane at her appeal on 16 May 2009.

6 Other information

6.1 Please do not send a covering letter with this form. You should add any extra information you want us to know here.

7 Your representative If you have a representative, please fill in the following.

7.1 Representative's name: Dan Fishman

7.2 Name of the representative's organisation: Hill, Wood & Co

7.3 Address:

Number or Name	Gillespie House, 13
Street	Highbury Street
✚ Town/City	London
County	
Postcode	NW2 1PE

7.4 Phone number:

7.5 Reference:

7.6 How would you prefer us to communicate with them?
(Please tick only one box)

E-mail   Post ✔

E-mail address:

Please read the form and check you have entered all the relevant information.
Once you are satisfied, please tick this box. ✔

Data Protection Act 1998. We will send a copy of this form to the claimant and Acas. We will put the information you give us on this form onto a computer. This helps us to monitor progress and produce statistics. Information provided on this form is passed to the Department for Business, Enterprise and Regulatory Reform to assist research into the use and effectiveness of employment tribunals. (URN 05/874)

REQUEST FOR ADDITIONAL INFORMATION, WRITTEN REASONS AND DISCLOSURE

London Employment Project
12 MALVERN ROAD, LONDON E8 3LT

Dan Fishman
Hill, Wood & Co, Solicitors
Gillespie House
13 Highbury Street
London NW2H 1PE

12 October 2009

Dear Sir

Re: Jenny Pennant v Strass Burger House Ltd – Case No: 20065/09/LC/A

I have now received your client's tribunal response.

Request for written answers and additional information
Please will you forward to this office on or before 26 October 2009[11] answers to the following questions:

1   Under paragraph 2 of the response, what was the precise date in the summer when it was decided that the Ashburton restaurant would be used for this alleged development, who made the decision, and who else was present at the time?[12]

2   Please state (a) the names of all other members of staff who were dismissed on the ground of redundancy as a consequence of this reorganisation, and (b) the selection method.[13]

3   Please state, with dates, the efforts made to secure the claimant alternative employment, who was responsible for this exercise, and the manner and extent of the enquiries made.[14]

4   Please state each and every vacancy within the company and the position and

---

11   State a time limit with which to comply; 14 days is fairly standard.

12   It is important to try to ascertain the precise date when the decision was reached to dismiss the employee. From this date the employer would be expected to consult with the employee and consider alternative employment.

13   This information is necessary to ascertain whether the worker was the only person dismissed and, if not, the other types of workers who were dismissed.

14   The failure to find alternative employment can make the dismissal unfair. The tribunal will have to consider the efforts made, in relation to the size and administrative resources of the employer's undertaking. This comparison cannot be made without this information.

salary attributable to the position in the period 1 January 2009 to 31 July 2009. Please state when each vacancy became available and when it was filled.[15]

Disclosure

Please will you also supply me, within 14 days, with the following documents:

5 A list of all chefs working for the company at any time between 1 January 2009 and 31 July 2009, with dates of employment, job title and location.[16]

6 A list of all job vacancies for kitchen staff within the company from 1 January 2009 to 31 July 2009, the job title, place of employment and the salary.[17]

7 All notes, minutes or memoranda of all meetings at which the reorganisation of the kitchen of the Ashburton restaurant was discussed.[18]

8 Copies of all documents which purport to evidence the claimant's contract of employment.

9 All other documents in your possession which relate in any way to these proceedings, whether or not they are of assistance to the respondent's case or assist the claimant.[19]

If you are unable to supply the above by 26 October 2009, please contact this office in order that a further extension of time can be agreed.[20]

Yours faithfully,

D Rocastle
The London Employment Project

cc Regional Office of the Employment Tribunal[21]

---

15 The period chosen starts on the date the employer says s/he first contemplated redundancy and ends on the date the employee's notice would have expired, had she been allowed to work it. On receiving the information, consider all the vacancies and list those which the employee could have been offered (ie, within his/her capability). If none of these jobs was offered it will be necessary to ascertain at the hearing the reason why not.

16 Needed to ascertain whether the selection of the worker was unfair. Length of service can be a relevant criterion, provided that it is not indirectly discriminatory in that workplace.

17 Needed for the purpose of determining the question of alternative employment.

18 Needed to ascertain when the decision to dismiss was made, who made it and how it was proposed to deal with those workers being dismissed.

19 This is a standard request to ensure the respondent holds nothing useful back of which the employee is unaware and also that the employee is not surprised by any problematic documents which the respondent first produces at the hearing.

20 This paragraph is optional. It puts pressure on the employer to reply voluntarily, but there is a risk in allowing extensions of time in a region where cases get listed swiftly for hearing.

21 It is useful to copy this letter to the tribunal.

REQUEST FOR ORDER FOR ADDITIONAL INFORMATION, WRITTEN ANSWERS TO QUESTIONS AND DISCLOSURE[22]

Under Sch 1 rule 11(3) of the Employment Tribunals (Constitution & Rules of Procedure) Regulations 2006, an application for an order must include an explanation of how the order would assist the tribunal in dealing with the proceedings efficiently and fairly. The difficulty is in providing sufficient explanation without revealing to the respondent all the arguments in the claimant's case.

London Employment Project
MALVERN ROAD, LONDON E8 3LT

The Assistant Secretary of the Tribunals
London Central Tribunal

12 November 2009

Dear Madam/Sir,

Re: Jenny Pennant v Strass Burger House Ltd – Case No: 20065/09/LC/A

On 12 October 2009 I requested from the respondent's solicitors additional information of the response, written answers to questions and disclosure of certain documents. Notwithstanding the time limit given, these have not been supplied. A copy of the request is attached. Please will you make an order under Schedule 1, rule 11(1) of the Employment Tribunal (Constitution and Rules of Procedure) Regulations 2006 for those matters sought in my letter of 12 October 2009. It is essential for my client's case to have this information, to establish that she has been unfairly dismissed.

An order for the requested information and disclosure will assist the tribunal in dealing with the proceedings efficiently and fairly for these reasons:
Item 1: This is relevant to the date when consultation with the claimant should have commenced.
Items 2 and 5: These are relevant as a general context for the redundancy and the fairness of the claimant's selection rather than others, eg, with shorter service..
Items 3 and 4: Alternative employment is relevant to the fairness of a redundancy dismissal.
Item 6: This is relevant as to the timing and reasoning behind the dismissal.
Items 8 and 9: These are standard items.

---

22 See para 20.67 for the requirements when requesting an order.

I am writing to the respondent today in accordance with rule 11(4) enclosing a copy of this letter.

Yours faithfully,

D Rocastle
The London Employment Project

cc Respondent

LETTER UNDER RULE 11(4) INFORMING RESPONDENT OF REQUEST TO TRIBUNAL FOR AN ORDER[23]

London Employment Project
MALVERN ROAD, LONDON E8 3LT

Dan Fishman
Hill, Wood & Co, Solicitors
Gillespie House
13 Highbury Street
London NW2H 1PE

12 November 2009

Dear Sir,

Re: Jenny Pennant v Strass Burger House Ltd – Case No: 20065/09/LC/A

I refer to my letter dated 12 October 2009 requesting additional information and disclosure, to which I have not had the courtesy of a reply. I have therefore written to the tribunal requesting an order for disclosure, copy attached. The reasons for the request are contained in that letter.

You must send any objection to my application to the employment tribunal office within seven days of receiving the application or if sooner, before the date of any case management hearing. Any objection to our application must be copied to the tribunal and myself.

Yours faithfully
D Rocastle

cc Employment tribunal

---

23 See para 20.69.

REQUEST FOR WITNESS ORDER[24]

In obtaining a witness order it is necessary to give the witnesses' full names and addresses (for the purpose of effecting service), a brief statement of their evidence, which must be material, and to state that they are not prepared to attend voluntarily.

London Employment Project
MALVERN ROAD, LONDON E8 3LT

The Assistant Secretary of the Tribunals
London Central Tribunal

18 November 2009
Dear Madam/Sir,

Re: Jenny Pennant v Strass Burger House Ltd – Case No: 20065/09/LC/A

I apply to the tribunal for a witness order for the following person to attend the hearing listed for 14 January 2010.

Patricia Reiss
23 Miller Court
London EC3

Patricia Reiss is employed by the respondent as a personal assistant to the Head of Human Resources. She can give evidence in respect of the respondent's decision to dismiss the claimant.
Ms Reiss is not prepared to attend voluntarily as she is still in the employ of the respondent.

Yours faithfully,
D Rocastle

The London Employment Project

---

24 See paras 20.75 – 20.76.

ADDITIONAL INFORMATION AND ANSWERS TO WRITTEN QUESTIONS

Hill, Wood & Co
GILLESPIE HOUSE, 13 HIGHBURY STREET, LONDON NW2H 1PC

D Rocastle
The London Employment Project
12 Malvern Road, London E8 3LT

15 December 2009

Dear Sir,

Re: Jenny Pennant v Strass Burger House Ltd – Case No: 20065/09/LC/A

You should by now have copies of the documents you requested. In reply to the employment tribunal order of 2 December 2009 to supply additional information and written answers to the claimant's letter of 12 October 2009:

1 The decision was made at a meeting on 10 February 2009 attended by Arthur Venger and Diana Deane. It was a decision reached as part of a reorganisation of the company which was felt to be in the best future interest of all concerned.
2 No other person was dismissed.
3 After 30 April 2009, Arthur Venger personally dealt with this matter. He decided to offer the claimant any future vacancy at head chef level in the larger restaurant. There was no point offering her any other position as she would not have accepted such an offer.
4 The respondent is a large organisation and the turnover of staff in the industry is high. There were many vacancies for other positions within the company, but they were not suitable. The respondent did not take these positions into consideration as they were not relevant.

Yours faithfully,

Dan Fishman

TERMS OF SETTLEMENT[25]

The respondent undertakes:

1 to pay the claimant on or before 2 February 2010 the sum of £7,500 in full and final settlement of all claims that she has arising out of her employment and the termination thereof, save for any claim for personal injury or industrial injury,[26]

2 to supply the following reference and only this reference, if requested for the same, and not to depart from it unless with the express permission of the claimant. If the reference is requested in writing, to supply the same on headed notepaper, dated and duly signed.[27]

'Jenny Pennant has been employed by Strass Burger House Ltd since January 1989 until her dismissal on the ground of redundancy on 30 April 2009. She was promoted on several occasions and at the time of her dismissal was employed as the senior head chef. Throughout her employment we found her to be honest, hard working and enthusiastic. Her timekeeping and attendance were exemplary. She had a pleasant personality and was liked by the other members of staff, as well as by management. We have no hesitation in recommending her for future employment in a similar capacity.'[28]

3 The above reference will also be supplied to the claimant as an open reference on or before 2 February 2010 on headed paper, dated and duly signed, and headed 'To whom it may concern'.

4 The claimant undertakes to withdraw her employment tribunal claim on receipt of the above sum and open reference, and in the meanwhile the case is adjourned generally.[29]

25 See paras 20.163-165 and settlement checklist on p738.
26 Always put in a date for compliance, and always insist that claims for personal injury are excluded with unfair dismissal claims. ACAS will encourage this exception. Also exclude pension rights if these exist.
27 A reference should form part of the agreement (see para 20.164 above), and this undertaking must be secured from the employer. Consider whether to permit leeway if a reference is sought in a different form or there are follow up questions.
28 Set out the reference in full. It helps when negotiating if the employee supplies the first draft of a reference for agreement. However, many employers only supply factual references nowadays.
29 If the worker undertakes to withdraw the claim only on receipt of the sum, it means that if there is non-payment the worker can return to the tribunal or sue for the agreed sum through the courts. If the worker returns to the tribunal s/he should apply for costs on the grounds of unreasonable conduct. See para 20.162 if the employer insists on adding a statement that the claim will be automatically dismissed on withdrawal.

Glossary

ACAS
The Advisory, Conciliation and Arbitration Service (ACAS) was founded in 1975 to work towards improving employment relations. An ACAS officer is appointed to ET cases to 'conciliate', ie, to act as an independent intermediary to facilitate the parties to settle. (See para 20.156.)

Admissible evidence
Evidence to the employment tribunal (ET) may be in documents or oral. Some forms of evidence will not be allowed by the ET and are termed inadmissible. The ET operates very lax rules of evidence. Most forms of evidence will be admissible although some may not be given much weight, eg, hearsay, written unsworn statements from absent witnesses, incomplete or unclear tape recordings.

Breach of contract
Breaking or not complying with one of the agreed terms of a contract (of employment). A fundamental or repudiatory breach of contract is an extremely serious breach going to the heart of the employment relationship. If done by the employer, it may entitle a worker to resign and claim constructive dismissal. If done by the worker, it may entitle the employer to dismiss without notice. (See para 6.33 for constructive dismissal.)

Burden of proof
This refers to which party (employer or worker) has the responsibility of proving matters, such as whether a dismissal took place or whether unlawful discrimination happened. The party with the burden of proof cannot simply make an allegation and ask the other party to disprove it. (See paras 9.1 and 16.1.)

Case management; case management discussion
Case management concerns the preparation of cases for hearings, eg, disclosing documents, obtaining additional information. A case management discussion (formerly known as a directions' hearing) deals with these matters at a private meeting with the ET, often in discrimination cases. Case management may also be known as interim matters. (See paras 20.52 and 21.42.)

Civil courts
Strictly speaking, civil courts are those dealing with civil law, eg, the county court, High Court, Court of Appeal and House of Lords as opposed to criminal law,

eg, the Magistrates' Court and Crown Court. Technically, employment tribunals are civil rather than criminal courts, but the term is sometimes used to distinguish the county court or High Court with their more formal processes, heavier costs risks and (sometimes) legal aid entitlement, from employment tribunals.

Civil Procedure Rules 1998 (CPR)

These are the rules of procedure applicable to the High Court, county courts and the civil division of the Court of Appeal. Although they are more formal than tribunal rules, they do have some influence in terms of understanding the scope of orders for documents and additional information (see chapter 20). The rules are available through the website for the Ministry of Justice at www.justice.gov.uk/civil/procrules_fin/index.htm

Claim

The worker's document which starts the ET proceedings, usually written on an ET1. Formerly known as Originating Application. (See paras 20.23 and 21.33.)

Claimant

The formal term for the worker in ET proceedings. Formerly known as the Applicant.

Closing submissions

See Final submissions.

Complainant

Another legal term for the worker, used in the questionnaire procedure under the SDA 1975, RRA 1976, DDA 1995, etc. Sometimes it is used to refer to the claimant in a discrimination case.

Compromise agreement

A settlement agreement through legal or other authorised representatives meeting specified requirements so as to be binding on the claimant in respect of ET claims (though others are often included). (See para 20.161.)

Conciliation, Conciliation officer

Normally refers to the role of an ACAS (Advisory, Conciliation and Arbitration Service) officer once a case has started in liaising between the parties or their representatives off the record, usually on the telephone, to help encourage a settlement (see para 20.156). ACAS now offers a conciliation service before the tribunal case has been lodged (see para 20.2). Conciliation is to be distinguished from mediation which involves different techniques and is not exclusively offered by ACAS.

Consolidation

Where separate cases with one or more of the same parties are combined for the purposes of preparation and a joint hearing. Strictly speaking the term consolidation is not used in the ET system and the phrase used is that the cases be 'considered together'.

Constructive dismissal

This is where an employee resigns due to the employer's fundamental or repudiatory breach of the employment contract. See para 6.35.

Contract workers

This is often used to refer to workers employed on fixed-term contracts who may or may not have unfair dismissal rights, according to whether they meet the eligibility criteria (see para 6.26). It is also a precise term with a slightly different meaning under the discrimination legislation (see para 13.14).

COT3

The standard form on which an ACAS conciliation officer records an agreement negotiated through him/her. (See para 20.158.)

DDP

DDP is short for the statutory minimum dismissal and disciplinary procedure under the statutory dispute resolution procedures. (See chapter 22.)

Directions; hearings for directions

See Case management and Case management discussions.

Discovery

See disclosure of documents.

Disclosure of documents

The process of one party disclosing relevant documents to the other. The term 'discovery' is sometimes used. (See paras 20.62 and 21.44.)

Discrimination strands

This is not a legal phrase, but it is often used to refer to the different areas of discrimination legislation, ie race, sex, disability, sexual orientation, religion/belief and age.

DL56

The standard form on which a questionnaire under the DDA 1995 is usually written. (See para 21.2.)

Domestic law

This term is usually used to distinguish the national law of an EU member state from European law, ie, law laid down by European legislation and case-law which applies to all member states.

EAT

Employment Appeal Tribunal, the first level of appeal from an ET decision.

Employee

Different categories of worker are eligible to claim different employment rights. Certain rights can only be claimed by employees. For a definition of employee under the ERA 1996, see section 229. The definition under discrimination law is wider, see DDA 1995 s68, RRA 1976 s78, SDA 1975 s82 etc.

ET

Employment Tribunal, formerly known as Industrial Tribunal (IT). Most employment cases are heard in ETs.

ET1, ET3

The ET1 (previously IT1) is the standard form on which the claimant's tribunal **claim** is written. The ET3 (previously IT3) is the standard form on which the employer's **response** is written. These documents are often referred to by the names of the forms rather than their full names. They are called ET1 and ET3.

Ex parte

This is when a procedural step is taken by one party in the ET without notifying the other party. Requests for interim orders are usually made ex parte and not on notice.

Evidence-in-chief

The evidence given in an ET hearing by a witness before s/he is cross-examined. The evidence is usually given to his/her own representative, who will be conducting an examination-in-chief.

Fact – questions of fact; fact findings

If something is a question of fact for the ET, it means that the issue is decided on the facts of the particular case as opposed to on the law alone. A fact finding is the ET's decision on where the truth lies between two conflicting pieces of evidence.

Final submissions

The closing speech in an ET hearing. The final submissions are sometimes put in writing. They may also be known as closing submissions.

Floating cases; floater

Many ET centres list more cases than they can possible hear, assuming that some will not go ahead, usually because they have settled at the last minute. This is to maximize the use of ET panels on any given day. So an ET case which has been set for a hearing date, but has been not allocated to a specific ET panel, is floating or a floater. The problem is that the case can be floating for anything between 5 minutes and all day; sometimes it may not even be heard that day, which can be very frustrating for unrepresented claimants who were not aware of this process.

Fundamental breach

See Breach above.

Grieve, Grievance, Grievance Procedure

Grievances are internal complaints made by workers to their employers, complaining that their employers have or have not done something in relation to the worker. The grievance may concerns the behaviour of a work colleague or manager. Employers should have their own grievance procedures for the bringing and investigation of such complaints. There is also the statutory minimum grievance procedure which must be followed in relation to employees under the **statu-**

tory dispute resolution procedures (see below). Occasionally, the horrible invented misuse of the verb 'grieve' is used to mean 'bring a grievance', especially under the statutory procedures. For a wonderful demolition of the use of this verb, see *Shergold v Fieldway Medical Centre* [2006] IRLR 76, EAT at para 17.

Held
Where something is held by a court or tribunal, this is its decision.

Indirect discrimination
This has a specific legal meaning under the RRA 1976 and other discrimination legislation (see para 13.52 onwards).

Interim
This refers to all procedural matters between lodging the claim and the hearing. An interim hearing deals with such matters and may, for example, be a case management discussion or a pre-hearing review.

Judgment
An ET decision deciding a case or particular issue in the case is a Judgment. A decision concerning an interim matter, eg, requiring a party to supply documents, is an Order. A Judgment can be given orally but must be confirmed in writing. Written reasons for a Judgment or Order are a separate matter. (See para 20.130.)

Jurisdiction
The ET may adjudicate only on certain claims brought by certain workers. These are matters 'within its jurisdiction'. The ET has no discretion to decide claims outside its jurisdiction, eg, where a worker has insufficient qualifying service.

Lay members
Otherwise known as wing members, these are the representatives from each side of industry (ie, CBI and Trade Unions) who sit on most ET hearings.

Liability; hearing on liability
The issue as to whether or not the worker wins his/her case, ie, whether the employer is found 'liable' for unfair dismissal, discrimination, etc, as distinct from the issue of what compensation or remedies the worker should receive.

Listing
When a hearing date is fixed, the case is 'listed' for hearing. (See para 20.77.)

Lodging documents
This usually refers to lodging the tribunal claim or lodging trial bundles at the ET. Usually it means delivering the relevant document to the ET by whatever means. The technical term for lodging the tribunal claim is presenting and the claim will not be accepted as presented if certain requirements are not met.

Mediation, Judicial Medication
A form of alternative disputes resolution. The parties and their representatives hold a meeting, often lasting a whole day, with a view to resolving their dis-

pute. The meeting is chaired by a neutral mediator who may speak to the parties separately or together and facilitate the discussions. The idea is that the parties will focus on what they want rather than the merits of the claim. Mediation is considered particularly suitable where the worker is still employed and in discrimination cases, but its success is very much dependent on the skill of the individual mediator. The risk is that claimants are pressurised by the situation to accept settlements below the true value of their case. Mediation is offered by ACAS or private organisations or free in some regions by the tribunal (see para 21.52 regarding judicial mediation).

Merits; merits hearing
This is the same as the hearing on liability (see above).

Mitigate; mitigation
Mitigation refers to reasonable steps which should have been taken or were taken by a worker to find fresh employment to mitigate (ie, reduce) the loss of earnings resulting from his/her dismissal. (See para 18.32.)

Motion, of its own
An ET has power to make interim orders and take other steps on its own initiative, ie, of its own motion, as well as at the request of either party.

Obiter
Where a higher court makes a statement of legal principle or interpretation, on which the decision in that particular case does not depend. It is therefore not a binding precedent but is of persuasive authority.

On notice
Where a party takes a procedural step in the ET having informed the other party, as opposed to **ex parte**.

Parties
The **claimant** and the **respondent** are collectively known as the parties to the case.

PHR
See **Pre-Hearing Review**

Pleadings; to plead
Pleadings are the documents which set out each party's case, ie, the ET1, ET3 and any additional information (in the technical sense – see paras 20.58–20.59). To plead something is to put it into any of these documents.

Precedent
The courts decide cases by applying and interpreting the law to given facts. There is a hierarchy of courts and tribunals for employment law purposes, ie, House of Lords, Court of Appeal, High Court, EAT, ET. Each level of court/tribunal is compelled to follow legal principles and interpretations set by higher level courts unless a case can be 'distinguished' on its facts. Where no higher level decision exists, the courts (except the ET) follow the interpretation of other courts of the same level. Precedent may also be referred to as 'authority'.

Pre-hearing review

A public hearing often conducted by the Employment Judge sitting alone, to deal with any interim or preliminary matter, eg, matters of jurisdiction which can be separated from the main issue (such as whether the claimant is an employee). It can also strike out parts of the claim or require a costs deposit as a condition of proceeding further. See para 20.89 onwards.

Presenting the tribunal claim

A claim is presented at the ET when it is arrives at the relevant regional ET. However, if the correct form is not used or the worker did not send a step 1 grievance letter to his/her employer when the statutory disputes resolution procedures apply, the tribunal will return the claim and it will not be taken as presented. (See para 20.45.)

Privilege

Certain verbal or written communications are private and need not be disclosed to the other side during a case. These are referred to as 'privileged'. The issue tends to come up on disclosure and the definitive rules are set out in the Civil Procedure Rules 1998. The rules can get very complicated, but the most well known form of privilege is communication between a party and his/her own solicitor. See also **Without prejudice**.

Questionnaire

A special procedure available under the RRA 1976, SDA 1975, DDA 1995, EqPA 1970, Employment Equality (Religion or Belief) Regulations 2003, Employment Equality (Sexual Orientation) Regulations 2003 and Employment Equality (Age) Regulations 2006 (see para 21.2).

Quantum

Financial compensation.

Recoupment

The process by which benefits claimed by the claimant are deducted from his/her award for loss of earnings in a successful unfair dismissal case and repaid by the employer to the DWP. See para 18.58 for precise details.

Remedies; remedies hearing

Remedies are the compensation in money and other forms which a worker receives if s/he wins. A remedies hearing is sometimes dealt with separately from the hearing on liability.

Repudiatory breach

See **Breach**.

Respondent

This is the legal term for the employer in ET proceedings.

Response

The employer's reply or defence, usually written on an ET3 form. Formerly known as the Notice of Appearance. (See para 20.47.)

Review

An ET can review a decision it has made on a number of specific grounds. This is different from appealing to the EAT and has a shorter time limit (see paras 20.134–20.135).

RR65

The standard form on which a questionnaire under the RRA 1976 is usually written. (See para 21.2.)

Schedule of Loss; Schedule of Remedies and Loss

During the preparation of a case, the claimant is often ordered to prepare a schedule setting out how much s/he has lost by way of earnings and the value of the claim generally. (See para 20.98).

SD74

The standard form on which a questionnaire under the SDA 1975 is usually written. (See para 21.2.)

Serving documents

Delivering or sending documents to the other party.

Skeleton argument

A written outline of a representative's final speech at the ET hearing, which s/he will hand to the ET panel and expand verbally.

Statutory dispute resolution procedures

In October 2004, the government introduced statutory minimum dispute resolution procedures which must be followed in most situations. There is a statutory minimum dismissal and disciplinary procedure, which an employer must follow when contemplating dismissal or relevant disciplinary action, and a statutory grievance procedure which an employee must start before s/he can bring an ET case regarding discrimination, unlawful deductions, minimum pay and many other matters. The procedures were abolished on 6 April 2009 but with transitional effects. (For full details, see chapter 22.)

Strands

See Discrimination Strands.

Submissions

An ET at the hearing may invite a representative to make submissions on a particular point. This usually means the representative is required to make comments or arguments on law or evidence. See also Final Submissions.

Summary dismissal

This occurs when an employee's conduct is sufficiently grave as to justify immediate termination of the employment contract without notice. The worker is not entitled to either notice or pay in lieu of notice when summarily dismissed.

TUPE

This abbreviation is commonly used by trade unions to refer to the Transfer of Undertakings (Protection of Employment) Regulations 2006. (See chapter 10.)

Unless Order

An order, eg for disclosure of documents, which – if it is not complied with by the claimant or respondent, will lead to the claim or response (as the case may be) being struck out on the date of non-compliance without further consideration by the tribunal.

Vicarious liability

This is where an employer is responsible for the unlawful acts of his/her employees as if s/he carried them out him/herself, regardless of whether s/he knew or approved of those acts. In the employment field, it is mainly relevant to discrimination law (see para 13.20).

Wing members

Otherwise known as lay members, these are the representatives from each side of industry who sit on most ET hearings.

Without prejudice

Negotiations between the parties for the purpose of settling a case are off-the-record from the viewpoint of the ET. To ensure this is so, it is traditional to introduce the conversation by saying the words 'can we speak without prejudice'? Letters regarding settlement should also be headed 'without prejudice'. See paras 9.19–9.20, 16.32, 20.151.

Witness order

An ET can issue a witness order to compel an unwilling witness to attend the hearing. (See para 20.75.)

Witness statement

A statement taken from each witness including the claimant, which it is intended to disclose to the other side in advance of the hearing or at the hearing itself. With the ET's permission, the witness statement may replace most or all of the witness's evidence-in-chief. Note that the witness must still attend the hearing unless the other side agrees that s/he need not do so. (See paras 20.101 and 21.61.)

Worker

Different employment rights have different eligibility requirements: some are available only to employees and others to 'workers' on a wider basis. These terms can themselves have different definitions according to the employment right concerned. See ERA 1996 s230 for definitions relevant to rights under that Act.

Redundancy payments table

READY RECKONER FOR CALCULATING THE NUMBER OF WEEKS' PAY DUE[1]

The redundancy payment due to each employee under the statutory redundancy payment scheme depends on his or her age and length of service (up to twenty years). This determines the number of weeks pay due, which is then subject to a limit on weekly pay.

To calculate the number of weeks pay due, you should use the following amounts –

- 0.5 week's pay for each full year of service where age during year less than 22
- 1.0 week's pay for each full year of service where age during year is 22 or above, but less than 41
- 1.5 weeks' pay for each full year of service where age during year is 41+

Employers using the above amounts to calculate an employee's entitlement to redundancy pay should note that where an employee's service crosses two bands, the figures in each band should be added together. For example -

Example 1 – if you are 25 with 7 years service, you will be entitled to 5 weeks' redundancy pay. The 5 weeks entitlement is based on 0.5 weeks' pay for each completed year of service between age 18 and 22 and 1 week's pay for each completed year of service between age 22 and 25. (The middle band of 1 weeks' pay only applies where an employee, who is entitled to a redundancy payment, has completed a year service at age 22 or above).

Example 2 – if you are 38 years old and have 12 years of service, you will be entitled to 12 weeks' redundancy pay. The 12 weeks is based on 1 week's pay for each completed year of service between age 26 and 38.

Example 3 – if you are 49 years old and have 15 years of service, you will be entitled to 19 weeks redundancy pay. The 19 weeks' entitlement is based on 1 week's pay for each completed year of service between age 34 and 41 and 1.5 weeks' pay for each completed year of service between age 41 and 49.

The maximum week's pay that an employee is entitled to under the statutory scheme is £350. The limit changes every February in line with the Retail Prices

1 This text and accompanying table is reproduced from BIS website at www.berr.gov.uk/whatwedo/employment/employment-legislation/employment-guidance/page33157.html Note that the maximum week's pay will increase to £380 on 1 October 2009 instead of February 2010, see para 18.17.

Index. However if you were made redundant on or before 31 January 2009 you will be entitled to the previous maximum amount of £330.

This page is intended only as a guide and shows how statutory redundancy pay is calculated for people who are entitled to receive it. Whether or not you are entitled to redundancy pay will depend on your individual circumstances.

Statutory redundancy pay table

To calculate the number of weeks redundancy pay, cross reference the person's age and years of service and then multiply that number by the weekly salary (maximum weekly salary is £350). Eg a person with a salary of £200 aged 22 with 4 years of service will be entitled to two weeks salary eg a total redundancy of £400.

17* - The table starts at age 17, as it is possible for a 17 year old to have 2 years service. Compulsory school leaving age can be 15¾ or 15⅓ where a child is 16 before 1 September. Particular care should be taken when calculating an individual's redundancy pay when they joined as an employee below the age of 16.

61* - The table stops at age 61 because for employees age 61 and over, the payment remains the same as for age 61.

The table has been changed to incorporate user comments received since the introduction of the Employment Equality (Age Regulations) in October 2006.

Statutory redundancy pay table

Service (Years)

Age	2	3	4	5	6	7	8	9	10	11	12	13	14	15	16	17	18	19	20
17*	1																		
18	1	1½																	
19	1	1½	2																
20	1	1½	2	2½	-														
21	1	1½	2	2½	3	-													
22	1	1½	2	2½	3	3½	-												
23	1½	2	2½	3	3½	4	4½	-											
24	2	2½	3	3½	4	4½ccc	5	5½	-										
25	2	3	3½	4	4½	5	5½	6	6½	-									
26	2	3	4	4½	5	5½	6	6½	7	7½	-								
27	2	3	4	5	5½	6	6½	7	7½	8	8½	-							
28	2	3	4	5	6	6½	7	7½	8	8½	9	9½	-						
29	2	3	4	5	6	7	7½	8	8½	9	9½	10	10½	-					
30	2	3	4	5	6	7	8	8½	9	9½	10	10?	11	11½	-				
31	2	3	4	5	6	7	8	9	9½	10	10½	11	11½	12	12½	-			
32	2	3	4	5	6	7	8	9	10	10½	11	11½	12	12½	13	13½	-		
33	2	3	4	5	6	7	8	9	10	11	11½	12	12½	13	13½	14	14½	-	
34	2	3	4	5	6	7	8	9	10	11	12	12½	13	13½	14	14½	15	15½	-
35	2	3	4	5	6	7	8	9	10	11	12	13	13½	14	14½	15	15½	16	16½
36	2	3	4	5	6	7	8	9	10	11	12	13	14	14½	15	15½	16	16½	17
37	2	3	4	5	6	7	8	9	10	11	12	13	14	15	15½	16	16½	17	17½
38	2	3	4	5	6	7	8	9	10	11	12	13	14	15	16	16½	17	17½	18
39	2	3	4	5	6	7	8	9	10	11	12	13	14	15	16	17	17½	18	18½
40	2	3	4	5	6	7	8	9	10	11	12	13	14	15	16	17	18	18½	19
41	2	3	4	5	6	7	8	9	10	11	12	13	14	15	16	17	18	19	19½
42	2½	3½	4½	5½	6½	7½	8½	9½	10½	11½	12½	13½	14½	15½	16½	17½	18½	19½	20½
43	3	4	5	6	7	8	9	10	11	12	13	14	15	16	17	18	19	20	21
44	3	4½	5½	6½	7½	8½	9½	10½	11½	12½	13½	14½	15½	16½	17½	18½	19½	20½	21½
45	3	4½	6	7	8	9	10	11	12	13	14	15	16	17	18	19	20	21	22
46	3	4½	6	7½	8½	9½	10½	11½	12½	13½	14½	15½	16½	17½	18½	19½	20½	21½	22½
47	3	4½	6	7½	9	10	11	12	13	14	15	16	17	18	19	20	21	22	23
48	3	4½	6	7½	9	10½	11½	12½	13½	14½	15½	16½	17½	18½	19½	20½	21½	22½	23½
49	3	4½	6	7½	9	10½	12	13	14	15	16	17	18	19	20	21	22	23	24
50	3	4½	6	7½	9	10½	12	13½	14½	15½	16½	17½	18½	19½	20½	21½	22½	23½	24½
51	3	4?	6	7½	9	10½	12	13½	15	16	17	18	19	20	21	22	23	24	25
52	3	4½	6	7½	9	10½	12	13½	15	16½	17½	18½	19½	20½	21½	22½	23½	24½	25½
53	3	4½	6	7½	9	10½	12	13½	15	16½	18	19	20	21	22	23	24	25	26
54	3	4½	6	7½	9	10½	12	13½	15	16½	18	19½	20½	21½	22½	23½	24½	25½	26½
55	3	4½	6	7½	9	10½	12	13½	15	16½	18	19½	21	22	23	24	25	26	27
56	3	4½	6	7½	9	10½	12	13½	15	16½	18	19½	21	22½	23½	24½	25½	26½	27½
57	3	4½	6	7½	9	10½	12	13½	15	16½	18	19½	21	22½	24	25	26	27	28
58	3	4½	6	7½	9	10½	12	13½	15	16½	18	19½	21	22½	24	25½	26½	27½	28½
59	3	4½	6	7½	9	10½	12	13½	15	16½	18	19½	21	22½	24	25½	27	28	29
60	3	4½	6	7½	9	10½	12	13½	15	16½	18	19½	21	22½	24	25½	27	28½	29½
61+	3	4½	6	7½	9	10½	12	13½	15	16½	18	19½	21	22½	24	25½	27	28½½	30

Bibliography and other resources

Textbooks and guides

Note: many of the following guides by Tamara Lewis are available on the Equality and Human Rights Commission (EHRC) website, via links on www.equalityhumanrights.com/advice-and-guidance/information-for-advisers/taking-discrimination-cases/. If you have any difficulty finding them, it sometimes works to search 'Tamara Lewis' on the EHRC site engine.

Butterworths Employment Law Handbook. Edited by Peter Wallington. All relevant statutes, regulations, codes and EU Directives fully reproduced. No commentary. The book is regularly reissued with latest statutes and amendments to existing statutes. It is invaluable, because it updates statutes and regulations with the amending legislation – something which cannot be found on the OPSI (Office of Public Sector Information) website.

Harvey on Industrial Relations and Employment Law. Published by Butterworths. Multi-volume loose-leaf, regularly updated. Also available on-line. The most authoritative academic text on employment law. Reviews case law and reproduces key statutes. Popularly known as 'Harvey', it is the textbook which is quoted in the courts and tribunals.

RRA Questionnaires: How to Use the Questionnaire Procedure in Cases of Race Discrimination in Employment. By Tamara Lewis. Published by Central London Law Centre. Guide to procedure and sample questionnaires for many situations. Latest edition available on EHRC website.

SDA and EqPA Questionnaires: How to Use the Questionnaire Procedure in Cases of Sex Discrimination in Employment. By Tamara Lewis. Published by Central London Law Centre. Guide to procedure and sample questionnaires for many situations. Latest edition available on EHRC website.

DDA Questionnaires: How to Use the Questionnaire Procedure in Cases of Disability Discrimination in Employment. By Tamara Lewis. Published by Central London Law Centre. Guide to procedure and sample questionnaires for many situations. Latest edition available on EHRC website.

Age Questionnaires: How to Use the Questionnaire Procedure in Cases of Age Discrimination in Employment. By Tamara Lewis. (2006) Published by Central London Law Centre. Guide to procedure and sample questionnaires for many situations. Latest edition available on EHRC website.

Discrimination Questionnaires: How to Use the Questionnaire Procedure in Cases of Discrimination in Employment. By Tamara Lewis. Published by Central London Law Centre. Guide to procedure and sample questionnaires for various discrimination strands, particularly sexual orientation, religion and belief. Latest edition available on EHRC website.

Proving disability and reasonable adjustments: A worker's guide to evidence under the DDA. By Tamara Lewis. Published Central London Law Centre. Latest edition available on EHRC website.

An Employer's Guide to Reasonable Adjustments under the Disability Discrimination Act. By Tamara Lewis. Published Central London Law Centre. Latest edition available on EHRC website.

How to recognise cases of age discrimination: An Adviser's Toolkit. By Tamara Lewis. (2006) Available free on TAEN's website at www.taen.org.uk/Publications/ad_guide_for_advisers.pdf

Redundancy Discrimination: Law and evidence for tribunal cases. By Tamara Lewis. Available on EHRC website.

Using the Data Protection Act and Freedom of Information Act in Employment Discrimination cases. By Tamara Lewis. Available on EHRC website.

Enforcing ET Awards and Settlements by Philip Tsamados. 2nd edn 2006. Published by Central London Law Centre. Telephone administrator on 020 7839 2998.

Claimant's companion: a client's guide to employment tribunal cases by Tamara Lewis. Published by Central London Law Centre. Hard copies or pdf at www.londonlawcentre.org.uk/publications are available to hand out to clients.

Law reports

Industrial Relations Law Reports (IRLR). Fully reproduced law reports. Essential if using cases in an employment tribunal, but you need to know what you are looking for. The other source of official law reports is Industrial Cases Reports (ICR). Technically these are the first choice reports to use in the tribunals, but they are less commonly used by advisers. Most judgments can now be found free on the internet (see below).

IDS Employment Law Brief (until issue 778, Apr 2005, IDS Brief). Abbreviated in this book throughout as IDS Brief. Published twice monthly by Incomes Data Services Ltd. Subscriptions include access to its website plus occasional specialist handbooks .Tel: 020 7449 1107.

Legal Action. Published by Legal Action Group. Tel: 020 7833 2931. Employment Law update in May, June, November and December issues written by Central London Law Centre's Employment Unit. Useful summary of key statutes and cases in the previous six months, selected from the worker's point of view and put into an understandable context.

Equal Opportunities Review (EOR). Published every month by Michael Rubenstein Publishing. Tel: 0844 800 1863. The legal content of this magazine has been reduced in favour of more news, features and reports on initiatives in the equal opportunities field. There are still some case-law round-ups and occasional legal updates, eg on tribunal awards, equal pay' and new equality legislation.

IDS Diversity at Work. Published monthly by Incomes Data Services Ltd. Tel: 020 7449 1107. Mix of equality good-practice case-studies and occasional case reports, similar to EOR. Some overlap with IDS Employment Law Brief.

UNIMAG. Published quarterly by Diversity Works Ltd. For subscription details, e-mail unimag@diversityworks.co.uk. Written by author of this book. Legal update available for UNISON branches. Summary of key legislation and cases in practical user-friendly style.

Websites

ACAS	www.acas.org.uk
Civil Procedure Rules 1998	www.justice.gov.uk/civil/ procrules_fin/index.htm
Council on the Tribunals	www.council-on-tribunals.gov.uk
Court of Appeal judgments	www.bailii.org/ew/cases/EWCA/ civ/toc-c.html To search by citation: http://alpha.bailii.org/ cgi-bin/find_by_citation.cgi

Department for Business Innovation & Skills – BIS (formerly Department for Business, Enterprise and Regulatory Reform – BERR, and before that, the DTI.)
At the time of writing, BIS is still using the BERR web address. The site used to publish regulations and government guidance in many areas of employment law. Unfortunately, much of the guidance previously on the site has been split between two other sites – Business Link for employers and Directgov for employees. These are still fairly informative. The links to particular topics can often still be found on the DBERR site.

www.berr.gov.uk
www.businesslink.gov.uk
www.direct.gov.uk

Employment Appeal Tribunal

Appeal forms, judgments and other information. www.employment appeals.gov.uk
Judgments going back several years at www.employmentappeals.gov.uk/ judgments/judgments.htm
Also on Baiili at www.bailii.org/uk/cases/UKEAT/

Employment Tribunals

General guidance on ET procedure and online ET1 and ET3 forms
www.employmenttribunals.gov.uk

Health and Safety Executive	www.hse.gov.uk
House of Lords Judgments	Judgments since 14 November 1996 www.parliament.the-stationery-office.co.uk/pa/ld199697/ldjudgmt/ ldjudgmt Also on Bailli at www.bailii.org/uk/cases/UKHL/
Information Commissioner	Covers Data protection and the Freedom of Information Act. The Scottish Information Commissioner has a separate site. www.informationcommissioner. gov.uk www.itspublicknowledge.info/ home/ScottishInformation Commissioner.asp
OPSI	Replacing HMSO. Publishes full text of all UK statutes and regulations since 1988 plus draft regulations. www.opsi.gov.uk/legislation
Parliamentary Bills	www.parliament.uk/bills/bills.cfm
Public Concern at Work	Informative site about whistleblow-ing law and cases www.pcaw.co.uk
The Stationery Office (TSO)	Online bookshop for most statutes, regulations and Codes www.tso.co.uk
TUC	www.tuc.org.uk
UNISON	www.unison.org/uk

Index

THE FIFTH WOMAN

Henning Mankell is the prize-winning and internationally acclaimed author of the Inspector Wallander Mysteries, now dominating bestseller lists throughout Europe. He devotes much of his time to working with Aids charities in Africa, where he is also director of the Teatro Avenida in Maputo.

Steven T. Murray has translated numerous works from the Scandinavian languages, including the Pelle the Conqueror series by Martin Andersen Nexø and three of Henning Mankell's Kurt Wallander novels. He is Editor-in-Chief of Fjord Press in Seattle.

ALSO BY HENNING MANKELL

Fiction

Faceless Killers
The Dogs of Riga
The White Lioness
The Man Who Smiled
Sidetracked
One Step Behind
The Return of the Dancing Master
Before the Frost
Chronicler of the Winds
Depths
Kennedy's Brain
The Eye of the Leopard

Non-fiction

I Die, But the Memory Lives On

Young Adult Fiction

A Bridge to the Stars
Shadows in the Twilight
When the Snow Fell